F. L. Bauer · F. L. De Remer
A. P. Ershov · D. Gries · M. Griffiths
U. Hill · J. J. Horning · C. H. A. Koster
W. M. McKeeman · P. C. Poole
W. M. Waite

Compiler Construction

An Advanced Course

Edited by F. L. Bauer and J. Eickel

Second Edition

Springer-Verlag
New York Heidelberg Berlin

Editors

Prof. Dr. F. L. Bauer
Prof. Dr. J. Eickel
Mathematisches Institut
TU München
Arcisstraße 21
8000 München 2/BRD

Originally published in the series
Lecture Notes in Computer Science Vol. 21
Springer-Verlag Berlin Heidelberg New York
First Edition: 1974
Second Edition: 1976

AMS Subject Classifications (1970): 00 A10, 68-00, 79-02
CR Subject Classifications (1974): 4.12

ISBN 0-387-08046-0 Springer-Verlag New York · Heidelberg · Berlin
ISBN 3-540-08046-5 Springer-Verlag Berlin · Heidelberg · New York

PREFACE

The Advanced Course took place from March 4 to 15, 1974
and was organized by the Mathematical Institute of the
Technical University Munich and the Leibniz Computing
Center of the Bavarian Academy of Sciences, in co-operation
with the European Communities, sponsored by the Ministry
for Research and Technology of the Federal Republic of
Germany and by the European Research Office, London.
Due to the great success of the first Course, a repetition
was held from March 3 to 15, 1975.

Contents

CHAPTER 1.: INTRODUCTION

CHAPTER 2.: ANALYSIS

CHAPTER 5.: ENGINEERING A COMPILER

CHAPTER 1.A

COMPILER CONSTRUCTION

W. M. McKeeman
The University of California at
Santa Cruz
U. S. A.

"If PL/I is the Fatal Disease,
then perhaps Algol-68 is
Capital Punishment".

An Anonymous Compiler Writer

1. DEFINITIONS

1.1. SOURCE AND TARGET LANGUAGES

A compiler is a program, written in an <u>implementation language</u>, accepting text in a
<u>source language</u> and producing text in a <u>target language</u>. <u>Language description</u>
<u>languages</u> are used to define all of these languages and themselves as well. The
source language is an algorithmic language to be used by programmers. The target
language is suitable for execution by some particular computer.

If the source and target languages are reasonably simple, and well matched to each
other, the compiler can be short and easy to implement (See Section 1.A.2 of these
notes). The more complex the requirements become, the more elaborate the compiler
must be and, the more elaborate the compiler, the higher the payoff in applying the
techniques of structured programming.

1.2. IMPLEMENTATION LANGUAGES

Compilers can, and have, been written in almost every programming language, but the use of structured programming techniques is dependent upon the implementation language being able to express structure. There are some existing languages which were explicitly designed for the task of compiler writing (FSL [Feldman 66], XPL [McKeeman 70], CDL [Koster 71b], and some for structuring (Pascal [Wirth 71], Algol 68 [van Wijngaarden 68]). The criterion for choosing an implementation language is quite straight forward: it should minimize the implementation effort and maximize the quality of the compiler. Lacking explicit knowledge of this kind, the compiler writer is advised to seek a language as close as possible to the ones mentioned above. The number, quality and availability of such languages is generally on the increase. It may be advantageous to write a compiler to run on a different machine than the target text will run on if better tools can thus be used (especially common for very small target machines). In any case, we shall simply assume an appropriate implementation language is available.

Since there are so many languages involved, and thus so many translations, we need a notation to keep the interactions straight. A given translator has three main languages (SL, TL, IL above) which are objects of the prepositions from, to and in respectively. A T diagram of the form

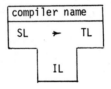

gives all three [Bratman 61]. If the compiler in Section 1.A.2 (below) is called Demo, then it can be described by the diagram

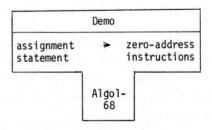

Now a compiler written in Algol-68 is of no use unless there is also a running compiler for Algol-68 available. Suppose it is on the Burroughs B5500. Then if we apply it to the T above, we will get a new T as follows:

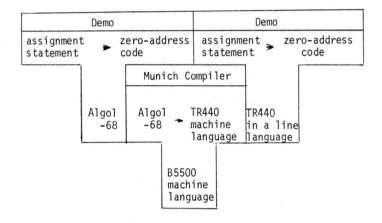

where the arms of the middle T must match the tails of the Ts to the left and right. Complicated, multistage, multilanguage, multimachine translation processes can be described by appropriate cascades of such T diagrams [McKeeman 70 pp. 16-18].

1.3 Language Defining Languages

Language defining languages are almost always based on grammars (see Chapter 2 of these notes) but frequently have additional features designed to define the target text (i.e., translation defining languages). Thus the distinction between language definition and implementation language has not always been very clear. There was a tradition at one point of time to define a programming language as "what the compiler would translate" but this turned out to be of no value to the user who was not prepared to explore the idiosyncrasies of a compiler to be able to write programs. The problem then has been to define languages without leaning on the compiler itself.

The ultimate solution is a definitional mechanism both clear enough for human reference and usable as input to a translator writing system which automatically creates the compiler.

2. Recursive Descent Compilation
2.1 Introduction

It is the intent of the following pages to give a concrete example of translation and also to review a particular, rather simple, rather successful, translation technique. The example, a translation of assignment statements to an assembly language for a stack machine, is trivial by contemporary standards but serves to elucidate the process. We can, in fact, present the entire translator as a whole without becoming mired in either detail or side issues. For the example, the source   text

$$A = - A + 5 * B / (B-1)$$

will be translated to the following zero-address target text
LIT A LIT A LOAD NEG LIT 5 LIT B LOAD MUL LIT B LOAD LIT 1 NEG ADD DIV ADD STORE
which closely approximates the instructions of the Burroughs B5500 computer [Organik 71] (See also Chapters 3.A and 3.E of these notes). The target text is executed, step by step, in Figure 2.1. Although the meaning of the target text is probably obvious to the reader, we will take a few words to describe it. There is an evaluation stack into which values can be pushed. Furthermore, the top values (hence the last ones pushed into the stack) are available to be used in computations. The LIT instruction pushes one value onto the stack. That value is either an address (e.g., the address of the variable A in LIT A) or a constant (e.g. the value 5 in LIT 5).

The LOAD instruction assumes the top value on the stack is an address. The address is removed from the stack and the value found in the indicated cell in memory is pushed onto the stack in its place. The STORE instruction must be supplied with two items at the stack top. One is the address of a cell in memory. The other is a value to be stored into the indicated cell (the address is below the value in the stack). After the STORE instruction has completed its action, both address and value are removed from the stack. The remainder of the instructions are arithmetic operations. NEG changes the sign of the top value on the stack and leaves it where it found it. ADD, MUL and DIV operate on the two top elements on the stack, removing them and then placing the result back on the stack.

Successive stack configurations during execution of the
translated version of A = - A + 5 x B / (B-1).

Note: memory (A) = 7, memory (B) = 6

Figure 2.1

The source text in the example can be described by the grammar in Figure 2.2.

```
Assignment = Variable '=' Expression;
Expression = Term
           | '-' Term
           | Expression '+' Term
           | Expression '-' Term;
Term = Factor
     | Term 'x' Factor
     | Term '/' Factor;
Factor = Constant
       | Variable
       | '(' Expression ')';
Variable = Identifier;
Identifier = 'A' | 'B' | ... |'Z';
Constant = '0' | '1' | ...'9';
```

A Source Text Grammar for Assignments

Figure 2.2

The target text in the example is described by the grammar in Figure 2.3.

```
Assignment = Variable Expression 'STORE';
Expression = 'LIT' Constant
           | Variable 'LOAD'
           | Expression 'NEG'
           | Expression Expression Operator;
Operator   = 'ADD' | 'MUL' | 'DIV';
Variable   = 'LIT' Identifier;
Identifier = 'A' | 'B' | ... | 'Z';
Constant   = '0' | '1' | ... | '9';
```

A Target Text Grammar for Assignments

Figure 2.3.

The translation problem is, then, to take a given source text and produce an <u>equivalent</u> target text. In case of assignments the condition for equivalence is easily expressed in terms of the so called parse tree. The two texts above are seen to be equivalent because the operators are associated with the properly corresponding operands in both parse trees (Figures 2.4 and 2.5).

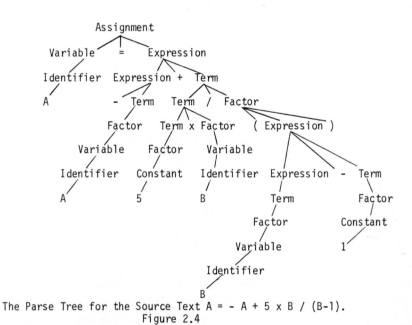

The Parse Tree for the Source Text A = - A + 5 x B / (B-1).
Figure 2.4

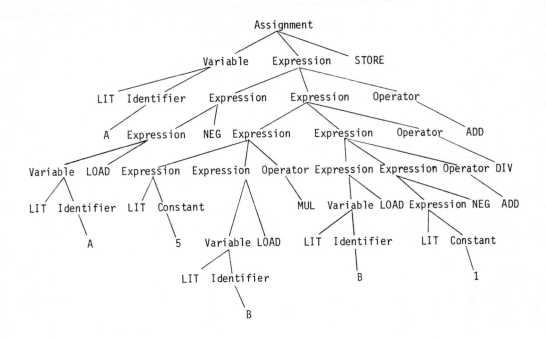

The Parse Tree for the Target Text for A = - A + 5 X B / (B-1)

Figure 2.5

That is not to say that we must build the parse tree as a part of translation. The most elaborate compilers may very well do so but it is not necessary for such a simple language as assignments. We can go directly from source text to target text without using any intermediate representations.

2.2 Writing a Recursive Descent Compiler

The technique of recursive descent translation [Lucas 61] is one of those ideas that is so simple that nobody ever bothers to write much about it. It is, however, in many cases the easiest method of writing good translators. The prerequisites are a grammatical definition of the source language and a recursive programming language in which to implement the compiler (Algol 68 in these notes).

The grammar serves much the same purpose as a flow chart. Given some experience, the compiler writer can produce a compiler such as that depicted in Figure 2.8 about as fast as he can write. It is easier to comprehend the writing process, however, if we use regular expression grammars to define the source text. The grammar in Figure 2.6 describes the same language as that in Figure 2.2. The grammar fragment (|'-') signifies that a minus sign may or may not be found (empty or present). The fragment (('+' | '-') Term)* signifies zero or more repetitions of either a plus or minus followed by a Term, and so on.

```
Assignment = Variable '=' Expression;
Expression = (|'-') Term (('+' | '-') Term)*;
Term = Factor (('x' | '/') Factor)*;
Factor = Constant | Variable | '(' Expression ')';
Variable = Identifier;
Identifier = 'A' | 'B'| ... |'Z';
Constant = '0' | '1'| ... |'9';
```

A Regular Expression Grammar Equivalent to the Grammar in Figure 2.2

Figure 2.6

A certain portion of the compiler is relatively independent of the source language to be translated and can be kept ready "on the shelf' so to speak. Such a partial compiler is called a skeleton and contains procedures for input and output, text scanning, error handling, etc. The compiler writer inserts his procedures into the skeleton (lines 27 to 85 in Figure 2.8). The symbol "token" contains the initial symbol of the source text and is to be replaced each time the current symbol has been processed.

Referring to Figure 2.6, we observe that we must find a variable, followed by the replacement operator ('='), followed by an expression. Without worrying about how the variable and expression are to be processed, we immediately write the procedure Assignment as depicted in Figure 2.7. Note that when the replacement operator is found, it is immediately discarded and the next symbol placed in token. If it is not found, an error message is generated.[†]

```
proc  Assignment = void:
begin Variable;
        if token = "=" then token := scan else error fi;
        Expression
end
```

A Procedure to Analyze Assignments

Figure 2.7

[†]The error response depicted is entirely inadequate for a compiler that will see any extensive service. Refer to Chapter 5.D of these notes.

```
01  proc   translate = void:
02  begin   co The variable token is used to communicate between the procedures that
03          follow.  co
04          string token;

05          co The two procedures, scan and emit, concerned with input and output,
06          are left undefined below to avoid introducing detail irrelevant to the
07          translation process.  co

08          co This procedure produces the next token from the input string each time
09          it is called.  co
10          proc scan = string:  skip;

11          co This procedure assembles one instruction of zero address machine code.
12          co
13          proc emit = (string op) void:  skip;

14          co The procedure constant returns the value true if its argument starts
15          with a digit.  co
16          proc constant = (string c) bool:
17                  charinstring (c[1] , "0123456789", loc int);

18          co The procedure identifier returns the value true if its argument
19          starts with a letter.  co
20          proc identifier = (string i) bool:
21                  charinstring (i[1] ,
22                  "ABCDEFGHIJKLMNOPQRSTUVWXYZ",
23                  loc int);

24          co The procedure error signals a violation of the input syntax.  co
25          proc error = void:
26                  print ("syntax error");
27          proc Assignment = void:
28          begin Variable;
29                  if token = "=" then token := scan else error fi;
30                  Expression;
31                  emit ("STORE")
32          end;

33          proc Expression = void:
34          begin string t;

35                  co First check for unary minus.  co
36                  if token = "-"
37                  then token := scan;
38                      Term;
```

```
39                          emit ("NEG")
40                  else Term
41                  fi;

42                  co Now process a sequence of adding operators.  co
43                  while token = "-" ∨ token = "+"
44                  do t := token;
45                     token := scan;
46                     Term;
47                     if t = "-" then emit ("NEG") fi;
48                     emit ("ADD")
49                  od
50          end;

51      proc Term = void:
52      begin
53              string t;
54              Factor;

55              co Now process a sequence of multiplying operators  co
56              while token = "x" ∨ token = "/"
57              do t := token;
58                 token := scan;
59                 Factor;
60                 if t = "x" then emit ("MUL") else emit ("DIV") fi
61              od
62          end;

63      proc Factor = void:
64      begin co First check for a constant.  co
65              if constant (token)
66              then emit ("LIT");
67                   emit (token);
68                   token := scan

69              co Second, check for a parenthesized subexpression.  co
70              elsf token = "("
71              then token := scan;
72                   Expression;
73                   if token = ")" then token := scan else error fi

74              co Finally, assume the token is an identifier.  co
75              else Variable;
76                   emit ("LOAD")
77              fi
78          end;
```

```
79          proc Variable = void:
80                  if identifier (token)
81                  then emit ("LIT");
82                       emit (token);
83                        token  := scan
84                  else error
85                  fi;

86          co The remaining code constitutes the body of the procedure
87          translate.  co

88          co Initialize the value of token.  co
89          token  := scan;
90          Assignment
91  end
```

A Recursive Descent Compiler for Assignments

Figure 2.8

Presuming that the procedure Variable actually produced the zero-address instruction stream

LIT A

and the procedure Expression produced the stream

LIT A LOAD NEG LIT 5 LIT B LOAD MUL LIT B LOAD LIT 1 NEG ADD DIV ADD we need only add the single instruction

STORE

to complete the process. This can be done by adding one line to procedure assignment (line 31 in Figure 2.8) after the invocation of procedure Expression.

Continuing in this manner, we observe, in Figure 2.6, that an expression has first an optional minus, a term, and then a sequence of operations and terms. If the first minus is there, a NEG operation must be placed <u>after</u> the instructions for the first term. The remainder of the terms (if any) must be processed and the corresponding target text operations placed <u>after</u> them. The result is the procedure Term (lines 51 to 62 in Figure 2.8). Note that a local variable t is used to save the information about whether a plus or minus is found. The remainder of the compiler is written similiarly.

2.3 Executing the Compiler

Execution begins with line 89 in Figure 2.8. Control soon passes to procedure assignment (line 90 then line 27) and onward. Figure 2.9 gives a complete history of the translation of A = - A + 5 x B / (B-1). The reader is advised to hand simulate the execution of the procedure translate, using the history as a check.

Active line in the top-down compiler	Value of token	Source text remaining	Target code produced
start 89	undefined	A=-A+5xB/(B-1)	
	A	=-A+5xB/(B-1)	
90 28 80			
	A	=-A+5xB/(B-1)	LIT A
83			
	=	-A+5xB/(B-1)	
29 30 36 37	-	A+5xB/(B-1)	
	A	+5xB/(B-1)	
51 54 63 64 70 75 80			
	A	+5xB/(B-1)	LIT A
76			
	+	5xB/(B-1)	LOAD
56			
	+	5xB/(B-1)	
39			

+	5xB/(B-1)	NEG

43
46

5	xB/(B-1)	

47
51
54
65

5	xB/(B-1)	LIT 5

56

x	B/(B-1)	

57
58

B	/(B-1)	

59
64
70
75
80

B	/(B-1)	LIT B

76

/	(B-1)	LOAD

60

/	(B-1)	MUL

56
57
58

(	B-1)	

59
64
70
71

B	-1)	

72
33
36
40
54
64
70
75
80

B	-1)	LIT B

83

-	1)	

76

-	1)	LOAD

60
56
58

1	)	

65
68

1	)	LIT 1

56

48		
	)	NEG
49		
	)	ADD
43		
73		
60		
		DIV
56		
47		
48		
		ADD
43		
31		
		STORE
91		

Summary of the Action of the Recursive Descent Compiler

Figure 2.9

2.4 Extending the Technique

The success of the recursive technique is due to several circumstances. First, it is so simple that an experienced programmer can do it quickly. Second, the programmer can insert his generator code between any two statements of the recognizer. This implies that whenever any structural entity of the source language has been recognized, the programmer has a convenient opportunity to attach an interpretation to it. Third, because the local variables of recursive procedures are in fact in a run-time stack, the programmer may associate temporary information with any source language construct (see the variables t in procedures Expression and Term, lines 34 and 53 without laboriously building stack data structures in his translator. One must reflect on the pervasive nature of stacks in translators to appreciate the value of getting them for "free". Perhaps the most important advantage of the recursive technique, aside from its simplicity, is the fact that it can handle complex languages without catastrophic costs in size or speed.

The recursive technique is of no particular help beyond the production of a source-langauge-specific code (e.g., zero-address code for assignments). Since the great bulk of the work in writing a compiler for the average modern computer comes in turning the source-language-specific code into good machine language, the helpful properties detailed above can look rather irrelevant to a hard-pressed implementor.

In addition to the need for a recursive language in which to write, the recursive technique has one serious disadvantage. The generator and parser are thoroughly mixed together, preventing the programmer from treating them separately for purposes of documentation, maintenance, memory management, testing, and so forth. In particular, it is not unusual to find target code dependencies in the source language recognizer, preventing the recognizer from being machine independent.

3. Modularization

The use of modular programming techniques depends upon exploiting the inherent structure of the translation process. Over a period of years there has been a certain amount of convergence in the form of source texts, and of target texts, and of translation sub-processes. One effect is that certain general structural outlines are applicable to most compilers. One should not therefore assume that all compilers should explicitly exhibit all of the structure. A very simple compiler (such as that of the previous section) is easier to write as a whole.

Before proceeding, we must recall at least four kinds of modularization. The documentation of the compiler, the programmer assignments during implementation, the source text of the compiler, and the executable machine language form of the compiler. Each kind of modularization is designed to simplify one or more processes but, as the processes are quite different, one should not expect the modularizations to be the same.

3.1 Modular Documentation

A body of descriptive literature grows up about a compiler, either by plan or by accident. It may well exceed the compiler in sheer volume of text and time of preparation. The documentation is, therefore, in need of structuring and is a candidate for modularization. The forms of the documentation can be expected to be technical prose with tables, appendices, indices and the like. The important point is that the documentation follow the inherent structure of the compiler so as to aid, rather than obscure.

For example, a particular module in the compiler may be the subject of a subsection of the documentation (e.g. The Parser). But more importantly, a more distributed concept may also be the subject (e.g. Module Interfaces). The documentation structure is designed for understanding, thus profits from any consistent theme, regardless of its mapping onto the compiler itself. Even such diverse topics as project history, source language definition, computer specifications, market survey, performance evaluation are properly included. The task of the organizer of the documentation is to find the proper orderings and groupings to minimize the size and cost and amount of crass referencing of the documentation while simultaneously increasing its effectiveness as a tool for understanding. One should not underestimate the importance of this task relative to the whole task of compiler implementations.

3.2 Modular Programmer Assignment

Large programming tasks, some compilers included, must be accomplished by a team of people over a period of time. The managerial task is to assign work to the team

members in a way that gets the job done, minimizing effort and maximizing quality
(See Chapter 5.B of these notes).

Each assignment (of a task to a group of programmers) is a module. These modules
are related by the dependencies of the resulting parts of the compiler. It is usually (always?) the case that part of the compiler structure evolves during the implementation hence the order of doing things is constrained by the order in which
decisions must be made. To quote an (old?) Irish proverb, the most general principle of structured programming is: "when crossing the bog, keep one foot on solid
ground". We may be able to proceed some distance into the swamp by top-down hierarchical decomposition of the task, and also some distance by bottom-up construction
of primitive functions. But, in the end, as does a schoolboy when proving a geometry
theorem, we proceed both ends to the middle to keep from sinking in a sea of unresolved decisions.

3.3 Modular Source Text

Another kind of modularization is found in the implementation language text of the
compiler (source text from the viewpoint of the compiler writer). The usual form of
a source text module is a set of related procedures together with a common data
structure private to them. Such a module also forms the basis for a good programmer
assignment module. The criteria for grouping procedures into modules is to minimize the module size while also minimizing intermodular communication. It would be
interesting to see if a theory of "best" modularization could be formulated [Parnas
71].

3.4 Modular Target Text

Running compilers tend to be large. If one is so large that it cannot fit in main
memory, then the target text form of the compiler must also be modularized. These
modules must be able to function for relatively long periods of time without requiring more than a few of the other modules be present simultaneously. The traditional
multipass compiler is a special case of run time modularization.

4. Intermodular Communication

4.1 Specification

No module exists in a vacuum; it must communicate with other modules. This requires
the specification, in the source text of the compiler, of intermodular data structures. Some languages, such as PL/I, have explicit linguistic facilities for
building external data structures. Intermodular communication also requires the
specification of the dynamic behavior of these same data structures. In both cases
grammars are useful. In the case of a static view of a data structure, such as a
table, gives the static structure. For example, a table of strings where the first
character position is used for the length which is followed by 8-bit character codes
can be described as follows in Figure 4.1.

```
string_table = string*;
string = length character*;
length = bit 8;
bit = '0' | '1';
character = a | b | c... | comma | ...;
a = '11000001';
b = '11000010';

        .
        .
        .

comma = '10101100';

        .
        .
        .
```

Grammatical Description of a String Table

Figure 4.1

When the compiler is running, the intermodular data structure goes through a sequence of states. If the states are viewed as terminal symbols, the sequence is a
language. Suppose, for example, the scanner is passing strings on to another
module coded as pointers into the aforementioned string table, together with some
auxiliary information for the error routine. Then the grammar in Figure 4.2
applies:

```
scan_output = string*;
string = pointer_into_string_table error_info;
pointer_into_string_table = bit 16;
error_info = record_number column_number;
record_number = bit 16;
column_number = bit 8;
bit = '0' | '1';
```

Grammatical Description of Scan Output

Figure 4.2

The advantages of using grammars in this manner are: (1) it is a familiar notation
(2) more precise and concise than natural language. It should be apparent to the
reader that the specification of these intermodular data structures, even just by
example, is a very useful step towards getting the job done.

Another interesting point arises when two module implementors who share a common
intermodular data structure give <u>different</u> specifications for that structure. The
difference probably represents source-text that is not seen to contain errors by the
earlier module, but fails to pass the stricter tests of the later module (e.g., the
scanner does not detect mismatched scope entry and exit, but the symbol table does).
The important point is that the consumer react to the wrong (to the consumer) intermodular communication with a meaningful message rather than silent disfunction.

For example, the intermediate language "characters" in Figure 4.5 is produced by the input module and consumed by the scanner. Figures 4.3 and 4.4 describe the differing views of the characters.

characters = character *;
character = letter | digit | separator;
letter + 'A' | 'B' | 'C' etc.
digit = '0' | '1' | '2' etc.
separator = ' ' | '(' | '+' etc.

The Character String (as produced)

Figure 4.3

characters = token_list;
token_list =
   list1 | list2 | list3 | list4;
list1 = (| list2 | list3 | list4) identifier;
list2 = (| list3 | list4) integer;
list3 = '| list1 | list2 | list4) string;
list4 = (| token_list) separator;
identifier = letter (letter | digit)*;
integer = digit +;
string = '''' string_character *'''';
string_character = '''' '''' | character;
character = letter | digit | separator;
letter = 'A' etc.
digit = '0' etc.
separator = ' ' etc., not including apostrophe.

The Character String (as consumed)

Figure 4.4

4.2 "Need to Know"

It is as important to shield the programmer from irrelevant detail, and also dangerous detail, as it is to insure he has an adequate task specification [Parnas 71] (Also Chapter 5.B of these notes). On the one hand he is saved the time it takes to assimilate the information he is not going to use. On the other hand he is prevented from "clever" use of "soft" detail. An example of the latter is when a programmer, knowing the internal label of some needed external routine, branches directly to it to avoid the overhead of a procedure call. The (negative) payoff comes when the label is changed (without notice because it was thought to be private). Proper modularization, and distribution of just the intermodular specifications, keeps each member of the team appropriately ignorant.

4.3 Test Environment

Although it is true, as Dijkstra says, a test only detects errors, we nevertheless
test our modules. A well-conceived test might form the basis for a proof of correctness but, more importantly, it is the quickest way to find and correct errors.

The specification of the intermodular communication is just the information we need
to "fake up" an environment which drives the module as though it were a part of the
whole compiler. It takes about as long to make up the test as it does to implement
the module but the effort pays off in early removal of loose ends detected by the
programmer as he builds his test.

Properly done, the test program is driven by a set of data so that more tests can
be prepared by a "Devils' Advocate". He prepares three kinds of tests: (1) a
simple test for correct functioning, (2) a test with a large number of incorrect
inputs to insure reasonable error behavior, (3) a test to overflow every internal
table to insure that limit failures are properly detected. There is an example of
some such tests in Chapter 3.D of these notes.

4.4 Feedback-Free

A particularly important kind of intermodular data flow is characterized as
feedback-free. It is this kind of flow that allows a multipass organization to be
used [McKeeman 72 and 74]. Compilers are particularly likely to have inherent
feedback-free structure because we tend to look at the process as a sequence of
forms that have the feedback-free property.

feedback-free form	comments
input records	just as the programmer prepared them
characters	control cards, card boundaries, comments removed
token, string-table	scanned symbols represented by pointer to a string table
parse tree (PT)	explicit links, leaves pointing to string table
abstract syntax tree (AST)	as above, nodes renamed, redundant structure removed
standard tree (ST)	transformed into standard form (See Chapter 2.E of these notes).
attribute collected tree (ACT)	declarative information pruned, replaced by symbol table
attribute distributed tree (ADT)	leaves replaced by attribute information
sequential expression tree (SET)	expression subtrees replaced by flat sequence of target text.
sequential control tree (SCT)	control subtrees replaced by target text control constructs
target text	whew!

Intermediate Forms

Figure 4.5

5. Vertical Fragmentation

Any module (or program) that can be broken into a multipass structure is said to be vertically fragmented. The previous section hinted at one (very elaborate) possible vertical fragmentation (Figure 4.5). A somewhat simpler one (that actually served as the basis for an implementation) is described below [McKeeman 72]. There are seven modules in the fragmentation in Figure 5.1.

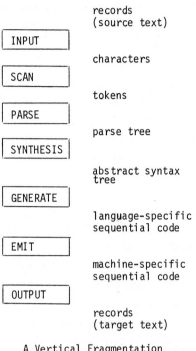

records
(source text)

INPUT

characters

SCAN

tokens

PARSE

parse tree

SYNTHESIS

abstract syntax
tree

GENERATE

language-specific
sequential code

EMIT

machine-specific
sequential code

OUTPUT

records
(target text)

A Vertical Fragmentation

Figure 5.1

The tasks of the modules are conventional. Each intermediate language must be specified (Recall Figures 3.1 and 3.2) but that is beyond the scope of these notes. Rather, we give a series of examples, one for each intermediate language in Figures 5.2a - 5.2h.

1 THEN X=53 + X

IF X <=

Source Text

Figure 5.2(a)

IF X <=1 THEN X=53 + X

Characters

Figure 5.2(b)

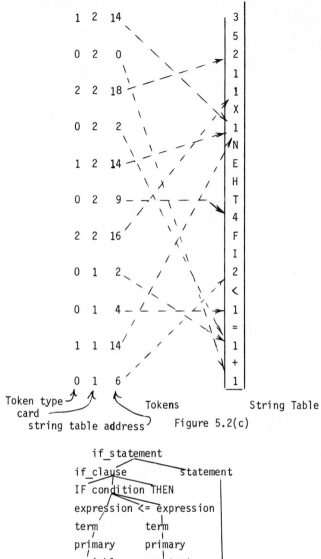

```
1  2  14                    3
                           5
0  2  0                    2
                           1
2  2  18                   1
                           X
0  2  2                    1
                           N
1  2  14                   E
                           H
0  2  9                    T
                           4
2  2  16                   F
                           I
0  1  2                    2
                           <
0  1  4                    1
                           =
1  1  14                   1
                           +
0  1  6                    1
```

Token type ↗
card ――――
     string table address ⌐   Tokens   String Table

Figure 5.2(c)

```
            if_statement
        if_clause        statement
        IF condition THEN
        expression <= expression
        term          term
        primary       primary
        variable      constant
        identifier       1   assignment
        X          variable = expression
        identifier expression + term
        X           term        primary
                  primary      variable
                  constant    identifier
                 53              X
```

Phrase-structure Tree
Figure 5.2(d)

```
              IF
             /  \
           LE     STORE
          /  \    /  \
         X    1  X   ADD
                     /  \
                   53    X
```

Abstract Syntax Tree

Figure 5.2(e)

LIT X;   LOAD; LIT 1; LE;
LIT $L1; BRANCH_FALSE; LIT X;
LIT 53;   LIT X; LOAD; ADD;
STORE; $LI:

Zero-address Code

Figure 5.2(f)

LOAD X;   SUB = 1;   BRANCH_POSITIVE $L1;
LOAD =53; ADD X;   STORE X; $L1:

Single-address Code

Figure 5.2(g)

5810D0405B10D0444740E124
411000375A10DC405010D040

Machine Code

Figure 5.2(h)

A more elaborate (and in some sense more powerful) fragmentation relies more heavily
on the tree form of the source text. In a very rough sense, the tree transforming
process consists of reshaping the tree, pruning information from the tree, and recording information in tabular terminal nodes. At each stage the remaining tree
structure represents work yet to be done. In the end, of course, the entire program becomes a purely tabular structure (sequential code for a conventional computer). The abbreviations in Figure 4.5 will be used below (i.e., PT, AST, ST, ACT,
APT, SET, SCT).

5.1 The Transformation PT ► AST
An AST is a condensed, renamed version of the PT. Most superfluous structure is
discarded, leaving a more convenient computational object. Because the PT is so
voluminous, we always specify the transformation PT ► AST as a part of the algorithm
that reduces the PT itself, avoiding ever forming the PT. This is accomplished by

the use of a transduction grammar [Louis 68, DeRemer 69]. The range of possibilities for an AST is therefore defined to be that set of trees that can be specified by transduction grammars. An example is given in Table 5.3 and Figures 5.4a and 5.4b.

```
E = E '+' T          =>          'ADD'
                                 E   T

  | E '-' T          =>          'SUB'
                                 E   T

  | T                =>          T;
T = T '*' P          =>          'MUL'
                                 T   P

  | P                =>          P;
P ='(' E ')'         =>          E
  | V                =>          'VAR'
                                   /
                                  V   ;

V ='x'               =>          'x'
  |'y'               =>          'y'
  |'z'               =>          'z'  ;
```

A Transduction Grammar for Expressions

Figure 5.3

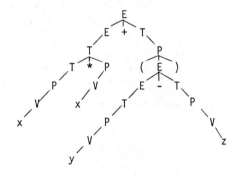

A Parse Tree for x*x + (y-z)

Figure 5.4a

```
                ADD
             MUL     SUB
          VAR  VAR VAR  VAR
           /    \   /    \
           x    x   y    z
```

An Abstract Syntax Tree for x*x + (y-z)

Figure 5.4b

5.2   The Transformation AST► ST

Programming languages sometimes allow more than one way to specify the same result. For example, attributes in PL/I may or may not be factored; certain expressions may or may not be parenthesized, etc. Some are more subtle, such as the assignment implied by parameter passing. The result is that there are classes of ASTs known to the language designer to be equivalent. The transformation AST► ST [Wozencroft 71] is designed to reduce members of the classes to single standard members, when it can be done by local renaming and reordering of tree nodes.

The semantic equivalence of two constructs can be precisely stated (not the semantics, but the equivalence) by mapping one construct into the other. For example, in the language PAL [Evans 68] we can write either

$$E1 \text{ where } x = E2$$

or

$$\text{let } x = E2 \text{ in } E1$$

where E1 and E2 are expressions. We state the equivalence of the constructs by the mapping in Figure 5.5 [DeRemer 74].

A Local Tree Transformation

Figure 5.5

Each transformation rule consists of two parts, an "input" template and an "output" template. These two corresponding to the left and right parts, respectively, or a production of a type 0 grammar. However, in this case the intent is to reorder, expand, and/or contract a local portion of a tree, rather than a local portion of a string.

To "apply" a transformation we first find a subtree that the input template matches. This establishes a correspondence between the "variables" in the input template and subtrees of the matched one. Then we restructure the part of the tree involved in the match, so that the ouput template will match it, maintaining the correspondence between variables and trees established by the input template match. In general, this will involve reordering, duplicating, and deleting the subtrees as dictated by the number and position of occurrences of each distinct variable in the input and output templates.

5.3   The Transformation ST► ACT

The attributes of variables are where you find them. From the compiler writer's viewpoint, they are best found collected in declaration statements clustered at the head of a variable scope. More generally attributes may depend upon the context in which variables are used or even more subtle conditions. In any case they must be gathered and tabulated before the translation of the corresponding executable portions of the program can proceed. Upon completion, the ACT may have the form defined in Figure 5.6.

```
program = ACT;
ACT = scope;
scope = symbol_table scope* command*;
symbol_table = (name attributes)*;
attributes= explicit_attributes
           | implicit_attributes;
```

Attribute-collected Tree
Figure 5.6

Within a scope we first have the table of local symbols, then an arbitrary sequence of nested scopes, and finally the executable (scope-free) commands. The transformation AST► ST may have been required to bring the tree into this form if a scope can be delimited by begin-blocks (as in Algol-60) as opposed to being exclusively identified with procedure declarations. Or the ACT can be more generally defined to allow for the less structured use of scopes.

Some attributes are explicitly supplied by the programmer. Other attributes are implicit. In particular, machine related attributes such as addresses are to be derived by the compiler as one of its major purposes. An important presumption is that there are no necessary attributes that cannot be derived prior to the processing of executable machine code. That is, properties of the machine, such as the relative location of certain instructions, are not allowed to effect the attributes of variables.

The algorithm can be implemented, of course, as an ad hoc tree searching algorithm along the lines commonly found in contemporary compilers. Some work has been done, however, on applying Knuth's concept of functions over trees [Knuth 68, Wilner 71] to this problem. It is a particularly attractive direction since declarative information is defined to be evaluable prior to the "main" computation (i.e., execution of the program). Knuth's functions can therefore be presumed to be evaluable for declaration processing without any great amount of iteration, hence efficiently.

The approach is to specify ST► ACT as a set of symbol-table-valued functions over the ST (as opposed to Knuth's functions over the PT) together with a standard ACT building process. We suspect that a reasonable restriction to put on declarative linguistic constructs is that they can be processed by Knuth's functions in one pass over the ST; i.e., going down the tree via function calls and then back up the tree via function returns.

To apply the functions to the tree we must be able to describe the nodes. Knuth used the names of the non-terminal symbols, numbering only for a repeated use of a name. When regular expressions are used it is simpler to use a purely numeric scheme. Zero designates the left part of a rule; 1, 2,...the items in the right part; -1, -2,...the same items numbered from right to left; (k,1), (k,2),...the items in each repeated term on the right, etc. For example, suppose we have a declarative subtree of the form shown in Figure 5.7.

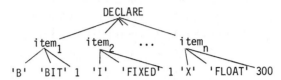

A Declarative Subtree of a ST for

DECLARE B BIT, I FIXED,...X(300) FLOAT;

Figure 5.7

The objective is to compute two functions, A and S, giving the relative offset and number of bits for each item. The grammar and functions in Figure 5.8 define A and S. Terminal nodes (name, type and dimension) have intrinsic values provided by a primitive function val.

$$DECLARE = item^+ \quad \Rightarrow \quad A(1,1) = 0,$$
$$A(1,I+1) = A(1,I) + S(1,I),$$
$$S(0) = A(1,-1) + S(1,-1);$$
$$item = name\ type\ dim \quad \Rightarrow \quad S(0) = T(2)*val(3)$$

$$T(2) \Rightarrow \begin{cases} val(2) = 'BIT'\ then\ 1 \\ val\ (2) = 'FIXED'\ then\ 16 \\ val(2) = 'FLOAT'\ then\ 32 \end{cases}$$

Declarative Functions over a ST

Figure 5.8

5.4 The Transformation ACT ► ADT

The implicit links by name between the leaves of the ACT and its symbol tables must be replaced by explicit attachment of the important attributes to the leaves themselves. The scope rules of most popular programming languages are identical, from the viewpoint of trees, thus the destination of the distributed information need not be specified by the compiler writer. What does need to be specified is which attributes are needed by the later modules.

If the distribution is to be accomplished by simply replacing the leaf names with pointers into the symbol tables, the transformations ST ► ACT ► ADT may as well be accomplished as one step. If the leaf names are to be replaced with attributes, the transformations need to be kept separate. A before-and-after view of a variable node is given in Figure 5.9.

```
     VAR                      VAR
      |          =>           / \
     'I'                    40  'FIXED'
```

Attribute Distribution for a Variable
of Type FIXED and Address Offset 40

Figure 5.9

The symbol table nodes are no longer needed and can be deleted.

5.5 The Transformation ADT► SET

The ADT is an executable form; that is, if we had tree executing hardware. But we do not, so we must reform the tree into equivalent sequential code. We expect rather long sequences of sequential code to be branch free. In particular, expressions (not including Algol-60 conditional expressions) have this property. We can replace each sub-tree representing an expression with its Polish form, say. Or we can go directly to single address code. Figure 5.10 shows an example of such a transformation.

```
        ASSIGN                          ASSIGN
        /    \                          /    \
      VAR    ADD           =>         VAR    POLISH
     / \     / \                      / \    /| | \
   40 'FIXED' VAR MUL               40 'FIXED'
            / \    \
          40 'FIXED'              VAR VAR CONST MUL ADD
                   \           40 'FIXED' 40 'FIXED' 3
                VAR CONST
               /|      \
             40 'FIXED'  3
```

Expression Flattening

Figure 5.10

Note that assignments are not included in the expression flattening, but this adds only one tier to the flattened expression trees. The reason assignments are left alone is two-fold: it avoids the ambiguity between variable addresses and values, and assignments need to be synchronized with some types of branching (parameters, returned values, index control for loops, etc.).

5.6 The Transformation SET► SCT

Having flattened the trees for everything except control constructs, we must finally provide a sequential representation for branch commands. There may be two kinds: implicit and labelled. The implicit branches (if-then-else, loops, case, etc.) merely require the replacement of tree links with branch links. Labels, on the other hand, must be found before the linking can be done. While ST► ACT could have collected this information, it is safely deferred to this stage. Most of the tree has been pruned, hence the search will not be over a very large data structure. For example, suppose we have been processing a procedure call

CALL P(x+3, 4)

and have arrived at the SET in Figure 5.11. x has offset 40 and the two formal parameters (now appearing explicitly in the tree) have offsets 60 and 64.

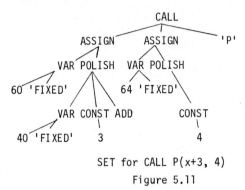

SET for CALL P(x+3, 4)

Figure 5.11

The only change needed is to replace 'P' with a pointer to the corresponding procedure definition. The tree has become a graph; all names have finally been pruned; we are ready to emit fully sequential code.

6. Horizontal Fragmentation

It is sometimes advantageous to specify modules that work in parallel. The simplest case is a subroutine that is occasionally called from the module. The subroutine may qualify as a module by virtue of its internal consistency and simple interface to the rest of the system yet not be feedback-free.

The particular example that led to the coining of this term [McKeeman 72] was the one hundred or so cases in interpreting the canonical parse [Wirth 66a] or phrase structure tree. The program that does the interpretation contains a switch, or case statement, containing over one hundred destinations (corresponding to over one hundred grammatical rules). Such a large construct is obviously a candidate for structuring.

On careful examination of a particular compiler for a rather conventional language, we found six categories of compilation actions as displayed in Figure 6.1. Each category, except the first, is of roughly equal complexity from the viewpoint of implementation. And each is nearly independent of the others, hence good candidates for explicit modularization.

Action Type	Comments
Null	These actions have no interpretation (e.g., term = factor)
Define	These actions come from the rules supplying information to the compiler (primarily declarations) for the symbol table.
Operand	These actions have to do with locating operands in expressions and assignments heavily dependent on symbol table.
Operator	These actions correspond to the operators in expressions.
Assignment	These actions correspond to assignments, either explicit or implicit such as parameter passing and returned values.
Control	These actions map onto the branching instructions of the target text.

Six Categories of Primary Compiler Actions

Figure 6.1

The use of this structure is fairly straight-forward. The unstructured case

```
        case rule_number of
            1:  case_1;
            2:  case_?;
                  .
                  .
          100:  case_100
        end
```

is transformed to a two level switch.

One first switches on category, then calls a processing procedure (module) for that category with a parameter which identifies the item in the category. The PASCAL type [Wirth 71]

   type category = (nulls, defines, operands, operators, assignments, controls)
allows the convenient PASCAL switch

```
        case kind (rule-number) of
            nulls:
            defines:  define (compact (rule_number));
            operands: operand (compact (rule_number));
            operators:  operator (compact (rule_number));
            assignments:  assignment (compact (rule_number));
            controls:  control (compact (rule_number));
        end
```

where array "kind" is filled with the appropriate values of type "category" and array "compact" renumbers the rules to a compact sequence of integers. The values in "compact" can be automatically derived from those in "kind".

7. Equivalence Transformations

As mentioned earlier, the sequences of states of the intermodular data structures can be viewed as languages (and grammatically described). Each such language is a candidate for equivalence transformations. There are two main reasons for such transformations: (1) making the remaining part of the compilation task easier, and (2) improving the resulting target text (See Chapter 5.E of these notes).

Each particular transformation can usually be done on any one of several intermediate languages. The major problems are deciding if a particular transformation is worthwhile and on which intermediate language it is most convenient to carry it out.

Translating a very complex language (e.g. the IBM PL/I) can be simplified by passing repeatedly over the token string, each time producing an equivalent token string with with fewer primitive concepts. The final set of primitives is usually taken to include GO TO, IF, assignments and other things that map directly onto a conventional instruction set.

Figure 7 displays three successive equivalence transformations on a PL/I program. Initially there is an array assignment which implies a loop (stage 2). The translator has had to create some new identifiers (which are started with '$' to avoid confusion). The control expressions of the do-loop are evaluated only once implying that the head of the loop contains only simple variables (stage 3). The loop itself can then be factored into IF and GO TO constructs (stage 4).

The advantages are the already mentioned reduction in overall translator complexity and also the fragmentation of the translator to aid in making each piece small enough to permit running in a small memory. It has some utility in documenting the meaning of language constructs where the transformations are simple enough to be easily understood.

The technique has some disadvantages. It can be slow since repeated passes over the token string are required. Clever methods of speeding things up may cancel the gain in simplicity that led to its use in the first place. There is also a lack of theory governing the transformations, leaving a potentially confusing series of ad hoc algorithms. Finally, the transformations may obscure relations that would have been useful to the generators. For instance, the fact that the example in Figure 7.1 can be accomplished with a single memory to memory block transfer instruction will never be recovered from the simplified form at stage 4.

```
DECLARE (A,B) (20) FIXED;
A = B;
--------------------------------
DECLARE (A,B) (20) FIXED;
DECLARE $I1 FIXED;
DO $I1 = LBOUND(A) TO HBOUND (A);
   A($I1) = B($I1);
END;
--------------------------------
```

```
DECLARE (A,B) (20) FIXED;
DECLARE ($I1, $I2, $I3, $I4) FIXED;
$I2 = LBOUND(A);
$I3 = 1;
$I4 = HBOUND(A);
DO $I1 = $I2 BY $I3 TO $I4;
   A($I1) = B($I1);
END;
-------------------------------
DECLARE (A,B) (20) FIXED;
DECLARE ($I1, $I2, $I3, $I4) FIXED;
$I2 = LBOUND(A);
$I3 = 1;
$I4 = HBOUND(A);
$I1 = $I2;
$I5: IF $I1 > $I2 THEN GO TO $I6;
   A($I1) = B($I1);
   $I1 = $I1 + 1;
   GO TO $I5;
$I6:
```

Successive Transformations of a PL/I Program Fragment

Figure 7.1

The computation tree, since it exhibits almost all of the meaningful source language structure, may also be a convenient host for equivalence transformations (See Chapter 2.E of these notes). Figure 7.2 depicts a before and after view of a small computation tree in which a (presumably expensive) multiplication has been transformed into additions.

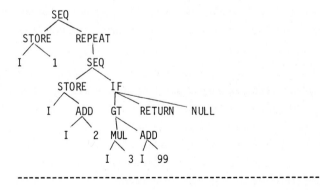

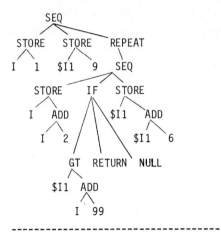

A Before and After View of the
Computation Tree for
I = 1;
DO FOREVER;
    I = I+2;
    IF I * 3 > I + 99 THEN RETURN;
END;

Figure 7.2

Tree transformations consume more computational resources than most other phases of translation both because the tree occupies a lot of memory and following the links takes a lot of time. It may also be that the transformation causes a new inefficiency to be introduced as a result of successfully ridding the program of the one being attacked. Thus the implementor must be careful in deciding which transformations are economically justified. Tree transformations are easier to carry out when the source language does not include a GO TO construct to break up sequences of code, thereby making difficult the detection of induction variables and the like.

Most computers have peculiarities that are utilized by assembly language programmers but are not directly available to the compiler, partly because the opportunities to make use of them do not become apparent until after the machine code itself has been emitted, and partly because they are special to the target machine in question [McKeeman 65]. Figure 7.3 shows a typical situation of this kind. At stage 1 we have a good machine code for the two statements. Because addition is commutative, the addresses of a pair, LOAD ADD, can be interchanged (stage 2) which permits the slow LOAD = 1 to be replaced with a fast load immediate LI 1 and also saves the cell containing the constant 1 (stage 3). In any pair, STORE X LOAD X, the LOAD can be dropped if it is not the destination of a branch (stage 4). Any pair of branches, where the first is a conditional skip and the second is unconditional can be reduced to a single conditional branch (stage 5). Finally, on a machine with an add-one-to-memory instruction, the sequence LI 1, ADD X, STORE X can be combined into one instruction (stage 6).

```
                LOAD X
                ADD = 1
                STORE X
        Stage 1 LOAD X
                LT = 3
                BRANCH_FALSE $L1
                BRANCH L
                $L1;
                ----------------
                LOAD = 1
                ADD X
                STORE X
        Stage 2 LOAD X
                LT = 3
                BRANCH_FALSE $L1
                BRANCH L
                $L1:
                ----------------
                LI 1
                ADD X
                STORE X
        Stage 3 LOAD X
                LT = 3
                BRANCH_FALSE $L1
                BRANCH L
                $L1:
                ----------------
                LI 1
                ADD X
                STORE X
        Stage 4 LT = 3
                BRANCH_FALSE $L1
                BRANCH L
                $L1:
                ----------------
```

```
              LI 1
              ADD X
              STORE X
     Stage 5  LT = 3
              BRANCH_TRUE L
              -----------------
              INDEX X
     Stage 6  LT = 3
              BRANCH_TRUE L
```

Machine-specific Transformations on
X=X+1; IF X < 3 THEN GO TO L
Figure 7.3

Innumberable such ingenuities can be applied. Since the savings can be dramatic (as in the last example), the technique is useful and popular. Nothing makes the hero-author of a compiler happier than producing really subtle correct code, beating the assembly programmer at his own game. One must, however, guard against introducing errors into the code as a result of not carefully considering the conditions under which the transformations leave the program invariant.

The algorithms that perform the equivalence transformations are feedback-free, and very isolated, hence excellent candidates for modularization.

8. Evaluation

In any substantial programming effort, there arise questions which start with the phrase: "Is it worth the effort to...". They must be answered. It would be nice if the answers had some scientific basis. In spite of a great deal of literature on the subject of evaluation, very little useful guidance is available. The intention of this section is partly to give that guidance, but more to show why it is so hard to do and to avoid giving false guidance.

The first problem is to decide what it is that is being evaluated. Generally speaking, it is a decision. From that decision will evolve two different World histories, one presumably more desirable than the other. The mere use of words such as "worth" and "value" imply an economic measure of desirability is to be applied. That is to say, of all the effects of the decision, some will benefit us, some will cost us, and some will be of no consequence. We can formalize this concept by hypothesizing a function which can be applied to a decision to give us its ultimate payoff:

value (decision)

where the units are monetary. For convenience, since we think of cost and benefit in quite different ways, we might split off the positive and negative components of value and express it in terms of two functions:

$$\text{value (decision)} = \text{benefit (decision)} - \text{cost (decision)}$$

Note especially that the functions are determined by a point of view: my benefit may well be your cost.

To keep things concrete, suppose the decision to be evaluated is: "Should compiler X be implemented?"; and our point of view is that of a user of the target text computer for compiler X. We know X will cost us a lot but we expect to need fewer programmers over years of using the computer, hence X will benefit us a lot. Suppose we can buy the compiler for $30,000 and we presently have a staff of assembly language programmers on a total annual budget of $100,000. Over the predicted 5 year lifetime of the computer, we must save about $30,000 in programmer salaries (i.e., 6%). But will we get 6% increased performance? Here is where evaluation gets hard. We need a priori data on human performance. Another problem also arises. Price is a matter of policy, not scientific fact. We may be able to determine what events will follow from our decision but the values are determined by what people are willing to pay and choose to charge. The point is that evaluations in computing is very tightly bound to rather difficult measures of human attributes. The worst, and most consistent error in the literature, is to ignore this fact.

Returning to the specific evaluation model, the alternative "World Histories" following from a decision are sets of events, H and H^1. We ascribe value to the events from our point of view. Some of the events have no value, and some are in both histories, hence can be ignored. The value of the decision can thus be expressed as the difference

$$\text{value (decision)} = \text{value (H)} - \text{value (}H^1\text{)}$$

where the value of a history is given by

$$\text{value (H)} = \sum_{h \in H} \text{value (h)}.$$

The first problem in evaluation is to pick out the classes of events of value (cost or benefit). The second problem is to quantify the occurences of those events. The third problem is to price them.

In compiler writing the events occur during compiler implementation, or compiler use, or use of the compiler output. We expect the costs to cluster in the implementation effort and the benefits (reduced costs with respect to having no compiler) to cluster in the compiler use. We may even find some benefits in the use of the target texts if the compiler has allowed less error-prone programs to be written.

In summary we can do somewhat better in our evaluation by listing out the events of importance and ascribing values to them. If nothing else it forces the decision maker to be specific about certain otherwise conveniently hidden values.

9. References

Bratman, H., An alternate form of the UNCOL diagram, CACM 4 (March 1961), 142.

DeRemer, F. L., Practical translators for LR(k) languages, Ph.D. Thesis, MIT, Cambridge, Massachusetts (1969).

DeRemer, F. L., Transformational grammars for languages and compilers, TR50, Computing Laboratory, University of Newcastle-on-Tyne, England (submitted for publication).

Evans, A., PAL, A language for teaching programming linguistics, Proc. 23rd National Conf. of the ACM (1968) 395-403.

Feldman, J. A., A formal semantics for computer languages and its application in a compiler-compiler, CACM 9 (January 1966).

Gries, D., Compiler construction for digital computers, John Wiley & Sons (1971) 452.

Knuth, D. E., Semantics of context-free languages, Math Systems Theory J., 2 No. 2 (1968) 127-146.

Louis, P. M. and Sterns, R. E., Syntax-directed transduction, JACM 15, No. 3 (July 1968) 465-493.

Lucas, P., Die strukturanalyse van formelubersetzern, Elektron. Rechenanl, 3 (1961) 159-167.

McClure, R. M., An appraisal of Compiler Technology, Proc. SJCC (1972) 1-9.

McKeeman, W. M., Compiler Structure, Proc. USA-Japan Computer Conference, Tokyo (October 1972) 448-455.

McKeeman, W. M. and DeRemer, F. L., Feedback-free modularization of compilers, Proc. Third Congress on Programming Languages, Kiel (March 1974).

McKeeman, W. M., Horning, J. J., Wortman, D. B., A compiler generator, Prentice Hall (1970).

Parnas, D. L., Information distribution aspects of design methodology, Computer Software, IFIP (1971) 26.

van Wijngaarden, A. (ed.), Report on the algorithmic language algol 68, Numerische Mathematick 14 (1969).

Wilner, W. T., Declarative semantic definition, STAN-CS-233-71, Ph.D. Thesis, Stanford, California (1971).

Wirth, The programming language PASCAL, Acta Informatica, 1, 1.

Wozencraft, J. M. and Evans, A., Notes on programming linguistics, Dept. E.E., MIT, Cambridge, Massachusetts (1971).

REVIEW OF FORMALISMS AND NOTATIONS

Franklin L. DeRemer
University of California
Santa Cruz, California, USA

1. Terminology and Definitions of Grammars [Aho 1972]

1.1. Unrestricted Rewriting Systems

A "grammar" is a formal device for specifying a potentially infinite "language" (set of strings) in a finite way. Strings in the lanaguage are generated by starting with a string consisting of one particular "start symbol" and successively rewriting the string according to a finite set of rewriting rules or "productions". Grammars of interest here impose a structure, called a "derivation tree", on the string generated. Formally, grammars are defined as follows.

A set of symbols is called a <u>vocabulary</u>. The notation $V*$, where V is a vocabulary, denotes the set of all strings composed of symbols from V, including the empty string. The <u>empty string</u>, denoted ε, consists of no symbols. The notation $V+$ denotes $V* - \{\varepsilon\}$. If α is a string then $|\alpha|$ denotes the length of (number of symbols in) α.

A <u>grammar</u> is a quadruple (V_T, V_N, S, P) where
V_T is a finite set of symbols called <u>terminals</u>,
V_N is a finite set of symbols called <u>nonterminals</u>
   such that $V_T \cap V_N = \emptyset$,
S is a distinguished member of V_N called the
   <u>start</u> <u>symbol</u> (or <u>goal</u> <u>symbol</u> or <u>axiom</u>), and
P is a finite set of pairs called <u>productions</u> such
   that each production (α, β) is written
   $\alpha \rightarrow \beta$ and the <u>left part</u> $\alpha \in V*$ and the
   <u>right part</u> $\beta \in V*$ where $V = V_T \cup V_N$.

By convention we use Latin capitals (A, B,..., Z) to denote nonterminals, lower case Latin letters (a, b,...,z) to denote terminals, and lower case Greek letters (α, β, ..., ω) to denote strings.

If $\alpha \rightarrow \beta$ is a production and $\gamma\alpha\rho$ is a string then $\gamma\alpha\rho \rightarrow \gamma\beta\rho$ is an __immediate deriva-__ __tion.__ A __derivation__ is a sequence of strings

α_0, α_1,...,α_n

where $n \geq 0$ such that

$\alpha_0 \rightarrow \alpha_1$, $\alpha_1 \rightarrow \alpha_2$, ..., $\alpha_{n-1} \rightarrow \alpha_n$;

it is written $\alpha_0 \rightarrow * \alpha_n$; or if $n \geq 1$ then $\alpha_0 \rightarrow^+ \alpha_n$.

Any string η derivable from the start symbol S, i.e. such that $S \rightarrow * \eta$, is called a __sentential form.__ Any sentential form consisting of terminals only is called a __sen-__ __tence.__ The __language L(G)__ generated by a grammar G is the set of all sentences; i.e. $L(G) = \{\eta \in V_T * | S \rightarrow^+ \eta\}$.

1.2 The Chomsky Hierarchy

An unrestricted rewriting system (grammar) as defined in 1.1 above is called a __type__ __0__ grammar, and it generates a __type 0 language.__ There are three successively more severe restrictions that can be placed on the form of productions which result in interesting classes of grammars.

A __type 1__ or __context-sensitive__ grammar (CSG) is one in which each production $\alpha \rightarrow \beta$ is such that $| \beta | \geq | \alpha |$. Alternatively, a CSG is sometimes defined as having productions of the form $\gamma A \rho \rightarrow \gamma \omega \rho$ where $A \in V_N$ and $\gamma \omega \rho \in V^+$, but $\omega \neq \epsilon$. A CSG generates a __type 1 language__ (CSL).

A __type 2__ or __context-free__ grammar (CFG) is one in which each production is of the form $A \rightarrow \omega$ where $A \in V_N$ and $\omega \in V^*$. Sometimes ω is not allowed to be the empty string ϵ. A CFG generates a __type 2 language__ (CFL).

A <u>type 3</u> or <u>regular</u> grammar (RG) is either <u>right linear</u>, with each production of the form A → a or A → aB, or <u>left linear</u>, with each production of the form A → a or A → Ba, where $A \in V_N$, $B \in V_N$, and $a \in V_T$. It is easy to show that allowing "a" to be in V_T^* does not change the essential idea behind, or computational complexity of regular grammars. An RG generates a <u>type 3 language</u> (RL).

1.3 Phrase Structure Implied By Context-Free Grammars

Let $G = (V_T, V_N, S, P)$ be a context-free grammar. Then a right derivation is one in which the rightmost nonterminal of each string is rewritten to form the next; i.e. if $\alpha_0, \alpha_1, \ldots, \alpha_n$ is the derivation, each step is of the form
$\alpha_{i-1} = \gamma A \rho \to \gamma \omega \rho = \alpha_i$ where $\rho \in V_T^*$, $\gamma \in V^*$, $A \in V_N$, and $\omega \in V^*$.

A "parse" of some sentential form η is an indication of how η was derived. In particular, a <u>right parse</u> is the reverse of the sequence of productions used in a right derivation of η. The LR techniques discussed in section 2.C below relate to right parses.

In a manner analogous to the above, one can define a <u>left derivation</u>. A <u>left parse</u> is the sequence of productions used in a left derivation. The left parse relates to the LL techniques discussed in section 2.B below.

One way to avoid questions of the order of the derivation or parse is to discuss the "derivation tree", variously called "parse tree" or "syntax tree". If we associate with each production $A \to X_1 X_2 \ldots X_n$, a tree structure of the form then we can associate a tree with the derivation of each sentence η in an obvious way. In parallel with the derivation of η we construct a tree. We start with the string S and, in parallel, the tree Ⓢ. Each time we rewrite a nonterminal in the string, we attach corresponding descendants to the corresponding node labelled with that nonterminal in the tree. At any given point in the derivation there is an ordered, left to right, one-to-one correspondence between the labels of the leaves of the tree and the symbols in the string. That is, the labels of the leaves when read left-to-right spell out the string.

Example Consider the context-free grammar
G_1 = ({+, (,), i}, {E, T}, E, P) where P consists of the following productions:

$$E \rightarrow E + T$$
$$E \rightarrow T$$
$$T \rightarrow (E)$$
$$T \rightarrow i$$

The right derivation of the sentence η = i + i in L (G_1) procceds as follows.

String derivation	Tree derivation
E	Ⓔ
E ≠ T	tree: E → (E)(+)(T)
E + i	tree: E → (E)(+)(T→i)
T + i	tree: E → (E→T)(+)(T→i)
i + i	tree: E → (E→T→i)(+)(T→i)

The right parse of η, then is

$\quad$ T → i, E → T, T → i, E → E + T.

The derivation tree of η is the last one above. The left parse would be

$\quad$ E → E + T, E → T, T → i, T → i.

Any production of the form A → Aω is called <u>directly</u> <u>left</u> <u>recursive</u>; such a production implies a left-branching tree. Similarly, A → ωA is <u>directly</u> <u>right</u> <u>recursive</u> and implies a right-branching tree. These terms are also applied to the nonterminal A. On a more subtle level, if a nonterminal A is not directly left (or right) recursive but if A → + A$\omega´$ (or A → + $\omega´$ A), then A is said to be <u>indirectly</u> <u>left</u> (or <u>right</u>) <u>recursive</u>. In either case, A is called <u>recursive</u>.

If A → + γ A ρ where neither γ = ε nor ρ = ε, then A is said to be <u>self-embedding</u>. If this occurs via the <u>self-embedding</u> <u>production</u> A → γ A ρ then it is <u>direct</u>, otherwise it is <u>indirect</u>.

1.4. Regular Grammars and Regular Expressions

The essential difference between regular and context-free grammars is that in regular ones there is no <u>self-embedding</u>. Consequently, regular grammars may at best describe sequences of symbols in which there are repetitions and alternatives but no nesting, such as between matched pairs of parentheses or <u>begin</u> ... <u>end</u> pairs, for example.

Thus, regular languages may also be described by <u>regular</u> <u>expressions</u> (REs). REs involve only the three notions of concatenation, alternation (union), and repetition (closure), represented respectively by the infix operators "blank" (i.e. nothing at all) and "|", and the postfix operator "*".

If M and N are RE's then

M N $\quad$ (concatenation; "M followed by N")

M | N $\quad$ (alternation; "either M or N"), and

M* $\quad$ (repetition; "zero or more M's"}

are also REs.

If M and N denote languages L_M and L_N, respectively, then

M N $\quad$ denotes the concatenation of the two languages L_M and L_N; i.e. L_{MN} =
$\quad$ $\{\alpha\beta \mid \alpha\varepsilon L_M$ and $\beta \varepsilon L_N\}$,

M | N $\quad$ denotes $L_M \cup L_N$, and

M* $\quad$ denotes the closure of L_M; i.e.
$\quad$ $L_M^* = \{\varepsilon\} \cup \{\alpha\beta \mid \alpha\varepsilon L_M$ and $\beta\varepsilon L_M^*\}$.

Except where altered by parentheses the precedence for these operators is as follows: closure is most binding, then concatenation, then alteration.

<u>Example</u> The regular expression a b* (c | de)* denotes
the language consisting of the following strings:

    a
    ab
    ac
    abb
    abc
    acc
    ade
    abbb
    abbc
    abcc
    abde
    accc
    acde
    adec
    .
    .
    .

i.e. a single "a" followed by zero or more "b"s followed by zero or more of either
"c" or "de".

Regular expressions can be mechanically converted into regular grammars and vice
versa. We will not go into those details here.

2.   Parsing

2.1. Syntactic Dominoes

Consider the problem of determining the derivation tree for a string η purported to
be in the language L(G) of a context-free grammar G, or alternatively, of determining that η is not in L(G). We may describe this problem as a game called "syntactic dominoes".

We play the game on a board with a "flat bottom" piece labelled with the start
symbol at the top of the board, and a sequence of "flat top" pieces at the bottom of
the board, each labelled with the successive symbols of η. Corresponding to each
production A → ω of G there are arbitrarily many "dominoes", all of the same shape:
at the top of the domino is a "flat top" labelled A and at the bottom is a sequence
of "flat bottoms" labelled with the successive symbols of ω. The connections between the top and bottoms of each domino are stretchy, but the order of the bottoms is fixed. Furthermore, the dominoes may not be played upside-down.

The game is played by positioning flat sides of dominoes against one another and the original flat sides on the board. The object of the game is to try to eliminate all flat sides. It is easy to see that if the player "wins", i.e. eliminates all flat sides, then the result is essentially a derivation tree. Furthermore, the player will be able to succeed if and only if η ε L(G).

<u>Example</u> Consider grammar G_1 of section 1.3 above. The distinct dominoes are as follows:

There are arbitrarily many of each. To <u>parse</u>, i.e. determine the derivation tree for, the string η = i + i we set up the playing board initially as follows:

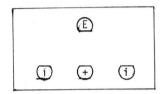

We might begin the game by playing a copy of domino (1) at the top of the board, resulting in:

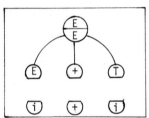

If we now play a copy of domino (4) at the right, we can match both the (T) and the (i) as well as the (+) resulting in:

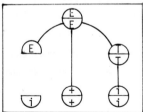

We must play two more dominoes, (4) and (2), to get the final result:

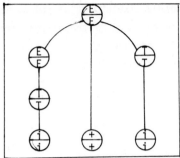

Thus, we have won this particular game. In doing so we have proven that $\eta \in L (G_1)$ and we have constructed its derivation tree.

Any algorithm that given a string determines its derivation tree, or equivalently its right or left parse, is called a parsing algorithm, parser, or analyser.

2.2. Parsing Strategies

Clearly we can devise various strategies, called parsing strategies, to win games of syntactic dominoes. Our strategy might be to try to determine the tree structure starting at the top and working down, or starting at the bottom and working toward the goal symbol at the top. Or we might mix top-down and bottom-up strategies. A good survey article covering early techniques in both top-down and bottom-up parsing is [Feldman 1968].

Independent of the vertical strategy there is the question of a horizontal approach. We might proceed from left-to-right (we usually do) or from right-to-left or we might alternate between the two in some fashion.

Numerous bottom-up parsing algorithms have been devised that depend upon relationships between symbols. Operator precedence parsers [Floyd 1963] make decisions based upon the precedence hierarchy of operator symbols in the language, in addition to matching parenthesis-like symbols. Simple precedence [Wirth 1966] and weak precedence [Ichbiah 1970] parsers work similarly, but depend upon precedence relations between all symbols, rather than just operators. Extended precedence [McKeeman 1966] and bounded context [Eickel 1963] parsers depend upon relationships between strings of symbols.

Top-down techniques are less numerous. Recursive descent parsing was illustrated in the elementary example given in the introduction. Most other top-down techniques involve guessing at parsing decisions and backing-up, or "back-tracking", to the last previous guess point when and if it becomes clear that the parser is on a path not leading to a solution. One survey article describing some of these techniques is [Floyd 1964].

Most bottom-up techniques have been <u>deterministic</u>; i.e. the parser makes a sequence of definite decisions leading directly to a correct parse of any string in L(G) and directly to an error message for any string not in L(G). In contrast, most top-down techniques have been <u>nondeterministic</u> in that they involve guessing. Of course deterministic techniques are usually more efficient in both space and time, than nondeterministic ones, thus much research in this area has been toward perfecting deterministic techniques.

The ultimate in deterministic, bottom-up parsers, were introduced in [Knuth 1965] and are called <u>LR</u> parsers. Analogous, deterministic, top-down parsers are called <u>LL</u> parsers [Lewis 1968]. The essence of nondeterministic parsers based on LR techniques is described in [Earley 1970]. LL and LR parsing techniques are discussed in detail below in sections 2.B and 2.C, respectively.

2.3. Ambiguity

Since the semantics and translations of programming languages are usually related to syntactic constructs, i.e. productions of a phrase structure grammar, an unambiguously defined and implemented language usually requires an unambiguous grammar.

A context-free grammar G is said to be <u>unambiguous</u> if and only if each sentence in L(G) has exactly one derivation tree; otherwise G is <u>ambiguous</u>. Equivalently, we may require that each sentence have a unique right parse (or left parse).

A sufficient condition for ambiguity is that a grammar contain a nonterminal A that is both left and right recursive; e.g. $A \rightarrow + A \gamma A$ for some $\gamma \varepsilon V^*$ guarantees that the grammar is ambiguous, as does $A \rightarrow + A$, as does $A \rightarrow + \alpha A$ with $A \rightarrow + A \beta$. For example, the grammar $G_2 = (\{i, +\}, \{E\}, E, P)$ where P contains the productions

$\quad E \rightarrow E + E$

$\quad E \rightarrow i$

is ambiguous since the sentence i + i + i has the two derivation trees:

2.4. Debugging A Grammar

The LL and LR techniques described below assume that all productions of each grammar are <u>useful</u>, i.e. that for each production $A \rightarrow \omega$ there exists a derivation $S \rightarrow * \gamma A \rho \rightarrow \gamma \omega \rho \rightarrow * \gamma' \omega' \rho'$ such that $\gamma' \omega' \rho' \varepsilon V_T^*$. This condition is easily checked. Presumably the language designer has erred in his phrase structure specification if his grammar contains useless productions.

Another condition that can be easily checked is the existence of an ambiguity due to some nonterminal being both left and right recursive. However, it is to be noted that this is a special case. In general, the question of ambiguity in context-free grammars is undecidable [Floyd 1962].

Other ways of discovering problems within grammars are discussed below relative to particular parsing and translating techniques.

3. Machines, Computational Complexity, Relation To Grammars

Corresponding to the Chomsky hierarchy of grammars is a hierarchy of machines [Hopcroft 1969]. A machine _recognizes_ a language L in the sense that, if it appropriately reads a sentence $\eta \in$ L, it will eventually halt and indicate that η is indeed in the language; i.e. it will _accept_ η. A machine M is said to be _equivalent_ to a grammar G if and only if L(G) is exactly the language recognized by M.

In this latter sense "Turing machines" are equivalent to type 0 grammars, both of which are equivalent, in a similar sense, to the most general (complex) computational systems known. Similarly, "linear bounded automata" are equivalent to context-sensitive grammars, "pushdown automata" are equivalent to context-free grammars, and finite-state machines are equivalent to regular grammars and regular expressions.

Proofs of the equivalences between the two hierarchies involve techniques of converting grammars into equivalent machines and vice versa. In essence, we arrange to get one system to simulate the other. These techniques are similar to the LL and LR parser construction techniques discussed below. Also, the techniques are used directly below in creating scanners based on finite-state machines.

The basic notion needed here from automata theory is that of "state". The state of a parser at any given time sums up the history of the parse for the purpose of making the next parsing decision. In addition, the parsers described here use a pushdown stack to remember more detail about left context (the parse history) for the purpose of matching left context against corresponding right context. Theoretically, our parsers are equivalent to deterministic pushdown automata.

4. Transduction Grammars

Translation can be formally defined via grammars with two right parts to each production rather than just one. We require a coordination between the two right parts. In particular, we require that each occurance of a given nonterminal in one right part have a corresponding occurance of that same nonerminal in the other right part. We do not, however, place any restriction on the relative orders of the symbols in the two right parts, nor do we put any restrictions at all on the terminals in either right part.

4.1 String-To-String Grammars

The formal definitions of grammars given in section 1 above can easily be extended to define such transduction grammars [Lewis 68]. In particular, we are interested here in context-free transduction grammars (CFTGs); i.e. those based on CFGs, and thus, having a single nonterminal as left part. The one-to-one correspondence between occurrances of nonterminals in the two right parts means that we can derive two strings simultaneously by rewriting corresponding nonterminals via these "parallel" productions.

Example Consider the following CFTG based on the CFG G_1 above. TG_1 = ({+, (,), i}, {E, T}, E,P) where P contains the following productions:

$$
\begin{array}{lcl}
E \rightarrow E + T & \Rightarrow & E\ T\ + \\
E \rightarrow T & \Rightarrow & T \\
T \rightarrow (E) & \Rightarrow & E \\
T \rightarrow i & \Rightarrow & i
\end{array}
$$

We have used the symbol => to separate the two right parts. TG_1 defines a translation from infix notation to postfix notation as is illustrated by the following parallel derivation.

E	E
E + T	E T +
E + (E)	E E +
E + (E + T)	E E T + +
E + (E + i)	E E i + +
E + (T + i)	E T i + +
E + (i + i)	E i i + +
T + (i + i)	T i i + +
i + (i + i)	i i i + +

Clearly, such string-to-string transduction grammars can be used to translate to prefix, postfix, and/or infix notation. The above example is simple in that the ordering of nonterminals in the two right parts is the same. Translation to postfix notation is naturally done by an LR parser; translation to prefix notation is naturally done by an LL parser, which can also translate to postfix but for a smaller class of grammars than LR techniques allow, as will be discussed below.

If the nonterminals are not in the same order in the two right parts, complex translations are defined which cannot be performed by deterministic pushdown automata. Rather than implementing such complex reorderings via string-to-string translators, one usually translates the strings at least partially into trees and then transforms

(reshapes) the trees. Such tree transformations can be defined via "transformational grammars" as described in section 2.E below.

4.2. String-To-Tree Grammars

If we use a tree as the second part of each production [DeRemer 1969], we can formally define the translation from strings to trees. For example, for the CFG G_1
of above we might write productions:

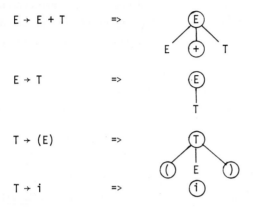

E → E + T	=>
E → T	=>
T → (E)	=>
T → i	=>

This "string-to-tree transduction grammar" obviously translates any string in the
language into its derivation tree. For the purposes of compilation, however, we are
not interested in all of the detail of the context-free grammar, but only in the
basic phrase structure and relations between operators and operands, key words and
phrases. That is, we are interested in the abstract syntax, not the concrete syntax. The derivation tree corresponds to the concrete syntax while a "computation
tree", or "abstract syntax tree", corresponds to the abstract syntax.

We can use the above technique to describe the translation to abstract syntax trees.
For example, for G_1 we might specify the following.

E → E + T	=>	
E → T	=>	T
T → (E)	=>	E
T → i	=>	(i)

A derivation via these productions is as follows:

E   E

E + T

E + (E)

E + (E + T)

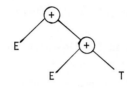

E + (E + i)

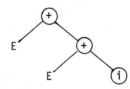

E + (T + i)

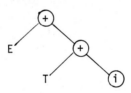

E + (i + i)

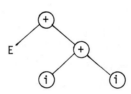

T + (i + i)

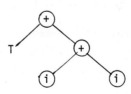

i + (i + i)

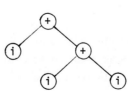

For very simple string-to-tree grammars such as the above, with no reordering of
nonterminals and at most one new node added to the tree per production, we may
abbreviate our rules by mentioning only the node name (if any) in the "tree part" of
each production. For example, the last grammar above could be abbreviated:

$$E \rightarrow E + T \qquad => \qquad +$$
$$E \rightarrow T$$
$$T \rightarrow (E)$$
$$T \rightarrow i \qquad => \qquad i$$

Finally, we note that in section 2.D on "lexical analysis" we use productions with
regular expressions in their right parts. For example

$$E \rightarrow T (+ T)^+ => +$$

means that E may be rewritten as T followed by one or more occurrances of +T and
that the corresponding tree is a + node with the (two or more) subtrees corresponding to the T's as descendants. Trees containing such nodes, having an arbitrary
number of branches, are sometimes called <u>bushes</u>.

5.   Meta-Grammars

5.1. Self-Describing Grammars

The notational conventions used above for specifying grammars, that is the written
forms, of course constitute a language themselves. If we are to implement LL and
LR grammar analysers as described below, we must adopt some well defined conventions
for the input format of these grammars, i.e. a language for grammars.

Rather than use the conventions used for formal purposes above, we prefer to use
standard programming language conventions. Our nonterminals are analogous to (even
sometimes called) variables so we choose to use identifiers to denote them. Terminals are constant strings so we choose to use quoted string constants to denote
them. In addition, we choose to use $(_1)$ "=" rather than "$\rightarrow$" to separate left part
from right part, $(_2)$ "|" to separate alternative right parts rather than require
separate productions for each, and $(_3)$ ";" to terminate the resulting "rules".

How can we describe this language for grammars? With our linguistic tools, of
course; i.e. with these very grammars. Thus, a grammar to define our grammatical
notation is a self-describing grammar. Correspondingly, our language processors
are usually self-implemented (i.e. "bootstrapped") to demonstrate both their use
and their capabilities.

There follows such a self-describing grammar. Note that its language is a set of
sequences of characters, such as might be punched on cards, including the new-line
character (or card boundary). Included is a description of comments (a sharp #

```
 7 |     # THE PHRASE STRUCTURE OF CONTEXT-FREE GRAMMARS.
 8 |
 9 |     Context_free_grammar
10 |        = Spaces                    # A NULL GRAMMAR.
11 |        | Context_free_grammar Rule Spaces
12 |        ;
13 |     Rule
14 |        = Left_part '=' Alternatives ';'
15 |        ;
16 |     Alternatives
17 |        = Right_part
18 |        | Alternatives '|' Right_part
19 |        ;
20 |     Right_part
21 |        = Spaces                    # AN EMPTY RIGHT PART.
22 |        | Right_part Terminal    Spaces
23 |        | Right_part Nonterminal Spaces
24 |        ;
25 |     Nonterminal = Identifier ;
26 |
27 |     Terminal    = String     ;
28 |
29 |
30 |
31 |
32 |     # THE LEXICON OF CONTEXT-FREE GRAMMARS.
33 |
34 |     Identifier
35 |        = Upper_case_letter
36 |        | Identifier Lower_case_letter
37 |        | Identifier Digit
38 |        | Identifier Underscore
39 |        ;
40 |     String      = Quote Any_characters Quote   ;
41 |
42 |     Spaces
43 |        = Separator
44 |        | Spaces Separator
45 |        ;
46 |     Separator
47 |        = Blank
48 |        | New_line
49 |        | Comment
50 |        ;
51 |     Comment     = Sharp Blank Any_characters New_line   ;
52 |
53 |     Any_characters
54 |        =                               # AN EMPTY RIGHT PART USAGE.
55 |        | Any_characters Character
56 |        | Any_characters Sharp 'N'   # NEW LINE CHARACTER.
57 |        | Any_characters Sharp 'Q'   # SINGLE QUOTE.
58 |        | Any_characters Sharp Sharp # SHARP.
59 |        ;
```

```
 60 |
 61 |
 62 |    # THE CHARACTER SET.
 63 |
 64 |    Character
 65 |        = Upper_case_letter
 66 |        | Lower_case_letter
 67 |        | Digit
 68 |        | Operator_symbol
 69 |        | Blank
 70 |        | Underscore
 71 |        ;
 72 |    Upper_case_letter
 73 |        = 'A' | 'B' | 'C' | 'D' | 'E' | 'F' | 'G' | 'H'
 74 |        | 'I' | 'J' | 'K' | 'L' | 'M' | 'N' | 'O' | 'P'
 75 |        | 'Q' | 'R' | 'S' | 'T' | 'U' | 'V' | 'W' | 'X'
 76 |        | 'Y' | 'Z'
 77 |        ;
 78 |    Lower_case_letter
 79 |        = 'a' | 'b' | 'c' | 'd' | 'e' | 'f' | 'g' | 'h'
 80 |        | 'i' | 'j' | 'k' | 'l' | 'm' | 'n' | 'o' | 'p'
 81 |        | 'q' | 'r' | 's' | 't' | 'u' | 'v' | 'w' | 'x'
 82 |        | 'y' | 'z'
 83 |        ;
 84 |    Digit
 85 |        = '0' | '1' | '2' | '3' | '4' | '5' | '6' | '7'
 86 |        | '8' | '9'
 87 |        ;
 88 |    Operator_symbol
 89 |        = '=' | '|' | ';' | '+' | '-' | '*' | '/' | '<'
 90 |        | '>' | ',' | '.' | '(' | ')'
 91 |        ;
 92 |    Quote      = '#Q' ;      # A USE OF THE QUOTE
 93 |                             # DENOTING CONVENTION.
 94 |    Underscore = '_'  ;
 95 |
 96 |    Sharp      = '##' ;      # A USE OF THE SHARP
 97 |                             # DENOTING CONVENTION.
 98 |    New_line   = '#N' ;      # A USE OF THE NEW-LINE
 99 |                             # DENOTING CONVENTION.
100 |    Blank      = ' '  ;
101 |
```

Note: This grammar has been mechanically confirmed to be LALR(1). (See the
       section on LR parsing.)

followed by a blank, then the comment goes to the end of the line). The sharp is the escape character inside strings; sharp followed by a Q denotes a single quote; sharp followed by N denotes the new line character; sharp followed by sharp denotes the sharp. The grammar is presented in three parts defining the phrase structure, the lexicon (how to construct words from characters), and finally, the character set.

5.2. Practical Applications

In practice it has proven to be advantageous to separate the lexical and syntactical specifications of languages into two grammars, a lexical grammar and a phrase structure grammar. Note for example that in the above self-describing grammar, spaces are required in places where they need not be (e.g. before a ";"). This problem can be solved with the addition of more productions, but when the phrase structure is more complex, as it usually is for programming languages, one tires of inserting "Spaces" in numerous productions. Furthermore, the insertions destroy the readability of the grammar.

Given next is a pair of grammars mutually describing themselves, in that one defines their lexicon and the other their phrase structure. The latter is significantly more complex than the above sample, as it includes regular expressions in right parts of productions and tree parts to describe trees.

The section below on lexical analysis discusses the mapping of the lexical grammar into a scanner, and the sections on LL and LR parsing discuss the mapping of phrase structure grammars into parsers.

Other lecturers use slightly different notations for grammars, and they define their notations in their lectures and notes.

```
 1 |#                      *******************************                      #
 2 |#                      *                             *                      #
 3 |#                      *      GRAMMAR LEXICON         *                      #
 4 |#                      *                             *                      #
 5 |#                      *******************************                      #
 6 |
 7 |
 8 |scanner Grammar_text:
 9 |
10 |   Pal_text = Text_id_num | Text_operator | Text_else;
11 |
12 |   # TEXT STARTING WITH AN IDENTIFIER OR NUMBER.
13 |   Text_id_num = (Identifier | Integer | Real) (Text_operator | Text_else)? ;
14 |
15 |   # TEXT STARTING WITH AN OPERATOR.
16 |   Text_operator = Operator (Text_id_num | Text_else)? ;
17 |
18 |   # TEXT STARTING WITH ANYTHING ELSE.
19 |
20 |   Text_else = Spaces (Text_id_num | Text_operator | Text_other)?
21 |             | Text_other ;
22 |
23 |   Text_other = (String | Punctuation | '#N') Pal_text? ;
24 |
25 |
26 |   # THE BASIC TEXTUAL ELEMENTS.
27 |
28 |   Identifier = Upper_case_letter (Lower_case_letter | Digit | '_')*
29 |                                                     => * 'IDENTIFIER'  ;
30 |   Integer = Digit +                                 => * 'INTEGER';
31 |   Operator = Operator_symbol +                      => * 'OPERATOR';
32 |   String = '#Q' Any_character * '#Q'                => * 'STRING';
33 |   Spaces = ' ' +                                    => 'IGNORE';
34 |   Punctuation = '('                                 => * '('
35 |               | ')'                                 => * ')'
36 |               | ';'                                 => * ';'
37 |               | ','                                 => * ',';
38 |
39 |
40 |   # CHARACTER SETS.
41 |
42 |   Any_character = Upper_case_letter | Lower_case_letter
43 |                 | Digit | Operator_symbol
44 |                 | ')' | '(' | ';' | ',' | '##' 'N' | '##' 'T' | '##' 'Q'
45 |                 | '##' '##' ;
46 |   Upper_case_letter = 'A' | 'B' | 'C' | 'D' | 'E' | 'F' | 'G' | 'H' | 'I'
47 |                     | 'J' | 'K' | 'L' | 'M' | 'N' | 'O' | 'P' | 'Q' | 'R'
48 |                     | 'S' | 'T' | 'U' | 'V' | 'W' | 'X' | 'Y' | 'Z'
49 |                     ;
50 |   Lower_case_letter = 'a' | 'b' | 'c' | 'd' | 'e' | 'f' | 'g' | 'h' | 'i'
51 |                     | 'j' | 'k' | 'l' | 'm' | 'n' | 'o' | 'p' | 'q' | 'r'
52 |                     | 's' | 't' | 'u' | 'v' | 'w' | 'x' | 'y' | 'z'
53 |                     ;
54 |   Digit = '0' | '1' | '2' | '3' | '4' | '5' | '6' | '7' | '8' | '9' ;
55 |
56 |   Operator_symbol = '+' | '-' | '*' | '<' | '>' | '&' | '.'
57 |                   | '@' | '/' | ':' | '=' | '~' | '|' | '$'
58 |                   ;
59 |end Grammar_text
```

```
 1 |#                    *******************************                    #|
 2 |#                    *                           *                      #|
 3 |#                    *    CONTEXT-FREE GRAMMARS   *                     #|
 4 |#                    *    WITH REGULAR EXPRESSIONS *                    #|
 5 |#                    *                           *                      #|
 6 |#                    *******************************                    #|
 7 |
 8 |parser Analysers:
 9 |
10 |     Analysers = ( Analyser ';' ) * Analyser                  =>   ';'            ;|
11 |
12 |     Analyser
13 |       = 'PARSER' 'IDENTIFIER' ':' T_grammar Ending           => * 'PARSER'
14 |       | 'SCANNER' 'IDENTIFIER' ':' T_grammar Ending          => * 'SCANNER'     ;|
15 |
16 |          Ending = 'END'                                      =>   'END'
17 |                 | 'END' 'IDENTIFIER'                                         ;|
18 |
19 |     T_grammar = T_rule +                                     =>   'PRODUCTIONS';|
20 |
21 |     T_rule = 'IDENTIFIER' '=' Right_part ';'                 =>   '='          ;|
22 |
23 |     Right_part = Pair ( '|' Pair ) +                         =>   'ALTERNATIVES'|
24 |                | Pair;
25 |
26 |     Pair =  Syntax_part
27 |          | Syntax_part '=>' Opt_star Tree_part               =>   '=>'         ;|
28 |
29 |        Opt_star =
30 |                 | '*'                                        =>   'OUTPUT'     ;|
31 |
32 |     Syntax_part =  Reg_term                                                   ;|
33 |
34 |     Tree_part = 'STRING' ?                                                    ;|
35 |
36 |     Reg_exp = Reg_term ( '|' Reg_term ) +                    =>   '|'
37 |             | Reg_term;
38 |
39 |     Reg_term =                                               =>   'NULL'
40 |              | Reg_factor Reg_factor +                       =>   '.'
41 |              | Reg_factor;
42 |
43 |     Reg_factor =  Reg_primary
44 |                | Reg_primary '*'                             =>   'ZERO_OR_MORE'
45 |                | Reg_primary '+'                             =>   'ONE_OR_MORE'
46 |                | Reg_primary '?'                             =>   'OPTIONAL'
47 |                | Reg_primary '**' Repitition_specification   =>   'REPEAT';
48 |
49 |     Repitition_specification =  'INTEGER'
50 |                              | '(' 'INTEGER' ')'             =>   'UP_TO_N'
51 |                              | '(' 'INTEGER' ',' ')'         =>   'N_OR_MORE'
52 |                              | '(' 'INTEGER' ',' 'INTEGER' ')'
53 |                                                              =>   'N1_TO_N2';
54 |
55 |     Reg_primary = 'IDENTIFIER'         # NONTERMINAL.
56 |                 | 'STRING'             # TERMINAL.
57 |                 | '(' Reg_exp ')'
58 |                 | ;
59 |
60 |end Analysers
```

References

[1] Aho, A.V., Ullman, J.D.: The theory of parsing, translation, and compiling. Englewood Cliffs (N.J.): Prentice-Hall 1972

[2] DeRemer, F.L.: Practical translators for LR(k) langauges. Ph.D. Thesis, M.I.T. Cambridge (Mass.) 1969

[3] Earley, J.: An efficient context-free parsing algorithm. Comm. ACM 13, 94-102 (1970)

[4] Eickel, J., Paul, M., Bauer, F.L., Samelson, K.: A syntax controlled generator of formal language processors. Comm. ACM 6, 451-455 (1963)

[5] Feldman, J.A., Gries, D.: Translator writing systems. Comm. ACM 11, 77-113 (1968)

[6] Floyd, R.W.: On ambiguity in phrase-structure languages. Comm. ACM 5, 526 (1962)

[7] Floyd, R.W.: Syntactic analysis and operator precedence. J. ACM 10, 316-333 (1963)

[8] Floyd, R.W.: The syntax of programming languages - a survey. IEEE Trans. Electronic Computers 13, 346-353 (1964)

[9] Hopcroft, J., Ullman, J.: Formal languages and their relation to automata. Reading (Mass.): Addison-Wesley 1969

[10] Ichbiah, J., Morse, S.: A technique for generating almost optimal Floyd-Evans productions of precedence grammars. Comm. ACM 13, 501-508 (1970)

[11] Knuth, D.E.: On the translation of languages from left to right. Information and Control 8, 607-639 (1965)

[12] Lewis, P.M., Stearns, R.E.: Syntax-directed transductions. J. ACM 15, 465-488 (1968)

[13] McKeeman, W.M.: An approach to computer language design. Ph.D. Thesis, Stanford University 1966

[14] Wirth, N., Weber, H.: EULER - A generalization of ALGOL and its definition. Comm. ACM 9, 13-25, 89-99 (1966)

CHAPTER 2.B.

LL(1) GRAMMARS AND ANALYSERS

M. GRIFFITHS

Laboratoire d'Informatique

UNIVERSITE DE GRENOBLE, FRANCE

I - INTRODUCTION -

Since this course is not solely concerned with syntax analysis, a choice
has had to be made amongst a large number of possible methods. We have chosen to
present the two methods which seem to be the most fundamental in theoretical terms.
The choice was, of course, much easier amongst top-down methods, of which there are
few. The LL(1) techniques described in this chapter were discovered by Foster
[Foster 68] and received a theoretical treatment in [Knuth 71]. The method is top-
down, deterministic with one character of look-ahead.

Before going into details of the method, we should consider the context
in which it will apply. Why are compiler-writers so interested in syntax ? It is
certainly not true that, in a given compiler, the syntactic part is that which
requires the most work. In fact, the pratical compiler writer should be able to
produce his compiler without even bothering much about the mechanics of syntax analysis. He is more interested in using the syntax as a framework on which to hang
semantics, since this gives the overall structure of the compiler. Essentially, for
the compiler writer, Backus normal form is a programming language.

This discussion shows us that, to be useful, a syntax analysis method
must be automated ; the user merely has to type his grammar and some program prepares
the appropriate analyser, which must also be efficient and allow easy interaction

with the semantics. This last point means that the method must be deterministic, but we will come back to that with the examples. We start with a non-deterministic method from long bygone days (a little over ten years ago), and then look at the problem of making it deterministic.

1.1 - Predictive Analysis -

Consider the following grammar, which describes an ALGOL block :

$$Block \rightarrow \underline{begin}\ DL\ \ ;\ \ SL\ \ \underline{end}$$

$$DL\ \ \ \rightarrow\ \ D\ \mid D\ ;\ DL$$

$$SL\ \ \ \rightarrow\ \ S\ \mid S\ ;\ SL$$

We will analyse the following program (considering declarations and instructions to be non-separable units for the time being) :

$$\underline{begin}\ \ D\ \ ;\ \ D\ \ ;\ \ S\ \ ;\ \ S\ \ \underline{end}$$

Analysis proceeds by comparing targets with the source text. The first target is the axiom of the grammar, and new targets are produced by replacing left-most terminal symbols by their possible expansions. Thoses targets which do not correspond to the text are rejected, leaving the others for further comparison, and so on. The successive states of the analysis of the given program are drawn up in the form of a table :

	Targets	Text
1.	Block	begin D ; D ; S ; S end
2.	begin DL ; SL end	begin D ; D ; S ; S end
3.	DL ; SL end	D ; D ; S ; S end
4.	D ; SL end D ; DL ; SL end	D ; D ; S ; S end
5.	; SL end ; DL ; SL end	; D ; S ; S end
6.	SL end DL ; SL end	D ; S ; S end
7.	S end S ; SL end D ; SL end D ; DL ; SL end	D ; S ; S end
8.	; SL end ; DL ; SL end	; S ; S end

and so on. State 8. is the same as state 5., except that some of the source text has been analysed between times. Resuming the rules of the game we see that :

a) - The initial state has the axiom as the unique target, and retains all the source text.

b) - Any target which begins with a non-terminal symbol is replaced by as many new targets as are necessary, each one being the original target with the non-terminal symbol replaced by one of its expansions.

c) - If all the targets begin with a terminal symbol, each of these symbols is compared with the left-hand member of the text. If the symbol does not match the text, the corresponding target is rejected, otherwise the decapitated target is passed to the next state, where the text also loses its first character.

d) - Analysis ends when a target and the text become empty simultaneously. If
several targets become empty at this point, the language is ambiguous, and if
no target becomes empty at this point, the text was not in the language. This
is also the case if no target exists at some moment.

e) - Left recursion causes the analyser to loop, since it becomes impossible to
obtain only targets starting with a terminal symbol.

A more formal presentation of predictive analysis is to be found in [Greibach 64].

1.2 - Efficiency -

Let us now consider state 4 of the analyser. The action leading to
state 5 was the matching of the declaration of the text with the first symbol of
each of the two targets. But the matching of a declaration is not in fact an instan-
taneous process, since a declaration consists of several, or, in the case of a
procedure declaration, of many characters. The two targets are retained during the
analysis of the complete declaration, which is thus analysed twice. Each statement
is also analysed twice, and this number is doubled each time statements are nested.
This obvious waste can easily be eliminated by choosing a different grammar, still
keeping the same analyser :

$$
\begin{aligned}
\text{Block} &\to \underline{\text{begin}} \ \text{DL} \ ; \ \text{SL} \ \underline{\text{end}} \\
\text{DL} &\to \text{D} \quad \text{X} \\
\text{X} &\to \epsilon \ | \ ; \ \text{DL} \\
\text{SL} &\to \text{S} \quad \text{Y} \\
\text{Y} &\to \epsilon \ | \ ; \ \text{SL}
\end{aligned}
$$

ϵ represents the null string, and we have simply factorised the rules. The analyser
now works as follows :

Targets	Text
Block	<u>begin</u> D ; D ; S ; S <u>end</u>
<u>begin</u> DL ; SL ; <u>end</u>	<u>begin</u> D ; D ; S ; S <u>end</u>
DL ; SL ; <u>end</u>	D ; D ; S ; S <u>end</u>
D X ; SL <u>end</u>	D ; D ; S ; S <u>end</u>
X ; SL <u>end</u>	; D ; S ; S <u>end</u>

and so on. The declaration is analysed once only. The obvious question is whether it is possible to obtain a grammar for which the analyser can always reduce the number of targets to one, and the answer is of course "Yes, in certain cases", otherwise there would be no story.

Of course, when the grammar presents alternatives, there must be some decision criterion, which in the case we are examining will always be the inspection of the leftmost character of the remaining source text. If the analyser can choose its target simply by looking at one character, the grammar is said to be LL(1). If k characters were necessary to reach a decision, the grammar would be LL(k). Measurements have shown that this sort of grammar transformation leads to a decrease of a factor of ten in the time spent to analyse relatively simple ALGOL 60 programs, and of course the improvement is exponential with the degree of nesting.

1.3 - Semantics -

As soon as the programmer uses a deterministic method of syntax analysis, it becomes possible to execute semantic routines during the syntax analysis process, thus saving a pass of the source text. This is easily understood in the case of an LL(1) analyser, since we see that when the analyser takes a decision, it is always the 'right' one. It can therefore call those semantic routines that the programmer has indicated, since it is sure of having correctly recognised a situation. Non-deterministic methods do not allow this, since back-tracking, for example, cannot apply to semantics ; alternatively if different routines were associated with two targets in the predictive analyser, it is not possible to decide which to execute.

Foster gives a simple example of the use of semantic functions :

$$\text{Integer} \rightarrow \text{Digit f1 X}$$
$$\text{X} \rightarrow \text{Digit f2 X} \mid \epsilon$$

f1 : result ← value (digit)
f2 : result ← 10*result + value (digit).

We suppose that the value of the integer is to be found in 'result' and that the procedure 'value' decodes the last digit. The addition of the names of semantic functions as a third type of object in the grammar is a technique which will be seen many times during this course. Compiler writers often consider the primary function of a syntax as being that of the skeleton on which they can hang semantics. The form of the semantics is, of course, very variable.

2 - LL(1) CONDITIONS -

We have seen that the analyser for an LL(1) grammar can decide which decision to take at any moment by looking at the leftmost character of the remaining source text. A decision is taken only when the first character of the target is a non-terminal character, and the decision is by which of its possible right-hand sides should the non-terminal be replaced. Thus any one terminal symbol should lead to only one expansion for a given non-terminal, and thus to each expansion corresponds a unique set of terminal symbols, which we will call the director symbols for that expansion.

Consider the following productions for a non-terminal A :

$$A \rightarrow \alpha_1 \mid \alpha_2 \mid \ldots \mid \alpha_n$$

The director symbols for α_i obviously contain all those terminal symbols which can occur at the left of any string generated by α_i. We call this set of symbols the 'starter symbols' of α_i, defined formally as :

$$S(\alpha) = \{a \in V_T \mid \alpha \overset{*}{\rightarrow} a \beta, \beta \in (V_T \cup V_N)^*\}$$

where α is any string (that is to say $\alpha \in (V_T \cup V_N)^*$). The starter symbols do not necessarily form the whole set of director symbols, since α_i can be, or can generate, the empty string, which has no starter symbol. Consider what could happen in this case, after a sequence of expansions starting with the axiom Z :

$$Z \rightarrow \ldots \rightarrow \beta A \delta$$

If A is the front character of the target, $\beta \in V_T^*$, $\delta \in (V_T \cup V_N)^*$.

If the expansion of A is to lead to the empty string, the character at the left of the source text is a starter of δ, and hence the starter set of δ is contained in the director symbols of that expansion of A which leads to the empty string. We note that there can be at most one such expansion, since otherwise the starters of δ would occur in more than one set of director symbols, and the analyser could not then decide which expansion to apply. The starters of all the possible strings which can follow A are called the followers of A :

$$F(A) = \{a \mid Z \rightarrow \beta A \delta, Z \text{ the axiom}, \beta, \delta \in (V_T \cup V_N)^*, a \in S(\delta)\}$$

where A is any non-terminal symbol $(A \in V_N)$.

We can now define the director symbols for the expansion α of a non-terminal A :

$$DS(A, \alpha) = \{a \mid a \in S(\alpha) \underline{\text{ or }} (\alpha \overset{*}{\rightarrow} \epsilon \underline{\text{ and }} a \in F(A))\}$$

We suppose the grammar to be clean throughout this presentation, which means that every non-terminal is accessible from the axiom (can occur in at least one string generated from the axiom) and that every expansion can lead to at least one string which contains no non-terminals.

It is now possible to give the necessary and sufficient condition that a grammar be LL(1), which is that the director symbols corresponding to the different expansions of each non-terminal should form disjoint sets. The justification of this condition is simple :

- the condition is necessary, since if a symbol occurs in two sets of director symbols the analyser can not decide which expansion to apply without further information

- the condition is sufficient, since the analyser can always choose an expansion in terms of the given symbol, and this choice will always be the right one. If the symbol is contained in no set of director symbols, the source text is not in the language and there is an error.

Knuth's original definition gave four conditions, which are equivalent to the one given above. One of the four deserves a little more attention, since it is the one which forbids left recursion. We have already noted that top-down analysers do not accept left recursive grammars ; these are also forbidden by the LL(1) condition, as shown by the following logic :

Consider a set of mutually left-recursive non-terminal symbols (such symbols form obvious closed sets), and in particular one of the symbols which presents alternative expansions (there must be one, otherwise, since the set is mutually left-recursive, the rules concerned cannot generate terminal strings). Consider its expansions:

$$A \rightarrow \alpha_1 \mid \alpha_2 \mid \ldots \mid \alpha_n$$

Suppose α_1 to be the left-recursive expansion. Thus we have

$$A \rightarrow \alpha_1 \overset{*}{\rightarrow} A \beta \rightarrow \alpha_2 \beta \qquad (\beta \in (V_T \cup V_N)^*)$$

then $D\ S(\alpha_1) \subseteq D\ S\ (\alpha_2)$, since $\alpha_1 \overset{*}{\rightarrow} \alpha_2 \beta$.

The director symbols are not disjoint. It is useful to test for left recursion independently of the LL(1) condition in order to avoid loops in the algorithms and also to give more informative error messages to the user.

3 - DECISION ALGORITHM -

The algorithm which decides whether or not a grammar is LL(1) simply deduces the director symbol sets for each expansion of a non-terminal and applies the condition described above. In order to find these sets we must first deduce the starter and follower sets for each non-terminal, together with the information as to whether or not the non-terminal can generate the empty string. It is for this last point that we give the first algorithm.

The algorithm requires a copy of the grammar and a vector V, with one entry per non-terminal in the grammar. The elements of V may take any one of three values : yes, no or undecided, saying whether or not the non-terminal can generate the empty string. We execute the following steps :

1) - Each element of V is initialised to 'undecided'.

2) - During a first pass of the grammar, the following two actions are performed :

a) - If any expansion of a non-terminal is the empty string, the corresponding element of V takes the value 'yes' and all the productions of the non-terminal are eliminated from the grammar.

b) - Any production containing a terminal symbol is eliminated from the grammar. If this action eliminates all the productions of a non-terminal, the corresponding value of V takes the value 'no'.

3) - The grammar is now limited to rules in which the right-hand sides contain only non-terminal symbols. Successive passes of the grammar obey the following actions, in which each symbol of each right-hand side is examined.

a) - If the corresponding entry of V has the value 'yes', the symbol is eliminated. If this leaves the empty string as right-hand side, the non-terminal for which this is an expansion can generate the empty string. The corresponding entry of V becomes 'yes', and the productions of the non-terminal are eliminated.

b) - If the corresponding entry of V has the value 'no', the production is eliminated. If all the productions of a non-terminal are eliminated in this manner, its entry in V takes the value 'no'.

4) If, during a complete pass of the grammar, no entry of V is changed and there are still undecided entries, the algorithm cannot terminate, and the grammar is not LL(1).

We must first of all prove that non-termination of the above algorithm is a sufficient reason to say that the grammar is not LL(1). In fact, in this case, it is both left-recursive and not clean, since there exist a number of pro-ductions consisting only of non-empty non-terminals, which cannot then generate strings which do not contain non-terminals. These productions must also be left recursive since they form a finite set, and thus the left-most members must loop. For any clean grammar we are therefore able to produce the vector V , indicating whether or not the non-terminals can generate the empty string.

The next step is the production of bit matrices which will indicate the starters and followers of each non-terminal. We first consider the starters, which are accumulated in a matrix with two fields:

```
    A  B  ...  Z    a  b    ...        z
A  ┌──────────────┬──────────────────────┐
B  │              │                      │
:  │              │                      │
:  │              │                      │
Z  └──────────────┴──────────────────────┘
```

During a pass of the grammar, the immediate starters are indicated in the matrix, for example, in the following rule:

$$A \;\rightarrow\; B\,c\,D \;|\; e\,f$$

(B, A) and (e, A) are set to 1.

Notice also that if B can generate the empty string (information found in V), c is also a starter of A, and (c, A) takes the value 1, and so on as long as the newly discovered starter is a non-terminal which can generate the empty string. The matrix of immediate starters is of course not sufficient, as is seen in the following trivial example :

$$A \;\rightarrow\; B\,c\,D$$
$$B \;\rightarrow\; b\,X$$

b is a starter of B, and hence a starter of A. The transitive closure of the immediate starter matrix gives us the complete starter matrix required to cal-culate the director symbols.

The complete starter matrix allows an immediate test for left recursion, since a 1
on the principal diagonal of the matrix indicates that a non-terminal is a starter of
itself. It is useful to give this diagnosis immediately to the user of the program.

We will not give details of the transitive closure algorithm in this text ; the
best-known efficient algorithm is described in [Warshall 62]. It is however to be
noted that a better algorithm can be written for this particular case since the
matrix is sparse, and the left-hand half of the matrix is not in fact required
(apart from the principal diagonal), since the tests only need the terminals which
are the starters of each non-terminal [Griffiths 69].

An immediate follower matrix should be produced during the pass over the grammar that
produced the immediate starter matrix. This matrix needs three fields, as is shown by
the following example:

$$A \rightarrow B\ C\ D\ |\ E\ f$$

Immediate deductions are:

- C follows B
- if C can generate the empty string, D follows B
- D follows C
- f follows E.

There is, however, a further problem. Consider a production containing A :

$$X \rightarrow Y\ A\ Z$$

Z follows A. But if we replace A by B C D , we obtain

$$X \rightarrow Y\ B\ C\ D\ Z$$

Z also follows D. Thus, the fact that D is the last symbol of A needs to be kept,
since all followers of A are followers of D (and if D can generate the empty
string, the same is true of C , and so on). The followers matrix has the form:

	A B ... Z	A B ... Z	a b ... z
A			
B			
...			
Z			

In the first field   (X, Y) = 1 means that X follows Y
In the second field   (X, Y) = 1 means that the followers of X are
       followers of Y , that is to say that Y is the last member of
       a production of X .

In the third field (x, Y) = 1 means that x follows Y.

For the first field, X follows Y means that all starters of X are followers of Y ; but these starters are to be found in the complete starter matrix, remembering that we are only interested in terminal starters and followers. Thus the corresponding line of the starters matrix is added into the third field of the followers matrix for each 1 in the first field. We now perform a transitive closure on the second and third fields to obtain a complete follower matrix.

We have now obtained complete starter and follower matrices which allow the calculation of the functions F and S of the preceeding paragraph. These in their turn allow the calculation of the director symbols and the application of the LL(1) condition.

The sets of director symbols are required in the generation of the analyser, since they form the decision criterion. If the condition gave a positive result, the analyser can be directly generated, otherwise the grammar needs modification before accepting it.

4 - PRODUCTION OF AN ANALYSER -

A grammar which is LL(1) allows the use of special forms of analysers. The most important of these is the method of recursive descent [Lucas 61], in which each non-terminal is made into a procedure. The analysis of a non-terminal is a call of the corresponding procedure. For example, consider an LL(1) grammar for the ALGOL 60 Block :

$$
\begin{aligned}
\text{Block} &\to \underline{\text{begin}} \ D \ ; \ X \ S \ Y \ \underline{\text{end}} \\
X &\to D \ ; X \ | \ \epsilon \\
Y &\to \ ; \ S \ Y \ | \ \epsilon
\end{aligned}
$$

A corresponding analyser, using primitives which we will subsequently define, would be the following :

```
ROUTINE BLOCK
        CHECK begin
        CHECK D
        CHECK ;
        CALL  X
        CHECK S
        CALL  Y
        CHECK end
    RETURN
```

```
            ROUTINE  X
                  DECIDE  D ,  11
                  EXIT
            11    CHECK  D
                  CHECK  ;
                  CALL   X
            RETURN

            ROUTINE  Y
                  DECIDE  ; ,  12
                  EXIT
            12    CHECK  ;
                  CHECK  S
                  CALL   Y
            RETURN
```

The different primitives have the following meanings:

ROUTINE   Procedure delimiters.
RETURN

CHECK   Confirms that the current character (the left-most character of the
            source text) is the same as the actual parameter, and moves on one
            character in the source text (hence calling the lexical analyser).
            If the current character does not conform, there is an error.

CALL   Procedure call.

DECIDE   If the current character is the same as the first parameter, then
            branch to the label in the second parameter, otherwise continue with
            the next instruction. The first parameter may be a list, and con-
            tains the starter set for the indicated expansion.

EXIT   Leaves the current procedure. Occurs when one of the expansions can
            generate the empty string, and the current character is not in the
            starter set of any expansion. It is not necessary to confirm that
            the character is in the follower set, since its correctness will be
            confirmed later.

ERROR   If the non-terminal cannot generate the empty string, then EXIT is
            replaced by ERROR at the end of the list of uses of DECIDE.

The procedure for a non-terminal has the following form:

```
ROUTINE    Name
     DECIDE    (Starter set of first expansion), 11
     DECIDE    (Starter set of second expansion), 12
     ...
```

```
        EXIT  or  ERROR    (Name generates the empty string or not)
11    First Expansion
      EXIT
12    Second Expansion
      EXIT
      ...
RETURN
```

The above primitives form a production language for LL(1) analysers. Ignoring the
necessity of character coding, the above form is suitable for rewriting as a set of
macros in any convenient system, the only long macro being CHECK, which obviously needs
to call the lexical analyser. The modern programmer may be shocked by the use of goto,
but he should realize that the analyser is generated by a program from the syntax,
and is never produced by hand. It can of course be written in any language allowing
recursive procedures:

```
        procedure block ;

        begin   check  ('begin') ;
                check  (' D ') ;
                check  (' ; ') ;
                x ;
                check  (' S ') ;
                y ;
                check  ('end')
        end ;

        procedure  x  ;

        begin   if  current character  =  ' D '
                then  begin  check (' D ') ;
                             check (' ; ') ;
                             x
                      end
        end ;
```

and so on. The analyser may also interpret the same information stored as a table,
as a transition diagram or as a transition matrix, using a modification of
[Conway 63].

5 - GRAMMAR TRANSFORMATION -

This section is intended to treat the problem which arises when a grammar is not LL(1) and is thus refused by the algorithm of paragraph 3. We have already seen that it is often possible to rewrite the grammar in a new form, the new grammar being LL(1). It is unfortunate that this process cannot be entirely automated, but help can be given to the user by the techniques which follow.

More formally, this problem can be looked at as one of decidability. While it is decidable whether or not a grammar is LL(1), it is undecidable whether or not a language is LL(1). This means that given an arbitrary grammar, it is not possible in general to say whether or not the grammar describes an LL(1) language [Rosenkrantz 69], and hence it is not possible to write a complete transformation algorithm. However, an algorithm which goes a long way can be written. We consider two different techniques.

5.1 - Elimination of left recursion -

The problem of eliminating left recursions is completely solvable, as was shown theoretically in [Greibach 65]. The practical algorithm given here is that of [Foster 68]. We first note that, in a given grammar, left recursive non-terminals fall into disjoint sets, the members of each set being mutually left recursive. (Obviously, if A is a member of two sets, A is mutually left recursive with all the members of the two sets, which are thus also mutually left recursive, by the transitivity of left recursion). Consider one such set :

$$H = \{X1, X2, \ldots, Xn\}$$

We may rewrite the rules defining the memebers of H in the following form :

$$X_i \rightarrow X1\ \beta_{1j} \mid X2\ \beta_{2j} \mid \ldots \mid Xn\ \beta_{ni} \mid \alpha_i$$

where α_i, $\beta_{ji} \in (V_T \cup V_N)^* \cup \phi$. $\alpha_i \not\Rightarrow Xi\ \delta$.

ϕ is a character which is not in the vocabulary, and thus strings containing ϕ are considered to be non-existent. It may have been necessary to rewrite the grammar to obtain this form, and there would be no loss of generality in rewriting α_i and β_{ji} as non-terminals, that is to say in adding the following rules to the grammar.

$$A_i \rightarrow \alpha_i$$
$$B_{ji} \rightarrow \beta_{ji}$$

The transformation to this 'canonical' form is not always trivial. Consider the following grammar :

$$A \rightarrow B \ A \ | \ ...$$
$$B \rightarrow \epsilon \ | \ ...$$

The left recursion of A must be made apparent. The transformation is, however, always possible, since there are known algorithms for producing ϵ-free grammars [Greibach 65].

The set of rules may be rewritten using the operators of multiplication and addition :

$$Xi = X1 \ B_{1i} + X2 \ B_{2i} + \ ... \ + Xn \ B_{ni} + A_i$$

These equations form a matrix equation :

$$X = X \ B + A$$

where $X = (X1 \ X2 \ ... \ Xn)$
$A = (A_1 \ A_2 \ ... \ A_n)$
$$B = \begin{pmatrix} B_{11} & B_{12} & \cdots & B_{1n} \\ B_{21} & B_{22} & \cdots & B_{2n} \\ \cdots & & & \\ B_{n1} & B_{n2} & \cdots & B_{nn} \end{pmatrix}$$

We may justify the use of these operators by noting that

- Multiplication (in fact concatenation) is associative, and the empty string serves as identity element.

- Addition (choice) is associative and commutative, with ϕ as identity element.

The identity matrix is

$$I = \begin{pmatrix} \epsilon & \phi & \phi & \cdots & \phi \\ \phi & \epsilon & \phi & & \phi \\ \cdots & & & & \\ \phi & \phi & \phi & \cdots & \epsilon \end{pmatrix}$$

with ϵ on the principal diagonal and ϕ elsewhere. A minimal solution of the matrix equation is :

$$X = A \ B^*$$

where $B^* = I + B + B^2 + \ ...$

Putting $Z = B^*$, and noting that $B^* = I + B \ B^*$, we obtain :

$$Z = I + B \ Z$$
$$X = A \ Z$$

Z is a matrix of new non-terminals :

$$Z = \begin{pmatrix} Z_{11} & Z_{12} & \cdots & Z_{1n} \\ Z_{21} & Z_{22} & \cdots & Z_{2n} \\ \cdots & & & \\ Z_{n1} & Z_{n2} & \cdots & Z_{nn} \end{pmatrix}$$

Let us illustrate this by a simple example :

$$P \rightarrow P\ a\ |\ Q\ b\ |\ c$$
$$Q \rightarrow P\ d\ |\ Q\ e\ |\ f$$

Thus :
$$X = (P\ Q)$$
$$A = (c\ f)$$
$$B = \begin{pmatrix} a & d \\ b & e \end{pmatrix}$$
$$Z = \begin{pmatrix} Z_{11} & Z_{12} \\ Z_{21} & Z_{22} \end{pmatrix}$$

The solution is :

$$(P\ Q) = (c\ f) \begin{pmatrix} Z_{11} & Z_{12} \\ Z_{21} & Z_{22} \end{pmatrix}$$

$$\begin{pmatrix} Z_{11} & Z_{12} \\ Z_{21} & Z_{22} \end{pmatrix} = \begin{pmatrix} \epsilon & \phi \\ \phi & \epsilon \end{pmatrix} + \begin{pmatrix} a & d \\ b & e \end{pmatrix} \begin{pmatrix} Z_{11} & Z_{12} \\ Z_{21} & Z_{22} \end{pmatrix}$$

That is to say :

$$P \rightarrow c\ Z_{11}\ |\ f\ Z_{21}$$
$$Q \rightarrow c\ Z_{12}\ |\ f\ Z_{22}$$
$$Z_{11} \rightarrow a\ Z_{11}\ |\ d\ Z_{21}\ |\ \epsilon$$
$$Z_{12} \rightarrow a\ Z_{12}\ |\ d\ Z_{22} \qquad\qquad (\phi \text{ disappears})$$
$$Z_{21} \rightarrow b\ Z_{11}\ |\ e\ Z_{21}$$
$$Z_{22} \rightarrow b\ Z_{12}\ |\ e\ Z_{22}$$

The transformations given here can fail if there exists a non-terminal A such that

$$A \overset{+}{\rightarrow} A$$

A discussion of this so-called 'empty word problem' is to be found in [Salomaa 69]. A reasonable solution to the problem is to reject such grammars, since such conditions are usually due to errors on the part of the compiler writer.

In all the other, 'reasonable' cases, the method has the advantage of not introducing new conflicts of the LL(1) condition, and the example is strictly LL(1). It is to be noted that the general case elimination produces a large number of new rules, and most users of the system prefer to write their grammars without left recursion. However, occasional cases may arise for semantic reasons, and one of these will be examined later.

5.2 - Factorisation and substitution -

The other standard technique which aims at creating LL(1) grammars is that of factorisation and substitution. An example of factorisation was seen in the grammar of an ALGOL block :

$$SL \rightarrow S \mid S ; SL$$

was replaced by

$$SL \rightarrow S Y$$
$$Y \rightarrow \epsilon \mid ; SL$$

Direct factorisation is not always possible:

$$A \rightarrow B C \mid D E$$
$$B \rightarrow b X \mid Z$$
$$D \rightarrow b Y$$

In this case, the expansions of B and D replace the B and D which are the starters of A :

$$A \rightarrow b X C \mid Z C \mid b Y E$$
$$\rightarrow b N \mid Z C$$

where $\quad N \rightarrow X C \mid Y E$

We consider also the following case:

$$A \rightarrow B C \mid D E$$
$$B \rightarrow b X \mid Y$$
$$D \rightarrow B Z$$

Substituting for B and D gives:

$$A \rightarrow b X C \mid Y C \mid B Z E$$

We must again substitute for B :

$$A \rightarrow b X C \mid Y C \mid b X Z E \mid Y Z E$$
$$\rightarrow b N1 \mid Y N2$$

where $\quad N1 \rightarrow X C \mid X Z E$
$$N2 \rightarrow C \mid Z E$$

And once again in N1

$$N1 \rightarrow X \quad N3$$
$$N3 \rightarrow C \mid Z \quad E \qquad \text{(the same as N2)}$$

However, if, in the original form, we had substituted for D only, this would have given:

$$A \rightarrow B \quad C \mid B \quad Z \quad E$$
$$\rightarrow B \quad N$$

where $\quad N \rightarrow C \mid Z \quad E$

which is much more efficient. This example shows that we must consider the order in which substitutions are made. This will be the subject of a subsequent paragraph.

This technique does not always resolve cases of non-disjoint starter sets.
For example:

$$A \rightarrow B \quad X \mid C \quad Y$$
$$B \rightarrow a \quad B \quad X \mid W$$
$$C \rightarrow a \quad C \quad Y \mid W$$

Substituting for B and C we obtain

$$A \rightarrow a \quad B \quad X \quad X \mid W \quad X \mid a \quad C \quad Y \quad Y \mid W \quad Y$$
$$\rightarrow a \quad N1 \mid W \quad N2$$

where $\quad N1 \rightarrow B \quad X \quad X \mid C \quad Y \quad Y$
$$N2 \rightarrow X \mid Y$$

N1 presents the same characteristics as A, except that the expansions are longer, and the algorithm either fails or loops.
Non-disjointness of director symbols is already difficult in the case of starters; in the case of followers it is worse. The obvious solution is to substitute for the non-terminal which can generate the empty string, but this often leads to other conflicts, since the empty string is usually present as a result of factorisation, which is immediately 'undone' by the substitution.

5.2.1 - ORDERING -

The following example showed up the problem of order :

$$A \rightarrow B \quad C \mid D \quad E$$
$$B \rightarrow b \quad X \mid Y$$
$$D \rightarrow B \quad Z$$

Since B is a starter of D, we should substitute for D first. In general, we should substitute first the non-terminal which needs the greater number of generations before reaching the common starter, since it may have the other as starter, but not the opposite. We define a partial ordering R of the non-terminals such that

$$B \in S(D) \Rightarrow R(B) < R(D)$$

Note first that this order always exists if there is no left recursion, since if $B \in S(D)$, $D \notin S(B)$ and $A \in S(B)$, $B \in S(C) \Rightarrow A \in S(C)$. We give an algorithm to find this ordering :

A vector V with one entry per non-terminal indicates whether or not the non-terminal has already been given its rank. The elements of V take the values 'yes' or 'no'.

1) - Initialise every element of V to 'no'

2) - $n \leftarrow 1$

3) - Find a non-terminal N which has no non-terminal starter for which the entry in V is 'no' (there must always be one, by the argument based on the lack of left recursion). $V(N) \leftarrow$ 'yes' ; $R(N) \leftarrow n$; $n \leftarrow n + 1$

4) - Repeat 3) until every element of V is marked 'yes'.

This algorithm can be carried out on the initial starter matrix by searching for an empty row, giving it the next rank and eliminating the corresponding column.

Many classic algorithms depend on orderings of this type, for example the search for precedence functions is a double ordering ; the ordering given here is that which allows transitive closure in a minimum number of steps.

6 - <u>SEMANTIC INSERTION</u> -

Compiler writers consider syntax as the skeleton on which to hang semantics, and in LL(1) directed methods they think of the analysis of a non-terminal as a procedure call (which is in fact its implementation in recursive descent) which has certain semantic results. We consider a number of examples from this point of view.

6.1 - Generation of postfixed notation -

Consider the following grammar of arithmetic expression :

$$
\begin{array}{rl}
E & \rightarrow \ E1 \ | \ E \ + \ E1 \ | \ E \ - \ E1 \\
E1 & \rightarrow \ E2 \ | \ E1 * E2 \ | \ E1 \ / \ E2 \\
E2 & \rightarrow \ Prim \ | \ E2 \ \dagger \ Prim \\
Prim & \rightarrow \ Variable \ | \ Constant \ | \ (\ E \ )
\end{array}
$$

The grammar expresses the priority of the different operators, and also the fact that operators of equal priority apply from left to right (since the grammar is left recursive). Note that this is one case where left recursion is required for semantic reasons, but forebidden for analysis reasons. We will come back to this problem.

We may add the generation of postfixed notation to this grammar very simply:

$$
\begin{array}{rl}
E & \rightarrow \ E1 \ | \ E \ + \ E1 \ f1 \ | \ E \ - \ E1 \ f2 \\
E1 & \rightarrow \ E2 \ | \ E1 * E2 \ f3 \ | \ E1 \ / \ E2 \ f4 \\
E2 & \rightarrow \ Prim \ | \ E2 \ \dagger \ Prim \ f5 \\
Prim & \rightarrow \ Variable \ | \ Constant \ | \ (\ E \ )
\end{array}
$$

f1 : output (+)
f2 : output (-)
f3 : output (*)
f4 : output (/)
f5 : output (↑)

It is supposed that 'variable' and 'constant' output the code corresponding to these operands. To convince the reader of the fact that this does in fact output the equivalent postfixed notation, we note that:

- For each non-terminal E, E1, E2, Prim, the following assertion is true: a call of the non-terminal provokes the output of the corresponding postfixed code.
- Consider, for example, E → E + E1 f1. The grammar is executed by recursive descent. But postfixed notation has the following property:

$$
PF \ (E \ + \ E1) \ = \ PF(E) \ || \ PF(E1) \ || \ +
$$

The sign || stands for concatenation. The calls of the non-terminals have exactly this effect, by the first assertion.

This short example shows up the advantages of the method. The grammar becomes the control structure of this pass of the compiler, and the programmer can express himself in a very compact form. The use of sequences of procedure calls also eliminates the need for an explicit stack, since the position in the grammar is the thing which 'remembers' which operator is applied. While writing the compiler, the programmer should note the semantic result of calling the non-terminal, preferably on the same line.

What should be done about the problem of left recursion? Leaving the semantic functions as they are, consider the grammar which includes their calls. First of all we factorise:

$$
\begin{array}{rcl}
E & \rightarrow & E1 \mid E \quad N1 \\
E1 & \rightarrow & E2 \mid E1 \quad N2 \\
E2 & \rightarrow & Prim \mid E2 \uparrow Prim \quad f5 \\
Prim & \rightarrow & Variable \mid Constant \mid (E) \\
N1 & \rightarrow & + \; E1 \; f1 \mid - \; E1 \; f2 \\
N2 & \rightarrow & * \; E2 \; f3 \mid / \; E2 \; f4
\end{array}
$$

The left recursions are all simple, of the form

$$
A \rightarrow A \; a \mid b
$$

The solution of this type of left recursion is:

$$
\begin{array}{rcl}
A & \rightarrow & b \; X \\
X & \rightarrow & a \; X \mid \epsilon
\end{array}
$$

The grammar becomes:

$$
\begin{array}{rcl}
E & \rightarrow & E1 \quad X1 \\
E1 & \rightarrow & E2 \quad X2 \\
E2 & \rightarrow & Prim \; X3 \\
Prim & \rightarrow & Variable \mid Constant \mid (E) \\
N1 & \rightarrow & + \; E1 \; f1 \mid - \; E1 \; f2 \\
N2 & \rightarrow & * \; E2 \; f3 \mid / \; E2 \; f4 \\
X1 & \rightarrow & N1 \; X1 \mid \epsilon \\
X2 & \rightarrow & N2 \; X2 \mid \epsilon \\
X3 & \rightarrow & \uparrow \; Prim \; f5 \; X3 \mid \epsilon
\end{array}
$$

This grammar has exactly the same semantic properties as the original, but is LL(1). Readers should convince themselves that the grammars have equivalent results by using them as generative grammars.

For each call of a semantic function we generate its name in the text as if it was a non-terminal. But since, in this sense, the two grammars generate the same language, the calls of semantic functions will occur at the same place in the text, and thus will have the same effect.

The new grammar is not very readable, and we should certainly never ask a programmer to write in this form. He should write in the original form, and the transformations will then be accomplished by a grammar transforming program. The transformed grammar should have the same status as the object code produced by a compiler - the user should never see it in other then exceptional circumstances.

It is only fair to indicate a process which would not work as easily, as the method has obvious limitations. If we wanted to produce prefixed notation, this would be more difficult, since the same semantic functions would be differently placed:

$$E \rightarrow E1 \mid f1 \ E + E1 \mid f2 \ E - E1$$

and so on. The factorisation no longer works. It is of course possible to write new semantic functions which generate prefixed notation, but they are considerably more complex. This is not strictly an LL(1) problem, but is due to the fact that the information arrives in the 'wrong' order.

6.2 - Symbol table insertion -

Consider a part of the syntax of ALGOL declarations :

```
Declaration → real Idlist f3 | integer Idlist f4 | ...
Idlist      → Id f1 Idrest
Idrest      → , Id f2 Idrest | ε
```

The grammar is written directly in LL(1) form ; we could have used left recursion. The corresponding semantic functions use the list processing primitives cons, hd and tl (these last two are called car and cdr in other languages) :

```
f1 : list ←   cons (last id, null)
f2 : list ←   cons (last id, list)
f3 : while  list ≠ null  do
     begin   put symbol table (real, hd(list), next displacement);
             list ← tl(list) ;
             next displacement ← next displacement + length of a real
     end
f4 : like f3 but with integer
```

'next displacement' is the next address that can be used for variables in the run-time storage model. Symbol table entries are supposed to be triplets of (type, name, run-time address). (See chapters 3.B, 3.D).

6.3 - Interpretation of postfixed expressions -

Grammars may be used to drive other passes of the compiler, and not only the input phase. Consider the following grammar for postfixed expressions :

```
        Ex  →  Ex  Ex  Binop  f2  |  Ex Unop  f3  |  Operand  f1
        Binop  →  +b  f4  |  -b  f5  |  * f6  |  ...
        Unop  →  +u  f4  |  -u  f5
   f1:  push  (value (last operand))
   f2:  pull  (second value) ;
        pull  (first value) ;
        case  i  of  begin    plus:  push (first value  +  second value) ;
                              minus:  push (first value  -  second value) ;
                       ...

                 end

   f3:  case  i  of  begin  plus :  ;
                            minus :  push ( - pull)
                 end

   f4:  i  ←  1
   f5:  i  ←  2
   f6:  ...
```

This is, of course, a highly artificial example, since it does not do type manipulation, but the idea is frequently used. '+b' and '+u' are the binary and unary addition operators, 'i' is present merely as an index to the case statement.

The above grammar is heavily left recursive, so for completeness we give the result of transforming this grammar to LL(1) form. The transformation would again, of course, be done by use of the transforming program.

```
        Ex  →   Operand  f1  X1
        X1  →   N1  X1  | ∈
        N1  →   Ex  Binop  f2  |  Unop  f3
        Binop  →   +b  f4  |  -b  f5  |  * f6  |  ...
        Unop  →   +u  f4  |  -u  f5
```

7 - GENERALISATION AND CONCLUSION -

This type of methodology forms the basis of most compiler-compiler construction, and will be talked about at a later stage during the course (chapter 4). We will thus restrict ourselves here to remarks of a strictly syntactic nature.

7.1 - Vienna Notation -

Classical Backus-Naur form [Backus 60] has been generalised in many directions. A simple improvement which eliminates many formal problems is that used in the Vienna language description documents [Alber 68]. In particular, the use of bracketing and of the repetition operator menas that the user writes many less recursive rules and also that the empty string requires less special treatment. For example, the example grammar of block used above might be written :

$$\text{Block} \quad \underline{\text{begin}} \; [\text{D} \; ;]^* \quad S \; \{; \; S\}^* \quad \underline{\text{end}}$$

The asterisk is the repetition operator, square brackets indicating that their contents must occur at least once and curly brackets that their contents may or may not be present. The unnecessary recursion has been replaced by iteration. [Bordier 71] shows how this notation may be transformed into an LL(1) analyser allowing recursive descent. The rule for block could generate :

```
procedure block ;
begin check ('begin') ;
        repeat D ;
               check (';')
        until current character ∉ starter set (D) ;
        S ;
        while current character = ';' do
        begin check (' ;) ;
               S
        end ;
        check ('end')
end
```

This is an example of a formalism which mirors more exactly the way in which we conceive things and which is more convenient than an artificial one. In this case, the programmer thinks of 'list of declarations', where 'list of' is in fact a repetition operator. Writing recursive rules does not express the concept in the same way.

7.2 - LL(k) Grammars -

We noted in the introduction that a recursive descent analyser could use k characters in order to make a decision, instead of using only one character. This generalisation is to 'strong LL(k)' grammars [Rosenkrantz 69], since LL(k) grammars in general are defined in a way analogous to LR(k) grammars (see chapter 2.c), and allow the analyser to take the past history of the analysis into account. Neither LL(k) nor strong LL(k) methods have been used in practice, although strong LL(k) grammars could be useful and not too inefficient. The following theorems are important in this respect :

- $\forall$ k $\geq$ 1, $\exists$ a language which is LL(k+1) and not LL(k) [Kurki-Suonio 69].

- $\forall$ k $\geq$ 2, $\exists$ grammars which are LL(k) and not strong LL(k) [Rosenkrantz 69]. For example, the following grammar is LL(2) and not strong LL(2) :

$$Z \rightarrow S \dashv \dashv$$
$$S \rightarrow X \mid b \: X \: a$$
$$X \rightarrow a \mid \epsilon$$

- All LL(1) grammars are strong LL(1), and hence there is no need to keep the history of the analysis in this particular case.

- All LL(k) languages are strong LL(k) [Rosenkrantz 69].

- The grammar transformation which deduces a strong LL(k) grammar which generates the same language as a given LL(k) grammar is known [Griffiths 74].

We see that the generalisation to strong LL(k) techniques allows the method of recursive descent to be applied to a wider class of languages. It is not, however, useful to go to general LL(k), since the analyser would be less efficient without a corresponding increase in the set of languages accepted. It is worth while repeating that, for the moment, this discussion is strictly academic, given that only LL(1) has been used in practice, and that there is no difference between LL(1) and strong LL(1).

8 - PRACTICAL RESULTS -

LL(1) analysers have been used to drive working compilers for a variety of languages since 1966. They are thus part of the scenery and have shown themselves to be extremely efficient, able to cope with the usual set of programming languages, and a practical proposition as for as inserting semantics is concerned. The first compiler-compiler based on the technique was that of [Foster 68] and it was used to implement a language called CORAL 66 [Currie 67] [Woodward 70].

To give some idea of space-time requirements, we quote figures from analysers used in conversational compilers for ALGOL60 and PL/1 [Berthaud 73]. The figures are for the executable modules produced from the macros of paragraph 4 by the IBM 360 assembleur, and include calls of semantic functions, but not the text of the functions. The ALGOL analyser occupied about 4 1/2 K characters, and the PL/1 about 12 K. Semantic calls amount to about 20 % of the text. In a batch environment on the 360 model 65 the PL/1 front end can process over 30 000 cards a minute. Since a large proportion of this time is spent in lexical analysis and semantic functions, the analyser was then running at over 100 000 cards a minute. These figures are, of course, approximate.

Using interpretable code instead of an executable text has the effect, on the 360, of dividing space requirements by a factor of two, and increasing analysis time by a factor of 1.5. All the figures can be improved upon by the use of known, simple optimisation techniques, but this has never been necessary in our experience.

K. ALBER - P. OLIVA - G. URSCHLER
Concrete Syntax of PL/1
IBM Vienna Laboratory, TR 25.084, 1968

J.W. BACKUS et al
Report on the Algorithmic Language ALGOL 60
CACM, Vol.3, N° 5, May 1960

M. BERTHAUD - M. GRIFFITHS
Incremental Compilation and Conversational Interpretation
Ann. Rev. in Aut. Prog., 7, 1973

J. BORDIER
Methodes pour la mise au point de grammaires LL(1)
Thesis, University of Grenoble, 1971

M.E. CONWAY
Design of a Separable Transition Diagram Compiler
CACM, Vol.6, N°7, July 1963

I.F. CURRIE, M. GRIFFITHS
A Self-Transferring Compiler
R.R.E. Malvern, Memo 2358, 1957

J.M. FOSTER
A Syntax Improving Device
Computer Journal, May 1968

S.A. GREIBACH
Formal Parsing Systems
CACM, Vol.7, N°8, Aug. 1964

S.A. GREIBACH
A New Normal Form Theorem for Context-Free Phrase Structure Grammars
JACM, 12, pps. 42-52, 1965

M. GRIFFITHS
Analyse Déterministe et Compilateurs
Thesis, University of Grenoble, Oct. 1969

M. GRIFFITHS - G. TERRINE
Submitted for publication, 1974

D.E. KNUTH
Top-Down Syntax Analysis
Acta Informatica, Vol.1, pp. 79-110, 1971

R. KURKI-SUONIO
Notes on Top-Down Languages
BIT 9, N° 3, 1969

P. LUCAS
Die Struckturanalyse vom Formelübersetzen
Elektron. Rechenanl. 3, 1961

D.J. ROSENKRANTZ, R.E. STEARNS
Properties of Deterministic Top-Down Grammars
ACM Symposium, Marina del Rey, 1969

A. SALOMAA
Theory of Automata
Pergamon, 1969

S. WARSHALL
A Theorem on Boolean Matrices
JACM, Vol.9, N°1, Jan. 1962

P.M. WOODWARD - P.R. WETHERALL - B. GORMAN
Official Definition of CORAL 66
H.M.S.O. London, 1970

Chapter 2.C.

LR GRAMMARS AND ANALYSERS

J. J. Horning

University of Toronto
Toronto, CANADA

1.   *INTUITIVE DESCRIPTION*

This chapter is concerned with a family of deterministic parsing techniques based on
a method first described by Knuth [1965]. These parsers, and the grammars acceptable
to them, share most of the desirable properties of the LL(k) family [Chapter 2.B.].
In addition, the class of LR(k)-parsable grammars is probably the largest class
accepted by any currently practical parsing technique. The techniques with which we
are mostly concerned are, in order of increasing power, LR(0), SLR(1), LALR(1) and
LR(1). Collectively, we call these four techniques the LR family [McKeeman 1970]
[Aho 1974].

Until recently, LR parsing techniques have not been as widely used as theoretically
less attractive methods. Early presentations of the method made the theory seem
forbiddingly difficult, although readable presentations are now appearing (e.g.,
[Aho 1974]). More seriously, direct implementations of Knuth's original method were
very inefficient, and the approach was not practically useful until a number of
optimizations were discovered (e.g., [Aho 1972 a, b] [Anderson 1973] [DeRemer 1971]
[Joliat 1973] [Pager 1970]). Now, however, LR is becoming the method of choice in a
large number of situations.

1.1.   DEFINITION OF LR(k)

Informally, a grammar is LR(k) if each sentence that it generates can be deterministically parsed in a single scan from left to right with at most k symbols of "lookahead."
This means that each reduction needed for the parse must be detectable on the basis of
left context, the reducible phrase itself, and the k terminal symbols to its right.
By contrast, LL(k) parsers must select the production to be used in a reduction on
the basis of left context, and the first k terminal symbols of the reducible phrase
combined with its right context. Thus, LR(k) parsers defer decisions until after
complete reducible phrases are found (a characteristic of "bottom-up" parsers), while
LL(k) parsers must predictively select a production on the basis of its first few
symbols. Both techniques share the property of using complete left context in making
decisions - a characteristic commonly associated with "top-down" parsers.

It is easily seen that any LL(k) grammar is also LR(k). It is less obvious that for
each k there are LR(1) grammars that are not LL(k). As we will see in Section 7.,
LR(1) also strictly dominates most other deterministic parsing methods, including the
widely-used precedence techniques.

1.2.   ITEMS

To talk about what happens within an LR parser, we need a notation for partly
recognized productions. An _item_ (also sometimes called a _configuration_) is a production
with a distinguished position in its right hand side. (Our usual notation will be to
place a period at the distinguished position.) If the productions are numbered, then
we can denote an item by a pair of integers [p,j], where p is the number of the
production and j is the number of the distinguished position.

For example, given the grammar

```
1    Block = 'begin' Declarations ';' Statements 'end' ;
2    Declarations = Dec
3                 | Declarations ';' Dec ;
4    Statements = St
5                 | St ';' Statements
```

We have the following correspondences

    [2,0]   Declarations = . Dec

    [2,1]   Declarations = Dec .

    [3,2]   Declarations = Declarations ';' . Dec

We will associate the following meaning to the use of an item [p,j] at some point in the parse:

The information collected so far is consistent with the possibility that production p will be used at this point in the parse, and that the first j symbols of p have already been recognised.

1.3. STATES

A _state_ is a collection of information about the progress of a parse, and may be represented by a set of items. LR parsing is based on the observation that for each LR grammar only a finite number of states need to be distinguished to permit successful parsing, and that all transitions between states (corresponding to parsing actions) may be tabulated in advance. Recall the example (Chapter 2.B., Section 1.1.) of parsing the sentence

    begin Dec ; Dec ; St ; St end

We start (see Figure 1.3.) in the state {[1,0]} = {Block = .'begin' Declarations ';' Statements 'end'}, which means that we expect the first production to apply, but that none of it has yet been recognized. We may immediately recognize the 'begin', and move to a new state containing the item [1,1] to record that fact, as well as [2,0] and [3,0] to record the possibility of starting either of those productions. Since the Dec at the head of the remaining text is consistent only with continuation of the [2,0] item, we move to a new state containing only the item [2,1].

Now we have a new situation: the item [2,1] (or Declarations = Dec.) indicates that we have recognized the complete right hand side of production 2. In general, any item with the period on the right - called a _completed item_ - corresponds to a possible reduction, in this case the replacement of Dec by Declarations. After the replacement the consistent items become [1,2] and [3,1].

In Figure 1.3. we have labelled each state in the stack by the terminal or non-terminal symbol whose recognition caused us to move to that state. Such labels are not a necessary part of the state, but simplify the process of understanding the progress of the parse. We have also indicated in the right-hand column the parsing action to which the various transitions correspond.

2.   INTERPRETING LR TABLES

Each LR parser has a <u>parsing action table</u> that controls its operation. Information about the parse is saved in a <u>state stack</u>, and at each step the next parsing action is selected on the basis of the top element of the state stack and the next symbol in the input. A parsing action may either consume one symbol from the input and place a new state on the stack (a <u>shift</u> action), or it may replace some of the top stack entries by a new state and signal a reduction (a <u>reduce</u> action).

2.1.   FORM OF ENTRIES

The parsing action table can be represented in many different ways. A simple (but not very efficient) representation of a parsing action table is shown in Figure 2.1. Each state is represented by a row of a matrix, each (terminal or nonterminal) symbol by a column. For any given combination of top state and input symbol the parsing

Stack			Remaining text	Action

1.   {[1,0]}   begin Dec; Dec; S; S end   Shift

2. begin   {[1,1][2,0][3,0]}   Dec; Dec; S; S end

          {[1,0]}   Shift

3. Dec   {[2,1]}   ; Dec; S; S end

   begin   {[1,1][2,0][3,0]}

          {[1,0]}   Reduce 2

4. Declarations {[1,2][3,1]}   ; Dec: S; S end

   begin   {[1,1] 2,0][3,0]}

               {[1,0]}   Shift

5. ;   {[1,3][3,2][2,0][3,0]}   Dec; S; S end

   Declarations {[1,2][3,1]}

   begin   {[1,1][2,0][3,0]}

               {[1,0]}

Figure 1.3.

	Name	Block	Declar-ations	State-ments	Dec	St	;	begin	end	$\perp$
1.	Initial	Halt						S2		
2.	begin		S5		S3					
3.	Dec						R2			
4.	Dec						R3			
5.	Declarations						S6			
6.	;			S9	S4	S8				
7.	;			S10		S8				
8.	St						S7		R4	
9.	Statements								S11	
10.	Statements								R5	
11.	end									R1

Figure 2.1.

action is found at the intersection of the corresponding row and column.

Entries take one of four forms:
- blank entries correspond to errors
- S entries correspond to shift actions
- R entries correspond to reduce actions
- Halt entries correspond to completion of parsing.

When the parser has looked up the next action
- if it is an error entry, recovery (described in Chapter 5.D.) is initiated.
- if it is a shift entry, the input symbol is discarded and the state number following the S is pushed into the state stack. (This will always be a state whose name is the same as the discarded input symbol.)
- if it is a reduce entry, the production whose number follows the R is determined. A number of states equal to the length of the right side of this production is popped (the names of these states will be precisely the right side of the production) and then the left side of the production will be treated as though it were the input symbol (the new action will always be a shift or halt - the net effect is to replace states named by the right side of the production by a single state named by the left side).
- if it is a halt entry, the parser quits.

Notice that Figure 2.1. contains an extra column for the symbol '$\bot$', which does not appear in the grammar. This is a special "end of input" symbol, whose insertion we will discuss later.

2.2   EXAMPLE

Consider the LR parsing action table given in Figure 2.1. and our familiar sentence
        begin Dec ; Dec; St ; St end
Starting from state 1 we have the following sequence of stacks, input symbols, and actions:

state	Name	input symbol	action
1	Initial	begin	S2
2	begin	Dec	S3
1	Initial		
3	Dec	;	R2
2	begin		
1	Initial		

state	name	input symbol	action
2	begin	Declarations	S5
1	Initial		
5	Declarations	;	S6
2	begin		
1	Initial		
6	;	Dec	S4
5	Declarations		
2	begin		
1	Initial		
4	Dec	;	R3
6	;		
5	Declarations		
2	begin		
1	Initial		
2	begin	Declarations	S5
1	Initial		
5	Declarations	;	S6
2	begin		
1	Initial		
6	;	St	S8
5	Declarations		
2	begin		
1	Initial		
8	St	;	S7
6	;		
5	Declarations		
2	begin		
1	Initial		

state	name	input symbol	action
7	;	St	S8
8	St		
6	;		
5	Declarations		
2	begin		
1	Initial		
8	St	end	R4
7	;		
8	St		
6	;		
5	Declarations		
2	begin		
1	Initial		
7	;	Statements	S10
8	St		
6	;		
5	Declarations		
2	begin		
1	Initial		
10	Statements	end	R5
7	;		
8	St		
6	;		
5	Declarations		
2	begin		
1	Initial		
6	;	Statements	S9
5	Declarations		
2	begin		
1	Initial		
9	Statements	end	S11
6	;		
5	Declarations		
2	begin		
1	Initial		

state	name	input symbol	action
11	end	$\bot$	R1
9	Statements		
6	;		
5	Declarations		
2	begin		
1	Initial		
1	Initial	Block	Halt

3.   CONSTRUCTING LR TABLES

If we can construct a parsing action table whose entries have all the following
properties
- error entries can never be encountered while parsing correct sentences,
- each shift entry specifies a state named by the input symbol,
- each reduce entry is only reached when the top states on the stack are named
  by precisely the symbols in its right hand side,
- halt entries can only be reached when the parse is complete,

then it should be obvious that an LR parser (operating in the manner described in the
previous section) will correctly parse any correct sentence, and detect at least one
error in each invalid one.

What is not so obvious is how to construct a table with all those properties. A
variety of algorithms have been developed to construct LR tables from grammars.
Although they differ in detail, they are all based on the same principles. We
describe first one of the simplest, the LR(0) algorithm, and then briefly sketch
various modifications to remove some of its inadequacies.

3.1.   THE LR(0) CONSTRUCTOR ALGORITHM

The LR(0) constructor works with states that are simply sets of items. After
initialization, it constructs the complete set of states that can be encountered
during a parse, by means of alternate "successor" and "closure" operations; finally
the parsing action table is derived from the items in the states (after which the
items themselves may be discarded).

3.1.1.   INITIALIZATION

First, the grammar is augmented with a new production 0 G' = G '$\perp$'; where G is the
goal symbol of the grammar. This explicitly brings the terminator symbol '$\perp$' into
the language, and gives us a starting point. The initial state starts with the item
[0,0], corresponding to the fact that production 0 will be used, but initially
nothing has been recognized.

3.1.2.   CLOSURE

If the distinguished point in an item precedes a nonterminal symbol, then each of the
productions for that nonterminal become possibilities at that point, and should be
included (with j = 0, since no part of them has yet been recognized) in any state
containing that item. The <u>closure</u> of a set of items is the result of repeatedly
applying this process until no new items are added. For example, given the grammar
of Section 1.1., the closure of {[0,0]} is {[0,0][1,0]}, the closure of {[1,1]} is
{[1,1][2,0][3,0]} and the closure of {[1,3][3,2]} is {[1,3][3,2][4,0][5,0]}.

3.1.3   SUCCESSOR STATES

The shift action moves from one state to a successor by "absorbing" a single symbol.
Only items in which the distinguished position immediately precedes the input symbol
remain viable, and the successor state will contain each of these items with the
distinguished position advanced by one ("the period moved across the input symbol").
We compute the <u>core</u> of the successor state for each symbol as this set of advanced
items; the state itself is the closure   of the core. For example, the state
{[1,3][3,2][4,0][5,0]} = {Block = 'begin' Declarations ';'. Statements 'end';
Declarations = Declarations ';'. Dec; Statements = . St ; Statements = . St ';'
Statements} has as the core of its St-successor the set {[4,1][5,1]} = {Statements
= St.; Statements = St. ';' Statements} and the core of its Statements-successor is
{[1,4]} = {Block = 'begin' Declarations ';' Statements . 'end'}

3.1.4   ACCESSIBLE STATES

Starting from the initial state we calculate the cores of each of its successors and
then complete them. These are the states that are directly accessible from the
initial state. The process is repeated until no new accessible states are found.
(States are distinct if and only if their cores are different.) Since, for any
grammar, there are only a finite number of items, there is also a finite bound on
the number of states. Therefore the process must terminate with a finite set of
accessible states, which are the only ones that can be encountered during the parse

of a correct sentence. Figure 3.1.4. shows the complete set of accessible states for our running example.

Core	Closure
{[0,0]}	{[0,0][1,0]}
{[1,1]}	{[1,1][2,0][3,0]}
{[2,1]}	{[2,1]}
{[3,3]}	{[3,3]}
{[1,2][3,1]}	{[1,2][3,1]}
{[1,3][3,2]}	{[1,3][3,2][4,0][5,0]}
{[5,2]}	{[5,2][4,0][5,0]}
{[4,1][5,1]}	{[4,1][5,1]}
{[1,4]}	{[1,4]}
{[5,3]}	{[5,3]}
{[1,5]}	{[1,5]}

Figure 3.1.4

3.1.5.   DERIVING THE PARSING ACTION TABLE

To convert the set of accessible states to a parsing action table is now straight-forward. For convenience, we number the states, and create a row of the action table for each state. The shift action corresponding to each successor state can most easily be entered in the appropriate column as the accessible states themselves are being calculated. The halt action is placed in the row of the initial state and the column of the goal symbol. After the reduce entries have been filled in, the remaining (blank) entries may all be treated as error entries.

Reduce entries are placed in rows whose states contain completed items. The various algorithms in the LR family differ primarily in the selection of the columns in which the reduce entries are placed. The LR(0) algorithm uses a particularly simple rule: place them in all columns headed by terminals. This rule is adequate for states that consist of a single item (the completed one), called LR(0) reduce states.

If a state has uncompleted items as well as the completed one, the LR(0) rule will cause some columns to have both shift and reduce entries (a shift-reduce conflict); if it has two or more completed items, terminal columns will have multiple reduce entries (a reduce-reduce conflict). States with either kind of conflict are called inadequate, because they do not lead to the generation of unambiguous parsing action tables. In our example, the state {[4,1][5,1]} = {Statements = St. ; Statements =

St. ';' Statements } is inadequate, because when the input symbol is ';' we do not know whether to shift or to reduce by production 4.

If there are no inadequate states, then the LR(0) constructor has succeeded and the grammar is said to be LR(0). Very few grammars for programming languages actually are LR(0), and it is generally necessary to resolve some inadequacies by one of the techniques described in the next section. However, most programming languages seem to be "almost" LR(0) in that only a small fraction of the states are actually inadequate. The LR(0) constructor thus provides a useful first approximation to the parsing action table.

3.2.   ADDING LOOKAHEAD

The inadequate state of our example is inadequate only because of our simple rule for placing reduce entries in the table. Simple inspection of the grammar shows that in a canonical parse reduction by Statements = St is only appropriate when the input symbol is 'end'. However, it is not always so simple to resolve conflicts and we need some more general mechanism for determining the columns in which to place reduce entries. In this section we will discuss a variety of such techniques.

3.2.1.   USING THE FOLLOWER MATRIX

Each reduce action places the nonterminal that is the left side of its production on top of the stack. If the input symbol cannot validly follow the nonterminal, then an error will be detected immediately after the reduction - thus, there was no real reason to have the reduce entry in that column of the parsing action table.

The SLR(1) constructor [DeRemer 1971] replaces the LR(0) rule for reduce entries by the more restrictive: for each completed item place reduce entries only in the columns of terminal symbols that are valid followers of the left side of the corres-ponding production. (An algorithm for computing the follower matrix was given in Chapter 2.B.3.) If the SLR(1) constructor removes all shift-reduce and reduce-reduce conflicts from the parsing action table, then the grammar is SLR(1). Note that we can apply the SLR rule to all completed items, or just to inadequate states, resulting in different parsing action tables, but not changing the class of SLR(1) grammars.

SLR(1) handles many more grammars (including our running example) than does LR(0). It is probably an adequate class of grammars for describing programming languages. The remaining refinements to be described do not greatly extend the class of acceptable grammars, but are somewhat more in the spirit of LR techniques. (By more carefully restricting the number of reduce entries they may also lead to smaller tables.)

3.2.2   USING THE SHIFT ENTRIES

For each state with a completed item it is possible to use the shift entries in the table to determine the state(s) that will be entered after a reduce action. Any columns of that state that contain only error entries should not have reduce entries in the original state. The problem is complicated by the possibility of encountering further reduce entries, but it is possible to construct an algorithm to trace through the parsing action table and find the minimum set of valid reduce entries for each completed item [Lalonde 1971]. If this algorithm succeeds the grammar is said to be LALR(1).

3.2.3.   ADDING CONTEXT TO ITEMS

The original LR(k) constructor algorithm [Knuth 1965], of which the LR(0) constructor is a special case, carries k symbols of right context with each item. For LR(1) this means that each item is augmented by a <u>lookahead set</u> of symbols that may validly be the input symbol when the item is completed. For example, the item [5,3], that may be validly followed by ';' and 'end' is denoted ([5,3] {';', 'end'}).

Recall that the items in an accessible state get there in two ways; they are either part of the core, arising from successor calculations, or they are added by closure. We must define the treatment of items in both cases. The first case is extremely simple - the symbols that may validly follow an item are unchanged by the successor operation, so the lookahead sets are carried over unchanged.

The second case is more subtle. If we add a new item (with j = 0), the symbols that may validly follow its completion may come either from the tail of the item that caused it to be generated, or (if the tail can produce the empty string) from the lookahead set of that item. We thus require the starter set and empty string computations of Chapter 2.B.3. to calculate closures. Items within a state with the same [p,j] but distinct lookahead sets are combined, and given the union of the lookahead sets.

In computing the set of accessible states, the lookahead sets may be treated in two different ways. If states with distinct lookahead sets are treated as distinct, the LR(1) algorithm results; if states are treated as distinct only if the LR(0) states are distinct, and the union of lookahead sets is taken when states are merged, then the result is equivalent to the LALR(1) algorithm previously described.

4. REPRESENTING LR TABLES

4.1. MATRIX FORMS

Thus far we have kept our parsing action tables in a very simple matrix form, for ease of comprehension. Although table lookup in a simple states x symbols matrix can be very efficient, programming language grammars may lead to tables with hundreds of states and symbols, and the space to store such a table may be a significant fraction of the total size of the compiler. In the next section we discuss an alternative form of the table, and in the following section a number of techniques that can be used to reduce the memory requirements of either form.

4.2. LIST FORM

Although it may not be obvious from our small example, large parsing action tables are typically very sparse, and various sparse matrix representations may be tried. One very useful form is to store lists of the non-error entries, organised either by rows or by columns. These two alternate forms of Figure 2.1. are shown in Figure 4.2.1.

Frequently, a pseudo-program notation that is equivalent to listing the terminal columns by row and the nonterminal columns by column is employed (cf. [Aho 1974]). Our example grammar is shown in this notation in Figure 4.2.2.

By Rows			By Columns		
State	Symbol	Action	Symbol	State	Action
1	Block	Halt	Block	1	Halt
	begin	S2	Declarations	2	S5
2	Declarations	S5	Statements	6	S9
	Dec	S3		7	S10
3	;	R2	Dec	2	S3
4	;	R3		6	S4
5	;	S6	St	6	S8
6	Statements	S9		7	S8
	Dec	S4	;	3	R2
	St	S8		4	R3
7	Statements	S10		5	S6
	St	S8		8	S7
8	;	S7	begin	1	S2
	end	R4	end	8	R4
9	end	S11		9	S11
10	end	R5		10	R5
11	⊥	R1	⊥	11	R1

Figure 4.2.1

by states

```
 1:  if Input = 'begin' then Shift (2) else Error
 2:  if Input = Dec then Shift (3) else Error
 3:  if Input = ';' then Reduce (2) else Error
 4:  if Input = ';' then Reduce (3) else Error
 5:  if Input = ';' then Shift (6) else Error
 6:  if Input = Dec then Shift (4)
       else if Input = St then Shift (8) else Error
 7:  if Input = St then Shift (8) else Error
 8:  if Input = ';' then Shift (7)
       else if Input = 'end' then Reduce (4) else Error
 9:  if Input = 'end' then Shift (11) else Error
10:  if Input = 'end' then Reduce (5) else Error
11:  if Input = ' ' then Reduce (1) else Error
```

by symbols

```
Block : if Stacktop = 1 then Halt else Error
Declarations : Shift (5)
Statements :  if Stacktop = 6 then Shift (9)
                else if Stacktop = 7 then Shift (10)
```

Figure 4.2.2.

4.3. EFFICIENCY TRANSFORMATIONS

There are many things that we can do to our parsing action tables, either to speed up parsing or to reduce the amount of storage required. This section discusses a few of the possible transformations that seem to be among the most effective. Some depend only on properties of the tables, and hence can be applied to any representations; others exploit properties of particular representations.

4.3.1. LR(0) REDUCE STATES

States that consist of a single completed configuration have the same reduce entry in all non-blank columns. At the cost of a slight delay in error detection (not involving reading another symbol), we can replace these LR(0) reduce rows by constants associated with the state. Better yet, by creating a new "shift-reduce" form of entry in the table we can replace all references to LR(0) reduce states in the table, quite typically effecting a 25-40% reduction in the number of states (and, in matrix form, in the size of the table). Figure 4.3.1. shows Figure 4.2.1. transformed to this form.

By Rows			By Columns		
State	Symbol	Action	Symbol	State	Action
1	Block	Halt	Block	1	Halt
	begin	S2	Declarations	2	S5
2	Declarations	S5	Statements	6	S9
	Dec	SR2		7	SR5
5	;	S6	Dec	2	SR2
6	Statements	S9		6	SR3
	Dec	SR3	St	6	S8
	St	S8		7	S8
7	Statements	SR5	;	5	S6
	St	S8		8	S7
8	;	S7	begin	1	S2
	end	R4	end	8	R4
9	end	SR1		9	SR1

Figure 4.3.1.

4.3.2. COLUMN REGULARITIES

All the shift entries in a column refer to states named by the symbol heading that column, a small fraction of the total. If states are sorted by name (and there is no reason for them not to be) then the shift entry for a given row need only select the correct state out of the small set of states with that name. Typically, this allows us to reduce the number of bits used to encode state numbers from around 8 to around 2.

4.3.3. ROW REGULARITIES

The number of distinct reduce entries in a row is generally small (usually 0 or 1). We may move the actual production numbers over to the margin to cut the width of reduce entries in the matrix.

4.3.4. DON'T CARES

By analysis, we can show that some of the error entries in the parsing action table will never be encountered, even in attempts to parse incorrect sentences. In particular, note that all blank entries in the nonterminal columns are really "don't cares" and could be replaced by anything. In particular, if a column contains no error entries, we can replace all the "don't cares" by the common entry, and then replace all occurrences of that entry in the column list by an else entry at the end of the list.

4.3.5.   COLUMN REDUCTION

If all the differences between two columns involve a "don't care" in one or the other of
them, then the two columns may be merged just by replacing the "don't cares." This
transformation is greatly facilitated by the transformation of Section 4.3.2. Note
that the freedom to re-number states may easily be exploited to make more mergers
possible.

4.3.6.   ROW REDUCTION

The preceding transformations will generally leave us with rows that differ only in
"don't care" positions, which can be combined for a further reduction in space. All
of these transformations are detailed by Anderson et al. [1973].

4.3.7.   LIST OVERLAPPING

It is generally the case that many of the lists formed in a list representation
contain identical sublists. By using a pointer plus length representation for lists,
and carefully ordering the elements, reductions in space by a factor of two or three
are generally possible [Lalonde 1971].

4.3.8.   MATRIX FACTORING

As we mentioned earlier, the matrix form of tables is generally preferred for fast
lookup. Joliat [1973] has taken the approach of retaining the matrix form, but
factoring it into a number of special-purpose matrices (e.g., a Boolean matrix that
merely indicates error entries). Although this initially multiplies the space
requirement, the new matrices mostly have very simple forms with many "don't care"
entries. By applying the various transformations seperately to each matrix, a very
compact form can be obtained. The LR parsers constructed by his techniques are
probably about as small and fast as any available table-driven parsers.

4.3.9.   ELIMINATING SINGLE PRODUCTIONS

For syntactic reasons, grammars for programming languages frequently contain productions
of the form X = Y, i.e., in which the right side is a single symbol. Furthermore,
these single productions do not generally have any semantic actions associated with
them, so that performing the corresponding reduction during a parse is pure waste motion.
Single productions may be eliminated from the parsing action table by replacing each
such reduce action in the table by the action that will be taken after the reduction.
The conditions under which this transformation preserves the correctness of the parser

are discussed by Aho and Ullman [1973]. This transformation typically doubles the speed of the parser [Anderson 1973].

5. *PROPERTIES OF LR GRAMMARS AND ANALYSERS*

LR analysers, and the grammars for which they can be constructed, have many desirable properties, some of which are shared by LL(1) grammars. This section reviews several of these properties that are of importance to compiler-writers, although formal proofs are not given (but see [Aho 1972, 1973]).

The first important property of the LR family is the existence of computationally feasible <u>constructor algorithms</u> for LR(0), SLR(1), LALR(1), and LR(1) (in increasing order of cost). These algorithms can construct a parsing action table for any given grammar and determine whether it contains any inadequate states. Computation times for typical programming language grammars range from a few seconds to a few minutes.

The next property is that each constructor algorithm is also a <u>decision algorithm</u> that determines whether the grammar is in the corresponding class. Each of the classes of LR grammars is <u>unambiguous</u>, so all ambiguous grammars are rejected. Each class also rejects some unambiguous grammars, but in practice (except for LR(0)) almost all rejections are for ambiguity. Since no general test for ambiguity is possible [Aho 1972], the various LR tests are about as good as we can do, and are often used to "debug" ambiguous grammars even when some other parsing algorithm (e.g., recursive descent) is ultimately to be used in the compiler.

The interpreters for LR tables in their various forms are all quite simple and easy to implement in almost any programming language (they don't even require recursion). Furthermore, the language parsed by an LR parser can be changed merely by changing the tables (perhaps even at run-time) without any change to the program at all. Most important, given tables without inadequate states, they share with LL(1) parsers the properties of <u>determinism</u> and <u>linearity</u>. The former means that they never make a mistake and have to backtrack, the latter, that the time to parse a sentence is directly proportional to the length of the sentence. (More general algorithms may require time proportional to the square or the cube of the length - clearly impractical for a compiler.)

Each LR parser can be guaranteed to <u>correctly parse</u> every correct sentence in its language and to <u>detect an error</u> in any incorrect sentence - properties that we ought to require of any parser (although some, e.g., operator precedence, do not possess the latter property). Moreover LR parsers are almost unique in that they guarantee to detect errors at the <u>first possible point,</u> i.e., before shifting the first symbol that cannot be a valid continuation of the input seen so far. This property is extremely important in error diagnosis and recovery (Chapter 5.D.), yet the only other well-known class of practical parsers that shares it is LL(1).

Semantic actions can readily be incorporated in LR parsing action tables. However, it is customary in "bottom-up" compilers [Wirth 1966][McKeeman 1970] to associate semantic actions only with the reduce actions, thereby allowing semantic modules to be cleanly separated from the parsing module. Since LR parsers have no difficulty with empty right sides, null productions can be inserted anywhere in the grammar as hooks on which to hang semantics. (If the grammar happened to be LL(1) to start with, inserting any number of such null productions will never cause an LR parser any difficulty.)

6. MODIFICATIONS TO OBTAIN LR GRAMMARS

Most unambiguous grammars for programming languages are SLR(1) - hence LALR(1) and LR(1) - in the form in which they are originally written. Thus there has been relatively little work on mechanical transformations to obtain LR grammars, corresponding to the transformations described in Chapter 2.B.5. for LL(1). However, there are a few situations in which "naturally occurring" grammars contain local ambiguities that must be eliminated to make them acceptable to LR constructors. This section discusses two examples.

6.1. MULTIPLE-USE SEPARATORS

The grammar in Chapter 2.B.1. uses the semi-colon as a separator in three different productions. It fails to be LR(1) because of shift-reduce conflict involving the second production DL→D. (which may be followed by the semi-colon in the first production), and the third production, DL → D ; DL (which contains a semi-colon). Two-symbol lookahead would resolve this problem (the grammar is SLR(2)). but a more practical solution is to transform the right recursion on DL into a left recursion, resulting in the grammar of Section 1.2. Note that while left recursion must be eliminated for LL(1) parsing, it causes LR parsers no difficulty. Right recursion is only a problem for LR parsers if the internal separator may also be a follow symbol.

6.2. COMPOUND TERMINAL SYMBOLS

Consider the grammar fragment:

```
St  = Var  ':' '=' Exp
    | Lab St ;
Var = Id ;
Lab = Id  ':' ;
```

Among the states for this grammar there will be one containing the completed item
Var = Id ., which has ':' as a valid follow symbol, and the uncompleted item Lab =
Id .':' , leading to a classical shift-reduce conflict. Again, one more symbol of
lookahead (to see if ':' is followed by '=') would solve the problem, but the usual
solution is to make ':=' into a single symbol - thereby forcing the scanner to do the
extra lookahead.

7.   COMPARISON WITH OTHER TECHNIQUES

Throughout this chapter we have compared properties of LR parsers with those of parsers
obtained by other techniques. In this section we summarize comparisons that may affect
the choice of a parsing technique.

7.1.   GRAMMAR INCLUSIONS

The LR(1) constructor accepts all grammars accepted by any of the other practical
canonical parsing techniques. In addition, each of the other techniques rejects some
grammars accepted by LR(1).

While it is hard to place a meaningful metric on these infinite sets, in practice it
turns out that the difference between LR(k) for k > 1 and LR(1) is not very significant,
nor is the difference between LR(1) and LALR(1) or SLR(1). However, both LR(0) and
LL(1) accept such significantly smaller classes of grammars that they are only
practically usable with mechanical transformations such as those described in
Chapter 2.B.5. The various precedence techniques also accept noticeably smaller classes
of grammars, and some transformations are generally required. Figure 7.1. summarizes
the inclusion relations among various classes of grammars.

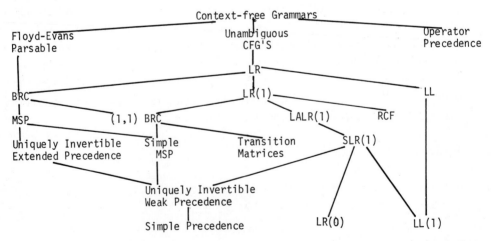

Figure 7.1.   Grammar Class Inclusion Hierarchy

7.2. *LANGUAGE INCLUSIONS*

In the last section we discussed the classes of grammars accepted by the various techniques. However, just because a technique rejects a particular grammar does not necessarily mean that it will reject all other grammars for the same language. Indeed, all our grammar transformation techniques aim to convert an unacceptable grammar into an acceptable one for the same language. It is interesting to determine the limitations of such transformations.

It has been shown that there are differences among the classes of languages recognized by the various parsing techniques. The largest practically recognizable class is called the <u>deterministic languages</u>, and it is precisely the class defined by the LR(k) grammars for any k $\geq$ 1, or by the LALR(1) grammars, or by the SLR(1) grammars. Thus, we do not sacrifice any <u>languages</u> when we restrict our attention to SLR(1) - in fact we can mechanically transform any LR(k) grammar to an SLR(1) grammar for the same language. Similar remarks hold for some of the more general precedence techniques (such as mixed-strategy precedence techniques [McKeeman 1970]), but not for Wirth-Weber Simple Precedence [Wirth 1966], which accepts a smaller class, the <u>simple precedence languages</u>.

It has been shown that the classes of LL(k) languages are distinct for every k, and properly contained in the deterministic languages. Thus there are some languages with SLR(1) (or even LR(0)) grammars that do not have LL(k) grammars at all! This is sometimes thought to prove the superiority of the LR approach, but, in practice, programming languages do not actually seem to fall in the gap between LL(1) languages and deterministic languages. Figure 7.2. summarizes the language inclusion hierarchy.

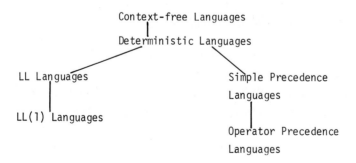

Figure 7.2.   Language Class Inclusion Hierarchy

7.3. ERROR DETECTION

One of the major reasons that LR and LL(1) parsers have been singled out for particular attention in this course is that their error detection and diagnostic capabilities are substantially superior to competitive techniques. Not only is the error detected at the earliest possible point, but the parsing action table contains, in a readily interpreted form, a list of the symbols that would have been valid continuations at that point. This information can be used to supply a highly meaningful diagnostic message, and may also be useful in error recovery (cf. Chapter 5.D.).

7.4. EFFICIENCY

Various studies ([Lalonde 1971][Anderson 1973][Joliat 1973]) have shown that LR parsers can be made as efficient as any technique of comparable generality, in both space and time. Compared to the demands of other processes within compilation, the requirements of LR parsers are quite modest.

Direct comparison of the efficiencies of LR and LL(1) parsers is difficult, because the usual implementation of the latter (recursive descent) imposes a substantial overhead in procedure calls and stack management that is not intrinsic in the technique. (If the compiling technique requires most of the procedure calls and stack management anyhow, then the added overhead due to parsing may be minimal.) Recursive descent tends to spread the parser out throughout the compiler, and it is difficult to determine the costs of parsing (e.g., the space and time costs of the procedure calls) in a machine-independent fashion. There is some reason to believe that comparable implementations of LL(1) and LR parsers (e.g., both non-recursive and table-driven) would have almost equal efficiencies.

8. CHOICE OF A SYNTACTIC ANALYSIS TECHNIQUE

The compiler-writer does not really want to concern himself with how parsing is done. So long as the parse is done correctly, without using too many resources, and with adequate hooks on which to hang semantics, he can live with almost any reliable technique. (In fact, he can probably switch techniques without affecting the rest of the compiler at all.) Thus, the choice of a particular technique is often made for reasons that have little to do with the intrinsic merits of the technique.

Probably the most important external factor is the availability of the appropriate constructor algorithm on an available machine. Only if more than one constructor is available are factors like speed, table size, class of grammars accepted, or even error detection, likely to be considered. A factor of some importance to the compiler-writer (though often neglected by authors of constructor programs) is the quality of diagnostic messages produced when problems are encountered in the grammar. If a good LR constructor is available, its wider classes of languages and grammars will probably be predominant factors.

If none of the available constructors is suitable, the balance shifts to LL(1) techniques. It is easier to quickly build an acceptably efficient LL(1) constructor than almost any other type. If even that imposes an unacceptable overhead, a recursive descent parser may be hand-constructed (and hand-checked for the LL(1) condition). This is somewhat less reliable and less flexible, but for an experienced compiler-writer may well be the quickest way to get the job done.

References

1. Aho, A.V., Johnson, S.C.: LR parsing. Computing Surveys (to appear 1974).
2. Aho, A.V., Ullman, J.D.: The theory of parsing, translation and compiling. Volume 1: Parsing 1972. Volume 2: Compiling 1973. Prentice-Hall.
3. Aho, A.V., Ullman, J.D.: Optimization of LR(k) parsers. J. Computer and System Sciences $\underline{6}$, 6 573-602 (1972).
4. Aho, A.V., Ullman, J.D.: A technique for speeding up LR(k) parsers. SIAM J. Computing $\underline{2}$, 2 106-127 (1973).
5. Anderson, T., Eve, J., Horning, J.J.: Efficient LR(1) parsers. Acta Informatica $\underline{2}$, 12-39 (1973).
6. DeRemer, F.L.: Simple LR(k) grammars. Comm. ACM $\underline{14}$, 453-460 (1971).
7. Feldman, J.A., Gries, D.: Translator writing systems. Comm. ACM $\underline{11}$, 77-113 (1968).
8. Joliat, M.L.: On the reduced matrix representation of LR(k) parser tables. University of Toronto, Computer Systems Research Group Techn. Rep. CSRG-28, 1973.
9. Knuth, D.E.: On the translation of languages from left to right. Information and Control $\underline{8}$, 607-639 (1965).
10. Lalonde, W.R.: An efficient LALR parser generator. University of Toronto, Computer Systems Research Group Tech. Rep. CSRG - 2, 1971.
11. McKeeman, W.M., Horning, J.J., Wortman, D.B.: A compiler generator. Prentice-Hall 1970.
12. Pager, D.: A solution to an open problem by Knuth. Information and Control $\underline{17}$, 462-473 (1970).

13. Wirth, N., Weber, H.: Euler: a generalization of Algol 60 and its formal description. Comm. ACM 9, 13-25, 89-99 (1966).

CHAPTER 2.D.

LEXICAL ANALYSIS

Franklin L. DeRemer
University of California
Santa Cruz, California, USA

1. Scanning, Then Screening

Early in the compilation process the source program appears as a stream of characters. The two subprocesses of "scanning" and "screening" constitute the process
known as lexical analysis.

Scanning involves finding substrings of characters that constitute units called
textual elements. These are the words, punctuation, single- and multi-character
operators, comments, sequences of spaces, and perhaps line boundary characters. In
its simplest form a scanner finds these substrings and classifies each as to which
sort of textual element it is.

Screening involves discarding some textual elements, such as spaces and comments,
and the recognition of reserved symbols, such as the key words and operators, used
in the particular language being translated. It is the output of this process,
usually called a token stream, that is the input to the parser.

For example, consider the following line from an Algol program represented as a
character stream:

After scanning, the program may be regarded as being in the following form:

where SP means "spaces", ID means "identifier", IN means "integer", and OP means "operator". After screening, the program would be represented by the following:

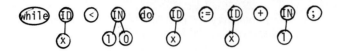

Of course, the parser reads only the names of the top nodes in this sequence, but the "subrosa information" (e.g. which particular identifier is meant for each ID node) is carried along through the parsing process for later processing.

2. Screening

We discuss screening first because it is simpler and consequently our discussion will be shorter. The screening process may be formally specified via a set of rules such as the following:

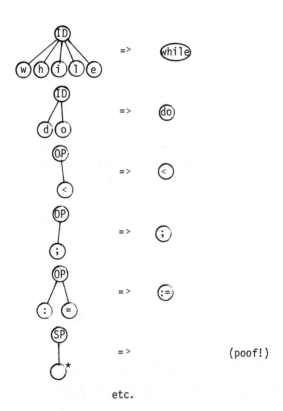

where the last rule means that an SP node, with any number of descendants, simply disappears (is erased). Formally, this set of rules constitutes a transformational grammar, as will be discussed in section 2.E below. Informally, it is simply a list of reserved words and reserved operators, plus a statement of which textual elements are to be ignored (e.g. spaces).

Perhaps the easiest implementation of a <u>screener</u> (reserved symbol processor) depends upon using a string table, which is undoubtedly used in the compiler anyway (see the section on "symbol tables" below). If in initializing the compiler we enter the reserved symbols first in the string table and remember the index r of the last one entered, then when the scanner finds an identifier, for instance, we may decide whether it is reserved by looking it up in the string table and asking if its index is less than or equal to r. We look up each identifier <u>anyway</u> so the compiler may work uniformly with indicies into the string table rather than with strings of non-uniform length. Thus, this reserved symbol process is extremely cheap.

Implemented thusly, the screener may be viewed as a table-driven processor. The reserved symbols constitute the tables. They are stored in the string table.

3. Scanning

3.1. Lexical Grammars

One can usually specify the textual elements of a programming language, i.e. its lexical level, with a regular grammar or a regular expression, or most conveniently with a mixture of the two in the form of a transduction grammar. For example, consider the following grammar, G_{LEX}:

```
Text       = ((Identifier | Integer) Spaces)* ;
Identifier = Letter (Letter | Digit | '_')*  => 'ID' ;
Integer    = Digit Digit *                    => 'IN' ;
Spaces     = ' ' (' ')*                        => 'SP' ;
Letter     = 'a' | 'b' | 'c' ;
Digit      = 'o' | '1' | '2' ;
```

(sometimes the notation D+ is used to mean D D *; i.e. one or more occurrances). This grammar describes a very simple lexicon containing identifiers, integers, and spaces. Identifiers and integers must be separated from each other by at least one space. The program can be empty (contain no characters); it cannot begin with spaces, but it must end with at least one space. We have limited the number of letters and digits so that we may use the grammar as a running example below.

3.1.1. Tokens

We require that the nonterminal vocabulary of a lexical grammar, such as G_{LEX}, be partitioned into three kinds of nonterminals:

(1) "textual element" nonterminals, or <u>tokens</u>, are the ones appearing as left parts of productions having a tree part; furthermore, all productions (alternatives) for tokens must have tree parts,

(2) nonterminals that generate terminal strings without ever generating any tokens, and

(3) nonterminals that <u>must</u> generate tokens to generate terminal strings in such a way that, for any such nonterminal A, every terminal string n that can be derived from A must be derivable in the form $A \to^+ \gamma \to^+ n$ such that γ is a string of tokens.

Thus, we have required a stratification of lexical grammars into levels. Let us call the three subvocabularies of nonterminals V_{token}, $V_{<tokens}$, and $V_{>tokens}$, respectively. In G_{LEX} we have

$$V_{token} = \{Identifier, Integer, Spaces\},$$
$$V_{<tokens} = \{Letter, Digit\}, \text{ and}$$
$$V_{>tokens} = \{Text\}.$$

3.1.2. A Regularity Condition

To further restrict lexical grammars, we require that no nonterminal be self-embedding. That is, if A is a nonterminal, then for every derivation $A \to^+ \gamma A \rho$ either γ or ρ must be ε. An easy way to satisfy this condition when constructing a lexical grammar is always to use either left or right recursion, or neither, but never to mix the two in one grammar. Given a purported lexical grammar it is easy to check that the condition of no self-embedding is satisfied.

It is well-known [Hopcroft 1969] that this condition is sufficient to guarantee that the grammar generates a regular language. Thus, we may freely use regular and finite-state techniques to process this lexical level of the language.

3.1.3. Converting Regular Grammars to Regular Expressions

Well known techniques exist for converting regular grammars to regular expressions [Hopcroft 1969]. Basically, one eliminates nonterminals from the grammar as one would eliminate variables from a set of linear equations. The technique is algebraic in nature and we are dealing with <u>regular algebra</u> [Kleene 1956].

Given a recursive nonterminal A with productions such as

$$A \to \alpha_1 \qquad A \to A\ \beta_1$$
$$\vdots \qquad \text{and} \qquad \vdots$$
$$A \to \alpha_n \qquad A \to A\ \beta_m$$

we can reduce these to one production, namely

$$A \to (\alpha_1\ |\ldots|\ \alpha_n)\ (\beta_1\ |\ldots|\ \beta_m)^*$$

or if m = 0 then simply $A \to \alpha_1\ |\ldots|\ \alpha_n$. Analogously, right recursion $(A \to \beta_i A)$ would produce

$$A \to (\beta_1\ |\ldots|\ \beta_m)^*(\alpha_1\ |\ldots|\ \alpha_n).$$

Having eliminated directly recursive productions in this way, we can next eliminate some occurrences of nonterminals by substituting production right parts for occurrences of the left part in other productions. In general, this will produce new directly recursive productions that will have to be eliminated as above.

This process can be iterated until one production remains whose left part is the start symbol, or stopped when desired. The process would get into an infinite loop if there were a self-embedding nonterminal in the grammar, since we have given no rule to eliminate this kind of recursion, hence the importance of the regularity condition given above.

3.2.   Generating Scanners Via LR Techniques

3.2.1. Using A Simplified LR Parser As A Scanner

To use LR parser construction techniques to generate scanners, we first use the latter conversion technique to eliminate all nonterminals from a lexical grammar except for the tokens and the start symbol, and we eliminate their recursion, if any. <u>Example</u> G'_{LEX}, the version of G_{LEX} that is to be mapped into a parser is as follows:

```
Text        = ((Identifier | Integer ) Spaces)*;
Identifier = ('a'|'b'|'c')('a'|'b'|'c'|'o'|'1'|'2'|'_')*
                                        => 'ID'  ;
Integer     = ('o'|'1'|'2')('o'|'1'|'2')*    => 'IN'  ;
Spaces      = ' ' (' ')*                 => 'SP'  ;
```

For G_{LEX}' we have

$$V_{token}' = \{Identifier, Integer, Spaces\},$$

$$V_{<tokens}' = \emptyset, \text{ and } V_{>tokens}' = \{Text\}.$$

Converting the grammar in this way means that the only reductions to be performed by the resulting parser will be to tokens or, at the end of the entire text, to the start symbol. On this last reduction the parser will enter the exit state, as usual. What state should the parser (scanner) enter after a reduction to a token? As in the case of context-free grammars and the LR parsers described in section 2.C above, this question is answered by restarting the parser in the state it was in at the be-ginning of the phrase being reduced and then causing it to read the token being re-duced to.

However, we do not need a stack to remember previous states as in the case of con-text-free grammars. Lexical grammars have no self-embedding, due to the regularity condition, thus no stack is needed to match left against right context. Furthermore, our restriction that the grammar be stratified, with the tokens being involved in generating all terminals but never other tokens, means that the parser will repeatedly read (scan) some characters and reduce them to a token until it reaches the end of the string, when it will quit. Thus, to restart after making a reduction all that the parser (scanner) needs to know is the state it was in after the previous reduc-tion.

To map our stratified, reduced lexical grammar into a parser (scanner) we must extend our LR parser construction techniques to deal with regular expressions. Since we already know how the machine is to make reductions, all we need are some rules for moving the LR marker (dot) through the regular expressions for the purpose of com-puting the parser states. The following three rules are what are necessary [Earley 1970].

During the computation of the closure of each set of items:

(1) If an item of the form $A \rightarrow \gamma \cdot (w_1 |\ldots|w_n)\rho$

appears, replace it with n items

$$A \rightarrow \gamma \ (\cdot w_1 |\ldots|w_n)\rho$$
$$\vdots$$
$$A \rightarrow \gamma \ (w_1 |\ldots| \cdot w_n)\rho$$

(2) If an item of the form $A \rightarrow \gamma \ (\ldots|w_i \cdot|\ldots)\rho$

appears, replace it with the item

$$A \to {}_\gamma (\ldots | w_i | \ldots) \cdot \rho$$

(3) If an item of the form $A \to {}_\gamma \cdot (w)* \rho$
or of the form $A \to \gamma (w\cdot)* \rho$ appears,
<u>replace</u> it with the two items

$$A \to \gamma (\cdot w)* \rho$$
$$A \to \gamma (w)*\cdot\rho$$

The idea behind these rules is to keep track of which parts of which productions are applicable at a given point in the input string, in a manner consistent with the LR construction technique and with the meanings of regular expressions. Note, in particular, that rule (3) returns the marker (dot) back to the beginning of the iterated phrase.

<u>Example</u>. We now construct the states of the LR parser for grammar G'_{LEX}. Note that to compute the parser we have added the terminator symbol (end of file) to the first production.

```
Start:       Text     = ·((Identifier | Integer) Spaces)* '⊥'      [Rule (3)]
             Text     = (·(Identifier | Integer) Spaces)* '⊥'      [Rule (1)]
             Text     = ((Identifier | Integer) Spaces)* · '⊥'  → EXIT
             Text     = ((·Identifier | Integer) Spaces)* '⊥'   → Identifier
             Text     = ((Identifier | ·Integer) Spaces)* '⊥'   → Integer
             Identifier = ·('a'|'b'|'c') (...)*                    [Rule (1)]
             Integer  = ·('o'|'1'|'2') (...)*                      [Rule (1)]
             Identifier = (·'a'|'b'|'c') (...)*                  → Letter
             Identifier = ('a'|·'b'|'c') (...)*                  → Letter
             Identifier = ('a'|'b'|·'c') (...)*                  → Letter
             Integer  = (·'o'|'1'|'2') (...)*                    → Digit
             Integer  = ('o'|·'1'|'2') (...)*                    → Digit
             Integer  = ('o'|'1'|·'2') (...)*                    → Digit
Identifier:  Text     = ((Identifier·|Integer) Spaces)* '⊥'       [Rule (2)]
             Text     = ((Identifier | Integer)·Spaces)* '⊥'    → Start
             Spaces   = ·' ' (' ')*                             → Blank
Integer:     Text     = ((Identifier|Integer·) Spaces)* '⊥'       [Rule (2)]
             Text     = ((Identifier|Integer)·Spaces)* '⊥'      → Start
             Spaces   = ·' ' (' ')*                             → Blank
```

(Integer is actually the same state as Identifier.)

```
Letter:      Identifier = ('a'·|'b'|'c') (...)*                    [Rule (2)]
             Identifier = ('a' |'b'·|'c') (...)*                   [Rule (2)]
             Identifier = ('a'|'b'|'c'·) (...)*                    [Rule (2)]
             Identifier = (...).('a'|'b'|'c'|'o'|'1'|'2'|'_')*     [Rules (3); (1)]
             Identifier = (...) (.'a'|'b'|...| '_')*             → Letter
             Identifier = (...) ('a'|·'b'|... |'_')*             → Letter
```

$\vdots$

```
          Identifier = (...) ('a'|'b'|...|.'_')*          → Letter
          Identifier = (...) ('a'|'b'|...|'_')* .          → Reduce
Digit:    Integer    = ('0'.|'1'|'2') (...)*              [Rule (2)]
          Integer    = ('0'|'1',|'2') (...)*              [Rule (2)]
          Integer    = ('o'|'1'|'2'.) (...)*              [Rule (2)]
          Integer    = (...).('o'|'1'|'2')*               [Rules (3); (1)]
          Integer    = (...) (.'o'|'1'|'2')*              → Digit
          Integer    = (...) ('o'|.'1'|'2')*              → Digit
          Integer    = (...) ('o'|'1' |.'2')*             → Digit
          Integer    = (...) ('o'|'1'|'2')* .             → Reduce
Blank:    Spaces     = ' ' .(' ')*                        [Rule (3)]
          Spaces     = ' ' ('.' ')*                       → Blank
          Spaces     = ' ' (' ')* .                       → Reduce
```

Note that in the above construction, states Identifier and Integer should really be one state since they have exactly the same transitions. This is becuase the three rules above say to __replace__ the original item. Note that the second two items listed in each of the two states are the same as those two in the other state, thus the two states are indeed identical; i.e. really just one state (call it I). In several other instances, for example relative to the transition from state Letter back to state Letter, this state identity has been recognized, but not emphasized in the construction above.

We emphasize that items with [Rule (i)] to their right above are not actually in the states, but have been replaced according to the indicated rule. __State identity is__ __determined__ __by__ __comparing__ __the__ __other__ __items__.

To display more clearly the structure of our scanner for grammar G_{LEX} we present its state diagram:

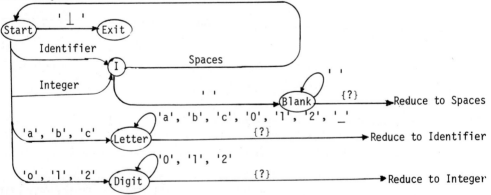

Note that we have indicated by {?} above that three of the states need look-ahead sets to determine read-reduce decisions. Look-ahead sets can be computed for this parser in essentially the same ways as for parsers for context-free grammars. In this particular case, the unique transitions under the tokens Spaces, Identifier, and Integer make it easy to see that the needed sets are:

$$\{'\underline{\quad}', 'a', 'b', 'c', 'o', '1', '2'\} \text{ for Spaces}$$
$$\{' '\} \qquad\qquad\qquad \text{for Identifier}$$
$$\{' '\} \qquad\qquad\qquad \text{for Integer.}$$

Such scanners can be implemented directly as executable programs, or interpretively via tables, as LR parsers usually are. However, it is noteworthy that these scanners frequently have states with direct loops, such as states Blank, Letter, and Digit, above. Such states should be implemented as fast as possible since they typically do the bulk of the scanning. (The "translate and test" (TRT) instruction of some models of the IBM 360 is useful for this purpose, for example.)

3.3. Hand-Written Scanners [Gries 1971]

Writing a scanner by hand is actually quite easy. In effect, we simply encode the state diagram into a program, preferably in the form of a <u>case</u> statement embedded in a <u>while</u> loop, as illustrated below.

This is not to imply that one need construct a state diagram for this purpose. On the other hand, in designing the lexicon of the language, it is important for both the human reader and the scanner to start each different kind of token with a symbol from a set distinct from the sets of symbols beginning other kinds of tokens. This should be readily apparent from the simplicity of the program structure illustrated below.

Several comments are appropriate before presenting the sample scanner:

We have related this program to G_{LEX} and the state diagram given above by inserting labels and comments and by using the names (constants) ID, IN, and SP. Note that the outer <u>while</u> loop implements the "major cycle" in the state diagram, while the inner <u>while</u> loops implement the "minor (direct) cycles". Note, however, that the program differs from the state diagram in that there is no check for a blank (' ') after identifiers and integers in the program fragment.

"Token_type" is intended to map characters into the appropriate case number. "Is_ identifier_character" and "Is_digit" are intended to map characters into truthvalues in an appropriate way. "Blank" and "End_of_file" are intended as constants whose values should be obvious.

```
c                                      c
c  A sample scanner program-structure.  c
c                                      c
Read (Next_character);                            c Read the very first
                                                    character.              c
Start:  while Next_character ¬= End_of_file       c Look for the end.      c
        do case Token_type (Next_character) in     c What kind of token
                                                      is next?              c
            Identifier:
              begin Read (Next_character);
                while Is_identifier_character (Next_character)
                do Read (Next_character) od;       c state Letter          c
                Make_token (ID)
              end,
            Integer:
              begin Read (Next_character);
                while Is_digit (Next_character)
                do Read (Next_character) od;        c state Digit           c
                Make_token (IN)
              end,
            Spaces:
              begin Read (Next_ character);
                while Next_character = Blank
                do Read (Next_character) od;        c state Blank           c
                Make_token (SP)
              end
            Error:
              begin ... RECOVERY ... end
          esac od
c We have not bothered with the detail of declarations          c
c because the intent should be clear from the choices of        c
c identifiers and the surrounding text.                         c
```

"Read" is assumed to read one character per call from the input stream and to treat line or card boundaries appropriately. "Make_token" is intended to construct tokens from the characters read since it was last called, except for the very last character, and perhaps to detect reserved symbols, and communicate the tokens to the parser in some way. We have specifically avoided irrelevancies, for our purposes here, of how these variables are implemented; e.g. whether the scanner and parser are coroutines or procedures, whether they operate in series or in parallel, whether "Next_character" is actually a character or a numerical code, etc.

3.4. Error Recovery

Little can be said about recovering from lexical errors for either the automatic or the hand written case. The problem is a lack of redundancy at the lexical level of language design.

While scanning a textual element, the scanner is always either in a context in which it has seen some left context that must be matched by some right context (e.g. the terminating quote on a string constant) or it is in a context that may legally end at any point (e.g. an identifier). In the latter case, characters in error show up as the beginning of the next textual element and can usually be skipped or replaced with a blank (' ') to recover safely. In the former case a scan to the end of the current line is usually in order to try to find the desired right context; if found the intervening text can be considered part of the current textual element; otherwise, the rest of the line is usually best skipped and the scanner is best restored to its start state.

4. On Not Including "Conversion Routines" in Lexical Analysers

Probably most compilers have been written with "conversion routines" embedded in and /or called by the lexical analyser. A call to such a routine usually occurs immediately after each token is discovered. Such routines usually convert digit strings to some "internal" integer representation, for example, or if a decimal point is encountered, to some representation of reals; or they may interpret special characters inside string constants; etc.

All too often the "internal" representation chosen is that of the machine on which the language is initially being implemented, with little or no thought that the compiler might later be moved to another machine or be modified to generate code for a different machine. Such decisions are usually made in the name of "efficiency", of course.

It is our thesis that such compiler design destroys modularity and portability. Ultimately, conversion must be made into the representations defined as part of the target language, i.e. target representations, and since the code generating parts of the compiler are already, and of necessity, intimately dependent upon those representations, that is the place where such routines should be placed and called. That is, dependencies on the target representations should be localized.

It is desirable to keep the entire front-end of the compiler independent of target representations, if possible. If constants are translated to target representations by the lexical analyser, tables of several different types usually must be mainained and some processors that do not need to know those representations, nonetheless must be programmed in terms of, or around them. For example, if constants are converted and an error message should relate to one, it must be converted back to source representation for printing.

In summary, we suggest that the scanner, screener, parser, standardizer (transform er), declaration processor, type checker, and flattener, should all be independent of target representations, if at all possible. (See section 2.E below on transformational grammars for a description of the compiler structure assumed in the previous sentence.)

References

[1] DeRemer, F. L.: Transformational grammars for languages and compilers, Technical Report No. 50, Computing Laboratory, University of Newcastle upon Tyne, England, July 1973

[2] Early, J.: An efficient context-free parsing algorithm. Comm. ACM 13, 94-102 (1970)

[3] Gries, D.: Compiler construction for digital computers. New York: John Wiley and Sons 1971

[4] Hopcroft, J. E., Ullman, J.D.: Formal languages and their relation to automata. Reading (Mass.): Addison-Wesley 1969

[5] Johnson, W. R., Porter J.S., Ackley S.I., Ross D. T.: Automatic generation of efficient lexical processors using finite state techniques. Comm. ACM 11, 805-813 (1968)

[6] Kleene, S.: Representation of events in nerve-sets. In: Automata Studies, Princeton (N.J.): Princeton Univ. Press 1956, pp. 3-42

TRANSFORMATIONAL GRAMMARS

F. L. DeRemer
University of California
Santa Cruz, California
U. S. A.

1. Language Processing as Tree Manipulation

One goal of researchers in the area of programming language translation techniques
has been, and will for some time be, to develop a language-description language such
that language descriptions can be mapped straight-forwardly into compilers. The
lessons of structured programming would lead us to expect each compiler to be a collection of modules, and correspondingly, each language description to be modular.

Some compiler modules would be expected to be language independent. Examples would
be input and output modules, as well as a symbol table module for collecting attributes associated with programmer-invented names. Such modules would, of course, not
be directly related to modules of any particular language description.

Other compiler modules would be expected to be, at least in part, directly specified
by modules of the language description. These might be table-driven modules, in
which all but the tables are language independent, or they might be totally rewritten for each language, depending upon implementation considerations. Examples of
such modules would be table-driven scanners, reserved word processors, parsers, and
as we shall see shortly, "transformers" and "flatteners".

Any programming system that aids in the construction of a translator (compiler) is
called a "translator writing system" (TWS). A system which takes as input programs

in a formally defined language-description langauge, and which is to produce a compiler (or equivalently, tables) as output, is called a "compiler compiler" (CC).

The ideal language-description language would be useable by a language designer who is not necessarily also a compiler writer. That is, this user should be familiar with the various levels of language description/processing, but need not be familiar with the systems programming techniques employed in implementing a compiler.

In [DeRemer 1973] we suggest that the ideal language description is a sequence of grammars that corresponds to the sequence of modules that appears conceptually, if not actually, in compilers. The corresponding phases or levels of language processing are illustrated in Figure 1.

(a) The PAL program "let x = 3 in x + 1" in character stream form.

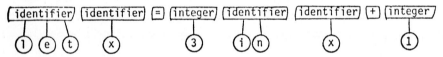

(b) The program after scanning; i.e., after finding and classifying separate textual elements.

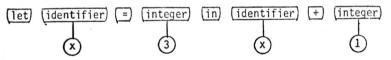

(c) The program after recognition of reserved words.

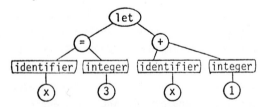

(d) The program after parsing; i.e., after determining the phrase structure.

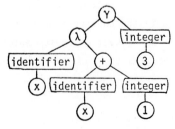

(e) The program after standardization.

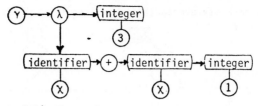

(f) The program after (partial) flattening.

Language Translation as a Tree-manipulating Process
Figure 1

1.1 Lexical and Syntactical Processing

Lexical and syntactical processing are assumed to produce an "abstract syntax" or
"computation" tree, as defined by corresponding lexical and syntactical specifications. Language processing to the point of producing such a tree is illustrated in
Figure 1, parts a - d, where we have used a PAL program as an example[Evans 1968,
Aho 1972]. PAL is particularly well suited for illustrations here, because it was
designed using a formalism similar to our own, albeit implicitly and informally.

The processing occuring between parts b and c of Figure 1, that of recognizing reserved words, can be conveniently described via transformations on the trees involved. For example:

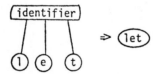

Of course, we already know how to implement an efficient processor corresponding to
such a transformation. In particular we would do so via a string-table look-up
mechanism, and in our compiler-writing language we would use strings rather than
trees to represent the words. But never mind the details; we are interested in the
processing on a conceptual, rather than an implementation level, for our purposes
here.

1.2 Standardization

Specification and processing beyond the syntactical level can usually be simplified
if the abstract syntax tree is transformed into a standard form according to language-specific rules. Since PAL is modelled on the lambda calculus [Wozencraft
1969] several constructs in the language can be mapped into applications (γ) of
lambda expressions (λ) to other expressions. The processing occuring between parts

d and e of Figure 1 implements this modelling via the transformation:

We emphasize that the reader need not understand the underlying semantics, but should be concerned only with the tree transformation.

Another PAL construct, the <u>where</u> expression, has the same meaning as the <u>let</u> expression. The following is an alternate for the program of Figure 1:

$$x + 1 \text{ } \underline{where} \text{ } x = 3$$

The semantic equivalence of the two constructs can be precisely stated (not the semantics, but the equivalence) by mapping both into γ and λ nodes:

Alternatively, we could have mapped one construct into the other; e.g.

In any case we may regard the resulting tree, after transformation, as being in a standard form.

1.3 Flattening

Part f of Figure 1 shows the program partially flattened into "pseudo code" ready to be further translated into "machine code". By "pseudo code" we mean the control structure (program) for an "ideal" machine, ideal in the sense of conceptual simplicity for defining the semantics of the language being translated. By "machine code" we mean the instructions for the actual (real) machine for which code is being compiled.

Pseudo code is typically prefix or postfix notation plus pointers. Expressions are typically flattened into the simple linear notation, but control constructs and procedures are linked together via pointers appropriately embedded in the linear notation. Looked at another way, the pointers link the lists of linear notation (expressions) together.

Grammars to specify the partial flattening of (standardized) trees into pseudo code are currently under research and are not a matter of main consideration here. However, for completeness we give a "flattening grammar" for PAL below. It is a "tree-to-string transformational grammar" and is described briefly below after we further describe and illustrate " subtree transformational grammars".

2. Description of Subtree Transformational Grammars

A transformational grammar consists of input and output vocabularies of node names, and a vocabulary of variables, and a finite set of transformations. Each transformation consists of two parts, an "input template" (tree pattern) and an "output template". These two correspond to the left and right parts, respectively, of a type 0 grammar [Chomsky 1959]. However, in this case the intent is to reorder, expand and/or contract a local portion of a tree, rather than a local portion of a string.

To "apply" a transformation we first find a subtree such that the input template matches its top. This establishes a correspondence between the "variables" in the input template and subtrees of the matched one. We have used uncircled nodes, labelled with identifiers, to indicate the variables above; i.e. X, E1, and E2. Finally, we restructure the part of the tree involved in the match, so that the output template will match it, maintaining the correspondence between variables and trees established by the input template match. In general, this will involve reordering, duplicating, and/or deleting the subtrees corresponding to variables in the initial match, as dictated by the number and position of occurrences of each distinct variable in the input and output templates. In summary, each application involves a structural match and then a structural change.

Example. Consider the "let transformation", indicated above, applied to the following tree:

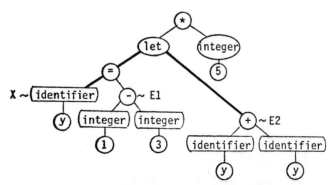

where we have indicated in an obvious way the subtrees matching the variables X, E1, and E2. After applying the transformation the tree looks like:

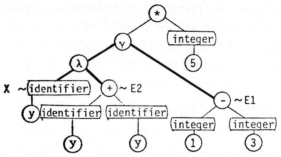

Order of application of transformations. It happens that for PAL, almost all of its modelling rules can be reasonably expressed via transformations. Furthermore, these transformations/have an innate bottom-up bent to them. The transformations may not

as a set

be applicable to one part of the tree until what is immediately below that part has been transformed to standard form. We shall see this below, relative to the standardization of PAL's <u>within</u> construct, in particular, and relative to the unfactoring of factored PL/1 attributes.

Thus, for PAL at least, and we suspect for other languages, there exists an important class of transformations which we describe as being "bottom-up". It is important, then, that any corresponding language processor, or "transformer", search the tree being standardized from the bottom up. In fact, even more "efficiency" may be gained if the transformer is "fed" or "driven" by some other mechanism already processing the tree in a bottom-up order, especially if that mechanism "knows" which nodes are to be transformed. We conclude that it makes sense to attach a bottom-up transformer to a bottom-up parser within our compiler. We emphasize, however, that by "bottom-up parser" we mean one that builds its abstract syntax tree from the bottom up, independent of the strategy it may use in parsing.

Some theoretical foundations for these transformational grammars already exist [Rosen 1973]. In particular, Rosen gives sufficient conditions for guaranteeing that, no matter what order of application of transformations is used, a unique standardized tree will result for a given set of transformations and a given initial tree, assuming infinite loops are avoided, of course.

A linear notation for trees   In light of the general lack of facilities for processing two dimensional languages, it behooves us to provide a linear notation for representing trees. In our application we have no a priori knowledge of the number of descendants associated with nodes labelled with any particular symbol. Furthermore, we do not even require that a given symbol always be associated with the same number of descendants; i.e. we do not limit ourselves to "ranked" trees.

An adequate convention for our purposes could be described as "Polish prefix notation with brackets, say <>, around interior branch nodes", sometimes called "Cambridge Polish". Consider the tree diagram:

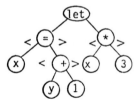

where we have added brackets around all nodes except the root and the leaves. The tree's linear representation is:

$$\text{'let' } < \text{'=' 'x'} < \text{'+ 'y' '1'} > > < \text{'*' 'x' '3' } >$$

Informally, an algorithm for "printing" the linear representation of a tree is as follows: starting at the root, traverse the tree from left to right printing the name of each node as you first come to it, except that if it is a branch node other than the root, print a left bracket < just before the name and print a right bracket > upon returning to the node for the last time.

[handwritten annotation: preorder]

Thus, our "let transformation" from above is written:

$$\text{'let' } < \text{'=' X E1 } > \text{E2} \Rightarrow \text{'y' } < \text{'λ' X E2} > \text{E1}$$

3. Compiler Structure

The implications regarding compiler structure of our examples and observations above are depicted in Figure 2. There we find the usual scanner module refined into two components: The part that actually scans the characters (a finite-state machine) and the part that recognizes reserved words (a trivial transformer). Similarly, we have two "phases" at the syntactic level: the actual parser (a "tree-building" deterministic pushdown automaton) and another transformer.

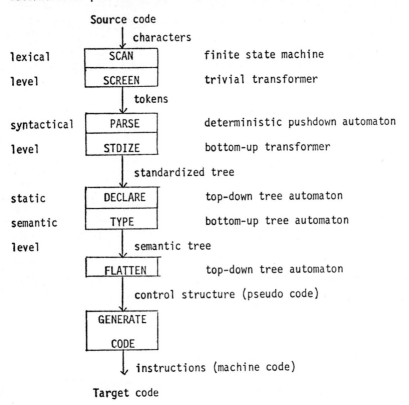

A Conceptual, if Not Actual, Compiler Structure

Figure 2

The transformations we envision happening at this second level are distinctly nontrivial. In fact, in most current compilers they happen only implicitly and are buried indistinguishably in that amorphous lump called the "code generator" or "synthesizer". One reason that this latter "semantic" phase of compilation is so complex is that we have not yet recognized that, indeed, part of what happens in that phase is really syntactic; i.e. is involved with changing, or working around, the original _form_ of the program.

We have little to say here about the "static semantic level" indicated in Figure 2. Let us merely note the following. The module called DECLARE is assumed to traverse the standardized tree from the top down, entering declarative information in a "symbol table" (better termed a "declaration table") and depositing that information at the leaves of the tree; i.e. this module checks scopes of definitions to see that each name is declared as it should be and associates declarative information with uses of names. The module called TYPE is assumed to process the tree from the bottom up, checking the type compatibilities of operators and operands (and perhaps transforming the tree by inserting "coercion operators") by using the declarative information distributed through the tree by DECLARE.

The "attribute grammars" of Knuth [Knuth 1968]appear to be an appropriate descriptive mechanism for specifying the declarative and type compatibility aspects of programming languages, and therefore, for specifying the modules DECLARE and TYPE. Other lecturers have more to say about these and similar grammars.

The module FLATTEN is intended to change the representation of the program into a mostly linear one. It also is a tree automaton that proceeds from the top of the tree to its bottom, flattening it mostly back into linear form.

In the module GENERATE CODE machine-dependent addresses are computed, registers are allocated and machine code is generated. A well designed compiler will have all dependencies on the target machine isolated in this module. As indicated in Figure 2 this module is a rather large one relative to the others found there. It appears that further splitting of this large module into smaller ones requires horizontal rather than vertical fragmentation; i.e. its internal modules seem to need to operate in parallel, even conceptually. Again, we leave further discussion of this point to other lecturers.

4. Further Examples of Transformations

4.1 Local Effects

The let and where transformations given above have strictly local effects on the trees to which they are applied. This is because they do not interact with themselves or other transformations to have a global effect through repeated application.

4.2 Global Effects

The within construct of PAL is standardized as follows:

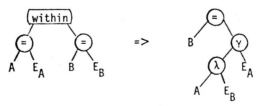

Note that the '=' node with left descendant B moves up the tree relative to the other nodes and subtrees. Furthermore, if in an actual tree, a given 'within' node is the right descendant of another one, the transformation will apply twice: first to the lower node and then to the upper one. Consequently, the (B, '=') pair will move up two levels. In general, the pair will "bubble" up the tree "through" any 'within' nodes above it.

Let us consider a specific example:

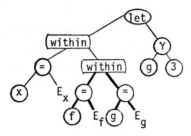

where E_x, E_f, and E_g denote subtrees whose internal structure is of no interest here. We have given above all the transformations that relate to our specific PAL example. Note that we have no choice of order of application in this case. We must apply the <u>within</u> transformation to the lower 'within' node.

The result is:

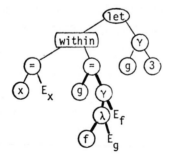

Next we may only apply the <u>within</u> transformation to the remaining 'within' node, giving:

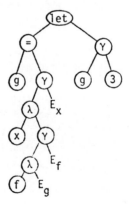

Finally, the <u>let</u> transformation produces:

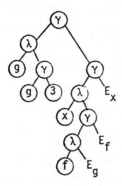

<u>Semantic motivation</u> The <u>within</u> construct defines an own variable "within" another definition. The name actually being introduced by this <u>let</u> construct is "g". Its scope of definition is the subtree which is the right descendant of the "let" node. Imagine how difficult it is to describe scopes of definition, in general, in the context of "within" nodes! However, after standardization, scopes of definition are easy to describe: the scope of a bound variable (left descendant of the 'λ' node) is the body of its lambda expression (right descendant of the 'λ' node)...with the usual stipulation that a contained lambda expression with the same bound variable defines a "hole" in the scope.

For the sake of the programmer/reader, it was convenient at the source code level to have "g" and "=" grouped with E_g. However, for the purposes of semantic-definition, translation, and evaluation (execution), it is convenient to have "g" grouped with both the subtree over which it is defined and its <u>total</u> definition, including own variables. Imagine the antics that would be necessary to get the desired effect via a stack-like symbol table if a compiler had to work with the program in its original order! The problem gets another order of magnitude more difficult when we add to the langauge the <u>and</u> construct described below (for "simultaneous" definitions).

On the other hand, if we appropriately standardize our abstract syntax trees before further processing, the addition of a new construct to a language is more likely to have a linear, than a multiplicative or exponential effect on the size of our compiler. In PAL's case, for example, the difference between the compilers for the language with and without the <u>and</u> construct need be only: (1) one extra transformation to recognize the reserved word <u>and</u>; i.e. one extra entry in the string table, plus (2) a few additional states in the parser, plus (3) one extra transformation to standardize each occurance of <u>and</u> into other constructs already in the language. A similar statement can be made about the <u>within</u>, <u>let</u>, and <u>where</u> constructs, since the lambda notation is directly available in PAL.

4.3 Iterative Transformations

In some cases a transformation must be applied to some of the same nodes it has just been involved in transforming. A case in point is the well known optimization which minimizes the number of registers necessary to sequentially compute nested sums. The optimization can be described as follows:

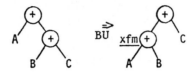

We have emphasized above that the transformation works most simply if it is applied in bottom-up (BU) order. Then, we can be sure that the subtree corresponding to "B + C", relative to the input template, has already been "optimized". Thus, we can guarantee that the subtree matching C does not have a '+' node as its root.

Still, the B subtree may have a '+' root. Thus, after the initial transformation, we must try to apply the transformation again, this time to the resulting "A + B" subtree. We have indicated this necessity above via the key word xfm. In general, the second application may result in the need for a third, and so on, until the tree is converted to a left-linear list of '+' nodes.

If, instead of using BU order, we apply the transformation first to the topmost '+' node of any connected set of '+' nodes, the initial application generates three points at which the transformation must be tried again. In particular, since in this case the tops of the three subtrees corresponding to A, B, and C may be '+' nodes, we must try again at the two '+' nodes constructed by the previous application, as well as at the top of the A subtree. Diagramatically:

Without going into details that are irrelevant to our purposes here, we note that in general the top-down (TD) version of this tranformation causes fewer structural changes to occur than the BU version when standardizing the same tree. In fact, the BU version is probably exponentially worse for large trees (probably irrelevant to compiler-writing practice since large expression trees are uncommon [Knuth 1971]).

The problem is basically that the BU version linearizes each subtree and then absorbs it into a containing subtree, one node at a time. The TD version, on the other hand, starts at the top and works only along the left edge of the tree, gradually absorbing nodes to the right into a longer and longer left edge. Thus, it does not unnecessarily linearize right subtrees, as the BU version does. The reader should get a feel for this by trying an example with, say, seven or nine nodes, initially arranged in a right list.

4.4 Extension to Regular Expressions

Given the linear notation used above, it seems natural to use regular notation, i.e.
Kleene closure (*) and union (|), to indicate even larger classes of trees. The
closure operator, or "star", allows us to describe "bushes": trees with nodes that
may have any arbitrary number of sons. The union operator, or "bar", allows us to
concisely describe trees with one of several alternate structures. The combination
of the two can substantially increase the linguistic power of our transofrmational
notation.
The following is a simple example using just a star:

'and' < '=' X E > * => '=' < ',' X * > < ',' E * >

or in a diagrammatic notation:

This transformation is intended to standardize the <u>and</u> construct of PAL, which expresses simultaneous definitions. (Semantics: In such, we evaluate all the expressions (Es) before making any name-value associations.)
In words, the transformation states that an 'and' node having zero or more sons,
each of which is an '=' node with two sons, called X and E, respectively, should be
transformed to an '=' node having two sons: (left) a ',' node with the X subtrees
as descendants, and (right) a ',' node with the E subtrees as descendants. For
example:

is one of an arbitrary number of specific transformations indicated by the above.
<u>PL/I Attributes</u> As a final substantial example, we give three transformations to
describe the unfactoring of factored attributes in PL/1 declarations. The transformations are described as they would operate in a bottom-up order. First we give a
sample tree to indicate what is to be standardized:

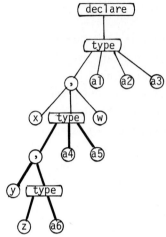

In the PL/1 program this would have appeared something like:

<u>declare</u> (x, (y, z a6) a4 a5, w) a1 a2 a3;

where the a_i denote attributes such as FIXED, BINARY, etc.
Compilation would be simpler for the equivalent form:

<u>declare</u> x a1 a2 a3,

y a4 a5 a1 a2 a3,

z a6 a4 a5 a1 a2 a3,

w a1 a2 a3;

We intend the two transformations given below to standardize the former to the latter. <u>First transformation</u>:

'type' < ',' ('type' N AN* | X)* > A*

=> ',' < 'type' N AN* A* |'type' X A* >*

or:

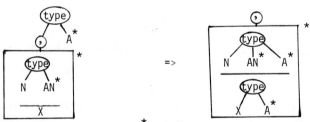

That is, distribute the attributes A* over the names X and N, the latter already having attributes AN*. Collect each name-attributes sequence under a "type" node, and collect all of those under a ',' node.

This transformation would first apply (BU order) to the middle 'type' node of the above tree, converting it to a ',' node:

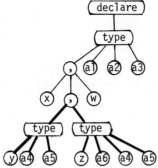

The <u>second transformation</u>, then causes a higher ',' node to absorb the members of lists below it:

$$',' < ',' \ X* \mid Y > * \quad => \quad ',' \ (X * \mid Y) *$$

or:

To implement the latter transformation, we must consider each   son   of the higher ',' node in turn. If it is itself a ',' node, we associate its sons with X; otherwise we associate the entire node with Y.   In the end, X is associated with a list of sublists and Y with a list of non-',' nodes. Furthermore, there is an interspersed ordering among the members of X and those of Y. To build the transformed tree, we build a ',' node whose descendants are the elements of Y and those of the sublists of X, in their original order.

All of that is presumably implied by that single transformation above! The result for our specific example above is:

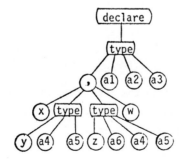

One more application of the first transformation is necessary to standardize this example, resulting in:

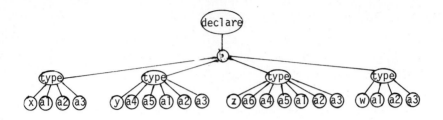

We challenge anyone to describe this, or an equivalent effect, in general, in only three lines (thirty is more likely) in any existing "compiler writing language". Of course we are a long way from knowing how to implement the above efficiently, as yet!

5. Summary and Conclusions

We have indicated the usefulness of a localized version of transformational grammars. They are relevant to the specification and processing of programming languages on several distinct levels. They may be used to describe: (1) the notion of reserved words, (2) the standardization of abstract syntax trees, (3) the insertion, if not the movement, of declarative information in trees, (4) the insertion of coercion operators, (5) optimizations involving the shape of trees; and probably others.

Transformational grammars can be mapped into tree-transforming modules, or "transformers". Several purposes may be served by such transformers. For example, (1) semantically equivalent but syntactically distinct constructs may be mapped into a single form, (2) inconveniently ordered or structured forms in the tree may be transformed to a more convenient form, (3) abbreviated constructs may be expanded in the style of macro substitutions, (4) redundant or useless information may be deleted from the tree, (5) distributed information may be collected, condensed, and even sorted, and (6) optimizing transformations may be performed at the source level, and after macro expansion, at lower levels.

We suggest that techniques such as "tree attributes" and "tree automata" are most useful and appropriate when applied to a standardized tree, rather than to a derivation tree of a context-free grammar that describes the concrete syntax of a language.

Much more research is needed to find the best combination of these techniques. The goal should be a technique of language description with a direct correspondence to techniques of efficient language implementation.

6. Appendix - Meta-grammars and PAL Grammars

The author of this section is currently supported by the National Science Foundation
of the United States to develop and implement a translator writing system based on
the conceptual framework presented in the current section and in the sections on LR
parsing and Lexical Analysis. /we presented two associated meta-grammars describing
          In chapter 2,A
the lexicon and phrase structure of an extended form of context-free grammars.
A third meta-grammar is presented next that describes the phrase structure of
subtree transformational grammars. We use the language defined by the previous
two meta-grammars to define this third one.

Following the meta-grammar are four grammars describing PAL's lexicon, phrase structure, standardization, and flattening into control structure. PAL's declaration processing and type checking are done at run-time so no attribute grammars for these
levels are given.

Unfortunately, we haven't the time nor the space to fully describe these grammars
here. Furthermore, the notations we are illustrating here are not fully developed
and perfected as yet.

Let us mention, however, that the "flattening grammar" for PAL should be interpreted
as a "tree-to-string transformational grammar". That is, the input template is to
be interpreted normally, but the output template should be interpreted as a string
rather than as a tree--unless this convention is specifically overridden by the
appearance of a pair of brackets < >, in which case a node is intended with name
and sons indicated by the contents of the brackets. When a variable appears in the
output template, the intention is to refer to the flattened form of the associated
subtree.

Another topic which we have not touched on at all above because it is still a matter
of research is the recursive definition of nested trees and re-entrant control
structures. Such definitions are marked in the grammars by the key words where and
rec.

We have included these grammars here more to illustrate the minimum possible sort of
input to a translator writing system than for their own sakes.

```
 3 |#NEW_PAGE                   ******************************    #|
 4 |#                     *                            *         #|
 5 |#                     *      TRANSFORMATIONAL      *         #|
 6 |#                     *          GRAMMARS          *         #|
 7 |#                     *                            *         #|
 8 |#                     ******************************         #|
 9 |
10 |parser Transformers:
11 |
12 |    Transformers = ( Transformer ';' )* Transformer        =>   ';'         ;|
13 |
14 |    Transformer
15 |       = 'TRANSFORMER' 'IDENTIFIER' ':' T_grammar Ending    =>   'TRANSFORMER'  |
16 |       | 'FLATTENER'   'IDENTIFIER' ':' T_grammar Ending    =>   'FLATTENER'    |
17 |       ;
18 |    Ending
19 |       = 'END'                                             =>   'END'
20 |       | 'END' 'IDENTIFIER'
21 |       ;
22 |    T_grammar
23 |       = T_rule +                                          =>   'TRANSFRMATIONS'|
24 |       ;
25 |    T_rule
26 |      = Input_template '=>' Output_template ';'            =>   '=>'
27 |      | Input_template '¬=>' Output_template ';'           =>   '¬=>'
28 |      ;
29 |    Input_template
30 |      = Definition_expression
31 |      ;
32 |    Output_template
33 |      = Definition_expression
34 |      ;
35 |    Definition_expression
36 |      = 'LET' Definition 'IN' Definition_expression        =>   'LET'
37 |      | Reg_exp ( 'WHERE' Definition ) +                   =>   'WHERE'
38 |      | Reg_exp
39 |      ;
40 |    Definition = Recursive? 'IDENTIFIER' '=' Reg_exp       =>   '='         ;|
41 |
42 |    Recursive = 'REC'                                      =>   'REC'       ;|
```

```
43 |#NEW_PAGE                                                               |
44_|_____|
45 |   Reg_exp                                                              |
46_|_____=_Reg_term_(_'|'_Reg_term_)_+._____=>____'|'_____|
47 |         | Reg_term                                                     |
48_|_____;_____|
49 |   Reg_term                                                             |
50_|_____=_____=>____'NULL'_____|
51 |         | Reg_factor Reg_factor +              => '.'                  |
52_|_____|_Reg_factor_____|
53 |         ;                                                              |
54_|___Reg_factor_____|
55 |     = Reg_primary                                                      |
56_|_____|_Reg_primary_'*'_____=>____'*'_____|
57 |       | Reg_primary '+'                        => '+'                  |
58_|_____|_Reg_primary_'++'_____=>____'++'_____|
59 |       | Reg_primary '?'                        => '?'                  |
60_|_____|_Reg_primary_'**'_Repetition_specification_____=>____'REPEAT'___|
61 |       ;                                                                |
62_|___Repetition_specification_____|
63 |     = 'INTEGER'                                                        |
64_|_____|_'('_'INTEGER'_')'_____=>____'UP TO N'_____|
65 |       | '(' 'INTEGER' ',' ')'                  => 'N OR MORE'          |
66_|_____|_'('_'INTEGER'_','_'INTEGER'_')'_____=>____'N1_TO_N2'_____|
67 |       ;                                                                |
68_|___Reg_primary_____|
69 |     = Subtree                                                          |
70_|_____|_'XFM'_Subtree_____=>____'TRANSFORM'_____|
71 |       | 'IDENTIFIER' ':' Reg_primary           => 'CALL'              |
72_|_____|_'COUNT'_Reg_primary_____=>____'COUNT'_____|
73 |       | 'STRING'                                                       |
74_|_____|_'('_Reg_exp_')'_____|
75 |       ;                                                                |
76_|___Subtree_____|
77 |     = 'IDENTIFIER'                                                     |
78_|_____|_'<'_Reg_exp_'>'_____=>____'NODE'_____|
79 |       ;                                                                |
80_|_____|
81 |end Transformers                                                        |
```

```
 1 |#NEW_PAGE                   ****************************       #|
 2 |#LOWER_CASE                 *                          *       #|
 3 |#                           *       PAL LEXICON        *       #|
 4 |#                           *                          *       #|
 5 |#                           ****************************       #|
 6 |
 7 |
 8 |scanner Pal_text:
 9 |
10 |    Pal_text = Text_id_num | Text_operator | Text_else:
11 |
12 |    # TEXT STARTING WITH AN IDENTIFIER OR NUMBER.
13 |    Text_id_num = (Identifier | Integer | Real) (Text_operator | Text_else)? ;
14 |
15 |    # TEXT STARTING WITH AN OPERATOR.
16 |    Text_operator = Operator (Text_id_num | Text_else)? ;
17 |
18 |    # TEXT STARTING WITH ANYTHING ELSE.
19 |
20 |    Text_else = Spaces (Text_id_num | Text_operator | Text_other)?
21 |                | Text_other ;
22 |
23 |    Text_other = (String | Punctuation | '#N') Pal_text? ;
24 |
25 |
26 |    # THE BASIC TEXTUAL ELEMENTS.
27 |
28 |    Identifier = Letter (Letter | Digit | '_') *          => * 'IDENTIFIER';
29 |    Integer = Digit +                                     => * 'INTEGER';
30 |    Real = Digit + '.' Digit + ('E' ('+' | '-')? Digit +)? => * 'REAL';
31 |    Operator = Operator_symbol +                          => * 'OPERATOR';
32 |    String = '#Q' Any_character * '#Q'                    => * 'STRING';
33 |    Spaces = ' ' +                                        =>   'IGNORE';
34 |    Punctuation = '('                                     => * '(';
35 |                  | ')'                                   => * ')';
36 |                  | ';'                                   => * ';';
37 |                  | ','                                   => * ',';
38 |
39 |
40 |    # CHARACTER SETS.
41 |
42 |    Any_character = Letter | Digit | Operator_symbol
43 |                  | ')' | '(' | ';' | ',' | '##' 'N' | '##' 'T' | '##' 'Q'
44 |                  | '##' '##' | ' ' ;
45 |    Letter = 'A' | 'B' | 'C' | 'D' | 'E' | 'F' | 'G' | 'H' | 'I'
46 |           | 'J' | 'K' | 'L' | 'M' | 'N' | 'O' | 'P' | 'Q' | 'R'
47 |           | 'S' | 'T' | 'U' | 'V' | 'W' | 'X' | 'Y' | 'Z'
48 |           ;
49 |    Digit = '0' | '1' | '2' | '3' | '4' | '5' | '6' | '7' | '8' | '9' ;
50 |
51 |    Operator_symbol = '+' | '-' | '*' | '<' | '>' | '&' | '.'
52 |                    | '@' | '/' | ':' | '=' | '~' | '|' | '$'
53 |                    ;
54 |end Pal_text
```

```
 3 |#NEW_PAGE              ****************************          #|
 4_|#                      *                          *          #|
 5 |#                      *    PA. PHRASE STRUCTURE  *          #|
 6_|#                      *                          *          #|
 7 |#                      ****************************          #|
 8_|                                                              |
 9 |parser P:                                                     |
10_|                                                              |
11 |    P  = ('DEF' D )+                        => * 'DEF'        |
12_|          |_E_;                                              .|
13 |    E  = 'LET' D 'IN' E                     => * 'LET'        |
14_|          | 'FN' D1                                           |
15 |          | Ew ;                                             |
16_|    Ew = Ev 'WHERE' Dr                      => * 'WHERE'      |
17 |          | Ev ;                                             |
18_|    Ev =  'VALOF' C                         =>   'VALOF'      |
19 |          | C ;                                             |
20_|                                                              |
21 |    # COMMANDS (STATEMENTS). *****************************************#|
22_|                                                              |
23 |    C  = Cl ';' C                           =>   ';'          |
24_|          |_Cl_;                                             .|
25 |    Cl = ( 'IDENTIFIER'  ':' ) + Cc         =>   ':'          |
26_|          |_Cc_;                                             .|
27 |    Cc = 'TEST'     B 'IFSO'  Cl 'IFNOT' Cl  => * 'IPSO-IFNOT'|
28_|          | 'TEST'   B 'IFNOT' Cl 'IFSO'  Cl => * 'IFNOT-IPSO'|
29 |          | 'IF'     B 'DO' Cl              => * 'IF'         |
30_|          | 'UNLESS' B 'DO' Cl              => * 'UNLESS'      |
31 |          | 'WHILE'  B 'DO' Cl              => * 'WHILE'       |
32_|          | 'UNTIL'  B 'DO' Cl              => * 'UNTIL'       |
33 |          | Cb ;                                             |
34_|    Cb = T ':=' T                           =>   ':='         |
35 |          | 'GOTO' R                        =>   'GOTO'        |
36_|          | 'RES' T                         =>   'RES'         |
37 |          | T ;                                             |
38_|                                                              |
39 |    # TUPLE EXPRESSIONS. *****************************************#|
40_|                                                              |
41 |    T  = Ta ( ',' Ta ) +                    =>   'TAU'        |
42_|          | Ta ;                                             |
43 |    Ta = Ta 'AUG' Tc                        =>   'AUG'        |
44_|          | Tc ;                                             |
45 |    Tc = B '->' Tc '|' Tc                   => * '->'         |
46_|          | B ;                                             .|
47 |                                                             |
48_|    # BOOLEAN EXPRESSIONS. *****************************************#|
49 |                                                             |
50_|    B  = B 'OR' Bt                          =>   'OR'         |
51 |          | Bt ;                                             |
52_|    Bt = Bt '&' Bs                          =>   '&'          |
53 |          | Bs ;                                             |
54 |    Bs = 'NOT' Bp                           =>   'NOT'        |
55 |          | Bp ;                                             |
56_|    Bp = A Rl A                             =>   'Rl'         |
57 |          | A ;                                             |
58_|    Rl = 'GR'                               =>   'GR'         |
59 |          | 'GE'                            =>   'GE'         |
60_|          | 'LS'                            =>   'LS'         |
61 |          | 'LE'                            =>   'LE'         |
62_|          | 'EQ'                            =>   'EQ'         .|
```

```
63 |        '=E'                                              =>    'NE'              |
64 |        '>'                                               =>    'GR'             |
65 |        '<'                                               =>    'LS' ;           |
66 |
67 | # ARITHMETIC EXPRESSIONS. ***************************************** #|
68 |
69 | A = A '+' At                                             =>    '+'               |
70 |     A '-' At                                             =>    '-'               |
71 |     '+' At                                               =>    'UNSHARE'         |
72 |     '-' At                                               =>    'NEGATE'          |
73 |     At ;                                                                         |
74 | At = At '*' Af                                           =>    '*'               |
75 |      At '/' Af                                           =>    '/'               |
76 |      Af ;                                                                        |
77 | Af = Ap '**' Af                                          =>    '**'              |
78 |      Ap ;                                                                        |
79 | Ap = Ap '@' 'IDENTIFIER' R                               =>    '@'               |
80 |      '$' R                                               =>    'UNSHARE'         |
81 |      R ;                                                                         |
82 |
83 | # RATORS AND RANDS (OPERATORS AND OPERANDS). **************************** #|
84 |
85 | R = R Rn                                                 =>    'GAMMA'           |
86 |     Rn ;                                                                         |
87 | Rn = 'IDENTIFIER'                                                                |
88 |      'INTEGER'                                                                   |
89 |      'REAL'                                                                      |
90 |      'STRING'                                                                    |
91 |      'TRUE'                                              =>    'TRUE'            |
92 |      'FALSE'                                             =>    'FALSE'           |
93 |      'NIL'                                               =>    'NIL'             |
94 |      '(' E ')'                                                                   |
95 |      'DUMMY'                                             =>    'DUMMY' ;         |
96 |
97 | # DEFINITIONS. ************************************************************** #|
98 |
99 | D = Da 'WITHIN' D                                        => * 'WITHIN'           |
100 |     Da ;                                                                        |
101 | Da = Dr ( 'AND' Dr ) +                                  => * 'AND'              |
102 |      Dr ;                                                                       |
103 | Dr = 'REC' Db                                           => * 'REC'              |
104 |      Db ;                                                                       |
105 | Db = Vl '=' E                                           =>   '='                |
106 |      'IDENTIFIER' Vb+ '=' E                             =>   'FUNCTION_FORM'    |
107 |      '(' D ')' ;                                                                |
108 | Dl = Vb Dl                                              => * 'LAMBDA'           |
109 |      Vb '.' E                                           => * 'LAMBDA' ;         |
110 |
111 | # VARIABLES. ************************************************************** #|
112 |
113 | Vb = 'IDENTIFIER'                                                               |
114 |      '(' Vl ')'                                                                 |
115 |      '(' ')'                                            =>   '()' ;             |
116 | Vl = 'IDENTIFIER' ( ',' 'IDENTIFIER' ) +               =>   'COMMA'            |
117 |      'IDENTIFIER' ;                                                             |
118 |
119 | end P                                                                           |
```

```
 2 |#NEW_PAGE                  ******************************          #|
 3 |#                          *                         *            #|
 4 |#                          *    PAL STANDARDIZATION  *            #|
 5 |#                          *                         *            #|
 6 |#                          ******************************          #|
 7 |                                                                  |
 8 |transformer Pal_standarization:                                   |
 9 |                                                                  |
10 |# PUT INTO STANDARD FORM.                                         |
11 |                                                                  |
12 | ( 'LET'    < '=' X E1 > E2                                       |
13 | | 'WHERE' E2           < '=' X E1 >) => 'GAMMA' < 'LAMBDA' X E2 > E1 ;
14 |                                                                  |
15 | 'AND' < '=' X E > *              => '=' < 'COMMA' X * > < 'TAU' E * >   ;|
16 |                                                                  |
17 | 'FUNCTION_FORM' F Vb+ E          => '=' F Lambdas                |
18 |                                      where rec Lambdas = E |     |
19 |                                         < 'LAMBDA' Vb Lambdas>  ;|
20 |                                                                  |
21 | 'LAMBDA' < ',' X* > E            => let T = 'NEW_IDENTIFIER' in  |
22 |                                      'LAMBDA' T Applys           |
23 |                                    where rec Applys = E |        |
24 |                                       < 'GAMMA'                  |
25 |                                          < 'LAMBDA' X Applys >   |
26 |                                          < 'GAMMA' T count X >   |
27 |                                       >                        ;|
28 |                                                                  |
29 | 'WITHIN' <'=' X Ex> < '=' Y Ey> => '=' Y <'GAMMA' < 'LAMBDA' X Ey > Ex> ;|
30 |                                                                  |
31 | 'REC' <'=' X E>                 => '=' X < 'GAMMA' 'Y' < 'LAMBDA' X E> > ;|
32 |                                                                  |
33 | ( 'IFSO_IFNOT' B E1 E2                                           |
34 | | 'IFNOT_IFSO' B E2 E1                                           |
35 | | '->' B E1 E2 )                => xfm < 'BETA' B E1 E2 > ;      |
36 |                                                                  |
37 | 'IF' B S                        => xfm < 'BETA' B S 'DUMMY' > ;  |
38 |                                                                  |
39 | 'UNLESS' B S                    => xfm < 'BETA' B 'DUMMY' S > ;  |
40 |                                                                  |
41 | ( 'RL' E1 Id E2                                                  |
42 | | '@' E1 Id E2 )                => 'GAMMA' < 'GAMMA' Id E1 > E2 ;|
43 |                                                                  |
44 | ':' N S                         => 'DELTA' < ',' < ':' N S > > S ;|
45 |                                                                  |
46 |#NEW_PAGE                                                         |
47 |                                                                  |
48 |# ADD IN A NEW LABEL.                                             |
49 |                                                                  |
50 | ':' N < 'DELTA' < ',' L * > S >  => 'DELTA' < ',' < ':' N S > L * > S ;|
51 |                                                                  |
52 |# COMBINE LABELS FROM LOWER IN THE TREE.                          |
53 |                                                                  |
54 | ';' < 'DELTA' < ',' Ll * > Sl > < 'DELTA' < ',' Lr * > Sr >      |
55 |                    => 'DELTA' < ',' Ll* Lr*> < ';' Sl Sr > ;     |
56 |                                                                  |
57 |# BUBBLE LABELS FROM THE LEFT OR RIGHT.                           |
58 |                                                                  |
59 | ( ';' < 'DELTA' Ls Sl > Sr                                       |
60 | | ';' Sl < 'DELTA' Ls Sr > )     => 'DELTA' Ls < ';' Sl Sr > ;  |
61 |                                                                  |
62 |# BUBBLE LABELS FROM THE STATEMENT.                               |
63 |                                                                  |
64 | ( 'WHILE' | 'UNTIL' ) E < 'DELTA' L S >                          |
65 |                    => 'DELTA' L < ('WHILE' | 'UNTIL') E S > ;    |
66 |                                                                  |
67 |# BUBBLE LABELS FROM THE RIGHT OR LEFT ARM OF THE CONDITIONAL, OR BOTH ARMS.|
68 |                                                                  |
69 | ( 'BETA' E Sl < 'DELTA' Ls Sr >                                  |
70 | | 'BETA' E < 'DELTA' Ls Sl > Sr )  => 'DELTA' Ls < 'BETA' E Sl Sr > ;|
71 |                                                                  |
72 | 'BETA' E < 'DELTA' <',' Ll * > Sl> <'DELTA' <',' Lr * > Sr> =>   |
73 |                    'DELTA' <',' Ll * Lr * > <'BETA' E Sl Sr> ;   |
74 |end Pal_standardization                                           |
```

```
 2 |#NEW_PAGE                        ******************************         #|
 3 |#                                *                          *           #|
 4 |#                  *    PAL CONTROL STRUCTURE     *                      #|
 5 |#                                *                          *           #|
 6 |#                                ******************************         #|
 7 |flattener Control_structure:                                             |
 8 |                                                                         |
 9 |     # THE APPLICATIVE CONSTRUCTS.                                       |
10 |     '_|_' Program                   => < 'DELTA' Program >             ;|
11 |                                                                         |
12 |     'GAMMA' Rator Rand              => 'GAMMA' Rator Rand              ;|
13 |                                                                         |
14 |     'LAMBDA' Bound_variable Body    => < 'LAMBDA' Bound_variable Body >;|
15 |                                                                         |
16 |     'BETA' Condition True_arm False_arm                                 |
17 |                                => < 'DELTA' True_arm  >                 |
18 |                                     < 'DELTA' False_arm >               |
19 |                                       'BETA'                            |
20 |                                       Condition                        ;|
21 |     # DATA STRUCTURES.                                                  |
22 |     'TAU' Expression *              => 'TAU' count Expression Expression*;|
23 |                                                                         |
24 |     'AUG' Tuple New_element         => 'AUG' Tuple New_element         ;|
25 |                                                                         |
26 |     # THE IMPERATIVE CONSTRUCTS.                                        |
27 |     ';' First_statement Rest_of_statements                             |
28 |                                => < 'DELTA' Rest_of_statements >        |
29 |                                     ';' First_statement               ;|
30 |                                                                         |
31 |     ':=' Address Value             => ':=' Address Value              ;|
32 |                                                                         |
33 |     'UNSHARE' Variable             => '$' Variable                    ;|
34 |                                                                         |
35 |     'WHILE' Condition Statements   => Cs where rec Cs =                 |
36 |                                       < 'DELTA'                         |
37 |                                         < 'DELTA' Cs ';' Statements_>   |
38 |                                         'DUMMY'                         |
39 |                                         'BETA'                          |
40 |                                         Condition                      |
41 |                                       >                                ;|
42 |     'UNTIL' Condition Statements   => Cs where rec Cs =                 |
43 |                                       < 'DELTA'                         |
44 |                                         'DUMMY'                         |
45 |                                         < 'DELTA' Cs ';' Statements_>   |
46 |                                         'BETA'                          |
47 |                                         Condition                      |
48 |                                       >                                ;|
49 |     'GOTO' Label                   => 'GOTO' Label                    ;|
50 |                                                                         |
51 |     'DELTA' Labels Block           => < 'DECLARE_LABELS' '¬' Labels Block >;|
52 |                                                                         |
53 |     'VALOF' Statements             => 'VALOF' Statements              ;|
54 |                                                                         |
55 |     'RES' Expression               => 'RES' Expression                ;|
56 |                                                                         |
57 |     # A MODULAR COMPILATION FEATURE.                                    |
58 |     'DEF' Definition               => < 'DEF' Definition >            ;|
59 |                                                                         |
60 |end Control_structure                                                    |
```

References

[1]   Aho, A.V., Ullman, J.D.:   The theory of parsing, translation, and compiling.
      Englewood Cliffs (N.J.):   Prentice-Hall 1972

[2]   Chomsky, N.:   On certain formal properties of grammars.   Information and Control
      2 (2), pp. 137-167, 1959

[3]   DeRemer, F.L.:   Simple LR(k) grammars.   Comm. ACM 14 (7), pp. 453-460, 1971

[4]   DeRemer, F.L.:   Transformational grammars for languages and compilers.   Techni-
      cal Report No. 50, Computing Laboratory.   University of Newcastle upon Tyne,
      England, July, 1973

[5]   Evans, Jr., A.:   A language designed for teaching programming linguistics.   Proc
      ACM 23rd Natl. Conf., Princeton, NJ, pp. 395-403, 1968

[6]   Feldman, J.A., Gries, D.:   Translator writing systems.   Comm. ACM 11 (2), pp.
      77-113, 1968

[7]   Ginsburg, S., Partee, B.:   A mathematical model of transformational grammars.
      Information and Control 15 (4), pp. 297-334, 1969

[8]   Hennie, F.C.:   Finite-state models for logical machines.   John Wiley & Sons, NY,
      1968

[9]   Johnson, W.R., Porter J.S., Ackley S.I., Ross D.T.:   Automatic generation of
      efficient lexical processors using finite state techniques.   Comm. ACM 11, 805-
      813 (1968)

[10] Kimball, J.:   The formal theory of grammar.   Prentice-Hall, Englewood Cliffs,
      NJ, 1973

[11] Knuth, D.E.:   On the translation of languages from left to right.   Information
      and Control 8 (October), pp. 607-639, 1965

[12] Knuth, D.E.:   Semantics of context-free languages.   Mathematical Systems Theory
      2 (2), pp. 127-146, 1968

[13] Knuth, D.E.:   An empirical study of FORTRAN programs.   Software Practice and
      Experience 1 (2), pp. 105-134, 1971

[14] Lewis, P.M., Stearns, R.E.:   Syntax-directed transduction.   J. Assoc. Comp.
      Mach. 15, 1968

[15] Peters, P.S., Ritchie, R.W.:   On the generative power of transformational
      grammars.   Info. Sci. 6, 1973

[16] Rosen, B.K.:   Tree-manipulation systems and Church-Rosser theorems.   J. Assoc.
      Comp. Mach. 20 (1), pp. 160-187, 1973

[17] Rounds, W.C.:   Mappings and grammars on trees.   Mathematical Systems Theory 4
      (3), pp. 257-287, 1971

[18] Wozencraft, J.M., Evans, Jr., A.:   Notes on programming linguistics.   Dept. of
      Electrical Engineering, Massachusetts Institute of Technology, Cambridge, MA
      1969

CHAPTER 2.F.

TWO-LEVEL GRAMMARS

C. H. A. Koster

Technical University of Berlin

Berlin, Germany

1.   Context sensitivity

1.1 On the borderline between syntax and semantics

In the definition of ALGOL 60, a clear distinction was maintained between the syntax
and the semantics of the language defined: syntax is concerned with the form of things,
semantics with their meaning.

The syntax was defined rather formally, in distinction to prose definitions which are
in use even now.

As an example, contrast the syntactic definition of arithmetic expressions now considered classical in section 3.3.1 of the ALGOL 60 Report [Naur 62] with the following
definition, taken from the description of the BASIC-System of a large computer manufacturer:

EXPRESSIONS

Two types of expressions are considered by BASIC, arithmetic and relational.
Arithmetic eypressions are rules for computing a value. Arithmetic operators may
not appear in sequence and must be explicitly stated. The following are invalid
arithmetic expressions:

.
.
.

OPERANDS

An operand itself is a valid expression.

There is no doubt that, for the compiler-maker, rigorous syntactic definition of the
language to be implemented is a help and not a hindrance, the use of CF grammars in
language definition has had a deep impact on the compiler-makers trade.

Formalization of semantics has clearly been less successful: the definitions of ALGOL 60, ALGOL W and ALGOL 68 all use some variant of the English language to state semantics in, with consequent trouble for the implementers.

Upon closer scrutiny the semantics in, e.g., the ALGOL 60 Report can be divided into two categories:

1) dynamic semantics: a definition of the effect and or value of some construct upon execution (Example: Paragraph 1 of section 3.3.3 of the ALGOL 60 Report). The dynamic semantics pertain to the execution phase of the program rather than its compilation phase, since the execution of a program generally depends on values supplied dynamically: In order to know what a program means, it has to be executed.

2) static semantics : admonitions, restrictions and other information about the form of the program, obviously directed at the compiler-maker (telling, e.g., how to treat borderline cases) or even at the programmer. (Examples: Section 2.4.3 of the ALGOL 60 Report, the "context conditions" in [van Wijngaarden 1969]).

Static semantics sails under false colours: it is syntax expressed verbally, because of impossibility to treat it in a formal way.
The restriction in 4.3.4 of the ALGOL 60 Report is syntactical in nature, having to do with matters which can be statically ascertained from the text of the program. It is also impossible to formalize by means of CF syntax. If the means would have been available, the authors of the ALGOL 60 Report would have included this restriction into the syntax, where it belongs.
In the revised version of the ALGOL 68 Report [van Wijngaarden 1974] the context conditions have disappeared from semantics and are now treated by syntax alone, making far more use of the syntactic mechanism.

It is difficult to draw the optimal borderline between syntax and semantics in any given language definition (indeed, cynics might argue that, at any point in time, that part of language definition which we can treat formally will be termed syntax and semantics starts where understanding ends). It is in the interest of compiler-makers that all matters syntactical are treated by one same helpful syntactical formalism. CF grammar is too weak for the purpose, a more powerful mechanism must be used.

2. Van Wijngaarden Grammars

Van Wijngaarden grammars arose from the need, felt in defining new programming
languages, for a type of grammar more powerful than context free grammar, allowing
the syntactic treatment of context dependencies. They are classified as "two-level-
grammars" because two superimposed syntactic levels can be discerned.

2.1 One-level van Wijngaarden grammars

As a first step in defining two-level van Wijngaarden grammar, we will introduce one-
level van Wijngaarden grammar.

2.1.1 Definition: 1VWG

A 1VWG is a 4-tuple
$$G = <S,T,E,P>, \text{ where}$$
S=<u>alphabet</u>, a finite nonempty set of <u>syntactic marks</u>, which does not contain the
<u>delimiters</u> $\bot$, , , : , ; or . .

T=<u>symbols</u>, a finite subset of S^+.

E = <u>initial notion</u> $\in S^+$.

P = <u>productions</u>, a finite subset of $(\bot(S^+-T)\bot) \times (\bot S^{*}\bot)^{*}$.

1.1.2 Notation

If $(\bot x\bot, \bot y_1 \bot \bot y_2 \bot ... \bot y_n \bot) \in p$, then we write x: y1, y2, ..., yn. .
When both $x:w_1$. and $x:w_2$. we write $x:w_1; w_2$. .

2.1.3 Terminology

A <u>protonotion</u> is any member of S^+.
A <u>notion</u> is any protonotion P such that
$$\exists y[P:y.]$$

A <u>member</u> is either a notion and is then termed <u>productive</u>, or is a symbol, or is some
other protonotion, which we will then term a <u>blind alley</u>.
A <u>list of notions</u> is a sequence of members separated by comma's.
A <u>direct production</u> of a notion X is a list of notions Y such that X:Y..
A <u>production</u> of a notion X is either a direct production of X or a list of notions
obtained by replacing in a production of X some productive member Y with a direct
production of Y.

A terminal production of a notion X is a production of X all of whose members are
either a symbol or empty.

A sentence of a 1VWG G is any terminal production of the initial notion of G. The
language of a 1VWG G is the set of sentences of G.

For every symbol, one or more graphics, its representations, are given.

2.1.4 Properties

The definition just given for a 1VWG is clearly functionally identical to that of a
Context Free grammar. The only unusual aspect is the insistence that the members are
denoted by strings rather than being treated as abstract elements of the set of pro-
tonotions. This property will be utilized in the definition of the second level.

2.1.5 Example

Following is a transscription in the present notation of section 4.2.1 of the
ALGOL 60 Report.

```
                left part: variable,becomes symbol;

                        procedure identifier, becomes symbol.

                left part list: left part;

                        left part list, left part.

                assignment statement:

                        left part list, arithmetic expression;

                        left part list, boolean expression.
```

Here, 'becomes symbol' is the only symbol.

Problem: an assignment statement consists of a left part list followed by an arithmetic or boolean expression, independent of the types of the variables in the left part list. Solved by static semantics in section 4.2.4.

2.2 two-level Van Wijngaarden grammars

The basic idea of 2VWG is to generate the productions of a 1VWG by means of a grammar.

2.2.1 Definition: 2VWG

A 2VWG is a 6-tuple
$$G = <M,S,T,E,R,P>, \text{ where}$$

M = meta alphabet, a finite set of metasyntactic marks, which does not contain the delimiters $\pm$, ι, $:$, $;$, , or . .
S = alphabet, a finite nonempty set of syntactic marks, which does not contain the delimiters $\pm$, ι, $:$, $;$, or . and such that $S_{\cap}M = \emptyset$.
T = symbols, a finite subset of S^+.
E = initial notion $\in S^+$.
R = metarules, a finite subset of
$$(\pm M^+ \pm) \times (S^+ U \pm M^* \pm)^* .$$
Let $L = \{x \in M^+ | \exists y [(\pm x \pm, y) \in R]\}$.
P = rules, a finite subset of
$$(\iota((Su \pm L \pm)^+ - T)\iota) \times (\iota(Su \pm L \pm)^* \iota)^*.$$

2.2.2 Notation

When $(\pm x \pm, \pm y_1 \pm \pm y_2 \pm \ldots \pm y_n \pm) \in R$, then we write

$$x::y_1 y_2 \cdots y_n .$$ Notation of metarules

When $(\iota x \iota, \iota y_1 \iota \iota y_2 \ldots \iota y_n \iota) \in P$, then we write

$$x: y_1, y_2, \ldots, y_n.$$ Notation of rules

When no ambiguity arises, the delimiter $\pm$ may be omitted. Indeed it is only introduced in this definition to assert unambiguous deconcatenability of rules and metarules.
When both x: w1. and x: w2. then we write x: w1; w2. .

2.2.3 Terminology

Observe that for every $m \in L$ the 4-tuple $G_m = (M, S^*, m, R)$ forms a 1VWG with as delimiter. In particular L(m) is the set of terminal productions of m. For string x,y and z, let subst (x,y,z) denote the result of substituting x for every occurrence of $\pm y\pm$ in z.

A <u>metanotion</u> is any member of L.

A <u>hypernotion</u> is any member of $(Su\pm L\pm)^+$.

A <u>protonotion</u> is any member of S^+.

A <u>notion</u> is any protonotion P such that there is a rule $(U,V)\in P$ and there are terminal productions $\bar{m}_1, \bar{m}_2, \ldots, \bar{m}_n$ of $m_1, m_2, \ldots, m_n\in L$ such that $subst(\bar{m}_1,m_1,subst(\bar{m}_2,m_2,\ldots subst(\bar{m}_n,m_n,U)\ldots))=P$.

A <u>member</u> is either a notion, and is then termed <u>productive</u>, or is a symbol, or is empty, or is some other protonotion, which we then term a <u>blind alley</u>.

A <u>list of notions</u> is a sequence of members separated by comma's.

A <u>direct production</u> of a notion X is a list of notions Y such that there is a rule $(U,V)\in P$ and there are terminal productions $\bar{m}_1, \bar{m}_2, \ldots, \bar{m}_n$ of the metanotions $m_1, m_2, \ldots, m_n$ such that

1) $subst(\bar{m}_1,m_1, subst(\bar{m}_2,m_2,\ldots subst(\bar{m}_n,m_n,U)\ldots)) = X$, and

2) $subst(\bar{m}_1,m_1, subst(\bar{m}_2,m_2,\ldots subst(\bar{m}_n,m_n,V)\ldots)) = Y$.

The terms <u>production</u>, <u>terminal production</u>, <u>sentence</u> and <u>language</u> can now be introduced for a 2VWG in the usual way.

2.2.4 Properties

Let us call a Finite State grammar, all of whose rules are of the form $A\rightarrow a$, where A is nonterminal and a is terminal, a Finite Choice grammar FC.

We thus have a hierarchy of grammars

$$FC \subset FS \subset CF \subset CS.$$

If in some 2VWG for every $m \in L$, G_m is a grammar of type T or weaker, we will indicate that 2VWG as a $\binom{T}{CF}$.

$$\binom{FC}{CF} \equiv CF$$

$$\binom{CF}{CF} \equiv \text{semiThue system } [\text{Sintzoff, 1967}]$$

It is extremely difficult to visualize a recogniser for general 2VWG; just ponder for instance over section 7.1.1. cc to jj of [van Wijngaarden, 1969].

Consider also the problem of finding out what rules are applicable after a certain rule, more precisely:

Referencing problem

Given a 2VWG G and two hypernotions U and V, is it decideable whether there are terminal productions $\bar{m}_i$ and $\bar{m}_i'$ of the metanotions m_i such that

$$\text{subst}(\overline{m}_1, m_1, \text{ subst}(\overline{m}_2, m_2, \ldots \text{ subst}(\overline{m}_n, m_n, U)\ldots)) =$$

$$\text{subst}(\overline{m}_1', m_1, \text{ subst}(\overline{m}_2', m_2, \ldots \text{ subst}(\overline{m}_n', m_n, V)\ldots)) \ ?$$

The referencing problem is undecideable because of the undecideability of the emptyness problem of the intersection of Context Free languages .

2.2.5 Example: assignment statement

Metasyntax:

        TYPE::ARITHMETIC; boolean.
        ARITHMETIC::real; integral.
        ARITHMETIC2::ARITHMETIC.

Syntax:

        TYPE left part: TYPE variable, becomes symbol;
                        TYPE procedure identifier, becomes symbol.
        TYPE left part list: TYPE left part;
                        TYPE left part list, TYPE left part.
        assignment statement:
                        ARITHMETIC left part list, ARITHMETIC2 expression;
                        boolean left part list, boolean expression.

The delimiter ± has as usual been elided.

This example introduces directly into the syntax the constraint given only verbally in the ALGOL 60 Report that the data types of all elements of a "left part list" must agree.

As it stands the example might have been written directly in context free notation, it would only have been more lengthy. Consider however the problem if ARITHMETIC had had an infinite number of terminal productions, as indeed the equivalent metanotion in ALGOL 68 has. Since there would need to be one "left part list" per terminal production of ARITHMETIC it would be quite impossible to write such a Context Free grammar. Either one uses the power of the 2VWG to impose the constraint syntactically or one must be content with a verbal statement of "static semantics".

2.2.6 Example: defining and applied occurrences

Consider a bare-bones language containing defining and applied occurrences of identifiers but nothing else:

```
program: statement sequence.
statement sequence:
      statement sequence, defining occurrence;
      statement sequence, applied occurrence;
      defining occurrence.
defining occurrence: define symbol, tag symbol.
applied occurrence : apply symbol, tag symbol.
tag symbol: letter symbol, tag symbol; letter symbol.
letter symbol: letter a symbol; ...; letter z symbol.
```

The above 1VW grammar allows us to write programs where the applied and defining occurrences of identifiers may appear in any order (except that one defining occurrence must come first). There might be multiple defining occurrences of the same identifier and perhaps some applied occurrence might have no corresponding defining occurrence.

Our goal is to impose two constraints on the language:

  (1) each applied occurrence of an identifier must correspond to some preceding defining occurrence
  (2) only one defining occurrence of each identifier is allowed.

To accomplish this we will proceed in several stages. First, a two-level grammar will be written whcih recognizes the same language as above but contains information about the occurring identifiers in the (nonterminal) notions themselves. Second, additional notions will be added to the grammar which yield ε if the constraint they represent is satisfied and otherwise are blind alleys and block the parsing of the program.

Metasyntax:

(A) TAGS :: TAGS TAG; TAG.

(B) TAG :: LETTER TAG ; LETTER symbol.

(C) LETTER :: letter ALPHA.

(D) ALPHA :: a;b;c;d;e;f;g;h;i;j;k;l;m;n;o;p;q;r;s;t;u;v;w;x;y;z.

Syntax:

 (a) program: TAGS statement sequence.

 (b) TAGS TAG statement sequence:

 (c)   TAGS statement sequence, TAG defining occurrence;

 (d)   TAGS statement sequence, TAG applied occurrence.

 (e) TAG statement sequence : TAG defining occurrence.

 (f) TAG defining occurrence : define symbol, TAG symbol.

 (g) TAG applied occurrence : apply symbol, TAG symbol.

 (h) LETTER TAG symbol : LETTER symbol, TAG symbol.

As promised this grammar recognizes exactly the same language as the foregoing. It does it however in the rather peculiar manner of having the initial notion produce an infinite number of alternatives, only one of which will not be a blind alley since the list of identifiers represented by that production of the metanotion TAGS will correspond exactly to the identifiers which actually appear in the input stream.

Say that we now want to introduce the constraint that an applied occurrence of an identifier must appear after its defining occurrence. This is equivalent to demanding in line(d) that the production for TAG must be a substring of the production for TAGS in that same line. (TAGS is the list of all the identifiers appear to the left of the one being applied). Let us modify that alternative so that it will recognize the input if and only if the condition is satisfied.

(b)   TAGS TAG statement sequence:

   ...

(d)   TAGS statement sequence, TAG applied occurrence, where TAG is in TAGS.

   ...

(i)   where TAG is in TAGSETY TAG TAGSETY2:EMPTY.

The production rule (i), which we call a <u>predicate</u>, needs some extra metasyntax to be complete:

(D)   TAGSETY2::TAGSETY.
(E)   TAGSETY::TAGS;EMPTY.
(F)   EMPTY::.

Observe that instances of the production rule (i) exist only when the left side TAG is embedded somewhere in the right side TAGSETY TAG TAGSETY2. This is insured by the Uniform Replacement Rule where the two occurrences of TAG must be replaced by the same (meta-)production. In the cases where an instance of (i) exists, the terminal production is the empty string and the parsing may continue. Otherwise this is a blind alley, the condition is not respected, and the parsing is blocked for that particular input string. Thus the permissible sentences of the language have been reduced to those where the first occurrence of an identifier is not an applied occurrence (and thus must be defining).

Multiple definitions are still possible. Let us eliminate those using the same technique:

(b)   TAGS TAG statement sequence:
(c)   TAGS statement sequence, TAG defining occurrence,
                where TAG is not in TAGS;

...   ...

The predicate we need here is just the inverse of the one we used before. This time it is little bit harder since we cannot exploit the Uniform Replacement Rule directly:

(j) where TAG is not in TAG2 TAGS :
        where TAG is not TAG2, where TAG is not in TAGS.
(k) where TAG is not in TAG2 : where TAG is not TAG2.

Hence an identifier is not in an identifier list when it is neither identical to the first element of the list nor somewhere in the rest of the list. We must use a meta-notion TAG2 here which again yields TAG directly. Since this kind of construction will be frequently needed let us impose the (metameta?) rule that any metanotion followed by a digit will produce that metanotion.

Now we need to verify if two identifiers are not identical:

(l) where LETTER TAG is not LETTER2 TAG2 :
        where LETTER symbol is not LETTER2 symbol ;
        where TAG is not TAG2.

They are not identical when either the first letters are not identical or the remainders of each identifier are not identical.

(m) where LETTER TAG is not LETTER2 symbol : EMPTY.
(n) where LETTER symbol is not LETTER2 TAG : EMPTY.

The two identifiers are certainly not identical if they have different lengths.

The job is done now if we can verify that two letters are different:

(o) where LETTER symbol is not LETTER2 symbol :
        where LETTER precedes LETTER2 in ALPHABET ;
        where LETTER2 precedes LETTER in ALPHABET .

ALPHABET is exactly what you think it is:

(G) ALPHABET :: abcdefghijklmnopqrstuvwxyz.

Now finally we can exploit the Uniform Replacement Rule to determine if one letter comes before another in the alphabet:

(p) where letterALPHA precedes letter ALPHA2
     in ALPHSETY ALPHA ALPHASETY2 ALPHA2 ALPHSETY3 : EMPTY.

This requires some more metysyntax:

(H) ALPHSETY :: ALPHAS ; EMPTY.
(I) ALPHAS :: ALPHA ; ALPHAS ALPHA.

Thus the last piece falls into place and we have defined a language obeying both of the initially proposed constraints. We have accomplished this purely within the bounds of the formal notation and hence have avoided the pitfalls inherent in a natural language presentation of "semantics".

3. Conclusion

We hope to have shown that two-level grammars allow to define precisely context-dependencies such as those that provide much of the compiler-makers daily sweat, and that even the forbidding armatory of van Wijngaarden grammars is understandable and usable by the normal compiler writer.
To conclude we should mention the fact that there exist other and rather different forms of two-level grammars, the most well known being Attribute Grammars [Knuth, 1968; Lewis et al, 1973; Bochmann, 1973; Rosenkrantz et al, to appear] which time and space do not allow us to treat here.

Acknowledgement the timely production of this lecture note would have been impossible without the help of Bruce Willis, who wrote the harder part.

References

G.V. Bochmann, Semantics evaluated from left to right, Publ 135, département d'Informatique, Université de Montreal (1973).

M. Griffiths, Relationship between Definition and Implementation of a language, in: Advanced Course on Software Engineering, Springer Verlag, 1973.

D. Knuth, Semantics of Context-Free Languages, Math. Systems Theory 2 (1968).

P.M. Lewis, P.J. Rosenkrantz, R.E. Stearns, Attributed Translations, Proc. Fifth Annual ACM Symposium on Theory of Computing (1973).

P. Naur (Editor), Revised Report on the Algorithmic Language ALGOL 60, Regnecentra-len, Copenhagen (1962).

Rosenkrantz et al., Compiler Design Theory, to appear at Prentice Hall, Englewood Cliffs, N.J. (1975).

M. Sintzoff, Existence of a van Wijngaarden syntax for every recursive enumerable set, Ann. Soc. Sci. de Bruxelles, 81 (1967).

M. Sintzoff, Grammaires superposées et autres systèmes formels, presented at the Journée d'Etude sur l'analyse syntaxique, Paris (1969).

R. Uzgalis, What every programmer should know about syntax, Lecture Notes UCLA (1972).

A. van Wijngaarden, Orthogonal Design and description of a Formal Language, Mathe-matisch Centrum Report MR 76, Amsterdam (1965).

A. van Wijngaarden (Editor), Report on the Algorithmic Language ALGOL 68, Numerische Mathematik, 14 (1969).

A. van Wijngaarden (Editor), Almost the Revised Report on the Algorithmic Language ALGOL 68, WG 2.1 Working Paper (1973).

CHAPTER 2.G.

SEMANTIC ANALYSIS

W. M. Waite

University of Colorado

Boulder, Colorado, USA

We have already seen how the syntax of a language allows us to analyze the structure of a program and display it as a tree, but this is only a part of the story. Structural analysis can be used to deduce the fact that the program contains a binary expression whose left operand is the identifier A, whose right operand is the identifier B and whose operator is +; it cannot tell us how to evaluate that expression. The purpose of the semantic analyzer is to derive an evaluation procedure from the structure of an expression and the attributes of its components.

An evaluation procedure is a sequence of primitive operations on primitive operands, and is completely specified by the definition of the source language. The semantic analyzer must deduce the attributes of the various components of a structure, ensure that they are compatible, and then select the proper evaluation procedure from those available. For example, if the semantic analyzer of an ANSI FORTRAN compiler sees a binary expression with integer operands and a + operator it selects the evaluation procedure for integer addition. When the operands are both real it selects the procedure for real addition, and if one is integer and the other real it signals an error [ANSI 1966, Section 6.1].

The input to the semantic analyzer consists of the structure tree (abstract program tree, abstract syntax tree) which specifies the algorithm, and the dictionary which provides attribute information. Two transformations, attribute propagation and flattening, must be performed to obtain the evaluation procedure.

Attribute propagation is the process of deriving the attributes of a tree from those of its components, while flattening (Chapter 3.E) transforms a tree into a sequence by making explicit the order in which the operators are executed. The result of the semantic analysis is an instruction sequence which may be thought of as a program for an abstract machine (source language machine, SLM) having the primitives of the source language [Newey 1972].

1. Tree Traversal

The structure tree may be subjected to various optimizing transformations, in addition to attribute propagation and flattening [Hopgood 1969]. These transformations may involve tree traversals, and are discussed in Chapter 5.E. Conceptually, each transformation takes place on the entire tree; practically, the scope of a particular transformation is quite limited. This property allows us to reduce the amount of random-access storage which must be devoted to the tree during semantic analysis.

During a particular traversal of the tree, each node might be encountered in three contexts:

a. As a descendent of another node (prefix)

b. After traversing a subtree descended from the node, when further subtrees remain to be traversed (infix)

c. After the last descendent subtree has been traversed (postfix)

If a node has only one subtree (e.g. the node for a unary operator), then no infix (type b) encounters occur. Many infix encounters will occur, however, if a node has many subtrees (e.g. the node for a conditional or a case statement.) Actions may be taken each time a node is encountered, and may depend upon the type of encounter as well as information contained in the tree.

The first "traversal" of the structure tree can be performed as it is being built: Each node of the tree corresponds to some production of the grammar for the source language. Suppose that the syntax analyzer can determine, without actually analyzing its components, that a particular production must derive a segment of the input text. (Such a determination would usually be made on the basis of some unique prefix, such as the if which begins on ALGOL conditional.) Making this determination is equivalent to a prefix encounter with a node in the structure tree. Any action which is appropriate to such an encounter, and which does not require the actual linkages of the tree, may therefore be taken. Similarly, if the completion of one component can be detected appropriate infix actions may be taken at that time; any postfix actions may be taken when the production is actually applied to reduce a segment of the input.

The evaluation procedures specified by the language definition, plus the degree and type of optimization desired, determine the number of traversals which must be made over the structure tree and the pattern in which they are to be made. This, in turn, determines the storage requirements of the semantic analyzer. For example, suppose that a small part of the tree must be traversed several times in sequence, no other part of the tree is examined during the sequence, and this part of the tree is not examined at any other time. If the entire tree is composed of subtrees with these properties, then random-access storage is required only for the largest subtree. Many existing compilers make such assumptions, although in some cases there is no theoretical limit to the size of the subtree which must be stored. The compiler then either accepts subtrees whose size depends upon the amount of storage which the user has allocated for the compiler during the current run, or it sets an arbitrary limit. Examples of the subtrees picked are FORTRAN statements and program units, ALGOL expressions, and PASCAL procedures.

When more extensive trees must be traversed several times, they are usually represented by some linear encoding and written to an intermediate file. The encoding is obtained from an initial traversal, which may be combined with the construction of the tree. Two basic strategies are available for processing a linearized structure tree, depending upon the manipulations which are required:

a. The fully-linked form of each relevant subtree can be reconstituted from the linearized intermediate form.

b. The linearized intermediate form can be used directly.

Care must be taken when using strategy (b) to ensure that the nodes of the tree are specified in the proper order.

One of the simplest linearizations of a tree is <u>postfix notation</u>: Prefix and infix encounters are ignored during the traversal which creates the linear encoding; a postfix encounter causes the specification of the node to be written to the intermediate file. In many cases the linearized form can be used directly, and recovery of the complete tree is a straightforward task.

Some operators influence the interpretation of their operands, but in a postfix string the operator is not encountered until after the entire operand has been processed. If a prefix encounter of a node in the structure tree causes output of the node specification, while infix and postfix encounters are ignored, each operator preceeds its operands in the linearized form. This <u>prefix notation</u> allows an operator to influence the processing of its operands when the linearized form is used directly, but considerably more storage is required to generate it. An arithmetic operator, for example, is not encountered in most source language text until after its first operand. To obtain the prefix notation, the subtree representing the entire expression would have to be built before any specifications were output.

Another useful representation of the structure tree is a list of <u>n-tuples</u>. Each node is represented by the n-tuple (operator, operand 1, ... , operand k, name.) "Name" is a unique identification associated with this node, and each operand is the name of a descendent node. Nodes with different numbers of descendents could be represented by different-length tuples, or by tuples of the same length with a special operand to indicate "no descendent." The most common case is n=4, with all tuples the same length.

Because each node of the tree is given an explicit name, the n-tuple notation can describe general directed graphs. This property is useful for certain kinds of optimization, such as common subscript elimination, but the presence of explicit names increases the bulk of the intermediate file and requires additional capabilities for cross-referencing. If the order of the n-tuples is fixed, the explicit name is unnecessary. Each descendent would then be represented by the index of the descendent tuple in the list, with 0 indicating that the descendent is absent.

2. Attribute Propagation

The declarative part of the program specifies the attributes of the leaves of the structure tree. These attributes must be used to deduce the attributes of entities resulting from the evaluation of subtrees. For example, consider the ALGOL 60 expression of Figure 2.1a. The syntax of the language allows us to create the structure tree of Figure 2.1b, and the mode indicated for each leaf is given in the declarative part of the program. By using the semantic rules stated in Section 3.3.4 of the ALGOL 60 Report [Naur 1963], we can deduce the modes of the subtrees as shown in Figure 2.1c.

A simple mechanism suffices for the case illustrated in Figure 2.1: Maintain a stack of modes (the semantic stack) which is updated as the structure tree is being built. A postfix encounter with a leaf places the mode of the corresponding entity onto the stack; a postfix encounter with an interior node causes the semantic analyzer to apply the appropriate rule to the two modes on top of the stack. These modes are removed and the proper result mode is entered in their place. (The result mode would also be used to modify the tree.)

Suppose that the rightmost leaf of Figure 2.1c were -2. According to Section 3.3.4.3 of the ALGOL 60 Report, the mode of k↑(-2) is real. Addition is defined for integer and real operands, but the result is integer only if both operands are; otherwise the result is real. This leads to a semantic error, because the result of an integer division is defined only if both of its operands are integer.

i ÷ (j+k↑2)   i,j,k <u>integer</u>

a) An ALGOL 60 expression

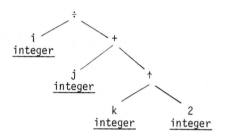

b) The structure tree for (a)

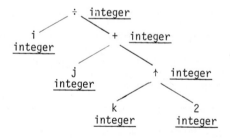

c) After attribute propagation

Figure 2.1

Attribute Propagation

Finally, suppose that the rightmost leaf were the integer variable n. The report states that the mode of k n depends upon the value of n: for n≥0 it is _integer_, and for n<0 it is _real_. Since the semantic analyzer has no way of determining the value of n, it cannot determine the mode of the result.

Even though the mode of the result cannot be determined precisely, it can be restricted to either _integer_ or _real_ (i.e. it is not _Boolean_, nor is it a string.) Thus the semantic analyzer could recognize a new mode (say, _arith_) which describes a value that might be either _integer_ or _real_. Such a mode is called a _union_ in ALGOL 68.

Application of the integer division operator to an operand of mode _arith_ may or may not constitute a semantic error. If this error is to be detected, a dynamic mode check must be included in the program. Unfortunately, most hardware does not permit a definitive mode check on values computed during execution (Chapter 3.A.) Another problem is that most computers would implement _integer_ and _real_ mode objects in different ways, and would have distinct instructions for performing addition on them. When one of the operands of + is an _arith_ mode object, the compiler will not be able to select the proper instruction.

So far, I have considered only the _bottom-up_ propagation of attribute information; _top-down_ propagation is also possible, and will solve our difficulties in Figure 2.1. The integer division operator requires operands of mode _integer_. Hence the result of the addition must be an _integer_, and this implies in turn that its operands must both be of _integer_ mode. If the rightmost leaf is replaced by n, then there is a semantic error unless n≥0. A dynamic check must still be inserted into the program, but now it tests the sign rather than a mode.

Top-down attribute propagation cannot generally occur as the tree is being built. (Suppose, for example, that the operands of the integer division were reversed in Figure 2.1a.) If the structure tree is represented in postfix notation, a backward pass over the linearized intermediate form can be used for top-down attribute propagation. The algorithm is virtually identical to that for the bottom-up case: A semantic stack is used to hold specifications of the required operand modes, which are then tested for compatibility with the modes derived previously.

3. Operator Identification and Coercion

Sections 3.3.4 and 4.2.4 of the ALGOL 60 report [Naur 1963] describe the relationship between operators and modes. For example, the mode of the result of an addition, subtraction or multiplication "will be integer if both of the operands are of integer type, otherwise real." There is no attempt to specify how this result is obtained, beyond the statement that the operators "have the conventional meaning."

When the compiler designer specifies evaluation procedures for these operators, he must use his knowledge of mathematics and of the structure of the target computer to implement "the conventional meaning" of each operator. One possibility would be to specify twelve distinct algorithms, four for each operator (e.g. integer + integer, integer + real, real + integer and real + real.) This approach is still feasible for ALGOL 60 because the number of combinations is not very large. As the number of modes and operators increase, however, the number of combinations rapidly becomes unmanageable.

The solution to the problem lies in the fact that most hardware offers only a limited number of algorithms for performing a given operation. For example, a target machine might provide only two add instructions: one implementing integer + integer and the other implementing real + real. The other two possibilities, integer + real and real + integer, would have to be implemented by converting the integer operand to a real and then performing real + real.

By stating "the conventional meaning" of addition, subtraction and multiplication in terms of two algorithms per operator and a single transfer function (Chapter 3.A., Section 1.3) which converts an integer operand to real, I can reduce the number of distinct algorithms from twelve to seven. This approach partitions the problem, reducing the rate at which the number of algorithms increases, but it introduces the possibility of semantic ambiguity.

Consider, for example, the ALGOL 60 expression of Figure 3.1a. Two possible evaluation procedures for this expression are shown in Figures 3.1c and 3.1d. (The expression to be evaluated at each step is enclosed in parentheses, with only the operand modes given. The result mode follows the parentheses; it is omitted if there is no result.) Note that there is no guarantee that these two evaluation procedures are equivalent. From the general considerations discussed in Chapter

```
a := i+j                          a real
                                  i,j integer
```

a) An ALGOL 60 expression

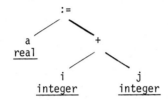

b) The structure tree derived from (a)

(integer+integer)integer; (integer)real; (real:=real);

c) A possible evaluation procedure

(integer)real; (integer)real; (real+real)real; (real:=real)

d) Another possible evaluation procedure

Figure 3.1

A Semantic Ambiguity

3.A, Section 1, we can conclude that Figure 3.1c might result in an overflow and Figure 3.1d might result in a loss of precision.

Semantic ambiguities such as this must be avoided in the language definition. The ALGOL 60 Report [Naur 1963] and the FORTRAN Standard [ANSI 1966] do so by specifying distinct algorithms for each operator and combination of operands. Each delimiter token, such as the + of ALGOL 60, may be considered to represent some set of algorithms, such as (integer + integer) integer, (real + real) real . Whenever this delimiter occurs in the structure tree, the semantic analyzer must select one of the algorithms in the set which the delimiter represents. In general, this selection (known as operator identification) depends upon both the modes of the operands and the context in which the entire subtree occurs. Once the algorithm has been selected, the operand modes which it requires are known. If the apriori modes of the operands do not agree with those required by the algorithm, then a sequence of transfer functions must be added to the structure tree. This process is known as coercion, and the sequence of transfer functions is called a coercion sequence.

It is important to note that the operator identification and coercion performed by the semantic analyzer are those specified by the language definition rather than by any particular hardware. In ALGOL 60, for example, there is no coercion associated with arithmetic operators; Section 3.3.4 of the report specifies distinct algorithms for each possible pattern of operand modes. A coercion is, however, associated with the ALGOL 60 assignment: "If the type of the arithmetic expression differs from that associated with the variables and procedure identifiers, appropriate transfer functions are understood to be automatically invoked." (Section 4.2.4 of the ALGOL 60 Report.) Further transfer functions may be inserted by the code generator in the course of implementing an algorithm on a particular target computer, but these transfer functions are machine-dependent and hence outside the scope of semantic analysis.

The operand modes of a language may be thought of as nodes in a directed graph [Hext 1967, Jorrand 1971]. Branches represent transfer functions which convert an object of one mode into an equivalent object of another mode (Chapter 3.A.) Operator identification is then performed by finding paths from the nodes representing the apriori modes of the operands to nodes representing the operand modes of <u>some</u> algorithm for the given delimiter. Each path defines a coercion sequence, and if more than one set of paths can be found a semantic ambiguity exists.

More than one graph may be specified for a given language. The semantic analyzer would then select a particular graph on the basis of context. In ALGOL 68 [van Wijngaarden 1969], for example, different graphs are used for the right-hand side of an assignation (a <u>strong</u> position) and for an operand of a formula (a <u>firm</u> position.) The latter is a subgraph of the former in the case of ALGOL 68, but such a relationship is not necessary.

I shall not discuss specific algorithms for operator identification and coercion, because most of those in use depend strongly upon the characteristics of a particular language [Hext 1965, Scheidig 1970, 1971, Woessner 1970, 1971].

References

ANSI: FORTRAN. X3.9-1966, American National Standards Institute 1966.

Hext, J.B.: Programming Languages and Compiling Techniques. Ph.D. Dissertation, University of Cambridge 1965.

Hext, J.B.: Compile-time type matching. Computer J. $\underline{9}$, 365-369 (1967).

Hopgood, F.R.A.: Compiling Techniques. MacDonald, 1969.

Jorrand, P.: Data types and extensible languages. SIGPLAN Notices $\underline{6}$, 75-83 (1971).

Naur, P. (ed.): Revised report on the algorithmic language ALGOL 60. CACM $\underline{6}$, 1-17 (1963).

Newey, M.C., Poole, P.C., Waite, W.M.: Abstract machine modelling to produce portable software. Software, Practice and Experience $\underline{2}$, 107-136 (1972).

Scheidig, H.: Anpassungsoperationen in ALGOL 68. Ph.D. Dissertation, Technical University of Munich 1970.

Scheidig, H.: Syntax and mode check in an ALGOL 68 compiler. In Peck, J.E.L. (ed.) ALGOL 68 Implementation. North-Holland 1971.

van Wijngaarden, A. (ed.): Report on the algorithmic language ALGOL 68. Num. Math. $\underline{14}$, 29-218 (1969).

Woessner, H.: Operatoridentifizierung in ALGOL 68. Ph.D. Dissertation, Technical

University of Munich 1970.

Woessner, H.: An identification of operators in ALGOL 68. In Peck, J.E.L. (ed.): ALGOL 68 Implementation. North-Holland 1971.

RELATIONSHIP OF LANGUAGES TO MACHINES

W. M. Waite

University of Colorado

Boulder, Colorado, USA

Selection of the proper interface between code generation and the analysis steps which preceed it is an engineering decision which balances two properties of the compilation:

a. Most of the structure of the program is determined solely by the source language.

b. Most of the representational details are determined solely by the target machine.

The interface should be chosen so that most of the structure is dealt with by the analysis steps, while most of the representational decisions are made by the code generation steps. This choice can be made in a way which is largely independent of a <u>particular</u> source language and target machine, if the fundamental concepts of programming languages and machine organization are understood.

We are interested in such features of the source language as the elementary data objects and operators which it provides, the methods available for constructing data aggregates and control structures, and the lifetime of objects during execution. The features of the target machine which are of interest are its register organization, its memory layout and addressing structure, and the facilities which it provides for instruction sequencing and environment specification. (We must regard the operating system, along with any software conventions in use by other systems, as a part of the target machine because they may act as constraints to fix the representation of certain data and operations.) It is not possible to explore all of these points in detail during this brief series of lectures; I shall therefore only attempt to outline the most important ones.

1. Data Objects

When we solve a problem on a computer, we use an algorithm to manipulate a set of objects which describe data that is relevant to the solution. The interpretation of these data objects depends upon the problem being solved. To implement the solution in a particular programming language, we must encode the data objects in terms of the primitive constructs available in that language; a further encoding is performed by the translator when it represents the data objects in terms of machine primitives. Most encodings are many-to-one, and hence we must distinguish two properties of each object: its value and the interpretation of that value. For example, consider the pattern of 32 bits specified in Figure 1.1a. If this pattern happened to be the contents of four consecutive bytes aligned on a fullword boundary in the memory of an IBM System/360 computer, it could be interpreted as any one of the values shown in Figures 1.1b-f. Unless the interpretation of the data item is known, it is impossible to choose the "correct" value from among those given.

1.1. Encodings. When an operator is applied to data objects, the interpretation of their values could be determined either by the operator or by the data objects themselves. For example, consider the addition of two integers. On Control Data

0100 0000 1000 0111 1001 0110 0101 1101

a) A 32-bit pattern

1 082 627 677

b) The pattern of (a) interpreted as a binary integer

-4 087 965

c) The pattern of (a) interpreted as packed decimal

.529 638 111 591 339 111 328 125

d) The pattern of (a) interpreted as a real

go)   (The first character is a space)

e) The pattern of (a) interpreted as a character string

STH   8,1629(7,9)

f) The pattern of (a) interpreted as an instruction

Figure 1.1

Interpretations of a Bit Pattern

6000 series machines, this could be done by executing the instruction IX6 X1+X2. X1 and X2 are registers containing 60-bit words. These words are interpreted according to the encoding of integers, and the encoding of the integer sum is placed in register X6. The interpretation of the words stored in X1 and X2 is determined solely by the operator IXX+X, and not by any property of the data objects. If the instruction FX6 X1+X2 had been executed with the same words in X1 and X2, they would have been interpreted according to the encoding of floating point numbers, and the encoding of the floating point sum would have been placed in X6.

In contrast, consider the fragment of an ALGOL program shown in Figure 1.2a. I and J are references to data objects which are interpreted according to the encoding of integers, and the encoding of the integer sum is the value of the formula I+J. The interpretation of the objects referred to by I and J is determined by the declarations of the identifiers I and J, and not by any property of the operator indication +. In Figure 1.2b the operands are interpreted according to the encoding of real numbers, and the encoding of the real sum is the value of the formula I+J.

Languages in which the interpretation of a data object is determined by the operator applied to it are called _typeless_ languages; those in which the interpretation is determined by the data object itself are called _typed_ languages. The attribute of a data object which specifies its interpretation in a typed language is called its _mode_. If the mode of a particular object can be deduced solely by examination of the program text, it is termed a _manifest_ mode. _Latent_ modes, on the other hand, cannot be deduced until the program is actually executed. An object whose mode is latent must therefore carry an explicit mode indication during execution. FORTRAN, COBOL and ALGOL 68 are examples of languages whose data objects have manifest modes: All variables are declared (either explicitly or implicitly) to have values of a certain mode, and there are different forms of denotation for constants of different modes. (The _union_ modes of ALGOL 68 are an explicit provision for controlled latency.) In contrast, SNOBOL4 has neither declarations nor implied mode specifications for its variables and hence the modes of its data objects are latent.

The major advantage of mode specification is that it enlarges the class of diagnosable errors to include inconsistent use of data objects. Such errors may

<u>integer</u> I, J;

... I+J ...

a) I and J interpreted as integers

<u>real</u> I, J;

... I+J ...

b) I and J interpreted as real numbers

Figure 1.2

Fixing Interpretation by Declaration

occur either when an object is created or when it is used. If the modes are manifest, then either kind of error is detected at the point of occurrence. When the modes are latent, however, both kinds are detected when the object is used incorrectly. Unfortunately, the actual error might have been the creation of an incorrect object. When an object forms part of a complex data structure, it is sometimes very difficult to determine the point at which it was created and the state of the computation at that point [Dunn 1973]. Thus the error-detection capabilities of a language will be enhanced if the modes are manifest rather than latent. Moreover, manifest modes can be checked statically by the translator, avoiding the necessity of a dynamic check which may be costly in execution.

Most machine languages are typeless, but in some cases mode information is carried by additional bits attached to each value [Iliffe 1972]. For example, on the Burroughs 5000 and 6000 series computers, descriptors (which represent addresses of various kinds) are distinguished from operands (which represent values.) A further distinction between single- and double-precision operands is made by the 6000 series. Even when the machine language of a particular computer is typeless, however, there may be redundancies in the encoding which make certain interpretations of certain data objects impossible. As a concrete example, consider the representation of decimal integers on a character-oriented computer. Not all bit patterns can be interpreted as valid digits, and hence an attempt to perform integer arithmetic on arbitrary character data may lead to a processor error. Other examples of this kind of redundant encoding are the addresses on IBM 1400 series computers and the packed decimal representation on System/360.

Mode specification and redundancy in machine language encoding of data items imply that machine-independent source languages must defer representational decisions by providing a variety of interpretations for data objects. This variety may be achieved in either a typed or a typeless language. In the former, many modes would be available; in the latter, many operators. I shall restrict my attention in these notes to typed source languages.

1.2. Primitive Modes. The set of all modes available in a typed language can be divided into two classes, the primitive modes and the derived modes. A data object whose mode is primitive has no internal structure which can be discussed in terms of the language. Derived modes, on the other hand, imply that the data object has components which can be accessed and manipulated explicitly within the language. In Section 2 I shall discuss the formation rules which allow the user of a typed language to construct objects with derived modes; here I shall review some of the data objects which have direct realizations in the hardware of current computers, and how these realizations are reflected in the primitive modes of current languages. The purpose of this review is to provide a basis for determining which decisions regarding representation of data objects should be taken during analysis of the source program, and which should be deferred until code for the target computer is being generated.

Integer data objects reflect the concept of counting which is fundamental to the design of current computers. They are used to index ordered sets of both data (arrays) and computations (iterations.) Every computer with which I am familiar provides hardware to implement addition and subtraction operations on non-negative integers. Usually there is also a natural interpretation of negative integers which is preserved by the addition and subtraction operations. Integer multiplication is often used in the mapping of a multidimensional array to a one-dimensional array, but this is really more dependent upon the implementation than upon the specification of the algorithm. On the Burroughs 5500, for example, two-dimensional arrays are represented as arrays of descriptors (Figure 1.3.) To reference such an array, the program places two subscript values in the stack and specifies the base descriptor. The first subscript value and base descriptor are used by the hardware to obtain a descriptor for the desired row, and the second value indexes the desired element. Arrays with more dimensions are treated in the same way; no integer multiplication is required for subscript calculations.

Integer arithmetic is exact. Integers can therefore be used to encode operands for business applications such as bank automation which require a larger range than that needed to (say) encode the indices of an array. Some hardware reflects this fact by distinguishing several lengths of integer (e.g. half- and full-word integers on the IBM System/360.) A machine-independent language should therefore permit the programmer to specify ranges of values which are relevant for his algorithm, leaving the choice of representation to the translator. Note that the

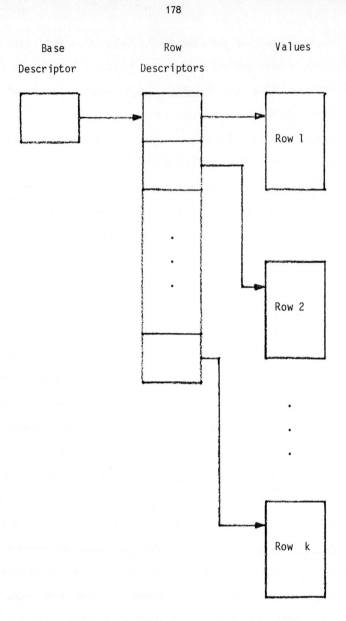

Figure 1.3

Array Storage on the B5500

set of possible ranges must not be fixed, since that would require a specification by the programmer which does not reflect the true needs of his algorithm. If the language is machine-independent, any fixed set of possibilities probably has no relevance for most target machines either!

The concept of a range of values must be distinguished from the concept of a mode. Range affects the manner in which a data object is accessed, but not its interpretation as an operand. This can be seen in the description of the halfword add instruction of the IBM System/360 [IBM 1967]: "The halfword second operand is expanded to a fullword before the addition by propagating the sign-bit value through the 16 high-order bit positions. Addition is performed by adding all 32 bits of both operands..." (The last sentence quoted and the remainder of the description is identical to that for a fullword add instruction.)

If a set has N elements, they may be placed in one-to-one correspondence with the integers 0,1, ... ,N-1. The definition of such a correspondence is a representational decision which might specify more properties of the set than necessary. For example, it would impose an irrelevant ordering on a set which was conceptually unordered. To avoid this problem, we must recognize the independent existence of finite sets. The programmer or language designer can then specify certain sets with exactly those properties needed, leaving the choice of encoding to the translator. Examples of such sets are {false, true} and the set of characters used in input/output communication. These occur so frequently that they are distinguished as Boolean and character modes respectively.

Most hardware does not make explicit provision for the encoding of Boolean mode objects. The representation should be chosen on the basis of the available instructions and storage access mechanisms, in an attempt to balance speed and space. You should realize that actual computation involving these objects is quite rare. In most cases, what appears to be a Boolean expression is really a test sequence which does not require any use of Boolean mode objects at all.

Different manufacturers use different encodings for characters, some of which (as I pointed out earlier) are not valid representations of integers. Hardware performs the conversion from external to internal representation, and special instructions are often available to manipulate these internal representations. In order to retain machine independence, the character set must be assumed to be unordered. Thus two character mode objects may be tested for equality but not for relative magnitude, nor is a successor function defined. Also, range is a meaningless concept because of the lack of order.

There is another important finite set whose characteristics are determined by the hardware and operating system of the target computer: the set of memory locations. A memory location is represented by an object of address mode, which may be encoded in many ways. As in the case of character encodings, an address may not be a valid representation of an integer. The set of memory locations must also be assumed to be unordered, due to the different storage allocation algorithms used in various situations. For example, on the Burroughs 5000 and 6000 series computers, arrays are allocated to different segments of memory. The relationship between the addresses of two segments may vary during execution, and hence no ordering of these addresses may be assumed. (The order of elements within a single array is defined, however, as discussed in Section 2.3.)

The lack of order in the sets of characters and memory locations precludes implementation of algorithms such as text sorting and most dynamic storage allocation. Each of these algorithms requires some additional ordering property which is not specified for the set. In the case of a sort, the desired order is fixed by the problem specifications and is independent of the internal representation of characters. The storage allocation problem, on the other hand, does not demand a particular order; it merely requires that there be some successor function defined on memory locations so that linear scans of the entire allocatable area are possible. Both kinds of order can easily be imposed by providing additional primitive functions on the elements of the set. These additional functions would be used to access the required property explicitly, and only when that property was relevant. Then implementation would vary from one machine to the next, depending upon the representation chosen for the set.

Most engineering and scientific applications require operands which have a larger range than can be economically provided by a single value interpreted as an integer. Also, most of these computations involve measurements which are subject to inherent errors. Precision may be traded for range without increasing the storage required for an object by interpreting it as a mantissa-exponent pair rather than a single integer. Precision is lost because some bits of the object are devoted to the exponent, thus leaving fewer available for the mantissa. This new interpretation of the object is distinguished as the primitive mode floating point. Floating point objects are ordered, but a successor function cannot be defined if machine-independence is to be preserved. Specification of explicit ranges is also impossible on the same grounds.

1.3. Mode Conversions. It is often useful to define an equivalence between values of different modes. For example, Section 2.2.3.1 (d) of the ALGOL 68 report [van Wijngaarden 1969] states: "Each integer of a given length number is equivalent to a real number of that length number." It goes on to say (in paragraph f of the same section) that there is a value of mode int equivalent to each character, but that the equivalence is "defined only to the extent that different characters have different integral equivalents."

Equivalent values of different modes generally have different hardware representations. This means that specific operations, called transfer functions, are usually required to implement the equivalences. Some transfer functions (such as int to real) may be provided as primitive actions in the instruction set of the target computer; others may be implemented by a sequence of instructions. (Note that when the objects of two different modes have identical encodings no target machine actions are needed to implement a transfer function.)

There are two distinct classes of transfer function: those which can be executed without loss of information and those which cannot. It is obvious that a general transfer function from floating point to integer cannot be managed without loss of information, because there are floating point objects (such as 3.14) which have no integer equivalent. A transfer function from integer to floating point does not have this problem, but remember that it must pack an integer exponent and an integer mantissa to form a floating point number. If the original integer has a larger range than that represented by the mantissa portion of a floating point object, then information would be lost in the conversion.

Some care must be exercised in selecting representations for the primitive modes of a language to ensure that the equivalences defined by the language are preserved by the transfer functions used to implement the necessary mode conversions. For example, on the IBM System/360 the range of an ALGOL 68 _int_ must be limited to the mantissa range of a floating point object (24 bits) rather than using the full range of an integer object (32 bits.) This limitation would be unnecessary for a FORTRAN or ALGOL 60 integer because the specifications for those two languages do not precisely define equivalence between integer and floating point objects.

2. Formation Rules

Program structure is provided by the formation rules of a language. They are concerned with the grouping of data objects into conceptual units, and the definition of control structures. In this section I shall not explore the full range of formation rules available to the user of the language, but rather shall concentrate upon those which are relevant for the analyzer/generator interface specification because they are reflected in the architecture of contemporary computers.

2.1. _Expressions._ The concept of an expression is borrowed from normal mathematics. It is a tree written in linear form (Figure 2.1), with each node representing an elementary computation. A leaf of the tree represents a computation which can be carried out independently of all other nodes in the tree, while an interior node represents a computation which requires as operands the results of the computations represented by its descendants. One possible evaluation procedure for this tree is the following:

a. Select _any_ leaf and perform the computation which it represents.

b. If the selected leaf is the root, then stop. The result of the computation is the value of the tree.

c. Otherwise, transmit the result to the parent of the leaf and delete the leaf from the tree.

d. Go to (a).

This evaluation procedure is strictly sequential, but nothing is said about the order in which the leaves are selected. In ALGOL 68 terminology, the elaboration is collateral. One could also specify evaluation procedures which performed parallel

(a+b)*c

a) A typical expression

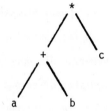

b) The equivalent tree

Figure 2.1

The Meaning of an Expression

computations or which selected leaves in some particular order.

The major reason for using an expression is to avoid naming each of the intermediate results created in the course of a computation: When a leaf of an expression is evaluated, the result is anonymous. The compiler is free to do what it will with these anonymous results because it has explicit control over the times at which they are created and the times at which they are no longer of interest; it does not need to worry about whether the programmer may access them unpredictably.

The concept of an anonymous operand appears in hardware as the register structure. Details vary widely, but five broad categories cover most computers:

a. No programmable registers. All instructions take their operands from memory and return their results to memory. (IBM 1400 series, IBM 1620)

b. A single arithmetic register. Unary operators take their operand from the register, binary operators use its content as their left operand and take their right operand from memory. All operators return their result to the register. The arithmetic register often has an extension, which does not have the full capability of the major register. (IBM 7090, Control Data 3000 series, many minicomputers)

c. Multiple arithmetic registers. Binary operators may take their right operand either from a register or from memory; all operators return their result to a register. Some registers may be paired to provide an analog of the extension in a single-register machine, but all have essentially the same capabilities. (IBM System/360)

d. Hierarchy. Both operands of a binary operator must be in registers, and all registers have essentially the same capabilities. All operators return their result to a register. This type of machine could be considered identical to type (a), with the registers and memory forming a two-level storage hierarchy. (Control Data 6000, 7000 series)

e. Stack. The top n locations of the stack hold the operands of an n-ary operator, with the rightmost at the top. They are removed by the operator, which pushes its result in their place. (ICL KDF9, Burroughs 5000 and 6000 series)

The number of anonymous operands may exceed the number of registers in all cases except (e). Excess operands must be stored in memory, thus effectively naming them. This is a representational decision which must be made on the basis of the target machine characteristics, and hence the interface should simply deal with anonymous results as such.

2.2. Names. A name is an object which refers to another object. This concept appears in hardware as the random-access memory: Each name defines a cell which may contain any object referred to by the name. The name has a definite lifetime, called its extent, during which the content of the defined cell may be changed without affecting the name itself. When the extents of two names overlap, those names must define disjoint cells.

Names can be represented by identifiers, and accesses to the cells which the names define are indicated by the appearance of these identifiers. A particular identifier is made to represent a particular name by means of a declaration. This declaration has a scope which defines the part of the program over which it is valid. Scope is a static property of the program, whereas extent is a dynamic property. Figure 2.2 illustrates the meaning of these two terms in the context of an ALGOL 60 program.

A single occurrence of an identifier may represent more than one name. For example, consider a local variable of a procedure in ALGOL 60. Conceptually, a new name is created each time the procedure is entered and an occurrence of the identifier represents each of these names in turn. The extents of the names represented by a local variable are not disjoint if the procedure is invoked recursively, according to Section 4.7.3 of the ALGOL 60 Report [Naur 1963].

Objects of address mode are used to implement names. When a particular occurrence of an identifier represents only one name, then the address used to implement that name can be completely specified by the translator. If the occurrence of the identifier represents more than one name, and if their extents do not overlap, then the translator can implement all of them by the same address. If the extents of any pair of names represented by the same occurrence of an identifier overlap, then the translator cannot specify a complete address to implement that occurrence of the identifier. There are three common mechanisms for providing the

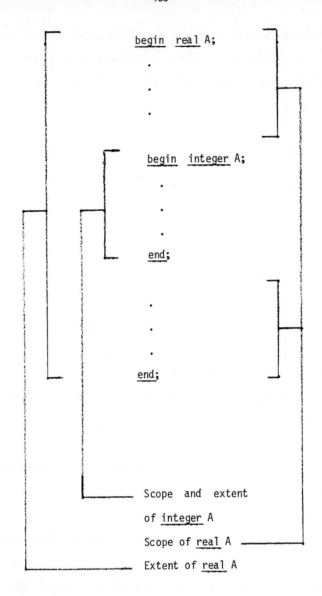

Figure 2.2

Scope and Extent in ALGOL 60

information to complete the specification at execution time:

a. Program modification. The complete memory address is computed by the program and placed into an instruction which is then executed. (IBM 1400 series, IBM 1620)

b. Indirect addressing. The complete memory address is computed by the program and placed into some memory location. The instruction references that location, and the hardware interprets its content as an address. (IBM 1620, Burroughs 6000 series, many minicomputers)

c. Address modification. The complete memory address is computed by the hardware at the time the reference is made. Part of the data required to compute the address is supplied by the referencing instruction, the remainder is obtained from one or more processor registers. (IBM System/360, Control Data 3000, 6000, 7000 series, Burroughs 5000, 6000 series)

Selection of a particular mechanism is obviously a representational decision which should be deferred until the characteristics of the target machine are known. This means that access information must be included in the specification of a named operand. For example, a local variable in ALGOL 60 might be distinguished from an own variable or a variable local to a containing block. The code generator might then use different mechanisms to complete the address specification in each case.

2.3. Aggregates. An aggregate is a single object which is made up of a number of distinguishable component objects. These components may be unordered or ordered, and may be of the same or different modes. (Most programming languages provide only for ordered aggregates in which all components are of the same mode.) If the components are unordered, then each is identified by a component name; if they are ordered, then each is identified by an integer index. Component names are not computable, and hence are specified literally in the source program. Indices, however, may be computed during the execution of the program.

In many programming languages, the indices of an aggregate are restricted to a range of integers. This restriction is unnecessary; any object which belongs to a finite set could be used to index an array which had one element for each object in that set. In order to allocate storage for the array and to access an element, a one-to-one correspondence must be established between the N elements of the set and the integers 0,1, ... ,N-1. This correspondence might not be implied by the definition of the set, and might not be a relevant property of the set for any operation except array indexing. Such constraints do not affect the use of the object as an index, although they would restrict the operations allowed in index expressions. For example, consider an array indexed by characters. On each computer, the character encoding used by the manufacturer provides an obvious one-to-one correspondence with a range of integers. The size of the array will vary from one machine to another, as will the particular element selected by a given character.

Each aggregate is usually implemented as a contiguous area of memory defined by a base, with the position of each component specified relative to that base. When the components are unordered, then the translator is free to rearrange them if this would be advantageous. The component name is translated into a displacement, defined in terms suitable for the target computer, which does not change during execution of the program. An aggregate with ordered components cannot be rearranged by the translator, but component references which do not change during execution can certainly be converted to displacements. Even if the index must be computed during execution, it may be possible to decompose the index expression into the sum of a constant and a variable part. The constant part can then be converted to a displacement by the translator. Thus a general reference to a component of a data aggregate consists of a base, a displacement and an index which must be combined at the time the program is executed. The hardware mechanisms listed in Section 2.2 are used to perform this combination.

It is important to distinguish all three parts of the reference because of the ways in which machines access these aggregates. For example, it may be that a particular machine instruction specifies an address and an index register whose content is to be added to that address when the instruction is executed. In this case, it is possible for the translator to combine the displacement with the base to obtain an effective base address. Such a strategy will not work, however, on a machine which addresses data aggregates indirectly. For example, on the Burroughs 6700 the base is the address of a descriptor which contains a pointer to the aggregate itself and specifies its size. In this case, even though the displacement is available at compile time, it must be added to the value of the index at run time to form an effective index. The hardware then combines this effective index with the descriptor to yield the final reference.

It may be that each component of an aggregate occupies only a part of an addressable memory location on the target computer. The number of memory locations which the entire aggregate occupies could then be reduced by packing the components instead of allotting one location to each. This usually leads to a tradeoff, because the components may be more difficult to access individually when the aggregate is packed. On the other hand, if the aggregate is heavily used as a unit, the difficulty of accessing individual components may be irrelevant. The optimum representation depends upon the number of aggregates involved, the size of each, the frequency of access to components and the frequency of use of the entire aggregate as a unit.

When an aggregate is packed, the access algorithms change: The displacement must specify the position within a memory location as well as the memory location itself. Some computers allow an instruction to specify the extraction of the relevant field directly as a part of the operand while a sequence of instructions may be required on others. In any case, the actual instruction would be constructed by the code generator on the basis of information about the structure of the aggregate and about the position of the relevant component.

2.4. Procedures. There are two aspects of procedure invocation: control interaction and data interaction. The control interaction is realized by instructions that transfer control to the procedure and back to the calling program, a process that involves saving status before the transfer and restoring it upon return. Data interaction is established when a procedure accesses global data or arguments passed by the calling program, and when it returns a value to the calling program.

It is useful to distinguish three components of the control interaction: call, entry and return. Implementation of a procedure invocation is distributed among these components, which occur at different points in the program and have access to different kinds of information. The status of the calling program (consisting of a program address and an environment specification) is passed to the procedure as an implicit argument. Like all arguments, its value is known only at the point of call. Transfer of control to the procedure requires establishment of only a minimal status (consisting of the program address and argument values.) Any further environment is established at the point of entry to the procedure, where such items as the lexicographic level and the amount of local storage are known. The status of the calling program is available at each point of return, since this status is an implicit argument of the procedure. If a value is to be returned explicitly, it is also known at this point. Restoring the caller's status returns control, and the value may be passed as though it were a parameter. Further action may be required at the point of call to incorporate this value into the caller's environment.

Control interaction is manifested in hardware by the mechanisms for status saving and transfer of control. There are four common methods:

a. Relevant status is placed on a stack by the hardware when a subroutine jump is executed. (Burroughs 5500, ICL KDF9)

b. Relevant status is placed in a register by the hardware when a subroutine jump is executed. (Data General NOVA, UNIVAC 1108, IBM System/360)

c. Relevant status is placed in memory by the hardware when a subroutine jump is executed. The memory location bears some fixed relationship to the target of the subroutine jump. (CDC 3000, 6000, XDS 940, UNIVAC 1108)

d. Separate instructions are provided for saving the relevant status and performing the subroutine jump. (GE 645)

The makeup of the "relevant status" depends entirely upon the computer. At the least, it contains the return address.

There are five common parameter mechanisms used to pass data to a procedure:

a. Call by value - The argument is evaluated and its value passed to the procedure. Assignments to the corresponding bound variable (if permitted) do not affect the argument value in the calling program.

b. Call by result - This mechanism is used to return values to the calling program. Before the call, an address is computed for the argument. As control is returned to the calling program, the value of the corresponding bound variable is assigned to the memory element specified by that address.

The assignment takes place upon a normal exit from the procedure, and hence is not made if a direct jump to a global label is executed within the procedure.

c. Call by value-result - This is a combination of (a) and (b). The argument value is passed to the procedure and the value of the corresponding bound variable is copied back into the calling program when control is returned.

d. Call by reference - The address of the argument is computed before the procedure is invoked, and this address is passed. Access to the corresponding bound variable from within the procedure is indirect, and thus the argument itself is being manipulated.

e. Call by name - The argument expression is converted to a parameterless procedure which, when invoked, yields the same result as the argument. Whenever the corresponding bound variable is accessed, this procedure is invoked.

Methods (a) and (b) are the basic ones; the other three can be synthesized from them.

Figure 2.3 illustrates the effect of the different parameter mechanisms. The program in Figure 2.3a is written in ANSI FORTRAN, except that the interaction between the main program and the function violates Section 8.3.2 of the standard [ANSI 1966] (if a bound variable becomes associated with an entity in COMMON, assignments to either within the function are prohibited.) The final values of M and N depend on the parameter mechanism that is used; possible values are listed in Figure 2.3b. (Call by result cannot be used in the example since that mechanism does not pass values to the function.) Most language standards do not explicitly state the parameter mechanisms which must be provided. By careful study of their effects, however, some of the possibilities can usually be eliminated as incompatible with various statements in the standard. Only method (c) or method (d) could be used in an implementation of ANSI FORTRAN, for example.

The element in the calling program that defines each argument sets up a value that is passed to the procedure. This value is an address in cases (d) and (e); the object program must therefore have the ability to manipulate addresses as values if either of these mechanisms is to be used. Call by result does not require that

```
FUNCTION I(J,K)
COMMON L
J = J + 1
L = L + K
I = J + L
RETURN
END
COMMON M
M = 1
N = I(M,M+3)
STOP
END
```

a) A FORTRAN Program

	N	M
Call by value	7	5
Call by value-result	7	2
Call by reference	12	6
Call by name	14	7

b) Possible results

Figure 2.3

The Effect of the Parameter Mechanisms

anything be passed <u>to</u> the procedure, but each argument must be updated when the invocation of the procedure has been completed.

The implementation of the data interaction may also be distributed over the call, entry and return components of the procedure invocation: Argument values must be set up at the point of call, and additional manipulations may be required after entry to the procedure. For example, if the call by value and call by value-result mechanisms pass addresses, then code must be generated to move the argument values into local storage. When call by result or call by value-result is used, values from local storage must be moved back to argument locations at the point of return. Generally, this will also require actions at the point of call after control has actually returned from the procedure.

Each of the three components of the procedure invocation must be distinguished in order to defer the representational decision until the characteristics of the target computer are known. The "point of call" is actually a broad area which begins just before the computation of the first argument value and ends just after any actions required to incorporate returned values into the caller's environment. It is necessary to distinguish both of these limits, since procedure invocations on some computers require distinct operations at each of them. (The "mark stack" and "enter" instructions of the Burroughs 6700 are an example of this situation.) Similarly, the "point of entry" must be considered to begin just before the first declaration of the procedure and end just before the first executable statement; both limits must be marked to permit flexibility in the choice of representation. A procedure may have several returns, each involving a sequence of actions. Again, both the beginning and end of such a sequence could be marked. In this case, however, my experience has been that a single return operation is sufficient.

References

ANSI: FORTRAN. X3.9-1966, American National Standards Institute 1966.

Dunn, R.C.: SNOBOL4 as a language for bootstrapping a compiler. SIGPLAN Notices $\underline{8}$, 28-32 (1973).

IBM: IBM System/360 Principles of Operation. Sixth Edition, IBM Corp. 1967.

Iliffe, J.K.: Basic Machine Principles. Second Edition, MacDonald 1972.

Naur, P. (ed.): Revised report on the algorithmic language ALGOL 60. CACM 6, 1-17 (1963).

van Wijngaarden, A. (ed.): Report on the algorithmic language ALGOL 68. Num. Math. 14, 29-218 (1969).

RUN-TIME STORAGE MANAGEMENT

M. Griffiths

Laboratoire d'Informatique

Université de Grenoble, France

I - <u>INTRODUCTION</u> -

This short course is an introduction to classical storage allocation and access techniques used by compilers (see [Randell 64], [Gries 71], [Griffiths 71]). It will be followed by a discussion of some more advanced features in chapter 3.C.

One of our aims will be to show which language features require different types of storage management, in which we distinguish a hierarchy. At the bottom end is the static allocation scheme for languages like FORTRAN, in which it is possible to know the address that each object will occupy at run time. The next level comes with the introduction of stack techniques for languages like ALGOL60, where space is allocated on a stack at block entry and released at block exit. The stack is not a sufficient model if the language allows store allocation and liberation in a non-nested fashion. List processing languages, like languages which allow parallel or pseudo-parallel processing, are in this category, and require more sophisticated treatment. Languages like PL/1 require all three types of storage management.

2 - <u>STATIC ALLOCATION</u> -

In a static allocation scheme it must be possible to decide at compile time the address that each object will occupy at run-time. In turn, this requires that the number and size of the possible objects be known at compile time, and also that each object may only have one occurrence at a given moment in the execution of the program. This is why, for example, in FORTRAN, arrays have constant bounds and procedures cannot be recursive.

The process through which the compiler goes in doing storage allocation for a static language is thus very simple. During a first pass of the text, the compiler creates a symbol table in which is kept the name, type, size and address of each object encountered. During code generation (which may be in the same or a subsequent pass), the address of each object is thus available for insertion into the object code.

Consider a FORTRAN program in which occur floating point variables A, B, a floating point array T of size 10 x 100, and fixed point variables I, J. We will suppose that floating point variables occupy four bytes and fixed point variables two. The symbol table could contain the following information :

Name	Type	Size	Address
A	float	4	0
B	float	4	4
T	float array	4000	8
I	fixed	2	4008
J	fixed	2	4010

The information under 'address' may, of course, be the absolute or the relative address of the object concerned, and will most often be a relative address, to be used, for example, as a displacement with respect to an implicit or explicit register.

The above is not meant to be a complete storage allocation scheme for FORTRAN, since no attempt has been made to trent COMMON statements or SUBROUTINES. The important thing is the basic principle, which states that the position of each object at run time can be foreseen at compile time, and any one object can always occupy one same storage address during the complete execution of the program. This does not mean that every FORTRAN compiler follows this principle, in particular the second part, since a particular compiler may, for other reasons, allocate, for example, different addresses to local variables during successive calls of a given SUBROUTINE.

3 - DYNAMIC ALLOCATION -

Modern programming languages allow recursive procedure calls, and this precludes any attempt at a static storage allocation scheme, since to a variable which is declared within a recursive procedure may correspond more them one value at a given moment during the execution of the programme. Note that recursive procedures are not the only perturbing factor, since the existence of arrays with calculated bounds means that it is no longer possible to know where each object starts and ends, since their size is unknown to the compiler.

The usual storage allocation model in these circumstances is a stack, on which entry to a block or a procedure causes a new allocation, the space being freed at exit from the block or procedure. The use of a stack to model nested structures is a standard device. Consider a program with the following block structure, where the blocks are numbered for convenience :

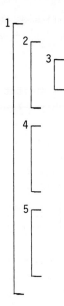

We consider the run-time stack at different moments during the execution of the program. Within block 4 :

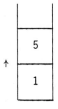

Direction
of growth ↑

The figures indicate that the zone contains the values of variables declared in the block of the same index.

Within block 5 :

↑

Notice that the values corresponding to variables declared in block 5 use the same physical space as those from block 4. Thus the stack allow the continual reutilisation of the available space.

We now suppose that block 2 is in fact a procedure, which is called from block 5. The stack will have the following form while the procedure is being executed :

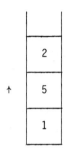

The order of occurrence of data zones in the stack is no longer that which indicates static inclusion (the procedure 2 is included in block 1 but not in block 5). We will say that the procedure is statically contained in block 1 and dynamically called from block 5. If procedure 2 calls itself, a further data zone, with new values corresponding to the same variables, is opened on the stack.

3.1 - Block Linkage -

At any moment in time, a base register B points at the start of the most recent data block in the stack (we will ignore hardware problems which may lead to slightly different solutions). B allows reference to be made to all those values which correspond to local variables. Consider the following simple program in ALGOL60 :

```
1. begin integer a, b, c ;
      ...
      2. begin integer x, y, z ;
            ...
            x := y + z ;
            a := b + c ;
            ...
         end
   end
```

When the execution of the program arrives at the two assignments, the form of the stack will be :

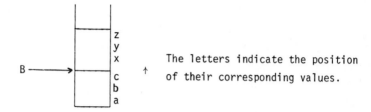

The letters indicate the position of their corresponding values.

x, y and z are accessible by their displacements from the value of B, say dx(B), dy(B), dz(B). This allows us to compile the first assignment, but not the second, since reference is made to a, b and c, which are not indicated by the base register. To solve this problem, the data zone corresponding to each block will indicate the start of the preceeding block, together with its own block number :

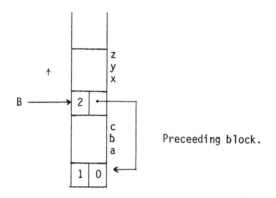

Preceeding block.

This pointer is simply the value of B before entry to the block. We see that the blocks are linked together on a chain (which always ends with block 1). When reference is made to a non-local variable, the compiler produces instructions which descend the chain looking for the block number, and positions a base register on the relevant data zone. The non-local value is accessed by displacement from this base register.

The same pointer in the stack serves both in searching for non-local variables, and in resetting the stack at block exit. As can be seen from the diagram, the base register points at the word which contains its preceeding value. At the end of a block, the stack is returned to its former state by replacing the base by this former value. The values declared within the block which has just been left are lost, and the space can be re-used.

However, in the case of a procedure, the two uses of this pointer do not necessarily indicate the same point, since reference to non-locals considers statically containing blocks, whereas procedure exit is to the dynamically calling block. Consider the following program :

1. <u>begin</u> <u>integer</u> a, b, c ;
    2. <u>procedure</u> f ;
      <u>begin</u> ...
          a := b + c ;
          ...
      <u>end</u> ;
      ...
    3. <u>begin</u> <u>integer</u> x, y, z
          ...
          f ;
          ...
      <u>end</u>
  <u>end</u>

When the program executes f the stack is as follows :

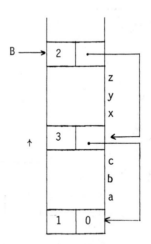

Within f, no reference can be made to x, y or z, and no purpose is served in examining block 3 on the chain when looking for non-local values. A second pointer should be included in the data zone of f, which indicates its statically containing block (block 1). In the particular example we give, this may seem to be simply an optimisation, but in certain cases this pointer becomes a necessity :

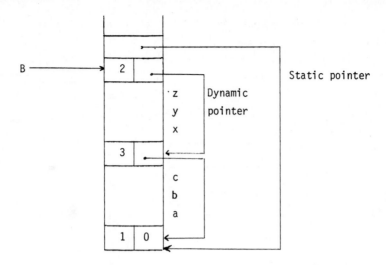

The static pointer is used in searching for non-locals, the dynamic pointer being used to reset the stack at exit from the procedure. The reason why this is unnecessary with blocks is that the two pointers would always have the same value.

3.2 - Displays -

References to non-local variables can be inefficient with the above method if nesting is deep. One way to avoid this is to use the DISPLAY introduced in [Dijkstra 60]. The idea is to have a table in which are kept pointers to the currently active data block corresponding to each block of the program. References to non-local variables are made by displacement from the value of the relevant display, which contains those values which would be inserted in the base register after searching down the chain for the relevant block level.

The simple DISPLAY defined above is thus a table with one entry per block :

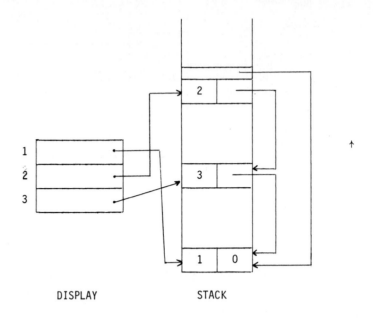

DISPLAY   STACK

Extra information needs to be kept in the stack to facilitate the resetting of the
DISPLAY at block or procedure exit.

An improvement to the above scheme is to create a new DISPLAY at each
block or procedure entry, and keep it in the stack. This time the table can contain
just those pointers which would be useful within the block, that is to say the
position in the stack of those data blocks to which reference may be made during
the execution of the current block or procedure. The data blocks referenced correspond to blocks in which are declared variables which are referred to as non-
locals in the current block. The values of the pointers can be deduced at block
entry by following the static chain, and this chain is thus followed only once per
block instedad of once per non-local reference. We consider an example :

```
1. begin integer a, b, c ;
        ...
2.       begin integer d, e, f ;
3.             procedure p(x) ; value x ; integer x ;
4.             begin integer i, j, k ;
                   i := a + d ;
                   ...
               end ;
               ...
               P(a)
         end
     end
```

The stack will have the following form when the assignment is executed as a result of the call of p at the bottom of the program :

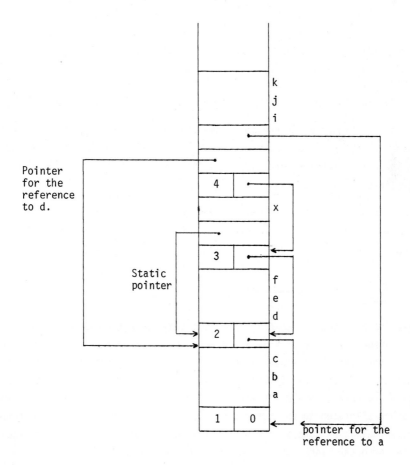

Since block 4 contains two non-local references (to a and d), two pointers are prepared, which indicate the corresponding data blocks.

3.3 Compaction of the Stack -

Consider the small ALGOL60 program that we have already seen :

1. begin integer a, b, c ;

      ...

2. ·   begin integer x, y, z ;

              ...

          end

      end

When block 2 is being executed, the form of the stack is always the following :

This means that it is not necessary to do the linkage joining block 2 to block 1.
Suppose that the base register points as usual, that a register S indicates the
first free space in the stack, and also that integers occupy one address. Just
before entry into block 2 we have.

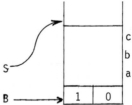

The addresses of a, b and c avec 1(B), 2(B) and 3(B). To enter block 2 it is sufficient to augment the value of S by 3 and refer to x, y and z as 4(B), 5(B), 6(B).
The base does not move, no linkage is done, and reference to non-locals is shorte-
ned in many cases. In general, if the inner block is not a procedure and the outer
block contains no array, this may always be done. Arrays are a problem, since the
amount of space allocated to the outer block is unknown at compiletime. The compac-
tion can nevertheless be done at the price of always keeping the space for simple
variables in the outer block. Consider the following program :

1. begin integer a, b, c ;
        array t [...] ;
        ...
2.   begin integer x, y, z ;
                array u [...] ;
                ...
            end
        end

In block 1 the stack has the form :

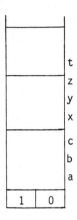

The space for t starts at 7(B), and the spaces for x, y, z are not used, but must be reserved. In block 2, we arrive at :

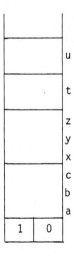

With this mechanism it becomes possible to allocate space for data of fixed size only at procedure level, as is suggested in [Gries 71] and [Wichmann 73]. Array space is allocated at block level, but only procedures need link information. The space for simple variables in inner blocks (x, y, z in the example) can be reused for parallel inner blocks, this part of the stack being modelled at compile-time.

3.4 - Parameter Linkage -

In chapter 3.1 the different methods of passing parameters were discussed. In terms of stack structure, the methods of value, result, reference or different combinations of them cause no problem. Parameters by name (or by procedure) are more difficult. The actual parameter corresponding to a formal parameter by name is re-evaluated at each reference to the formal, and the evaluation takes place in the environment of the call of the procedure. For example :

```
1.   begin procedure f(x) ; integer x
2.         begin ...
                  x

                  ...

          end ;
3.        begin integer a, b ;
                  ...

              f(a+b)

                  ...

          end
     end
```

Procedure f is statically contained in block 1. However, the reference to x requires re-evaluation of a+b, and hence reference to variables of block 3. The stack will have the following form :

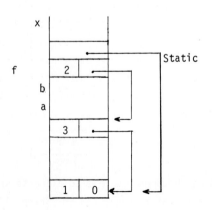

Since block 3 is not on the static chain of f, a and b cannot be referenced. In fact, the evaluation of actual parameters corresponding to formal parameters by name is by creation of a parameterless procedure (called a 'thunk') which is linked to the calling block.

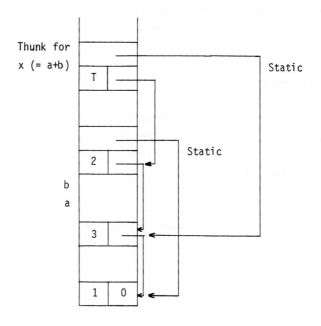

The static pointer of a thunk points to the data zone towards which points the dynamic pointer of the procedure of which the formal is a parameter. This allows access to a and b, and ensures the correct environment in all circumstances.

3.5 - Labels -

Whether he approves of goto or not, the compiler writer usually has to implement it. A goto a non-local label requires that the stack be in the right state on arrival. Since the scope of a label, like the scope of any variable, is known at compile-time, and thus has a block number, finding the right environment is simply a matter of descending the static chain. That is to say that the local base register points at the level of data which corresponds to the block in which the label occurs. As usual, all data at a higher level is lost and the space can be reused.

4 - AGGREGATES -

We have already seen that the definition of arrays has a considerable influence on storage allocation algorithms, since it may be that the size of an array is unknown at compile time, which means that some part of the storage alloca- tion mechanism must be dynamic. But arrays are not the only way of forming aggre- gates, and we will also consider storage allocation for structures.

4.1 - Arrays -

If the size of an array is known at compile time, its space can be allocated statically, as in FORTRAN. Arrays may follow each other in the run-time data zone, and the compiler can always foresee the address of each one. In a lan- guage in which the limits can be calculated at run-time, allocation must be dyna- mic. On an ALGOL60 stack, for example, arrays are stored in two parts. One space will be allocated by the compiler in the same way as those allocated to simple variables ; this space will contain a pointer to the actual location of the array. Space for the array is seized at block entry, after calculation of the amount neces- sary, and this on top of the stack. For example :

```
1.    begin integer n ;
             read (n) ;
2.           begin integer array p[1 : n], q[1 : 10, 1 : n] ;
                 ...
             end
      end
```

When the program is being executed, and inside block 2, the stack will have the following form :

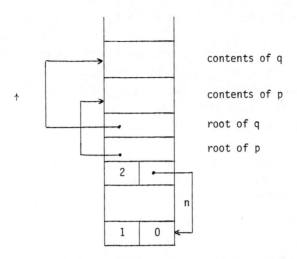

contents of q

contents of p

root of q

root of p

We call the pointer which indicates the address of an array, its 'root'.

In the following paragraphs, we will discuss different ways of ordering the elements of arrays in order to facilitate references to different elements.

4.1.1 - Reference by multiplication -

The definition of FORTRAN, which will be used as an example of this method, specifies the order in which array elements are stored, and chooses to store them with the first subscript varying the most rapidly. This is the opposite of usual mathematical convention, but in most cases the order is of no importance. Consider an array defined by

DIMENSION A(5, 10)

A is a matrix of size 5 x 10, and will occupy 50 consecutive storage locations in the order :

A(1, 1), A(2, 1), ..., A(5, 1), A(1, 2) ..., A(5, 2), ..., A(1, 10), ..., A(5, 10).

When making a reference, element A(I, J) is to be found in position

$$(J - 1) * 5 + I - 1$$

from the start of the array. In general, given an array T with bounds B_i :

DIMENSION $T(B_1, B_2, ..., B_n)$

Element $T(I_1, I_2, ..., I_n)$ is to be found at position :

$$(\ldots \; ((I_n - 1) * B_{n-1} + I_{n-1} - 1) * B_{n-2} + \ldots + I_2 - 1) * B_1 + I_1 - 1$$

This sequence of calculations must be made at run-time by the instructions generated for each reference to an array element. Note that, if any I_i is a constant, parts of the calculation may be done at compile time. A displacement address is of course calculated by multiplying the position by the size of each element, and adding the result to the address of the first element of the array.

The case of FORTRAN is the simplest possible, but other languages may equally well be treated by the same method. ALGOL60 is a typical example, in which an array declaration has the form :

$$\underline{\text{integer array}} \; t \; [l_1 : u_1, \; l_2 : u_2, \; \ldots, \; l_n : u_n]$$

Both lower and upper bounds are given, and both may be calculated at run-time. Consider a reference :

$$t \; [i_1, \; i_2, \; \ldots, \; i_n]$$

If the elements are stored as in FORTRAN (ALGOL60 leaves the decision to the compiler writer), the position of the element is found by replacing $(I_j - 1)$ by $(i_j - l_j)$ and B_j by $(u_j - l_j + 1)$, which gives :

$$(\ldots \; ((i_n - l_n) * (u_{n-1} - l_{n-1} + 1) + i_{n-1} - l_{n-1}) * (u_{n-2} - l_{n-2} + 1)$$
$$+ \ldots + i_2 - l_2 * (u_1 - l_1 + 1) + i_1 - l_1.$$

Whereas in FORTRAN the bounds are constants known at compile time, in ALGOL60 they are calculated at run-time, at block entry, and must therefore be stored in the stack. For each dimension, the quantity $(u_j - l_j + 1)$ is also calculated at block entry and stored in the stack in order to improve the speed of references. Thus the diagram given in § 4.1 was incomplete, and in practice, the stack will look like :

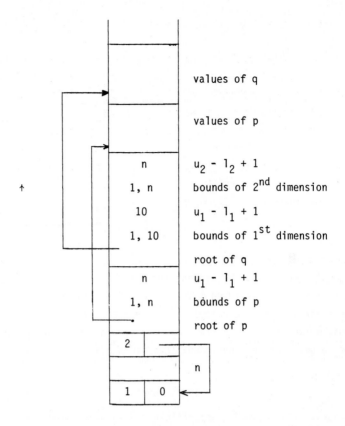

The compiler will once again take advantage of each time bounds or subscripts are constants to optimise the calculations.

However, since ALGOL and similar languages leave a choice, another method is often used which follows pointers instead of doing arithmetic :

4.1.2 - Reference by Code Words -

A better title for this methode would be repeated indexing, since a matrix is treated as a vector of vectors, a three-dimensional array as a vector of matrices, each of which is a vector of vectors, and so on. The method will be illustrated by an example :

<u>integer</u> <u>array</u> t [3 : 10, - 5 : 7] ;

The root of t points at a vector of pointers to the vectors of elements :

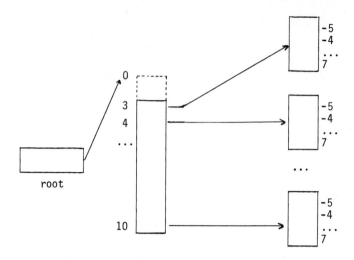

Every pointer points at the element zero of the next vector (whether this element exists or not), thus avoiding substraction of the lower bound. The sequence of instructions for a reference calculates the address by adding the first subscript to the root, which gives an address. Add the second subscript to the contents of that address to get another, and so on. That is to say, in general, an element is found by :

$$(\ldots \text{contents (contents (contents (root)} + i_1) + i_2) \ldots + i_n)$$

This sequence can be coded very efficiently in many computers.

4.1.3 - Range Testing -

An important source of errors in certain types of program is that resulting from using subscripts which are outside the declared bounds. A good compiler will allow the programmer to specify whether he wishes the object code to test subscripts, since this testing is a process which may slow down considerably the running program. A compromise which is useful in the multiplication method is just to test if the final address is in fact part of the array, thus avoiding the overwriting of instructions of the program, for example.

This need to test subscripts is, for some people, a criticism of current language design, since in most cases it is clearly wasteful. It would be more efficient to write

    for i index of t do t[i] := ...

than the standard step - until construction, the compiler handling bounds.

4.2 - Structures -

Structures are sets of named fields which are variously defined in different languages, for instance in PL/1 or ALGOL68 :

```
DCL   1  POINT
          2   X, Y   FIXED ;
struct point (integer x, y) ;
```

References are made by

```
POINT.X   or   x of point
```

Other languages have other definitions. In the run-time memory, a zone is created which will contain the successive fields of the structure. Structure references are resolved at compile time, since at least the address of the root of each field is known.

The quantity of memory given to each field depends on the type of the field. If a field is of simple type (as in the above example), space is directly reserved for the corresponding value ; otherwise a pointer serves as a root, as in the method of storing arrays.

The fields of a structure may themselves be structures or arrays, but this causes no inconvenience with the methods that have already been described.

5 - LISTS -

It is not always possible to manage store as a stack, since this requires that storage be released at known moments, in the opposite order from its allocation, and in a completely nested manner. Languages which allow the use of heavily - structured data and the manipulation of pointers do not follow this rule. Examples of language features of this type are own in ALGOL60, the list-processing primitives hd, tl and cons, reference in ALGOL W, ref ref in ALGOL68. In all these cases, the programme requires allocation of memory as the result of the execution of statements, and this in unforeseeable quantities ; the allocation lasts as long as some live pointer references the element of memory, and liberation can take place when no live pointer allows access to the object. Allocation and liberation are at arbitrary moments.

As an example, let us add the list primitives to ALGOL60, which allows the writing of programs like :

```
l := null ;
    for l := cons (hd (a), l) while tl(a) ≠ null do
    a := tl(a)
```

Which transfers the contents of list a to l, supposing that a contains at least one element. Each execution of the function cons causes the allocation of a new space in memory, which will have the form :

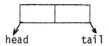

head   tail

Thus the list (a (b c) d) is represented as follows :

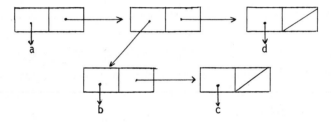

The diagonal stroke represente null, the end of a list or the empty list. The statement

```
l := cons (a, cons (cons (b, cons (c, null)), cons (d, null)))
```

would create the above list structure, and a pointer would be placed in the memory space corresponding to l.

New manipulations may mean that some or all of the elements of a list structure are no longer accessible ; the space can them be recovered by a technique called 'garbage collection'.

5.1 - Free Lists and Garbage -

The storage spaces seized by cons have to be taken from a special zone, for which we will use the ALGOL68 term 'heap'. Since, in the example seen above, the space seized was always the same size, it is possible to cut the space available for the heap into elements of this size. These elements are initially linked together in a special list called the 'free list'. When space is required within cons, an element is taken from the free list and used by the routine. When the free list is empty, no more space is available. However, as we have already seen, it is usually possible to recover space as a result of the inaccessibility of no longer used elements by the process of garbage collection.

Garbage collection is a process which usually works in two phases, the first being to mark all useful elements and the second to recover space at the same time as removing the marks. Marking requires that the algorithm consider in turn each pointer defined in the program ; the pointer is followed, marking each accessible element. If the element marked contains pointers, these also must be followed, and so on. A bit may be available within the element to be marked, or otherwise a heap model is kept which consists of one bit per heap word. When marking is complete, the whole heap space is examined. Marked words have their marks removed, and unmarked words are put into the free list.

The main problems of garbage collection are its inefficiency, and the fact that it logically takes place when there is no space left in the memory, and so the garbage collection algorithm has no work space. Sufficient space must therefore be kept in reserve.

5.2 - Storage Collapse -

Many languages allow space to be taken from the heap in elements of arbitrary and differing sizes. In this case the idea of a free list no longer works, and the following problem can arise. Consider a memory in which the unused spaces are shaded :

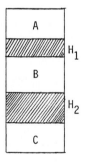

The memory is shared between three items, A, B and C, which leave two holes H_1 and H_2. If we now wish to store an item D of size greater them that of H_1 or H_2 but less than their sum, them a difficulty has arisen. The existing items must be

moved towards one end of the memory in order to leave a consecutive piece of store
of large enough size. This process is called 'storage collapse'.

It may be necessary to use storage collapse even if the heap consists
of elements of like size, for example if, in a fixed storage space, the stack
grows from one end and the heap from the other. When the two meet, garbage collection with a free list would not allow the stack to expand, and so the heap must be
collapsed.

Storage collapse is preceeded by a marking algorithm, but is even less
efficient than was the use of a free list, since items are moved. In this case, all
pointers to a moved item must be updated, which is a costly process. It is usual to
use a mixture of free list and storage collapse techniques in order to keep a certain level of efficiency. In particular, since objects may be moved, it may be practical to direct all pointers to these objects via individual pointers which are
themselves in a zone which is garbage collected by free list techniques. Only these
individual pointers need updating, since they themselves are not moved :

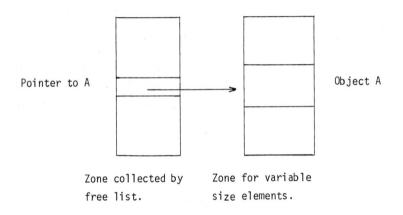

Pointer to A   Object A

Zone collected by   Zone for variable
free list.   size elements.

All references to A are to the pointer in the pointer zone and not to A itself.

A complete garbage collection method will be given in chapter 3.C.

6 - PARALLEL PROCESSES -

Another situation in which it is not possible to use a stack is that
in which the time-scale of the execution of a program is not that indicated by consecutive execution of the instructions, for instance in the control of real-time

processes, or in their simulation. A given task may activate a second one, activation which looks like a procedure call, except that the relative order of evaluation of the two tasks is unknown. Thus it is possible for the calling task to finish before the called task, which is in contradiction with the necessity of a completely nested calling structure. What is more, the called task may need access to data furnished by the calling task, and thus, at its completion, the calling task may not be able to liberate its data space.

Consider an example from an operating system. A routine P can activate an input-output operation as a task, in order to transfer data to be found in the data zone of P. But P may well terminate before the input-output operation ; in this case, the data space of P cannot be liberated, since the input-output task continues to make use of the space.

We see that compilers for languages which allow parallel processing, or which simulate such processes, must use a storage allocation technique which allows storage recovery by methods similar to those used for lists; space is seized at block or procedure entry, the space being taken from the heap. At any one moment, the different active tasks indicate their data zones. Within each zone exist pointers to those zones to which access may be required, exactly as in the case of the second type of display seen above. When it is necessary to recover storage, a garbage collection algorithm can follow the pointers from the different tasks in order to mark their data zones. These zones is their turn point to any other data zones to which the task may make reference, and these zones are also marked. Space can then be recovered by storage collapse :

Description blocks

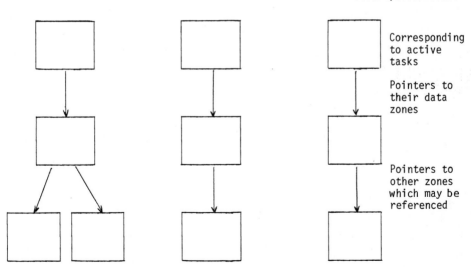

Corresponding to active tasks

Pointers to their data zones

Pointers to other zones which may be referenced

This represents only one method of keeping track of used and unused store, and there exist many variations on the same theme.

7 - CONCLUSION -

The generation of executable machine code is obviously completely conditioned by the storage allocation techniques which are to be used at run-time. We have tried to give some idea of the basic storage allocation mechanisms, without going into too much detail. It should be noted that an extremely wide variety of techniques exist, and many interesting ideas have not been discussed here. However, most of the variety stems from efforts to improve the basic themes that we have developped, or to adapt them to particular machines.

One point of importance is the very close relationship between storage allocation mechanisms and the type of operations which may exist in the language. Small changes in language design can lead to large changes in the architecture of the compiler and in the complexity of the run-time system.

REFERENCES

J.W. BACKUS et al.
Report on the Algorithmic Language ALGOL60
CACM, Vol.3, N°5, May 1960

E.W. DIJKSTRA
ALGOL60 Translation
Supplement, ALGOL Bulletin 10, 1960

D. GRIES
Compiler Construction for Digital Computers
Wiley, 1971

M. GRIFFITHS
Langages Algorithmiques et Compilateurs
Course Notes, University of Grenoble, 1971

I. B. M.
PL/1 Language Specifications
IBM Form C28 - 6571, 1965

B. RANDELL, L.J. RUSSELL
ALGOL60 Implementation
Academic Press, 1964

B.A. WICHMANN
ALGOL60 Compilation and Assessment
Academic Press, 1973

A. van Wijngaarden et al.
Report on the Algorithmic Language ALGOL68
Num. Math. 14, pp. 79-218, 1969

N. WIRTH, C.A.R. HOARE
A Contribution to the Development of ALGOL
CACM, Vol.9, N° 6, June 1966

CHAPTER 3.C.

SPECIAL RUN-TIME ORGANIZATION TECHNIQUES FOR ALGOL 68

Ursula Hill

Technical University of Munich

Munich, Germany

1.   *INTRODUCTION*

In the previous lectures, in particular those of W. M. Waite and of M. Griffiths, basic concepts like *mode* and *object* etc. in higher programming languages were introduced and their equivalents in the machine discussed. Especially, I refer to the presentation of the principles of data storage management, such as *static* and *dynamic* [1] *storage allocation, procedure calls*, realization of more *complex data structures*, and the illustration by examples of storage allocation models for FORTRAN and ALGOL 60.

The intention of this lecture is to discuss the realization of those principles for a more ambitious language, ALGOL 68. This language requires the study of a great deal of the general principles, although some important concepts, coroutines or partial parametrization for instance, are missing. There are still other restrictions in connection with modes - e.g., there are no arrays of arrays [2] - and the manipulation of data - e.g., changing the length of flexible arrays by joining new components is not possible - as examples which should simplify the handling for the compiler without being inconvenient for the user of the language. On the other hand, ALGOL 68 contains features of questionable usefulness which can only be integrated into the general storage mechanism with special additional provisions.

This discussion is based on the concrete Munich implementation of ALGOL 68 for the Telefunken TR4 [9]; the basic design of the compiler was developed by G. Goos [5], [6]. Many of the details to be mentioned can be realized in different ways. Especially, I should call your attention to the work of the Brussels ALGOL 68 implementation group which, at the same time, in some cases came to the same, in others to quite different solutions, and which published detailed descriptions [2].

---

[1] Throughout this lecture the term *static* is connected with tasks which can be carried out at compile-time, whereas *dynamic* means that the execution is only possible at run-time; the attribute dynamic is used, in particular, for run-time stack operations.

[2] Instead of the ALGOL 68 technical term *multiple value* we shall mostly use the more usual term *array*.
Furthermore, we shall use the terms *block* and *procedure* in the following sense: a block corresponds to a serial clause containing at least one declaration or generator, a procedure is an object the mode of which begins with *proc*.

1.1. SHORT OUTLINE OF DATA STORAGE PRINCIPLES

Our first task is to give a summary of data storage allocation principles applicable to ALGOL 68. We begin with a brief survey of basic concepts such as handling objects of more usual modes and the mechanisms for run-time stack and heap [7], [8], [9].

1.1.1. FIXED AND VARIABLE PARTS OF OBJECTS

Each object consists of a fixed and a variable part. In this context *fixed* means that the size of the needed storage area is known at compile-time, whereas for the *variable* part this size can only be determined at run-time. The variable part may be empty. In any case, it is not empty if the considered object is, or contains as subvalue, a dynamic array or a string. At run-time, fixed and variable part may be stored in disjoined data areas, furthermore, the variable part can consist of several components which need not stand in consecutive storage cells (see Figure 1).

It is essential that within the fixed part relative addressing is possible at compile-time.

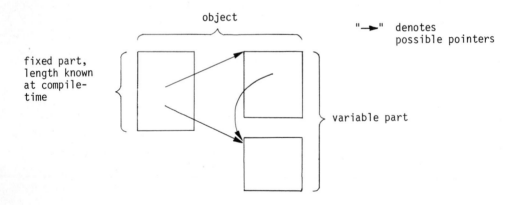

Figure 1. Fixed and variable part of an object

1.1.2. MODES AND OBJECTS IN ALGOL 68

ALGOL 68 contains several primitive standard modes as *int*, *real*, *char*, etc. Objects of these modes have only a fixed part of constant length (depending on the machine). Furthermore, there are standard modes *string*, *bits*, and *bytes*, which can be considered as special array modes. Objects of these modes need not be handled like general multiple values: for objects of modes *bits* or *bytes* the length normally is restricted to one or two machine words:

bits: | ... *1101* | , bytes: | *BYTES ...* |

An object of mode *string* is of flexible length. It can be represented as a fixed part, which is nothing more than a (internal) pointer, and a variable part composed of the length as a particular entry and the actual string (see Figure 2).

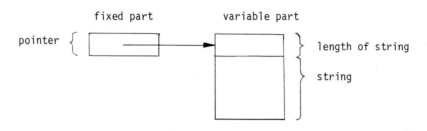

Figure 2.   String

Starting from the standard modes, new modes can be defined. Most important (and also known from other languages) are *references*, *multiple values* (arrays) and *structured values* (records).

An object of a reference mode consists of a fixed part containing an address (see also 3.2).

A multiple value consists of a descriptor (information vector) as fixed part and the set of the elements as variable part, which at least in the case of a subvalue, need not be stored in consecutive storage cells (see Figure 3). The length of the descriptor depends only on the dimension. For arrays with fixed bounds the set of elements can be considered to belong to the fixed part; but we don't go further into the discussion of such optimization possibilities.

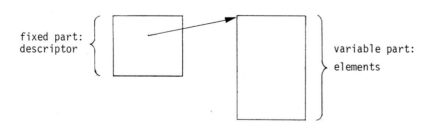

Figure 3.   Multiple value (array)

A structured value is the collection of the objects of the component modes. The fixed part is the sequence of the fixed parts of the components, the variable part is the collection of the appropriate variable parts. In particular, the length of the fixed part is $\sum_i Li$, where Li = length of fixed part of i-th component.

An example is given in Figure 4.

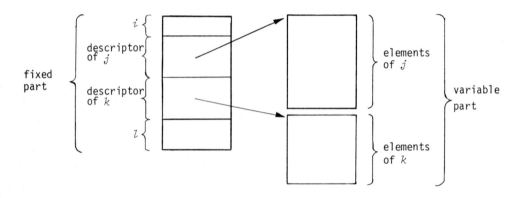

Figure 4. Object of mode *struct* (*int* i, [l_1:u_1] *real* j, [l_2:u_2]*real* k, *compl* l)

Objects of procedure modes can be handled quite simply. They only require a fixed space for the reference to the corresponding code in the program storage part together with a reference to (the beginning of the data storage of) the static predecessor. See also 4.1.

Other, more special objects are treated in section 2.

We conclude the paragraph with a remark on one of the most widely discussed features of the ALGOL 68 mode declarations: modes in ALGOL 68 can (with certain restrictions) be defined recursively and, by consequence, modes can be "infinite".

For example

$$\text{\underline{mode} } m = \text{\underline{struct} } (\text{\underline{int} } i, \text{\underline{ref} } m \ j \ ) \qquad \text{implies}$$
$$m = \text{\underline{struct} } (\text{\underline{int} } i, \text{\underline{ref} } \text{\underline{struct} } (\text{\underline{int} } i, \text{\underline{ref} } \text{\underline{struct} } (\ldots$$

Now, the mode conditions guarantee that objects of "infinite" modes are always finite, that means the storage needed is finite. There may occur only more or less complicated cycles but only through references, as e.g., with the above mode $\underline{m}$:

$\underline{m}$ x, y; x:= (1,y); y:= (2,x)   delivers: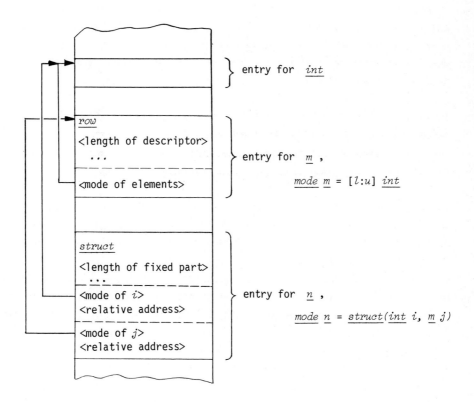

For every object occurring in an ALGOL 68 program the mode is known at compile-time. For all these modes representations are stored in a mode-table. For the further handling of modes and objects in the compiler it is convenient to store together with each mode the length of the fixed part of an object of this mode (note that this length only depends on the mode). In the case of a structured mode the relative addresses of the fixed parts of the components are also stored. See Figure 5.

Figure 5.   The mode-table. Example

The mode-table is used for a number of purposes, amongst them code generation at compile-time and interpretation of complicated operations or garbage collection at run-time.

Access to subvalues is in general more expensive but no more complicated than in ALGOL 60. For each fixed part of an object a pair consisting of relative address and base register is known at compile-time. Code can be generated for accessing the elements of a multiple value by means of the descriptor in the usual ways. For accessing a component of a structured value a simple relative addressing within the fixed part is sufficient.

1.1.3. *STATIC AND DYNAMIC DATA STORAGE AREAS*

Our main task is to discuss the storage allocation for the objects occurring in an ALGOL 68 program. At first we can distinguish two cases: There are objects given by denotations (constants in the sense of ALGOL 60 for instance); these objects are stored in a constant-list at compile-time (with the exception of procedures, of course) and we can forget about them. All other objects are created during run-time, e.g., by copying values from the constant-list or by building structures from other objects. We shall concentrate on this case where storage requirements are determined explicitly by generators and declarations, or implicitly by intermediate results.

In ALGOL 60 ([7], [8]), for each block the fixed parts of the local data can be collected into the *static data area*, the variable parts form the *dynamic data area*. Length and structure of static data areas are determined at compile-time. These areas can be handled according to the block structure.

In a procedure-oriented (as opposed to the usual block-oriented) stack organization, to the main program and to each procedure corresponds one static data area consisting of the static data areas of the local blocks joined or overlapped according to the tree structure inherent in block structure, and of certain items required for organizational purposes (see Figure 6). The organization of dynamic data areas is still block-oriented. We use a vector of block pointers (stacktop locations) for the main program and each procedure whose length is given by the respective maximum local block level. Dynamic composition of procedural static and dynamic data area gives the runtime stack. Base registers (displays) for addressing all accessible data are allocated according to the static procedure level structure. The contents of these registers are kept in the organizational storage parts of procedures to allow eventually necessary reloadings of the base registers. Details may be taken from the Figures 7 and 8.

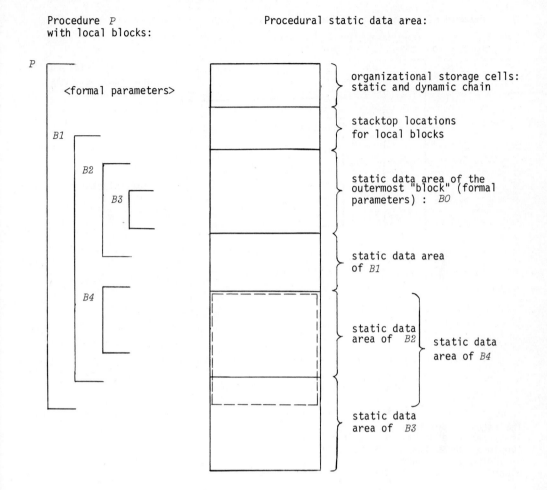

Figure 6.   Procedural static data area

Example of a program structure:

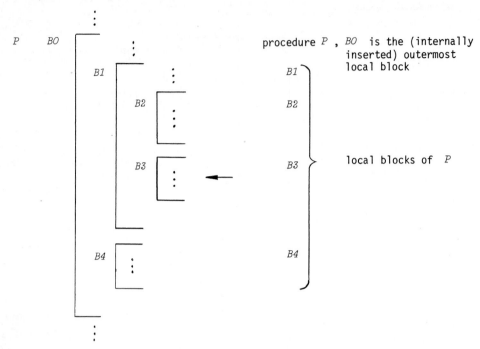

procedure P , BO is the (internally inserted) outermost local block

local blocks of P

Run-time stack at the moment denoted by " ← "

The stacktop pointer is stored in a stack-top location at the beginning of an inner block.

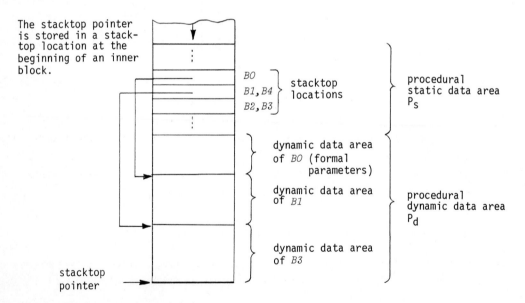

Figure 7. Procedural static and dynamic data areas

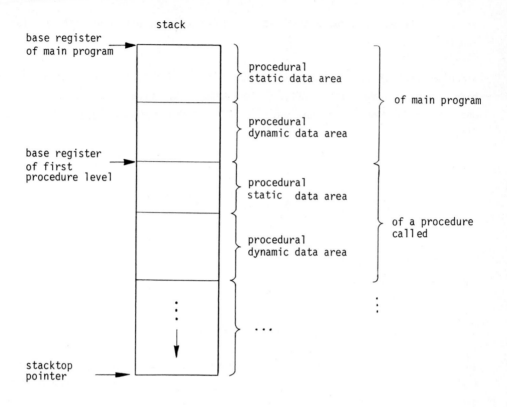

Figure 8.   Procedure-oriented organization of the run-time stack

In principle, the above used terms and the stack organization can be applied to ALGOL 68. Deviations concern mainly the fact that in ALGOL 68 the static data area of a block needs not contain all local fixed parts, the corresponding fact holds for the dynamic data areas (see 4.2). Nevertheless, these areas can be defined and handled as for ALGOL 60, but with the mentioned modifications and with the observation that there are still other parts of objects (which form what may be called heap-areas) to be stored on the heap.

1.1.4.   THE HEAP

The heap is realized as a portion of unstructured free storage. There are diverse mechanisms of allocating storage needed for an object on the heap and of releasing it, e.g., the boundary tag method [10], or the use of an additional bit list for marking free or used words.

Since in ALGOL 68 objects and subvalues of any mode and length may be stored on the heap, storage in the area provided for the heap is allocated in consecutive locations. When the whole area is used up, the heap is collapsed by the garbage collector (see Figure 9).

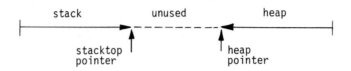

Figure 9. Data storage at run-time

1.2. GENERATIVE AND INTERPRETATIVE HANDLING

In compiler theory generation and interpretation are well-known terms. In practice it seems that only compilers of mixed forms exist with more or less tendency to either generative or interpretative handling. Pure interpreting is out of the question (not only) for ALGOL 68. And most of the so-called interpreters for other languages are based on material collected in prepasses, and thus are "partial"-interpreters only. Sometimes, it is a matter of taste how far to go with generation and interpretation.

In the case of ALGOL 68 a more generative handling seems appropriate. All information necessary for handling objects is known at compile-time. Apart from the "actual modes" of union objects for each ALGOL 68 object the mode is kown statically. Difficulties for code generation result only from the immense work to be done for general modes. Obviously, the code for, e.g.,

$a := b$ where mode of a is $\underline{ref}$ $\underline{m}$,   mode of b is $\underline{m}$ and
$\underline{m}$ = [...] $\underline{struct}$ (..., [...] $\underline{struct}$ (...)...)

is expensive; nested loops must be generated. This is, of course, possible. The same holds for the implementation of declarations of such objects, for parameter transfers etc. In our implementation we decided to use a partly interpretative method in these cases. Certain preparations, such as coercions, are performed at compile-time. But the code generated consists (for general modes) of a macro or subroutine call of the form   ASSIGNATION $(a,b,$ mode (a), mode $(b))$

where the first two parameters deliver the actual storage addresses, the last ones are references to the corresponding entries in the mode-table mentioned above. The subroutine ASSIGNATION is designed in a way enabling it to handle all possible objects and modes.

A more generative method could mean that instead of the general subroutine a special subroutine is generated at compile-time for each actually occurring mode.

Different possibilities exist analogously for the garbage collector. The Munich implementation contains a general garbage collection program applicable to all ALGOL 68 programs. Another proposal, made by Branquart et al. [2], provides for generating special garbage collector parts for the actually occurring modes.

2. SPECIAL OBJECTS IN ALGOL 68

In this section special ALGOL 68 objects are briefly considered.

2.1. FLEXIBLE ARRAYS

Subscript bounds in array declarers may contain the symbol _flex_. Objects declared by means of such declarers are called flexible arrays. (Note, however, that in ALGOL 68 _flex_ does not belong to the mode.)

Example:

$$\underline{mode}\ \underline{m} = [1\ \underline{flex}\ :\ 3\ \underline{flex}]\ \underline{int};$$
$$\underline{m}\ x;\quad \underline{struct}(\underline{int}\ i,\ \underline{m}\ j)\ y$$

The values referred to by x and j $\underline{of}$ y are flexible arrays.

The bounds cannot be changed by using "out of bounds" components, but only through assignations to the whole array.

2.2. OBJECTS GENERATED BY SLICING

Slicing of an array means a) selecting a single component (subscripted variable in ALGOL 60), and b) selecting a subvalue which is itself an array. We consider here the second case: The result of slicing a given array is an object consisting of a new descriptor as fixed part and of the set of selected elements as variable part, which are not copied (see Figure 10).

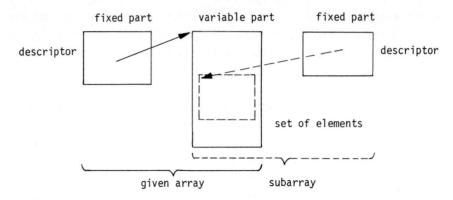

Figure lo. Slicing

2.3. *OBJECTS GENERATED BY ROWING*

Objects may be rowed to arrays. Some different cases are to be distinguished:
Rowing a vacuum means generation of a descriptor referring to an empty variable part.
If the given value is not an array and the result is not a reference, then an object
is generated consisting of a descriptor and of the given value as only component.
If the given value is an array the result of rowing is a new array of higher dimension.
At least a new descriptor must be generated.
If the mode of the result begins with *ref*, only a new descriptor is generated; the
variable part of the new object is the value referred to by the given object, or its
variable part if the given object is already an array (see Figure 11).

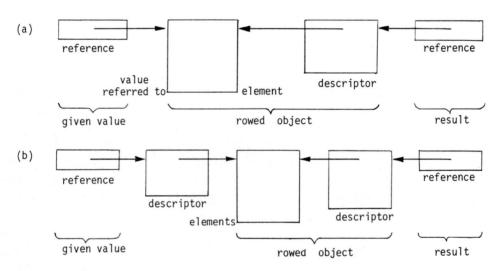

Figure 11. Rowing, where the result is of reference mode

2.4.   OBJECTS OF UNION MODES

An object of a union mode is actually an object of one of the component modes. It consists of a fixed part containing the fixed part of the actual value and a mode information, that is a reference to the corresponding entry in the mode-table, and of the
actual variable part. Sufficient storage place must be reserved for actual values of
any possible component mode; in consequence, it is reasonable to reserve as fixed part
the maximum storage needed, as shown in Figure 12.

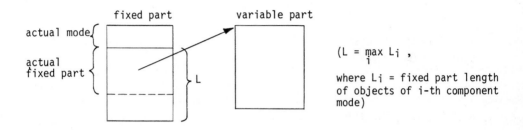

Figure 12.   Object of union mode

A variable part exists only if the actual value is or contains an array. The storage
area needed is , in general, not known at the moment of elaboration of declaration;
it is reserved in connection with assignations.

3.   SCOPES OF VALUES (LIFE-TIME)

Up to now we have discussed the overall structure of the data storage, of run-time
stack and heap, and we considered the representation of objects of the different modes.
Our next task is to study in which part of storage the objects and in particular where
fixed and where variable parts can be placed. This does not only depend on the modes
of the considered objects but also on the *scopes*. There is a close relation between
scopes and storage allocation; of course, at least during its life-time, storage must
be reserved for any object. In this section we give at first the definition of scopes.

3.1.   DEFINITION

The scope of a value is some block or the entire program; it covers the proper life-
time which, however, begins with the generation of the object.

In detail:

The scope of a primitive object is the entire program.
The scope of a composed value (array or structure) is the minimum of the scopes of its elements; the scope of a subvalue of an array is the scope of the array.
The scope of a generator (reference) in the case of a global generator is the entire program and otherwise the block containing the (local) generator.
For procedures see 4.1.

Access to a value is, of course, only possible within its scope (or more exactly during its life-time).

For scopes two conditions must be observed:

1) The scope of the result of a block (or procedure) must strictly contain the block (or procedure).

2) For assignations the scope of the left hand value must be contained in the scope of the right hand value.

3.2. CHECKING THE SCOPE CONDITIONS

In simple cases, the scope conditions can be checked statically, otherwise checks at run-time must be provided [5].

Static checkings:

In general, it is not possible to determine at compile-time for each expression and subexpression the block which is the scope of its value. One can give only estimates, that means we define a minimum and a maximum scope for each expression (which are, in the worst case, an innermost block, and the entire program, resp.). At compile-time, to each block and procedure B a block level number $bl(B)$ can be attached, with the property

$$bl(B_1) < bl(B_2) \quad \text{if} \quad B_1 \neq B_2 \quad \text{for blocks or procedures} \quad B_1, B_2.$$

These block level numbers can be used for static checkings (provided that identifications have been made correctly). We denote the block level number of the minimum (maximum) scope by bl_i (bl_a).

(1) For a result r of a block or procedure B:
   if $bl_i(r) < bl(B)$ then correct else
   if $bl_a(r) \geq bl(B)$ then incorrect,
   otherwise dynamic checking is necessary.

(2) For an assignation $lhv := rhv$:

if $bl_a(lhv) \stackrel{>}{=} bl_i(rhv)$ then correct else

if $bl_i(lhv) < bl_a(rhv)$ then incorrect,

otherwise dynamic checking is necessary.

Dynamic checkings:

At run-time the use of block level numbers is not sufficient, since there may exist several incarnations of one block with different life-times. In our implementation the absolute addresses of the stacktop locations $blst$ in the run-time stack are a suitable representation of the corresponding blocks or scopes.

For two active blocks B_1 and B_2

$blst(B_1) < blst(B_2)$ if the life-time of B_1 is greater than the one of B_2.

Thus, the dynamic checkings reduce to comparisons of addresses $blst$. The checks are necessary for objects of reference modes, and these objects are conveniently represented by a pair of addresses:

address of the object referred to
$blst$ of the block which is the scope

(The scope is known at the moment when the reference is generated).

4.   SCOPES AND DATA STORAGE ALLOCATION

We already stated that there is a connection between scope and storage allocation. There are two groups of objects to be handled, that is *local* and *global* ones. We said that two data storage areas are available and we shall examine in section 4.2 where to store the different objects.

But, at first, we consider another consequence of the scope definition in ALGOL 68 which concerns the general stack mechanism.

4.1.   SCOPE OF ROUTINES AND ALLOCATION OF BASE REGISTERS

The scope of a routine is the smallest of those embracing blocks which contain the declarations (defining occurrences) of identifiers, indications and operators used but not defined within the routine, or eventually the entire program. The allocation of the base registers for the stack organization depends on these scopes:

In ALGOL 60 static predecessors, static chains, procedure levels and the corresponding allocation of base registers are directly given by the text of the program. As may be seen from the example in Figure 13, for ALGOL 68 these correspondences are possible in the same manner only after each procedure has been lifted to the level of the block which is its scope (together with appropriate replacements). Otherwise the static chain could have gaps which would require a modification of the stack organization (especially of procedure calls).

Program example: Procedure levels

$$(\quad proc(int)int \ P \ ;$$

$$proc \ Q \ = \ (int \ i) \ proc(int)int \ :$$

$$(proc \ R \ = \ (int \ j) \ proc(int)int \ :$$

$$(\ ..... \ ;$$

$$| \ ((int \ k) \ int \ : \ k \ \uparrow \ 2)| \ );$$

$$int \ x \ := \ R(0)(1) \ ; \ .....$$

$$R(2) \qquad);$$

$$P \ := \ Q(3) \ ; \ .....$$

$$P(4);$$

$$..... \ )$$

1

2

3

a) 4?

b) 2?

procedure level $i \leftrightarrow$ base register BR_i.

Static chains

when executing	when executing
$R(0)(1)$	$P(4)$

a)
$BR_1 \rightarrow$ main program
$BR_2 \rightarrow$ procedure Q
$BR_4 \rightarrow$ procedure $R(0)$

$BR_1 \rightarrow$ main program
$BR_4 \rightarrow$ procedure $R(2)$

b)
$BR_1 \rightarrow$ main program
$(\ BR_2 \rightarrow)$ procedure Q
$BR_2 \rightarrow$ procedure $R(0)$

$BR_1 \rightarrow$ main program
$BR_2 \rightarrow$ procedure $R(2)$

Figure 13.   Static chains and base registers

Dynamic scope checking (see 3.2) requires that the objects of procedure modes too contain information on their scope. We represent these objects in the form:

address of code
address of the beginning of the data storage of the static predecessor
blst of the block which is the scope

4.2.   STORAGE FOR DATA

We have pointed out that the size of the storage area needed for any object depends on its mode and on actual subscript bounds, if any. Furthermore, we stated that the scope of an object must have an influence on where to store its fixed and variable part, in the data stack or on the heap.

For this aspect of data storage allocation we distinguish four classes of objects.

4.2.1.   LOCAL OBJECTS GENERATED IN THE BLOCK WHICH IS THEIR SCOPE

These objects correspond to the ALGOL 60 objects; the usual simple stack mechanism applies. See Figure 14.

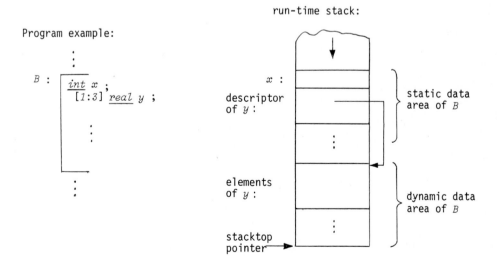

Figure 14.   Local objects

4.2.2. LOCAL OBJECTS GENERATED IN AN "INNER" BLOCK

There are local objects (that means objects, the scope of which is a block) which are not generated in the block defining their scope, but in an inner block. Such objects must be stored on the heap, since they don't fit into the stack mechanism.

This in particular concerns

descriptors of slices whose mode begins with *ref*

and rowed expressions whose mode begins with *ref*

(see Figure 15).

Program example:

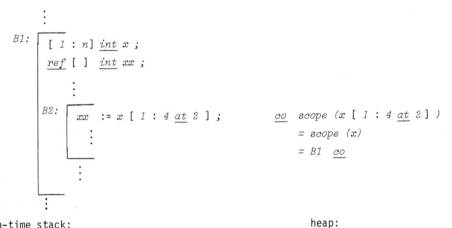

```
B1:    [ 1 : n] int x ;
       ref [ ]  int xx ;
          ⋮
   B2:    xx  := x [ 1 : 4 at 2 ] ;        co  scope (x [ 1 : 4 at 2 ] )
             ⋮                                  = scope (x)
                                                = B1  co
             ⋮
       ⋮
```

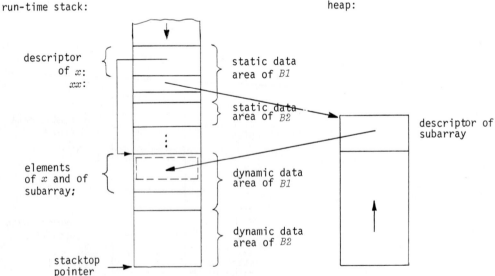

Figure 15. Local objects generated in an "inner" block

4.2.3.   LOCAL OBJECTS WITH FLEXIBLE LENGTH

For these objects the need of storage for the variable part changes during life-time
(flexible array or string). For the variable part the storage must be allocated on the
heap, whereas the fixed part can be placed in the stack. By the way, the same is true
for variable parts of union objects. In the case of a string the fixed part is an internally introduced pointer to the heap. See Figure 16.

Program example:

B:
$$[\ 1\ :\ 2\ \underline{flex}\ ,\ 1\ :\ 2\ \underline{flex}\ ]\ \underline{int}\ a\ ;$$
$$a\ :=\ ((1,2)\ ,\ (3,4))\ ;$$ ①

$$a\ :=\ ((1,2,3)\ ,\ (4,5,6)\ ,\ (7,8,9));$$ ②

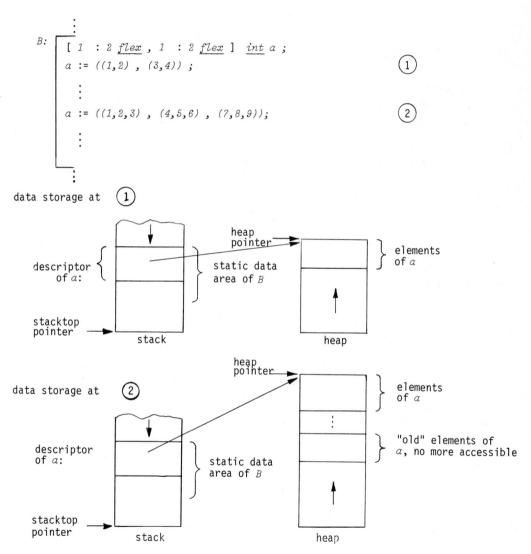

Figure 16. Local objects with flexible length

4.2.4. GLOBAL OBJECTS

Apart from constants which can be stored in a constant list at compile-time, and multiple values with unrestricted scope, global objects must be stored on the heap. Yet for each such entry on the heap an internal pointer is inserted in the stack within the storage area for the block in which the global object is generated. See Figure 17.

Program example:

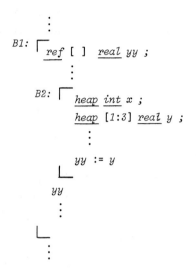

run-time stack: heap:

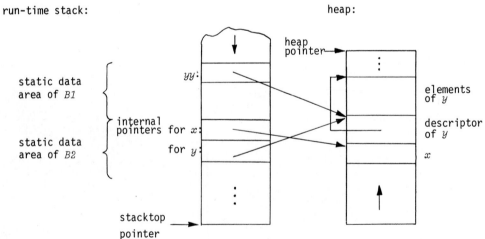

Figure 17. Global objects

5.   SPECIAL TOPICS

Though in principle for ALGOL 68 the well-known mechanisms for run-time stack and heap can be used, some special problems arise for which special provisions are to be considered. In certain more or less obvious points a modification of the storage allocation scheme is necessary.

5.1.   RESULTS OF BLOCKS AND PROCEDURE CALLS

In ALGOL 68, blocks and procedure calls may have results of any general mode. Moreover, it may occur that such a result is stored in the data area of the block concerned, and is lost, if storage is released by the usual simple reloading of the stack pointer. These results must be saved as illustrated by Figure 18.

Program example:

```
        ⋮
  B1: ⌐
       [ 1 : 4 ]  int x ;

       x :=
  B2:              ( [ 1 : 3 ]  struct (int i , [ 1 : 4 ] int j ) a ;
                     ⋮
                 j of a [1]    co result of block B2 co  ) ;

   └  ⋮
      ⋮
```

run-time stack at the end of B2 :

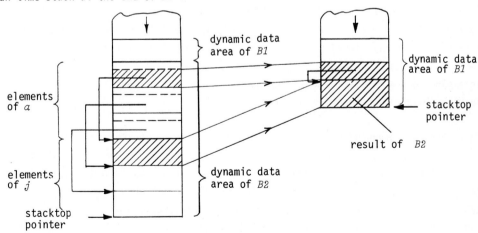

Figure 18.   Result of a block

This saving can be interpreted as

> assignment to an intermediate variable declared in an outer block

or as

> a certain garbage collection-like collapsing of the data area of the top block
> in the stack which preserves only the compacted block result, with resetting
> of the stack pointer to the last word of the result.

In order to avoid overwriting this transfer requires already a suitable storage scheme
for objects of general modes. In particular it is possible that the variable parts of
objects are not   stored in consecutive storage cells (e.g., in the case of subvalues
of multiple values).

A simple solution of the problem is the transfer of the objects to the heap.

5.2.   GENERAL ACTUAL PARAMETERS

Actual parameters in ALGOL 68 may contain e.g. blocks and jumps which cause certain
modifications for the stack operations.

One of the points to be considered is how to insert blocks occurring in actual parameters into the block and procedure structure of the whole program. According to the
semantics of the ALGOL 68 procedure call the actual parameter is transferred into the
(copy of the) routine where it is elaborated during elaboration of the routine. Thus,
blocks in actual parameters are local blocks of the procedure called. For the static
chain (used for reaching non-locals) this is, however, not true. Since actual parameters are in effect value-parameters (with the restriction that the formal parameters
pack contains no semicolon) they should be elaborated before actually entering the
routine called. In our implementation this is done and the values of the actual parameters are directly stored in the places for the formal parameters.

In a block-oriented stack scheme special provision must be made for the static chain
such as shown for the example in Figure 19.

In a procedure-oriented version the same modification of the static chain is necessary,
because procedures, too, may occur in actual parameters. But there are still other
difficulties in handling the dynamic storage areas of blocks in actual parameters.
Among other possibilities are a special handling of block ends concerned or the insertion of those blocks into the static block level structure of the calling procedure together with an additional stacktop location for the call (see Figure 20).

program example: run-time stack:

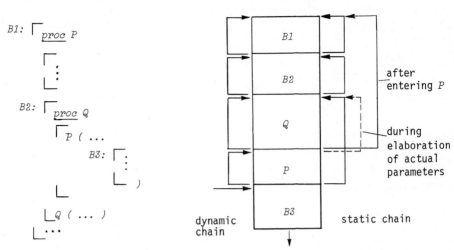

Figure 19. Actual parameters. Block-oriented run-time stack

5.3.   *LOCAL GENERATORS*

Storage for local generators cannot be reserved in a static data area in general, because the number of objects actually generated in the same block depends on program flow.

Local generators occurring as actual parameters in identity declarations, e.g., *ref real x = loc real* := *3.1* , cause no problems. In the Munich implementation we restricted the handling of local generators to those cases. Otherwise, difficulties arise in storage allocation and scope checking [3]. (Moreover, in most cases the use of global generators is more reasonable.)

A case in point is the occurrence of a local generator in an actual parameter of a procedure call. Consider, for example

B: *begin real y;*
        proc P = (ref ref real x) : ... *x* := *loc real;* ... ;
        P (loc ref real := *y)*
                                    (ref ref real x = loc ref real := *y;*
                                    ... *x* := *loc real;* ...*)*
    end

Program example:

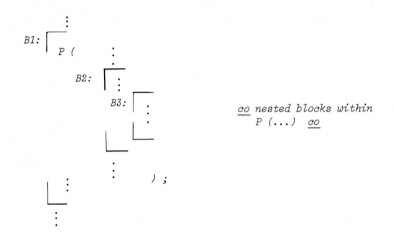

_co_ nested blocks within
P (...) _co_

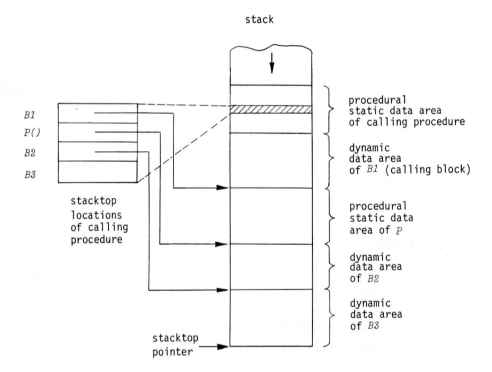

Figure 20.   Stacktop locations for calls

The scope of a local generator is the innermost range (block) containing it. The call mechanism prescribes the call to be replaced by the routine, that is a block containing identity declarations derived from formal and actual parameters. This block contains the generator and, in consequence, the scope and thus the stacktop location representing it, is in general determined only dynamically, depending on the routine called. A call *P(xx := loc real := ...)* for instance, where *xx* is of mode *ref ref real* and declared in the calling block, is undefined. The general storage allocation scheme leads to reserving space in the dynamic area for the local (or even actual) parameters, where the generator must be kept until the routine is left.

5.4.   GENERAL MODE DECLARATIONS

In a mode declaration the actual declarer may contain actual bounds. Each applied occurrence of the defined mode indication must be replaced by the actual declarer. For example:

$$mode \; m = [1:n] \; \; real \; ;$$
$$m \; x \; ; \; \; struct \; \; (m \; i, \; ...)$$
$$\underbrace{\qquad\qquad} \quad \underbrace{\qquad\qquad}$$
$$[1:n] \; real \quad [1:n] \; real$$

Therefore, in generating code, this insertion is conveniently done by calling a closed subroutine derived from the mode declaration.

These subroutines may contain procedure calls and thus become even (implicitly) recursive:

$$proc \; P = (int \; x) \; int:$$
$$\lceil mode \; m = [1:...P(1) \; ... \;] \; \; real; \; ...\rfloor$$

The easiest way to deal with this fact is to handle mode declarations with actual bounds like procedures without parameters with all consequences concerning base registers and storage allocation. Our previous definition of procedures, therefore, must be supplemented. A scope definition is not necessary since modes cannot be handled like other data.

5.5.   "EMPTY" FLEXIBLE ARRAYS

At the time of elaboration of a declaration for a flexible array the space initially required for the elements may be empty. This causes problems when the elements again may contain arrays.

For example: [1 : 0 flex] struct ([m : n] int i, ...) x
                        x has initially an empty set of elements.

Normally the values of *m* and *n* are stored in descriptors contained in these elements.

m and n are furthermore needed when assignments to x are made, e.g. Since a subsequent access to m and n would be rather cumbersome, we decided to reserve store for just one element where the necessary local information can be held.

6.   GARBAGE COLLECTION

In this section we consider an ALGOL 68 garbage collector; we restrict ourselves to the storage collapse technique used in the Munich implementation. Possible optimizations of the underlying principle are not discussed here.

The garbage collector works in 3 phases:
(1) Marking phase:
All objects or subvalues stored on the heap can be reached by reference chains starting in static data areas in the run-time stack.

One of the tasks is now to find all static areas of active blocks and procedure calls in the stack. This is possible by means of the dynamic chain for procedure calls. Furthermore, we introduce a (static) numbering of all blocks and procedures. This number is stored, together with the stacktop pointer, in the stacktop location of the block (procedure) concerned. Thus, the number of all active incarnations of blocks and procedures can be found (see Figure 21).

Each static data area must be examined whether it contains pointers leading into the heap (possibly, through dynamic areas). For static data areas the structure is known at compile-time (and it is the same for any incarnation). That is, a storage allocation list can be set up at compile-time for each static data area, which specifies for each item whether or not its content is relevant for the garbage collector. To these lists the aforementioned block number can be attached. A model of such a list is given in Figure 22. For each item in a static data area it contains

> a sequence of n zeroes (0) if the item needs n storage cells and is or
> contains no pointer,
> a one (1) if the item is or contains a pointer; in addition a reference
> to the entry of the mode table for the item concerned is given.

These lists allow us to analyze at run-time all chains in a partly interpretative manner with regard to modes. All objects (storage cells) on the heap reached in this way are marked (in our case by using a marking bit list).

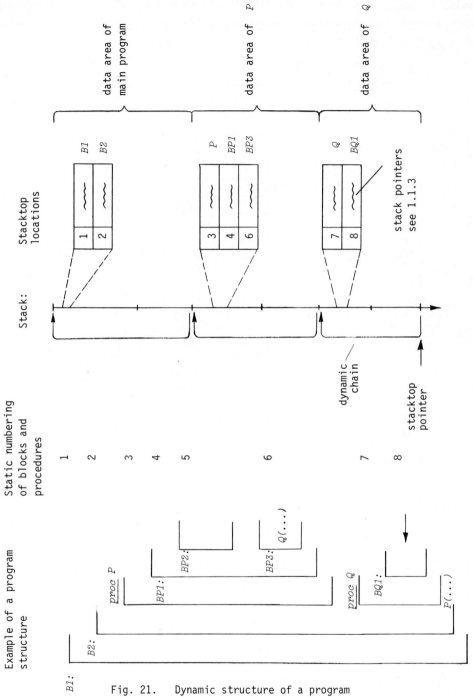

Fig. 21. Dynamic structure of a program

Example:

...

B: <u>begin</u> <u>real</u> a;
        [l : u] <u>ref</u> <u>real</u> b;
        <u>heap</u> <u>real</u> c;
        <u>int</u> d;
        ⋮

    <u>end</u>

...

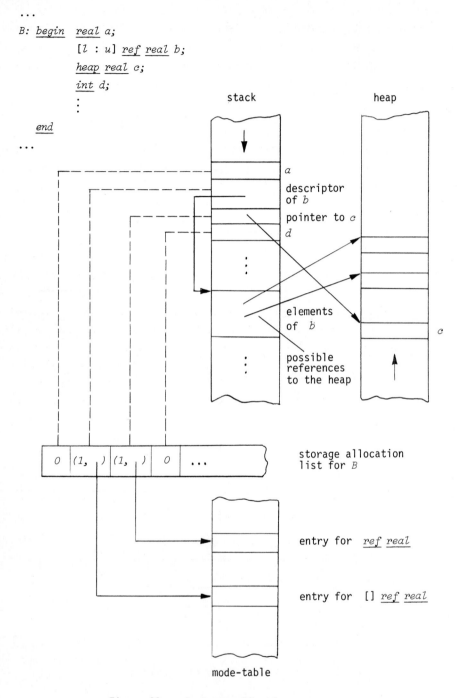

Figure 22.   Garbage collection

(2) Compactification phase:

In the compactification phase all (sequences of) storage cells marked on the heap are joined into an uninterrupted sequence. A special requirement of ALGOL 68 is that even if only a subvalue of an array is marked, then in general the whole array is kept, with the exception that dynamic parts of the irrelevant elements of the original array are discarded. This was deemed advisable, in particular, since redefinition of descriptors would be necessary, otherwise.

(3) Addressing phase:

Collapsing requires (almost) all pointers into the heap (possibly within the heap) to be changed according to the transfers performed. The problem is to find all these pointers, which would require a great deal of the work done in phase (1) to be repeated. Instead, during phase (1) a list of all respective pointers can be set up which facilitates the work of this phase.

One of the problems in garbage collection is posed by the storage which the collector itself needs for lists and for the stack used for analyzing modes and composed objects.

Two additional remarks should be made: The use of storage allocation lists does not allow objects of different non-primitive modes to be stored in the same storage cells of one static data area. Thus, the use of a "number cellar" for intermediate results is only possible for objects of primitive (irrelevant for garbage collection) modes. Furthermore, the initialization of storage cells with a suitable skip-value is necessary at each block begin, dynamic storage allocation, and procedure call and return; otherwise, the garbage collector might work with undefined values.

References

[1] Branquart, P., Lewi, J.: On the implementation of local names in ALGOL 68. MBLE Research Lab., Brussels, Report R121, 1969

[2] Branquart, P., Lewi, J.: A scheme of storage allocation and garbage collection for ALGOL 68. MBLE Research Lab., Brussels, Report R133, 197o

[3] Branquart, P., Lewi, J., Cardinael, J. P.: Local generators and the ALGOL 68 working stack. MBLE Research Lab., Brussels, Technical Note N62, 197o

[4] Fites, P. E.: Storage organization and garbage collection in ALGOL 68. In [12]

[5] Goos, G.: Eine Implementierung von ALGOL 68. TU München, Report Nr. 69o6, 1969

[6] Goos, G.: Some problems in compiling ALGOL 68. In [13]

[7] Grau, A. A., Hill, U., Langmaack, H.: Translation of ALGOL 60. Handbook for Automatic Computation, Vol. 1/Part b. Berlin-Heidelberg-New York: Springer 1967

[8] Gries, D.: Compiler Construction for Digital Computers. New York: John Wiley & Sons 1971

[9] Hill, U., Scheidig, H., Wössner, H.: An ALGOL 68 Compiler. TU München. Internal Report, 1973

[10] Knuth, D. E.: The Art of Computer Programming, Vol. 1. Reading (Mass.): Addison-Wesley 1968

[11] Marshall, S.: An ALGOL 68 garbage collector. In [13]

[12] Peck, J. E. L. (Ed.): Proceedings of an Informal Conference on ALGOL 68 Implementation. University of British Columbia, Vancouver (B.C.) 1969

[13] Peck, J. E. L. (Ed.): ALGOL 68 Implementation. Amsterdam: North-Holland 1971

[14] van Wijngaarden, A., Mailloux, B. J., Peck, J. E. L., Koster, C. H. A.: Report on the Algorithmic Language ALGOL 68. Numerische Mathematik 14, 79-218 (1969)

[15] Wodon, P. L.: Methods of garbage collection for ALGOL 68. In [13]

SYMBOL TABLE ACCESS

W. M. McKeeman

University of California at

Santa Cruz, U.S.A.

> "The butterfly collector likes to
> catch elusive little things and
> line them up in rows. He should
> enjoy symbol tables."

1. INTRODUCTION

During the translation of many programming languages it is necessary to associate each occurrence of an identifier with its collected attributes. This is
accomplished by means of a symbol table which holds relevant information about all
active identifiers encountered in the source text. Information required for translation, and held in the symbol table, may include the name, type, location, diagnostic information, scope nesting, etc. An entry is made into the symbol table when a
new identifier is declared. When an identifier is otherwise used the symbol table
is interrogated for the information on which to base translation decisions.

If the same identifier has been declared in nested scopes, the declaration in the innermost scope controls its use. As a result the symbol table search mechanism must insure that the first occurrence found will be the innermost.

All entries local to a scope (e.g., local variables to a procedure) become irrelevant upon exit from that scope and are removed from the symbol table. This serves the dual function of freeing space in the symbol table and "uncovering" any previous use of those symbols in outer scopes.

Symbol tables access consumes a major portion of the processor time during translation. For example, a study of an efficient translator for the PL-like language XPL revealed that one-fourth of its translation time was spent interrogating the symbol table when a linear search method was employed. Changing to a hashed table lookup algorithm, a faster access method for this application, saved nearly all of that time.

There are four methods for symbol table access presented here for evaluation and comparison (linear, hash, sorted, and tree). None are new and all have their merits depending on the application for which they are being used.

2. OPERATIONS

Certain programming languages, such as ALGOL-60 and PL/I, have nested scopes of application for their identifiers. A scope is delimited by matching bracketing symbols (such as begin-end). The appearance of a declaration for an identifier within the brackets makes the identifier local to that scope (i.e., not available outside the brackets). When a single identifier is declared in more than one level of nested scopes, the innermost declaration takes precedence (see Figure 2.1).

```
1    /* A PL/I PROGRAM FRAGMENT */
2    BEGIN;
3       DECLARE (A, B) FIXED;
4       A = 1;
5       BEGIN;
6          DECLARE (C, A) FIXED;
7          A, B, C = 1;
8          BEGIN;
9             A = 1;
10         END;
11         BEGIN;
12            DECLARE A FIXED;
13            A = 1;
14         END;
15         A = 1;
16      END;
17      A = 1;
18   END;
```

A Program Exhibiting Nested Scopes

Figure 2.1

The symbol table for a nested language holds a record of identifiers and the information associated with them. Upon encountering the declaration of an identi - fier (explicit or implicit), a translator must first check that there has been no previous declaration of it in the present scope and then enter it into the table. Upon encountering the use of an identifier, the translator must find the symbol table entry for the corresponding declaration to make available the associated in- formation. The scope bracketing symbols must also cause the translator to react appropriately.

The simplest table organization for symbols in a nested language is a stack. Upon scope entry the stack must be marked to delimit the new scope; upon encounter- ing a declaration the new identifier is stacked; upon encountering the use of an identifier the stack is searched from newest entry to oldest to find the most re- cently declared occurrence of that name; upon scope exit the identifiers local to the scope must be discarded.

The speed with which the above operations can be accomplished is often a criti- cal design criterion for the symbol table mechanism. There are several access methods that can be superimposed on the stack organized table to improve performance. The choice between them is based on various considerations of table size and fre- quency of access; several choices are given below. In each case there are four procedures corresponding to the four access actions as noted in Figure 2.2.

Two other auxiliary functions are needed to deal with the attributes associated with each symbol: "new-attribute" and "old-attribute' . The first records a newly discovered attribute and checks that it does not conflict with previously recorded information. The latter simply retrieves an attribute from the symbol table.

Let "id" be the character string form of a name, "n" be its location in the symbol table, "atr" be the designation of an attribute, and "atrval" the value of the designated attribute. The the following six lines are the standard calls of the six functions (in PL/I).

```
n = new_id (id);
n = old_id (id);
call enter_scope;
call exit_scope;
call new_attribute (n , atr, atrval);
atrval = old_attribute  (n, atr);
```

procedure name	action accomplished
new_id	An identifier has just been declared. Check that no previous conflicting declaration has been given and then enter the symbol into the table.
old_id	An identifier has just been used. Find the table location corresponding to its most recent declaration.
scope_entry	A beginning bracket for a scope has been encountered. Prepare a new local naming scope.
scope_exit	An ending bracket for a scope has been encountered. Discard identifiers no longer accessible and reestablish the next outer scope.

Symbol Table Access Primitives
Figure 2.2

3. Method of Presentation

The presentation here is primarily in terms of some running programs written in XPL. The advantage of presenting complete programs is in immediate transfer to a working translator. All of the details are spelled out so that the user can simply translate into his implementation language and use the algorithms. Another advantage is in immediate comparison of the four algorithms presented. They have been made as similar as possible so that the differences will stand out.

The running programs contain the implementation of the four access primitives that are needed to define the symbol table module (See Section 1.A .5 of these notes). The "language" that drives the symbol table module is given by the grammar in Figure 3.1.

define_actions = scope-entry action_list scope-exit
action_list=(new_id |old_id| define_actions)*

The Intermodular Communication
with the Symbol Table Module
Figure 3.1

The test programs read in a stylized example of the intermodular communication and obey the implicit commands. Other tests (See Section 1.A.4.3 of these notes) can be presented to the program by simply changing the input. The code words in the data correspond to the actions as listed below:

IN   scope_entry
OUT   scope_exit
NEW   new_id
OLD   old_id

The trace output prints the driving input data as well as all the table contents at each stage. The output is a bit cryptic but, since the program that produced it is there, it should be understandable.

4. LINEAR SYMBOL TABLE ACCESS

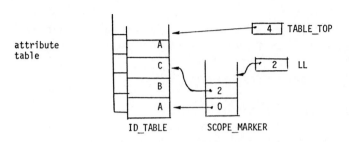

Linear Access Method
Symbol Table Configuration
Figure 4.1

The diagram in Figure 4.1 depicts the linear search method symbol table as it would appear after a translator has processed lines 1-6 of the program fragment in Figure 2.1. ID_TABLE holds the identifiers A, B, C, and A while SCOPE_MARKER signifies that the first two are in the outer scope and the second two are local to the inner scope. The variables LL and TABLE_TOP point to the next available cell in their respective tables. The attributes of the identifiers are held in another table which is accessed by the same pointer as ID_TABLE allowing the translator to first locate an identifier then use its location to sample or add to the associated attributes.

The linear access method is expressed and tested in the following XPL program. (The language XPL is close enough to PL/I so that the reader should easily understand the meaning of its constructs.) The output of the program consists of a series of snapshots of the table contents and pointers after each action triggered by the program in Figure 2.1. INDEX records the location found by the procedure

invoked. The signals IN and OUT correspond to scope entry and exit caused by
BEGIN and END; NEW A signifies the declaration of the identifier A and OLD A the
use of A. The table configuration in Figure 4.1 is reached after the seventh
event in the test run.

```
1             /* S Y M B O L  T A B L E  A L G O R I T H M S */
2             /* L I N E A R  S E A R C H  M E T H O D      */
3
4    /*  DATA STRUCTURE DEFINITIONS:
5
6      ID_TABLE() HOLDS THE IDENTIFIERS.
7      TABLE_TOP POINTS TO THE NEXT AVAILABLE CELL IN ID_TABLE().
8      TABLE_LIMIT IS THE BOUND ON TABLE_TOP.
9
10     SCOPE_MARKER POINTS TO THE FIRST ENTRY IN EACH SCOPE.
11     LL IS THE PRESENT LEVEL OF PROGRAM NESTING.
12     LL_LIMIT IS THE BOUND ON LL.
13
14     INDEX IS THE SYMBOL TABLE LOCATION FOUND BY THE ACCESS PROCEDURES.
15   */
16
17  DECLARE TABLE_LIMIT LITERALLY '100', TABLE_TOP FIXED,
18     ID_TABLE(TABLE_LIMIT)  CHARACTER ;
19  DECLARE LL_LIMIT LITERALLY '10', LL FIXED, SCOPE_MARKER(LL_LIMIT)  FIXED;
20  DECLARE INDEX FIXED;
21
22  ERROR: PROCEDURE; OUTPUT, OUTPUT = 'ERROR'; CALL EXIT; END ERROR;
23
24  NEW_ID:
25     PROCEDURE(IDENTIFIER);
26       DECLARE IDENTIFIER CHARACTER;
27       DECLARE SB FIXED;
28
29       /* SEARCH FOR DUPLICATE DECLARATION */
30       SB = SCOPE_MARKER(LL-1);
31       INDEX = TABLE_TOP;
32       DO WHILE INDEX > SB;
```

```
33        INDEX = INDEX - 1;
34        IF IDENTIFIER = ID_TABLE(INDEX) THEN CALL ERROR;
35   END;
36
37   /* CHECK FOR ID TABLE OVERFLOW  */
38   IF TABLE_TOP = TABLE_LIMIT THEN CALL ERROR;
39
40   /* ENTER NEW IDENTIFIER */
41   INDEX = TABLE_TOP;  TABLE_TOP = TABLE_TOP + 1;
42   ID_TABLE(INDEX) = IDENTIFIER;
43 END NEW_ID;
44
45 OLD_ID:
46   PROCEDURE(IDENTIFIER);
47      DECLARE IDENTIFIER CHARACTER;
48
49      /* SEARCH ID_TABLE FOR THE IDENTIFIER */
50      INDEX = TABLE_TOP;
51      DO WHILE INDEX > 0;
52         INDEX = INDEX -1;
53         IF IDENTIFIER = ID_TABLE(INDEX) THEN RETURN;
54      END;
55
56   /* RECORD FAILURE TO FIND THE IDENTIFIER */
57   CALL ERROR;
58  END OLD_ID;
59
60 SCOPE_ENTRY;·
61   PROCEDURE;
62      /* MAKE SURE PROGRAM TEXT IS NOT TOO DEEPLY NESTED */
63      IF LL = LL_LIMIT THEN CALL ERROR;
64      SCOPE_MARKER(LL) = TABLE_TOP;   /* POINT TO FIRST LOCAL */
65      LL = LL + 1;   /* INCREASE LEXIC LEVEL */
66   END SCOPE_ENTRY;
67
68 SCOPE_EXIT:
69   PROCEDURE;
70      LL = LL -1;
71      TABLE_TOP = SCOPE_MARKER(LL);
72   END SCOPE_EXIT;
73
```

```
74   /* TEST PROGRAM FOR SYMBOL TABLE  ALGORITHMS */
75   DECLARE (CARD, LINE) CHARACTER;
76   DECLARE I FIXED;
77   OUTPUT = '     SIMULATION OF EVENTS DURING TRANSLATION ' ;
78   OUTPUT = ' ';
79   OUTPUT = 'EVENT:    TABLE STATUS:';
80   OUTPUT = ' ';
81   LL = 0;  TABLE_TOP = 0;
82   DO WHILE LL  >= 0;
83
84     /* PRINT STATUS OF TABLES AND POINTERS */
85     OUTPUT = '         TABLE_TOP='||TABLE_TOP||'  LL='||LL||'  INDEX='||INDEX;
86     LINE = '         ID_TABLE()=  ';
87     DO I =  0 TO TABLE_TOP -1;
88        LINE = LINE   || ID_TABLE(I) || ' ';
89     END;
90     OUTPUT = LINE;
91     LINE = '    SCOPE_MARKER() = ';
92     DO I =  0 TO LL-1;
93        LINE = LINE || SCOPE_MARKER(I) || ' ';
94     END;
95     OUTPUT = LINE ;
96
97     /* SIMULATE ACTIONS OF A TRANSLATOR */
98     CARD, OUTPUT = INPUT ;
99     IF SUBSTR(CARD,0,2) = 'IN' THEN CALL SCOPE_ENTRY ;
100    ELSE IF SUBSTR(CARD,0,3) = 'OUT' THEN CALL SCOPE_EXIT;
101    ELSE IF SUBSTR(CARD,0,3) = 'NEW' THEN CALL NEW_ID(SUBSTR(CARD,5,1));
102    ELSE IF SUBSTR(CARD,0,3) = 'OLD' THEN CALL OLD_ID(SUBSTR(CARD,5,1));
103  END;
104  EOF EOF
```

Test Module for Linear Access

Figure 4.2

EVENT: TABLE STATUS:

```
            TABLE_TOP = 0  LL = 0  INDEX = 0
            ID_TABLE() =
            SCOPE_MARKER() =
```

IN

```
            TABLE_TOP = 0  LL = 1  INDEX = 0
            ID_TABLE() =
            SCOPE_MARKER() = 0
```

NEW A

```
            TABLE_TOP = 1  LL = 1  INDEX = 0
            ID_TABLE() =      A
            SCOPE_MARKER() = 0
```

NEW B

```
            TABLE_TOP = 2  LL = 1  INDEX = 1
            ID_TABLE() =   A B
            SCOPE_MARKER() = 0
```

OLD A

```
            TABLE_TOP = 2  LL = 1  INDEX = 0
            ID_TABLE()  = A B
            SCOPE_MARKER() = 0
```

IN

```
            TABLE_TOP = 2  LL = 2  INDEX = 0
            ID_TABLE()=    A B
            SCOPE_MARKER() = 0 2
```

NEW C

```
            TABLE_TOP = 3  LL = 2  INDEX = 2
            ID_TABLE() =   A B C
            SCOPE_MARKER() = 0 2
```

NEW A

```
            TABLE_TOP = 4  LL = 2  INDEX = 3
            ID_TABLE() =  A B C A
            SCOPE_MARKER() = 0 2
```

OLD A

```
            TABLE_TOP = 4  LL = 2  INDEX = 3
            ID_TABLE() =  A B C A
            SCOPE_MARKER() = 0 2
```

OLD B

```
            TABLE_TOP = 4  LL = 2  INDEX = 1
            ID_TABLE() =  A B C A
            SCOPE_MARKER() = 0 2
```

OLD C

        TABLE_TOP = 4 LL = 2 INDEX = 2
        ID_TABLE() = A B C A
        SCOPE_MARKER() = 0 2

IN

        TABLE_TOP = 4 LL = 3 INDEX = 2
        ID_TABLE() = A B C A
        SCOPE_MARKER() = 0 2 4

OLD A

        TABLE_TOP = 4 LL = 3 INDEX = 3
        ID_TABLE() = A B C A
        SCOPE_MARKER() = 0 2 4

OUT

        TABLE_TOP = 4 LL = 2 INDEX = 3
        ID_TABLE() = A B C A
        SCOPE_MARKER() = 0 2

IN

        TABLE_TOP = 4 LL = 3 INDEX = 3
        ID_TABLE() = A B C A
        SCOPE_MARKER() 0 2 4

NEW A

        TABLE_TOP = 5 LL = 3 INDEX = 4
        ID_TABLE() = A B C A A
        SCOPE_MARKER() = 0 2 4

OLD A

        TABLE_TOP = 5 LL = 3 INDEX = 4
        ID_TABLE() = A B C A A
        SCOPE_MARKER() = 0 2 4

OUT

        TABLE_TOP = 4 LL = 2 INDEX = 4
        ID_TABLE() = A B C A
        SCOPE_MARKER() = 0 2

OLD A

        TABLE_TOP = 4 LL = 2 INDEX = 3
        ID_TABLE() = A B C A
        SCOPE_MARKER() = 0 2

OUT

        TABLE_TOP = 2 LL = 1 INDEX = 3
        ID_TABLE() = A B
        SCOPE_MARKER() = 0

OLD A

```
        TABLE_TOP = 2  LL = 1   INDEX = 0
        ID_TABLE() =    A B
        SCOPE_MARKER() = 0
```

OUT

```
        TABLE_TOP = 0  LL = 0   INDEX = 0
        ID_TABLE() =
        SCOPE_MARKER() =
```

OUT

Trace Output: Linear Access

Figure 4.3

5. SORTED SYMBOL TABLE ACCESS

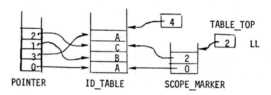

Sorted Table Access Methoa

Symbol Table Configuration

Figure 5.1

If a table is ordered and we can locate the middle item, half of the table can be discarded with a single comparison. The remaining half can be treated similarly, etc., until only one item remains. Since the requirement of nested language scope predetermines the table order, a second ordering is imposed via a table of pointers.

Figure 5.1 depicts the sorted table method after processing lines 1-6 of Figure 2.1. The order:

```
ID_TABLE(POINTER(1))   =  A
ID_TABLE(POINTER(2))   =  A
ID_TABLE(POINTER(3))   =  B
ID_TABLE(POINTER(4))   =  C
```

is in increasing collating sequence allowing the subdivision to be accomplished.
Multiple entries are handled by always taking the higher one (e.g., ID_TABLE
(POINTER(2)) for A in this instance).

Exercise   Verify that the simulation output corresponds to the
correct symbol table actions.

Exercise   Hand simulate the look-up implied by action 8 (OLD A)
of the simulation.

```
1          /*  S Y M B O L  T A B L E  A L G O R I T H M S  */
2          /*  S O R T E D  T A B L E  A C C E S S  M E T H O D  */
3
4     /*  DATA STRUCTURE DEFINITIONS:
5
6      ID_TABLE() HOLDS THE IDENTIFIERS,
7      TABLE_TOP POINTS TO THE NEXT AVAILABLE CELL IN ID_TABLE(),
8      TABLE_LIMIT IS THE BOUND ON TABLE_TOP,
9
10      SCOPE_MARKER POINTS TO THE FIRST ENTRY IN EACH SCOPE,
11      LL IS THE PRESENT LEVEL OF PROGRAM NESTING,
12      LL_LIMIT IS THE BOUND ON LL,
13
14      INDEX IS THE SYMBOL TABLE LOCATION FOUND BY THE ACCESS PROCEDURES.
15   */
16
17 DECLARE TABLE_LIMIT LITERALLY '100', TABLE_TOP FIXED,
18      ID_TABLE(TABLE_LIMIT)  CHARACTER;
19 DECLARE LL_LIMIT LITERALLY '10', LL FIXED, SCOPE_MARKER(LL_LIMIT) FIXED;
20 DECLARE INDEX FIXED;
21
```

```
22     /* POINTERS FOR INDIRECT SORT */
23  DECLARE POINTER(TABLE_LIMIT) FIXED;
24
25  ERROR; PROCEDURE; OUTPUT, OUTPUT = 'ERROR'; CALL EXIT; END ERROR;
26
27  NEW_ID:
28     PROCEDURE(IDENTIFIER);
29        DECLARE IDENTIFIER CHARACTER;
30        DECLARE (R, M, T) FIXED;
31
32        /* SEARCH FOR DUPLICATE DECLARATION */
33        B = -1; M, T = TABLE_TOP;
34        DO WHILE B+1 <  T;
35           M = SHR(B+T, 1);
36           IF IDENTIFIER < ID_TABLE(POINTER(M)) THEN T = M;
37           ELSE B = M;
38        END;
39        IF B = M THEN
40           IF IDENTIFIER = ID_TABLE(POINTER(M)) THEN
41              IF POINTER(M) >= SCOPE_MARKER(LL-1) THEN CALL ERROR;
42
43        /* CHECK FOR ID_TABLE OVERFLOW */
44        IF TABLE_TOP = TABLE_LIMIT THEN CALL ERROR;
45
46        /* ENTER NEW IDENTIFIER */
47        INDEX = TABLE_TOP; TABLE_TOP = TABLE_TOP + 1;
48        ID_TABLE(INDEX) = IDENTIFIER;
49
50        /* KEEP THE POINTER TABLE IN ORDER */
51        T = INDEX;
52        DO WHILE B+1 < T;
53           POINTER(T) = POINTER(T-1);
54           T = T-1;
55        END;
56        POINTER(T) = INDEX;
57     END NEW_ID;
58
59  OLD_ID:
60     PROCEDURE(IDENTIFIER);
61        DECLARE IDENTIFIER CHARACTER;
62        DECLARE (R, M, T) FIXED;
```

```
63
64      /* SEARCH ID_TABLE FOR THE IDENTIFIER */
65      IF TABLE_TOP = 0 THEN CALL ERROR;
66      B = -1; M, T = TABLE_TOP;
67      DO WHILE B + 1 < T;
68         M = SHR(B+T, 1);
69         IF IDENTIFIER < ID_TABLE(POINTER(M)) THEN T = M;
70         ELSE B = M;
71   END;
72
73      /* RECORD FAILURE TO FIND THE IDENTIFIER */
74      IF B < 0  THEN CALL ERROR;
75      INDEX = POINTER(B);
76      IF IDENTIFIER = ID_TABLE(INDEX) THEN CALL ERROR;
77   END OLD_ID;
78
79 SCOPE_ENTRY:
80   PROCEDURE;
81      /* MAKE SURE PROGRAM TEXT IS NOT TOO DEEPLY NESTED */
82      IF LL = LL_LIMIT THEN CALL ERROR;
83      SCOPE_MARKER(LL) = TABLE_TOP;  /* POINT TO FIRST LOCAL */
84      LL = LL + 1;  /* INCREASE LEXIC LEVEL */
85   END SCOPE_ENTRY;
86
87 SCOPE_EXIT:
88   PROCEDURE;
89      DECLARE (SB, B, T) FIXED;
90
91      LL = LL -1;
92      /* DISCARD POINTERS INTO LIMBO */
93      T, B = 0; SB = SCOPE_MARKER(LL);
94      DO WHILE T < TABLE_TOP;
95         IF POINTER(T)  < SB THEN
96            DO; /* SAVE GOOD ONES */
97               POINTER(B) = POINTER(T);
98               B = B + 1;
99            END;
100        T = T + 1;
101     END;
102     TABLE_TOP =  SB;
```

```
103    END SCOPE_EXIT;
104
105    /* TEXT PROGRAM FOR SYMBOL TABLE ALGORITHMS */
106   DECLARE (CARD, LINE, LINE1) CHARACTER;
107   DECLARE I FIXED;
108   OUTPUT = '   SIMULATION OF EVENTS DURING TRANSLATION ';
109   OUTPUT = ' ' ;
110   OUTPUT = 'EVENT:      TABLE STATUS:';
111   OUTPUT = ' ' ;
112   LL = 0; TABLE_TOP = 0;
113   DO WHILE LL >= 0;
114
115      /* PRINT STATUS OF TABLES AND POINTERS */
116      OUTPUT = '     TABLE_TOP = ' ||TABLE_TOP||' LL = ' ||LL|| '  INDEX='||INDEX;
117      LINE = '     ID_TABLE() =     ';
118      LINE1 = '      POINTER() =      ';
119      DO T = 0 TO TABLE_TOP-1;
120         LINE = LINE ||ID_TABLE(I) || ' ' ;
121         LINE1 = LINE1   || POINTER(I) ||  ' ';
122      END;
123      OUTPUT = LINE;
124      OUTPUT = LINE1;
125      LINE = '      SCOPE_MARKER() = ';
126      DO I = 0 TO LL-1;
127         LINE = LINE || SCOPE_MARKER(I) ||  ' ';
128      END;
129      OUTPUT = LINE;
130
131      /* SIMULATE ACTIONS OF A TRANSLATOR */
132      CARD, OUTPUT = INPUT;
133      IF SUBSTR(CARD, 0,2) = 'IN' THEN CALL SCOPE_ENTRY;
134      ELSE IF SUBSTR(CARD,0,3) = 'OUT' THEN CALL SCOPE_EXIT;
135      ELSE IF SUBSTR(CARD,0,3) = 'NEW' THEN CALL NEW_ID(SUBSTR(CARD,5,1));
136      ELSE IF SUBSTR(CARD,0,3) = 'OLD' THEN CALL OLD_ID(SUBSTR(CARD,5,1));
137   END;
138   EOF EOF
```

Test Module for Sorted Access

Figure 5.2

```
EVENT:          TABLE STATUS:

                TABLE_TOP = 0  LL = 0  INDEX = 0
                ID_TABLE() =
                POINTER() =
                SCOPE_MARKER() =
IN
                TABLE_TOP = 0  LL = ·1  INDEX = 0
                ID_TABLE() =
                POINTER() =
                SCOPE_MARKER() = 0
NEW A
                TABLE_TOP = 1  LL = 1  INDEX = 0
                ID_TABLE() =    A
                POINTER() =     0
                SCOPE_MARKER() =0
NEW B
                TABLE_TOP = 2  LL = 1  INDEX = 1
                ID_TABLE()  =    A B
                POINTER()  =     0 1
                SCOPE_MARKER() =  0
OLD A
                TABLE_TOP = 2  LL - 1  INDEX = 0
                ID_TABLE() =     A B
                POINTER() =      0 1
                SCOPE_MARKER() =  0
IN
                TABLE_TOP = 2  LL = 2  INDEX = 0
                ID_TABLE() =     A B
                POINTER() =      0 1
                SCOPE_MARKER()  = 0 2
NEW C
                TABLE_TOP = 3  LL = 2  INDEX = 2
                ID_TABLE() =     A B C
                POINTER() =      0 1 2
                SCOPE_MARKER() =  0 2
```

```
NEW A
                TABLE_TOP = 4  LL = 2  INDEX = 3
                ID_TABLE() =    A B C A
                POINTER() =     0 3 1 2
                SCOPE_MARKER() = 0 2
OLD A
                TABLE_TOP = 4  LL = 2  INDEX = 3
                ID_TABLE() =    A B C A
                POINTER() =     0 3 1 2
                SCOPE_MARKER() = 0 2
OLD B
                TABLE_TOP = 4  LL = 2  INDEX = 1
                ID_TABLE() =    A B C A
                POINTER() =     0 3 1 2
                SCOPE_MARKER() = 0 2
OLD C
                TABLE_TOP = 4  LL = 2  INDEX = 2
                ID_TABLE() =    A B C A
                POINTER() =     0 3 1 2
                SCOPE_MARKER() = 0 2
IN
                TABLE_TOP = 4  LL = 3  INDEX = 2
                ID_TABLE() =    A B C A
                POINTER() =     0 3 1 2
                SCOPE_MARKER() = 0 2 4
OLD A
                TABLE_TOP = 4  LL = 3  INDEX = 3
                ID_TABLE() =    A B C A
                POINTER() =     0 3 1 2
                SCOPE_MARKER() = 0 2 4
OUT
                TABLE_TOP = 4  LL = 2  INDEX = 3
                ID_TABLE() =    A B C A
                POINTER() =     0 3 1 2
                SCOPE_MARKER() = 0 2
IN
                TABLE_TOP = 4  LL = 3  INDEX = 3
                ID_TABLE() =    A B C A
                POINTER() =     0 3 1 2
                SCOPE_MARKER() = 0 2 4
```

NEW A

    TABLE_TOP = 5 LL = 3 INDEX = 4
    ID_TABLE() =   A B C A A
    POINTER() =   0 3 4 1 2
    SCOPE_MARKER() = 0 2 4

OLD A

    TABLE_TOP = 5 LL = 3 INDEX = 4
    ID_TABLE() =   A B C A A
    POINTER() =   0 3 4 1 2
    SCOPE_MARKER() = 0 2 4

OUT

    TABLE_TOP = 4 LL = 2 INDEX = 4
    ID_TABLE() =   A B C A
    POINTER() =   0 3 1 2
    SCOPE_MARKER() = 0 2

OLD A

    TABLE_TOP = 4 LL = 2 INDEX = 3
    ID_TABLE() =   A B C A
    POINTER() =   0 3 1 2
    SCOPE_MARKER() = 0 2

OUT

    TABLE_TOP = 2 LL = 1 INDEX = 3
    ID_TABLE() =   A B
    POINTER() =   0 1
    SCOPE_MARKER() = 0

OLD A

    TABLE_TOP = 2 LL = 1 INDEX = 0
    ID_TABLE() =   A B
    POINTER() =   0 1
    SCOPE_MARKER() = 0

OUT

    TABLE_TOP = 0 LL = 0 INDEX = 0
    ID_TABLE() =
    POINTER() =
    SCOPE_MARKER() =

OUT

                Trace Output: Sorted Access
                      Figure 5.3

6. TREE SYMBOL TABLE ACCESS

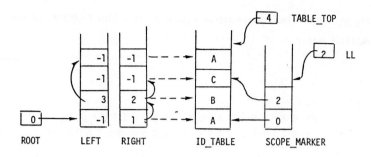

Binary Tree Access Method

Symbol Table Configuration

Figure 6.1

An access tree is a structure that has nodes corresponding to each identifier
in the table (Figure 6.1). Starting from some root position, an identifier is compared with the identifier at the root and either the left or right branch taken
(unless marked with -1, signifying the node is a leaf of the tree). The tree
corresponding to the table configuration above (which itself corresponds to the
processing of lines 1-6 of Figure 2.1 as usual) is more readily understood from
the diagram in Figure 6.2.

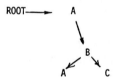

Figure 6. 2

A is at the root. Since nothing will sort "<" than A, everything else hangs off
the right branch of the tree. The next node, B, allows the second A to sort left
and the C to sort right where the tree terminates in leaves. Because the tree is
grown from oldest entry out to recent entries at the leaves, the last entry

found is the correct one.

Exercise   Hand simulate the access algorithm for action 8 (OLD A) of the
simulation output.


```
1            /* S Y M B O L   T A B L E   A L G O R I T H M S */
2            /* B I N A R Y   T R E E   A C C E S S   M E T H O D */
3
4   /* DATA STRUCTURE DEFINITIONS:
5
6     ID_TABLE() HOLDS THE IDENTIFIERS
7     TABLE_TOP POINTS TO THE NEXT AVAILABLE CELL IN ID_TABLE(),
8     TABLE_LIMIT IS THE BOUND ON TABLE_TOP,
9
10    SCOPE_MARKER POINTS TO THE FIRST ENTRY IN EACH SCOPE,
11    LL IS THE PRESENT LEVEL OF PROGRAM NESTING,
12    LL_LIMIT IS THE BOUND ON LL,
13
14    INDEX IS THE SYMBOL TABLE LOCATION FOUND BY THE ACCESS PROCEDURES.
15   */
16
17 DECLARE TABLE_LIMIT LITERALLY '100', TABLE_TOP FIXED,
18      ID_TABLE(TABLE_LIMIT) CHARACTER;
19 DECLARE LL_LIMIT LITERALLY '10', LL FIXED, SCOPE_MARKER (LL_LIMIT) FIXED;
20 DECLARE INDEX FIXED;
21
22 /* DATA STRUCTURES FOR TREE ACCESS */
23 DECLARE (LEFT, RIGHT)(TABLE_LIMIT) FIXED, ROOT FIXED;
24
25 ERROR: PROCEDURE; OUTPUT, OUTPUT = 'ERROR'; CALL EXIT; END ERROR;
26
27 NEW_ID:
28   PROCEDURE (IDENTIFIER);
29     DECLARE IDENTIFIER CHARACTER;
30     DECLARE (I, K) FIXED;
31
```

```
32       /* SEARCH FOR DUPLICATE DECLARATION */
33       K = ROOT; INDEX = -1;
34       DO WHILE K  = -1;
35          IF IDENTIFIER = ID_TABLE(K) THEN INDEX = K;
36          I = K;
37          IF IDENTIFIER < ID_TABLE(K) THEN K = LEFT(K); ELSE K = RIGHT(K);
38       END;
39       IF INDEX   >= SCOPE_MARKER(LL-1) THEN CALL ERROR;
40
41       /*  CHECK FOR ID_TABLE OVERFLOW */
42       IF TABLE_TOP  = TABLE_LIMIT THEN CALL ERROR;
43
44       /* ENTER NEW IDENTIFIER */
45       INDEX = TABLE_TOP;  TABLE_TOP  = TABLE_TOP + 1;
46       ID_TABLE(INDEX) = IDENTIFIER;
47       IF ROOT =-1 THEN ROOT = INDEX;
48       ELSE IF IDENTIFIER < ID_TABLE(I) THEN LEFT(I) = INDEX;
49       ELSE RIGHT(I) = INDEX;
50       LEFT(INDEX), RIGHT(INDEX) = -1;
51    END NEW_ID;
52
53 OLD_ID:
54    PROCEDURE(IDENTIFIER);
55       DECLARE IDENTIFIER CHARACTER;
56       DECLARE K FIXED;.
57
58       /* SEARCH ID_TABLE FOR THE IDENTIFIER */
59       K = ROOT;   INDEX = -1;
60       DO WHILE K    = -1;
61          IF IDENTIFIER = ID_TABLE(K) THEN INDEX = K;
62          IF IDENTIFIER < ID_TABLE(K) THEN K = LEFT(K); ELSE K = RIGHT(K);
63       END;
64
65       /*  RECORD FAILURE TO FIND THE IDENTIFIER */
66       IF INDEX = -1 THEN CALL ERROR;
67    END OLD_ID;
68
69 SCOPE_ENTRY:
70    PROCEDURE;
```

```
71      /* MAKE SURE PROGRAM TEXT IS NOT TOO DEEPLY NESTED */
72      IF LL = LL LIMIT THEN CALL ERROR;
73      SCOPE_MARKER(LL) = TABLE_TOP;   /*POINT TO FIRST LOCAL */
74      LL = LL + 1; /* INCREASE LEXIC LEVEL */
75   END SCOPE_ENTRY;
76
77 SCOPE_EXIT:
78   PROCEDURE;
79      DECLARE I FIXED;
80      LL = LL -1;
81      TABLE_TOP = SCOPE_MARKER(LL);
82      /* DISCARD LEAVES CORRESPONDING TO LOCAL IDENTIFIERS */
83      IF ROOT >= TABLE_TOP THEN ROOT = -1 ;
84      ELSE
85         DO I = 0 TO TABLE_TOP -1;
86            IF LEFT(I)   >= TABLE_TOP THEN LEFT(I) = -1;
87            IF RIGHT(I)  >= TABLE_TOP THEN RIGHT(I) = -1;
88         END;
89   END SCOPE_EXIT;
90
91   /* TEST PROGRAM FOR SYMBOL TABLE ALGORITHMS */
92 DECLARE (CARD, LINE, LINE1, LINE2) CHARACTER;
93 DECLARE I FIXED;
94  OUTPUT = ' SIMULATION OF EVENTS DURING TRANSLATION ';
95 OUTPUT = ' ';
96 OUTPUT = 'EVENT:    TABLE STATUS: ' ;
97 OUTPUT = ' ' ;
98 LL = 0; TABLE_TOP = 0;
99 ROOT = -1;
100 DO  WHILE LL > = 0;
101
102    /* PRINT STATUS OF TABLES AND POINTERS */
103    OUTPUT = '    TABLE_TOP = ' ||TABLE_TOP|| ' LL = ' ||LL||' INDEX='||INDEX;
104    LINE = '   ID_TABLE() =     ';
105    LINE1= '    LEFT() =        ';
106    LINE2 = '    RIGHT() =      ';
107    DO I = 0 TO TABLE_TOP-1;
108       LINE = LINE  ||ID_TABLE(I) || ' ';
109       LINE1 = LINE1 ||LEFT(I) ||  ' ';
```

```
110      LINE2 = LINE2  ||RIGHT(I)||  ' ' ;
111   END;
112   OUTPUT = LINE ;
113   OUTPUT = '         ROOT = ' || ROOT;
114   OUTPUT = LINE1;
115   OUTPUT = LINE2;
116   LINE = '          SCOPE_MARKER() = ';
117   DO I = 0 TO LL-1;
118        LINE = LINE || SCOPE_MARKER(I) ||  ' ';
119   END;
120   OUTPUT = LINE ;
121
122   /* SIMULATE ACTIONS OF A TRANSLATOR */
123   CARD, OUTPUT = INPUT;
124   IF SUBSTR(CARD, 0,2) = 'IN' THEN CALL SCOPE_ENTRY;
125   ELSE IF SUBSTR(CARD,0,3) = 'OUT' THEN CALL SCOPE_EXIT;
126   ELSE IF SUBSTR(CARD,0,3) = 'NEW' THEN CALL NEW_ID(SUBSTR(CARD,5,1));
127   ELSE IF SUBSTR(CARD,0,3) = 'OLD' THEN CALL OLD_ID(SUBSTR(CARD,5,1));
128 END;
129 EOF EOF
```

Test Module for Binary Tree Access
Figure 6.3

EVENT: TABLE STATUS:

                    TABLE_TOP = 0 LL = 0 INDEX = 0
                    ID_TABLE() =
                    ROOT = -1
                    LEFT() =
                    RIGHT() =
                    SCOPE_MARKER() =
IN
                    TABLE_TOP = 0 LL = 1 INDEX = 0
                    ID_TABLE() =
                    ROOT = -1
                    LEFT() =
                    RIGHT() =
                    SCOPE_MARKER() = 0

NEW A

```
TABLE_TOP = 1  LL = 1  INDEX = 0
ID_TABLE() =
ROOT = -1
LEFT() =
RIGHT() =
SCOPE_MARKER() = 0
```

NEW B

```
TABLE_TOP = 2  LL = 1  INDEX = 1
ID_TABLE() =        A B
ROOT = 0
LEFT() =           -1 -1
RIGHT() =           1 -1
SCOPE_MARKER() = 0
```

OLD A

```
TABLE_TOP = 2  LL = 1  INDEX = 0
ID_TABLE() =        A B
ROOT = 0
LEFT () =          -1 -1
RIGHT() =           1 -1
SCOPE_MARKER() = 0
```

IN

```
TABLE_TOP = 2  LL = 2  INDEX = 0
ID_TABLE() =        A B
ROOT = 0
LEFT() =           -1 -1
RIGHT() =           1 -1
SCOPE_MARKER()      0 2
```

NEW C

```
TABLE_TOP = 3  LL = 2  INDEX = 2
ID_TABLE() =        A B C
ROOT = 0
LEFT() =           -1 -1 -1
RIGHT() =           1  2 -1
SCOPE_MARKER() =    0 2
```

NEW A

```
TABLE_TOP = 4  LL = 2  INDEX = 3
ID_TABLE() =        A B C A
ROOT = 0
LEFT() =           -1 3 -1 -1
RIGHT() =           1 2 -1 -1
SCOPE_MARKER()  =   0 2
```

OLD A

```
TABLE_TOP = 4  LL = 2  INDEX = 3
ID_TABLE() =      A B C A
ROOT = 0
LEFT() =          -1 3 -1 -1
RIGHT() =          1 2 -1 -1
SCOPE_MARKER() =   0 2
```

OLD B

```
TABLE_TOP = 4  LL = 2  INDEX = 1
ID_TABLE() =      A B C A
ROOT = 0
LEFT() =          -1 3 -1 -1
RIGHT() =          1 2 -1 -1
SCOPE_MARKER() =   0 2
```

OLD C

```
TABLE_TOP = 4  LL = 2  INDEX = 2
ID_TABLE() =      A B C A
ROOT = 0
LEFT() =          -1 3 -1 -1
RIGHT() =          1 2 -1 -1
SCOPE_MARKER() =   0 2
```

IN

```
TABLE_TOP = 4  LL = 3  INDEX = 2
ID_TABLE() =      A B C A
ROOT = 0
LEFT() =          -1 3 -1 -1
RIGHT() =          1 2 -1 -1
SCOPE_MARKER() =   0 2 4
```

OLD A

```
TABLE_TOP = 4  LL = 3  INDEX = 3
ID_TABLE() =      A B C A
ROOT = 0
LEFT() =          -1 3 -1 -1
RIGHT() =          1 2 -1 -1
SCOPE_MARKER() =   0 2 4
```

OUT

```
TABLE_TOP = 4  LL = 2  INDEX = 3
ID_TABLE() =      A B C A
ROOT = 0
LEFT() =          -1 3 -1 -1
RIGHT() =          1 2 -1 -1
```

```
                    SCOPE_MARKER() =    0 2
IN
                    TABLE_TOP = 4  LL = 3  INDEX = 3
                    ID_TABLE() =        A B C A
                    ROOT = 0
                    LEFT() =            -1 3 -1 -1
                    RIGHT() =           1 2 -1 -1
                    SCOPE_MARKER() =    0 2 4
NEW A
                    TABLE_TOP = 5  LL = 3  INDEX = 4
                    ID_TABLE() =        A B C A A
                    ROOT = 0
                    LEFT() =            -1 3 -1 -1 -1
                    RIGHT() =           1 2 -1 4 -1
                    SCOPE_MARKER() =    0 2 4
OLD A
                    TABLE_TOP = 5  LL = 3  INDEX = 4
                    ID_TABLE() =        A B C A A
                    ROOT = 0
                    LEFT() =            -1 3 -1 -1 -1
                    RIGHT() =           1 2 -1 4 -1
                    SCOPE_MARKER() =    0 2 4
OUT
                    TABLE_TOP = 4  LL = 2  INDEX = 4
                    ID_TABLE() =        A B C A
                    ROOT = 0
                    LEFT() =            -1 3 -1 -1
                    RIGHT() =           1 2 -1 -1
                    SCOPE_MARKER() =    0 2
OLD A
                    TABLE_TOP = 4  LL = 2  INDEX = 3
                    ID_TABLE() =        A B C A
                    ROOT = 0
                    LEFT() =            -1 3 -1 -1
                    RIGHT() =           1 2 - 1-1
                    SCOPE_MARKER() =    0 2
OUT
                    TABLE_TOP = 2  LL = 1  INDEX = 3
                    ID_TABLE() =        A B
                    ROOT = 0
                    LEFT() =            -1 -1
```

```
                        RIGHT() =              1 -1
                        SCOPE_MARKER() =       0
OLD A

                        TABLE_TOP = 2  LL = 1  INDEX = 0
                        ID_TABLE() =           A B
                        ROOT = 0
                        LEFT() =              -1 -1
                        RIGHT() =              1 -1
                        SCOPE_MARKER() =       0
OUT

                        TABLE_TOP = 0  LL = 0  INDEX = 0
                        ID_TABLE() =
                        ROOT = -1
                        LEFT() =
                        RIGHT() =
                        SCOPE_MARKER() =
OUT
```

Trace Output: Binary Tree Access
Figure 6.4

    Scope exit and removal of identifiers from the tree symbol table de-
picted in Figure 6.1   requires a linear search of the left and
right pointers to delete the entries greater than the SCOPE_MARKER. This is a
linear process.   A faster variation is shown in Figure 6.5. A table of pointers
corresponding to each entry in the ID_TABLE is maintained. Each entry in this
table points to the entry in the LEFT/RIGHT table for the corresponding identifier
in the ID_TABLE. Scope exit removal of identifiers from the symbol table would be
accomplished by deleting all entries in the LEFT/RIGHT table pointed to by entries
in the POINTER table above the SCOPE_MARKER being returned to. This method would
be an $N' \log_2 N$ process and the additional memory required for the backward
pointers would be the cost.

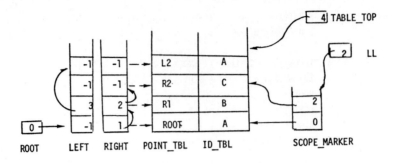

Binary Tree Access Method

With Backward Pointers

Figure 6.5

7. HASH SYMBOL TABLE ACCESS

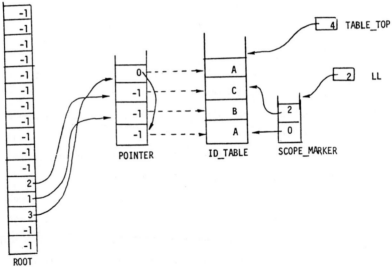

Hash Access Method

Symbol Table Configuration

Figure 7.1

A hash or scramble is an integer valued function on the identifier itself. A good hash will give an even distribution of integer values over the set of identifiers actually presented to the translator, effectively separating them into a large number of small classes. The access method only examines members of the hash class which reduces search time by roughly a factor equal to the range of scrambled values (in this case, 16).

The diagram in Figure 7.1 depicts the table as it would appear after the translator had processed lines 1-6 of Figure 2.1 (refer to the previous example).

Two arrays, ROOT AND POINTER, appear in addition to the identifier table and scope marker. Each entry in ROOT points to the first identifier in its hash class (or is -1 if the class is empty). Each entry in POINTER points to the next number of the hash class (or is -1 if there are no more). To access an identifier, we scramble it, look into ROOT then follow the pointers until we find the identifier or come to the end of the chain. The pointers are arranged to point from new to old so that the first match found is correct.

<u>Exercise</u>   Verify that the simulation output corresponds to the correct symbol table actions.

<u>Exercise</u>   Hand simulate the algorithm for action 8 (OLD A) in the simulation.

```
1           /* S Y M B O L   T A B L E   A L G O R I T H M S  */
2           /* H A S H   S E A R C H   M E T H O D          */
3
4     /* DATA STRUCTURE DEFINITIONS
5
6       ID_TABLE() HOLDS THE IDENTIFIERS,
7       TABLE_TOP POINTS TO THE NEXT AVAILABLE CELL IN THE ID_TABLE(),
8       TABLE_LIMIT IS THE BOUND ON  TABLE_TOP,
9
10      SCOPE_MARKER POINTS TO THE FIRST ENTRY IN EACH SCOPE,
11      LL IS THE PRESENT LEVEL OF PROGRAM NESTING,
```

```
12      LL_LIMIT IS THE BOUND ON LL,
13
14      INDEX IS THE SYMBOL TABLE LOCATION FOUND BY THE ACCESS PROCEDURES.
15   */
16
17 DECLARE TABLE_LIMIT LITERALLY '100', TABLE_TOP FIXED,
18      ID_TABLE(TABLE_LIMIT) CHARACTER;
19 DECLARE LL_LIMIT LITERALLY '10', LL FIXED, SCOPE_MARKER(LL_LIMIT) FIXED;
20 DECLARE INDEX FIXED;
21
22  /* DATA STRUCTURES REQUIRED FOR HASH ACCESS METHOD */
23 DECLARE HASH_SIZE LITERALLY '15', ROOT(HASH_SIZE) FIXED,
24      POINTER(TABLE_LIMIT) FIXED;
25
26 SCRAMBLE:
27   PROCEDURE(IDENTIFIER) FIXED;
28      DECLARE IDENTIFIER CHARACTER;
29      /* FIND A NUMBER BETWEEN 0 AND 15 */
30      RETURN (LENGTH(IDENTIFIER) +BYTE(IDENTIFIER)) & HASH_SIZE;
31   END SCRAMBLE;
32
33 ERROR: PROCEDURE; OUTPUT, OUTPUT = 'ERROR' ; CALL EXIT; END ERROR ;
34
35 NEW_ID:
36   PROCEDURE(IDENTIFIER);
37      DECLARE IDENTIFIER CHARACTER;
38      DECLARE (SB, K) FIXED ;
39
40      /* SEARCH FOR DUPLICATE DECLARATION */
41      K = SCRAMBLE(IDENTIFIER) ; INDEX = ROOT(K);
42      SB = SCOPE_MARKER(LL-1);
43      DO WHILE INDEX  > =  SB;
44         IF IDENTIFIER = ID_TABLE(INDEX) THEN CALL ERROR;
45         INDEX = POINTER(INDEX);
46      END;
47
48      /* CHECK FOR ID_TABLE OVERFLOW */
49      IF TABLE_TOP = TABLE_LIMIT THEN CALL ERROR;
50
51      /* ENTER NEW IDENTIFIER */
```

```
52      INDEX = TABLE_TOP;   TABLE_TOP = TABLE_TOP + 1;
53      ID_TABLE(INDEX)  = IDENTIFIER;
54      POINTER(INDEX) = ROOT(K);  ROOT(K)  =  INDEX;
55   END NEW_ID;
56
57 OLD_ID:
58   PROCEDURE(IDENTIFIER);
59      DECLARE IDENTIFIER CHARACTER;
60
61      /* SEARCH ID_TABLE FOR THE IDENTIFIER */
62      INDEX = ROOT(SCRABLE(IDENTIFIER));
63      DO WHILE INDEX ¬ = -1;
64         IF IDENTIFIER = ID_TABLE(INDEX) THEN RETURN;
65         INDEX = POINTER(INDEX);
66      END;
67
68      /* RECORD FAILURE TO FIND THE IDENTIFIER */
69      CALL ERROR;
70   END OLD_ID;
71
72 SCOPE_ENTRY:
73   PROCEDURE;
74      /* MAKE SURE PROGRAM TEXT IS NOT TOO DEEPLY NESTED */
75      IF LL = LL_LIMIT THEN CALL ERROR;
76      SCOPE_MARKER(LL) = TABLE_TOP;   /*POINT TO FIRST LOCAL*/
77      LL = LL + 1;  /*INCREASE LEXIC LEVEL */
78   END SCOPE ENTRY;
79
80 SCOPE_EXIT:
81   PROCEDURE ;
82      DECLARE K FIXED;
83      DECLARE K FIXED;
84      INDEX = TABLE_TOP;
85      LL = LL -1;
86      TABLE_TOP = SCOPE_MARKER(LL);
87
88      /*DE-LINK IDENTIFIERS BEING DISCARDED */
89      DO WHILE INDEX  >  TABLE_TOP;
90         INDEX = INDEX -1;
91         K = SCRAMBLE(ID_TABLE(INDEX));
```

```
 92          ROOT(K) = POINTER(ROOT(K));
 93      END;
 94   END SCOPE_EXIT;
 95
 96   /* TEST PROGRAM FOR SYMBOL TABLE ALGORITHMS */
 97 DECLARE (CARD, LINE, LINE1) CHARACTER;
 98 DECLARE I FIXED;
 99 OUTPUT = '   SIMULATION OF EVENTS DURING TRANSLATION  ';
100 OUTPUT = ' ' ;
101 OUTPUT = 'EVENT:   TABLE STATUS :';
102 OUTPUT = ' ';
103 DO I = 0 TO HASH_SIZE;
104      ROOT(I) = -1;  /* MARK ALL HASH CLASSES EMPTY */
105 END;
106
107 LL = 0;  TABLE_TOP = 0;
108 DO WHILE LL >= 0;
109
110     /* PRINT STATUS OF TABLES AND POINTERS */
111     OUTPUT = '    TABLE_TOP ='  ||TABLE_TOP||  ' LL=' ||LL||' INDEX='||INDEX;
112     LINE = '         ID_TABLE() =    ';
113     LINE1 = '        POINTER() =     ';
114     DO I = 0 TO TABLE_TOP-1;
115       LINE = LINE || ID_TABLE(I) || ' ';
116       LINE1 = LINE1|| POINTER(I)||  ' ';
117     END;
118     OUTPUT = LINE;
119     OUTPUT = LINE1;
120     LINE = '          SCOPE_MARKER() = ';
121     DO I + 0 TO LL-1;
122       LINE = LINE || SCOPE_MARKER(I) || ' ';
123     END;
124     OUTPUT = LINE;
125     LINE = '        ROOT() =       ';
126     DO I = 0 TO HASH_SIZE;
127       LINE = LINE || ROOT(I)||  ' ';
128     END;
129     OUTPUT = LINE;
130
131     /*SIMULATE ACTIONS OF A TRANSLATOR */
```

```
132  CARD, OUTPUT = INPUT;
133  IF SUBSTR(CARD, 0,2) = 'IN' THEN CALL SCOPE_ENTRY;
134  ELSE IF SUBSTR(CARD,0,3) = 'OUT' THEN CALL SCOPE_EXIT;
135  ELSE IF SUBSTR(CARD,0,3) = 'NEW' THEN CALL NEW_ID(SUBSTR(CARD,5,1));
136  ELSE IF SUBSTR(CARD,0,3) = 'OLD' THEN CALL OLD_ID(SUBSTR(CARD,5,1));
137  END;
138  EOF   EOF
```

Test Module for Hash Access
Figure 7.2

EVENT: TABLE STATUS:

                TABLE_TOP = 0 LL = 0 INDEX = 0
                ID_TABLE() =
                POINTER() =
                SCOPE_MARKER() =
                ROOT() =   -1 -1 -1 -1 -1 -1 -1 -1 -1 -1 -1 -1 -1 -1 -1 -1
IN
                TABLE_TOP = 0 LL = 1 INDEX = 0
                ID_TABLE() =
                POINTER() =
                SCOPE_MARKER() = 0
                ROOT() =   -1 -1 -1 -1 -1 -1 -1 -1 -1 -1 -1 -1 -1 -1 -1 -1
NEW A
                TABLE_TOP = 1 LL = 1 INDEX = 0
                ID_TABLE() =   A
                POINTER() =   -1
                SCOPE_MARKER() =   0
                ROOT() =   -1 -1 0 -1 -1 -1 -1 -1 -1 -1 -1 -1 -1 -1 -1 -1
NEW B
                TABLE_TOP = 2 LL = 1 INDEX = 1
                ID_TABLE() =   A B
                POINTER() =   -1 -1
                SCOPE_MARKER() =   0
                ROOT() =   -1 -1 0 1 -1 -1 -1 -1 -1 -1 -1 -1 -1 -1 -1 -1
OLD A
```
```

```
                    TABLE_TOP = 2  LL = 1  INDEX = 3
                    ID_TABLE() =        A B
                    POINTER() =         -1 -1
                    SCOPE_MARKER() =    0
                    ROOT() =            -1 -1 0 1 -1 -1 -1 -1 -1 -1 -1 -1 -1 -1 -1 -1
IN
                    TABLE_TOP = 2  LL = 2  INDEX = 0
                    ID_TABLE() =        A B
                    POINTER() =         -1 -1
                    SCOPE_MARKER() =    0 2
                    ROOT() =            -1 -1 0 1 -1 -1 -1 -1 -1 -1 -1 -1 -1 -1 -1 -1
NEW C
                    TABLE_TOP = 3  LL = 2  INDEX = 2
                    ID_TABLE() =        A B C
                    POINTER() =         -1 -1 -1
                    SCOPE_MARKER() =    0 2
                    ROOT() =            -1 -1 0 1 2 -1 -1 -1 -1 -1 -1 -1 -1 -1 -1  -1
NEW A
                    TABLE_TOP = 4  LL = 2  INDEX = 3
                    ID_TABLE() =        A B C A
                    POINTER() =         -1 -1 -1 0
                    SCOPE_MARKER() =    0 2
                    ROOT() =            -1 -1 3 1 2 -1 -1 -1 -1 -1 -1 -1 -1 -1 -1 -1
OLD A
                    TABLE_TOP = 4  LL = 2  INDEX = 3
                    ID_TABLE() =        A B C A
                    POINTER() =         -1 -1 -1 0
                    SCOPE_MARKER() =    0 2
                    ROOT() =            -1 -1 3 1 2 -1 -1 -1 -1 -1 -1 -1 -1 -1 -1 -1
OLD B
                    TABLE_TOP = 4  LL = 2  INDEX = 1
                    ID_TABLE()          A B C A
                    POINTER() =         -1 -1 -1 0
                    SCOPE_MARKER() =    0 2
                    ROOT() =            -1 -1 3 1 2 -1 -1 -1 -1 -1 -1 -1 -1 -1 -1 -1
```

OLD C

```
TABLE_TOP = 4  LL = 2  INDEX = 2
ID_TABLE() =        A B C A
POINTER() =         -1 -1 -1 0
SCOPE_MARKER() =    0 2
ROOT() =            -1 -1 3 1 2 -1 -1 -1 -1 -1 -1 -1 -1 -1 -1 -1
```

IN

```
TABLE_TOP = 4  LL = 3 INDEX = 2
ID_TABLE() =        A B C A
POINTER() =         -1 -1 -1 0
SCOPE_MARKER() = ٬  0 2 4
ROOT() =            -1 -1 3 1 2 -1 -1 -1 -1 -1 -1 -1 -1 -1 -1 -1
```

OLD A

```
TABLE_TOP = 4  LL = 3  INDEX = 3
ID_TABLE() =        A B C A
POINTER() =         -1 -1 -1 0
SCOPE_MARKER() =    0 2 4
ROOT() =            -1 -1 3 1 2 -1 -1 -1 -1 -1 -1 -1 -1 -1 -1 -1
```

OUT

```
TABLE_TOP = 4  LL = 2  INDEX = 4
ID_TABLE() =        A B C A
POINTER() =         - 1 -1 -1 0
SCOPE_MARKER() =    0 2
ROOT() =            -1 -1 3 1 2 -1 -1 -1 -1 -1 -1 -1 -1 -1 -1 -1
```

IN

```
TABLE_TOP = 4  LL = 3  INDEX = 4
ID_TABLE () =       A B C A
POINTER()  =        -1 -1 -1 0
SCOPE_MARKER() =    0 2 4
ROOT() =            -1 -1 3 1 2 -1 -1 -1 -1 -1 -1 -1 -1 -1 -1 -1
```

NEW A

```
TABLE_TOP = 5 LL = 3  INDEX = 4
ID_TABLE() =        A B C A A
POINTER() =         -1 -1 -1 0 3
SCOPE_MARKER() =    0 2 4
ROOT() =            -1 -1 4 1 2 -1 -1 -1 -1 -1 -1 -1 -1 -1 -1 -1
```

OLD A

```
                TABLE_TOP = 5  LL = 3  INDEX = 4
                ID_TABLE() =        A B C A A
                POINTER() =         -1 -1 -1 0 3
                SCOPE_MARKER() =    0 2 4
                ROOT() =            -1 -1 4 1 2 -1 -1 -1 -1 -1 -1 -1 -1 -1 -1 -1
```

OUT

```
                TABLE_TOP = 4  LL = 2  INDEX = 4
                ID_TABLE() =        A B C A
                POINTER() =         -1 -1 -1 0
                SCOPE_MARKER() =    0 2
                ROOT() =            -1 -1 3 1 2 -1 -1 -1 -1 -1 -1 -1 -1 -1 -1 -1
```

OLD A

```
                TABLE_TOP = 4  LL = 2  INDEX = 3
                ID_TABLE() =        A B C A
                POINTER() =         -1 -1 -1 0
                SCOPE_MARKER() =    0 2
                ROOT() =            -1 -1 3 1 2 -1 -1 -1 -1 -1 -1 -1 -1 -1 -1 -1
```

OUT

```
                TABLE_TOP = 2  LL = 1  INDEX = 2
                ID_TABLE() =        A B
                POINTER() =         -1 -1
                SCOPE_MARKER() =    0
                ROOT() =            -1 -1 0 1 -1 -1 -1 -1 -1 -1 -1 -1 -1 -1 -1 -1
```

OLD A

```
                TABLE_TOP = 2 LL = 1  INDEX = 0
                ID_TABLE() =        A B
                POINTER() =         -1 -1
                SCOPE_MARKER() =    0
                ROOT() =            -1 -1 0 1 -1 -1 -1 -1 -1 -1 -1 -1 -1 -1 -1 -1
```

OUT

```
                TABLE_TOP = 0  LL = 0  INDEX = 0
                ID_TABLE() =
                POINTER() =
                SCOPE_MARKER() =
                ROOT() =            -1 -1 -1 -1 -1 -1 -1 -1 -1 -1 -1 -1 -1 -1 -1 -1
```

OUT

Trace Output: Hash Access

Figure 7.3

7.1 Hash Functions

Numerous algorithms can be developed for scrambling the bits of an identifier to produce an index for entering a symbol table lookup. Some standard methods employed in these algorithms include concatenation of N select bits of the identifier where N is the size of the required index, or multiplication of a portion of the identifier, usually a machine word, by a constant value and selecting the middle bits of the product as the index.

Execution speed of the algorithm and the distribution of the indices across the range of the table are the considerations for selecting an algorithm for calculating the hash index. In order to choose the most efficient hashing algorithm, the trade-off between the time taken to produce the hash and flatness of the distribution of indices over the hash table must be found for each candidate algorithm and evaluated in respect to the specific application.

Concerning the speed of an algorithm, when dealing with filing systems of large size, where the hash tables tend to be large and not always resident in primary store it may be necessary to carefully develop an efficient hash in order to minimize the need to fetch tables. In translators the complete hash and symbol tables reside in primary store and the time spent in developing the hash is a factor in the overall efficiency of the hash algorithm. The accuracy of the hash produced is not critical as long as it is sufficiently distributive. In this case the faster the hash algorithm the faster will be the symbol table access. However, the speed of the hash algorithm tends to become unimportant as the average number of symbols to be interrogated during each symbol table access increases. If more than one symbol is to be looked at the time taken in development of the hash will be masked out by the time spent in the comparison of each symbol. In the examples of the hash algorithms given in the next section the average number of symbols looked at was slightly less than two and the overall access speed was only slightly effected by the faster algorithms.

Concerning the randomness of the distribution of an algorithm the ideal case is the algorithm which, given a table length L with positions $E_1E_2....E_L$, produces hash keys to cover the entire range of L without any predictable grouping.

Consider implementation on an IBM 360 of a hash table of 256 positions which would require an index of 8 bits length. The identifier is presented as the key and the hashing algorithm consists of the least significant four bits of the first letter plus the length shifted left four bits all masked to 8 bits. The indices produced by this algorithm will cover a range of only 144 numbers out of the possible 256; 112 of the table locations would never be used. The reason is that the least significant four bits of the hexadecimal code for letters maps into only 9 of the entire range of 16 possible numbers. The least significant four bits of the key would always be 0-9 instead of 0-F.

A test of six hash algorithms was performed on an IBM 360/40 using as input the actual identifiers taken from a student translator interpreter program. The intent was to determine the overall efficiency of each algorithm, speed, against distribution, using data representative of a normal programming problem.

The algorithms are shown imbedded in the actual procedures used in the test program. In each procedure the parameter ID contains the identifier to be hashed and the procedure returns an index value of the range 0 to 255.

```
1
2
3    ALGORITHM_1 :
4       PROCEDURE (ID) FIXED;
5          DECLARE ID CHARACTER;
6          IF LENGTH (ID) = 1 THEN
7             ID = ID || ' ' ;
8          RETURN ((BYTE(ID)&"0F")+(BYTE(ID,1) & "0F")+SHL(LENGTH(ID),4))&"FF";
9       END ALGORITHM_1;
10
11   /* ALGORITHM_1 PRODUCES AN INDEX FROM THE SUM OF THE LOW ORDER
12      FOUR BITS OF THE FIRST TWO CHARACTERS CONCATENATED WITH THE LENGTH
13      OF THE IDENTIFIER AS THE HIGH ORDER FOUR BITS OF THE INDEX.
14 */
```

```
15
16
17
18    ALGORITHM_2:
19       PROCEDURE (ID) FIXED;
20          DECLARE ID CHARACTER, L FIXED;
21          L = LENGTH(ID);
22          RETURN((BYTE(ID) &"3F")+(BYTE(ID,L-1)&"3F") + SHL(L,4))& "FF";
23       END ALGORITHM_2;
24
25    /* ALGORITHM_2 PRODUCES AN INDEX FROM THE SUM OF THE LOW ORDER
26        SIX BITS OF THE FIRST AND LAST CHARACTERS AND THE LENGTH OF THE
27        IDENTIFIED SHIFTED LEFT FOUR PLACES.
28    */
29
30
31
32    ALGORITHM_3:
33       PROCEDURE (ID) FIXED;
34          DECLARE ID CHARACTER;
35          RETURN (BYTE(ID) + LENGTH(ID)) & "FF";
36       END ALGORITHM_3;
37
38    /* ALGORITHM_3  PRODUCES AN INDEX FROM THE PRODUCT OF THE LENGTH
39        OF THE IDENTIFIER TIMES THE FIRST CHARACTER OF THE IDENTIFIER.
40    */
41
42
43    ALGORITHM_4:
44       PROCEDURE (ID) FIXED;
45          DECLARE ID CHARACTER, L FIXED;
46          L = LENGTH(ID);
47          RETURN(BYTE (ID) + BYTE(ID,L-1) + SHL(L,4) & "FF";
48       END ALGORITHM_4;
49
50    /* ALGORITHM_4   PRODUCES AN INDEX FROM THE SUM OF THE EIGHT BITS
51        OF THE FIRST AND LAST CHARACTER AND THE LENGTH OF THE IDENTIFIER
52        SHIFTED LEFT FOUR PLACES.
53    */
54
```

```
55
56
57    ALGORITHM_5:
58      PROCEDURE (ID) FIXED;
59        DECLARE ID CHARACTER, L FIXED;
60        L = LENGTH(ID);
61        RETURN (BYTE(ID) + SHL(BYTE(ID,L-1),3) + SHL(L,4) & "F";
62      END ALGORITHM_5;
63
64   /* ALGORITHM_5   PRODUCES AN INDEX FROM THE SUM OF THE FIRST
65      CHARACTER AND THE LAST CHARACTER SHIFTED LEFT THREE PLACES AND
66      THE LENGTH OF THE IDENTIFIER SHIFTED LEFT FOUR PLACES.
67   */
68
69
70
71    ALGORITHM_6:
72      PROCEDURE (ID) FIXED ;
73        DECLARE ID CHARACTER ;
74        RETURN (SHR((BYTE(ID)*"5B5C3D5A"),20) + SHL(LENGTH(ID),4))& "FF";
75      END ALGORITHM_6;
76
77   /* ALGORITHM_6   PRODUCES AN INDEX BY MULTIPLYING THE FIRST CHARACTER
78      OF THE IDENTIFIER BY A CONSTANT AND EXTRACTING THE MOST RANDOM BITS
79      OF THE PRODUCT TO SUM WITH THE LENGTH OF THE IDENTIFIER IN THE
80      HIGH ORDER OF FOUR BITS.
81   */
82
83
84
85
```

Hashing Algorithms
Figure 7.4

The results of the symbol table test on each algorithm is shown in Figure 7.5.

ALGORITHM #	BUCKETS USED	SYMBOLS INTERROGATED	SECONDS CONSUMED
1	183	27,969	29.32
2	202	27,428	26.58
3	151	36,044	28.01
4	203	27,428	24.20
5	198	26,823	26.15
6	182	28,564	25.42

Table 7.5 Symbol Table Test Results

The results of the tests are inconclusive. Thus we conclude that even
a   fair hash is pretty close to optimal.

7.2 Secondary Store

The technique of superimposing an access method on the basic table has
allowed for quite uniform programs with nevertheless different attributes. A more
serious test of the technique comes when the strings of identifiers themselves
cannot be kept in main memory. If the characters are on secondary store, then
every comparison (line 34 of Figure 4.2, for example) implies an access to secondary store. That is unacceptable.

An interesting solution, involving a second hash, can be applied to all of
the methods already proposed. Instead of having the characters available for comparison, keep a suitably short code for each one of them in main memory (say eight
bits). The code is to be generated by a second hash function and recorded when
the symbol is first placed onto secondary store (by new_id). Now, when another
occurrence of the identifier appears, we first look through the table to see if the
second hash function of the new occurrence matches that already recorded. Only if
the codes are the same can the two symbols be the same. We then must actually look
at the symbol on secondary store to verify that the comparison holds, and continue

on with the look-up if it turns out to have been an accidental match of the codes.

In the case of hash access, where we were already looking at only 1/N of the identifiers (those in the same hash class) we now look at only $1/N^2$ (assuming both hashes have a range of N).

Exercise Modify one of the symbol table algorithms to add a secondary store and secondary hash to keep the number of accesses down. What is the cost? In memory accesses? In secondary accesses? In memory residence?

8. EVALUATION OF ACCESS METHODS

The choice between the four methods presented (or others) depends upon which is the most economical, a criterion easier to state than to measure. In a practical situation one simply tries likely algorithms and measures gross performance against an actual computational load. We can also analyze the algorithms to give a reasonable predictive analysis to eliminate those not even near the optimum. The critical resource is memory and the two bottlenecks are memory access and memory residence. The most meaningful parameters are t, the average number of symbols in the table, t', the average number of symbols in the most local scope, t", the largest number of identifiers the algorithms must be prepared to tabulate at one time, H, the range of the hash function, and f_1, f_2, f_3, f_4, the predicted relative frequency of the actions scope entry, scope exit, declaration of an identifier, and use of an identifier.

We want to predict the load on the mechanisms of memory residence and memory access due to the symbole table activity. We need not consider the load on the other devices of the computer (e.g.,CPU) since they are largely idle and we can choose not to tabulate loads common to all methods (such as calling the access procedures). We will assume that the appearance of an identifier is equivalent to a memory access and that certain loops in the algorithms are terminated on the average after 1/2 their maximum run. On that basis Figure 8.1 defines the memory access load for each primitive symbol table action. (lnt stands for the logarithm of t to the base 2).

ACCESS METHOD	SCOPE ENTRY	SCOPE EXIT	DECLARATION	USE
Linear	7	5	$7t'+14$	$3t+2$
Hash	7	$19t'+7$	$(8/H)t'+32$	$(3.5/H)t+10$
Sort	7	$13t+9$	$4t+(11)lnt+20$	$(11)lnt+12$
Tree	7	$10t+8$	$(16)lnt+31$	$(15)lnt+4$

Memory Access Counts

Figure 8.1

Counting the actions in one of the small test programs for the symbol table algorithm and extrapolating for a somewhat larger program, we predict the actual access actions in the numbers:

Program Size	f_1 Entry	f_2 Exit	f_3 Declaration	f_4 Use
Small	5	5	20	100
Medium	10	10	100	700

Symbol Table Actions

Figure 8.2

Then for each action we need to evaluate the formulas of Figure 8.1 with weights given in Figure 8.2. The resulting formula

$$M = f_1M_1 + f_2M_2 + f_3M_3 + f_4M_4$$

simplifies to the formulae given in Figure 8.3.

M_{linear}	=	335t		+ 540
M_{hash}	=	25.6t		+ 1710
M_{sort}	=	145t	+ 1320lnt	+ 1680
M_{tree}	=	50t	+ 1820lnt	+ 1095

"Small program"

Memory access as a function of table contents

Figure 8.3

In calculating the equations in Figure 8.2 we have assumed t' = t/4 and H = 256. It might be more realistic to assign t' a constant value (such as 10) since it is not necessarily valid to assume that the number of variables declared locally in a program will increase with the size of the program. The effect of assigning a constant term would be to remove the linear term from the Linear and Hash equations. Their graph lines represented in Figure 8.4 would then slope slightly downward. One can get a feeling for which algorithm makes the least demand on the memory access circuitry by a graph of the functions (Figure 8.4) over a reasonable range (t = 1, 100).

Observing Figure 8.4, we conclude that except for very small table sizes the hash scheme places the least load on the memory access mechanism. It does not make sense to extrapolate the curves further since they are based on frequency counts from small programs, but the analysis can be repeated with new figures for the larger load as suggested in Figure 8.2. The disappointing performance of the sorted table is due to the term 145t in the equation which is due to the necessity to re-sort upon scope exit and each new addition to the table. The larger weights reduce the importance of both actions so we should expect some improvement there. The tree algorithms should gain even more radically. We conclude that algorithm performance is sufficiently dependent upon environment that it is meaningless to ask which is "best" overall but performance can be estimated once the environment is specified.

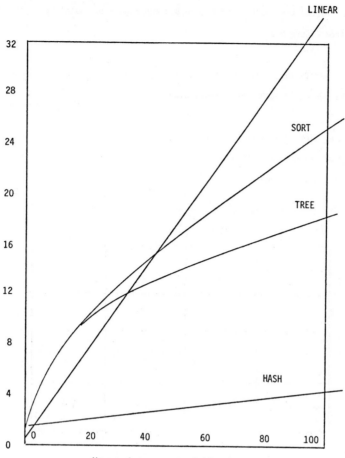

Memory Accesses vs. Active Contents

Figure 8.4

Exercise   Repeat the analysis of Figure 8.3 and Figure 8.4 with the "medium" figures from Figure 8.2

Exercise   Verify in detail the formulae in Figure 8.1 by counting the potential memory references in each symbol table algorithm.

Another view of what has just been described is shown in Table 8.5. Here the _order_ of the number of memory accesses caused by each symbol table operation is given for the four methods.

	SCOPE ENTRY	SCOPE EXIT	DECLARATION	USE
LINEAR	0	0	t''	t
HASH	0	t''	$\frac{t''}{H}$	$\frac{t}{H}$
SORT	0	t	t''	lnt
TREE	0	t''lnt	lnt	lnt

Table 8.5 Memory Accesses

Memory access is not the whole picture; memory residence is also expensive. If it were not we would simply increase the size of the hash function so as reduce cost of hash access arbitrarily far. Ignoring the difference in actual program size, the extra memory required over the symbol table itself is given in Figures 8.6 and 8.7.

Linear		Linear	
Hash	t" + H	Hash	356
Sort	t"	Sort	100
Tree	2t"	Tree	200

(Linear = 0, Linear = 0)

Figure 8.6   Figure 8.7

Extra Memory Required   Extra Memory Cells Occupied

Assuming modest value of 100 for maximum table size and 256 for an 8-bit hash, we
see that the speed of the hash algorithm is paid for in used memory. The combination of the figures for memory residence and memory access depends upon the computer
organization in a way that cannot be predetermined. It depends upon where the
critical resource is and what will happen to idle resources (e.g., can some other
process use them via multiprogramming).

Exercise   Pick a computer you are familiar with and attempt to weigh the considerations of memory access vs. memory residence to make a choice of symbol table
algorithms for a translator that is going to handle streams of small student jobs.

Exercise   Gather an actual set of numbers f_1.... f_4 by modifying an existing compiler, writing a special processing program or doing some manual examination of
the input set to some compiler. Also obtain estimates of t, t', t". How does the
ratio f_4/f_3 vary with t and t'? What implication does this have on the choice of
algorithms? State a mathematical analysis which allows a comparison of the algorithms over the distribution of values you have determined. Would a policy of
using one algorithm for small programs and another for large programs pay large
dividends?

CHAPTER 3.E.

CODE GENERATION

W.M. WAITE

Dept. of Electrical Engineering

University of Colorado

BOULDER, COLORADO USA

A source language definition specifies the evaluation procedures for the constructs of the language in terms of a set of primitive operators and operands provided for this purpose. If the source language is machine-independent, then these primitives are necessarily abstractions, as discussed in Chapter 3.A. Code generation is the process of implementing an evaluation procedure in terms of the primitives of a particular target computer. The basic approach is to simulate the evaluation procedure in the environment (register organization and addressing structure) provided by the target computer: A description of the run-time contents of the environment is maintained by the code generator. When the evaluation procedure indicates that the contents should be altered, then code to perform the alteration is emitted and the description is updated.

The data for the code generator consists of the structure tree, as modified during the semantic analysis, and the dictionary. These two components can be considered as one, since the dictionary is simply a means of recording the attributes of certain structure tree nodes. (In the GIER ALGOL compiler [Naur 1964], for example, the attributes of each identifier were recorded in the intermediate text at every occurrence of that identifier.) The evaluation procedures specify the sequence in which the nodes of a structure tree are to be considered when performing the evaluation, and this sequence is largely independent of the particular target computer. I shall therefore assume that the structure tree is traversed by the semantic analyzer or by an optimizer which considers entire subtrees before deciding upon the best sequence of operations to perform. (This is the flattening process mentioned in Chapter 2.G.) Thus the code generator input is a sequence of tokens specified by the nodes of the structure tree. Conceptually, the input is derived from an intermediate text file; actually, it may be specified by a sequence of procedure or coroutine calls upon the code generator by another module. Regardless of the source of the input stream, it is assumed to represent a program which is correct. (Any errors detected during analysis must be patched up by the analyzer, and not passed on to the code generator.)

1. A Model for Code Generation

I have assumed that the code generator does not have arbitrary access to the structure tree, and must therefore operate on the basis of limited information. The model which I advocate [Wilcox 1971] consists of two parts:

a. A pushdown store transducer, which maintains the contextual information that can be derived from the sequence of input tokens.

b. A target machine simulator, which maintains the run-time contents of the environment and produces sequences of target computer instructions to implement the abstract primitives.

(Wilcox terms these components the translator and the coder, respectively.) The transducer passes a sequence of commands to the simulator, each consisting of an

abstract operator and its associated operands. Each command is interpreted by the simulator in the light of the environment which will exist at that point in the execution of the program. It generates appropriate code and then updates the environment to reflect the effect of that code.

1.1. <u>The Transducer</u>. A pushdown store transducer has four components: an input tape, an output tape, a finite-state control and a pushdown store. In our case the input tape models the stream of tokens which encodes the structure tree, and the output tape models the abstract instructions which will be delivered to the simulator. The finite-state control and the pushdown store encode the limited contextual information derived from the sequence of input tokens.

Information pertaining to the ancestors of the current node, and the status of the current node itself, is encoded by the finite-state control. This information can be used to distinguish regions of the program in which a particular construct may have different meanings. For example, a string expression appearing as the argument of a LENGTH function in PL/1 and the same expression appearing as the right hand side of a string assignment should be translated differently. In the former case, we are not interested in the actual string produced by the expression, but merely in its length; hence concatenation operators should be translated as additions. Similar situations arise with expressions appearing in array subscripts (where we wish to do linear subscript optimization) and on the left hand side of assignment statements (where we need to obtain an address rather than a value.)

The pushdown store contains information derived from subtrees which have been completely traversed. After all subtrees whose roots are descendants of a particular node have been traversed, their entries are deleted from the pushdown store and replaced by a single entry for the entire tree rooted at that node. Information from the pushdown store is used to identify the operands of an operator.

State information may also be retained in the pushdown store during the traversal of the subtree rooted in a given node. When this is done, the state would be entered into the pushdown store at the prefix encounter with the node and removed during processing of the postfix encounter. The sequence of actions which implements the postfix encounter would be: remove subtree entries, remove state, insert result entry.

During the flattening of the structure tree by the semantic analyzer, encounters with interior nodes result in input tokens for the transducer only if the evaluation procedure requires it. These tokens are the operators and delimiters of the input stream, and I shall discuss specific examples in Section 2. Operand tokens are always created for leaves of the tree. The transducer has four basic actions which it may perform, singly or in combination, for each token:

    a. Request simulation of a given token with given arguments, accepting a description of the result if one exists.

    b. Remove the top k entries of the pushdown store (k>0).

    c. Insert a given entry into the pushdown store.

    d. Make the state of the control a given value.

The first action allows the transducer to supply information to the simulator. Its arguments may include the value of the transducer state, and the top k entries of the pushdown store. (This is a violation of the strict definition of a pushdown store transducer, but it is a reasonable assumption for any practical implementation.) In action (c) the "given entry" may be the current value of the transducer state, and in action (d) the "given value" may be the top entry of the pushdown store.

1.2. The Simulator. In order to interpret the primitives of the source language in terms of the target machine, the simulator must maintain descriptions of the values being manipulated (value image) and of the target machine environment (machine image.) A particular value may be represented in many different ways in the target computer, and the purpose of the value image is to specify the current representation of each value. Similarly, the registers of the target machine may contain many different values during the course of execution, and the purpose of the machine image is to specify the current contents of each register. The relationships between values and the registers which contain them are expressed by cross-linkages between the two images. I shall discuss the detailed structure and contents of the images in Section 3.

A value comes under the control of the code generator when the transducer requests simulation of an operand token, giving the current transducer state as an argument. At that point the simulator creates an entry for the operand in the value image and, if appropriate, links it to the machine image.

Values pass out of the control of the code generator when they are used as operands (but see Section 1.3.) This is signalled when the transducer requests simulation of an operator token giving the current state and one or more values as arguments. At that point the simulator deletes the operand entries from the value image, breaking any linkage to the machine image. If a result is specified, a description of the result value is created and linked to the appropriate entry in the machine image.

1.3. Common Subexpressions. The model which I have presented above is based on the representation of a program as a structure tree in which the leaves correspond to named operands or constants. These entities lie outside of the ken of the code generator. Their values are obtained when the corresponding leaves are encountered, and the values so obtained are then treated as distinct entities which are under the code generator's total control. In effect, the code generator deals only with anonymous results (Chapter 3.A, Section 2.1.)

Common subexpression elimination is an optimization which creates a directed acyclic graph rather than a structure tree to describe the program (Figure 1.1). This graph can be represented by an equivalent tree which contains an additional named operand, as shown in Figure 1.1c. The new operand, however, is not one which was named by the programmer. Control of this operand should therefore be the responsibility of the code generator. Since it is not anonymous, however, it will be used more than once and hence it cannot be modelled by an entry in the transducer's pushdown store.

This problem can easily be circumvented if we realize that the value image maintained by the simulator may encompass more than just the contents of the transducer's pushdown store. In general, the pushdown store contains a subset of the values being managed by the code generator at any given instant. When the simulator creates a value image entry for an operand, it might set a counter to indicate the number of uses left for that value. Each time the value appears as an argument this count would be decremented; the entry would be deleted only when it reaches zero.

$$4-3*(I+J)+(I+J)\uparrow 2$$

a) An expression with a common subexpression

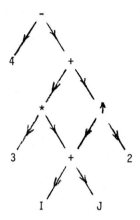

b) The directed acyclic graph for (a)

T1:

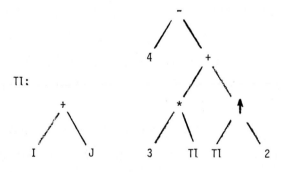

c) An equivalent tree

Figure 1.1

Representing Common Subexpressions

2. Sequencing and Control

An operator is <u>postfix-translatable</u> if code for its operands can be generated in the same state as code for the operator/operand combination, and if the semantics of the operator do not require prologue code or intervening code between operands. These conditions imply that the transducer will never take action (d) (Section 1.1), and only postfix encounters with interior nodes of the structure tree will result in transducer input tokens. Most infix operators in current programming languages satisfy these constraints, provided that certain kinds of optimization are not required.

As an example of the problems caused by optimization, consider the two expressions (I+J)*K/L and (I+J+K)/L. Using an appropriate syntax for expressions, these two could be translated to the postfix forms IJ+K*L/ and IJ+K+L/ respectively. Note that the translations are identical over the first four characters; in particular the summation of I and J is the same in both. If we assume that the operators are postfix translatable, then the code generated from IJ+ must be the same in both expressions because we have no information about text to the right of this subexpression.

Let us now consider the translation of these two expressions into object code for the IBM System/360. Integer multiplication on this machine is specified as follows [IBM 1967]: "Both multiplier and multiplicand are 32-bit signed integers. The product is always a 64-bit signed integer and occupies an even/odd register pair. Because the multiplicand is replaced by the product the register field of the instruction must refer to an even numbered register ... the multiplicand is taken from the odd register of the pair. The content of the even numered register replaced by the product is ignored unless that register contains the multiplier." Integer division is defined as follows: "The dividend is a 64-bit signed integer and occupies the even/odd pair of registers specified by the ... instruction. ... A 32-bit signed remainder and a 32-bit signed quotient replace the dividend in the even numbered and odd numbered registers respectively. The divisor is a 32-bit signed integer." Given these instruction definitions, the best code for each of the two expressions is shown in Figure 2.1. Notice that the operator following K determines the register in which I+J is computed.

```
L       RI,I
A       RI,J
M       R0,K
D       R0,L
```

a) Code for the expression ((I+J)*K/L)

```
L       R0,I
A       R0,J
A       R0,K
SRDA    R0,32
D       R0,L
```

b) Code for the expression ((I+J+K)/L)

Figure 2.1

Optimum Instruction Sequences for System/360

To produce the optimum code, the code generator could recognize that it is processing the first operand of a division. In other words, the two operands of the division would be translated in different states of the code generator. A further change in state when the first operand is an expression containing a multiplication would guarantee that the multiplicand is left in the proper register of the pair. Alternatively, the registers could be allocated but not assigned on a first pass, with a second pass substituting the actual register numbers [Beatty 1974].

Figure 2.2 is a flow chart showing the basic sequencing algorithm for postfix-translatable operators. It assumes that the input tape to the code generator consists of a sequence of identifier and operator tokens, plus a distinguished terminator. The assumption that the token stream is correct makes it unnecessary to provide an exit for an unrecognizable token. In Figure 2.2 I use Wilcox' notation O(IT,S) to denote the action of simulating the operand token IS with the current state S of the transducer as its argument, and R(IT,S,Z) to denote the action of simulating the n-ary operator token IS with the current state S of the transducer and the current contents Z of the pushdown store as its arguments. Each of these is an action of type (a), which constructs the description of a result value. It is this value description (denoted by "d" in Figure 2.2) which is inserted into the pushdown store before the next symbol of the token stream is read.

The algorithm of Figure 2.2 assumes that the number of operands is known for each operator, which is not always the case. (For example, the FORTRAN intrinsic functions MAXO and MINO could be considered to be postfix-translatable operators with two or more operands.) Figure 2.3a illustrates possible ambiguities which could arise unless extra information is included in the token stream to delimit the operand list of a variadic operator. As Figure 2.3b shows, the addition of the single delimiter token "(" is sufficient to resolve this ambiguity. This token is considered an operand, and the function O("(",S) creates a special descriptor to mark the beginning of the operand list. When IT represents a variadic operator, R(IT,S,Z) scans the pushdown store for this marker and thus determines the value of n. The value of n is set to one more than the number of operands in this case, to ensure removal of the marker. (I should perhaps note that the example of Figure 2.3 is somewhat contrived; it would probably be more satisfactory to translate MINO into

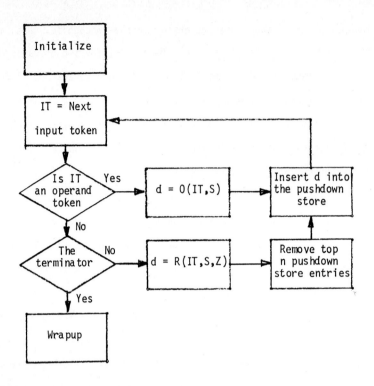

Figure 2.2

Sequencing for Postfix-Translatable Operators

A B C MINO D MAXO

a) A sequence of input tokens

MAXO(A,MINO(B,C),D)

MAXO(MINO(A,B,C),D)

b) Possible interpretations of (a)

(A (B C MINO D MAXO

c) Forcing the first interpretation

Figure 2.3

Correction of Ambiguity due to Variadic Operators

a sequence of dyadic MIN operators.)

Array referencing can be treated as a postfix-translatable operator in a single-state language, but not in a language whose transducer uses multiple states. Again, a simple example is provided by the PL/1 LENGTH function: The prefix operator LENGTH switches the code generator into the "length" state, in which only the length of string variables is of interest. The subscript of the array reference in LENGTH(A[I]), however, should not be evaluated in this state. Hence, the array-reference operator must be prefixed in order to change the state to one suitable for evaluation of the subscript. Upon completion of the subscript, the previous state of the code generator is restored. Similar problems arise with function invocations, in which it is necessary to mark parameters uniquely.

Figure 2.4 shows the basic sequencing algorithm for prefix operators. $D(IT,S)$ denotes the simulation of a prefix operator token IT with the current state S of the transducer as its argument. Like $O(IT,S)$, it constructs a description which is to be entered into the pushdown store. Instead of an operand value, however, this description specifies the current state of the transducer. The action of resetting the transducer state is denoted by $S=N(IS,S)$. Note that N does not depend explicitly upon the contents of the pushdown store. This reflects the fact that the state is used to encode information pertaining only to the current node and its ancestors. Finally, $T(S,Z)$ denotes the action of simulating the postfix encounter with the node. In addition to constructing a description of the result value, it restores the state from the information originally created by $D(IS,S)$ at the prefix encounter. Thus $T(S,Z)$ includes both type (a) and type (d) actions.

Figure 2.4, like Figure 2.2, assumes that the number of arguments is known for each operator. An obvious modification is to have a delimiter token ")" to mark the end of a variable length argument list: When IT=")", control would transfer directly to the $T(S,Z)$ action.

A hybrid code generation scheme which permits both prefix and postfix operators requires a delimiter token to flag the end of an intermediate operand for a prefix operator. This delimiter signals an infix encounter with the node representing the prefix operator; if it were not present the code generator would continue to process the stream of tokens, under the assumption that sooner or later a postfix operator

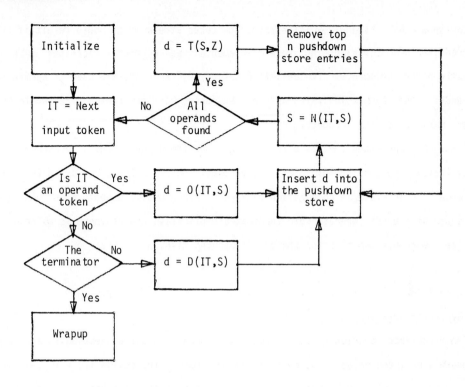

Figure 2.4

Sequencing for Prefix-Translatable Operators

would show up. Figure 2.5 illustrates the token stream which would result if the Fortran intrinsic function MIN0 were implemented as a prefix operator with a variable number arguments. Two delimiter tokens, "," and ")", are used to terminate operands: The former indicates an infix encounter with the parent node, while the latter marks a postfix encounter.

Figure 2.6 describes the basic sequencing algorithm which accepts a stream of input tokens consisting of prefix operators, postfix operators, delimiters and operands. It is a simple combination of Figures 2.2 and 2.4, except that now the operands of a prefix operator are terminated explicitly. Hence there is no need to loop on the completion test for the prefix operand list.

3. Generator Data Structures

The three data structures used by the code generator model of Section 1 are the pushdown store, the value image and the machine image. In Section 1.3 I argued that the pushdown store contained entries for a subset of the elements of the value image. If the transducer and the simulator coexist in memory, then the pushdown store could be formed simply by linking appropriate elements of the value image. Each element of the value image would carry information for both the transducer and the simulator, and would have provision for the necessary linkage. Wilcox calls these elements value descriptors; I shall discuss their structure in Section 3.1.

Not all of the pushdown store entries specify value information. Recall that the state of the transducer may also be saved on the pushdown store during the processing of a subtree. This state is of no interest to the simulator and does not resemble a value descriptor. Practically speaking, there is no reason to use the same pushdown store for values and transducer states; only an ardent theoretician would object to the use of a separate state stack.

The transducer and simulator need not coexist in memory. Action (a) of Section 1.1, which requests the simulation of a token with arguments, could simply write that request to a file which would be scanned by the simulator in another pass. In this case the pushdown store and value image would be disjoint. Only the information relevant to the transducer would appear in a pushdown store entry, and

A*MINO(B,C-D,E)

a) A typical expression

A MINO B , C D - , E)

b) Input stream for the expression of (a)

Figure 2.5

Input for a Hybrid Code Generator

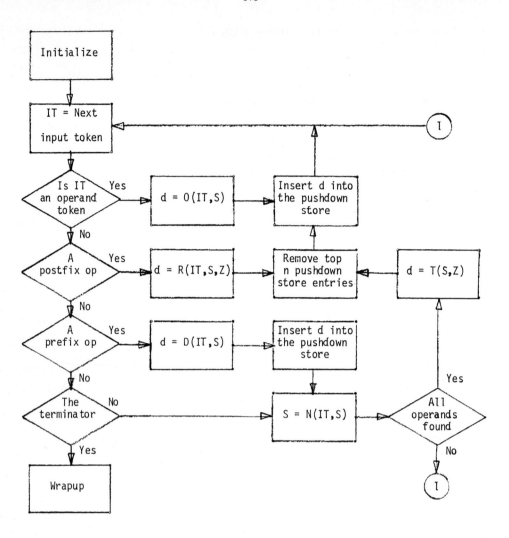

Figure 2.6

Sequencing for a Hybrid Input Stream

only that relevant to the simulator would be held in the value descriptor. It might still be useful, however, to have a separate state stack for the transducer.

Each target computer requires a machine image based upon the peculiarities of its internal organization. Accessible processor components would be represented by various elements capable of holding their status. I shall lump all of these together under the title register descriptor, although they might not actually represent registers. The machine image contains representations not only of processor components, but also of temporary storage. These memory locations are used by the code generator when the number of values which it must manage exceeds the capacity of the target computer's registers, and when it must store the values of literal constants. They are represented by descriptors which might correspond to individual elements of storage or entire areas. The number of such memory descriptors might be fixed, or it might grow and shrink as storage was allocated and released.

Named operands are modelled by certain entries in the translator's dictionary, which specify all attributes of these operands. Three general attribute classes can be distinguished:

    a. Source language: Mode, scope, associated identifier. These are maintained by the semantic analyzer.

    b. Target computer: Encoding, size, environment. These are maintained by the code generator.

    c. Memory image: Memory address, reference chains, defined origin. These are maintained by the assembler.

The values of named operands are not managed by the code generator, since it does not have complete control over the manner in which they are changed.

3.1. Value Descriptors. An access function is a procedure for obtaining the contents of the cell defined by a name; it exists at all points within the scope of the declaration which associates an identifier with that name. When the access function of a name is realizable within a given addressing structure, we say that the object referred to by the name is addressable. If an object required by the computation is not addressable, then the code generator must issue instructions which manipulate the environment in order to make it addressable before it can be used.

The manipulations of the environment required to make an object addressable can be divided into two groups, those required by source language constructs and those required by limitations on the addressing structure of the target computer. Implementation of a reference through a pointer variable would be an example of the former, while loading a value into an index register illustrates the latter. The exact division between the groups is determined by the structure of a value descriptor. When an operand token is encountered in the input stream, a value descriptor is constructed for that operand. If the operand is not a constant, then the value descriptor must specify a location at which the operand may be found. This means that the value descriptor must realize some addressing structure, and if the operand is not addressable within that structure then primitive operators must be used to make it addressable. When an operator is applied to an operand described by a value descriptor, it may happen that the operand location is not addressable with the single target machine instruction which implements the operator. In that case, the function which is processing the operator must emit further addressing code. Thus we see that addressing code may appear both at the point where the reference to a variable was first encountered in the structure tree, and at the point where it was finally used as an operand.

Value descriptors should employ a uniform addressing mechanism to insulate the operator processors from the original source language form of the operand. We have already seen (Chapter 3.A, Sections 2.2 and 2.3) that a base, index and displacement can provide such a mechanism for addressing locations in memory: The base is a name which refers to an area of memory, and which may be computed at execution time. It would be represented in the value descriptor by a pointer to the dictionary (if its value were known at compile time) or to another value descriptor (if its value were computed.) The index is always a computed value, and is therefore represented by a pointer to another value descriptor; the displacement is simply an integer value. This mechanism can easily be extended to cover constants and values held in registers.

Initially, a constant value has no location; the value descriptor must therefore specify the constant itself. This permits the code generator to perform certain machine-dependent optimizations (such as implementing multiplications by shifts.) The constant value would also be required if evaluation of constant expressions were left to the code generator. Most such expressions would probably be handled by the optimizer, since it can combine evaluation with other optimizations such as strength reduction, but the simulator should have this capability in order to handle constants introduced during code generation.

On most computers, constants must be stored in memory unless they are small integers which can be placed in the address fields of certain instructions. When the constant is used, the code generator will decide whether it must be placed in memory. Thus the value descriptor for a constant must provide space for a memory reference as well as for the constant value. If the constant has no location, this fact would be indicated by a null pointer in the base field.

If a value is held in a register, then the base field of its descriptor contains a pointer to the descriptor for that register. Note that this case cannot be confused with that of an indirect reference to memory through an address held in a register: When the reference is indirect, the base field of the value descriptor points to another value descriptor which describes the address. (Figure 3.1 illustrates the distinction.)

In addition to the location and value specifications, a value descriptor must define the encoding of the operand and provide some housekeeping information. Figure 3.2 is an example of a typical value descriptor layout, adapted from Wilcox' description of the PL/C compiler [Wilcox 1971]. (PL/C is a variant of PL/1, and the compiler runs on the IBM System/360 [Conway 1973].)

3.2. Register Descriptors. There is one register descriptor for each target computer register which could be of interest to the code generator. This includes dedicated registers whose contents might be used as operands, as well as registers that are actually managed by the code generator. Each register descriptor contains all of the information needed to use the register as an operand, and to control its allocation. The code generator specifies a register simply by a pointer to the register descriptor.

When a value is in a register, the value descriptor contains a pointer to the register descriptor. The register descriptor must point to the value descriptor

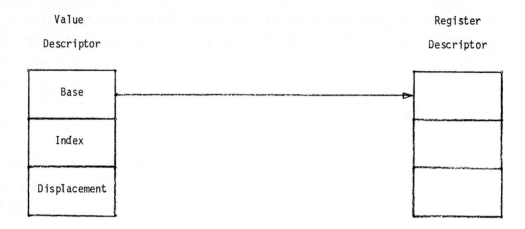

a) Value is in a register

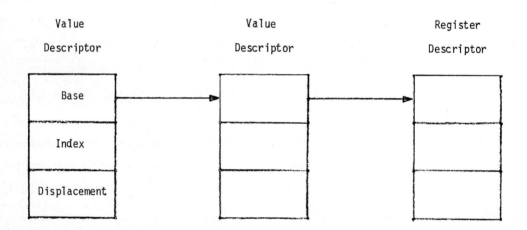

b) Value is in memory, address is in a register

Figure 3.1

Indirection

```
1 VALUE_DESCRIPTOR  UNALIGNED BASED(P)

  2 DESCRIPTOR_MANAGEMENT

    3 STATUS

      4 USES_LEFT  FIXED BIN(7)        /*USED BY OPTIMIZER*/

      4 VALUE  BIT(1) INIT(1)          /*1 INDICATES A VALUE DESCRIPTOR*/

      4 STORAGE  BIT(1)                /*0 INDICATES ITEM IN A REGISTER*/

      4 TEMPORARY  BIT(1)              /*1 INDICATES A TEMP IS ALLOCATED*/

      4 IMAGE  BIT(1)                  /*1 INDICATES ANONYMOUS OPERAND*/

      4 OTHER_FLAGS  BIT(20)

    3 FORWARD_LINK  POINTER

    3 BACK_LINK  POINTER

  2 ACCESS_FUNCTION

    3 BASE  POINTER

    3 DISP  FIXED BINARY(31)

    3 INDEX  POINTER

  2 ATTRIBUTES

    3 MACHINE_TYPE

      4 S360_STORAGE  BIT(8)

      4 SCALE  FIXED BINARY(7)         /*RADIX POINT POSITION*/

      4 PRECISION  FIXED BINARY(7)     /*SIGNIFICANT DIGITS*/

    3 SOURCE_TYPE  BIT(8)

  2 VALUE  BIT(64)                     /*IF KNOWN*/
```

Figure 3.2

PL/C Value Descriptor

also, since it may be necessary to free the register by storing the value which it contains. This action would normally be taken in response to a request which had nothing to do with the value currently in the register, and hence the value descriptor for the evicted operand must be accessible from the register descriptor.

In some cases the content of a register is duplicated in some memory location managed by the code generator. If it becomes necessary to free a register, one whose content is also available in memory need not have that content stored again; all that is necessary is to reset the value descriptor to refer to the memory location. This requires that we provide space to store a base, index and displacement in the register descriptor. When a register is loaded, the value descriptor's location specification could be copied into the register descriptor. Similarly, when a value is stored from a register the register descriptor would be set to address the target location of the store.

Note that the linkage between the register descriptor and storage is quite independent of any particular value descriptor. It represents a condition which happens to exist in the run-time environment, and which is not connected with the particular values currently being used in the computation. This is particularly important in connection with address modification. Consider a reference to a variable local to a containing block in ALGOL 60. In order to access that variable, it may be necessary to load a register with the base address of the containing block's local storage. This value is not relevant to the computation once the reference has been made, and hence no value descriptor will be retained for it. However, if the register is not needed, its descriptor will remain linked to the memory location containing the base address. When another reference occurs to a local variable of the same block, the base register load can be avoided by checking the register contents. This is done in the PL/C compiler, which uses the register descriptor defined in Figure 3.3. Note the close similarity between it and the value descriptor of Figure 3.2.

```
1 REGISTER_DESCRIPTOR  UNALIGNED BASED(P)

  2 DESCRIPTOR_MANAGEMENT

    3 STATUS

        4 USES_LEFT  FIXED BIN(7)        /*USED BY OPTIMIZER*/

        4 VALUE  BIT(1) INIT(0)          /*0 INDICATES A REGISTER DESCRIPTOR*/

        4 DEDICATED  BIT(1)              /*0 INDICATES MANAGED REGISTER*/

        4 GENERAL  BIT(1)                /*0 INDICATES FLOATING PT REG*/

        4 PAIRED  BIT(1)                 /*1 INDICATES USE IN A PAIR*/

        4 SAVED  BIT(1)                  /*1 INDICATES COPY IN MEMORY*/

        4 OTHER_FLAGS  BIT(3)

        4 REGISTER_INFORMATION

          5 REGNUM  BIT(4)

          5 ALLOCATION_CLASS  BIT(4)

          5 STORE_OP  BIT(8)

      3 FORWARD_LINK  POINTER

      3 BACK_LINK  POINTER

  2 CONTENT_ADDRESS

    3 OLD_BASE  POINTER

    3 OLD_DISP  FIXED BINARY(31)

    3 OLD_INDEX  POINTER

  2 CONTENT_ATTRIBUTES

    3 MACHINE_TYPE

      4 S360_STORAGE  BIT(8)

      4 SCALE  FIXED BINARY(7)

      4 PRECISION  FIXED BINARY(7)

    3 SOURCE_TYPE  BIT(8)

  2 CONTENT_DESCRIPTION  POINTER       /*VALUE DESCRIPTOR FOR CONTENT*/
```

Figure 3.3

PL/C Register Descriptor

4. Instruction Generation

Synthesis of the actual instruction encodings acceptable to the control unit of the target machine is an assembly task, as is the allocation of target computer storage. The simulator generates a sequence of specifications for machine instructions and assembly directives, which it passes to the assembler [Capon 1972]. Conceptually, an intermediate file is used for this communication; actually, the simulator may call assembly procedures directly or the two may interact through a coroutine linkage.

The simulator is generating an assembly language program and, like a human programmer, it must maintain its image of the environment within which the generated code will operate. For a given target computer, the operations one uses to maintain the machine image (such as register management and storage area management) are independent of the particular assembly language program being generated. The simulator routines which perform such functions can therefore be written without regard for the source language, and could form the basis for many different simulators.

If value descriptors are not used to implement the transducer's pushdown store, then they are also independent of the source language. Each represents a target machine value, and the mapping from the source language to the target machine is carried out when the descriptor is constructed. No information regarding the source language attributes is required by the simulator, since the evaluation procedure is chosen by the transducer on the basis of those attributes. Thus the value descriptor management utilities can also be used in many simulators.

To create a simulator for a particular source language, we must specify the evaluation procedures in terms of sequences of machine instructions, assembly directives and simulator functions. These procedures tend to be bulky because they perform extensive analysis of special cases in an attempt to generate good code, but most of their execution time is spent in the various utilities. An evaluation procedure is thus a prime candidate for interpretation: The sequence is encoded in a compact form which is scanned by a central control routine. This routine sets up parameters for the simulator utilities specified by the sequence, and calls them to perform the actual operations.

4.1. <u>Primitive</u> <u>Operations</u>. Table 4.1 is a typical set of simulator primitives. I present it as a concrete basis for discussion, not as an exhaustive list of possibilities. (Remember that the particular operations which are relevant depend upon the target machine.) My purpose is to explain the major tasks, and to indicate specific operations which are useful.

Instruction generation always results in a call on an assembly procedure. Before this call is made, however, the simulator guarantees that the operand of the instruction is addressable within the structure of the target machine. This may involve generation of additional instructions to load base and index registers. Some care must be taken to ensure that allocating these registers does not free other registers needed by the instruction.

Assembly directives are used for the actual allocation of target computer memory and definition of symbols. The assembler also has facilities for multiple storage areas (Chapter 3.F, Section 3.2), with allocation and initialization. It does not usually provide complex recovery strategies for use in temporary storage areas, and those are best handled within the simulator.

The LOCK operation of Table 4.1 allows an evaluation procedure to guarantee that a particular register will not be reallocated. Normally, the register manager would base its reallocation policy on the <u>allocation</u> <u>state</u> of the register, which specifies whether the register is in use and whether a copy of its content can be found in memory. (The memory reference for the content is also considered part of the allocation state.)

LINK is used to attach a value descriptor to a register descriptor, linking the two and setting the allocation state. This operation does not generate instructions to load the value into the register, it simply updates the relevant descriptors. Presumably it would be preceeded or followed by the appropriate LOAD instruction.

There is no "delink" operation. When the content of a register has been stored, the register's allocation state can be set to "not in use, copy in memory at reference --" if this is the intent. However, the value remains in the register, and that is the most accessible copy. Hence the value descriptor stays linked to the register descriptor. If the register is now reallocated and another value linked to it, the old value descriptor is altered to reference memory. Thus

Table 4.1

Simulator Operations

Instruction Generation

    Generate 15-bit instruction   Generate 30-bit instruction

Storage Management

    Create storage area   Establish default area

    Allocate element   Free element

    Define location

Register Management

    Allocate   Free

    Lock   Unlock

    Link   Set allocation state

    Save   Restore

                                        Join

Descriptor Management

    Create   Destroy

    Protect   Release

    Copy descriptor   Make working copy

"delinking" is a function of the LINK operation, and is only done when a new value is brought into the register.

On most machines a transfer of control does not alter the contents of the registers. Consider the implementation of the if-then-else-fi construct in ALGOL 68 [van Wijngaarden 1969]. The contents of the registers will be the same just before then and just after else; they may differ just before else and just before fi. These facts can be reflected in the evaluation procedure by the use of SAVE, RESTORE and JOIN, each of which operates on the complete register status and the contents of a specified register status save area in the simulator (Figure 4.1.)

Wilcox defines JOIN as follows [Wilcox 1971]: "For each currently managed register, if its [allocation state] differs from that recorded in [the specified register status save area] it is marked empty. If they agree, it remains unchanged." Thus none of the three operations generate code in his simulator, and memory must contain copies of the contents of all registers in use at else and fi. A simple modification allows JOIN to generate only necessary STORE instructions at fi, but all active registers must still be saved at else (unless an extra jump is inserted.) A backwards pass of a multiple-pass code generator could be used to move the necessary information from JOIN B to SAVE B, thus eliminating redundant STOREs at else also.

When a value is no longer needed by an evaluation procedure, its descriptor is RELEASEd. This frees all resources (register, storage) allocated to the value, unless the descriptor indicates that uses are left. PROTECT increments the count of uses left.

Sometimes it is necessary to have a copy of a value which can be destroyed. For example, on the IBM System/360 an ADD instruction replaces its first operand with the result. If the first operand is a value which will be needed again (i.e. one which indicates that uses are left), then another copy of that value must be used in the ADD. This new copy inherits all of the attributes of the original except the number of uses left.

4.2. Interpretive Coding Language. The primitive operations of Figure 4.1 form the nucleus of an interpretive coding language (ICL) suitable for describing the manipulation of values necessary to implement evaluation procedures. Since each

```
if                    ...

   .                     °
   .                     .
   .                     .
                      SAVE   A
then                  CJMP   LI

   °                     .
   °                     °
   °                     °
                      SAVE   B
else                  UJMP   L2
                 LI:  RESTORE  A
   .                     °
   °                     .
   °                     .

fi               L2:  JOIN   B
```

Figure 4.1

Saving Register Status

value under the control of the code generator is represented by a value descriptor, value descriptors are the basic problem-oriented operands of this language. Algorithm-oriented operands (e.g. integers, booleans, finite sets, labels) and operators (e.g. transfer of control, declaratives) are also required if the ICL is to have a conventional structure.

An assembly language is one obvious tool to use for describing sequences of machine instructions. In conventional assembly languages, each line is a statement made up of four fields:

a. The location field may contain a symbol or be empty.

b. The operation field must contain a symbol

c. The content and layout of the operand field depends upon the symbol in the operation field.

d. The comment field is for documentation only; its content is ignored.

The operations which the language provides include all of the machine instructions, plus a set of pseudos which access the compile-time facilities of the assembler. The particular pseudos supplied vary widely; the following four will, however, be available in even the simplest assembler:

a. END. Causes the assembler to wind up its processing of this program.

b. DATA. Causes the assembler to initialize the contents of a block of memory.

c. RESERVE. Causes the assembler to reserve a block of memory without initializing its contents.

d. DEFINE. Causes the assembler to define the value of a symbol.

As we study the assembly process, I shall present additional pseudos which are useful for the simulator [Mealy 1967].

The assembly language for a particular computer can serve as a starting point for the design of an ICL for that computer: It is familiar to the system programmers who must construct simulators, and it provides access to the assembly procedures for instruction encoding and storage allocation. Additional pseudos can be provided to access the simulator utilities discussed in Section 4.1 and to provide the algorithm-oriented facilities mentioned above. The ICL statements must be translated into a compact sequence of data items, which is then incorporated into the compiler. This translation is simplified by the structure of an assembly language. (If the assembler for the target machine has a macro facility, then appropriate macros allow the existing assembler to perform the translation.)

Several authors have employed the basic strategy of using an ICL to create a description of the final code generation process [IBM 1968, Arden 1969, Elson 1970, Wilcox 1971]. Most of these languages were based on assembly code, and some were actually implemented by macro definitions for a conventional assembler

References

Arden, B.W., Galler, B.A., Graham, R.M.: The MAD definition facility. CACM $\underline{12}$, 432-439 (1969).

Beatty, J.C.: Register assignment algorithm for generation of highly optimized object code. IBM J. Res. Dev. $\underline{18}$, 20-39 (1974).

Capon, P.C., Morris, D., Rohl, J.S., Wilson, I.R.: The MU5 compiler target language and autocode. Computer J. $\underline{15}$, 109-112 (1972).

Conway, R.W., Wilcox, T.R.: Design and implementation of a diagnostic compiler for PL/I. CACM $\underline{16}$, 169-179 (1973).

Elson, M., Rake, S.T.: Code Generation Techniques for large-language compilers. IBM Systems J. $\underline{9}$, 166-188(1970).

IBM: IBM System/360 Principles of Operation. Sixth Edition, IBM Corp. 1967.

IBM: IBM System/360 Operating System FORTRAN IV (H) Compiler Program Logic Manual. Fourth Edition, IBM Corp. 1968.

Mealy, G.H.: A generalized assembly system. In Rosen, S. (ed.) Programming Systems and Languages. McGraw-Hill 1967.

Naur, P.: The design of the GIER ALGOL compiler. Ann. Rev. in Automatic Programming $\underline{4}$, 49-85 (1964).

van Wijngaarden, A. (ed.): Report on the algorithmic language ALGOL 68. Num. Math. $\underline{14}$, 29-218 (1969).

Wilcox, T.R.: Generating Machine Code for High-Level Programming Languages. Ph.D. Thesis, Cornell University 1971.

CHAPTER 3.F.

ASSEMBLY AND LINKAGE

W. M. WAITE

Dept. of Electrical Engineering
University of Colorado
BOULDER, COLORADO USA

Assembly is the final step in the translation to machine code. Instruction specifications are converted into the actual patterns recognized by the control unit of the computer, and these patterns are placed into a memory image. Some of the instruction specifications normally contain references to other items in the program; during assembly, these references are replaced by the addresses in the memory image of the referenced items.

In many respects, assembly is machine-dependent: The number and layout of fields within an instruction, the length of an instruction and the representation of a memory address are all items which vary from one computer to another. Nevertheless it is possible to derive a general model of the overall assembly process which highlights its basic machine-independence. By studying the model, we can identify important interfaces and specify a collection of procedures which can be used to carry out an assembly. These procedures are machine-dependent only in their detailed operation; their functions and interconnections are independent of any particular computer or class of computers.

It is often convenient to split an assembly into several passes. The most common reason is to permit separate translation of modules in a large program. Each module is partially assembled, and the text placed in a file. When the program is to be executed, the files for all modules are combined in a final assembly pass. This final pass is usually termed "loading", "linkage editing" or "binding", but in reality is a completion of assembly.

1. A Model for Assembly

Figure 1.1 summarizes the major data structures used during assembly, and shows how they are interconnected. MEM is the memory image which is being created by the assembly, LCNTR is the location counter which indicates the current position of the assembly in MEM, and DICT is the dictionary, which is used to retain certain constant values and positions in MEM. I assume that the assembly procedures may access MEM and DICT randomly, and that LCNTR may address any "relevant position" in MEM. (The "relevant positions" are determined by the architecture of the target computer.) At the completion of assembly, the contents of MEM can be executed immediately by the target computer; no further processing is required.

The data structures of Figure 1.1 are manipulated by a collection of procedures which can be grouped into the classes shown in Figure 1.2. Procedures in the object, reference and definition classes provide an interface to the assembly data structures, while statement procedures interface to the remainder of the translator. Each basic instruction generation step is a call on a statement procedure, passing arguments which describe the desired instruction. The interpretation of these arguments depends entirely upon the statement procedure which is called.

1.1. Object and Statement Procedures. Object procedures insert information into MEM and maintain LCNTR. They are called by the code generator, and their functions

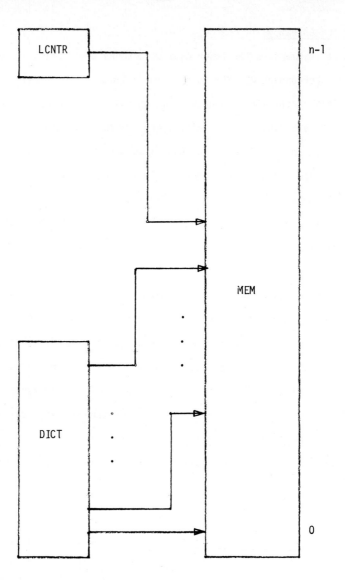

Figure I.1

Assembly Data Structures

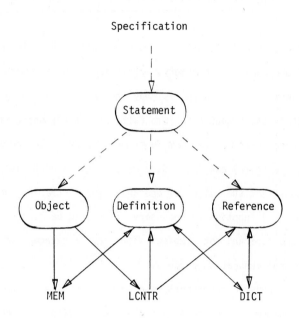

Specification

Statement

Object   Definition   Reference

MEM   LCNTR   DICT

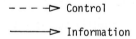

- - - ▷ Control

——— ▷ Information

Figure 1.2

Procedure Classes

can be placed into the following broad categories:

a. Enter a given item into MEM.

b. Advance LCNTR by a given amount.

c. Advance LCNTR if necessary to address an element of a particular storage class.

Category (c) reflects the fact that in some computers certain information must fall on particular "boundaries" in memory. For example, on a computer which can store several instructions in each word it may be necessary to guarantee that an instruction which is the target of a jump falls at the beginning of a word.

Some object procedures may perform functions in more than one category, the most usual combination being (a) and (b). Care must be taken with category (c) functions because LCNTR can affect the values of operands used in the instruction. This means that if a category (c) function is necessary, it should be carried out before the instruction is generated and not combined with (say) a category (a) function carried out at the end of the generation process.

A statement procedure interprets and processes its argument, calling upon procedures in the other classes to obtain the desired effect. For example, consider the processing of an instruction which specifies an address and an index register. The statement procedure called would be one which processes instructions with index and address fields; the arguments passed would specify the operation code for the particular instruction, the number of the index register, and the address. After building the instruction pattern required by the control unit, the statement procedure would call an object procedure to place the instruction into MEM at the address specified by the location counter. This object procedure would probably update the location counter to address the space immediately following the instruction.

I shall assume for the moment that each statement procedure can determine the proper object procedures to use simply by examining its arguments. This seems at first glance to be a trivial assumption, but consider a computer which provides jump instructions of several lengths: The short jump is used when the jump target is within (say) 128 locations of the jump instruction, while the long jump is used when the jump target is more distant. It would be useful to simply specify that a jump was required, and let the statement processor sort out which to use [Richards 1971]. This means, however, that the statement processor cannot determine the proper object procedure from its arguments alone, because the instruction length depends upon the position of the instruction and the position of the jump target.

There will be one statement procedure for each distinct class of instruction patterns, because the statement procedure must know how to interpret and pack the fields which specify its arguments. At least two procedures are needed to provide direct access to category (a) and (b) object functions. These procedures are used to specify arbitrary data items (patterns which cannot be expressed as instructions) and to reserve blocks of storage. Sometimes it is useful to provide a third procedure to access category (c) functions; this depends strongly upon the target computer organization.

1.2. Cross Referencing. Some of the operands of an instruction may depend upon the location of other instructions. An obvious example is the address field of a jump instruction, which depends upon the location of the jump target. Such operands present a cross-referencing problem which is solved through the use of the dictionary: Each operand is associated with an entry in the dictionary holding the value of LCNTR at the defining occurrence of the operand. Access to these entries is provided by procedures in the reference and definition classes.

The only problem which arises in providing cross-references is that of a forward reference: An operand for which one or more applied occurrences preceed the defining occurrence. It is possible (at some cost in convenience) to eliminate forward references to data objects by re-arranging the source program. Forward references to instructions, however, can only be eliminated in certain simple cases; thus we must deal with the forward reference problem.

A conceptually simple solution to the problem is to make two passes over the input specifications. During the first pass, the statement routines request only object functions in categories (b) and (c). Thus they maintain the value of the location counter, but place no information into MEM. Applied occurrences of all operands are ignored, but definition procedures are called to process defining occurrences. At the end of this pass, the dictionary contains the values of all cross-referenced symbols. A second pass is now made in which defining occurrences of operands are ignored and all categories of object functions are used. (Note that this solution is possible only because of the assumption made in Section 1.1. If the length of a jump instruction depended upon the position of its target, we would not be able to decide which object function to use during pass I.)

In order to show that a second pass can be avoided, we must first show that it is possible to remember each location where information must be supplied, and what information is required, in an amount of space which grows with the number of distinct items rather than the number of references. The basic strategy is the following [Wilkes 1957]:

a. Consider an instruction which makes a forward reference. We do not know what to put into the field containing the forward reference, and hence this field may be used (temporarily) to hold anything.

b. In particular, it may be used to address the last forward reference to the same location by setting it equal to the difference between the current address and the address at which the last reference occurred. (If this is the first reference, the field would contain 0.)

c. The dictionary entry contains the address of the most recent forward reference.

This technique is called back chaining. The back chains are constructed by the procedure invoked when an undefined identifier is referenced, and the values are filled in by the procedure invoked when an identifier is defined.

An obvious problem with back chaining is that the field containing the forward reference must be large enough to address the last forward reference to the same symbol. In practice, it is usual to allow forward references only in address fields because this is where they are most useful. Unfortunately, a restriction of forward references to address fields does not always solve the problem completely. Consider, for example, a computer which permits several instructions to be stored in one word, but in which an address field of an instruction is only large enough for a word address. Thus it is not possible for a back chain to specify which address field of a given word contained the last forward reference to the same symbol. In this case, however, it is usually true that the number of possible positions for an address field is small. (On CDC 6000 series computers the address field of an instruction must appear in one of three positions.) It is therefore feasible to maintain a separate back chain for each address field position in the word.

A somewhat more challenging example is the class of machines with short address fields in which the effective address is constructed by using the contents of the address field and the contents of a base register. The simple case is that in which the base register is the location counter. Here the address distance between the first forward reference to a symbol and the definition of the symbol must be repesentable in the short address field. Since all entries on the back chain lie between the first reference and the definition, all links must be representable in short address fields.

If the base register is not the location counter, then it may be impossible to maintain all of the links of the back chain in the address fields of the instruction making the forward references. One possible solution is to use several back chains, starting a new one for each reference which is too far from the preceeding one to permit the normal linkage. Although this violates the one-pass criterion, it is usually successful because the references tend to cluster and hence the number of back chains is much smaller than the number of references. When using this technique, only the head of the most recent back chain is kept in the dictionary entry. Earlier back chain headers are kept in a pushdown list accessible from the dictionary entry. This means that the reference procedure needs to take special action only when it discovers that linkage to the previous entry of the current back chain is impossible. (Note that the full address of the last entry in the chain must be kept in the dictionary.)

There is a more serious problem with machines (such as the IBM System/360) having a number of base registers: The base register which must be used for any given reference may depend both upon the symbol being referenced and upon the point at which the reference occurs.

The effects of these complexities are localized in the reference and definition procedures, and in the structure of the dictionary. If it is necessary to cater for link fields of several sizes which fall into several positions with respect to the location counter, then more than one reference procedure might be specified. Each of these procedures would have access to the location counter and to the dictionary entry for the forward reference; knowing the peculiarities of its particular fields, it would be able to construct appropriate link values and dictionary modifications.

When a forward-referenced operand becomes defined, then the back chain must be followed and the proper values filled in. This task can be split into two parts: following a chain and performing a certain action at each element. It would be useful to implement the two parts of the task by separate procedures if you anticipated tracing the back chain for purposes other than definition (one example would be to print a list of references to an undefined symbol at the end of the assembly.) Even if the task is implemented as a single procedure, however, a conceptual split can help in understanding the design.

The back-chain trace procedure must visit every entry, in any order. At each entry it must provide the action procedure with both the value of the location counter at the time the entry was made and the type of field in which the entry resides. (Type information could be given implicitly by calling an action procedure which was specific to that particular type of field.) If the action procedure is defining the operand, then it must have access to the definition as well as the field specification.

The dictionary entry for a symbol must not only specify whether that symbol has been defined, but also whether it has been referenced. A reference procedure uses the "referenced" flag to control initialization of the back chain, and a definition procedure uses it to control the filling of a back chain. It is needed because a dictionary entry may be created for a symbol before a valid reference to that symbol, one in which a back chain link could be stored, actually exists.

1.3. Assembly under a Storage Constraint. I shall now show that the assembly can be carried out even if the entire object program cannot be held in memory. To do this, I must postulate another program, a loader, which is capable of performing the "back chain fill" function of a definition procedure. The necessary information is provided by means of loader directives, which are encodings of the relevant dictionary entries. (Loader directives are written to the same file as the object text, and it must be possible for the loader to distinguish them.)

The program is processed exactly as before, until there is no further space for object code; at that point the existing object code may still contain unfilled back chains, but these will be processed later by the loader. The current object code is output to a file; the assembler continues to process the program, re-using the same memory area. A definition procedure may now attempt to follow a back chain into the object code which is no longer in memory. When this happens, an appropriate loader directive is written to the object file to enable the loader to continue processing of the back chain. Note that this loader directive immediately follows the object code to which it applies.

Suppose that the translator's memory does not fill a second time. At the completion of the assembly, no unfilled back chains will exist in the portion of the object program which remains in memory. This absolute block of text is then written to the object file. When the loader is called to process the object file, it reads the text for the first part of the program into memory. (This text must fit, because the loader is smaller than the translator and needs no dictionary.) It then reads the directives and fills the specified back chains. The entire text is now absolute; the loader may read the remainder of the object text and execute the program, or it may create an absolute object file for later execution by writing out the text held in core and copying the remainder from the other file.

If the translator's memory fills several times, then there may be several blocks of object text separated by loader directives. Only the last block is guaranteed to be absolute. In this case, the loader may not be able to store all of the object text which must be updated. More than one pass by the loader will therefore be needed to complete the processing of the object code. It can be shown that each pass increases the amount of text which follows the last loader directive, and is hence guaranteed to be absolute.

If a loader is to be used, there is actually no need for the translator to retain any object code or to fill any back chains. Object text is written as it is generated, and when a symbol definition is encountered the proper loader directive is emitted. This approach is useful on small machines with limited peripheral capacity, where it is desirable to retain the object program for repeated execution.

1.4. _Operand Expressions_. Figure 1.3 gives several examples of the use of expressions as operands in assembly code statements. These expressions are made up of symbols and constants, using the four basic arithmetic operators and the

```
LENGTH    DEFINE    80              Input line length
WORK      RESERVE   LENGTH          Work area for line
BUFFER    RESERVE   2*LENGTH        Double buffer for I/O
```

a) Blocks keyed to a certain constant

```
SETXR     BUFFER+LENGTH,1    Second buffer
```

b) Placing an address into an index register

```
TABLE     RESERVE   0               Start of table
          DATA      1               Data items in the table
          DATA      2
          DATA      3
SIZE      DEFINE    *-TABLE         * means "current address"
```

c) Length keyed to table contents

```
SETXR     A1+A2-A3          A1,A2 and A3 addresses
```

d) An apparently meaningless expression

Figure 1.3

Operand Expressions

parentheses. The meaning of these operators is clear when all of the operands are integers; let us consider their meanings with address operands.

A computer memory is made up of one or more ordered sets of locations called segments. The result of adding an integer, n, to an address, A, is the address of the nth location beyond the one addressed by A. If this location would lie outside the segment addressed by A, then the result is undefined. Similarly, A is the address of the nth location beyond the one addressed by A-n.

If A1 and A2 are addresses no reasonable interpretation can be placed upon the result of A1+A2, and hence such an expression is meaningless. Since multiplication by an integer is simply a shorthand notation for repeated addition, A*n is also meaningless. The only useful operation involving two addresses is A1-A2, which yields an integer giving the directed distance from A2 to A1 . Figure 1.3c illustrates such an expression, which automatically redefines SIZE when data declarations are added to or removed from the table.

The usual associative and commutative laws hold when an expression contains more than one operator. Thus a valid interpretation can be placed upon the expression of Figure 1.3d, even though it contains the sum of two addresses as a subexpression.

An expression containing a forward reference cannot be evaluated at the time it is encountered, because the value of the forward reference is unknown. A back chain entry cannot be created for later update, because that would require storing the entire unevaluated expresson in the address field of the instruction. Let us approach the solution to this problem obliquely, first asking whether it really is a problem.

Consider an expression as the operand of a DEFINE directive. Since this directive does not actually generate code, it could be placed anywhere in the program. In particular, it could be placed at the end (or at least at some point after all of the components of its operand expression had become defined.) Thus we can arrange that the operand of a DEFINE directive never contains a forward reference.

Suppose that the programmer wishes to use an expression containing forward references as the operand of some instruction which cannot be moved. He can avoid using the expression (and yet achieve the same effect) by substituting a new identifier which does not appear anywhere else in the program. He then adds a DEFINE directive at the end of the program which defines this new identifier as the value of the desired expression. By this strategem he makes it unnecessary to store the complete unevaluated expression in the address field; only a reference to a single undefined identifier, using a normal back chain, is required.

The effect of adding a new identifier and inserting a DEFINE can be achieved by the assembler: When it encounters a forward reference in an address expression, it adds an entry to the dictionary which cannot be accessed via the normal lookup mechanism. This entry represents the "new identifier," and obviously cannot appear anywhere else in the program. A forward reference to the new entry replaces the address expression, which is stored in the dictionary as an unevaluated DEFINE directive. The directive is represented by an element which has two components:

   a. A pointer to the entry for the identifier being defined.

   b. An encoding of the expression which is the operand of DEFINE.

In order to allow the assembler to evaluate all such directives at the end of the program, a third component is also required:

   c. A pointer to the entry for the previously-stored directive (if one exists). The assembler keeps a pointer to the most-recently stored directive, and from that it can reach all previous ones.

Any convenient encoding can be used for the expression. It is important to realize that some of the operands of the expression must be dictionary references (for if they were not, then all operands would be known and the expression would be evaluable.) Thus the encoding must include a means of distinguishing dictionary references from constants.

Consider a symbol which has not been defined, and which has been used only in address expressions. This symbol must appear in the dictionary, because the encoded expressions must point to it. There is, however, no back chain associated with it because it has never been referenced directly in an instruction. Hence this symbol would not have its "referenced" flag (Section 1.2) set.

You should note that all of the code required to handle operand expressions is localized in a single routine. If forward references are allowed in operand expressions, then the END statement processor must also be changed to evaluate the expressions which have been deferred and to call definition procedures to fill the back chains.

2. Two-Pass Assembly

The one-pass assembler places information into fixed locations in memory. Often it is advantageous to translate a block of instructions without knowing exactly where it will be placed. In this case, addresses can only be specified relative to the start of the block; an extra pass would be necessary to make those relative addresses absolute. Several blocks containing relative addresses can also be combined to yield a larger block in which the addresses are still relative.

2.1. Relative Symbol Definition. In section 1.4 I discussed the specification of operands by expressions containing forward references. Suppose that such an expression were used as the operand of a RESERVE directive, as shown in Figure 2.1a. Since the amount of storage reserved cannot be computed immediately, it is not possible to specify the absolute location of the instructions which follow the RESERVE directive. There is, however, no difficulty in determining their values relative to the end of the reserved area (Figure 2.1b.)

RESERVE directives such as those of Figure 2.1 can be avoided by suitable re-arrangement of the source code. However, they serve as models for variable-length instructions such as the short and long jumps discussed in Section 1.1. Thus if we can process these directives, we can relax the assumption made in that section which prevented the assembler from selecting the proper jump instruction automatically. The techniques developed in this section also form the basis for implementation of multiple, independent storage areas.

Let the first absolute memory location beyond the reserved space be denoted by X. Every symbol which follows the RESERVE directive can then be given a value of the form X+C, where C is an integer. In particular, FIRST = X+100 and LAST = X+150. The RESERVE directive itself allows us to define X by X = 15+(LAST-FIRST). At the end of the assembly, when all symbols have been defined, the values of FIRST and LAST can be substituted into this expression to yield an equation in X:

$$X = 15+((X+150)-(X+100)) = 15+50 = 65$$

```
START                                    ⎫
                                         ⎬  15 locations
                                         ⎭
AREA      RESERVE   LAST-FIRST
                                         ⎫
                                         ⎬  100 locations
                                         ⎭
FIRST                                    ⎫
                                         ⎬  50 locations
                                         ⎭
LAST
```

a) An assembly language program

SYMBOL	ADDRESS	RELATIVE TO
START	0	Zero
AREA	15	Zero
FIRST	100	End of reserved area
LAST	150	End of reserved area

b) Symbol values

Figure 2.1

Relative Symbol Definition

This value of X can then be substituted into all of the definitions which depended upon it, and a second pass completes the assembly.

Assume a more complex program than that of Figure 2.1, in which there are n RESERVE directives whose operands contain forward references. This means that there will be n X's and n groups of symbols whose values have the form X+C. Each RESERVE directive contributes an expression which defines an X in terms of integers and X's. Moreover, the rules for address arithmetic discussed in Section 1.4 guarantee that these expressions are linear in the X's. Thus a system of linear equations in n unknowns is available; there are well-known methods for obtaining a solution (or showing that no solution exists.) The solution may be obtained at the end of one pass, and assembly completed in a second pass.

A relative address is still an address, and obeys the rules for address arithmetic discussed in Section 1.4: When an integer is added to or subtracted from a relative address the result is an address relative to the same point; relative addresses may not be added together, nor may they appear as operands of multiplication operators. However, the result of the difference of two relative addresses is defined only if the addresses are relative to the same point; the difference of two addresses relative to separate points is unevaluable, but does not necessarily represent an error. Figure 2.2 illustrates a correct program in which this situation occurs. Note that the operand of the second RESERVE directive is undefined even though definitions of all symbols appearing in it have previously been encountered.

Suppose that our assembler is already equipped to handle expressions containing forward references, as discussed in Secton 1.4. To accommodate relative symbol definition we must expand the dictionary entry for each symbol to specify an origin as well as a value. In two ways, an origin acts as though it were a symbol: It may be used in expressions, and it may eventually take on a value relative to some other origin. Thus it is reasonable to represent an origin by a symbol entry in the dictionary, and to specify the origin on which a symbol is based by giving a pointer to this entry.

If the operand of a RESERVE directive is an unevaluable expression, then it will be represented by a new symbol, as discussed in Section 1.4. Let us denote this

```
START
                                        }   10 locations

        RESERVE    S3-S2
                                        }   20 locations

ST
                                        }   30 locations

        RESERVE    ST-START
                                        }   40 locations

S2
                                        }   50 locations

S3
```

a) An assembly language program

$$X1 = 10 + (S3-S2) = 10 + (X2+90-(X2+40))$$
$$X2 = X1+50 + (ST-START) = X1+50 + (X1+20-(0))$$

b) Simultaneous equations derived from (a)

Figure 2.2

Additional Complexity

created symbol by E, the current origin by A and the current offset from that origin by I. The RESERVE procedure must therefore create an origin whose value will be the value of the expression A+I+E. In effect, the new origin is a symbol, N, defined by:

```
N    DEFINE    A+I+E
```

In section 1.4 I explained how such directives were created by the assembler and stored in the dictionary.

In addition to setting up an expression entry in the dictionary and creating a new symbol to represent the origin, the RESERVE procedure must reset the current origin to this new symbol and make the current offset from that origin equal to 0. Subsequently-defined symbols will then specify the new origin, and the value of the offset will be updated to reflect the code generated.

When all of the origins in a program are defined by RESERVE directives, no operations on pairs of equations are required to solve for the origin values. This means that we simply need to evaluate the expressions in the proper order to obtain a solution; if no such order exists, then no solution exists. Unfortunately, the expressions have been chained in the reverse order of occurrence (Section 1.4), and Figure 2.2 illustrates the fact that this ordering is not necessarily the proper one.

Even if the ordering of the chain is not the correct one, all expressions may be evaluated by repeated passes over the chain. At least one expression is evaluated and removed from the chain on each pass. If a pass is made without evaluating an expression, then no solution to the set of equations exists.

As expressions are evaluated, the origin on which symbols are based may change. For example, in Figure 2.2 the origin of S1 changes from X1 to 0 when S3-S2 is evaluated. This change must be noted on the second pass over the list of expressions in order to evaluate S1-START. Thus it must be possible, given an origin entry, to find all of the symbols based directly upon that origin entry. By including one more pointer field in each symbol entry, we can construct a chain which begins at an origin entry and links all of the symbols defined relative to this origin. When the origin becomes defined relative to another origin, we can scan over the chain and update all of the symbol entries. The chain (including the origin entry) is then added to that of the new origin.

2.2. Multiple Location Counters. The memory image of a running program can usually be partitioned into several distinct regions, each holding information of a particular type. For example, instructions, contants and working storage locations often occupy different areas of memory. This partitioning may be required by the hardware of the target computer, but translators tend to construct separate regions even if the hardware does not require them.

So far we have considered assembly under the control of a single location counter; a single point at which information can be entered into the memory image. If only one location counter is provided, then the partitioning discussed in the previous paragraph must be done in the source code: All instructions must be written first, followed by all DATA directives which establish constants, followed in turn by all RESERVE directives declaring the working storage.

Instead of providing only a single location counter, allow the translator to define as many as it needs. Each location counter specifies the point at which information can be entered into a given region of the memory image, and also the origin of the region. A region may, of course, contain RESERVE directives whose operands cannot be evaluated; in that case the region would be made up of several related blocks of information. The origin of each of these blocks must eventually be defined relative to the origin of the region (Section 2.1), but as yet we have no mechanism for defining the relationship of the regions to one another.

Perhaps the simplest way to define the relative positions of several regions is to have them follow one another in the order in which they were declared.   This is satisfactory in most cases, but sometimes the user may wish to combine them differently (when designing overlays, for example.) If we consider the location counter name to be a symbol representing the origin of the region, then the normal DEFINE directive can be used to specify the location of that origin relative to some symbol in another region. In the absence of an explicit declaration, the region could be assumed to follow the region declared before it.

A location counter actually consists of two symbols: one represents the beginning of the region, the other represents the current position in the region. The state of each location counter is completely specified by the second symbol:

Its origin pointer indicates the current base for relative addresses, its symbol pointer remembers the last symbol defined under this location counter, and its offset field is the present relative address. Thus LCNTR can be a pointer to this symbol entry, and a change of location counters is merely a change of the pointer.

Assuming that the assembler already provides relative symbol definition, the only added mechanism required to support multiple location counters is a directive, USE, which specifies that subsequent assembly should be under the control of a different counter. The operand of USE is the location counter name, which provides access to the first of the two symbol entries associated with the counter. In order to actually perform the change, access to the second symbol entry is required. Thus a location counter entry is normally a composite of the two symbol entries. Such an entry is created by USE when its operand has not previously been encountered.

3. Partial Assembly and Linkage

Separate translation of modules requires that assembly be carried only to a certain point, and sufficient information written in a file to permit completion at a later time. In this section I examine the question of information flow in partial assembly, basing my discussion on the complete assembly algorithms presented in earlier sections of this chapter. You should be aware that translations of partial programs written in some higher level languages may require information (such as mode indications for procedure parameters) beyond that discussed in this section.

Consider first a program which contains no relative symbol definition. Suppose that we assemble this program using the algorithms of section 1 with two slight changes: An address-valued symbol is always represented by a dictionary pointer, and the definition procedure for an address-valued symbol records the value in the dictionary and marks the symbol defined but does not fill the back chain. (The back chain of a symbol with a constant value would be filled.) These changes reflect the fact that the actual address depends upon the position at which the program is loaded; the definition of the symbol simply provides a relative address.

Upon reaching the end of the program we have a body of text containing back chains and a dictionary containing all of the symbols referenced. These symbols can be divided into three classes:

    a. Symbols which have been defined as constants.

    b. Symbols which have been defined as addresses.

    c. Symbols which remain undefined.

Those in class (a) are of no further interest, since their values have already been substituted into the text; values for the remaining symbols must be determined in a subsequent pass. Thus the output of the partial assembly consists of the text and specifications for the symbols in classes (b) and (c).

The value of a class (b) symbol depends only upon the value of the text origin. Thus these symbols can be represented by directives which specify the back chain and address relative to the origin. A directive representing a class (c) symbol, on the other hand, must specify the back chain and the name of the symbol. Since this name generally refers to a class (b) symbol in another program, the names of certain class (b) symbols must be known to subsequent passes.

An extra assembly directive, ENTRY, is needed to specify which class (b) symbol names should remain known after a partial assembly. This directive might result in the output of a new directive similar to DEFINE, or it might simply expand the normal directive for a class (b) symbol to include the symbol name.

A subsequent assembly pass might complete the assembly, or it might simply combine several partially-assembled blocks to form a larger block. In the latter case, additional ENTRY directives must be input to specify symbols whose names are to be retained for future passes.

When two passes are used for the partial assembly (Section 2), another strategy becomes available for representing the output program: Place the proper relative address in each address field and attach a flag specifying the origin. (This flag is usually termed "the relocation bits" of the field.) Back chaining must still be used if the symbol is defined by an expression which contains operands not defined in the program unit being assembled. Specifications for the class (c) symbols and class (b) symbols whose names must be retained can appear either before or after the text; back chain headers and generated DEFINE's should follow the text.

References

Barron, D.W.: Assemblers and Loaders. Second Edition, MacDonald 1972.

Richards, D.L.: How to keep the addresses short. CACM 14, 346-348 (1971).

Wilkes, M.V., Wheeler, D.J., Gill, S.: The Preparation of Programs for an
        Electronic Digital Computer. Second Edition, Addison-Wesley 1957.

CHAPTER 4.A.

INTRODUCTION TO COMPILER COMPILERS

M. Griffiths

Laboratoire d'Informatique

UNIVERSITE DE GRENOBLE, France

1 - MOTIVATION -

Historically, the existence of compiler-compilers is a result of using syntax-directed compiling techniques in order to structure the compiler. Syntax becomes a language in which parts of the compiler may be written, and the concept is extended to semantics by including a compatible programming language, usually general purpose, which allows classical programming methods for those parts of the compiler not susceptible to treatment by syntax. We will divide the subject in two parts, dealing first with those compiler-compilers whose formal treatment is limited to context-free grammars, and subsequently with extensions of these formalisms by one method or another. This division is strictly arbitrary, but corresponds to a practical fact, which is that the former class can be used, and indeed are being used, in a commercial environment to produce efficient compilers more easily than by ad hoc methods. The second group includes a series of promising ideas which are at different stages of development, but for which it is as yet not possible to make a reasonable evaluation.

Compiler compilers depend very much on language definition techniques, since, for example, it is difficult to use syntax-directed methods for a language which has no syntax. It may even be said that the compiler-compiler is the tool which takes a formal language definition together with a machine description and produces a compiler. We may consider them to be satisfactory when it is no longer necessary for a programmer to intervene to achieve this goal. At the present moment we are a long way from it, mainly because our definitional tools are not yet sufficient.

2 - COMPILER-COMPILERS BASED ON CONTEXT-FREE SYNTAX METHODS -

The first of a large number of compiler-compilers of this generation is described in [Brooker 62] ; most of them have certain characteristics :

- Based on a particular method of syntax analysis.

- Calls may be made during syntax analysis to semantic functions, which are procedures written in some programming language. These calls appear in the tables used by the analyser, or in the analysis program produced by the compiler-compiler.

- Some compiler-compilers use specially created 'production languages' (for example, that of Floyd and Evans [Floyd 61]).

A survey has been made of many of the methods used [Feldman 68], but, unfortunately, the methods treated do not include some interesting European contributions.

2.1 - Syntax -

There exist few top-down analysis techniques, and the principal one has already been described (Chapter 2.B). The method is heavily used, since it is relatively simple to implement and allows semantic functions to be placed at different points in the grammar. There exist many more bottom-up methods, of which one (Chapter 3.C) has already been described in some detail. Perhaps the most frequently used methods are those of precedence, while bounded context [Floyd 64] represents a convenient special case of LR for use with some forms of production language.

Whichever analysis method is used, the compiler-compiler must include a certain number of sub-programs, which will perform the following tasks :

- Test that the grammar is well-defined and clean (all symbols defined, all productions useful, no parasites, and so on)

- Test whether the grammar can be used with the method chosen (LL(1), precedence, LR, ...)

- If the grammar does not conform, try to transform it so that it does

- Production of an analyser in the relevant form, together with the interface which provides the 'hooks' for the semantic functions.

Examples of the implementation of these functions have already been given in the relevant chapters ; we will not repeat the text here. Reasons which may lead to a particular choice among the different analysis methods have also been given (Chapter 3.C).

2.2 - Languages for Compiler Writing -

The language in which a compiler is written must be considered in two parts, the production language, which is generated by the compiler-compiler and which includes the syntax analyser with semantic hooks, and the language in which the semantics are written, the 'hand-coded' part.

2.2.1 - Production Language -

One production language has already been seen in connection with the LL(1) analyser. It consists of a small number of primitives which can readily be coded in any suitable language. Alternatively, the same information can be stored in tables, as was done in the LR analyser. Semantic hooks may be associated with all or with certain entries in the table. In addition to these methods, we must also mention the Floyd-Evans production language [Floyd 61], both because of its historical interest and subsequent frequent use and because it can be used to express analysers which are based on different bottom-up techniques, for example bounded context or precedence. This multiplicity of application of Floyd-Evans productions is due to the fact that these different bottom-up techniques are closely related. The productions are simply descriptions of the state of the analysis stacks when a reduction or a shift is to take place. For example, consider the grammar of an ALGOL60 block previously used to demonstrate LL(1) analysis, changed slightly to facilitate a bottom-up technique :

$$
\begin{aligned}
\text{Axiom} &\rightarrow \ \vdash \text{Block} \dashv \\
\text{Block} &\rightarrow \textbf{begin } \text{DL SL } \textbf{end} \\
\text{DL} &\rightarrow \text{D ; } | \text{ D ; DL} \\
\text{SL} &\rightarrow \text{S } | \text{ S ; SL}
\end{aligned}
$$

An analyser for this grammar, written in Floyd-Evans productions, could have the following form, with Z|— the start point :

```
Z|—     |— begin          | * Zb
        error
Zb      begin D            | * ZD
        error
ZD      D ;                | * Z;
        error
Z ;     D ; S |→ DL S  | ZDL
        D ; D              | * ZD
        S ; S              | * ZS
        error
ZDL     D ; DL S |→ DL S|  ZDL
        begin DL S         | * ZS
        error
ZS      S end |→ SL end |  ZSL
        S ;                | * Z;
        error
```

```
ZSL    S ; SL end |→ SL end      | ZSL
       DL SL end                 | * Ze
       error
Ze     begin DL SL end ⊣ |→ B ⊣ | ZB
       error
ZB     |— B —|                   | finish
       error
```

A production has the form : l1 character list1 | → character list2 | * l2 f

      l1 is the label of the production. If the top of the stack is the same as the first character list, it is replaced by the second and control is passed to label l2, having read a character if the star is present and having executed, if one is given, the semantic function f. If the first character list is not the same as the top of the stack, the following production is examined. The first label, the replacement clause, the asterisk and the semantic function may be individually omitted. This brief description is simply meant to give some idea of the form of the production language.

2.2.2. - Machine Oriented Languages -

      Production languages are relatively simple, since they have few primitives and their subject matter can be formalised. This is not true of the languages in which are written semantic functions, which need to be more general, while retaining compatibility with the production language. A great deal of interest has been shown recently about this subject ([van der Poel 74] [Rain]), and the current trend is towards the use of special-purpose languages for the production of software in general, and not only compilers

      A wide variety of machine oriented languages has already been published, and some of the characteristics which are considered to be important by their authors are amongst the following :

- Complete control of the computer and its instruction set (this will usually mean that the language is machine-dependent)

- Existence of high-level language constructs for the flow of control (loops, procedures, case, ...), usually in their simpler forms.

- Possibility to define a wide range of data structures and addressing mechanisms

- Constructions which could lead to less than efficient object code are suppressed.

The aim of many of these languages is to retain all the advantage of low-level programming, while allowing a programming style which is high-level. The resulting gain in ease of programming, speed of error correction and communicability is not offset by a lack of efficiency. Indeed, in most cases, there is an improvement in performance, since the programmer has a better overall view of his algorithms and can more easily improve their logic.

3 - CURRENT RESEARCH -

Several interesting improvements or developments of the compiler-compiler principles outlined above are the subject of research in different laboratories; some of these new ideas are already being applied to the production of usable compilers or programming systems.

A first glance at any of the projects which will be indicated provides a striking confirmation of the close relationship there must be between language definition methods and compiler implementation techniques. If we are convinced that compiler improvement depends on formalisation, them we are soon convinced that the formalisation must occur in the language definition. The formal definition of a language should, to a great extent, indicate the implementation method to be used. On a trivial level, if the language is to be compiled using an LL(1) compiler compiler, it is a good thing to have an LL(1) grammar to start off with. However, the remark goes much deeper, in particular if we wish to use more sophisticated techniques.

Let us consider the different types of information contained in a language definition. They may be separated into three categories - syntax, static semantics, and dynamic semantics. Syntax is concerned with the form of the text, and is comparatively well-understood. Static semantics are the static constraints which must be imposed on this text, for example, that each use of an identifier corresponds to one and only one definition of the identifier, and so on. Having achieved a moderate degree of success in the automation of syntax, research workers are now proposing ways of treating static semantics in a similar manner. Of course, this leaves the difficult part of the problem unresolved, that being dynamic semantics, which describe the effects of the different language constructs. Dynamic semantics is difficult because of the fact that it is here that we are required to know something about machines and their operations. A more detailed discussion of this topic is to be found in [Griffiths 73].

In clarifying the definition of static semantics, methods which have been used include that of extension of context-free syntax methods (see, for example, W-grammars, chapter 2.F). The point of difficulty is finding formal methods which are also implementable in practical machines. Chapter 4.B discusses a practical method of compiler-compiler which is a descendant of double grammars, and the attributes of [Knuth 67] form a related and very promising method. In the author's view, the use of attributes to describe static semantics is feasible and would constitute an advance in both definitional and implementation methods if it was adopted.

3.1 - Extensible Languages -

Dynamic semantics requires a description of operations in terms of some machine, either real or abstract. In practice this means in terms of another language, presumably of a lower level. The lower level language is always difficult to define, since if it is too close to a particular machine, it is useless for others, whereas if it is too for removed, it is unimplentable (see the discussion on implementation languages).

The idea behind extensible languages is to take some lower-level language, called the 'base language' which is supposed to be implementable and clearly understood, and to define the higher-level language in terms of the base language by means of extension mechanisms which are themselves contained in the base language. ALGOL68 is said to use extension techniques when it allows the definition of new modes and operators. A powerful device, which allows the creation of new syntatic forms, as well as the possibility of defining the meaning of phrases using these forms in terms of previously existing ones, is that of syntax macros. We illustrate the idea with an example which uses the formalism of [Schumann 70] :

$$\underline{macro}\ statement_o\ \rightarrow\ \underline{while}\ Ex_1\ \underline{do}\ statement_1$$

$$\underline{where}\ type\ (Ex_1)\ =\ boolean$$

$$\underline{means}\ 11\ :\ \underline{if}\ Ex_1\ \underline{then}\ \underline{begin}\ statement_1\ ;\ \underline{goto}\ 11\ \underline{end}$$

The macro defines the 'while-statement' in terms of a condition and a branch statement. The formalism permits the confirmation of static semantics ('where') as well as giving the equivalence. Readers interested in this subject may consult the proceeding of two consecutive ACM special interest group conferences [SIGPLAN 69], [SIGPLAN 71].

3.2 - Formal Semantics -

Compiler writers are also encouraged by the number of efforts being made towards the formalisation of semantics, which should eventually lead to the automation of new implementation levels. One idea is to create a model machine, and give the effect of each construct in terms of this machine. The machine is often represented as a tree manipulation program. The semantics of ALGOL68 are defined in terms of an abstract machine, and the formal definition of PL/1 [Lucas 71] goes further, since all the operations are symbolically defined. For the moment, neither of these definitions is directly exploitable, and it seems probable that both the definitional and the implementation experts will need to make progress before these formalisms are directly useful.

Efforts are also being made to introduce language definition on an axiomatic basis, by static assertions. This technique is like that used by advocates of structured programming and program proving. An example is to be found in [Wirth 73]. Methods of this type require research before we will be able to make use of them. In particular, the relationships between static assertions and their equivalent programs are only just being brought to light, and then only in the sense of proving equivalences between a given static and a given dynamic description. Whether a program can be deduced from a set of assertions is considered in ABSYS [Foster 69], but the results are not yet satisfactory as far as compiler construction is concerned.

4 - CONCLUSION -

It may seem misleading to talk so much about language definition methods when we wish to examine the state of the art in compiler-compilers, but the one is directly dependent on the other. Compiler implementers have always complained that the language definers ignore their problems, but both sides should listen more carefully to what the other has to say.

The present situation as regards the mechanical production of compilers is that the classical methods, based on context-free syntax drivers, are well established and well understood, even though certain industrial compiler producers have yet to see the light. Methods which take their formalisation further than context-free grammars are promising subjects of research (or in some cases development) and some time will elapse before they are applicable in the industrial arena. It seems likely that the introduction of new implementation techniques will have a large influence not only on language definition tools, but also on the contents of languages.

REFERENCES

A. BROOKER - D. MORRIS - J.S. ROHL
The Compiler Compiler
Ann. Rev. in Aut. Prog., 1962

J. FELDMAN - D. GRIES
Translator Writing Systems
CACM, Vol 11, N°2, Feb. 1968

R.W. FLOYD
A Descriptive Language for Symbol Manipulation
JACM, Vol. 8, April 1961

R.W. FLOYD
Bounded Context Syntax Analysis
CACM, Vol 7, N°2, Feb. 1964

J.M. FOSTER - E.W. ELCOCK
ABSYS 1 : An Incremental Compiler for Assertions
Machine Intelligence 4, Edinburgh Univ. Press, 1969

M. GRIFFITHS
The Relationship between Language Definition and Implementation
In Advanced Course in Software Engineering,
Ed. F.L. BAUER,
Notes in Economic and Mathematical System,
Springer Verlag, 1973

D.E. KNUTH
The Semantics of Context-Free Languages
Mathematical Systems Theory, Vol.2, 1967

P. LUCAS - K. WALK
On the Formal Definition of PL/1
Ann. Rev. in Aut. Prog., 1971

M. RAIN (editor)
Machine-Oriented Languages Bulletin

S.A. SCHUMANN
Specifications de langages de Programmation et de leurs
Traducteurs au moyen de Macros-Syntaxiques
Proc. Congrès AFCET, 1970

Proceeding of the Extensible Languages Symposium
SIGPLAN Notices, Aug. 1969

Proceedings of an Extensible Languages Symposium
SIGPLAN Notices, Dec. 1971.

W.L. van der POEL (editor)
Proceedings of a Conference on Machine-Oriented Language,
Trondheim, 1973
North Holland, 1974

N. WIRTH, C.A.R. HOARE
An Axiomatic Definition of the Programming Language PASCAL
International School, Marktoberdorf, 1973

CHAPTER 4.B.

USING THE CDL COMPILER-COMPILER

C. H. A. Koster

Technical University of Berlin

Berlin, Germany

0.   Introduction

In this sequence of lectures one compiler compiler is going to be highlighted by
means of somewhat larger examples, preceded by a discussion of ideas underlying it.

This does not imply that this particular compiler compiler is the best available:
even though it has been around for two years now, it has still not been evaluated
sufficiently in practice. Nor is it very typical: Other compiler compilers embody
quite different ideas.

The intention is to give an insight into the way of working with a compiler compiler.
Instead of, as a demonstration, carrying through a total implementation of a compiler, which would then of necessity be very simple, it was decided to first show the
full implementation of an interpreter-like object (a small editor) and then treat
in greater detail some parts out of a realistic compiler.   In the course of
these examples we will find the opportunity to discuss some farther going questions
(such as machine dependence and efficiency).

4 B 1. Affix grammars and CDL

The Compiler Description Language CDL is based on an equivalence between grammars and specific programs, viz. the corresponding analyzers.

It is possible to make a two-level extension of CF grammars which has its analogue for the corresponding analyzers. These Affix Grammars [Koster 1971] can therefore, after the addition of some syntactic sugar, be considered as a programming language with peculiar grammarlike characteristics, which lends itself well for writing compilers in.

1.1 CF grammar as a programming language

Suppose we want to translate programs written in some language including, among other objects, numbers, with the following CF syntax (written in van Wijngaarden's notation):

$$\text{number: digit, number; digit.} \qquad \text{G1}$$

If we want to use this rule to construct a top-to-bottom parser we will have to bring it into LL(1) form introducing an auxiliary rule to obviate backtrack:

$$\begin{aligned}&\text{number: digit, number tail.}\\&\text{numbertail: digit, numbertail;}\end{aligned} \qquad \text{G2}$$

Now we can very simply translate these syntactic rules into two procedures which answer the question whether the next symbols of some input form a number, provided only such a procedure is also written to recognize digit. In ALGOL 68 we might write:

$$\begin{aligned}&\underline{proc}\ number = \underline{bool}:\ \underline{if}\ digit\ \underline{then}\ numbertail\ \underline{else}\ \underline{false}\ \underline{fi};\quad \text{P2}\\&\underline{proc}\ numbertail = \underline{bool}:\ \underline{if}\ digit\ \underline{then}\ numbertail\ \underline{else}\ \underline{true}\ \underline{fi};\end{aligned}$$

More abstractly, such recognizing procedures for number and numbertail may be seen as realization of the syntax diagrams

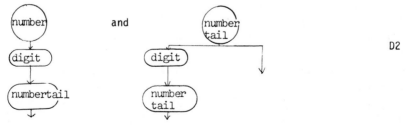

and

D2

where the ovals denote invocations of other rules (or, alternatively, recognizers).
Notice that the ordering of the alternatives in numbertail is important, in distinction to the usual interpretation of CF grammars. This comes from the fact that a
procedure corresponding to some rule is of necessity executed deterministically
from left to right. In assigning to CF grammars an interpretation as a program one
must be aware of this difference. We will, at a later point, show some advantages
of this non-standard interpretation of grammars, in particular the fact that it
allows to include error treatment in the syntax.

The two boolean procedures in P2, and in general all procedures realizing the diagram D2, could be obtained from the two rules in G2 by a more or less mechanical
process of transcription. We will call a boolean procedure obtained from a rule by
such a transcription a predicate; under certain conditions (such as the fact that
the grammar must be LL(1)) these predicates serve as recognizers for the corresponding rules, working by the method of recursive descent.

Since we are going to the trouble of recognizing number, we may just as well try
do something useful, and compute their meaning. The meaning of a number, clearly,
is its value. As a side effect of recognizing the number we want to derive its value.
We can do so by introducing semantic actions into the syntax:

number: digit, action1, numbertail.

numbertail: digit, action2, numbertail; .
$\qquad$ G3

where action1 performs *val:=last digit read* and action2 performs *val:=10×val+last
digit read*, with the effect that the value *val* is computed globally. In a diagram,
enclosing the invocations of actions by a rectangle to distinguish them from those
of predicates:

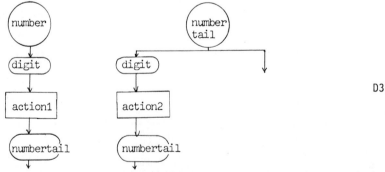

$\qquad$ D3

This scheme is not very satisfactory because it presupposes some environment in
which the actions are performed, and no way to access that environment is available,
nor is it clear how to define the semantic actions. We will have to extend CF
syntax in order to remove these problems.

1.2. Extending CF grammar

1.2.1 Affixes

We will show, in a sequence of steps, the extension of CF grammars to the compiler description language CDL, stressing the motivation for each change.
We will allow predicates to have both parameters and local variables, and extend CF syntax accordingly by adding a second level. Parameters and local variables will be indicated in the grammar by identifiers associated with the nonterminal symbols; we will term them Affixes. .
We will suppose digit to have one parameter which gets the value of the last digit read. We therefore have to invoke digit with one parameter, e.g.: digit+d, using, for historical reasons, the infix-plus rather than parentheses. The corresponding predicate is supposed to have the following properties:

1) If the next symbol of the input is a digit, then it returns the value <u>true</u> after having assigned to its parameter the value of that digit and advanced the input by one symbol.

2) If the next symbol of the input is not a digit, then it returns the value <u>false</u>. (The value of the parameter is irrelevant.)

The rule for number uses a parameter val to compute the value in, and to pass that value to the outside. We will indicate this in the left hand side of the rule:

number+val:

Parameter correspondence is to be by name or by reference.

The rule for numbertail needs both a parameter val and a local variable d, the latter to hold the values of individual digits. We will indicate this in the left hand side of the rule, using an infix minus as separator:

numbertail+val-d:

Employing these extensions, we can now write:

number+val: digit+val, numbertail+val.
numbertail+val-d: digit+d, action2, numbertail+val; .   G4

Here action2 performs *val:=10×val+d*. The value of the number is now computed locally. A corresponding piece of program in ALGOL 68 might be:

proc number = (ref int val) bool:
if digit(val) then numbertail(val) else false fi;
proc numbertail = (ref int val) bool:
begin int d;   P4
    if digit (d)
    then val := 10×val+d; numbertail(val)
    else true
    fi
end

Thinking of affixes as local variables and parameters is intuitively quite satisfactory; a more precise and formal definition can be found in [Koster 1971A] .

1.2.2 Primitive actions and predicates

The introduction of action2 is still unsatisfactory: we want to be able to define such primitives in a way which allows harmonious insertion in a predicate.
In P4 we have used a very simple device: textual substitution in the framework of the predicate. This smacks of macros: A macro is a rule for replacing each piece of text which satisfies a given pattern by another text, the macro body, possibly after replacing in that text a number of parameters. We will introduce a simple macro system. Macros should be invoked in exactly the same way as predicates, e.g.,

one more digit+val+d

where the pattern has 2 parameters.
Introducing some syntactic sugar, we can define action2 as

'macro''action' one more digit = *'1':=10×'1' +'2'* .

Here *'1'* stands for the first parameter, etc. The expansion of the macro invocation one more digit+val+d is therefore *val:=10×val+d*, which in the languages ALGOL 60, ALGOL W and ALGOL 68 happens to have one same meaning. This Macro definition is therefore useful in conjunction with predicates written in any of those 3 languages, but not with predicates in, e.g., 360 Assembler. The body of a macro is not inherently meaningful, but becomes so only by association with transcription of the rules to a specific language. By this macro definition we have introduced into our grammar arithmetic capabilities by borrowing them from the target language of the compiler compiler. Macros provide a limited extensional facility, with, as we shall see, profound consequences.

Thus we can give a new approximation to the definition of number:

```
'macro''action' one more digit = '1':='1'*10+'2'.
number val: digit+val, numbertail+val.
numbertail+val-d:
        digit+d, one more digit+val+d, numbertail+val; .
```
                                                                    G5

with P4 as a transcription into ALGOL 68.
Similarly, we can introduce primitive predicates by macros, like:

```
'macro''predicate' less = '1'<'2',
                   equal = '1'='2',
                   lseq = '1'≤'2'.
```

allowing us e.g. to let the effect of a predicate depend upon some values.

1.2.3. Actions

The concepts of primitive predicates and primitive actions lead to the idea of having, besides predicates, also non-primitive actions. Intuitively, an action is a rule transcribed to a <u>proc</u> <u>void</u> instead of to a <u>proc</u> <u>bool</u>. We will visualize actions as predicates whose value is uninteresting because it is always *true*. An example is numbertail, whose transcription may or may not do some further parsing, but always returns *true*. We will indicate by an action-specification that we regard this rule as defining an action:

```
'action' numbertail.
number+val: digit+val, numbertail+val.
numbertail+val-d:
        digit+d, one more digit+val+d, numbertail+val; .
```
                                                                    G6

with as a transcription:

$$\underline{proc}\ number = (\underline{ref}\ \underline{int}\ val)\ bool:$$
$$\underline{if}\ digit(val)$$
$$\underline{then}\ numbertail(val);\ true$$
$$\underline{else}\ \underline{false}$$
$$\underline{fi};$$

```
proc numbertail = (ref int val) void:
begin int d;
    if digit(d)
    then  val:=10*val+d; numbertail(d)                          P6
    else skip
    fi
end
```

We will now attempt to define digit. We presuppose an environment containing an *int*
buffer *char* holding, at any moment, the code of the first character of the input
that has not yet been consumed, and an action nextchar reading the code of the next
character of the input into that buffer. We suppose the characters are encoded as
small integers, and in particular the digits zero to nine have the codes 100 to 109.
We can then write:

```
'macro''predicate' is a digit = '1' ⩾ 100 ∧ '1' ⩽ 109.
'macro''action' convert to dig = '2' := '1' - 100.                G7
digit d: is a digit+char, convert to dig+char+d, nextchar.
```

with as an ALGOL 68 transcription:

```
proc digit = (ref int d) bool:
if char ⩾ 100 ∧ char ⩽ 109
then d := char - 100; nextchar; true                             P7
else false
fi
```

1.2.4 Repetition

The example G6 is still unrealistic in that the number is recognized recursively.
A number is not inherently a recursive object: it consists merely of a sequence of
digits, and any systems programmer would compute its value in a loop, not by recursion.
We will allow labels and jumps within a rule. Now don't start laughing or cursing.
I know the literature on structured programming just as well as you do: hear me out.
We will use label identifiers and write the jump to the label next: as :next. A jump
can only occur as the last member of an alternative. Only jumps to "visible" labels
are allowed where a label is visible from a jump only if, in the syntax diagram,
there is a path directed from the labelled point to the jump. In this fashion, forward jumps and all manner of other dangerous phenomena are forbidden: the jump is
tamed. The equivalent syntax diagram are, of course, ordered trees with additional
arcs from descendants to ancestors:

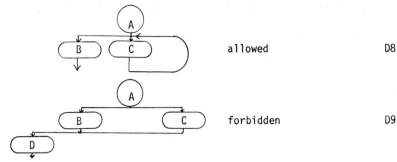

allowed	D8
forbidden	D9

In a linear notation, these diagrams read:

> A:
> rep:(B;
>   C, :rep).   G8

generating C^*B, and

> A: B, rest: D;
>   C, :rest.   G9

which is forbidden, and has to be written as

>   A : B,D; C,D.
> or   A : Q,D.   G9'
>   Q : B;C.

Using this notation, we can write:

> numbertail+val-d:
>   rest: digit+d, one more digit+val+d, :rest; .   G10

with a transcription

> *proc numbertail = (ref int val) void:*
> *begin int d;*
> *rest: if digit (d)*   P10
>   *then val := 10∗val+d; goto rest*
>   *else skip*
>   *fi*
> *end*

which should put the hearts of the efficiency fiends at rest.

1.2.5 Grouping

In order for the grammar G1 to be backtrack free, we had to rewrite in into G2, introducing an auxiliary rule. This is something of a nuisance, all the more so because what we want to achieve is so simple: having found one digit, we take it into account, and then expect either further digits, or no further digits.

We will allow the grouping of alternatives by means of parentheses:

number+val-d:
    digit+val,   G11
      rep: (digit+d, one more digit+val+d, :rep;).

with a transcription.

$$proc\ number = (\underline{ref}\ \underline{int}\ val)\ \underline{bool}:$$
$$\underline{begin}\ \underline{int}\ d;$$
$$\underline{if}\ digit(val)$$
$$\underline{then}$$
$$rep:\ \underline{if}\ digit(d)$$
$$\underline{then}\ val := 10{\times}val+d;\ \underline{goto}\ rep \qquad\qquad P11$$
$$\underline{else}\ \underline{true}$$
$$\underline{fi}$$
$$\underline{else}\ \underline{false}$$
$$\underline{fi}$$
$$\underline{end}$$

1.2.6 Data types

In turning CF grammars into a full-fledged programming language we have to choose what data types we will allow. We must choose them such that they are primitive for every present day computer and suitable for expressing the data usually manipulated by compilers. It is highly important that they should not be so elaborate as to re-quire large run-time support.

The philosophy adopted is to have as basic data types only the <u>machine-word</u> and the <u>linear array of machine words</u> of fixed length. More fancy data structures are to be expressed algorithmically in terms of those basic data types. More about this in 4B2.3.

A variable to hold a machine word is termed a <u>pointer</u>. As an example, a one-word buffer can be declared

        'pointer' buffer.

In principle such a word is uninterpreted, and any interpretation as, e.g., an inte-ger or even an address, is at the discretion and the risk of the compiler writer by his choice of macros. CDL provides only for the declaration facility and the para-meter passing (by name, or by reference, which are equivalent in this case) and gives no means of looking at the value of a word.

A linear array of machine words is termed a <u>list</u>. As an example, an input buffer of 200 words can be declared by

        'list' inbuf (1:200).

CDL gives only the means to declare the list. A means for accessing it has to be provided explicitly, e.g. for ALGOL W

$$\text{'macro''action' get = '3' := '1' ('2'),}$$
$$\text{put = '1' ('2') := '3'.}$$

allowing, e.g.,   get+inbuf+p+nextsym

Pointers can of course also be introduced by macros. As an example, one should of course never mention one constant as upper bound of a list whose length may have to be varied, but give a manifest constant (named constant), e.g.:

$$\text{'macro''pointer' maxbuf≠200.}$$
$$\text{'list' inbuf (1:maxbuf).}$$

Finally, in spite of all hope to the contrary, it turns out that a compiler spends its time mainly doing arithmetic, which forces us to allow integral constants to be denoted directly: an unsigned sequence of digits can be used as actual parameter. As an example set to+777 passes a word with the value 777 on to the predicate set to.

1.3 Affix grammars

A contextfree grammar extended with affixes, primitive predicates and primitive actions is called an Affix grammar [Koster 1971A] , a two-level grammar not unlike van Wijngaarden grammar (see 2F). Affix grammars are also equivalent to semi- Thue systems, and it is a simple exercise to write down an affix grammar generating, e.g., only the prime numbers. In distinction to van Wijngaarden grammar a number of important practical questions are solvable. In particular, for an affix-grammar that satisfies a number of lenient and realistic restrictions, the parsing-problem is solvable.

Affix grammars are, in a sense, a more natural extension of CF grammar than context-sensitive grammar is, because practically all techniques for parsing or for "improving" the grammar which are applicable to CF grammars can be applied with slight modification to affix grammars.

1.4 From language definition to Compiler Description

The present knowledge of compiler compiler techniques should have a profound influence on the definition of future programming languages. A very successful language like FORTRAN was standardized and precisely defined only after it was in widespread use for a number of years. The, in Europe, moderately successful language ALGOL 60 was only implemented and given to the users after a precise definition, and this course of events was intellectually much more satisfactory. Since then, the history of ALGOL 68 has shown that for such an intricate language a highly precise definition is necessary but not sufficient: both the difficulty of implementation (which was foreseen) and the long time lag in the arrival of implementations (which was not foreseen) have turned much initial enthusiasm of some people to frustration and have enforced the, often unfounded, distaste of others. The history of PASCAL has shown that a language for which a good implementation is available immediately, can be a success, even if that implementation differs from the (none too precise) definition of the language and is not available on IBM computers.

The lesson to be learned from these observations is that a language definition must be precise and must be constructive in the sense that it must be possible to directly derive from the definition a correct implementation on any computer. A language definition must be of use to the user and the implementor as well as to the language theorist.

The syntactic and semantic techniques employed in a language definition should therefore consist of a description of a machine-independent compiler or interpreter, given in a sufficiently well-defined formal system to suit the language theorist, accompanied by humanly understandable pragmatics systematically giving motivation, explanation and consequences of the various language elements.

The compiler-maker's task then consists of turning this description into a correct, efficient, helpful and well-documented implementation on a specific machine. In this task he should have a set of mechanical tools at his disposal.

It is in this spirit that the compiler description language has been designed.

4 B 2.   The CDL Compiler Compiler

In this chapter, the problem of implementing CDL, and some properties of the existing compiler compiler, are discussed, as well as some techniques in making use of it.

2.1 Extensional mechanisms

Indicating, in the usual fashion, a compiler written in the implementation language I translating from the source language S to the target language T by

we mean by a __CDL compiler compiler__ some compiler

where M is some directly executable language, e.g. FORTRAN, ALGOL or the machine code of our machine.

This compiler compiler can translate a CDL program correctly only if the bodies of macros occurring in that CDL program are written in T. To make this dependence explicit we will indicate a CDL program which is a compiler from A to B and has macrobodies in T , by

allowing us to produce:

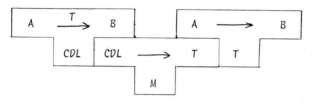

In this way, we have made the first extensional mechanism explicit: the borrowing of concepts from some target language by means of macros.

This is still not all of the picture: the product of the compiler compiler, a piece of text written in T, need not be intended to run on the bare T machine, but will run in some <u>environment</u>, containing e.g. the interface with the operating system. Now it is clearly not within the scope of CDL to define that interface too, we will have to be content with assuming its existence and knowing its properties. This is a spur to keep the interface as small as possible, containing just the primitives necessary for the communication of our compiler with the system, e.g.:

      'external''action' resym, prsym, pusym, exit.

where resym allows input one character at a time, assigning the next character of input to its parameter, prsym outputs one character to a printfile, pusym outputs one character to the file that should hold the code generated, and exit aborts the program and returns control to the operating system. It is the responsibility of the compiler writer that such procedures are linked and loaded together with the program.

The extensional mechanisms, especially the macro system, give CDL its power, and the possibility to write compilers in a machine-independent fashion and still obtain efficient results on any machine. Machine dependence is a question of style, but the necessary tools are provided. Some examples of their use can be found in 4 B 2.3, 3, 4 and 5.

2.2 Realizing the CDL machine

There are two versions of the CDL compiler compiler in current use: a high-level
version (which translates to a high level language like ALGOL 60 or ALGOL W, or even
PL/1, by mapping CDL constructs into corresponding constructs in the target language)
and a low-level version (which is intended to translate to various assemblers, and
has been used to generate code for a 360/67 and a DEC PDP 10).
Since the possibility to map CDL into a high level language is so obvious as to be
unenlightening, we will describe in this section a simple abstract machine, suitable
for executing CDL programs, and easily mappable onto any existing computer.
We assume the underlying computer to have one linear homogenous addressable store M,
one index register p which will serve as a stack pointer, a condition register C
capable of holding at least one bit, a subroutine jump instruction, a sufficient
number of further registers to perform arithmetic, and a facility for symbolic
addressing of instructions and data words, such as present in practically all assemblers.

On any computer satisfying these assumptions, CDL can be realized easily.

2.2.1 Some instructions

Consider the definition of the following CDL predicate, where pred, pred1 and pred2
are predicates and act is an action.

>   pred+p1+p2-l1:
>   pred1+p1+l1, act+p1+p2;
>   pred2.

We want to translate this piece of text into a sequence of instructions for a suitable
abstract machine. This machine will have one stack.
We will first define and explain some instructions of an abstract machine for CDL,
and then show a translation of the piece of text into a sequence of those instructions.

Instruction	Meaning

1) *procdeclare+label*   *label:*

   It is assumed upon entry that the address of all parameters are on the stack,
   with the return address λ on top.

2) *loadzero* $M[p]:=0; \; p:=p+1$

   Used to reserve space for one local variable and initialize it to zero.

3) *loadpar+offset* $M[p]:=M[p-offset]; \; p:=p+1$

   The address of some parameter is copied on top of the stack.

4) *loadloc+offset* $M[p]:=p-offset; \; p:=p+1$

   The address of some local variable is copied on top of the stack.

5)   *call+label* $M[p] := instructioncounter+1;\ p:=p+1;$

       A stacking subroutine call to the label. $instructioncounter := label$

6)   *negjump+label* $if \neg C\ \underline{then}\ instructioncounter := label$

       A conditional jump inversely dependent on C.

7)   *lab declare+number* $L\ number:$

       Putting a numbered label.

8)   *return+npar+nloc* $p := p-npar-nloc-1;$

                                                            $instructioncounter := M[p+npar]$

On the stack the room for *npar* parameters, *nloc* locals and 1 link is freed, after which a return is made utilizing the link (which is still on M, albeit possibly beyond p). In this way, each procedure can remove its own debris from the stack.

9)   *set true* $C := \underline{true}$

10) *set false* $C := \underline{false}$

       The setting of the condition C.

Using only 8 of these 10 instructions, we can make our translation of *pred* into a procedure *pred*. At the moment of entry into *pred* we assume the following stack structure: p points to the first free place in the stack. On top of the stack we find the link λ with underneath it the addresses of the two parameters *p1* and *p2*.

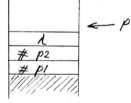

a) *procdeclare+pred*   pred+p1+p2

b) *loadzero*   -11:

c) *load par+4*

d) *load loc+3*   pred1+p1+l1

e) *call+pred1*

f) *negjump+1*   ,

g) *load par+4*

h) *load par+4*   act+p1+p2

i) *call+act*

j) *return+2+1*

k) *lab declare+1*   ;

l) *call+pred2*   pred2

m) *return+2+1*   .

After line b the stack picture is

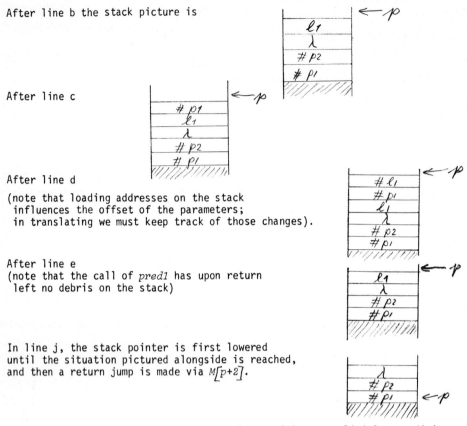

After line c

After line d
(note that loading addresses on the stack
 influences the offset of the parameters;
 in translating we must keep track of those changes).

After line e
(note that the call of *pred1* has upon return
 left no debris on the stack)

In line j, the stack pointer is first lowered
until the situation pictured alongside is reached,
and then a return jump is made via $M[p+2]$.

Observe that we at no place had to set the condition C explicitly: condition setting
is done by tests in macros, and for the rest is practically always done correctly
as a side effect of predicates called.

2.2.2 Parametrization

Since it is parametrization which distinguishes affix grammars most from CF grammars,
we will look at it more closely.
We must distinguish between three types of calls that can be parametrized:

- rules
- system macros
- user macros.

By <u>system macros</u> we mean the macros corresponding to the instructions of the abstract
CDL machine, by <u>user macros</u> we mean the macros particular to some CDL text. We will
see that all three might have to be parametrized by different mechanisms.

2.2.2.1 Parametrization of rules
In the model given here (other models are certainly conceivable) a rule corresponds

to a closed subroutine, called with addresses of the actual parameters.
On machines with a palatable stack-facilitiy, the parameters and return address can
be passed via the stack. On machines with a 360-like architecture (many registers
and a fast multiple-store instruction) it is faster to pass them in registers and
store them on top of the stack en bloc upon procedure entry. Removal from the stack
is in both cases achieved by a subtraction from the stack pointer without reloading
the registers: the calling environment is either unaffected or on the stack anyway,
so it need not be restored explicitly.

2.2.2.2 Parametrization of system macros

For parametrizing macros in the low-level version, simple textual substitution of the
identifiers of actual parameter gives some difficulty, since in most assemblers there
is no symbolic addressing mechanism for globals, locals and formal parameters to fall
back on. The system will have to invoke different macros to, e.g., load an address
on top of the stack, depending on the class of actual parameter, so that for each of
them text substitution will work.

Apart from macros corresponding to the instructions *loadloc* and *loadpar* already
mentioned, they are:

11) *loadglob+idf* $M[p]:=\underline{addr}\ Gidf;\ p:=p+1$

> To load the address of a global variable, the address of a word labelled *Gidf*
> in a data segment is loaded on top of the stack.

12) *loadcons+n* $M[p]:=\underline{addr}\ Cn;\ p:=p+1$

> To load the address of a constant, the address of a word initialized to n and
> labelled *Cn* in a data segment is loaded in top of the stack.

13) *loadlist+idf* $M[p]:=\underline{addr}\ Gidf;\ p:=p+1$

> To load the address of a list, the address of the first word of part of a
> data segment, reserved for that list, is loaded on top of the stack.

By choosing the appropriate macro and substituting for its parameter the appropriate
piece of text (an identifier in some cases, an offset in others), the system macros
can use textual substitution for parametrization.

2.2.2.3 Parametrization of user macros

For a user macro like, e.g., *make* to perform the assignment, whose body can be expressed so concisely in ALGOL as *'1':='2'*, we get into trouble when attempting to use
textual substitution, e.g. (for some hypothetical assembler-like target language)

```
            'macro''action' make =
                fetch acc, '1'
                store acc, '2'.
```

The trouble is that for each of the various types of parameters mentioned, we would have to substitute different pieces of text, e.g., for a bound parameter we would have to supply something like M[M[p-offset]] , indirectly addressing via the stack. If the architecture of the target machine is flexible and systematic enough to allow this kind of address calculation with every type of instruction, then there is no problem, but an important machine like the 360 is definitely deficient in these respects.

Three methods of parametrization for user macros, in order of decreasing preferability, are

a) by text substitution. Needs a machine with well designed indirect addressing, like the DEC PDP 10.

b) by index registers, passing the addresses of all parameters in corresponding registers. Needs a machine with a sufficient number of registers that can also serve as index registers, like the 360.

c) by stack, passing the parameters on top of the stack. A slow but secure method when everything else fails.

It is clearly important that user macros be relatively large units of action, for the following reasons:

a) parametrization by registers or by stack gives,for small macros, a relatively large overhead

b) small units of action lead to large interdependencies between actions, where the information is unnecessarily stored from registers at the end of one unit and restored at the beginning of the next.

c) The larger the macro, the better the chances to apply local optimizations and shortcuts in it.

2.2.2.4 Suggested ameliorations

The previous discussion shows that it might be helpful to have a more powerful macro mechanism,where, depending on the type of parameters, different macro bodies can be chosen. In this way, unnecessary indirections can be weeded out, which will lead to an appreciable condensation of the code generated.

Furthermore, it is clearly advantageous to introduce a distinction between parameters called by address and parameters called by value, so that, e.g., a horror like   make+3+4

is prevented, which is pedantically correct if the doctrine is accepted that all parameters are passed by address.

A revision of CDL is being undertaken in which this and other matters will be ameliorated.

2.3 Data structures and Data access

In CDL only two types of data are handled (the <u>word</u> and the <u>linear array of words</u>) which, at first sight, seems to be a shocking lack of expressional power, and in contrast to tendencies, even in systems implementation languages intended to run in an essentially empty environment, to provide for ever better structured and more helpful data structures.

CDL allows the formulation of algorithms in such a way that they are highly machine-independent and can be ported easily. If we can define data structures by means of algorithms, then their portability is assured by the same mechanism.

From the point of view of CDL, a data structure is an access discipline, a set of cooperating access algorithms, providing access to a primitively structured collection of data in an orderly fashion. Thus, a stack consists of a linear array of words and a stack pointer, accessible (after initialization) through two access algorithms stack and unstack and in no way else.

The access algorithms provide a cleancut interface, independent of whether they are made to correspond to some facilities supplied by the run time environment or whether they are broken down laboriously in terms of smaller and smaller algorithms, e.g., in porting a compiler which uses a stack one can choose between simulating that stack or making use of a stack facility already present. If a compiler is ported which has say a characterwise I/O interface, then one can initially utilize this interface, and later on speed up the compiler by taking a more complicated level of interface, and program the necessary algorithms in Assembler.

As an example of the philosophy of providing data access algorithms instead of data structures, consider the following.
In some compiler we build, for each identifier, a chain of defining occurrences, stating in which blocks it has been defined and with what types.
We need something like:

$$\underline{mode}\ \underline{defchain} = \underline{struct}\ (\underline{int}\ bnmb,$$
$$\underline{type}\ type,$$
$$\underline{ref}\ \underline{defchain}\ link).$$

In CDL we might write (choosing some fixed maximal size to this table, and letting pdef point to the first free place):

```
'macro''pointer' max def=1000.
'pointer' pdef.
'list' defch (1:maxdef).
'macro''action' get bnmb='2':=defch['1'], put bnmb=defch['1']:='2',
    get type='2':=defch['1'+1], put type=defch['1'+1]:='2',
    get link='2':=defch['1'+2],put link=defch['1'+2]:='2'.
'macro''pointer' def element size=3.
```

Assuming now that with every identifier a chain is associated whose head is held by a specific pointer (initially zero), we can append a new cell b,t to the front of the chain pointed at by p by:

append def+b+t+p-1:
    make+1+p, make+p+pdef, add+pdef+def element size+pdef,
        (less+max def+pdef, report def full and quit;
        put bnmb+p+b, put type+p+t, put link+p+1).

The algorithm ensures that, if we run out of space, this is signalled in some orderly fashion. Notice that it works for any value of max def and def element size, provided we do not forget to initialize this administration at the start of the program, by

    prepare def: make+pdef+1.

Now suppose we want to pack the type and the block number together into one word. The only changes needed are suitable redefinitions of get bnmb, put bnmb, get type and put type, as well as

    'macro''pointer' def element size = 2.

This kind of memory economy does not bring much gain in the design and test phases of a compiler, or in porting it, but once a compiler is running correctly it can be adapted without endangering its correctness.

The advantages of making use of data access algorithms instead of data structures can be summed up as follows:

a) no runtime system. Having such data-structures as stacks, records, queues and files would ask for a fairly large runtime memory management system, which would lessen the portability of compilers written in CDL.

b) machine independence. By a judicious use of the technique, the question of machine-dependence of data representations is shifted to the man who adapts a portable compiler to his machine, and who therefore can be supposed to have the intimate knowledge and the patience necessary to turn a correct but academic compiler into one suitable for production purposes.

c) structured programming. The benefits of structured programming (and, in a wider sense, software engineering) are until now essentially confined to algorithms. To those algorithms various methodologies for design and proof can be applied much more easily than to data structures.

2.4 The CDL compiler compiler as a tool

In spite of its syntactical background, CDL is more like an implementation language than like the usual syntax-driven compiler generating system, because it provides a technique to describe, in a homogenous fashion, not only the parsing part of the

compiler, but the full table administration and generation of code as well. In implementing a major language, this is at least one third of the work (the other two
thirds being taken up by design and implementation of the run-time system, run-time
environment and documentation), whereas parsing is something like 10 percent of the
work.

In porting a compiler, these proportions stay more or less the same, but the total
amount of work is much less.

In this section, we will go into three aspects of using the CDL compiler compiler
as a tool. Other aspects will have to come from the examples following it: the proof
of the pudding is in the eating.

2.4.1 High-level and low-level version

It is useful to have access to two versions of the compiler compiler, a high-level
version, generating e.g. an ALGOL 60 program, and a low-level version, generating a
program in Assembler.

We can then develop and debug compilers using ALGOL 60 for the macros, and run the
resulting program in the knowledge that it will not collapse in a mysterious fashion,
as machine-code programs are wont to do, but that all static and dynamic debugging
aids plus the inherent security of the high level language are at our disposal. We
can then if necessary try an improvement by patching the ALGOL text, only recompiling
the CDL program by the time we are sure of what has to be done.

For production purposes it is of course intolerable to put a compiler first through
the ALGOL compiler before running it, and also use of ALGOL may lead to unnecessary
overhead. Once we dispose of a correct compiler we can rewrite the macros in Assembler and then use the low-level version of the compiler compiler to generate an equivalent assembler program, which we need never look at: assembly language is not fit
for human eyes.

The same considerations hold in porting a compiler: it is advantageous to first get
a high-level language version running, and only then spend a thought on efficiency.

2.4.2 Syntactic debugging aids

All versions of the compiler compiler have a number of built-in debugging aids. The
most interesting one of them consists of a collection of error messages concerning
the syntactic structure of the program.

Consider the following rule, where all identifiers denote predicates:

        p: q; d.
        q: a,b; c.

Under the assumption that the grammar is LL(1), the input for which p should deliver
true is $ab \cup c \cup d$; for any other input it should deliver false. Now consider the equivalent syntax diagram

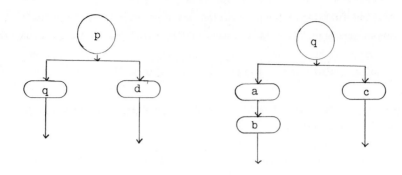

and imagine its realization as a set of procedures. Suppose the input contains *ad*, so a returns true but b returns false so q returns false; next d is tried and (since the input has not been repositioned) returns true: the input is accepted even though it should not.

The point is that, upon finding that *a* was there and *b* was not, the side effect of a had to be undone. In general, whenever an alternative returns false, it should have had no side effects. Since it is obviously impossible to undo all side effects (e.g., those of *print*) only one other way remains: once an alternative has had a side effect, it should not be allowed to return false any more.

The compiler compiler keeps track of side effects, under the assumption that a flag never has a side effect, and a predicate or action always has a side effect. Whenever in an alternative after some side effect has been noticed a test follows (be it a predicate or a flag) the warning

backtrack?

appears, e.g., in our example:

q: a,b;
backtrack?   c.

meaning that, when b is false, either *a* must be undone, or the missing b must be signalled, thus:

q: a, (b; signal missing b); c.

where we assume signal missing b to be an action.

Taking an example from a programming language, which allows declarers $\underline{long}^n\underline{int}$ and $\underline{long}^n\ \underline{real}$ for $n \geqslant 0$, we might have:

declarer: int symbol;
real symbol;
long symbol, declarer.

We are promptly told that declarer may cause backtrack, and are forced to write

```
declarer: int symbol;
          real symbol;
          long symbol,
            (declarer;
             report declarer missing).
```

The resulting grammar is robust against input errors since we have extended it to describe also all incorrect input. Notice the important use we are making here of the ordering of alternatives !

Another warning message is given when a predicate never returns false, which is an invitation to scrutinize it and possibly to specify it as an action.

In this way, our syntax for number needs a specification 'action' numbertail., which also rids us of a backtrack warning.

Two further warning messages make the system complete:

They warn when any other than the last alternative of a rule always returns true (which would make the remaining alternatives superfluous) or when an action, considered as a predicate, could return false.

By this system of warnings, the most insidious structural errors in the grammar are exposed, and ways of correcting them suggested.

2.4.3 Efficiency of the resulting compiler

A compiler obtained with the help of the CDL compiler compiler is, of course, longer and slower than one obtained by clever assembler programming, but it is much more likely to be bug free. Some overhead in space and time is paid. As usual one should distinguish between distributed and localized overhead. The overhead in using CDL is essentially distributed all over the program, and CDL does not contain any costly features, nor are there aspects to a compiler badly expressible in CDL.

Once a low-level version of the compiler is running correctly, if its speed and size compare badly to other compilers one can tune it in various ways. Mostly, this tuning will be unnecessary because the inherent simplicity of CDL (simple procedure mechanism and parameter passing, etc.) means that a straightforward implementation will be satisfactory. Tuning should encompass only those parts of the compiler where most time is spent, and should essentially entail a better choice of algorithm rather than piecemeal shortcuts and optimizations, choosing, e.g., a hashed symbol table instead of a linear one, etc.

In order to reduce distributed overhead, the CDL system will include in future two optimizations:

a) Various transformations will be applied to the CDL text to reduce the physical size of the corresponding program and consequently raise its speed.

b) A more sophisticated macro system will allow local optimization of the code generated.

Some research is also going on as regards models for CDL on machines with different architectures, in particular microprogrammed machines.

2.4.4 Conclusion

It should be obvious that the technical problems of size and speed can be overcome, making implementation languages like CDL not only equal but even superior to assembly languages in all aspects of the writing of large system programs like compilers.

The next step is for compiler makers to start concentrating on the problems of design of abstract machines for realizing high level languages, relying on the use of software writing tools to perform the more menial tasks.

4 B 3   Example   : A simple Editor

Our first example will be the design in full of a simple interpreter-like object: an editor. While not being a compiler in the strict sense, it displays some important properties of compilers (some syntactic structure to the input; table up-keep by semantic actions) while not necessitating the treatment of code generation techniques.

This example is intended to bring out another property of CDL which is essential for implementation languages: it lends itself well as a vehicle for structured programming. In the course of teaching CDL [Koster, 1974] and ALEPH, a variant of CDL [Grune, 1973] , to students it was gradually realized that CDL has a tendency to enforce good programming habits.

The suitability of CDL for structured programming derives from the following properties:

- The basic programming construct, the rule, possesses a control flow graph which is a tree with additional arcs from terminal nodes back to their ancestors. Any node of the tree may be decomposed in the same way. This encourages top-down-programming, and ensures that individual rules remain short and uncomplicated.

- The control structures are very simple, allowing the shortest possible notation of conditional and return. Also the use of jumps and labels, with the restriction mentioned, is just an unusual notation for the repetition and in no way distorts program structure.

- All objects defined by rules and all macros are named, and there is no upper limit to the length of such identifiers. The programmer has to name even the simplest operations. This fact in conjunction with the low degree of complexity of each individual object seduces even the more stupid programmers to choose helpful mnemonic names.

- The overall simplicity of the language helps to prevent tricky programming. In particular the utter simplicity of the data structures encourages the programmer to think in terms of algorithms, including data access algorithms.

CDL helps in writing programs by a process of stepwise refinement, top-down programming with some timely interludes of bottom-up programming to get the feet back on earth. In unfolding this last example we will try to demonstrate the naturalness of this "yoyo-programming" (a term coined at the Trondheim Working Conference on Machine Oriented High Level Languages in 1973).

3.1 Specification of a simple editor

We will construct an editor which allows to establish, update and display a document consisting of (not necessarily consecutively) numbered lines, in the order of increasing line number. Initially the document consists of no lines at all. It can be manipulated by the following commands:

I.   n = entry ↵

    where: n is some number, the line number,

            = serves to indicate the beginning of an entry, and

            entry is some sequence of characters not containing the ↵, and

            ↵ is the end of line character.

The effect of such a command is the following:

A) If a line with line number n was not yet present in the document, then the entry is inserted with line number n.

B) If a line with line number n was already present, then that line is replaced by the entry with line number n.

This allows both insertion and change in a very simple fashion.

II.   d n ↵

    where: d is the letter d,

            n is some number, and

            ↵ is the end of line character.

The effect of this command is:

A) If a line with line number n was present in the document, then it is deleted.

B) If such a line was not present, then an error is reported, but editing is not terminated.

III.   l ↵

    where: l is the letter l, and

            ↵ is the end of line character.

    Effect: all lines of the document are listed in the order of increasing line numbers, after which the editing is ended.

From this specification we will deduce a syntax of the input language of the editor:

    input:

        spaces to end of line, input;

        fresh line, input;

        deletion command, input;

        list command.

    spaces to end of line:

        space char, spaces to end of line; end of line char.

```
fresh line:
     number, equals char, rest of line.
rest of line:
     end of line char;
     any character, rest of line.
deletion command:
     letter d char, number, spaces to end of line.
list command:
     letter l char, spaces to end of line.
number:
     space char, number;
     digit, (number;).
```

Notice that we built into the syntax a number of degrees of freedom as regards lay-out that are not mentioned in the original specification, but are highly necessary because of the fallibility of humans: a good compilermaker should have a great pragmatic insight, foreseeing and forestalling the input errors that are going to be made.

3.2 Environment, and arithmetic macros

As contact with the environment we need solely an action resym reading one character and an action prsym printing one character as well as an action exit to terminate the editor, e.g. in case of some list overflow.

Of course resym and prsym must make use of one same character encoding, where we will require the digits zero to nine to have consecutive increasing codes, as well as the letter a to z. We need to know the codes for these characters and a few more. To that end, we will introduce some macro pointers:

```
     'external''action' resym, prsym, exit.
     'macro''pointer' spacechar=105,
               end of line char=110,
               digit zero char=54,
               digit nine char=63,
               letter d char=31,
               letter l char=39,
               equals char=86.
```

We will also presuppose a, more or less standard, set of macros for arithmetic and testing. As a goal language for the design and test phase we will choose ALGOL W for the 360/67.

3.3 Table administration strategy

Now we will choose a strategy for the tables and their administration. We will have
to remember lines associated with their numbers (keys). We will combine those keys
into a directory, telling at any point in time what keys are present, and indicating
the associated texts in a list text, which will contain lines stripped of their
number and equals symbol. The directory will therefore consist of two lists key and
ptr. In a picture:

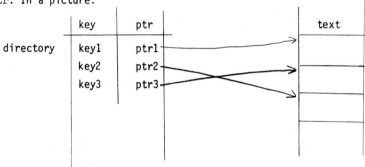

The three lists mentioned must have one access action each for putting and getting a
word. The first free place in the directory will be pointed at by pdir, the first
free place in text by ptext. Obviously the lists in the directory must have one same
length. Choosing some sensible lengths for the lists, we write:

```
'macro''pointer' max dir=50.
'list' lkey(1:max dir), lptr(1:max dir).
'pointer' pdir.
'macro''action' get key='2':=lkey('1'), put key=lkey('1'):='2',
                get ptr='2':=lptr('1'), put ptr=lptr('1'):='2'.
'macro''pointer' max text=2000.
'list' text(1:max text).
'macro''action' get text='2':=text('1'), put text=text('1'):='2'.
'pointer' ptext.
```

We must not forget to initialize pdir and ptext to 1 at the start of the program.

Since we intend to search the directory for a specific key a number of times and in
the end want to list all lines in order of increasing keys, the keys in the directory
had better be ordered. Rather than explicitly sorting them, we will take care that
the keys are kept ordered at any point in time. This will entail moving part of the
keys up or down the directory when inserting or deleting a line, but this overhead
is distributed over the editing process.
So much for the directory.

We must also decide how the entries in text will be stored. We will have to indicate
the end of such an entry in some fashion. We could store, at the beginning of each

entry, its length. We do not know that length until we have stored the whole entry, so we would have to leave a place open at the beginning of the entry for storing the length. (It would not be advisable to extend the directory with a third list containing lengths of entries, because when inserting or deleting lines this information would also have to be moved.)

Alternatively, we could add to each character a bit indicating whether it was the last one of the entry - but this might entail too high an overhead in space.

A third alternative is to store a special character at the end of the entry. The natural choice for such a terminating character here seems to be the end-of-line character, which is used for that same purpose during input. In outputting an entry we can then output also this terminating character saving an explicit newline statement. We will prefer it over the first two alternatives, especially because it saves us the trouble of counting.

We will now design the low-level primitives for entering entries into text. The characters of the entry will become available in one long burst. In order to simplify the initial version of the editor, we will not now tackle the problems of packing more than one character into a word, but will at first store one character per text word. We will choose the text entering actions such that we can, in adding character packing later on, keep the same interface. We choose stack text as the lowest action, stacking its parameter under control of ptext, we choose add to text to add one more character to the current text entry and finish text to complete the current entry.

> 'action' add to text, finish text, stack text.
> add to text+x:
>   stack text+x.
> finish text:
>   add to text+end of line char.
> stack text+x:
>   lseq+ptext+maxtext, put text+ptext+x, incr+ptext;
>   text overflow, exit.

We make a note that we will have to define the error reaction text overflow giving e.g. some suitable message.

Another question to be solved is what to do when deleting an entry, either by an explicit deletion command or by redefining the entry belonging to some given key. In redefining we could overwrite the previous entry provided the new entry was of the same length as the old entry (or at any rate not longer), but we do not know the length of an entry until we have read it completely. We could of course reserve as much space for each entry as its maximal length, but that would be unsatisfactory for various reasons. It would entail a probably large waste of space; and if the input is from paper tape then there is no hard maximum to the length. We take the simple way out: we will not try to reuse the space in text freed because we suppose

that the deletion of an entry is a rather infrequent action. If this retention strategy turns out to be a real bother in practice, we will let text overflow perform a
garbage collection and continue if space was salvaged.

3.4 ˙Input and output primitives

Now we will choose a reading strategy. A one character buffer should suffice, because
we do not envisage any back-up-over the input stream.

   'pointer' char.

In order to have a record of the editing done, we will output each character immediately upon its consumption before reading the next one:

   'action' nextchar.

   nextchar: prsym+char, resym+char.

We will need a predicate asking for specific characters, and another one asking for
a digit; the latter one should also provide the value of the digit.

    is+x: equal+char+x, nextchar.

    digit+d: was digit+char, conv char to dig+char+d, nextchar.

The macro was digit should test whether the value of its parameter is the code of
some digit, and the macro action conv char to dig should convert the code of a digit
into the numeric value of that digit:

    'macro''flag' was digit=('1' ≥digit zero char)

       ' and '('1' ≤digit nine char).

    'macro''action' conv char to dig='2':='1'-digit zero char,

       conv dig to char='2':='1'+digit zero char.

We must not forget to read one character into the buffer at the start of the program!
Finally, we define a predicate to read a number and two actions to skip spaces and to
skip to the end of a line:

    is number+x-d:

     skip spaces, is digit+x,

      rst: (is digit+d, append digit+x+d,:rst;).

    'macro''action' append digit='1':=10✳'1'+'2'.

    skip spaces:

     skp: is+space char,:skp;

    skip to next line:

     skp: is+end of line char;

      nextchar,:skp.

On output we will need, apart from prsym to print one character, an action to output
one number and an action to give a new line. We will define an auxiliary action
prdig to output one digit.

```
    'action' out number, prdig, new line.
out number+x-head-d:
        less+x+10, prdig+x;
        remove digit+x+head+d, out number+head, prdig+d.
    'macro''action' remove digit='2':='1'' div '10; '3':='1'' rem '10.
    prdig+x-c:
        conv dig to char+x+c, prsym+c.
    new line: prsym+end of line char.
```

Higher level input and output will be developed later on as needed.

3.5 The works

We have laid a sufficient foundation, and are by now rather fed up with working
bottom-up, so it is time to construct the bold lines of our design.
We want to construct a simple editor. It must, after some as yet unspecified preparation, proceed to consume an input sequence consisting of fresh lines and deletion
commands, terminated by a list command. At the beginning of a line we are willing to
skip any number of blanks. Furthermore we are willing to overlook blank lines without
protest. If the input line is not a correct command, we issue a message.

```
        simple editor:
            preparation,
          rst: skip spaces,
                (fresh line,:rst;
                 deletion command,:rst;
                 list command;
                 is+end of line char,:rst;
                 incorrect line, skip to next line,:rst).
```

A fresh line starts with a number (the key of the line) followed by an equals symbol,
possibly preceded by some number of spaces, followed by the entry for that key. Now
we must distinguish two possibilities: either this key was already present in the
directory, in which case we discard the previous entry by overwriting the ptr belonging to the key; or it was not yet there, in which case we will have to make room for
it in the directory. While searching for a key in the directory we will, as a side
effect, compute the offset in the directory of the slot where the key has been or is
to be inserted:

<u>case a</u>   key = 111

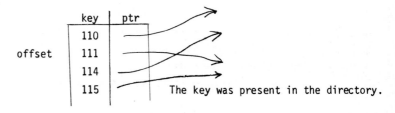

The key was present in the directory.

case b   key = 112

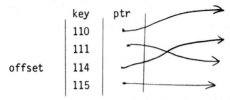

key	ptr
110	
111	
offset 114	
115	

The key was not present in the directory. The directory entries for keys $\geq$ 114 must be moved up by one position. The offset is that of the key 114, which is where 112 should come instead.

case c   key = 120

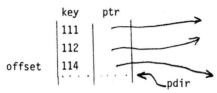

key	ptr
111	
112	
offset 114	

The key was not present in the directory. This is just a special form of case b and should be handled by the same mechanism.

We program this as follows:

```
fresh line→key→offset:
    is number→key, obtain offset→key→offset, rest of line→offset.
obtain offset→key→offset:
    already there→key→offset;
    shift up from→offset, put key→offset→key.
```

In order to find whether a key was already there we will search the directory linearly, until we either find the key, or give up because it is absent.

```
already there→key→offset-there:
    make→offset+1,
      srch:less→offset→pdir, get key→offset→there,
            (equal→there→key;
              less→there→key, incr→offset,:srch).
```

We will now define shift up from, making sure that the directory does not overflow.

```
shift up from→p-q:
    less→pdir→max dir, make→q→pdir,
      shft: (equal→p→q, incr→pdir;
              decr→q, copy up→q,:shft);
    dir overflow, exit.
  'macro''action' copy up=
    lkey ('1'+1):=lkey('1'); lptr('1'+1):=lptr('1').
```

The action directory overflow should provide some sensible reaction when the directory becomes too small. Notice that case c is handled correctly (nothing is shifted). While we are at it, we may likewise define the action shift down to for use by the deletion command:

            shift down to+p-q:
                make+q+p,
                    shft: (equal+pdir+q, decr+pdir;
                                incr+q, copy down+q,:shft).
            'macro''action' copy down=
            lkey('1'-1):=lkey('1'); lptr('1'-1):=lptr('1').

Now we define what to do with the rest of the line. We check the presence of the equals sign after the number. We then cause the ptr of the key to point to the first free place in text and proceed to read characters until we reach the end of line, adding each of them into the text as we go along.

            rest of line+offset:
                check equals sign, put ptr+offset+ptext,
                    rst: add to text+char,
                                (is+end of line char, finish text;
                                nextchar,:rst).

In checking for the equals sign we are willing to skip any number of blanks preceding it. If the equals sign is missing we will signal an error by the action equals sign missing, but continue editing

            check equals sign:
                skip spaces,
                    (is+equals char;
                    equals sign missing).

A deletion command consists of a letter d followed by a number, the key of the line to be deleted. If this key is present in the directory then the corresponding directory entry is obliterated by shifting the upper part of the directory down one place; if it is not present, an error is reported by the action impossible to delete.

            'action' delete.
            deletion command-key:
                    is+letter d char,
                        (is number+key, delete+key, skip to next line;
                        missing number, skip to next line).
            delete+key-offset:
                already there+key+offset, shift down to+offset;
                impossible to delete.

That leaves us with the list command.

      'action' list entry, list text.

      list command-p:

            is+letter l char, make+p+1, newline,

          lst: (equal+p+pdir, skip to next line;

                list entry+p, incr+p,:lst).

      list entry+offset-key-ptr:

          get key+offset+key, out number+key,

          prsym+equals char,

          get ptr+offset+ptr, list text+ptr.

      list text+p-c:

      lst: get text+p+c, prsym+c,

          (equal+c+end of line char;

          incr+p,:lst).

Finally, we program preparation combining various initializations:

      preparation:

          make+ptext+1, make+pdir+1, resym+char.

This completes the design of the editor, apart from some reordering to combine related pieces of program into one section headed by a comment and supplying the necessary 'action' specifications.

3.6 Packing more characters into a word

It is rather a waste of storage not to pack the characters in the text array: practically all computers can store considerably more than one character per word. Of course, for debugging purposes packing one character into a word is convenient, but after the editor is running correctly we would like to tune it up so that it gets some semblance of usefulness.

We will define new versions of the two actions add to text, which packs one more character into text, and finish text, which serves to round off the packing process. At every point in time, ptext will point to the first free place in text and we will have a word under construction, word containing charcount characters. Whenever charcount threatens to exceed the machine-dependent number of chars per word we stack the word into text and start constructing the next word.

      'action' add to text, finish text.

      'macro''pointer' chars per word=4, nix=1.

      'macro''action' pack onto='1':=256*'1'+'2',

                  unpack from='2':='1'' div '16777216;

                      '1':=256*('1'' rem '16777216).

      'pointer' word, charcount.

```
        add to text+x:
                equal+charcount+chars per word, stack text+word,
                        make+word+x, make+charcount+1;
                pack onto+word+x, incr+charcount.
        finish text:
            fill: equal+charcount+chars per word, stack text+word,
                    make+word+0, make+charcount+0;
                pack onto+word+nix, incr+charcount,:fill.
```

The action pack onto shifts the first parameter 8 bits to the left and then adds the second. Of course, the ALGOL W version given here works correctly only if overflow into the sign bit cannot occur or is ignored, which we happen to be sure of because our code is a 7-bit-code. The reason we still choose to partition the (/360) 32 bit word into groups of 8 bits is that we did not want to shock IBM by having 7-bit bytes. Notice that the last word must, if necessary, be padded with nix.

We now have to redefine the preparation in order to initialize the word and charcount administration:

```
        preparation:
                make+ptext+1, make+pdir+1, resym+char,
                make+word+0, make+charcount+0.
```

Finally, we have to rewrite list text to reflect the new situation:

```
        'action' list text, get from text.
        list text+p-q-x:
                make+q+p, make+charcount+0,
                1st: get from text+q+x, prsym+x,
                        (equal+x+end of line char;
                            :1st).
        get from text+q+x:
                equal+charcount+0, get text+q+word, make+charcount+
                    chars per word,
                    incr+q, get from text+q+x;
                unpack from+word+x, decr+charcount.
```

Another candidate for tuning is the predicate already there which can be speeded up substantially by performing binary search instead of linear search. This is left as an exercise to the reader. This one example of tuning should show the technique of improving the algorithm while retaining the interface.

3.7 Various target languages

This editor , including the packing of text, was written by the author, using ALGOL W as a target language, in one sunday morning and keyed into the terminal and debugged in two evening sessions. Debugging took 3 runs, in which the following errors were removed:

1) Because ALGOL W uses it as a reserved identifier, the identifier is had to be changed into char is.
2) The Modulo-operator in ALGOL W is written rem, not mod as I thought in my innocence.
3) The initialization of ptext and pdir was overlooked.
4) The analogy between shift up and shift down had caused a programming mistake, which had to be caught by "proving" that the editor could not do what it did.

This is certainly not a record of brilliant programming, but, considering the rather sloppy programming style of the author, it shows that CDL is decidedly helpful in avoiding errors.

Afterwards, the editor was translated by one student to /360 Assembly language.

In translating to /360 Assembler, the bulk of the work was in rewriting the macros. Of the 27 macros, many could either be taken over from another program or were very similar to one another, so that essentially 8 macros had to be invented. With some perusal of IBM manuals, the writing of the macros took him a good half hour.

The time spent debugging the ensemble was 8 hours, during which the following errors were repaired:

1) 4 clerical errors in macros, of which 3 were found statically and one dynamically.
2) One of the macros invoked itself recursively, because of identity of a string to be output with the macro name.
3) One 'macro''flag' set its condition wrongly. With the 2 condition bits of the /360, it is difficult to model a one-bit C-register.
4) A /360-System macro had an unforeseen side effect on a register.
5) An error was found in the CDL program, viz. the fact that a last word of an entry has to be padded out until it contains max nmb chars characters. Because in the ALGOL W version, zero was the code of a nonprinting character, this was only discovered in the assembler version. A good example of the pitfalls in writing machine-independent programs - mea culpa.

A comparison between the programs obtained in this fashion is very difficult: comparison of speed is rather useless because of the character of the editor, but other experience shows that the /360 Assembler version of CDL programs is at least a factor 3 faster than the ALGOL W version. In this comparison it should be noted that the ALGOL W compiler produces the fastest code for CDL among all high-level language compilers available on our 360.

A comparison of the length of the code generated by the assembler version (2924 bytes = 736 words) with that generated by the ALGOL W compiler is not given because we could not with certainty deduce that length from a listing of entry points, but we suspect the ALGOL W object code is actually shorter.

A cross compilation to the DEC PDP 10 was not completed in time for these lecture notes.

A tentative conclusion from these experiences is that first writing in CDL and debugging a high-level version and only then constructing an assembler version is highly preferable over writing in assembly language direct as far as the manpower necessary is concerned. Conclusions about efficiency in time and space can not be drawn at this point.

Acknowledgement
The /360 Assembler version was prepared by one student, Jost Müller, at his own initiative and in his own spare time.

4 B 4. Example 2: Symbol table administration

This example and the one in Section 4 B 5 are connected: we will attempt to treat a large chunk out of a realistic compiler, encompassing all of the lexical scan and some parsing and treatment of static semantics.

The presentation will not be topdown, as in the first example, but bottom up layer-wise, knowing by hindsight (having written the whole compiler) what each layer should contain.
This is of course not exactly the way this program originated, because that was a process of yoyo programming, but it allows the consecutive display of segments of the compiler as a sequence of stills, which can each be understood in full.

The language, for which this example provides the lexical analysis, is assumed to have the outward appearance and the complexity of ALGOL 68.
Seen from the viewpoint of lexical analysis, the compiler reads a text with following syntax:

>   text:
>   end of file symbol;
>   comment, text;
>   item, text.
>   comment:
>   comment symbol,
>   rest comment: (comment symbol;
>   character,:rest comment).

A text consists of items, with comments interspersed which are discarded.

>   item:
>   layout, item;
>   tag;
>   bold symbol;
>   denoter;
>   special symbol.
>   layout:
>   space character, (layout;);
>   nlcr character, (layout;).

An item is, apart from layout which is disregarded, of one of four kinds of symbols.

>   tag: letter,
>   rest tag: (letgit,:rest tag;).
>   bold symbol: bold letter,
>   rest bold: (bold letter,:rest bold;).

```
special symbol:
    semicolon character; comma character;
    open character,(slash character; );
    slash character,(close character; ) .
denoter: digit,
    restden:(layout, restden;
              digit,:restden; ).
```

The special symbols include the two compounded symbols (/ and /) . For bold letter
we will use the capital letters, instead of the more usual underlined or enclosed
letters.
The next lower level consists of the characters, including the letters, letgits
(= letter or digit) and bold letters, which we will not enumerate.

It is the purpose of the lexical analysis to split the text up into items, discarding
comments and layout, and translate each item into a key, a small integral number
with the property that equal items get equal keys, unequal items get unequal keys,
and the key allows us to output that item again.
We will now present that part of the compiler which performs this task, starting with
the details, until we have laid the foundation for the parsing and table handling in
the next example. It is divided into four parts,
- the environment
- storing representations
- output, and
- input
of which the last section is the longest.

Because of the size of the compiler, we will keep the number of explanatory remarks
to the minimum, hoping its text speaks for itself.

4.1 The environment

In this section we will treat the interface with the machine, as well as the encoding
of characters and the usual macros for arithmetic and testing.

4.1.1. Interface with the machine

(**********INTERFACE WITH THE MACHINE)

'EXTERNAL''ACTION' RESYM,PRSYM,EXIT.

We will read characterwise from one file, and print characterwise on another. If it
becomes necessary to abort the program, exit is called.

4.1.2 Character encoding

```
( *********CHARACTER ENCODING )

'MACRO''POINTER'
     DIGIT 0 CHAR = 68,
     CLOSE CHAR   = 89,
     COMMA CHAR   = 94,
     MINUS CHAR   = 92,
     OPEN  CHAR   = 82,
     SEMICOL CHAR = 90,
     SPACE CHAR   = 78,
     SLASH CHAR   = 93,
     NIX          = 1,
     NLCR CHAR    = 10,
     EOF CHAR     = 5.

'MACRO''FLAG'
     IS LETTER =('1'>=16)'"AND"'('1'<=41),
     IS BOLD LETTER =('1'>=42)'"AND"'('1'<=67),
     IS DIGIT =('1'>=68)'"AND"'('1'<=77),
     IS LETGIT =('1'>=16)'"AND"'('1'<=41)
        '"OR"'('1'>=68)'"AND"'('1'<=77).
```

It is assumed that the digits 0 to 9 have consecutive increasing codes, as have the letters a to z and the bold letters A to Z. The nix is used to pad out words containing padded-out characters, and is nonprinting.

4.1.3 The basic macros

```
( *********BASIC MACROS )

'MACRO''ACTION'
     MAKE       = '1':='2',
     INCR       = '1':='1'+1,
     INVERT     = '1':=-'1',
     ADD        = '3':='2'+'1',
     ADD BYTE = '1':='1'*256+'2',
     OBTAIN BYTE = '2':='1''"/"'16777216;'1':=('1''"MOD"'16777216)*256,
     DIVREM10 = '2':='1''"/"'10; '3':='1''"MOD"'10,
     SET        = '1':=1,
     RESET      = '1':=0.

'MACRO''FLAG'
     EQUAL      ='1'='2',
     LESS       ='1'<'2',
     LSEQ       ='1'<='2',
     MARKED     ='1'<0,
     HOLDS      ='1'=1,
     FALSE      ='"FALSE"'.
```

The complementary macros add byte and obtain byte are used in packing characters into a word. To use a pointer as a flag, the macros set and reset are provided, as well as holds to test such a flag.

4.2 Storing representation

In order to retain representations of symbols for later use we build up one table
containing the representation of each symbol. Each entry into this repr table consists of a static and a dynamic part.

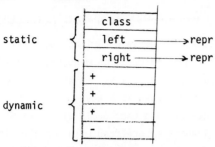

The static part consists of three elements, the class of the symbol and two pointers
left and right which are used to connect repr entries into a binary tree for fast
searching.

The dynamic part consists of some number of words, at least one, all but the last of
which are positive, the last being marked by a negative sign. The dynamic part contains the individual characters of the symbol, packed some number to a word, e.g.:

class
left
right
+a m s t
+e r d a
−m ⊠ ⊠ ⊠

where ⊠ stands for the padding character nix.

4.2.1 The repr table

(**********REPR-TABLE)

```
'MACRO''POINTER'
      MIN REPR=100000, FIX PART OF REPR ENTRY=3,
      FIRST REPR=100000+3+1,MAX REPR=100000+20000.

'POINTER'
     PREPR.

'LIST'
      REPR (MIN REPR:MAX REPR).

'MACRO''ACTION'
      GET CLASS = '2':=REPR(/'1'-3/)   , PUT CLASS = REPR(/'1'-3/):='2',
      GET LEFT  = '2':=REPR(/'1'-2/)   , PUT LEFT  = REPR(/'1'-2/):='2',
      GET RIGHT = '2':=REPR(/'1'-1/)   , PUT RIGHT = REPR(/'1'-1/):='2',
      GET REPR  = '2':=REPR(/'1'  /)   , PUT REPR  = REPR(/'1'  /):='2'.
```

```
'MACRO''FLAG'
    IS REPR = ('1'>=MIN REPR)'"AND"'('1'<=PREPR).

'ACTION' STACK REPR.

STACK REPR+X:
      PUT REPR+PREPR+X,INCR+PREPR,
        (LESS+PREPR+MAX REPR;
         ABORT+MSG OVERFLOW+MSG OF+MSG REPR+MSG TABLE+PREPR).
```

The macro pointer first repr points at the dynamic part of the first entry, and its
value will be the key of the first symbol entered. In general, we will use the index
of the first word of the dynamic part of a symbol as its key. The test is repr serves
to determine whether the value of some integer is a key.

The action abort outputs its 5 parameters and then calls exit - we will define it
later. We shall take care that an identifier prefixed with msg identifies a pointer,
whose value is a key to a symbol whose representation is suggested by the identifier;
e.g., outputting msg overflow will cause the text overflow to be printed, etc.

4.2.2 Building a repr table element

```
( *********BUILDING A REPR TABLE ELEMENT)

'ACTION'
    INIT REPR ENTRY,ADD TO REPR ENTRY,CLOSE REPR ENTRY.

'POINTER'
      WORD,BYTECOUNT.

'MACRO''POINTER'
      BYTES PER WORD=4.

INIT REPR ENTRY:
      ADD+PREPR+FIX PART OF REPR ENTRY+PREPR,
        (LSEQ+PREPR+MAX REPR,
           PUT CLASS+PREPR+0,PUT LEFT+PREPR+0,PUT RIGHT+PREPR+0;
         ABORT+MSG OVERFLOW+MSG OF+MSG REPR+MSG TABLE+PREPR).

ADD TO REPR ENTRY+BYTE:
      EQUAL+BYTE COUNT+BYTES PER WORD,STACK REPR+WORD,
        MAKE+WORD+BYTE,MAKE+BYTE COUNT+1;
      ADDBYTE+WORD+BYTE,INCR+BYTECOUNT.

CLOSE REPR ENTRY:
REP:  (EQUAL+BYTECOUNT+BYTES PER WORD,
          INVERT+WORD,STACK REPR+WORD,MAKE+WORD+0,MAKE+BYTECOUNT+0;
       ADD BYTE+WORD+NIX,INCR+BYTECOUNT,:REP).
```

In this section we find the machinery for packing characters into a word. The number
of bytes per word, and the packing operators add byte, must be chosen in such a way
that the sign bit of each word is left free for marking purposes. Alternatively, a
special list of marking bits can be added. The three actions init repr entry,
add to repr entry and close repr entry control the building of a table element on
top of the repr table.

4.2.3 Entering an element into the repr table

```
( **********ENTERING AN ELEMENT INTO REPR TABLE)

'ACTION' ENTER REPR.

ENTER REPR+IT-OLDENTRY:
      CLOSE REPR ENTRY,
         (IS IN REPR+IT+OLD ENTRY,
            MAKE+P REPR+IT,MAKE+IT+OLD ENTRY;
          INIT REPR ENTRY).

'MACRO''FLAG'
      LIES TO THE LEFT = ABS('1')<ABS('2').

IS IN REPR+IT+RESULT ENTRY-NEW ENTRY-X1-X2-W1-W2:
      LESS+FIRST REPR+IT,MAKE+RESULT ENTRY+FIRST REPR,
NEXT ENTRY:
      (MAKE+X1+IT,MAKE+X2+RESULT ENTRY,
NEXT WORD:  (GET REPR+X1+W1,GET REPR+X2+W2,
            (LIES TO THE LEFT+W1+W2,GET LEFT+RESULT ENTRY+NEW ENTRY,
              (EQUAL+NEW ENTRY+0,
                 PUT LEFT+RESULT ENTRY+IT,(FALSE);
               MAKE+RESULT ENTRY+NEW ENTRY,:NEXT ENTRY);
             EQUAL+W1+W2,
               (MARKED+W1;
                INCR+X1,INCR+X2,:NEXT WORD);
             GET RIGHT+RESULT ENTRY+NEW ENTRY,
               (EQUAL+NEW ENTRY+0,
                  PUT RIGHT+RESULT ENTRY+IT,(FALSE);
                MAKE+RESULT ENTRY+NEW ENTRY,:NEXT ENTRY)))).

IS SAME SYMBOL+P+Q-X-Y-WX-WY:
     MAKE+X+P,MAKE+Y+Q,
REP:  (GET REPR+X+WX,GET REPR+Y+WY,
         EQUAL+WX+WY,
         (MARKED+WX;
          INCR+X,INCR+Y,:REP)).
```

The reading strategy is such that the representation of each symbol is first stacked
on top of the repr table as its characters are read, under the assumption that it is
different from all previous symbols; then in enter repr a check is made whether this
symbol was already present in the repr table. If it was not, then the new symbol is
linked into the binary tree, but if it was, the candidate entry is deleted. The key
obtained is that of of the old entry equal to the symbol, if such an entry was present, and otherwise that of the new entry.

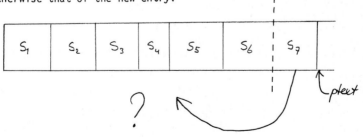

The repr table is kept as a binary tree in order to facilitate searching and insertion. Each entry contains a pointer left to all entries lexicographically preceding it (zero if there are none), and a pointer right to all those lexicographically following it, if any. The key of the root of the tree is the value of the pointer first repr.

As an example, the binary tree for the symbols *DD, AD, AE, EE, CD, DE, EG* can be depicted as

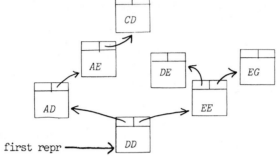

Notice that the structure of the tree obtained depends heavily on the order in which the symbols arrive.

The lexical ordering is defined using the test to the left which, disregarding the sign bit used for marking, compares the numerical value of words packed full of characters. The assumption underlying this method is that the leftmost character has been packed into the most significant part of the word, and that the ordering of character codes is an acceptable ordering for the characters.

The predicate is same symbol tests for equality of repr entries without attempting to link the topmost entry into the tree. It is used in skipping comments.

4.3 Output

```
( *********OUTPUT )

'ACTION'
    OUT TEXT,OUT M WORD,NEWLINE,LINE TAB,OUTINT,OUTINT1.

'MACRO''POINTER' EMPTY = 100000.

OUT TEXT+X-PTR-W:
    EQUAL+X+EMPTY;
    IS REPR+X,PRSYM+SPACE CHAR,MAKE+PTR+X,
NWD: GET REPR+PTR+W,
        (MARKED+W,INVERT+W,OUT M WORD+W;
        OUT M WORD+W,INCR+PTR,:NWD);
    ERROR+MSG OUTPUT ERROR+MSG INCORRECT PREPR+X+EMPTY+EMPTY.

OUT M WORD+W-BYN-C:
    MAKE+BYN+1,
REP:   OBTAIN BYTE+W+C,PRSYM+C,
        (LESS+BYN+BYTES PER WORD, INCR+BYN,:REP; ).
```

```
OUTINT+X:
      LESS+X+0,PRSYM+MINUS CHAR,INVERT+X,OUTINT1+X;
      EQUAL+X+0,PRSYM+DIGIT 0 CHAR;
      OUTINT1+X.

OUTINT1+X-Q-R:
      EQUAL+X+0;
      DIVREM10+X+Q+R,OUTINT1+Q,ADD+R+DIGIT 0 CHAR+R,PRSYM+R.

NEWLINE:
      PRSYM+NLCR CHAR.

LINE TAB:
      PRSYM+NLCR CHAR,PRSYM+NLCR CHAR,PRSYM+NLCR CHAR.
```

The action out text serves to output the symbol with a given key, outint prints a
number, newline and tabline provide for vertical layout.

4.4 Input

The following part constitutes the lexical scan proper and consists of a number of
layers. It is not suggested that the reader of these notes should plod through each
layer in order, but he may skim through them and look at details only when necessary.

4.4.1 A one character stock

(*********INPUT)

(*********A ONE CHARACTER STOCK)

```
'POINTER'
      CHAR STOCK.

'POINTER'
      CHAR IN STOCK.

'ACTION'
      REMEMBER.

REMEMBER+C:
      HOLDS+CHAR IN STOCK,
         ABORT+MSG OVERFLOW+MSG OF+MSG CHAR+MSG STOCK+EMPTY;
      MAKE+CHAR STOCK+CHAR,MAKE+CHAR+C,SET+CHAR IN STOCK.
```

For reading composed symbols like (/ it is useful to have some look-ahead facility.
The strategy used here is to have a stock for one character which is normally empty.
Initially, char in stock does not hold. If we have read one character too far (e.g.,
in order to inspect the character following an opening bracket), we remember this
character by putting it into the stock and causing char in stock to hold.

4.4.2 Reading a single character

(*********READING A SINGLE CHARACTER)

'POINTER'
    CHAR,LINE NUMBER.

'POINTER'
     SOURCE DISPLAY WANTED.

'ACTION'
    NEXT CHAR.

NEXT CHAR-C:
     HOLDS+CHAR IN STOCK,MAKE+CHAR+CHAR STOCK,RESET+CHAR IN STOCK;
     MAKE+C+CHAR,RESYM+CHAR,
       (HOLDS+SOURCE DISPLAY WANTED,
        (EQUAL+C+NLCRCHAR,NEWLINE,INCR+LINE NUMBER,
         OUT INT+LINE NUMBER;
        PRSYM+C);).

We read characters one at a time by resym, keeping track of the line number of input,
and displaying the source text as we are reading along if source display wanted holds.

4.4.3 Recognizing characters

(*********RECOGNIZING CHARACTERS)

'ACTION'
    SCAN ANY CHAR, SKIP LAYOUT,SKIP ILLEGAL CHAR.

SCAN ANY CHAR:
    ADD TO REPR ENTRY+CHAR,NEXT CHAR.

LETTER: IS LETTER+CHAR,SCAN ANY CHAR.

BOLD LETTER: IS BOLD LETTER+CHAR,SCAN ANY CHAR.

DIGIT: IS DIGIT+CHAR,SCAN ANY CHAR.

LETGIT: IS LETGIT+CHAR,SCAN ANY CHAR.

SKIP ILLEGAL CHAR:
    NEWLINE,PRSYM+CHAR,
    ERROR+MSG ILLEGAL+MSG CHAR+MSG IN THIS POSITION+MSG CODE+CHAR,NEXT CHAR.

END OF FILE:
     EQUAL+CHAR+EOF CHAR.

SKIP LAYOUT:
N CHAR: EQUAL+CHAR+SPACE CHAR,NEXT CHAR,:N CHAR;
        EQUAL+CHAR+NLCR CHAR,NEXT CHAR,:N CHAR; .

In this section the primitives are introduced for recognizing the input characters.
Notice that scan any char adds the representation of the character just recognized
to the repr table.

4.4.4 Recognizing a symbol

(**********RECOGNIZE A SYMBOL)

```
TAG:
    LETTER,
       N CHAR:(SKIP LAYOUT,(LETGIT,:NCHAR; )).

BOLD SYMBOL:
    BOLD LETTER,
    N CHAR:(BOLD LETTER,:N CHAR; ).

SPECIAL SYMBOL:
       EQUAL+CHAR+SEMICOL CHAR,ADD TO REPR ENTRY+SEMICOL CHAR,NEXT CHAR;
       EQUAL+CHAR+COMMA CHAR,ADD TO REPR ENTRY+COMMA CHAR,NEXT CHAR;
       EQUAL+CHAR+OPEN CHAR,ADD TO REPR ENTRY+OPEN CHAR,NEXT CHAR,
          (EQUAL+CHAR+SLASH CHAR,ADD TO REPR ENTRY+SLASH CHAR,NEXT CHAR; );
       EQUAL+CHAR+SLASH CHAR,NEXT CHAR,
          (EQUAL+CHAR+CLOSE CHAR,NEXT CHAR,
             ADD TO REPR ENTRY+SLASH CHAR,ADD TO REPR ENTRY+CLOSE CHAR;
          REMEMBER+SLASH CHAR);
       EQUAL+CHAR+CLOSE CHAR,ADD TO REPR ENTRY+CLOSE CHAR,NEXT CHAR.

DENOTER:
       DIGIT,
N CHAR: (SKIP LAYOUT,(DIGIT,:N CHAR; )).

 'ACTION'
    RECOGNIZE.

RECOGNIZE+IT:
       SKIP LAYOUT,MAKE+IT+PREPR,
N CHAR: (TAG,PUT CLASS+IT+X TAG,ENTER REPR+IT;
          BOLD SYMBOL,ENTER REPR+IT;
          DENOTER,PUT CLASS+IT+X DENOTER,ENTER REPR+IT;
          SPECIAL SYMBOL,ENTER REPR+IT;
          END OF FILE,MAKE+IT+EOF SYMBOL;
          SKIP ILLEGAL CHAR,:N CHAR).
```

Four kinds of symbols are distinguished. Notice the liberal attitude towards the presence of layout within a tag or denoter. The action recognize attributes to each tag the class x tag and to each denoter the class x denoter. Other symbols do not obtain a class at this point, but obtain their class differently. This corresponds to the fact that, in an ALGOL 68-like language, one can define the class of newly introduced bold and specials symbols by a mode- or operator-declaration.

In an initialization not shown here, all delimiters (i.e., those bold an special symbols which belong to the kernel of the language) are given classes like x decl token for *struct*, etc. Upon reading a symbol with the same representation as some symbol already encountered before, the new symbol gets the same class as the old symbol (automatically, since no new entry is made).

4.4.5 Reading items

(********** READING ITEMS)

'ACTION' NEXT ITEM,BACKTRACK,SKIP COMMENT.

'POINTER' ITEM,CLASS,ITEM STOCK,CLASS STOCK,ITEM IN STOCK.

ITEM WAS+IT: EQUAL+ITEM+IT,NEXT ITEM.

CLASS IS+IT: EQUAL+CLASS+IT.

```
NEXT ITEM:
      EQUAL+ITEM+EOF SYMBOL,
        ABORT+MSG EOF+MSG BEFORE+MSG LOGICALEND+MSG OF+MSG PROGRAM;
      HOLDS+ITEM IN STOCK,
        MAKE+ITEM+ITEM STOCK,MAKE+CLASS+CLASS STOCK,RESET+ITEM IN STOCK;
REP:  RECOGNIZE+ITEM,
        (EQUAL+ITEM+BEGIN COMMENT SYMBOL,SKIP COMMENT,:REP;
         GET CLASS+ITEM+CLASS).

BACKTRACK+IT:
      HOLDS+ITEM IN STOCK,
        ABORT+MSG OVERFLOW+MSG OF+MSG ITEM+MSG STOCK+EMPTY;
      MAKE+ITEM STOCK+ITEM,MAKE+CLASS STOCK+CLASS,SET+ITEM IN STOCK,
        MAKE+ITEM+IT,GET CLASS+IT+CLASS.

SKIPCOMMENT-OLD PREPR:
REP: (MAKE+OLD PREPR+PREPR,
      (BOLD SYMBOL,MAKE+PREPR+OLD PREPR,
       (IS SAME SYMBOL+PREPR+END COMMENT SYMBOL;:REP);
       MESSAGE,MAKE+PREPR+OLD PREPR,
       (IS SAME SYMBOL+PREPR+EOF SYMBOL,
           ABORT+MSG EOF+MSG IN+MSG COMMENT+EMPTY+EMPTY;:REP);
       NEXT CHAR,:REP)).
```

The pointers item and class hold at each moment the current item and its class. There is a one-item stock allowing to backtrack by one item if such is found necessary. The apotheosis of all these definitions lies in the action next item and the predicates item was and class is. The test item was checks whether the current item is equal to a given item, and if true as a side effect inputs the next item. The test class is checks whether the current item is of a given class, but has no such side effect.

4.5 The work table

The work table is used as a stack to hold information gleaned from the program, of two kinds:

        a) block structure
        b) defining occurrences of identifiers

```
( **********WORK TABLE )

'MACRO''POINTER'
     MIN WORK=200001, MAX WORK=200001+9999.

'POINTER'
     PWORK.

'LIST'
     WORK (MIN WORK:MAX WORK).

'MACRO''FLAG'
     IS WORK=MIN WORK<='1'''"AND"'''1'<=PWORK.
```

The test is work serves to find out whether some integer can be a pointer into the
work table.

4.5.1 The block administration

```
( **********BLOCK ADMINISTRATION )

'MACRO''POINTER'
     BLOCK TABLE ENTRY LENGTH=1.

'POINTER'
     CURR BNMB.

'MACRO''ACTION'
GET PREDEC ='2':=WORK(/'1'/), PUT PREDEC =WORK(/'1'/):='2'.

'ACTION'
     UP BLOCK,DOWN BLOCK.

UP BLOCK-P:
     MAKE+P+PWORK,ADD+PWORK+BLOCK TABLE ENTRY LENGTH+PWORK,
        (LSEQ+PWORK+MAX WORK,
           PUT PREDEC+P+CURR BNMB,MAKE+CURR BNMB+P;
        ABORT+MSG WORK+MSG TABLE+MSG OVERFLOW+EMPTY+EMPTY).

DOWN BLOCK:
     GET PREDEC+CURR BNMB+CURR BNMB.
```

In order to uniquely characterize each block with an integral number, its block
number, we have a pointer curr bnmb to which we assign, at the beginning of a block,
the current value of the pointer pwork which points at the lowest free word in work.
Since we at the same time stack the blocknumber of the directly surrounding block
into the work table, we achieve two goals
   1) it is assured that different blocks get different block numbers
   2) at the end of a block we can very easily restore the block number to be that
      of the directly surrounding block.

4.5.2 Symbol table

(**********SYMBOL TABLE)

```
'MACRO''POINTER'
        SYMBOL TABLE ENTRY LENGTH=3.

'MACRO''ACTION'
GET BNMB ='2':=WORK(/'1'  /), PUT BNMB=WORK(/'1'  /):='2',
GET MODE ='2':=WORK(/'1'+1/), PUT MODE=WORK(/'1'+1/):='2',
GET LINK ='2':=WORK(/'1'+2/), PUT LINK=WORK(/'1'+2/):='2'.
```

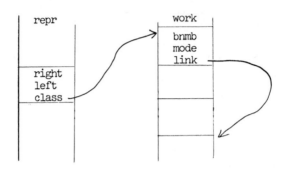

The work table contains also chains of defining occurrences, in the following fashion:
As long as an identifier has had no defining occurrence, its class is x tag ; if it
has some number of defining occurrences, these are chained together in a chain of
triples (bnmb, mode, link) in the work table, and the class of the identifier is a
pointer to that chain, e.g.:

```
'ACTION'
        DEFINE IDENTIFIER,ADD TO DEF CHAIN,APPLY IDENTIFIER.

DEFINE IDENTIFIER+IDF+MODE-P:
        MAKE+P+PWORK,ADD+PWORK+SYMBOL TABLE ENTRY LENGTH+PWORK,
        (LSEQ+PWORK+MAX WORK,
            PUT BNMB+P+CURR BNMB,PUT MODE+P+MODE,
            ADD TO DEF CHAIN+IDF+P;
        ABORT+MSG WORK+MSG TABLE+MSG OVERFLOW+EMPTY+EMPTY).

ADD TO DEF CHAIN+IDF+DEF-LINK-SUCC:
        GET CLASS+IDF+LINK,
            (IS REPR+LINK,PUT LINK+DEF+0,PUT CLASS+IDF+DEF;
            IS GOOD SUCCESSOR+LINK+IDF,
              PUT LINK+DEF+LINK,PUT CLASS+IDF+DEF;
            REP:
              (GET LINK+LINK+SUCC,
                  (EQUAL+SUCC+0,PUT LINK+DEF+SUCC,PUT LINK+LINK+DEF;
                  IS GOOD SUCCESSOR+LINK+IDF,
                      PUT LINK+DEF+SUCC,PUT LINK+LINK+DEF;
                  MAKE+LINK+SUCC,:REP))).

IS GOOD SUCCESSOR+LINK+IDF-NBNMB:
        GET BNMB+LINK+NBNMB,
            (LESS+NBNMB+CURR BNMB;
            EQUAL+NBNMB+CURR BNMB,
                ERROR+MSG IDENTIFIER+IDF+MSG DECLARED+MSG TWICE+EMPTY).
```

Great care is taken that the elements in such a chain are kept in order of decreasing blocknumber, which makes the converse process of finding, for an applied occurrence, the mode of the defining occurrence which it identifies, a whole lot easier.

```
APPLY IDENTIFIER+IDF+MODE-LINK-TRY BNMB-DEF BNMB:
        GET CLASS+IDF+LINK,
        (IS REPR+LINK,ERROR+MSG IDENTIFIER+IDF+MSG NOT+MSG DECLARED+EMPTY,
          MAKE+MODE+ERRONEOUS;
        MAKE+TRY BNMB+CURR BNMB,
NEXT DEF:(GET BNMB+LINK+DEF BNMB,
NEXT SURR:  (LESS+DEF BNMB+TRY BNMB,
                GET PREDEC+TRY BNMB+TRY BNMB,:NEXT SURR;
              EQUAL+DEF BNMB+TRY BNMB,GET MODE+LINK+MODE;
            GET LINK+LINK+LINK,
              (EQUAL+LINK+0,
                ERROR+MSG IDENTIFIER+IDF+MSG NOT+MSG DECLARED+EMPTY,
                MAKE+MODE+ERRONEOUS;
              :NEXT DEF)))).
```

4.6 Conclusion

We have laid the foundation for the next example, in the form of parsing predicates and some table administration, which is sufficient to handle languages of the intricacy of ALGOL 68.
In the next example we will try to put to work the algorithms defined until now, in particular the actions up block, down block and define identifier, as well as the predicates item was and class is.

4 B 5 Example 3: Treatment of declarations

In this example we build, on the basis laid in the previous example, a recognizer
for a language with some of the characteristics of ALGOL 68.
The example is intended to show the relationship between syntax and parser, metasyntax and table administrations, and also show within a small framework techniques
which are also vital to the construction of life-size compilers.

5.1 The language to be recognized

The language to be recognized consists essentially of identifier definitions (with
an ALGOL 68-like syntax) and identifier applications (of the most trivial form) embedded in a block-structure.
In three instalments of syntax and metasyntax we will give a very informal syntactic
definition of the language. The starting symbol of its grammar is closed clause.

5.1.1 Closed clauses

a) closed clause:

  begin symbol, serial clause, end symbol.

b) serial clause:

  identifier definition, semicolon symbol, serial clause;
  series.

c) series:

  unit, semicolon symbol, series;
  unit.

d) unit:

  closed clause;

  identifier application.

e) identifier definition:

  MODE declarer, MODE identifier.

f) identifier application:

  MODE identifier.

With the closed clause a blockstructure is associated in the usual fashion, with the
usual scope rules for identifiers. The appearance of MODE in identifier definition
and identifier application is there to remind us of the fact that a definition establishes the identifier with a given mode (viz. the mode of the declarer) and every
applied occurrence of an identifier must identify one defining occurrence and obtain
a mode from it.

Example:

>   *begin* *real* a; *bool* b;
>   a;   #*real identifier*#
>   *begin* *int* a;
>   a;   #*int identifier*#
>   b   #*bool identifier*#
>   *end*;
>   a   #*real identifier*#
>   *end*

5.1.2 Modes

A)   MODE::
         PRIMITIVE;
         reference to MODE;
         LONGS INTREAL;
         PROCEDURE;
         structured with FIELDS;
         ROWS of MODE;
         union of MODES mode.

C)   PRIMITIVE::
         INTREAL; bool; char; void.

D)   INTREAL::
         int; real.

E)   LONGS::
         long LONGS; long.

F)   PROCEDURE::
         procedure PARAMETY MODE.

G)   PARAMETY::
         with PARAMETERS; EMPTY.

H)   EMPTY::

I)   PARAMETERS::
         PARAMETER and PARAMETERS;
         PARAMETER.

J)   PARAMETER::
         MODE parameter.

K)   FIELDS::
         FIELD and FIELDS;
         FIELD.

L)   FIELD::
         MODE field TAG.

M)   ROWS::row ROWS; row.

N)   TAG::

    letter LETTER;

    TAG letter LETTER;

    TAG digit DIGIT.

O)   LETTER:: a;b; ... ; z.

P)   DIGIT:: 0;1; ... ; 9.

Q)   MODES::

    MODE and MODES; MODE.

We call each terminal production of the metanotion MODE a <u>mode</u>. Clearly, there are countably many modes, and we will have to construct some mechanism for storing modes.

The construction principle of the modes should speak for itself, as well as their interpretation. Otherwise, a full treatment of a similar system can be found in [van Wijngaarden 1974].

5.1.3 Declarers

a) MODE declarer: MODE declarator.

    At this point in syntax, mode indicants can be added.

b) PRIMITIVE declarator:

    PRIMITIVE symbol.

    Example: *real* is a real declarator.

    For each primitive mode, there is one symbol, such as the real symbol with re-presentation *real*, etc.

c) long INTREAL declarator:

    long symbol, INTREAL declarator.

d) long LONGS INTREAL declarator:

    long symbol, LONGS INTREAL declarator.

    Example: *long long int* is a long long int declarator.

    We distinguish between an arbitrary number of lengths of reals and integers.

e) reference to MODE declarator:

    reference to symbol, MODE declarator.

    Example: *ref char* is a reference to char declarator.

f) PROCEDURE declarator:

    procedure symbol, PROCEDURE plan.

g) procedure with PARAMETERS MODE plan:

    open symbol, PARAMETERS part, close symbol, MODE result.

h) MODE parameter part: MODE declarer.

i) MODE parameter and PARAMETERS part:

    MODE declarer, PARAMETERS part.

j) procedure MODE plan: MODE result.

k) MODE result: MODE declarer.

Examples: *proc (real) real* is a procedure with real parameter real declarator, and *proc ref int* is a procedure reference to int declarator.

l) structured with FIELDS declarator:

structure symbol, open symbol, FIELDS part, close symbol.

m) MODE field TAG part:

MODE declarer, TAG.

n) MODE field TAG and FIELDS part:

MODE declarer, TAG, comma symbol, FIELDS part.

We omit the syntax for TAG which allows the syntactic handling of identifiers.

Example: *struct (real re, real im)* is a structured with real field letter r letter e and real field letter i letter m declarator.

o) ROWS of MODE declarator:

sub symbol, ROWS rower, bus symbol, MODE declarer.

p) row rower: .

q) row ROWS rower: comma symbol, ROWS rower.

Example: [,,] *char* is a row row row of char declarator.

r) union of MODES mode declarator:

union of symbol, open symbol, MODES declarer list, close symbol.

s) MODE declarer list: MODE declarer.

t) MODE and MODES declarer list:

MODE declarer, comma symbol, MODES declarer list.

Example: *union (real, bool)* is a union of real and bool mode declarator.

The syntax shows how the mode of a declarer can be deduced from its outward appearance.

5.2 Recognizing closed clauses

As a first step in obtaining a recognizer from this language definition, we will build a parser for the overall structure, leaving the treatment of declarers out of consideration for the moment. From the syntax in 5.1.1 a recognizer written in CDL can be obtained by trivial rewriting of the rules, but this text, as it stands, will elicit 6 backtrack messages (where?).

In order to get rid of those messages, it is sensible to turn series and serial clause into actions, by the addition of suitable error messages, since e.g. after a begin symbol there is no question that a serial clause must follow, and if it does not, the program is wrong.

A backtrack free formulation is

(**********CLOSED CLAUSES)

'ACTION'
        SCAN SERIAL CLAUSE,SCAN SERIES,MUST BE UNIT,MUST BE IDENTIFIER.

CLOSED CLAUSE:
        ITEM WAS+BEGIN SYMBOL,
            UP BLOCK,
            SCAN SERIAL CLAUSE,
            DOWN BLOCK,
            (ITEM WAS+END SYMBOL;
             ERROR+END SYMBOL+MSG EXPECTED+EMPTY+EMPTY+EMPTY,
                SKIP TO NEXT CLOSER,NEXT ITEM).

SCAN SERIAL CLAUSE:
REP: IDENTIFIER DEFINITION,
            (ITEM WAS+GO ON SYMBOL,:REP;
             ERROR+GO ON SYMBOL+MSG EXPECTED+EMPTY+EMPTY+EMPTY,
                SKIP TO NEXT SEPARATOR,
                (ITEM WAS+GO ON SYMBOL,:REP;));
        SCAN SERIES.

SCAN SERIES:
REP: MUST BE UNIT,
            (ITEM WAS+GO ON SYMBOL,:REP;).

IDENTIFIER DEFINITION-IDF-MODE:
        DECLARER+MODE,
            MUST BE IDENTIFIER+IDF,
            DEFINE IDENTIFIER+IDF+MODE,
            TRACE+MSG DEFINING+MSG IDENTIFIER+IDF+MSG MODE+MODE.

MUST BE IDENTIFIER+IDF:
        IDENTIFIER+IDF;
        ERROR+MSG IDENTIFIER+MSG EXPECTED+EMPTY+EMPTY+EMPTY,MAKE+IDF+DUMMY.

MUST BE UNIT:
        CLOSED CLAUSE;
        IDENTIFIER APPLICATION;
        ERROR+MSG INCORRECT+MSG UNIT+EMPTY+EMPTY+EMPTY,
            SKIP TO NEXT SEPARATOR.

IDENTIFIER APPLICATION-IDF-MODE:
        IDENTIFIER+IDF,
            APPLY IDENTIFIER+IDF+MODE,
            TRACE+MSG IDENTIFIER+IDF+MSG MODE+MODE+EMPTY.

IDENTIFIER+IDF:
        IS TAG+CLASS,MAKE+IDF+ITEM,NEXT ITEM.

IS TAG+CL:
        IS WORK+CL;
        EQUAL+CL+X TAG.

Notice that the actions have been named by identifiers starting with scan or must be.

The action trace is called in order to leave a record of the recognition process; its definition is omitted here.

5.3 Storing modes

We want to store modes, and to obtain a <u>key</u> for each mode, a small integer with the property that equal modes get equal keys, unequal modes get unequal keys and the key allows printing the modes. The strategy we will followed is suggested by the meta-syntax in 5.1.2 and the syntax in 5.1.3: As a representative of a mode we will store a declarer in a list decl (with stack pointer pdecl), in a form reminiscent of LISP, viz. *(head, tail)* pairs where *head* and *tail* each can be the key of a symbol or a pointer into the decl table.

This idea is elucidated by the following table. In the right hand side, either an arrow or overlining is used to indicate a pointer, and a symbol stands for its key.

mode	representation
int	*(int,0)*
real	*(real,0)*
bool	*(bool,0)*
char	*(char,0)*
void	*(void,0)*
reference to MODE	*(ref,*$\overline{\text{MODE}}$*)*
long MODE	*(long,*$\overline{\text{MODE}}$*)*
procedure PARAMETY MODE	*(proc,* ↶↗ *(PARAMETY,*$\overline{\text{MODE}}$*)*
structured with FIELDS	*(struct,*$\overline{\text{FIELDS}}$*)*
FIELD and FIELDS	*(*$\overline{\text{FIELD}}$*,FIELDS)*
MODE field TAG	*(*$\overline{\text{MODE}}$*,*$\overline{\text{TAG}}$*)*
row of MODE	*(row,*$\overline{\text{MODE}}$*)*
row ROWS of MODE	*(row,*$\overline{\text{ROWS of MODE}}$*)*
union of MODES mode	*(union,*$\overline{\text{MODES}}$*)*
MODE and MODES	*(*$\overline{\text{MODE}}$*,*$\overline{\text{MODES}}$*)*

We store *(head, tail)* pairs by the action enterd into the decl table, obtaining the index in decl where the pair is stored as a key. We take care that no pair is entered twice, by searching the decl table and, in case the pair was already there, not entering it again but returning the index of the old pair. For the language under consideration, this solves all problems of equivalence of modes (if we agree that *union (real,char)* is not equivalent to *union (char,real)*. For a language which includes mode declarations and circular modes this is a good heuristic approach even though it does not fully prevent entering equivalent declarers.

```
( *********DECLARER TABLE )

'ACTION' ENTERD.

'MACRO''POINTER'
      MIN DECL=300001, DECL ENTRY LENGTH=2,
      MAX DECL=300001+1000*2-1.

'LIST' DECL(MIN DECL:MAX DECL).

'POINTER' P DECL.

'MACRO''ACTION'
GET HEAD='2':=DECL(/'1'/),PUT HEAD=DECL(/'1'/):='2',
GET TAIL='2':=DECL(/'1'+1/),PUT TAIL=DECL(/'1'+1/):='2'.

'MACRO''FLAG'
      IS DECL=MIN DECL<='1'''"AND"'''1'<=PDECL.

ENTERD+D1+D2+MODE-I-I1-I2:
      LSEQ+PDECL+MAX DECL,
         MAKE+I+MIN DECL,
REP:       (LESS+I+PDECL,
            (GET HEAD+I+I1,EQUAL+I+D1,
               GET TAIL+I+I2,EQUAL+I2+D2,MAKE+MODE+I;
            ADD+I+DECL ENTRY LENGTH+I,:REP);
         PUT HEAD+PDECL+D1,PUT TAIL+PDECL+D2, MAKE+MODE+PDECL,
            ADD+PDECL+DECL ENTRY LENGTH+PDECL);
      ABORT+MSG OVERFLOW+MSG OF+MSG DECL+MSG TABLE+EMPTY.
```

Clearly, enterd can be speeded up tremendously by replacing the linear search by some faster algorithm.

5.4 Recognizing declarers

It is not so easy to rewrite the syntax in 5.1.3 into CDL, because of some features of 2VWG: The first problem is, that many left hand sides of rules in that section are just particularizations of MODE declarator, so in affix grammars those rules would have to be combined into one fat rule. This problem can be solved by changing the overall structure to something starting as follows:

```
        declarer + mode:
            primitive declarator + mode;
            reference declarator + mode;
            long declarator + mode;
            procedure declarator + mode;
            structure declarator + mode;
            rows declarator + mode;
            union declarator + mode.
```

The second problem is that the original grammar is intended to be used generatively: in parsing, the information comes available strictly from left to right. The solution taken is to turn the mode of each declarator into an output parameter, and to let each declarator enter the information it obtains in a postfix fashion, i.e., making sure the *head* and the *tail* are both in decl before entering *(head, tail)*.

(**********DECLARERS)

```
'ACTION' MUST BE DECLARER,PROCS RESULT,PARAMETERS,PLAN,
REST STRUCTURE DECLARATOR,REST ROWS DECLARATOR,FIELD,FIELDS,
REST DECL LIST PACK,REST UNION DECLARATOR.

'POINTER'
        INT,REAL,BOOL,CHAR MODE,FORMAT,VOID.

MUST BE DECLARER+MODE:
        DECLARER+MODE;
        ERROR+MSG DECLARER+MSG EXPECTED+EMPTY+EMPTY+EMPTY,MAKE+MODE+ERRON
                                                              EOUS.
DECLARER+MODE:
        CLASS IS+X DECL TOKEN,
                (STRUCTURE DECLARATOR+MODE;
                 REFERENCE DECLARATOR+MODE;
                 PROCEDURE DECLARATOR+MODE;
                 UNION DECLARATOR+MODE);
        PRIMITIVE DECLARATOR+MODE;
        ROWS DECLARATOR+MODE;
        LONG DECLARATOR+MODE.

PRIMITIVE DECLARATOR+MODE:
        CLASS IS+X PRIMITIVE,
                (ITEM WAS+INT SYMBOL,MAKE+MODE+INT;
                 ITEM WAS+REAL SYMBOL,MAKE+MODE+REAL;
                 ITEM WAS+BOOL SYMBOL,MAKE+MODE+BOOL;
                 ITEM WAS+CHAR SYMBOL,MAKE+MODE+CHAR MODE;
                 ITEM WAS+FORMAT SYMBOL,MAKE+MODE+FORMAT;
                 ITEM WAS+VOID SYMBOL,MAKE+MODE+VOID).

LONG DECLARATOR+MODE-M1:
        ITEM WAS+LONG SYMBOL,
                (ITEM WAS+INT SYMBOL,ENTERD+LONG+INT+MODE;
                 ITEM WAS+REAL SYMBOL,ENTERD+LONG+REAL+MODE;
                 LONG DECLARATOR+M1,ENTERD+LONG+M1+MODE).

REFERENCE DECLARATOR+MODE-M1:
        ITEM WAS+REF SYMBOL,MUST BE DECLARER+M1,ENTERD+REF+M1+MODE.
```

The next problem is to insert error reporting and error recuperation in the right places, with some help from the backtrack messages that keep coming as long as some backtrack possibility was overlooked.

```
STRUCTURE DECLARATOR+MODE:
        ITEM WAS+STRUCT SYMBOL,REST STRUCTURE DECLARATOR+MODE.

REST STRUCTURE DECLARATOR+MODE-M1-M2-M3-IDF:
        ITEM WAS+OPEN SYMBOL,
                FIELD+M1+IDF,ENTERD+M1+IDF+M2,FIELDS+M1+M3,ENTERD+M2+M3+M3,
                ENTERD+STRUCT+M3+MODE;
        ERROR+MSG INCORRECT+MSG STRUCTUREDWITH+MSG DECLARATOR+EMPTY+EMPTY,
        MAKE+MODE+ERRONEOUS.

FIELD+MODE+IDF:
        MUST BE DECLARER+MODE,MUST BE IDENTIFIER+IDF.

FIELDS+M1+MODE-M2-M3-IDF:
    AGN:ITEM WAS+COMMA SYMBOL,
            (IDENTIFIER+IDF,ENTERD+M1+IDF+M2,FIELDS+M1+M3,ENTERD+M2+M3+MODE;
             FIELD+M1+IDF,ENTERD+M1+IDF+M2,FIELDS+M1+M3,ENTERD+M2+M3+MODE);
        ITEM WAS+CLOSE SYMBOL,MAKE+MODE+0;
        ERROR+MSG INCORRECT+MSG FIELDS+MSG PACK+EMPTY+EMPTY,
            SKIP TO NEXT CLOSER,NEXT ITEM.
```

The action skip to next closer performs the error recuperation its identifier suggests.
Notice that an erroneous declarer gets a special mode erroneous which can be of help
in preventing multiple signalling of one same error. The remaining declarators
present no new problems.

```
PROCEDURE DECLARATOR+MODE:
        ITEM WAS+PROC SYMBOL,PLAN+MODE.

PLAN+MODE-M1-M2:
        PARAMETERS+M1,PROCS RESULT+M2,ENTERD+M1+M2+M1,ENTERD+PROC+M1+MODE.

PARAMETERS+MODE: DECLARER LIST PACK+MODE; MAKE+MODE+0.

PROCS RESULT+MOID:
        MUST BE DECLARER+MOID.

DECLARER LIST PACK+MODE-M1-M2:
        ITEM WAS+OPEN SYMBOL,MUST BE DECLARER+M1,REST DECL LIST PACK+M2 ,
                ENTERD+M1+M2+MODE.

REST DECL LIST PACK+MODE-M1-M2:
    AGN:ITEM WAS+COMMA SYMBOL,MUST BE DECLARER+M1,REST DECL LIST PACK+M2,
                ENTERD+M1+M2+MODE;
        ITEM WAS+CLOSE SYMBOL,MAKE+MODE+0;
        ERROR+MSG INCORRECT+MSG DECLARER+MSG LIST+MSG PACK+EMPTY,
            SKIP TO NEXT CLOSER,NEXT ITEM.
```

```
ROWS DECLARATOR+MODE-M1:
          ITEM WAS+SUB SYMBOL,
               REST ROWS DECLARATOR+M1,ENTERD+ROW+M1+MODE.

REST ROWS DECLARATOR+MODE-M1:
     RST: ITEM WAS+COMMA SYMBOL,
               REST ROWS DECLARATOR+M1,ENTERD+ROW+M1+MODE;
          ITEM WAS+BUS SYMBOL,MUST BE DECLARER+MODE;
          ERROR+MSG INCORRECT+MSG ROWOF+MSG DECLARATOR+EMPTY+EMPTY,
               SKIP TO NEXT CLOSER,NEXT ITEM.

UNION DECLARATOR+MODE:
          ITEM WAS+UNION SYMBOL,REST UNION DECLARATOR+MODE.

REST UNION DECLARATOR+MODE-M1:
          DECLARER LIST PACK+M1,ENTERD+UNION+M1+MODE;
          ERROR+MSG INCORRECT+MSG UNIONOF+MSG DECLARATOR+EMPTY+EMPTY,
          MAKE+MODE+ERRONEOUS.
```

5.5 Conclusion

As a bonus to all readers who have shown the patience to follow the argument so far,
we end by giving some output obtained from the recognizer described.

```
          1BEGIN REF PROC INT a;
           ----> DEFINING IDENTIFIER a MODE REF PROC INT

          2      BEGIN STRUCT ((//)REAL b)b;
           ----> DEFINING IDENTIFIER b MODE STRUCT ( ROW REAL b )

          3           INT b;
           ====> ERROR: IDENTIFIER b DECLARED TWICE

           ----> DEFINING IDENTIFIER b MODE INT

          4           b;
           ----> IDENTIFIER b MODE INT

          5           a;
           ----> IDENTIFIER a MODE REF PROC INT

          6           d
          7      END
           ====> ERROR: IDENTIFIER d NOT DECLARED

           ----> IDENTIFIER d MODE ERRONEOUS
          ;
          8a;
           ----> IDENTIFIER a MODE REF PROC INT

          9b
          10END
           ====> ERROR: IDENTIFIER b NOT DECLARED

           ----> IDENTIFIER b MODE ERRONEOUS
```

If we add a driving program, error reporting, and various odds and ends, what have we obtained? In biblical terms, a colossus on gold feet, silver legs, iron thighs topped with a clay head. Those parts of a compiler which are the hardest to invent, especially code generation, machine-independent and dependent optimization are missing. Still the parts we have shown here are sufficiently general to be a sizeable part of any compiler design. This should show the possibility of "off the shelf" compiler components.

By all standards of judgement, the only way one should not write compilers is the one still used most: to write it in assembly language.

We hope to have made clear that it is possible to design a language, intended solely for the writing of compilers, which is of undisputed help in all phases of compiler construction. Time, and the interest taken by others, will have to decide whether CDL is going to contribute to the availability of good compilers for all languages on each machine.

Acknowledgements

The skeleton compiler presented was written over a period of two months by one student, Christoph Oeters, who managed to put it in good shape in spite of my frequent changes of specifications.

My thanks go out to Ute Szêll, who typed those 6 lecture notes competently and cheerfully in spite of their typographic complexity and the erratic flow of my inspiration.

References

[1] Crowe, D.: Generating parsers for affix grammars. Comm. ACM 15, 728-734 (1972)

[2] Bosch, R., Grune, D., Meertens, L.: ALEPH, a language encouraging program hierarchy. Proc. Intern. Computing Symposium Davos 1973. Amsterdam: North-Holland 1974, p. 73-79

[3] Koster, C.H.A.: Affix grammars. In: Peck, J.E.L. (ed.): ALGOL 68 implementation. Amsterdam: North-Holland 1971

[4] Koster, C.H.A.: A compiler compiler. Mathematisch Centrum Amsterdam, Report MR 127, 1971

[5] Koster, C.H.A.: Portable compilers and the UNCOL problem. In: Proc. of a Working Conference on Machine Oriented High Level Languages. Amsterdam: North-Holland 1974

PORTABLE AND ADAPTABLE COMPILERS

Peter C. Poole

University of Colorado

Boulder, Colorado, USA

1. BASIC CONCEPTS

1.1. Portability and Adaptability

To say that a program is "portable" implies that it is a relatively easy and straight forward task to move it from one machine to another; if the effort to move the program is considerably less than the effort required to write it initially, then we can say that the program is "highly portable". An "adaptable" program, on the other hand, is one that can readily be modified to meet a wide range of user and system requirements; again, if the effort to vary the characteristics or behaviour of the program is much less than that required to produce a specialized program for the same task, then the program is "highly adaptable".

Portability is clearly a property possessed by programs written in high level languages. In theory at least, if a translator for the language is available on the target machine, then the program can easily be transferred, compiled and executed. Adaptability is a less obvious property but is exemplified in a situation where say an operating system is being generated to suit a particular machine configuration.

Based on the above definitions, we can say that a "portable and adaptable compiler" is one that can easily be moved to a new machine and modified to interface with its operating system. However, the situation is not quite as simple as this. Suppose we have a compiler for language A operating on machine X and we wish to move it to machine Y. By one means or another, we make the transfer and the compiler becomes available on Y. It accepts, as input, source statements in A; unfortunately, it will still produce code for the original machine X. Thus, just a straight transfer of the program does not give the desired result. We must also modify the algorithm so that it produces the correct code for the new machine. Usually, with portable software, this is just the thing we are trying to avoid. e.g. if we transfer a text editor, we expect it to behave on the new machine exactly as it did on the old one without us having to alter the program in any way. With a compiler, we must be concerned not only with the transfer to the new machine but also with the modifications that will enable it to produce correct output.

The advantages that accrue from making software portable and adaptable are largely economic ones. If the effort involved to move the software is much less than the effort required to reprogram, then the cost of making the software available on a new machine will be greatly reduced. If the transfer process is a fairly mechanical one so that the probability of introducing new errors is small, then users of the software on the new machine will benefit greatly since it will be tried

and tested. Portable and adaptable compilers provide a two-fold benefit
- the development of new software is not impeded by compiler errors and
the transfer of old software is greatly facilitated.

1.2. Problems with Current Compilers

With the development of FORTRAN and other high level languages in the
early 60's, people began to predict quite confidently that the era of
"machine independence" would soon be with us. Programs no longer would
be locked to the particular machines on which they were developed;
installations would no longer have to bear the heavy expense of re-
programming for a new machine. All software would be written in high
level languages and programs could easily be transferred from one
machine to another once the compiler for the particular language became
available.   Although it was recognized that it would be necessary to
expend considerable effort to make the compilers widely available, it
was assumed that it was merely a question of time and money. A decade
later, we are all only too well aware that these early predictions have
not become reality. High level languages have found ready acceptance in
the user community and have been largely responsible for the tremendous
growth in the use of computers that has occurred in the last few years.
However, it is still no easy task to move programs from one computer to
another even when they are written in a high level "machine-independent"
language.

The reasons for the present difficulties in transferring software are
partly historical and partly economic. The first of the high level
languages to find wide spread acceptance was FORTRAN. This language was
developed by IBM and, as it became more and more popular, other

manufacturers were forced to follow suit by providing compilers for the language that is, if they wished to continue to compete with IBM in the market place. Invariably, such compilers accepted slightly different languages to the one processed by the IBM version, partly because the language was not well defined and partly because each manufacturer tended to add new features in an attempt to make his system more attractive to a potential customer. Even moving a FORTRAN program from one IBM machine to another could be fraught with difficulties since compilers developed by different implementation groups even for the same machine might not necessarily be compatible.

The key to the difficulty appeared to be standardization. If a well defined standard for the language could be constructed and published, then there might be fewer discrepancies between compilers produced by different manufacturers since there would be pressure from customers on them to adopt the standard. Accordingly, in 1962, a group was set up by the American Standards Association to prepare a standard for FORTRAN. In 1966, the first ASA standard for FORTRAN IV was published [FORTRAN 66] and was followed by revisions and clarifications in 1969 [FORTRAN 69]. These documents have gone a long way towards setting up the necessary standards for the language. However, differences between compilers still occur. The existence of a standard does not prevent a manufacturer from adding extra features to the language over and above what the standard sets out in order to attract new customers or keep existing ones locked to his machine once they have made use of some non-standard feature. Programmers are usually guided by manuals supplied by the manufacturer and most are unaware of the details of the standard, even, in many cases, of its very existence. Hence, they can easily make use of some convenient feature available locally and not appreciate the difficulties it will cause them when subsequently they try to move the program to another machine. For example, a permissible subscript in IBM FORTRAN IV is

$$\text{variable} \pm \text{variable}$$

which is obviously more general, efficient and convenient than

$$\text{variable} \pm \text{constant}$$

the only form permitted by the standard. Any attempt to move a program containing such constructs to say a CDC machine could involve many changes and considerable effort. Further, the implementation of non-standard features can still lead to discrepacies between two compilers from the same manufacturer and operating on the same machine since they can be implemented in slightly different ways. For example, mixed mode arithmetic involving reals and integers is not permitted by the ASA FORTRAN IV standard. However, both FORTRAN compilers for the CDC 6000 series accept expressions containing such mixtures. Unfortunately, the algorithms used in the two compilers differ slightly. One of the compilers only switches to real arithmetic when it encounters an operand of this type; the second compiler, on the other hand, first searches the expression for the dominant mode and performs all arithmetic operations in that mode i.e. if the expression contains a real operand, then only real arithmetic is used during its evaluation as all integer operands are first converted to real ones . It is not difficult to construct expressions which will produce slightly different results according to which of the two algorithms is used. Thus, the result of a calculation could depend on which compiler produced the object program, hardly a very satisfactory situation.

Even when an attempt is made to implement the standard exactly, there still remains a strong possibility that the finished compiler will not be error-free. Residual errors could be due to the implementation or ones due to a misinterpretation of the published standard. The document which defines FORTRAN, although it uses English as the meta-language, is not an easy one to read. The definition is very rigorous and must be thoroughly understood before any attempt is made to translate it into the design of a compiler. It should be noted that the standard is only concerned with the syntax and semantics of FORTRAN; it says nothing about how the language should be translated. There are therefore many possibilities for introducing errors during the construction of a working compiler. Most of these will ultimately be corrected but some will be allowed to remain, either because they are not considered troublesome or because they could be very expensive to correct. Users of a particular compiler soon learn to avoid its trouble spots. The difficulties only arise when an attempt is made to transfer software between machines.

To illustrate the type of error that has been allowed to remain in existing compilers, consider the FORTRAN program in Figure 1.1. The compiler has obviously mistaken the statement labelled "10" as a FORMAT statement even though FORMAT has been dimensioned as an array at the beginning of the program. Some FORTRAN compilers are designed to treat words like GOTO, IF, FORMAT, etc. as reserved words even though the standard does not define them as such since this simplifies the construction process. However, it cannot be argued that the CDC

```
RUN VERSION NOV 71 D  13:39 74/01/04
                PROGRAM OUCH(OUTPUT,TAPE6=OUTPUT)
000003          DIMENSION FORMAT(2),J(2)
000003          INTEGER FORMAT
000003          FORMAT(1)=1
000004          J(1)=2
000005     10   FORMAT(1)=J(1)
000005          WRITE(6,100) FORMAT(1)
000013    100   FORMAT(23H VALUE OF FORMAT(1) IS ,I1)
000013          END


VALUE OF FORMAT(1) IS 1
```

a) successful compilation under RUN but incorrect execution

```
PROGRAM     OUCH      CDC 6400 FTN V3.0-P363 OPT=1  74/01/04  13.39.10.

                PROGRAM OUCH(OUTPUT,TAPE6=OUTPUT)
                DIMENSION FORMAT(2),J(2)
                INTEGER FORMAT
                FORMAT(1)=1
        5       J(1)=2
           10   FORMAT(1)=J(1)
                WRITE(6,100) FORMAT(1)
          100   FORMAT(23H VALUE OF FORMAT(1) IS ,I1)
                END

CARD NO.  SEVERITY         DIAGNOSTIC

     6      FE      15 CD 6 PRECEDING CHARACTER ILLEGAL AT THIS POINT
                          IN CHARACTER STRING. ERROR SCAN FOR THIS
                          FORMAT STOPS HERE.
```

b) unsuccessful compilation under FTN

Figure 1.1
Varying Behaviour of Equivalent Compilers with Same Program

compiler belongs to this class with FORMAT as a reserved word since it accepts as legal the assignment statement at the beginning of the program. One can only conclude that FORMAT is taken to be a reserved keyword if it is followed by a left parenthesis and the statement is terminated by a right parenthesis. Notice also that the same error occurs in both CDC compilers although the RUN compiler does not check the format specification as does FTN. Thus the latter compiler not only accepts an assignment statement as a format statement but also proceeds to inform the programmer that the specification is incorrect. It could be argued that anyone who uses the word FORMAT as an identifier is asking for trouble. However, it is permitted by the standard and could have a very valid mnemonic meaning in a particular program. Clearly the RUN compiler could create a puzzling situation if a program which contains the identifier FORMAT is transferred from a machine in which it is accepted to a CDC computer. The program would compile as legal but would execute to produce incorrect results.

Another example of an error is shown in Figure 1.2a where a perfectly legal FORTRAN program fails to compile. The offending statement is a GOTO and the error message indicates that there is an illegal reference to a DO loop terminator. It is clear from an examination of the text that this is not so since the labelled GOTO statement is in the extended range of the DO as defined by Section 7.1.2.8.2 of the FORTRAN standard. If, now, we move the GOTO statement to a position before the DO loop, then the program compiles successfully as shown in Figure 1.2b. Apparently, the compiler only permits an extended range if it occurs before the DO statement. This does not conform to the standard which does not specify any position relative to the DO loop for an extended

```
RUN  VERSION NOV 71 D    13:56 74/01/04.

                PROGRAM FORTES3(INPUT,OUTPUT)
  000003    30   DO 10 I=1,9
  000005         IF(I.EQ.1)GOTO 20
  000007    10   CONTINUE
  000011         STOP
  000013    20   GOTO 10
****GTF**********
  000013         END

GT*******ILLEGAL REF. TO DO LOOP TERMINATOR FROM OUT OF LOOP
      000013
```

a) unsuccessful compilation under RUN

```
RUN  VERSION NOV 71 D    13:56 74/01/04.

                PROGRAM FORTES4(INPUT,OUTPUT)
  000003    20   GOTO 10
  000004    30   DO 10 I=1,9
  000006         IF(I.EQ.1)GOTO 20
  000010    10   CONTINUE
  0000012        STOP
  000014         END

SPACE REQUIRED TO COMPILE -- FORTES4
032000
```

b) successful compilation under RUN

Figure 1.2
Varying Behaviour of Same Compiler with Equivalent Programs

range.

1.3. Portable and Adaptable Standards

Pressure for the definition of and adherence to standards must, in the long run, come from computer users. It is their interests which are best served by the easy transfer of software from one machine to another. To some extent, manufacturers gain from forward portability i.e. the ability to move existing software but they have little to gain by making it easy for a customer to transfer his programs to a competitor's machine. Hence, users must be provided with a readily accessible yardstick against which they can compare the compiler supplied by the manufacturer. Such a measure could be provided in the shape of a standard compiler, one that is both portable and adaptable.

Let us suppose that the standards committee in addition to publishing a meta-linguistic description of the language also makes available a standard compiler and a comprehensive set of test programs. The compiler would have to be both portable and adaptable so that it could be readily transferred to many machines and easily tailored to a variety of systems. An implementation guide would also be required so that any manufacturer could make the language (or a standard subset) available on his machine. The purpose of the suite of test programs is two-fold. In the first place, any implementor of the compiler would need such a set in order to validate his implementation. A second and perhaps even more important function is to provide the customer with a means for checking the manufacturer's compilers. One would certainly expect the portable standard to be available on any machine. However, there would be nothing to stop a manufacturer providing his own compiler as well, perhaps to gain extra efficiency. The test programs could be used to check this compiler as well as the standard. If the testing can be carried out successfully to show that the two compilers are compatible, then the user will have a high degree of confidence that his programs will be easily transferred to other machines. Of course, if the manufacturer out of the goodness of his heart, adds extra features to the language and makes these available in his compiler, then the onus is on the user to beware of such "goodies". Any difficulties he encounters in moving software are on his own head.

As will be seen during the course of these lectures, the technology for creating such portable and adaptable standards is already here; whether the current political situation favours such an approach is another question. Apart from discouraging noises that might emanate from manufacturers, there is still a considerable gap between the language designers who specify the syntax and semantics of the language and the software engineers who build the compilers. Hence, there is always the possibility that a standard will be misinterpreted or even consciously modified because some particular feature is very difficult to implement. What we would like to achieve is a situation in which the definition of the language could be used to produce the compiler automatically. The compiler would then be the physical realization of the standard for the language.

2. SURVEY OF TECHNIQUES

Let us now consider what is actually involved in transferring a compiler from one machine to another and the ways in which this might be achieved. Obviously, if the compiler is written in the assembly code of machine A, then no transfer to machine B is possible unless B is very similar to A, for example, both A and B are members of a range of machines. Hence, we must assume that the compiler is described in some machine independent language. We will consider first the case where a general purpose language is used to describe the compilation algorithm. Later, we will mention techniques which use special purpose languages to describe the language to be compiled and to assist in the production of the compiler.

2.1. Portability through High Level Language Coding

Suppose we have a compiler for language A written in language B which is running on machine X and producing code for that machine. Suppose, now, that we wish to transfer the compiler to machine Y. If the compiler for B is available on Y, then the transfer would be quite straight forward, provided the compilers were compatible. Of course, as we have already noted, the compiler would still be translating A into code for X. Hence, the code generation routines would have to be rewritten and, whether this is possible or not, will depend on the existence of a well defined interface and the availability of good documentation. Provided these conditions are fulfilled, then, in principle, there should be no difficulty in transferring the compiler.

Some of the early attempts at producing portable compilers made use of FORTRAN, the most widely distributed high level language. Unfortunately, FORTRAN is not a language well suited to the writing of compilers and these usually proved to be rather large, slow and cumbersome. The situation has improved somewhat of late with the availability of languages like BCPL [Richards 69a] and Pascal [Wirth 71a] which are much more suitable for the writing of compilers than was FORTRAN. However, whatever the language, there is still the need to modify the code generating routines for the new machine.

2.1.1. <u>Bootstrapping</u>. The more usual situation is one in which there is no compiler for language B on machine Y and we are faced with the task of "bootstrapping" the compiler onto the new machine. There are two approaches that can be taken to solve this problem. The first approach involves both the donor and the target machine. Firstly, the compiler for B on the donor machine X is modified to produce symbolic assembly code for Y. Then, the compiler for A written in B is modified to produce code appropriate to a production compiler on machine Y. When a satisfactory version of this compiler has been produced, it is taken to machine Y, assembled and tested. Errors result in changes to the source text of the compiler held at the donor machine and the cycle is continued until a working version of the compiler is available on the target computer. A minor variation to the approach occurs when A and B are the same language i.e. the compiler for A is written in A. In this situation, the compiler can be modified to produce symbolic assembly code for Y instead of code appropriate to the final version. The latter can then be developed entirely on the target machine.

The above strategy, sometimes called "half-bootstrapping" [Halstead 62] or "pushing", can suffer from a slow debugging loop and communication difficulties. If both machines are close together and accessible to and understood by the implementatation personnel, then the method can be quite effective. However, this is not the usual case and there is evidence which indicates that when the machines are geographically remote and different groups are attempting to communicate, then the success rate is not very high. A large number of iterations is usually required and a long time may be needed to bring the compiler up on the target machine.

In the second approach, all the work to implement the compiler on the new machine is carried out on that machine. This strategy is often referred to as "full bootstrapping" [Waite 69] or "pulling". The implications are that the compiler is available in a symbolic form, that there are tools available to assist the implementation and that the whole process is supported by good documentation. In practice, this turns out to be the better of the two approaches since the communication problems are much less severe. It appears that one is much more certain of a successful implementation if one describes to people who understand the target machine and its system the method for implementing the portable software rather than trying to inform the developers of the software about the idiosyncracies of the target machine.

To illustrate the full bootstrap approach, suppose that, in addition to the compiler for language A written in B, there also exists a compiler for language B written in FORTRAN. If FORTRAN is available on machine Y, then this version of the compiler can be readily transferred (providing that the FORTRAN's are compatible). It will still translate language B into assembly code for machine X and the code generators must therefore be modified to produce assembly code for machine Y. Again, we assume that the compiler has been suitably structured so that this is a straight forward process. Now, what we have is a compiler for language B running on machine Y and producing code for that machine. Since it is written in Fortran, it is likely to be very slow and inefficient and would hardly suffice as a production compiler. However, it only has one task in front of it, namely, to translate the compiler for A written in B into assembly code for Y and it really does not matter how long this process takes. The resultant assembly code version of the compiler for A still produces code for machine X but, at least, the process is an efficient one. What we must do now is modify the code generators of this compiler. Once these modifications have been checked out and the compiler interfaced to the system, then we have achieved our goal - a compiler for A operating on machine Y. Notice that all the work has been carried out on the target machine - an essential point of the full bootstrap approach.

2.1.2. <u>Language-Machine</u> <u>Interface</u>. It is clear from the above discussion that a key factor controlling the portability of a compiler is the existence of a suitable program structure. In order to move the compiler, we must be able to rewrite the code generating routines to suit the new machine. For this to be a not unreasonable task, there must be a well defined interface such that the compiler can be divided into two parts, one dependent on the language and the other on the target machine. Providing there is a clear separation, only the part dependent on the new machine will need to be modified to effect the transfer. The part of the compiler which depends only on the characteristics of the language we will call the language-dependent translator (LDT); the part which depends only on the target computer will be referred to as the machine-dependent translator (MDT). The communication between these two parts can either be in the form of procedure calls or as a symbolic program in an intermediate assembly code.

The LDT breaks the source code into tokens, and contains the formation rules that express the way the tokens may be combined in a program to form sentences in the language. If the program's syntax does not conform to that of the language, appropriate error diagnostics must be reported. After the LDT has analyzed the program for syntactic errors, it determines what actions are required to execute the program. Collectively, the actions are semantically equivalent to the source program. To keep the LDT machine-independent, the actions it produces must not rely on a particular target computer; they are the fundamental operations that must be implemented on any computer. As the LDT determines what fundamental operations are needed, it calls upon the MDT to convert each operation into executable code for the target computer. Thus, the information flow is generally from the LDT to the MDT. The information passed back to the LDT from the MDT involves characteristics of the target machine which are needed to generate the proper fundamental operations. For example, the LDT must be able to perform address calculations in terms of the target machine's address unit.

If a compiler is written in a high-level language and structured as described above, then in principle, there should be no difficulty in moving it from one machine to another. Often such compilers are written in their own languages and once the first compiler is available, the half-bootstrap technique can be used to effect the transfers. However, as we have already noted, this is not without its attendant difficulties. We would prefer to use the full-bootstrap approach. We will now consider how this might be achieved with no assumptions made about the software available on the target machine.

2.2. <u>Portability through Abstract Machine Modelling</u>

The information flow between the two parts of a compiler is composed of the fundamental operations of the language in one direction (LDT to MDT), and the information about the target machine in the other (MDT to LDT). The fundamental operations are the instruction set for a computer which is designed for the programming language (e.g. a Pascal machine). The information flow from the MDT to the LDT is represented by pseudo operations in the computer's assembly language. This computer is called the <u>abstract machine</u>.

An abstract machine is based upon operations and modes that are primitive in the programming language. The LDT translates a program into abstract machine code by breaking constructs of the language into a sequence of primitive operations on the primitive modes. The primitive modes of the abstract machine can be types in the language (e.g. REAL in Pascal), or modes that are used to construct the more complex types of the language (e.g. structured types in Pascal). The primitive operations of the abstract machine are the simplest and most direct operations that will describe a program in the language. A primitive mode and a primitive operation form a pair which describe an instruction; some modes and operations cannot be paired because they would have no meaning in the language.

The architecture of the abstract machine forms an environment in which the modes and operations interact to model the language. Unlike a real machine whose architecture is governed by economic considerations and technical limitations, the abstract machine has a structure which facilitates the operations required by a given programming language. The designer of the abstract machine must plan the architecture so that it can be efficiently implemented on a real machine.

The abstract machine can be embedded into the LDT by a series of interface procedures, one for each abstract machine instruction. When the LDT determines that a certain abstract machine instruction is needed, a call is made upon the corresponding procedure. The effect of the procedures is dependent on the method chosen to implement the MDT.

The use of an abstract machine allows the LDT and the MDT to be separated by a well-defined interface. The separation permits one to refine either part of the compiler without affecting the other. A move to a new machine will require extensive modifications to the MDT, while the LDT will need little change.

Another advantage of using an abstract machine is the choice it allows in implementing the MDT. The LDT's interface procedures could produce a symbolic assembly code for the abstract machine. The MDT would then be an abstract machine assembler which could be implemented by using a macro processor, either the one provided with the real machine's assembler or a machine-independent macro processor.

Another implementation of the MDT is to place it within the interface procedures. When the LDT makes a call upon one of these procedures, the MDT gains control and produces the target machine equivalent of the abstract machine instruction corresponding to the procedure. The equivalent code could be in the target machine's assembly language, relocatable binary, or absolute binary.

2.2.1. A Standard Abstract Machine. A standard abstract machine is an abstract machine which has been carefully designed around a model that can be used for many programming languages. Many LDTs can produce assembly code for the standard abstract machine, and one assembler could be used to translate this assembly code for the target machine.

The standard abstract machine language should be extensible to allow new operations and modes that appear in a new programming language. When several compilers use the same abstract machine, many of the operations and modes will recur in several of the compilers. A new compiler will require only a few new operations and modes. The more differences there are between two languages, the harder it is to design an abstract machine which will be suited to both. For example, an abstract machine designed for Pascal could with a few modifications be adapted to ALGOL60. However, major modifications might be necessary to make the machine useful for LISP1.5.

The amount of work necessary to design and implement a particular abstract machine decreases as the library of operations and modes grows.

Moving a standard abstract machine version of a compiler to a new machine requires only the implementation of the operations and modes not in the new machine's abstract machine library. The result is less work and faster initial implementation of the compiler.

A family of abstract machines called Janus [Coleman 73] has been developed at the University of Colorado in order to study the problems of producing portable software and in particular portable compilers. Figure 2.1b illustrates the role of Janus in the translation process: The translator is split along the interface of Figure 2.1a. A small module attached to the analyzer encodes the information normally passed across the interface from left to right. The encoded information constitutes a symbolic program, which can then be transmitted to another computer. Janus specifies the structure of this symbolic program, but says nothing about the particular set of operators and modes which can be used.

The symbolic Janus code is translated to the assembly language of the target computer by a program such as STAGE2 [Waite 70b]. Simple translation rules are supplied by the user to describe the various Janus constructs and the primitive modes and operators. Final translation to object code is provided by the normal assembler of the target computer.

The design for the Janus family of abstract machines is based upon the relationship between existing languages and existing hardware. Each component of Figure 2.2 models a specific language characteristic; the precise form of the model was chosen to simplify the generation of machine code from symbolic Janus.

Depends upon source language

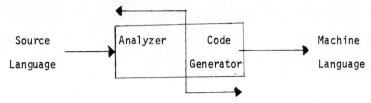

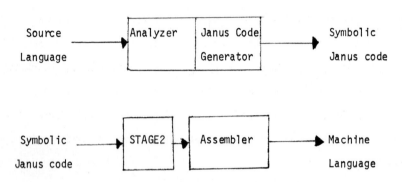

Depends upon target computer

a) A conventional translator

b) Janus as an intermediate language

Figure 2.1

The Translation Process

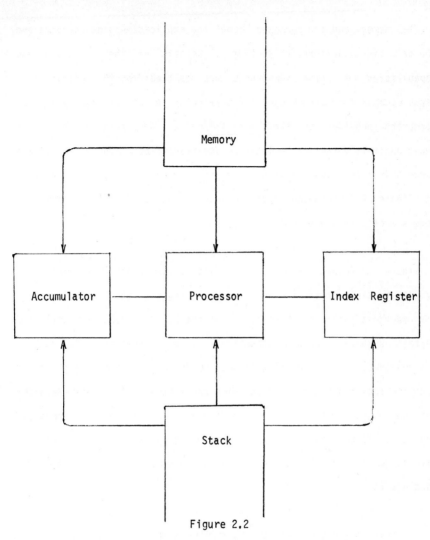

Figure 2.2

The Architecture of the Janus Family of Abstract Machines

The memory and the processor model the explicitly-named operands and the primitive operators, respectively. Details of the structure and capabilities of these components are omitted from the definition of Janus because they depend upon the particular set of primitve modes and operators provided by the abstract machine. An expression is used to avoid explicitly naming the intermediate results of a computation, and hence this introduces anonymous operands. The accumulator and the stack of Figure 2.2 model anonymous operands in the same way that the memory models explicitly-named operands.

Figure 2.2 favors target computers with a single arithmetic register, or with multiple arithmetic registers and register/storage arithmetic. For machines with a register file or stack, it is necessary to expand certain symbolic Janus instructions into sequences of machine instructions. This expansion is easy to do, because the code generator need not consider the context in which the instruction occurs. Machines with no programmable registers have no provision for anonymous operands, and hence all operands must be given names by the code generator. Correct çode can always be produced by simulating a machine with a single arithmetic register.

An array or structure is an aggregate which is recognized as a distinct entity, but whose components may be used individually as operands. Access to a component is provided by an index, which defines a location within the aggregate. Again, the organization of Figure 2.2 favors computers with explicit index registers. This class seems to represent the mainstream of computer architecture, although there exist other mechanisms for component addressing. However, the model chosen provides enough information to generate correct code in each case without retaining contextual information. Figure 2.2 thus reflects the use of expressions to form complex operations from primitive operators, and the use of arrays and structures to create complex data items from primitive modes. Since there appears to be widespread agreement about how these particular formation rules should be implemented in hardware, Figure 2.2 also reflects the organization of contemporary computers.

There is less agreement regarding the hardware realization of conditionals, iterations, and procedures. It appears that these formation rules do not have a strong influence on the overall organization of a machine; they are reflected in the set of operators provided.

For conditionals, the critical questions here are whether the abstract machine should have an explicit condition code, and whether a comparison should destroy the contents of the accumulator. Janus takes a middle course and provides both destructive and non-destructive comparison operators which set a condition code destroyed by any instruction other that a conditional transfer. The accumulator is destroyed by any transfer of control except one following a non-destructive comparison.

An iteration may proceed under count control, or it may continue until a certain condition holds. The former is a special case of the latter, but it is sufficiently important such that some computers have special instructions which will modify a register, test it and transfer control if some condition is met. Although this indicates that the abstract machine model might be provided with an iteration counter which can be incremented and tested by a transfer instruction, it has not been incorporated because of the difficulties in formulating the instructions to manipulate it in such a way that they apply to most computers.

A procedure invocation involves both parameter passing and status saving. Because of the diversity in status saving methods, one must use a high level model for a procedure call. Janus employs three instructions:

1) _Return jump_ is used in the calling program to actually invoke the procedure.

2) _Link_ appears as the first executable instruction of the procedure body.

3) _Return_ is used in the procedure body to actually return from the procedure.

These instructions are interdependent, a fact which may be used by the implementor to match any one of the status saving methods.

Parameter mechanisms (reference, value, etc.) are primarily determined by the source language. The location of parameters in the calling sequence is system-dependent; there are three common techniques:

1) Parameters are stored in the calling program in the vicinity of the return jump.

2) Parameters are stored in a fixed area of the called program.

3) Parameters are stored in registers or on a stack.

A diversity of parameter mechanisms, like the diversity of status saving methods, demands a high level model. Janus uses two special pseudos:

1) CALL marks the beginning of the code required to compute arguments at run time. (For example, to obtain the address of A(I) when arguments are passed by reference.)

2) CEND marks the end of a set of storage reservation pseudos which define the argument list.

These pseudos, in conjunction with the three procedure call instructions discussed above, can be used to create procedure calls conforming to a wide variety of conventions.

Reference modes are represented by addresses or by descriptors. A primitive mode ADDR may be used to describe either representation. A "load immediate" instruction creates an entity of ADDR mode which references the operand of the instruction, and leaves it in the accumulator. A pseudo which allows one to preset a reference in memory is also required.

2.2.2. Janus Assembly Language Formats. The symbolic Janus program is an encoding of the information which passes across the interface of Figure 2.1a. The design goal was to present the information in a form which would simplify the process of producing assembly language for the target computer. Although it would certainly be possible for a human programmer to write Janus, such an approach is not advocated. It is assumed that the code will always be produced as the output of some translator.

Janus has two basic formats for executable instructions:

    operator model mode2
    operator mode reference

The first of these is used for instructions which may be broadly classed as mode conversion (fix, float) and value conversion (negate, truncate) operations which modify the contents of the accumulator. Model and mode2 are the initial and final modes, respectively, of the accumulator contents. The second instruction format is used when an operand other than the accumulator must be specified. Three major classes of references may be distinguished: references to explicitly-named operands, references to anonymous operands, and references to constant operands.

Each reference to an explicitly-named operand specifies a symbol and an index. Normally, the attributes of each symbol would be specified by declaration and stored in a dictionary by the translator. However, dictionary lookup is a time- and space-consuming process for STAGE2 and it was desired to avoid this if possible.

Examination of the usual attributes of an operand revealed two - category and address - which influenced the translation of the reference into machine code. The category tells what sort of operand is being represented. For example, categories can be used to distinguish arguments, formal parameters, and particular storage areas (local, global, dynamic, etc.) Often these operands will require different translations. Such special treatment can be provided only if it is possible to distinguish the operands which require it.

On most machines the value of the address does not affect the sequence of instructions needed to accomplish the reference. Provided that the symbol in the Janus instruction is acceptable to the target machine's assembler, it may be used unchanged in the output code. Under these circumstances no dictionary lookup is required to establish the address during the STAGE2 run.

It is useful to separate the index of an aggregate reference into two parts: the fixed offset (whose value may be obtained from the program text) and the variable offset (whose value must be determined during execution.)   On many computers the base address and fixed offset may be combined at translation time to form an "effective base address." The final address is then obtained at run time by addition of the variable offset.

Instructions which reference explicitly-named operands therefore have the following general form:

    operator mode category symbol(fixed)variable

Either or both of the offset specifications may be omitted.

A reference to an anonymous operand is a reference to the top element of the stack. If the target computer does not have a hardware stack, then the Janus stack must be simulated in memory. All references to anonymous operands are in the same category, and hence the category field of the instruction can be used to indicate that the operand is anonymous. The address specifies a location within the current frame of the simulated stack. The only problem is that entities of different modes require different amounts of storage and, in some cases, must be aligned on different address boundaries. It would be wasteful to simulate the stack by an array of fixed-size elements, and hence the actual address corresponding to a particular operand must be determined by the contents of the stack at the time the operand is pushed onto the stack. Most of the bookkeeping associated with this storage allocation can be performed by the analyzer; only the actual address assignment must be deferred until the characteristics of the target machine are known.

If the address and size of the previous element on the stack are known, then these can be combined to determine the first address beyond the previous element. The alignment of the new item can be used to determine the proper boundary. The address of the new element is then assigned to the symbol for the anonymous operand, which would be used to provide the address of the previous element for the next new element. (Note that both the size and alignment of an item can be determined from its mode.)

Instructions which reference anonymous operands therefore have the following general form:

   operator mode STACK symbol(size)previous

Both "size" and "previous" would be omitted if the operand were the first on the stack.

A reference to a constant operand may or may not involve a memory reference on the target machine. The value can often be incorporated into the instruction itself if the constant satisfies certain machine-dependent constraints. When this cannot be done, the constant must be placed in memory. All references to constant operands are in the same category, and hence the category field of the instruction can be used to indicate that the operand is a constant. It is also useful to associate a symbol with the constant in case the target machine's assembler is incapable of handling literals.

There are four types of constants:

(1) An <u>as-is</u> constant is independent of the target computer, and its value can be placed directly into the Janus code.

(2) An <u>expression</u> constant is usually associated with the addressing structure of the target computer. Its complexity is limited by the translator. Each Janus mode identifier is assumed to be a variable whose value is the number of target machine address units occupied by an entity of the corresponding mode.

(3) A <u>symbolic</u> constant provides for machine-dependent constants which are unrelated to the addressing structure. Their values are preset in the memory of the translator by a pseudo, and are substituted into the Janus instruction.

(4) A <u>character code</u> constant could be handled via a symbolic reference, but this requires excessive amounts of translator memory. It is a simple matter for the translator to compute the integer equivalent of a character [Waite 73], and hence such constants are treated separately.

Instructions which reference constant operands therefore have the following form:

    operator mode CONST symbol() type value

Storage for an operand can be reserved if one knows the mode of the operand, whether it is an array, and the number of array elements. If the contents of the reserved area are to be initialized, most assemblers require that the initial values be presented at the time the storage reservation is made. The storage requirements of the entire array should be stated in a single pseudo so that a descriptor for the array can be constructed. If all elements have the same initial value, that value can be attached to the pseudo. Otherwise, the pseudo is flagged to indicate that initialization follows. The initial values can then be defined by a sequence of pseudos, each of which sets or skips a block of elements.

The storage reservation pseudo therefore has the following general form:

    SPACE mode category symbol(elements)flag type value

If "flag" is present, initial value specifications follow this pseudo; "symbol" and "flag" will both be omitted on those specifications.

2.2.3. _Some_ _Janus_ _Examples._ Figure 2.3 contains several storage reservations, both with and without initialization. The constant types are flagged by "A" (as-is), "E" (expression), "M" (symbolic) and "C"

```
SPACE INT LOCAL G1() .           SIMPLE VARIABLE
SPACE INT LOCAL G2(3) .          THREE-ELEMENT ARRAY
```

a) Reservation without initialization

```
SPACE INT LOCAL G3() C X.        CHARACTER C DE
SPACE REAL LOCAL G4() M LNBASE.  SYMBOLIC CONSTANT
SPACE INT LOCAL G5(15) A 6.      FIFTEEN IDENTICAL ELEMENTS
```

b) Reservation with initialization

```
SPACE INT LOCAL G6(4)+ .         DECLARE ARRAY, INITIALIZATION FOLLOWS
SPACE INT LOCAL (1) A 0.         FIRST ELEMENT IS INITIALIZED
 PACE INT LOCAL (1) .            SECOND ELEMENT IS NOT
SPACE INT LOCAL (2) A 1.         THIRD AND FOURTH ARE
```

c) Separate initialization of array elements

Figure 2.3

Use of the SPACE Pseudo

(character code). A plus is used as the "initialization to follow" flag.

The procedure of Figure 2.4 calculates the square root of a positive real number, using Newton's iteration. The algorithm has been simplified somewhat in order to concentrate on the features of Janus.

The first line specifies the mode of the result and the number of parameters, as well as the name of the routine. This information is included to ease the implementation of certain linkage conventions.

A SPACE declaration is given for each parameter. These declarations may or may not reserve storage. They serve to identify the mode of the parameter and to associate a symbol with the parameter position. Declarations of parameters are distinguished by the category PARAM, and hence may be treated specially by the translator.

LINKN is a special form of LINK, which conveys the additional information that this procedure does not invoke other procedures. Some optimization may be possible in this case if parameter addresses are passed in registers.

The remainder of the program is quite straight forward with the exception of CMPNF. This is a non-destructive comparison which checks the contents of the accummulator without destroying it. The F indicates that the value of the accummulator is only used on the "fall-through" path. The LOC pseudo defines a label and also indicates whether the contents of the accumulator and index register are significant at that

```
BEGIN REAL PROC SQRT(1)   .    SQRT RETURNS A REAL AND HAS ONE PARAMETER
SPACE REAL PARAM G92()   .     DECLARE THE FORMAL PARAMETER
SPACE REAL LOCAL G93()   .     DECLARE A LOCAL VARIABLE
LINKN REAL PROC SQRT(1)   .    PERFORM LINKAGE DUTIES IF NECESSARY
LOAD REAL PARAM G92()   .      ACCESS THE VALUE OF THE FORMAL PARAMETER
CMPNF REAL CONST G22() A 0E0.DOES NOT DESTROY THE ACCUMULATOR CONTENTS
JLT,I INSTR CODE G99()   .     ABORT THE RUN ON A NEGATIVE ARGUMENT
LOC REAL VOID G98.             ACCUMULATOR CONTENTS REAL, INDEX IRRELEVANT
STORE REAL LOCAL G93()   .     SAVE THE CURRENT GUESS
LOAD REAL PARAM G92()   .      RECALL THE VALUE OF THE FORMAL PARAMETER
DIV REAL LOCAL G93()   .       DIVIDE BY THE CURRENT GUESS AT THE ROOT
ADD REAL LOCAL G93()   .       AVERAGE THE RESULT WITH THE CURRENT GUESS
DIV REAL CONST G88() A 2E0.  TO GET A NEW GUESS
CMPN REAL LOCAL G93()   .      DOES NOT DESTROY ACCUMULATOR CONTENTS
JNE,I INSTR CODE G98()   .     REFINE THE GUESS AGAIN IF NECESSARY
RETURN REAL PROC SQRT(1)   .   ELSE RETURN WITH RESULT IN ACCUMULATOR
LOC VOID VOID G99.             ACCUMULATOR AND INDEX CONTENTS IRRELEVANT
MSG STRNG CONST G100() A NEGATIVE ARGUMENT FOR SQRT.
ABORT REAL PROC SQRT(1)   .    ABANDON THE EVALUATION OF THE PROCEDURE
END SQRT.
```

Figure 2.4

A Janus Procedure

point.

One of the problems with procedure calls is that of insuring modularity [Dennis 73]: In order to run programs written in Janus with those written in other languages one must be able to translate a Janus procedure call into the standard calling sequence assumed by the other languages. Thus it is extremely important to be able to recognize parameter setup and parameter use in the Janus code. If these constructs can be recognized, then translation rules can be written to match virtually any conventions.

As a concrete example, consider the procedure call of Figure 2.5a. The first and third arguments are to be passed by value, while the second and fourth are to be passed by reference. Computation is required to obtain the third and fourth arguments. It is assumed that the procedure returns a value in the accumulator.

Figure 2.5b shows the Janus version of the call with variable names instead of generated symbols for clarity. Two specifications of the arguments are given. The first, lying between CALL and RJMP, shows how they are computed. The second, lying between RJMP and CEND, is a list of argument addresses.

The translation of D[I+3] reflects the fact that an array index is an integer which must be multiplied by the number of address units per element before being used. Multiplication of the fixed offset can be carried out at translate time; a separate Janus instruction performs the multiplication of the variable offset. (The "+" in the variable offset

F(1,A,B+C,D[I+3])

a) A procedure call

```
CALL REAL PROC F()
ARGIS INT CONST C1() A 1
ARGIS,I REAL LOCAL A()
LOAD REAL LOCAL B()
ADD REAL LOCAL C()
STARG REAL TEMP T1()
LDX INT LOCAL I()
MPX INT CONST C2() E REAL
LOAD,I REAL LOCAL D(3*REAL)+
STARG ADDR ARG L1(3*ADDR)
RJMP REAL PROC F()
SPACE ADDR ARG L1(4)+
SPACE ADDR ARG (1) A C1
SPACE ADDR ARG (1) A A
SPACE ADDR ARG (1) A T1
SPACE ADDR ARG (1)
CEND REAL PROC F()
```

b) Janus code for (a)

Figure 2.5

Example of a Procedure Call

field of the reference specifies an anonymous operand in the index register.)

This procedure call can readily be translated for various interface conventions including stack (both hardware and software), list of addresses following the jump to the procedure, list of addresses within the procedure body, list of values within the procedure body. The calling sequence will not easily handle the case in which values are stored following the jump to the procedure. However, this form is unlikely to be used in practice: Access to the arguments from within the procedure body would involve some kind of indexing or indirection, and space to store the arguments would be needed at every call.

Janus has now been implemented, via the STAGE2 macro processor, on two computers. It is estimated that approximately two man-weeks of effort are required to construct the macros for a new machine. This would be the effort required to implement the first piece of Janus software; subsequent software would require only the additions to the original set of macros.

2.2.4. Realizing the Abstract Machine by Interpretation. Another method of implementing the abstract machine on the real machine is by interpretation i.e. a program is written in the language of the real machine to simulate the operation of the abstract machine. The data supplied to the interpreter is the program for the abstract machine, usually after it has been translated in one way or another to some binary representation. The writing of such an interpreter is usually a fairly straightforward task and consequently, the effort required to move the program can be quite small.

At first sight, it might appear that realizing abstract machines by interpretation produces portable programs at the cost of efficiency. The term "interpreter" usually conjures up visions of a very slow program. How is it then that this technique can be used to produce software of an acceptable efficiency. Let us first examine the structure of a simple interpreter.

Interpreters usually consist of:-

(a) A main routine to carry out instruction fetching and decoding

(b) A number of routines to perform the instructions of the machine being simulated

For a simple machine, the logic of the main routine is as follows :-

1. Fetch the next instruction to be obeyed

2. Increment the simulated program counter

3. Separate the operation code from the operands

4. Select the appropriate function routine on the basis of the operation code and jump to it

Each of the function routines must be terminated by a jump back to the start of the main loop of the interpreter. If we assume that the program being interpreted has been thoroughly checked so that there is no need to test for program counter or operand out of range, then the overhead introduced by interpretation is about 5 operations. If a particular function routine carries out a very simple operation e.g.

add the contents of a memory location to the simulated accumulator, then the overhead is relatively very high. On the other hand, if the function is a complex one so that the routine involves many operations, then the overhead introduced by the interpretation is only a small fraction of the total number of operations performed. Hence, the overall efficiency could be quite acceptable. Of course, the more complex the operations of the abstract machine, the greater the efficiency and the lower the portability. The goal of the designer is to choose the correct level of complexity so that he has a convenient language available for writing the program, yet can still obtain acceptable efficiency without having to expend too much effort implementing the interpreter.

2.3 Portability through Generation

Another approach to producing portable compilers involves the use of programming systems which attempt to automate the writing of translators of programming languages. These range in complexity from ones which automatically construct recognizers from the grammar of the language to those in which an attempt is made to handle both the syntax and the semantics, e.g. to use a compiler-compiler, one first expresses the formal syntax in a syntatic meta-language and inputs this to the syntax loader. This constructs tables which will control the recognition and parsing of programs in the language. Similarly, the semantics described in a semantic meta-language are fed into the semantic loader to produce another table containing a description of the meaning of statements in the language. When the loaders are discarded, the remaining program is a table driven compiler for the language.

The mechanical production of compilers and the use of compiler-compilers is being treated elsewhere in this course [Griffiths 74, Koster 74] and will not be discussed in any detail here. It should be noted, however, that many of the problems associated with the moving of compilers written in high-level languages still exist. For example, the kernel of a compiler-compiler includes such facilities as input-output, code generation routines and other facilities used by all the translators. Thus the portability of the individual compilers is dependent on the portability of the compiler-compiler itself. Similarly, if a syntax analyzer generator is itself not portable, then the new compiler must be developed on the old machine. Even with the difficulties that this can cause, it may still be a better proposition than attempting to write the analyzer by hand for the new machine. The output phase of the generator must be modified to produce code for the target computer but, once this has been accomplished, the analyzer can be generated from the meta-linguistic description of the syntax which, hopefully, has already been proven.

2.4 Adaptability

The two properties of portability and adaptability are very closely interrelated since the latter can enhance the former. If a portable program is created containing many facilities, then there is a risk that it will be rejected by an installation on the grounds that it is too large. Conversely, omission of some facilities may still result in the program being rejected because it does not satisfy the needs of the users of the installation. A portable program stands a much better chance of being accepted if the implementor is given some control over the way in which it utilizes system resources.

Techniques for producing adaptable software have already been discussed in some detail in a previous course [Poole 73]. Broadly speaking, they fall into two classes

(a) parameterization and selection

(b) translation

The former involves constructing the original software in such a way that it can be tailored to meet a specific application by the setting of parameters and the selection of components. For example, the portable text editor MITEM [Poole 69a] was written in such a way that from the original body of text one can generate one of six different versions, each of which can include a number of optional features. The choice of version and options is left to the implementor and is made on the basis of what facilities are to be provided for users and what system resources would be required. Adaptability through translation, on the other hand, is dependent on the characteristics of the translator and implies that the type of code generated can be varied according to the form of optimization required i.e. optimization for space as opposed to optimization for speed. For example, the production of a hybrid version of MITEM consisting of a mixture of interpretive and directly executable code was only made possible by the fact that the translator STAGE2 possessed highly adaptable code generators.

If the above techniques are applied to the production of a compiler, then, we might expect it to possess the following properties:

(a) compilers for standard subsets of the language can readily be generated from the original source statements.

(b) the source code is well parameterized so that the implementor has control over any facility which affects the amount of storage used by the compiler e.g. size of symbol table.

(c) the implementor can choose the appropriate balance between optimization for space and optimization for speed to assist in fitting the compiler into the space he wishes to make available to it, e.g. code to handle little used facilities in the language might be optimized for space to reduce the size of the compiler.

Finally, we would like the compiler itself to be able to apply different forms of optimization to the code it generates in response to requests from the user. We can envisage a situation in which a user first gathers statistics on which parts of his program are used most frequently. He then tells the compiler to optimize these for speed and the remainder of the program, for space. The resultant program being smaller in size and only slightly less efficient in terms of CPU utilization may be cheaper to run or provide a better turn around depending on the scheduling and costing algorithms of the particular installation.

3. CASE STUDIES

We will now consider a number of case studies involving portable compilers and the methods used to move them from one machine to another. The list is not intended to be exhaustive; rather, each study has been chosen in an attempt to illustrate one of the techniques discussed above.

3.1 AED

AED-0 [Ross 69] is a high level language developed by the M.I.T. Computer-Aided Design Project. It is based on ALGOL60 and is aimed at providing a convenient and effective language for creating specialized computer aided design systems for a wide variety of application areas. The original AED-0 compiler written in a bootstrap compiler language became operational on an IBM 709 machine in 1963. Subsequently, it was moved to CTSS of M.I.T.'s Project MAC operating on an IBM 7094. Further developments were then made in this system to produce a fairly stable language by late 1964. By this time, the compiler existed in its own language and all further system changes and improvements were carried out in AED-0 itself.

In 1967, considerable emphasis was placed on machine independence and the problem of moving the AED system to third generation machines. Successful transfers were made to a Univac 1108 and to an IBM system 360 in 1967 and 1968 respectively. In 1969, work was underway to move the system to DEC and GE machines.

Published details on the method of transferring the AED system are sparse. However, it appears that the compiler is moved via a half-bootstrap technique. Once, the compiler has been set up on the new machine, then the remainder of the AED software can be brought across. Estimates of the amount of effort required to make the move are not readily obtainable. However, all of the successful transfers of the AED system have been made by the people who developed it and who are therefore very familiar with it. To date, there does not appear to have been any move of the system made by other people. Such evidence supports the comment made earlier in this course about the difficulties that can be encountered when a half-bootstrap approach is used to port software.

3.2. LSD

LSD (Language for Systems Development) [Calderbank 71] is a low level systems programming language designed to provide programmers with some of the facilities of high level languages . The design goals for the language were object code efficiency and portability. The purpose behind the LSD project was to provide a language for implementing software on small machines, in particular, a suite of data acquisition programs being developed by a group of physicists. As a large time sharing machine was also available, the LSD compiler was set up in a test bed on this machine to provide facilities for the developers of the software to test their programs online. Once the programs were checked out, they could be transferred to the small machine providing a translator was available for that machine. However, the LSD compiler in the test bed did not produce machine code for either of the two machines. Instead, it output an intermediate code which was then interpreted. This facilitated the inclusion of many useful debugging features in the test bed, e.g., break point, trace, register dump etc. Since the intermediate code produced by the compiler was machine independent, there was no need to rewrite the code generators when the compiler was moved to a new machine. Of course, the interpreter itself would have to be rewritten in order to make the transfer.

Once the LSD program was tested and debugged on the large machine, it was translated into the assembly code of the small machine. The compiler used for this translation was the STAGE2 macro processor. The design of the LSD language was strongly influenced by the decision to use STAGE2 to make the language portable. STAGE2 is not a very fast translator and the more complex the language the slower the translation process. It should be noted that the speed of STAGE2 was of no consequence during the development of software written in LSD since all compilations required during the testing and debugging phase were carried out in the fast compiler in the interactive test bed.

The compiler for LSD, as one might expect, was itself written in LSD. STAGE2 and the appropriate set of macros formed the bootstrap compiler for the initial implementation on the large machine.

To move the LSD compiler, one would first implement STAGE2 on the target machine and then develop a set of macros to translate LSD into the machine code of the new machine. The LSD translator could then be compiled and set up on the new machine using this full bootstrap procedure. Given that the implementor was familiar with STAGE2, experience gained from moving LSD a number of times indicated that about one man-month of effort was required to implement about 95% of the language on a new machine. This included all the common and most frequently used facilities. The remaining 5% required about another man-month of effort.

Clearly this technique could be applied to other languages and compilers, i.e. use a portable general purpose macro processor as the translator to perform the bootstrap. Since one assumes that the compiler being moved has been debugged (except for the code generator) then the speed of the bootstrap translator is not a critical factor. It can, of course, be quite troublesome if the bootstrap compiler is also used to develop the main compiler initially. Translation speeds are very important when one is in the testing and debugging phase of software development.

3.3 BCPL

BCPL is a general purpose programming language which was originally developed as an aid to compiler writing. It has proved itself to be a very useful language in this area and in other systems programming applications. It is an ALGOL-like language based on CPL which was developed by the Cambridge and London Universities in the mid 60's. Although BCPL is block structured and permits recursion, it is a much less complex language than CPL, the most significant simplification being that it has only one data type - the binary bit pattern. The BCPL compiler which is written in BCPL is a highly portable program [Richards 71] and has been moved successfully to a number of different machines. It requires about 1 - 2 man-months of effort to make the move.

BCPL is a fairly simple language to compile. The compiler is quite straight forward and produces reasonably efficient object code at an acceptable speed. The language has a simple underlying semantic structure which is organized around an idealized abstract machine. The compiler can therefore be divided into two sections: one which translates BCPL into the language of the intermediate machine and the other which translates this intermediate language into the machine code of the target computer. This intermediate language called OCODE is a macro-like low level language which contains 56 different statement types. It can be thought of as the assembly language of the abstract machine defined by the BCPL language. OCODE is a very simple language since there is only one data type i.e. all values in the language have the same size. This allows for a very simple addressing structure as well as a stack whose operations do not need to be concerned with type.

The format of OCODE is that of an assembly code with a keyword specifying one of the possible statements. This is followed by arguments whose number depends upon the particular keyword. An OCODE program is coded as one statement per line.

Since BCPL permits recursion, all arguments, anonymous results and most variables are allocated space on a run time stack and are addressed relative to a pointer which indicates the start of the currently active portion of the stack. The instructions in OCODE are logically grouped in the following way:

1. Local variable access i.e. to variables in the active portion of the stack.

2. Global variable access similar to FORTRAN common.

3. Static variable access which is similar to own variables in ALGOL or local variables in FORTRAN.

4. The loading of constants.

5. Diadic expression operators.

6. Monadic expression operators.

7. Command operators.

8. Function and routine calling.

The BCPL compiler is moved to another machine via a distribution tape containing the compiler written in BCPL and the corresponding OCODE version. Both compilers generate OCODE as output. A working version of the compiler is created by translating each statement in OCODE into the corresponding sequence of assembly code instructions via a macro processor. This gives us a running compiler on the target machine which will translate OCODE. However, as OCODE is a simple language, there is little chance for optimization and the compiler is a rather inefficient one. More efficient code generators for translating OCODE into the machine language of the target machine can now be written and added to the compiler written in BCPL at the OCODE interface. Note that these code generating routines could largely be written in BCPL. There is considerable room for optimization during this process so that a reasonable level of local optimization can be obtained. This can be done by simulating the state of the run time stack and delaying the generation of code as long as possible. Instructions are only output when it becomes necessary to simplify the simulation. This method was used in BCPL code generators for machines like the 7094, 360, XDS Sigma5 and proved to be quite satisfactory. One advantage of this form of simulation is that it is largely independent of the machine. Hence a large portion of the code generator written for one machine could be used in a code generator for another. Once the BCPL compiler with the optimizing code generators is available then it can be put in service and the less efficient versions discarded.

Although the BCPL compiler proved to be highly portable, the amount of effort required to move it seemed to be larger than was really necessary. As it is of little importance just how inefficient the bootstrap version of the compiler is, Richards designed an interpretive machine code called INTCODE to ease the initial bootstrapping of BCPL onto a new machine. The main advantage of the language is that it is very compact; the assembler and interpreter are both very short and easy to write. Together they are almost an order of magnitude smaller than a typical BCPL code generator translating OCODE into assembly language and can therefore be implemented in machine code in a few days. The OCODE version of the compiler was translated into INTCODE and this became the distributed version. The interpreter for INTCODE can be expressed in BCPL and, even though no BCPL is available on the target machine, it can serve as a documentation aid and be translated by hand into some other high level language or assembly code.

The BCPL compiler composed of the INTCODE version, plus the interpreter is about the factor of 10 to 1 slower in execution speed than the directly executable one. However, again, we must remember that this is no great drawback since we are only involved in the first stage of the bootstrap process. The steps are still as outlined above, i.e., write code generators which translate OCODE into machine code and develop this compiler using the interpretive INTCODE version. With the

BCPL available in INTCODE, the transfer time is about one month.

The portability of BCPL illustrates the use a hierarchy of abstract machines [Poole 71]. The OCODE machine reflects the characteristics of the language and is well suited to executing programs written in BCPL. It is further removed from real machines than the INTCODE machine and hence requires a larger amount of effort to realize it on the actual computer. Its function in the hierarchy is efficiency rather than portability. The INTCODE machine, on the other hand is much closer in structure to that of real machines. It has a store consisting of equal size locations addressed by consecutive integers from 0 upwards. The central registers of the machine are A and B, accumulators, C, a control register, D, an address register, and P, a pointer used to address the local work area and function arguments. The form of an instruction on the INTCODE machine consists of four fields:

1. Operation code specifying one of eight possible machine functions.

2. Address field specifying an integer in the range 0 - 8191 which is the initial value of D in the evaluation of the effective address.

3. P bit is a single bit to specify whether the stack base is to be added into D at the second stage of the address evaluation.

4. I bit is an indirection bit which determines whether D is replaced by the contents of the location addressed by D at the last stage of the address evaluation.

There are 8 machine functions: load, store, add, jump, jump if true, jump if false, call a function and execute. The latter allows an auxilliary operation to be executed and effectively extends the number of operation codes available on the machine. The address D specifies which of the operations are to be carried out. There are in fact 24 such operations and the effective number of instructions on the machine is therefore about 30. It is clear that this machine is much closer to real machines and much further removed from BCPL, i.e., there are no stack operations. The stack itself is simulated in the linearly addressed memory. Hence the function played by INTCODE in the transfer of BCPL is portability rather than efficiency.

3.4. Pascal

There are two reasons why Pascal was chosen for this project [Webber 73]:

1. It is easier to move the LDT to a new machine if the translator is written in the language that it translates; the Pascal compiler that was available was written in Pascal.
2. The burden of writing any program is lessened if the implementation language is suited to the task and Pascal is well suited to writing a compiler.

3.4.1. Structure of Pascal. Pascal is fairly complete in terms of the programming tools it gives to the programmer. It is an ALGOL-like language with features found normally in more complex languages such as ALGOL 68 or PL/I. The language provides a rich set of data types and structuring methods that allow the programmer to define his own data types.

Two important features of the language are the RECORD and the CLASS. These two structuring methods are used to build the symbol table. (A CLASS is an execution-time allocatable memory area, and a RECORD is a collection of fields.)

Pascal is a procedure-oriented language. A procedure is the basic unit of a program and each is always defined within another procedure. The main program is considered to be a procedure without parameters which is defined in and called from the software system. A data area for local variables associated with every procedure invocation may be active or inactive. (An active data area is one whose variables are accessible to the executing procedure.) The data area for the main program containing global variables is always active.

There are two kinds of scalar data types in the Pascal language: predefined and defined. There are five predefined scalar types: INTEGER, REAL, CHAR, ALFA and BOOLEAN. The second kind of a scalar data type is one defined by the programmer. These are formed by specifying either a subrange of another scalar or enumerating the elements of the scalar.

A non-scalar type may be defined by specifying a structuring method and the component type of the structure. e.g. an ARRAY is a structure with all elements of one type and a component selection mechanism for selecting any element. A RECORD is a made of a series of fields, each of which may be of any type. A field of the RECORD is selected by the name of the field. A SET is a structuring method which indicates the inclusion or exclusion of every element in the domain of the SET. A

FILE is a sequence of components which are all the same type. The CLASS has components which are allocated during the program's execution. The components may be of any type except a CLASS or FILE. A pointer is the address of a component that was dynamically allocated in a CLASS. The component is allocated by the standard procedure NEW which returns a pointer to the component.

The assignment statement in Pascal allows the assignment of a scalar value to a scalar variable or an ARRAY or RECORD variable to a similarly structured variable. Other statements in the language include a GOTO statement for transferring control to another place in the program. Conditional statements are the IF statement which allows a two-way branch and the CASE statement which allows an n-way branch depending on the value of the case-expression. Pascal also allows repetitive statements such as the FOR, WHILE, and REPEAT statements. The compound statement allows a series of statements to be used as a single statement. The WITH statement allows the programmer to omit the description of the RECORD of a field within the WITH statement's component statement.

The reader should note that if the FOR statement has a final value which must be computed (i.e. an expression), it must be possible to save the value for the test preceding each execution of the component statement. Similarly, the RECORD variable of a WITH statement must be saved if its value is not constant (e.g. an array of RECORDs). This need to save run time values between statements must be reflected in the abstract machine.

3.4.2. **The Abstract Machine for Pascal.** The Pascal abstract machine has seven primitive modes. Five of these (INT, REAL, CHAR, ALFA and BOOL) arise from the predefined scalar types INTEGER, REAL, CHAR, ALFA and BOOLEAN respectively, and the primitive mode SET is derived from the Pascal SET structure. The seventh primitive mode of the abstract machine is ADDR. It represents a target machine address, and is required to handle two Pascal constructs:

1. Pointer variables
2. Parameters passed by reference

The memory of the abstract machine is divided into a number of areas or categories. The variables declared by the main program are called global variables and are assigned the category GLOBAL. All variables that are not declared in the main program are called non-global variables and are kept in the run time variable stack (RTVS). Every time a nested procedure begins its execution, an area of memory is allocated in the stack for its local variables. The RTVS has areas on it which are accessible to the executing procedure; these areas are said to be active. The areas on the stack which are not accessible are said to be inactive.

A display is used to identify the active data areas on the RTVS. It contains, for each nesting level, the base address of the active RTVS area for that level. To access a variable in RTVS the abstract machine first accesses the display to locate the active data area containing the variable, and then uses the given offset as an address within this area. Operands on RTVS are distinguished by the category DISP.

There is a high probability that a procedure will access its own data area, which is the last allocated data area on the RTVS. A significant optimization is possible if these references can be distinguished, and hence they use the category LOCAL instead of DISP.

Before calling a procedure, the calling procedure must set up a parameter area. This area is called PARAM in the abstract machine. When the procedure is entered, PARAM becomes part of the LOCAL data area.

Every mode, whether primitive or derived, has two characteristics which are relevant for storage allocation: size and alignment. These depend upon the target machine and cannot be determined by the LDT. Many machines use different amounts of storage for data depending upon the mode. The target machine may also require that an item of a certain mode must reside on a particular word boundary. The LDT cannot plan for any space that must be inserted between variables or fields in order to make an item reside on the correct boundary.

On the IBM 360, for example, a CHAR could be assigned a byte and an INT could be assigned four bytes. For efficient use of the hardware, the address of the first byte of an INT must be divisible by 4. The following PASCAL RECORD would then require nine bytes of memory:

```
RECORD
      A:INTEGER;
      B:INTEGER;
      C:CHAR
END
```

In contrast is the following RECORD which contains the same information but would require twelve bytes of memory if implemented in a staightforward manner:

```
RECORD
    A:INTEGER;
    C:CHAR;
    B:INTEGER
END
```

Although the LDT needs to know the sizes of structured types, it does not have enough information about the target machine to compute them. A possible solution, and the one chosen for the Pascal LDT, is to include in the abstract machine a way of mapping Pascal structures into the target machine. This requires the abstract machine to compute the size of the structure and pass the value back to the LDT.

Although there can be no physical flow of information from the MDT to the LDT, information flow can exist because the LDT does not have to numerically manipulate the size of a structure which is passed to it from the MDT. The latter can compute the size of the structure and associate the size with the symbol. Every time the LDT wants to use that size, it can pass the symbol to the abstract machine. If the MDT is implemented within the interface procedures of the LDT, the MDT could then actually pass back a numeric value of the size.

Two pseudo operations are used to compute the size of a record. The REC pseudo specifies the symbol that corresponds to the size of the record. It also specifies the boundary that the record must be on. The

REC pseudo is followed by a SPACE declaration for each field in the record; the symbol that is specified in the SPACE declaration is set to the offset of the field from the beginning of the record. An ENDR pseudo terminates the abstract machine record. Figure 3.1 illustrates the relationship between a Pascal RECORD and an abstract machine record.

A variable in the abstract machine is defined by four quantities:

1. Level of the Pascal procedure which defined the variable.
2. The offset from the beginning of data area.
3. The data area containing the variable.
4. The type of the variable.

The level of a variable is the level of the procedure which declared the variable. The problem of finding the offset of a variable is the same as finding the offset for a field in a RECORD; the size of the entire data area is needed so that storage can be allocated on the RTVS. The size of a data area and the offset for each variable are determined by treating the procedure's variables as a RECORD. Figure 3.2 shows how a Pascal VAR declaration is mapped into the abstract machine.

The type of a Pascal variable is determined in the declaration of that variable. The LDT translates all variable references in a source program to their equivalents in the abstract machine. The type of an abstract machine variable can be:

1. A primitive mode of the abstract machine
2. A block of data with a size equal to an integral number of elements of a primitive mode

```
RECORD

        A:ALFA;

        B:-10..10;

        C:BOOLEAN;

        D:REAL

    END;
a) A PASCAL RECORD
```

```
REC ALFA RECORD S1().

SPACE ALFA RECORD SA(1).

SPACE INT RECORD SB(1).

SPACE BOOL RECORD SC(1).

SPACE REAL RECORD SD(1).

ENDR ALFA RECORD S1().

b) The equivalent abstract machine record
```

Figure 3.1

A Pascal RECORD compared to an abstract machine record.

```
PASCAL:

        VAR

                A,B:REAL;

                C:CHAR;

                I,J,K:INTEGER;


JANUS:

        REC REAL RECORD S1().

        SPACE REAL RECORD SA(1).

        SPACE REAL RECORD SB(1).

        SPACE CHAR RECORD SC(1).

        SPACE INT RECORD SI(1).

        SPACE INT RECORD SJ(1).

        SPACE INT RECORD SK(1).

        ENDR REAL RECORD S1().
```

Figure 3.2

Mapping a Pascal VAR

declaration into an abstract machine record

The block of data is either a RECORD or an ARRAY; the need for describing a block of data arises from the Pascal construct that allows a RECORD or ARRAY to be assigned or compared to another RECORD or ARRAY.

In general there are three parts to every Pascal abstract machine instruction: the operation code, the operand mode, and the operand address. If the instruction references a constant, then a fourth field is to specify the constant.

The operation code and the operand mode are used collectively to specify the operation. The operand address is composed of four parts: a memory area, a base address, a fixed offset, and a variable offset. The memory area of an operand can be the CODE memory, the GLOBAL memory, or the RTVS.

The base address can have two meanings. If the category is CODE or GLOBAL, then the base address is the location of an instruction or data. For a non-global variable, the base address indicates the level of the procedure which declared that variable. A non-global variable reference uses DISP to find the active data area on the RTVS for the level of the variable. As noted earlier, the LOCAL category is considered a quick way to access an active area on the RTVS which ordinarily would be accessed via DISP.

The fixed offset part of an address is an LDT determined value that is included in the address computation of the operand. This value is the distance from the beginning of the data area to the variable in address units. If the operand is a field of a record, then the offset includes the distance from the beginning of the record to the field. Figure 3.3 shows an example of how the fixed offsets computed for the variables shown in Figure 3.2 are used in several Janus instructions.

The variable offset allows an execution-time determined value to be included in the address computation. If a variable offset is indicated, the contents of the abstract machine's index register are added to the address.

3.4.3. Incorporating the Abstract Machine into the LDT. The symbol table has an entry for every type, variable, constant, field of a RECORD and procedure defined by the programmer or predefined in the language. An entry for a type must contain the amount of storage required for a variable (or field) of that type. A size is represented by two things:

1. a primitive mode and
2. an integer value (or symbol that the MDT associates with an integer value).

The integer value times the primitive mode is equal to the storage required for the type. For example, if the integer is ten and the primitive mode is REAL then the size is equal to the storage required for ten REALs. The size also indicates that variables of that type must be aligned (in the target machine) on the same memory boundary as the primitive mode.

An entry for a variable must indicate a type and an address for the variable. The type is a pointer to the symbol table entry for the type of the variable; the address of a variable is composed of three parts.

PASCAL:

    J:=I+1;

JANUS:

        LOAD INT LOCAL D2(SI).
        ADD INT CONS S4() 1.
        STORE INT LOCAL D2(SJ).

                        Figure 3.3
                Accessing variables in the
            active data area for level two

The first part is the integer level of the procedure which declared the variable. (A level of zero indicates a global variable.) The second part of an address is an offset in address units from the beginning of the procedure's data area to the variable, and the third part is the category of the variable.

A entry for a constant contains a type and a value. The type is a pointer to the symbol table entry for the type of the constant; the value part contains the value of the constant. An example of a symbol table entry for a constant is an element of an enumerated scalar. The entry contains a pointer to the type of the scalar and a value equal to the non-negative integer mapping for that element.

An entry for a field in a record is similar to an entry for a variable. The address specifies an offset which is equal to the distance from the beginning of the record to the field. It also contains an offset which is used if the field is in the variant part of the record. This extra offset facilitates addressing a field of a record that may have been allocated in a CLASS structure.

Procedures require several kinds of information in their symbol table entries. Every procedure has a CODE category entry point address, which specifies the first executable instruction of the procedure, and two data areas. The two data areas are the parameter list and the local variable data area, allowing the LDT to produce instructions that will make appropriate adjustments to the RTVS on entry and exit to the procedure. Before a procedure is entered, the calling procedure allocates space on the RTVS for the called procedure's parameters. Upon entry to the procedure, the called procedure allocates space for its local data area. The parameter list becomes part of the local data area at this time.

If the procedure is a function, its value is left in the RTVS. The symbol table entry for the function contains an address in the RTVS for the returned value and the value's type.

The LDT translates phrases in the source program into their abstract machine equivalents; the MDT takes the abstract machine instructions and produces code for the target machine. The translation of source code into abstract machine instructions is accomplished through a set of interface procedures in the LDT, one procedure for every abstract machine instruction. As the LDT determines the appropriate abstract machine instructions for the phrase, it will make calls upon the proper procedures. The parameters of each procedure contain the same information as the operands of the corresponding abstract machine instruction.

The function of the interface procedures is to interact with a particular implementation of the MDT; their results will vary depending on the implementation of the MDT. Symbolic abstract machine language can be done away with by having the procedures produce target machine instructions that are equivalent to abstract machine instructions.

3.4.4. <u>Measurements</u>. There are various measures of efficiency that could be applied to the compiler produced on this project. Clearly, by dividing the compiler into two sections, one could introduce inefficiencies which would not otherwise be there if the compiler were to produce machine code directly. These inefficiencies involve both execution speed and core occupancy. Since the Pascal compiler modified in this project was the 6400 compiler, the necessary standard was available to make comparisons. Another factor of interest is the time taken to implement the MDT on a new machine as this gives some measure of the portability of the approach.

The MDT has been implemented on the 6400 via a set of STAGE2 macros. Although a full implementation has not been completed as yet, the effort required to implement about 90% of the abstract machine was one man-week. One short cut taken was to use the FORTRAN input-output system available on the machine. The implementor estimated that about another one man-week of effort would be required to make a full implementation. Currently, it appears that given the existence of STAGE2 on the target machine, about one man-month of effort would be required to implement a working and usable version of the Pascal compiler via a full bootstrap technique. Such a compiler could then be put into service while work was being carried out to optimize the compiler by moving the macro definitions into procedures.

With the macros available to translate Janus to 6400 assembly code, it is then possible to write test programs in Pascal and compare execution time and core occupancy for the object code produced by both the modified and unmodified compilers. A test package was constructed consisting of the basic mathematical functions and a main program to call them 10,000 times. The code produced by the modified compiler proved to be about 10% slower than that from the unmodified one. The size of the object code was the same in both cases. At the time the project was carried out, it was suspected that the mechanism for procedure entry and exit was not as efficient for the abstract machine as it might have been. Accordingly, timing tests were carried out on procedure calls and these showed that the modified compiler produced code that was about 30% slower. With a more efficient mechanism, one is led to believe that the modified code could be brought to within about 5% of the code produced from the unmodified compiler. This is not a very heavy price to pay for the high portability both of the compiler itself and of the object code it produces. Note that an applications program written in Pascal could now be transported to another computer in Janus and implemented on that machine via STAGE2.

3.5. IBM S/360 FORTRAN(G) Compiler

The IBM Fortran IV G-level compiler exemplifies an approach to compiler portability in which the abstract machine is implemented on the real machine via an interpreter. Although the compiler has probably never been moved to another computer, in principle it could be, since the technique used to construct it would facilitate such an operation.

The compiler is written in the language of an abstract machine called POP whose design is well suited to the implementation of compilers. As one might expect, POP is a machine organized around a number of last in - first out queues i.e. push down stacks. The instructions of the machine are set up to operate on these stacks as well as on a linearly organized memory. There are two stacks, WORK and EXIT which are an integral part of the machine so that access is efficient. The remainder of the stacks are created dynamically as required by the particular program. The language of the POP machine available to the compiler writer is a one-address symbolic assembly code comprising an operation code and an operand. Since there are about 100 instructions in the abstract machine, the operation code can be represented in one byte. The language has been organized so that the operand which represents either a value or a relative address can also be represented in one byte. Hence each POP instruction occupies 16 bits on the System/360. For a full description of the machine, the reader is referred to the Program Logic Manual [FORTRAN 67]. Some idea of the structure may be gained by considering the various classes into which the instructions have been divided :-

(a) transmissive

(b) arithmetic and logical

(c) decision making

(d) jump

(e) stack control

(f) code producing

(g) address computation

(h) indirect addressing

The compiler is divided into five phases:-

Parse   Phase 1 translates the Fortran source text into polish notation and creates various in-core tables for use in later phases.

Allocate   Phase 2 allocates storage for the variables defined in the source module.

Unify   Phase 3 optimizes the usage of general registers within DO loops.

Gen   Phase 4 uses the polish notation and the memory allocation information to produce the code for the object module.

Exit   Phase 5 completes the output for the object module and winds up the compilation process.

From the description of the various parts of the compiler, it appears likely that phases 1 and 2 are largely machine independent although 2 could reflect some of the structure of S/360. Phase 3 obviously depends on the register structure of the 360 and is machine dependent as are phases 4 and 5. These phases would have to be rewritten to transfer the compiler to another machine. However, it should be noted that this rewrite can be carried out in the POP language.

The Fortran compiler written in POP is translated for the S/360 by defining each instruction type as a macro and using the standard macro-assembler. Each instruction produces a pair of address constants of size 2 bytes. The POP interpreter written in S/360 assembly code fetches a half word according to the current value of the simulated program counter, separates it into a 1-byte opcode and a 1-byte operand and then transfers control to the appropriate function routine. Since access to the WORK and EXIT stacks must be efficient, the pointers to these stacks are maintained in general registers. The remaining stacks are referenced via pointers stored in memory.

As was pointed out in Section 2.2.4, the efficiency obtainable when an abstract machine is realized through interpretation depends on the relationship of the overhead introduced by the main loop of the interpreter and the number of operations involved to perform each of the instructions. Thus the time required to execute the POP instruction

ADD G

which adds the contents of the memory location G into the top cell of the WORK stack is probably somewhat shorter than that required to execute the main loop. Hence, if all instructions were such simple ones, then the resulting program would be very inefficient. On the other hand, consider the instruction

QSA G

which compares character strings and advances a pointer along a line if the strings are equal. Clearly, this could involve many operations and the time required would be large compared with that of the main loop. If the program spends most of its time executing instructions of comparable complexity, then the overall efficiency could be quite high.

References

Calderbank, V.J., Calderbank, M.: LSD Manual. CLM-PDN 9/71, Culham Laboratory UKAEA, Abingdon, Berkshire (1971).

Coleman, S.S., Poole, P.C., Waite, W.M.: The Mobile Programming System: Janus National Technical Information Center PB220322, U.S. Dept. of Commerce, Springfield, Va., 1973. (To appear in Software, Practice and Experience.)

Dennis, J.B.: Modularity. Advanced Course on Software Engineering. Bauer, F.L. (ed.), Springer-Verlag, Berlin, 1973.

USA Standard FORTRAN (USAS X3.9-1966), USA Standards Institute, New York, 1966.

IBM FORTRAN IV (G) COMPILER, Program Logic Manual, 1967.

Clarification of FORTRAN Standards: Initial Progress, CACM, 12 (May, 1969).

Griffiths, M.: 4.A. Introduction to Compiler-Compilers, Advanced Course on Compiler Construction, 1974.

Halstead, M.H.: Machine Independent Computer Programming, Spartan Books, Washington, D.C., 1962.

Koster, C.H.A.: 4.B. Using the CDL Compiler-Compiler, Advanced Course on Compiler Construction, 1974.

Poole, P.C., Waite, W.M.: A Machine Independent Program for the Manipulation of Text. Tech. Rept. 69-4. Computing Center, University of Colorado, 1969.

Poole, P.C.: Hierarchical Abstract Machines. Proc. Culham Symposium on Software Engineering (April 1971).

Poole, P.C., Waite, W.M.: Portability and Adaptability, Advanced Course on Software Engineering, Springer-Verlag, 81, 183-278 (1973).

Richards, M.: BCPL: A Tool for Compiler Writing and Systems Programming, Proceedings of the Spring Joint Computer Conference, 34, 557-566 (1969).

Richards, M.: The Portability of the BCPL Compiler, Software, Practice and Experience, 1, 135-146 (1971).

Ross, D.T.: Introduction to Software Engineering with the AED-0 Language, Report ESL-R-405, Softech (October 1969).

Waite, W.M.: The STAGE2 Macroprocessor, Tech. Report 69-3-B, Computing Center, University of Colorado, 1969.

Waite, W.M.: The mobile programming system: STAGE2. CACM, 13, 415-421 (July 1970).

Waite, W.M.: Implementing Software for Non-Numeric Applications. Prentice-Hall, Englewood Cliffs, N.J., 1973.

Weber, L.B.: A Machine Independent Pascal Compiler. MS Thesis, University of Colorado, Boulder, 1973.

Wirth, N.: The Programming Language Pascal. Acta Informatica, 1, 35-63 (1971).

CHAPTER 5.B.

STRUCTURING COMPILER DEVELOPMENT

James J. Horning

University of Toronto

Toronto, Canada

1. GOALS OF COMPILER DEVELOPMENT

Each compiler is developed in a particular environment, in response to certain needs, and that environment will shape not only the form of the completed compiler, but also the process by which it is developed. This chapter is concerned with ways in which the development process can be structured to meet given objectives.

An explicit set of goals should be formulated at the outset of any compiler project; although they may change with time, they provide guidelines for major decisions and are the basis for evaluation. Merely stating goals does not ensure their attainment, but without goals no coherent product can be developed.

1.1. TYPICAL COMPILER GOALS

1.1.1. CORRECTNESS

"Of all the requirements that we might place on a program, first and foremost is that it be correct. In other words, it should give the correct outputs for each possible input. This is what we mean when we say that a program 'works,' and it is often and truly said that 'any program that works is better than any program that doesn't.'...

"If a program doesn't work, measures of efficiency, of adaptability, or of cost of production have no meaning. Still, we must be realistic and acknowledge that probably no perfect program was ever written. Every really large and significant program has 'just one more bug.' Thus, there are degrees of meeting specifications - of 'working' - and evaluation of programs must take the type of imperfection into account.

"Any compiler, for example, is going to have at least 'pathological' programs which it will not compile correctly. What is pathological, however, depends to some extent on your point of view. If it happens in your program, you hardly classify it as pathological, even though thousands

of other users have never encountered the bug. The producer of the compiler, however, must make some evaluation of the errors on the basis of the number of users who encounter them and how much cost they incur...." [Weinberg 1971]

One goal of every compiler is to correctly translate all correct input programs and to correctly diagnose all incorrect ones [see Chapter 5.D.]. However, compilers are seldom absolutely correct; perhaps "reliability" is a more feasible goal, i.e., keeping the number of errors encountered acceptably small.

What constitutes an acceptable error rate will depend on the expected cost of errors in the environment. The cost of an error, in turn, depends on the way in which the compiler has deviated from its specification. It may be worse, for example, to incorrectly translate a correct program than to incorrectly diagnose a faulty one. Many compilers deliberately deviate from the specifications of their source languages, either accepting prohibited constructs ("language extensions") or rejecting permitted ones ("restrictions"); the costs of such deviations may be justified by advantages gained elsewhere. Errors or deviations that produce warning messages are generally more tolerable than those that go unreported.

1.1.2.   *AVAILABILITY*

Even a correct compiler that cannot be run is of very little use. Thus, a very important aspect of any compiler project is its schedule. If the compiler is worth anything, then any delay in its production will incur a real cost. Similarly, the compiler must run on the right (i.e., available) machine in the right configuration with the right operating system.

Unfortunately, scheduling is one of the least understood aspects of managing software development. Teams seldom have a chance to undertake projects similar to what they have done before, so past experience is not a sufficient guide. Most often, project deadlines are set by external constraints, with little appreciation for technical realities.

As Weinberg [1971] notes, "Conceptually, there is a minimum expertise and a minimum time necessary to produce a given system. Because these quantities cannot be clearly defined - and because of the uncertainties involved in program estimation - managers often form a team which any reasonable judgement would indicate cannot perform the designated task in the allotted time. Inevitably, the team is given an extension when the time limit is reached and the reality must be faced. Had it been faced earlier, the work could probably have been organized differently - in recognition of the longer schedule - and thus produced, in the end, more quickly."

It should be recognised that man-months is a measure of cost, not of productivity. A compiler that can be produced by a team of four in two years can certainly not be produced by a team of sixteen in much less than a year, nor by a team of a hundred in a lifetime!

1.1.3. GENERALITY AND ADAPTABILITY

Although some special-purpose compilers are produced to compile single programs, most compilers must be planned to handle a large number of programs, and to evolve over a considerable lifetime to meet changing requirements. Compiler-writers are frequently surprised at the uses to which their compilers are put, and often find that they persist longer than was planned during their construction.

The design of a compiler should not make unnecessarily restrictive assumptions about the programs it will compile that will rule out new classes of users (e.g., that a fast "student" compiler will only be used for small programs), nor should it limit the compiler to particular equipment configurations (e.g., exactly 64K of memory and one disk). It should rather contain a number of parameters that allow the compiler to be tailored to particular environments with a minimum of redesign.

During the lifetime of a compiler, requirements and specifications may change many times (often, even before it is completed!). Unless special care is taken during its construction to ensure adaptability, responding to these changes may be both traumatic and expensive.

1.1.4. HELPFULNESS

Chapter 5.D. contains a catalogue of features that separate a "bare-bones" compiler from a truly useful one. None of these features comes by accident, and few are likely to be included unless "helpfulness" is among the design goals of the compiler. The kind and amount of help that is most appropriate will depend on the intended users: beginning students need careful explanations of simple errors in small programs, while system programmers are more concerned with the detection of subtle errors in large programs, or the location of efficiency "bottlenecks."

In addition to error detection and diagnosis, the compiler may assist with various other parts of the program development process, such as documentation, updating source programs, and maintenance of program libraries. The general aim is to reduce the cost of program development in a specific environment.

1.1.5.   *EFFICIENCY*

Efficiency is both a frequently-stated and easily-misunderstood goal in compiler
development. The usual two-dimensional classification into "space efficiency" (memory
usage) and "time efficiency" (processor usage) is greatly over-simplified. Space and
time interact, and in different environments different balances are appropriate.
Furthermore, there are several other dimensions of efficiency to be taken into account:
- efficiency of the compiler development process
- efficiency of program development using the compiler (including efficiency of
  compilation)
- efficiency of target programs produced by the compiler.

There are some environments in which the first dimension is relatively unimportant
(because a single compiler will have many users), or the third dimension is relatively
unimportant (because program development costs overshadow execution costs), but
environments in which the second dimension can be neglected are much less common.
Most compiler projects must aim for at least acceptable efficiency in all three
domains.

1.2.   *THE EFFECTS OF TRADE-OFFS*

Having picked a set of goals, the compiler-writer must recognise that they cannot all
be optimised simultaneously. There is a general "trade-off" phenomenon: improvements
in one area can only be made by sacrificing something in another. (This is sometimes
known as the TANSTAAFL Law: There Ain't No Such Thing As A Free Lunch.) The rare
occasions in which a new technique allows an improvement without a corresponding cost
represent significant advances in the theory of compilers.

Serious compiler-writers attempt to make trade-offs rationally, but face immense
difficulties in doing so. Success in meeting a goal is difficult to measure quantita-
tively (and even harder to predict); even where measurements can be made, the units do
not lend themselves to comparison (e.g., should a compiler be speeded up from 8600
cards/minute to 9200 cards/minute if the reliability would drop from 99.995% to
99.992%?). In theory, all trade-off decisions are economic, and the appropriate units
are monetary ones, derived from cost-benefit analysis. In practice, they are usually
taken intuitively, based on simple rankings of the goals (e.g., yes/no, because speed
is considered more/less important than reliability). This section mentions several
trade-offs that generally occur within any compiler project.

1.2.1. COMPILATION EFFICIENCY VS. EXECUTION EFFICIENCY

For most languages and most machines, the simplest and most easily produced translation of a program will not be optimum in execution efficiency. Thus, the compiler-writer is faced with the choice of whether to invest effort at compile-time to save effort at run-time, as well as choices that allow him to trade space for time. There is a spectrum between very efficient compilers and compilers that produce very efficient target code, and the appropriate point on this spectrum depends on whether compilation or execution is expected to be the dominant cost. (Caution: Installations that have done careful measurements have generally been surprised at the high proportion of computer time actually spent on compilation.)

The topic of optimisation is discussed more fully by Cheatham [Chapter 5.E.]. Here we merely note that some local optimisations (e.g., "peephole" optimisations [McKeeman 1965]) are so cheap that their inclusion is almost always justified, while most global optimisation techniques are appropriate only to execution-intensive environments, and that the inclusion of optimisation will also affect other goals, such as schedule and efficiency of compiler development.

1.2.2. COMPILATION EFFICIENCY VS. HELPFULNESS

It is clear that a "stripped-down" compiler that makes no attempt at careful error-checking or diagnosis can be smaller and faster than a more helpful one. Such "efficiency" is often illusory, however, since the faster compiler may have to compile programs many more times before they are completely debugged.

1.2.3. GENERALITY VS. EFFICIENCY

"If our primary concern in a particular application is efficiency, the first step should always be to look for areas in which the specifications can be changed to suit computer efficiency rather than user convenience.... The effect of slight differences in source language on compiler efficiency can be striking. Typically, if the compiler writer can choose 10 percent of the language which he will not implement, he can produce a 50 percent faster compiler." [Weinberg 1971] "The addition of features to a language is not a linear process as far as the translator is concerned. Constructs interact with each other, and the addition of a single feature may, in some cases, double the size of the translator." [McKeeman 1970]

Highly specialized compilers can be tuned to be extremely effective in limited environments. However, every bit of tuning that is done for a particular environment reduces the possibility of effectively transferring the compiler to some other environment.

Thus, it is extremely useful to delimit in advance the intended range of application of the compiler (and hence, the allowed tunings).

1.2.4. *RELIABILITY VS. COMPLEXITY*

Every decision provides an opportunity for error, and generally the reliability of programs declines rapidly with size. Many of the techniques of software engineering are designed to cope with unreliability, but even they can only delay, not eliminate, this phenomenon. Thus, when reliability is an important goal it may be necessary to keep the compiler structure very simple and to ruthlessly restrict its size.

1.2.5. *DEVELOPMENT SPEED VS. EVERYTHING ELSE*

It is generally recognized that when a programming team is under time pressure all other aspects of its work suffer. Weinberg [1972] contains striking experimental evidence of the deleterious effect on four other factors (core usage, output clarity, program clarity, program size) of the simple instruction "try to complete this assignment as quickly as possible." It is not surprising that the best compilers are generally the work of small teams relatively free of external time pressures.

2. *PROCESSES IN DEVELOPMENT*

The construction of a compiler (or any large software system) involves several conceptually distinct processes: specification, design, implementation, validation, evaluation, and maintenance. Several processes may involve the same people, many of them may procede concurrently, and the whole cycle may be repeated several times, yet it is useful to remember that they have distinct aims and produce different products. This section briefly reviews the function of each process - more thorough treatments will be found in Metzger [1973], Bemer [1969], and Aron [1970].

2.1. *SPECIFICATION*

In an initial phase of the project, a set of goals should be chosen and their implications explored. The compiler specification document should include
- a precise specification of the source language to be compiled
- a definition of the target language or machine
- an indication of the relative importance of various goals
- design targets for such features as compiler size and speed and degree of optimisation
- a list of diagnostic and other features to be included in the compiler

and perhaps
- a scheduled completion date and/or budget
- a choice of the language in which the compiler is to be written.

At this stage, the specification is the principal interface between the compiler project and the potential users (customers). Great care should be taken that it is complete and unambiguous, and that both groups are satisfied with the same interpretation.

2.2. DESIGN

The design of a compiler should be started well before the specifications are frozen, since it will generally reveal the possibility of trade-offs that can best be evaluated by the customers. It will also continue well into implementation; indeed, in many projects it is impossible to draw a precise boundary between design and implementation.

The design process should structure the compiler into major components (passes, phases, modules), allocate functions and responsibilities among them, and define their interfaces. Its result should be one or more design documents, describing the overall structure (and the reasons why it was chosen) and the specifications of the major components.

Since design works from a specification and produces specifications for components, it may be treated as a recursive process, with each component being designed in the same way that the compiler itself was. The recursion terminates at a level where a specification is simply an executable program. Some designers prefer to use a non-compilable language (e.g., English) for the higher levels of a design, doing only the bottom level in a programming language; others have found it convenient to express the structure at all levels in a programming language, using macro or procedure names for the components.

2.3. IMPLEMENTATION

Regardless of the design technique used, at some point the compiler must be written in an already implemented language, translated into machine code, and executed. Because of the size of compilers, implementation is usually the process in which the most people are involved. However, the ability to parcel out pieces of a compiler to different programmers depends critically on the success of the design in separating those pieces cleanly, with well-specified interfaces and no implicit interactions.

2.4.   VALIDATION

After the compiler has been written, it is necessary to verify that it in fact works correctly. Such over-all testing is normally preceded by smaller tests of individual program modules as they are written ("unit testing," "debugging") and as they are collected into successively larger subsystems ("system integration"). It may well be followed by an independent "acceptance test" performed by the customer.

Thorough testing is greatly facilitated if each level of specification is accompanied by a carefully designed set of test data, to be supplemented by test data supplied by the person (generally the programmer) most familiar with the internal structure of the component. Such data should be permanently associated with the program as part of its documentation, and should be updated with every change of specification, and re-run after every modification [Poole 1973].

2.5.   EVALUATION

Throughout the lifetime of a project, trade-offs are continually forcing evaluation of various aspects of the compiler. After the compiler has been validated it is useful to attempt a global evaluation of the compiler to see how well it has met its original (or modified) goals, how appropriate were various decisions taken during its development, and whether the specifications were reasonable. A careful cost-benefit analysis may well indicate the desirability of repeating some of the previous processes to produce a new product.

2.6.   MAINTENANCE

The compiler-writer generally feels that his troubles are over when the compiler has been accepted and released. However, it is not uncommon for the maintenance process of a successful (widely-used) compiler to consume as much manpower as all the others combined. Demands for maintenance may arise for a variety of causes
- change of language specifications
- detection of errors
- detection of inefficiencies
- new environments
- need for new facilities.

It is largely because of the unpredictable (but predictably large) demands of maintenance that careful and extensive documentation of previous processes is required. Belady and Lehman [1971] give a theory that predicts maintenance costs.

3. MANAGEMENT TOOLS

Because compilers are large programs, their construction generally involves several people, and thus, necessarily, management. This section is devoted to some social structures that assist the human activity of compiler development.

3.1. PROJECT ORGANIZATION

Conway's First Law [1968] states that every program has the same structure as the organization that produced it. This principle can be used to structure the implementation group, given a particular design. Alternatively, it can warn against the choice of certain designs, given existing group structures. (It is no accident that small teams generally produce single-pass compilers, or that the largest computer company recently produced an 87-phase compiler!)

Baker and Mills [1973] have advocated the production of structured programs by means of highly structured groups, called Chief Programmer Teams. (The CPT concept also includes a number of other tools that will be treated later.) Each CPT contains several members with clearly defined roles. The chief programmer has overall design responsibility, writes the top-level program, specifies components, and checks the programming of all other team programmers. The backup programmer monitors the work of the chief programmer, performs his functions in his absence, and assumes responsibility for major subsystems. Up to five junior programmers work on the development of components defined by the chief programmer; in large projects they may also serve as the chief programmers of subsidiary CPT's. The programming librarian modifies source programs as instructed by programmers, submits runs at their request (programmers may not submit their own runs), logs all runs,(together with listing, predicted result, and actual result), and generally maintains project records. The results obtained by CPT's are impressive - 10,000 lines of "debugged" source program per man-year, with a mean of one bug later detected per 10,000 lines of debugged program - but how much is due to project organisation, and how much to other factors, is hard to determine.

Weinberg [1971] has proposed another organisation: the "egoless programming" group, based on the observation that a programmer is the person least likely to spot errors in his own work. In egoless programming, programs are the property of the group, rather than the individual, and all programs are passed around for checking by one or more other programmers. The approach certainly seems applicable to compiler development, although it may not generalize to extremely large projects.

One thing that should be kept in mind when trying a new project organisation is the

"Hawthorne effect": workers involved in any experimental situation may take such pride in their work that their performance improves temporarily, whether or not the new situation is superior. (Smart managers sometimes exploit this fact by trying arbitrary experiments.)

3.2. INFORMATION DISTRIBUTION AND VALIDATION

The design and implementation of a system progresses by a series of decisions. Each decision must be checked to ensure that it is consistent with system specifications and earlier decisions. Furthermore, each decision results in information about the system that is potentially useful in making further decisions. System documentation should record and communicate these decisions.

It is common in compiler projects to maintain a project workbook containing the current state of the design and implementation, generally in loose-leaf form to make updating easy. Each member of the project has an up-to-date copy of the workbook, to which he can refer for information as needed. As pages are replaced, they may be filed in a special section to provide project history. A workbook is most useful if it concentrates on recording the reasons for decisions, rather than simply listing the decisions themselves.

Both the Chief Programmer Team [Baker 1973] and "egoless programming" [Weinberg 1971] methodologies rely heavily on converting programming from a "private art" to a "public practice." By ensuring that all programs are checked by at least two people, and that program listings are public (project) documents, they greatly reduce the probability of programming errors escaping notice for long periods. They also cut down a project's vulnerability to the loss of a programmer - someone else has already read and understood the modules he has produced.

For very different reasons, Parnas [1971] has advocated that management provide techniques for restricting the flow of information within a project. He argues that in well-structured systems each module will make only a few clearly-specified assumptions about the rest of the system. On the other hand, "a good programmer makes use of the usable information given him." The conclusion that he draws is that each programmer should receive documentation only of those design decisions that he is intended to assume in the production of his current module. Systems produced under such a discipline should be more reliable and more adaptable, although, as Weinberg [1971] points out, most actual information flow in a social system takes place outside management-defined channels in any case.

3.3.   PROGRAMMER MOTIVATION

The goals of an individual programmer are not necessarily those of the group. Many projects have ended disastrously or been substantially delayed because some members were working at cross-purposes to the project. Weinberg [1971] has pointed out several pitfalls in the usual management techniques for motivating programmers: salary and threats.

Perhaps the strongest single motivation to project members is participation in establishing project goals, and the imposition of goals from outside the project is often ineffective. Groups that coalesce into teams also exert strong social pressures on each other to ensure that each member "pulls his weight," particularly in situations where everyone's contribution is available for public inspection. One company has found that substantial rewards (up to $10,000) for error-free programming contributes to the establishment of a Zero-Defects psychology.

4.   TECHNICAL TOOLS

Not all of the problems involved in compiler development are human problems. There is a growing body of software engineering practice and experience that indicates the utility of a variety of technical tools, some of which are mentioned here.

4.1.   COMPILER COMPILERS

Most compilers have many tasks in common: lexical analysis, syntactic analysis, semantic analysis, code generation. When some (or all) of these problems are solved in general form, the compiler-writer can be relieved of some part of his job. This is the goal of compiler compilers, as described by Griffiths [Chapter 4.A.], Koster [Chapter 4.B.], McKeeman et al. [1970], and Feldman and Gries [1968].

Every compiler-writer should certainly consider the compiler compilers available to him before deciding to write his own complete compiler. If he finds one that acceptably meets his requirements, he may gain in a number of respects:
- the compiler will be produced more quickly, with less manpower
- the compiler will probably contain fewer errors
- the compiler will be more flexible and adaptable
- the compiler may well contain useful features that would not otherwise have been included
- since it uses well-tested techniques, the compiler may even be more efficient.

Not every compiler compiler offers all these advantages, of course, and there are not

yet good compiler compilers for all environments. Some languages may be beyond the
scope of existing compiler compilers.

4.2. STANDARD DESIGNS

Even if no compiler compiler is suitable, the compiler-writer need not start from
scratch. Many different designs, suitable for various languages and environments
have been published. McClure [1972] and Gries [1971] survey a number of these. We
may mention designs
- for COBOL [Conway 1963]
- for Algol 60 [Randell 1964]
- for PL/I subsets [McKeeman 1970]
- for Algol 68 [Peck 1971].

The user of a standard design
- saves time
- avoids pitfalls
- perhaps increases compatability with other compilers.

4.3. DESIGN METHODOLOGIES

For components that he chooses to design himself, the compiler-writer may find it
advantageous to adopt one of the current design methodologies, such as those described
by Zurcher and Randell [1968], Liskov [1972], and Graham [1973]. These promise
- better control of the design process
- earlier evaluation of the system
- more adaptable designs.

4.4. OFF-THE-SHELF COMPONENTS AND TECHNIQUES

Virtually every technique mentioned in this course has been described in the open
literature, frequently in the form of an algorithm. Most of them have been implemented
on one or more machines, and frequently these implementations are available from their
originators. Many compiler-writers choose to combine research with development, but
there is no real need to do so.

A word of caution is in order. Algorithms are much more portable than programs. Even
if a program module is available "free" from its implementor, unless it has been
constructed with portability and adaptability in mind, it may be easier to write a
new program based on the same design than to adapt the old program to the new environment. (Interface specifications are particularly troublesome.)

4.5. *STRUCTURED PROGRAMMING*

Programming need not be the undisciplined art form that it once was. Systematic techniques for decomposing a problem and constructing a program to solve it are now becoming accepted practice. Particularly when combined with management tools (e.g., in Chief Programmer Teams) these disciplines have proved to be very effective in increasing programmer productivity, retaining adaptability, and ensuring reliability. Very readable expositions are contained in Dahl, Dijkstra and Hoare [1972], Wirth [1971], Mills [1972], and Naur [1969].

4.6. *STRUCTURED PROGRAMS*

It is very helpful for programs to retain the structure that guided their construction. This contributes to reliability, and particularly to maintainability. It is now generally accepted that the replacement of <u>go to</u> statements by more structured control constructs (e.g., <u>if-then-else</u>, <u>case,do-while</u>) contributes to this structure [SIGPLAN 1972].

Careful use of procedures and macros to modularize the program is another extremely helpful technique. Ideally, every decision in the design and implementation of the compiler would be stated in one place only, and each module would isolate the consequences of an independent decision.

4.7. *APPROPRIATE LANGUAGES*

Our languages control the way we think and the rate at which we work. The choice of an appropriate language can reduce the cost of compiler by an order of magnitude. This is due to two effects: in the right language, the source text of the compiler will be much shorter, and a suitable language will reduce the opportunities for error and assist in the detection of errors that do occur.

We may identify a number of requirements of a language suitable for writing compilers:
- it must be easily readable and understandable
- it must have appropriate data objects (e.g., Booleans, integers, characters) and operations on them
- it must have simple yet powerful control and data structures (e.g., iteration, vectors, selection)
- it must contain enough redundancy for substantial compile-time checking
- it must support modularisation (e.g., by means of macros, procedures, and data type definitions), preferably with secure separate compilation
- it must allow separate and checkable specification of module interfaces

- it must map efficiently into machine code.

Assembly languages are unsuitable on almost all counts, but many high-level languages are also unsatisfactory. Probably the best candidates currently are the so-called Machine-oriented Languages (MOL's) [van der Poel 1974].

References

1. Aron, J.D.: Estimating resources for large programming systems. In Buxton, J.N., Randell, B. (eds.): Software engineering techniques 68-79. NATO Science Committee, Brussels 1970.

2. Baker, F.T., Mills, H.D.: Chief programmer teams. Datamation December 1973 58-61.

3. Belady, L.A., Lehman, M.M.: Programming system dynamics or the meta-dynamics of systems in maintenance and growth. IBM Research Report RC3546, Yorktown Heights, 1971.

4. Bemer, R.W.: Checklist for planning software system production. In Naur, P., Randell, B. (eds.): Software engineering 165-180. NATO Science Committee, Brussels 1969.

5. Conway, M.E.: Design of a separable transition-diagram compiler. Comm ACM $\underline{6}$, 7 396-408 (1963).

6. Conway, M.E.: How do committees invent? Datamation April 1968.

7. Dahl, O.-J., Dijsktra, E.W., Hoare, C.A.R.: Structured programming. Academic Press 1972.

8. Feldman, J.A., Gries, D.: Translator writing systems. Comm ACM $\underline{11}$ 2 77-113 (1968).

9. Graham, R.M.: Performance prediction. In Bauer, F.L. (ed.): Advanced course on software engineering 395-463. Springer-Verlag 1973.

10. Gries, D.: Compiler construction for digital computers. John Wiley & Sons, Inc. 1971.

11. Liskov, B.H.: A design methodology for reliable software systems. Proc FJCC $\underline{41}$ 191-199 (1972).

12. McClure, R.M.: An appraisal of compiler technology. Proc SJCC $\underline{40}$ 1-9 (1972).

13. McKeeman, W.M.: Peephole optimisation. Comm ACM $\underline{8}$ 443-444 (1965).

14. McKeeman, W.M., Horning, J.J., Wortman, D.B.: A compiler generator. Prentice-Hall 1970.

15. Metzger, P.W.: Managing a programming project. Prentice-Hall 1973.

16. Mills, H.D.: Mathematical foundations of structured programming. IBM Federal Systems Division, Report FSC72-6012, Gaithersburg 1972.

17. Naur, P.: Programming by action clusters. BIT $\underline{9}$ 3 250-258 (1969).

18. Parnas, D.L.: Information distribution aspects of design methodology. Computer Software 26-31 IFIP Congress, Ljubljana 1971.

19. Peck, J.E.L. (ed.): Algol 68 implementation. North Holland 1971.

20. Poole, P.C.: Debugging and testing. In Bauer, F.L. (ed.): Advanced course on software engineering 278-318. Springer-Verlag 1973.

21. Randell, B., Russell, L.J.: Algol 60 implementation. Academic Press 1964.

22. SIGPLAN: Special issue on control structures in programming languages. SIGPLAN Notices $\underline{7}$ 11 (1972).

23. van der Poel, W. (ed.): Machine-oriented languages. Proceedings of an IFIP working conference, to appear 1974.

24. Weinberg, G.M.: The psychology of computer programming. Van Nostrand 1971.

25. Weinberg, G.M.: The psychology of improved programming performance. Datamation November 1972 82-85.

26. Wirth, N.: Program development by stepwise refinement. Comm ACM $\underline{14}$ 4 221-227 (1971).

27. Zurcher, F.W., Randell, B.: Iterative multilevel modelling - a methodology for computer system design. Proc IFIP Congress 1968 138-142.

Chaper 5.C

PROGRAMMING LANGUAGE DESIGN

W. M. McKeeman

University of California at

Santa Cruz, U.S.A.

"It is as important to
forbid non-sense as it is
to permit good sense"

1. WHO SHOULD (NOT?) DO IT?

I can still find no better way to express my thoughts on this subject than the following [McKeeman 66]: "The universe and its reflection in the ideas of man have
wonderfully complex structures. Our ability to comprehend this complexity and per-
ceive an underlying simplicity is intimately bound with our ability to symbolize and
communicate our experience. The scientist has been free to extend and invent language whenever old forms became unwieldy or inadequate to express his ideas. His
readers however have faced the double task of learning his new language and the new
structures he described. There has therefore arisen a natural control: a work of
elaborate linguistic inventiveness and meager results will not be widely read."

"As the computer scientist represents and manipulates information within a machine,
he is simulating to some extent his own mental processes. He must, if he is to make
substantial progress, have linguistic constructs capable of communicating arbitrarily
complicated information structures and processes to his machine. One might expect
the balance between linguistic elaboration and achieved results to be operable. Unfortunately, the computer scientist, before he can obtain his results, must successfully teach his language to one particularly recalcitrant reader: the computer itself. This teaching task, called compiler writing, has been formidable."

"Consequently, the computing community has assembled, under the banner of standardization, a considerable movement for the acceptance of a few committee-defined
languages for the statement of all computer processes. The twin ideals of a common
language for programmers and the immediate interchangibility of programs among
machines have largely failed to materialize. The main reason for the failure is that
programmers, like all scientists before them, have never been wholly satisfied with
their heritage of linguistic constructs. We hold that the demand for a fixed standard programming language is the antithesis of a desire for progress in computer
science. That the major responsibility for computer language design should rest with
the language user will be our central theme."

While a great deal of programming language design has gone on in the meantime, much
of it has been at cross purposes. On the one hand the designer has been trying to
facilitate the messy process of human understanding; on the other hand he has had to
insure efficient use of modern computers. His language constitutes the impedance
match between grossly different representations. In some sense the designer has been
limited to the top of a tower of languages that starts at bits in computer memory and
build up through stages to his higher level language. Between each stage there must
be an automatic translation program. As might be expected, there is only a limited
amount of variation possible under these constraints. The major concepts that have
arisen are the variable and structures composed of variables which are, in fact and
intent, ways of using computer memory; finite functions over data structures; and

sequence control. Programming languages are still a long way from the patterns of
human thought.

A simple analogy will illustrate the point. Suppose we were designing languages for
expressing recipes. We might very well succeed in saving some ingredients, and even
some footwork by the cook. But we would probably not help the master chef invent a
new dish, nor the gourmet to enjoy one. Their patterns of thought, about exactly
the same subject, are on a different plane altogether.

The fact that programming costs now exceed computer costs has forced the langauge
designer to concentrate more on structuring the programming process than the program
itself. There is as much to save by reducing the pre-inspiration flailings of a programmer as there is in eliminating a redundant STORE in the inner loop.

Two additional levels of language appear to be forming on top of the more traditional programming structures (Figure 1.1). One is characterized by a top-down analyses of the program structure. The other is characterized by predicates over various abstract data structures. At the highest level we now see, we have statements of things that must be true, perhaps at specific points in the computation. Once we established these restrictions, we fragment the program hierarchically into the most natural units possible. Only then do we map the program onto machine-related constructs. These topmost mappings are probably not done automatically; it is easier to do them by hand than to formalize the mapping process. Paradoxically, we no longer care very much about the structure of the higher level language program if we can understand it easily with reference to the even higher level descriptions.

Again, since it is the programming process that is being facilitated, we observe that progress down the tower of abstraction may well run into problems, causing lower level obstacles to be solved by changing higher level descriptions. It is an iterative process involving all the levels of abstraction.

Thus we in one sense put to rest the issue of "Who should do it?". At the level of meaty thoughts, the programmer necessarily invents his symbolism. Either in one wrenching step, or in a series on smaller steps, he transforms the program to the top of the automatically translatable series and then turns the problem over to the compiler.

The substantive questions are what structures are useful at each of the various levels of abstraction. The new viewpoint is that it is not necessary to mix all the levels into one notation. Or, to put it differently, it was a mistake to assume we could think effectively in a (single) programming language.

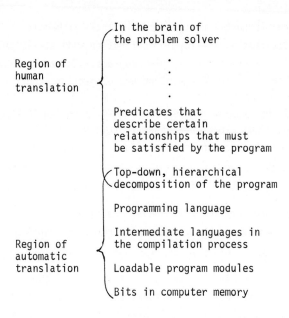

Levels in the
problem solving language tower.

Figure 1.1

2. DESIGN PRINCIPLES

There are a lot of reasons to design computer languages but the point of view expressed here is that there is a special application area which needs a special language. The designer is attempting to put such a language together without secretly
trying to upstage the designers of Algol-68 (or any other general purpose language).

The first question, as a practical matter, is how to do it. And the first rule, as
a practical matter, is how to Keep It Simple. The major error by beginning designers
and compiler writers is overambition. The result may be a great design but will
surely be an unfinished project. As Wirth says, the hardest decisions are what to
leave out.

Use established constructs as much as possible. The remaining sections of this
chapter are concerned with the most useful models for languages.

Having decided not to do very much, and to copy most of it, the problem reduces to
achieving the necessary features (Figure 3.1) in a consistent manner. The simplest
way to proceed is to write some programs. That is, let your new language invent itself naturally. A small program will generally exercise a large part of the language.

Then attempt to use the standard language defining tools (grammars) to specify the language concisely. The restrictive form of definition will surely suggest changes in the language, then, in turn, in the sample programs. Iterate the process until both the programs and the language description are elegant and understandable.

One might suspect that the language would not improve by having to conform to a restrictive defining tool. But experience shows that it does. In some sense there is no art unless there is a restriction of the medium. In some perverse way, the human mind, in coping with restriction, produces its best results. And grammars, the very formalization of nested definition, are a rich medium.

Involution is a desirable property for a language. Having added a facility, it pays to use it everywhere it makes sense. The use of <expression> in Algol is an example.

Orthogonality is a desirable property. The facilities that are there should be highly independent. For example, if there are features for sequence control, then there should not be an additional set of sequence controlling features down inside expressions.

Adequacy is a desirable property. It should be able to express the solutions to all problems to be solved in it. But that is not the same as generality, or completeness. There is no reason to be able to compute an arbitrary function if we know ahead of time that only certain simple classes of functions are going to be used.

Translatability is a desirable property. There is not much point in designing a neat language that cannot be translated, eventually, to machine language. Although we have made the point that some translations are best done by the human hand, they must be doable. For those that are going to be automatically translated, the language designer had better have some translator writing experience. A number of our most spectacular modern computer languages concealed hidden snags that defeated the compiler writers.

Another important property of the language is that it mirror human thought patterns. The go-to controversy is an excellent example. When one human is giving another another commands, he rarely says "Now go to step 3" or the like. More likely he will say "Do X and then Y and then Z." While you are doing Z, if P happens, then quit doing Z and start all over." That is, naming, abstraction, sequencing, repeating, quitting, and the like are natural modes of thought. Unfortunately, early programmers were more concerned with giving commands to computers, leaving us with an anachronistic, inhuman go-to heritage. The solution is not to get rid of the go-to, it is to get it out of our sight and mind. It belongs at some convenient point below the highest level language the human is going to deal with in the tower in Figure 1.1.

3. MODELS FOR LANGUAGES

There are an enormous number of useful language models upon which the designer might base his new language. Each must have some merit or it would not have survived the "natural control" mentioned in Section 1 of this chapter. For the problem solver the measure of merit is in how much the language helps him to discover a good solution.

In each linguistic model there are some of these necessary, human-engineered facilities. Figure 3.1 gives a brief list of important features. Again, it is not necessary (or even advisable) to have all features in one level.

Assertions	A facility to state propositions that should hold regardless of the details of implementation. (Also called predicates, invariants, properties).
Hierarchical decomposition	A facility to express a top-down analysis of the programming task. Tasks and subtasks. Structures and substructures. May or may not imply sequencing.
Modular decomposition	A facility to express program units that may be semi-independently written or executed. Sequencing not implied. Intermodular interfaces necessarily simple in both form and dynamic behavior.
Data structuring	A facility to express sets of values. A program is a function over a domain consisting of all values of its global variables (including input). Reducing the variability of the range through data definition reduces the needed complexity of the function (program).
Abstraction	A facility more general than hierarchical decomposition. The ability to take any internally consistent theme of a program, describe it, name it, and use only the name subsequently.
Sequencing	A facility to control the sequence of events during computation, fully or partially.

| Data manipulation | A facility to carry out primitive operations on the data. Except for its interaction with sequencing, highly application dependent. |
| Redundancy | The facility to guide programming by detecting and diagnosing inconsistencies of the programmer. Includes paragraphing, required declaration, type checking, etc. |

Programming Language Features.

Figure 3.1

3.1 THE ALGOL FAMILY AS MODELS

The Algol family of languages (Algol-58, Algol-60, Euler, Algol-W, PL/1, Pascal, Simula-67, Formula Algol, Algol-68, to name a few), serves as an excellent repository of notations for scientific problem solving. A few of them are reviewed below. Some constructs are the incarnation of more than one different features out of Figure 3.1.

The facility of Algol for hierarchical decomposition of the programming process is the procedure. Procedures can be defined in terms of other procedures to an arbitrary depth. We can write

```
          procedure program;
          begin
               initialization;
               main process;
               termination
          end program;
```

having left out the details of the three parts. Continuing we write

```
          procedure initialization;
          begin
               read user directions;
               prepare tables;
               print headings;
          end initialization;
```

again without making any commitments to details of data structures and other low level details. And so on.

The use of the procedure in this manner has one disadvantage: it is decidedly sequential. Some hierarchical decompositions do not have any implied sequencing. For example, the perfectly reasonable decomposition

```
procedure scientific subroutines;
begin
    floating point routines;
    fixed point routines;
    text routines
end scientific subroutines
```

does not make any sense.

The facility in Algol for modular decomposition is also the procedure. The necessary discipline on the intermodular interface is achieved by requiring all communication to take place through the parameter list (no global or up-level addressing).
Since procedure definitions can be nested, modules can be further refined. The problem with this kind of refinement is that the inner procedures cannot be used outside of the containing procedure, an effect not always desired. Another important
feature of modularization, the ability to restrict the access to the global data
structure for any given module to the appropriate variables is not generally possible in Algol. The only scope restriction available is through nesting. Thus it
is impossible to have three modules A, B and C, and three variables AB, AC and BC,
where A is restricted to exactly AB and AC, B is restricted to exactly AB and BC,
and C is restricted to exactly AC and BC.

The facilities in Algol for sequencing have proven most successful. Recent designs
have tended to minimize the elaborate looping constructs, eliminate the go-to, and
add procedure and loop exit constructs.

The most general form of the Algol decision making (conditional, if, case, etc.)
facility can be expressed as [from rumors about the Dijkstra New Mexico lectures,
1/74]:

```
if
    guard:  action;
    guard:  action;
    guard:  action;

      . . .

fi
```

where one action is selected from among those which are "unguarded". The traditional if-then-else construct has two guards that are mutually exclusive. For example:

$$\text{if } a > b \text{ then S1 else S2}$$

is expressed

```
if
    a < b:   S1;
   ¬ a < b:  S2
fi
```

The case statement of Pascal

```
case i of
begin
    c1:      S1;
    c2:      S2;
    c3:c4:   S3;

      . . .

end;
```

is expressed

```
if
    i = c1:        S1;
    i = c2:        S2;
    i = c3 ∨ i = c4:S3;
fi
```

The general notation has several important properties. First, it is general. Second, the possibilities of more than one guard simultaneously satisfied, or zero guards satisfied now occur, giving the opportunity for new semantics. Third, the notation is order-independent (in contrast to if-then-else, the original case statement of Hoare, the LISP conditional). Fourth, and perhaps most important, the guards are in the form of assertions, forming a possible link to a higher level assertion definition of the program.

Exactly the same form can be used for looping.

```
loop
    guard:  action;
    guard:  action;
    guard:  action;

      . . .

pool;
```

with the obvious interpretation that all guards passed are executed in some unknown order, and all guards failing terminates the loop.

Again, one can imagine using the same form for events. The guards are to be "continuously" evaluated and, whenever one becomes true, the computation is interrupted and the corresponding action carried out.

An argument against all of the above can be based on the inefficiency of evaluating all of the guards every time the construct is entered, and the possibility of side effects causing the guards to be ill-defined. Both are based on traditional intuition as to how such constructs might be implemented on contemporary computers. I suspect the solution is an interesting, but not very difficult, problem for compiler writers.

The facilities in Algol for redundancy include required declarations of variables. This allows the compiler to not only check for spelling errors but also certain semantics implied by type restrictions. The type facilities of Pascal are much stronger in this regard by eliminating the need for coding a host of little messages as integers which have then lost their unique identity in the program for checking purposes. It was the lack of such a facility that caused many errors in the XPL compiler.

Long, mnemonic identifiers are also redundant, both for the compiler and the human reader, as are paragraphing conventions, enforcing the matching of begin-end pairs and other similiar rules [McKeeman '65].

Facilities for data structuring finally appear in the Algol languages in Algol-W, and then in Pascal (Algol-68 has, of course, everything). We start with certain sets from mathematics (integers, reals, etc.) and other user defined sets (types). Then the concepts of sets, ordered sets and graphs are used to build more complex combinations. It is important to realize that the path from the original idea to the ultimate programming language data structure is a long one. Algol does not give us much guidance, for example, on representing veal cordon bleu.

3.2 MATHEMATICS AS A MODEL

The notations of mathematics are a second, though certainly not independent source of concepts. Mathematics is a lot less constrained than Algol. About all that is necessary is that the notation facilitate formal manipulations and that it can be written down. And, in addition, it has hundreds of years of evolution behind it. The lack of constraint is not all of positive value. A great deal of mathematics deals with concepts that are noncomputational in nature (the law of excluded middle, extrapolation to the limit, infinite sets, etc.). What is always finite is the sequence of formal manipulations the mathematicians go through to prove their results.

There is not much point in trying to review mathematics here. To date it is the most primitive concepts that have been most used in programming languages. To some extent this is a result of the more complex mathematical concepts failing to work. There is, for example, a great deal of theory about functions of a real variable, most especially analytic functions. But computer represented functions are always finite in both range and domain. The result is that algorithms that depend upon convergent series, or the finer properties of the real field, may be erratic. In computing it always seems best to do a lot of something simple than a little bit of something clever.

3.3 STREET LANGUAGE AS A MODEL

Although we have placed it last, it should be clear that past formalisms are not the source of new ideas. It is the undisciplined ramblings of human communication that are most likely to lead to real linguistic progress. If there is a special application, then the sample programs (of Section 2) may well show special primitives. The language of a bank teller at a computer console, for example, might be described by the grammar

```
teller = command *;
command = deposit
        | withdrawal
        | transfer
        | open_account
        | close_account;
```

and so on. Such a language is matched firmly to the application. We expect it, no matter how far from our heritage, to be better for the application than all of the neat constructs of numerical analysis (or astronomy for that matter).

4. REFERENCES

1. W. M. McKeeman, Algol 60 Reference Language Editor, Comm. ACM, Vol. 8, No. 1 November 1965, pg 667.
2. W. M. McKeeman, An Approach to Computer Language Design, Ph.D. Thesis, Stanford University, April 1966.

CHAPTER 5.D.

WHAT THE COMPILER SHOULD TELL THE USER

James J. Horning

University of Toronto

Toronto, Canada

0.   INTRODUCTION

> "When I use a word," Humpty Dumpty said, in a rather scornful tone,
> "it means just what I choose it to mean - neither more nor less."
> "The question is," said Alice, "whether you can make words mean so
> many different things."
> "The question is," said Humpty Dumpty, "which is to be master -
> that's all."
>
> — Lewis Carroll, Through the Looking Glass.

The emphasis of this course has been on the process of translation from high-level
to low-level languages: man-machine communication. It is all too easy to neglect
the importance of communication in the other direction, but without effective
machine-man communication, compilers are useless. Furthermore, if we are to be
truly masters of our machines, we must insist that both parts of this dialogue be
conducted in languages acceptable to us.

Koster [1972] identifies several tasks of a compiler:
- to check whether the source program is correct
- if it is not correct, to give all useful information for correcting it
  (treatment of static errors)
- if it is correct, to translate the program into an equivalent object code
  program
- to cause the object program to be executed
- to report any errors occurring during execution.

This chapter is concerned with the design of appropriate communication from the compiler to the user regarding each of these tasks. It is motivated by the warning that "the naive programmer is only too willing to confuse the properties of the language with those of the compiler" [Koster 1972].

Since conversations with the compiler are initiated by the user, compiler responses may conveniently be thought of as feedback. It is useful to have both negative feedback (warnings of detected errors), and positive feedback (indications that certain types of errors were not found). Compiler output has both immediate uses (e.g., debugging) and deferred uses (e.g., maintenance, documentation). A well-engineered compiler will take all of these into consideration, without drowning the user in paper.

1. NORMAL OUTPUT

Most of this chapter is devoted to compiler responses to various sorts of errors, but it is worth noting that a basic requirement on any compiler is that it produce suitable output for correct programs. Since error messages and diagnostics are generally in addition to normal output, they constitute a small fraction of the total compiler output, even though errors are detected in most programs.

1.1. HEADINGS

Every compiler should clearly identify itself at the start of each compilation. Failure to provide such identification is one of the most common (and inexcusable) errors of amateur compiler-writers. Useful information includes the
- source language
- target machine
- compiler (name and version)
- date when the compiler was created
- time of the current compilation
- options in effect, and options suppressed.

As illustrated in Figure 1.1., such a heading need not consume much space, and is not hard to generate.

```
TOOLCOM/390 - UNIVERSITY OF TORONTO  VERSION 4.2 (1985 MARCH 22)
SOURCE LANGUAGE: TOOLKIT - TARGET MACHINE: SYSTEM/390 - TIME: 1985 MARCH 29, 14:38
OPTIONS: ON (PARAGRAPH, CROSS-REFERENCE, PROFILE) - OFF (TARGET CODE, TRACE, DUMP)
- - - - - - - - - - - - - - - - - - - - - - - - - - - - - - - - - - - - - - - -
    1 |   << SOURCE PROGRAM STARTS HERE >>
```

Figure 1.1. A Sample Heading

Headings are perhaps neglected because they don't seem to be too helpful as immediate feedback to the user debugging his program. By and large he treats them as so much noise to be ignored at the top of every listing. However, in the deferred uses of compiler output some piece of identifying information may well be crucial, and extremely hard to reconstruct after the fact.

1.2.   LISTINGS

Almost all compilers make provision for listing source programs when they are compiled.
A listing enables the programmer to verify that the program was input correctly,
provides a framework for error messages and diagnostics, and serves as an essential
component of documentation. It rarely makes sense to suppress the source listing.

A good listing contains more than just the source text. It must establish a co-ordinate system within the program by which program elements can be identified, both for
human communication and for association with (compile-time and run-time) error messages.
It is common to number either every line or every statement of a program; some compilers
use an additional co-ordinate (e.g., code location) to simplify run-time messages.
Other useful information (particularly measures of cost) may be included in any extra
space remaining on each line.

Much time is spent reading listings (although perhaps not as much as should be). A
corresponding amount of thought should be given to their layout and appearance.
Few compiler-writers can agree on precise formatting rules, but any user can spot
the difference between a haphazard listing and a well-considered one. One non-
obvious point learned from hard experience is that the part of each line containing
source text should be separated from the rest by visible delimiters, avoiding visual
ambiguity.

The placement of source text within the available space can substantially affect
the readability and understandability of programs. Careful programmers use blank
lines and spaces to improve readability by making visual structure reflect logical
structure. The key to effective "paragraphing" is the consistent application of
simple rules (e.g., indent the body of each nested structure, such as a _for_ loop or
a _begin_ block). Various paragraphing styles have evolved, many of them algorithmically
expressable. Automatic paragraphing of source listings is now becoming a popular
compiler option.   There are many reasons for doing this:
- it relieves the programmer of a tedious chore
- it simplifies the process of modifying programs (since the source deck need
  not be re-paragraphed)
- it assures an exact correspondence between logical and visual structure, not
  subject to programmer error
- it ensures a uniform paragraphing style within a group
- it allows programs to be automatically reformatted to new page sizes (e.g.,
  for publication)
- it allows the consistent use of extended character sets (e.g., upper and lower

```
1        context Portion_of_the_timer_manager;

2            type Timer_interrupt_type = (Calender_clock_update_alarm,
3                Cpu_scheduler_alarm,Primitive_manager_calender_clock_alarm,
4                Flush_interrupt);

5            type Alarm_type = (End_of_time_slice, Run_clock_alarm);

6            type Timer_element =
7                record
8                    pointer to Process_or_capability_description_type (
9                        Process),
10                   pointer to Timer_element (Next_element),
11                   Alarm_type (Alarm_reason),
12                   Timer_units (Time)
13               end;

14           /*        Insert - - this puts element in its correct place in the *
15            * queue and adjusts the interval.                                */

16           macro Insert(Element);

17               begin
18                   open Element@;

19                   if Time < First_timer_element@.Time;
20                       then:  Next_element := First_timer_element;
21                           First_timer_element := Element;
22                           Next_element@.Time := Next_element@.Time - Time;
23                       else:

24                           begin
25                               declare
26                                   pointer to Timer_element (E);
27                               E := First_timer_element;
28                               Time := Time - E@.Time;

29                               cycle

30                                   .... exit when Time < E@.Next_element@.Time
31                                       | E@.Next_element = End of queue;
32                                   E := E@.Next_element;
33                                   Time := Time - E@.Time
34                               end;

35                               Next_element := E@.Next_element;
36                               E@.Next_element := Element
37                           end;

38                           if Next_element    = End_of_queue;
39                               then: Next_element@.Time :=
40                                   Next_element@.Time - Time
41                           end

42                   end

43               end
44           end macro;

45       -|-
```

Figure 1.2.1   An Automatically Paragraphed Listing

case)   available on printers, but not keypunches, to add further visual structure
Figure 1.2.1. shows the output of a typical automatic paragrapher. Further details
may be found in Gordon [1974].

Listings of target programs are not needed nearly as frequently as source listings.
They are sometimes demanded by users who do not really trust their compilers, but
their most common use is to assist the compiler-writer himself in debugging or maintaining the compiler. The provision of a capability to list the target code generated
for specified sections of source code is thus a good investment, but the emphasis
should be on simplicity and clarity, rather than on the provision of elaborate
features. Figure 1.2.2 shows one possible style.

1.3.   SUMMARIES

Although a source listing contains theoretically complete information about a
program, it is generally useful to collect some information in a more compact form.
The compiler's symbol table is the repository of much of this information, and provision should be made to print it in a convenient form, either at the end of compilation,
or at the end of each major unit (e.g., procedure). For ease of access, it should
be sorted alphabetically, and for each symbol should indicate at least:
- its type and size
- the co-ordinate where it was defined (declared)
- the number of times it was used

and possibly:
- the co-ordinates of all uses of the symbol (a cross-reference table)
- the (absolute or relative) memory address associated with the symbol (a
  memory map).

The compiler should indicate the memory requirement (code, and, if possible, data)
for each major program unit. Depending on the language and the environment, various
other statistics gathered about the program may be helpful. Finally, the number of
warnings and error messages printed must be displayed in a conspicuous place, so
that the programmer can easily verify that he has not missed any. (If no errors are
detected, do not make the mistake of telling the programmer that his program does
not contain any errors.)

Compilers should also collect statistics on their own performance. A few lines at
the end of compilation indicating the amount of time used by major compiler components,
the size of various tables, etc., will not only warn the user who strains various
compiler limits, but will also guide the person who wishes to optimize compiler performance.

X P L   COMPILATION -- STANFORD UNIVERSITY -- XCOM III VERSION OF MAY 7, 1969.

TODAY IS AUGUST 10, 1969.

```
1  |                                                                    1286
2  |     /*  INTERLIST $EMITTED CODE  */                                1286
3  |                                                                    1286
4  |     DECLARE I FIXED, J BIT(16), K BIT(8),                          1286
5  |         ALPHA CHARACTER INITIAL('MESSAGE'),                        1286
                                          24: DESC = 6, 160
                                         160: CHARACTER = D4
                                         161: CHARACTER = C5
                                         162: CHARACTER = E2
                                         163: CHARACTER = E2
                                         164: CHARACTER = C1
                                         165: CHARACTER = C7
                                         166: CHARACTER = C5
6  |         BETA (3) BIT(64) ;                                         1286
7  |                                                                    1286
8  |     CALL TRACE ; /* BEGIN TRACING */                               1286
                                        1286: CODE = STM  1,124(3,11)
                                        1290: CODE = LA   1,12(0,0)
                                        1294: CODE = BALR 12,15
                                        1296: CODE = LM   1,124(3,11)
9  |     I,J,K = 2 ;                                                  | 1300
                                        1300: CODE = LA   1,2(0,0)
                                        1304: CODE = STC  1,1346(0,11)
                                        1308: CODE = STH  1,1344(0,11)
                                        1312: CODE = ST   1,1340(0,11)
10 |     BETA(I) = ALPHA ;                                            | 1316
                                        1316: CODE = L    1,1340(0,11)
                                        1320: CODE = L    2,24(0,13)
                                        1324: CODE = SLL  1,2
                                        1328: CODE = ST   2,2811,13)
```

Figure 1.2.2.   Interlisting Emitted Code.

2.   REACTION TO ERRORS

In an ideal world, where neither humans nor machines ever made mistakes, the
compiler-writer could limit his attention to correctly translating correct programs
(and some naive compiler-writers do so). In reality, however, most of the programs
processed by any compiler will be to some degree incorrect - simply because correct
programs need not be recompiled - and most compilers themselves contain hidden
errors. Unless the compiler-writer has planned for them, some errors may have
catastrophic consequences.

2.1   STYLES OF REACTION

We may broadly classify a compiler's response to a particular error into one of six
categories.

2.1.1   CRASH OR LOOP

Although every compiler should respond reasonably to any possible input, all too
often some unforeseen combination of circumstances will place a compiler in a non-
terminating loop or cause it to lose control and be terminated abnormally.

2.1.2.   PRODUCE INVALID OUTPUT

Sometimes a compiler will apparently operate correctly, yet produce output that is
invalid because of an undetected error. It can be argued that such a reaction is
potentially more damaging than one in the previous category, since the user is given
no indication that anything is wrong.

2.1.3.   QUIT

While it is at least honest, a compiler that quits upon first detecting an error will
not be popular with its users. Many runs may be required just to remove trivial
keypunching errors from a program. (Some puritans argue that this strict discipline
will encourage better habits on the part of programmers, however.)

2.1.4.   RECOVER AND CONTINUE CHECKING

A compiler may continue looking for errors even after it has abandoned compilation
of a program. In order to do so, however, it must somehow get past the original
error in such a way that further problems it reports are likely to be symptoms of
new errors.

2.1.5   REPAIR AND CONTINUE COMPILATION

An incorrect program may be transformed into a "similar" but valid program, which
is then compiled. If carefully done, such transformations may permit the detection
of more errors than simple recovery techniques do, and they may also make it
possible to guarantee that some parts of the compiler need only deal with valid
programs. However, there is no guarantee that the transformed program represents
the user's intent.

2.1.6.   "CORRECT"

True error correction - the replacement of incorrect programs by the programs the
user intended - is substantially beyond the current state of the art of both
language design and compiler design. "Error correcting" compilers to date merely
repair and hope. Unfortunately, they may also mislead the user who believes that
they have really corrected his errors.

2.2   ENSURING CHOSEN REACTIONS

The less desirable reactions (crash or loop, produce invalid output, quit) may be
produced accidentally. Even at this level, however, some planning is required to
ensure consistent responses to a variety of errors. Compilers never perform well
at recovery or repair unless considerable forethought has gone into the design of
their error-handling mechanisms.

A compiler should be a total function. To ensure that no possible input can cause
the compiler to loop unboundedly or crash, it is necessary to demonstrate that no
module ever loses control, regardless of its inputs, and that every loop either has
an a priori bound, or involves the consumption of some input. We may call these
properties error immunity.

Compilers should attempt to detect and report as many errors as possible. Two
obstacles block our desire to strengthen this to "all errors": 1) Some errors transform valid programs into other valid programs (e.g., replacement of "I := I + 1"
by "I := I + I"). Errors are more likely to be detected in languages with high
redundancy than in those designed for conciseness. 2) Although "correctness is a
compile-time property," some errors manifest themselves only under particular
dynamic conditions, which can only be determined by the compiler by simulating
complete executions of the program. Fortunately, syntactic errors, to which we will
devote a great deal of attention, can all be detected by the compiler. There is no
excuse for failing to report a syntactic error.

All error detection is based on redundancy. Thus, the symptom of an error is always an inconsistency between two (or more) pieces of information that are supposed to agree. For recovery, it is sometimes sufficient to ignore the inconsistency. Repair requires that at least one of them be changed to achieve consistency. Correction would require sufficient redundancy to determine (with high probability) which item is in error and what its intended value is.

2.3   ERROR SOURCES, DETECTORS AND SINKS

Before we can deal effectively with errors, we need to determine where they come from, where they are noticed, and how they are removed.

An error can enter a program in many different ways. The original specifications for the program may be wrong; the programming may not accurately reflect the design (a "logic error"); the source program may not be what the programmer intended (a "keypunch error"); or the compiler itself may introduce an error by incorrect processing. Errors from different sources may frequently exhibit some of the same symptoms within the compiler, but (except for compiler errors) the compiler's chances of dealing properly with an error increase somewhat as we move down the list, due to the kinds of redundancy available to it.

Explicitly or implicitly, each of the analysis phases of the compiler compares its input with a set of specifications. Since not all inputs are valid, there is a possibility of conflict (error detection). Frequently, if somewhat inaccurately, we name errors by the analyser that detects them. Thus we speak of lexical errors, syntactic errors, and semantic errors.

After detecting and reporting an error, a module may either attempt to repair it (so it is not seen by subsequent modules) or pass it along. Each approach has its problems. If a module is to be truly an error sink, it must ensure that none of the effects of the error it has repaired can propagate. Conversely, if it does not filter out all errors, then all subsequent modules must be prepared to deal reasonably with them (without generating too many further messages). In many compilers, a single error can trigger a whole avalanche of messages on the unsuspecting user; this is very nearly as unacceptable as quitting after the first error.

3. SYNTACTIC ERRORS

Syntactic analysis not only plays a central role in the organisation of compilers, it is also the focal point of error detection and recovery within compilers. Because syntactic specifications are precise, it is possible to develop parsers that accept exactly the specified languages; because they are formal, it is possible to prove that the parsers detect any syntactically invalid program. Typically, syntax provides the most stringent single structure within a programming language; more keypunch errors and coding errors will be caught as violations of the syntactic specifications than by all other tests combined.

Recovery from syntactic errors is particularly difficult (and especially important) because of their non-local effects. The omission of a single begin or the insertion of an extra parenthesis may radically change the interpretation of a large section of the program being compiled. By contrast, errors detected during lexical analysis or semantic analysis frequently have only local effects.

3.1. POINT OF DETECTION

Different parsing techniques will in general respond differently to an error that causes a program to be syntactically invalid. Many ad hoc techniques and some of the older formal methods (e.g., operator precedence) will actually fail to detect any errors at all in suitably chosen gibberish. Other methods (e.g., precedence) guarantee to eventually detect some error in every invalid program, but the point of detection may be arbitrarily delayed.

One of the principal merits of the LL(1) and LR parsing techniques [Chapters 2.B and 2.C] is that they guarantee to report error at the earliest point at which it can be determined that an error has occurred, i.e., before accepting the first symbol that cannot be a valid continuation of the portion of the program that has already been read and partially parsed. This early detection makes it much easier to produce meaningful diagnostic messages, improves the chances of successful recovery, and ensures that later compiler modules never partially process source text that turns out to contain a syntactic error.

3.2. RECOVERY TECHNIQUES

A syntactic error is discovered when the parser can take no further valid parsing actions, given the current state of the parse (the stack) and the current input symbol. Recovery thus requires changing the stack, the input, or both. The changes may take the form of deletions or insertions (a substitution is simply a deletion and an insertion). Various combinations of these four kinds of changes have been used in compilers, and the optimal recovery strategy is still a matter for debate.

Arguments can be advanced against each class of change. Gries [1971], for example, points out that changes to the stack are particularly dangerous, since semantic routines will have been invoked for the parsing actions leading to the current stack, and the parser cannot safely undo or modify the effects of these actions. The argument against deleting source text is that some part of the input will thereby not be checked. Source text inserted for recovery purposes is unlikely to correspond exactly with the programmer's intent, and errors detected in the inserted text during semantic analysis may lead to confusing diagnostics. Neither insertion nor deletion by itself is sufficient to recover from all errors; in particular, a parser that attempts recovery solely by insertion may loop unboundedly on some inputs.

3.3.   SYSTEMATIC RECOVERY STRATEGIES

Compilers using ad hoc parsing techniques generally rely on ad hoc recovery techniques, i.e., the compiler-writer attempts to supply a "reasonable" recovery action at each point where an inconsistency may be detected. Compilers using formal parsing techniques are more likely to adopt some overall strategy that is expected to cope "reasonably" with any error encountered. No totally satisfactory strategy has yet been demonstrated (and some of the theoretically more attractive ones have not yet been tried in practical compilers). Each strategy can be opposed by particular counter-examples that cause it to perform badly, and comparisons between strategies often rest on undocumented assumptions about which kinds of errors are really the most common (or the most important to recover well from).

Probably the most widely used strategy is also one of the least effective. Panic mode (the term is due to Graham and Rhodes [1973]) has generally been adopted for its simplicity. It merely involves discarding source text until something "solid," such as a statement delimiter, is found, and then discarding stack entries until something that can validly precede the solid token is found. The only merit (besides simplicity) that this method has is that it avoids infinite looping. Almost all the criticisms of the previous section apply.

Two interesting techniques have been reported for using precedence parsing tables to isolate and recover from syntactic errors. Leinius [1970] tries to find the smallest potential phrase containing the point of error that is required by its context to reduce to some unique non-terminal (e.g., <statement>), and then to make the required replacement. Graham and Rhodes [1973], also use precedence relations to isolate the troublesome phrase, but rely more heavily on its internal "resemblance" to some right

hand side of a production in choosing a substitute. Both methods suffer from the
delayed error detection capabilities of precedence parsers, and violate the criterion
of not modifying the stack.

Gries [1971] has proposed an untested scheme for synthesizing a terminal string that
will allow the parse to continue based on the context of the error and the productions
of the grammar. If no such string can be found, an input symbol is deleted and the
search repeated. It is not clear how effective the strategy would be in general,
although it does avoid most of the specific problems mentioned in the previous section.

Several authors [e.g., Aho and Johnson 1974, Leinius 1970, Wirth 1968] have considered
augmenting the syntactic description of a language by a number of error productions,
describing common errors, so that recovery can be (at least partially) subsumed under
normal parsing. For this strategy to be effective, several problems must be dealt with:
the compiler-writer must ensure that he has really included enough error productions
to cover the common errors; since so many different errors are possible, the error
productions may substantially enlarge the grammar (and hence the parser); it is
difficult to include error productions without making the grammar ambiguous.

Aho and Johnson [1974] have proposed a strategy for LR parsers that seems to be a
promising combination of the error production technique with the error isolation ideas
of Leinius. Error productions are restricted to the form A→error, where error is a
special terminal symbol and A is a "major" non-terminal. When the LR parser encounters
an error, it reports it and then replaces the current input symbol by error. Elements
are then discarded from the stack until a state is reached with a parsing action for
the symbol error. The parser can then read error and reduce by the corresponding
error production. Finally, input is discarded until a symbol that can be read in the
new state is found.

3.4. REPAIR TECHNIQUES

Some diagnostic compilers, notably PL/C [Conway 1973], do a reasonably successful job
of transforming programs containing syntactic errors into programs that are both valid
and similar. The PL/C technique is somewhat ad hoc, and is based on its authors' long
experience with diagnosing errors in students' programs. This section will describe
a similar, but somewhat more systematic, method developed for the SP/k compiler by
Holt [1973].

Repair is divided into three levels, each with its own delimiters:
- the program level
- the statement level

- the token level

At the program level, if the logical end of the program is not immediately followed by a job control card, input text is discarded until a job control card is found. If a job control card is found before the logical end of the program, input text is generated (by a process to be explained later) until the logical end of the program is generated.

At the statement level, if a semi-colon (or then) is expected, but not found, input text is discarded until a statement delimiter (a semi-colon, then, or a statement-starting keyword - such as begin or else) is reached. If an unexpected statement delimiter is found in the input, input text is generated to complete the current statement.

At the token level, if the current input token is not permitted by the parsing tables, one input symbol is generated. The current input symbol is also discarded unless the generated symbol is a parenthesis or operator and the current input symbol is an identifier or constant.

Generation is controlled directly by the LL(1) parsing tables. If a number is required, "1" is generated; if an identifier is required,"$NIL" is generated; any other terminal symbol is generated for itself when required. If a non-terminal symbol is required, one of its alternatives (generally the most common, or "default" alternative) is selected. The generation process is continued by the parser until repair has been completed at the controlling level, and normal parsing can be resumed.

Although more sophisticated repair strategies can be designed, Holt's simple strategy works surprisingly well. It frequently makes the obvious "correction," and seldom generates avalanche errors; the source text it produces is generally an adequate diagnostic message.

The following figures summarize observations on SP/k's error repair in 83 student programs containing 102 syntactic errors:

errors	"corrections"	Symptom
33	30	missing or unbalanced parenthesis
13	13	missing procedure or end
9	8	missing semi-colon
8	6	misspelled keyword
39	15	miscellaneous
102	72	

4. OTHER ERRORS

4.1 LEXICAL ERRORS

Certain errors can be detected purely by lexical analysis. For example, many languages do not utilize the full character set of the computer on which they run (except, perhaps, in character strings and comments). Thus, the detection of an illegal character can be reported immediately; the usual recovery is either to ignore the offending character, or to treat it as a blank. Some classes of tokens (e.g., numbers, identifiers) are formed of restricted character sets. Characters that are invalid in the current token, and that cannot validly follow the current token, may be detected as invalid, even if they are valid in other contexts.

More generally, each token class has its own formation rules, any violation of which must be reported. Many errors can be classified as "delimiter errors" involving tokens that start and end with particular symbols (e.g., comment and semicolon, "/*" and "*/", quotation marks). Failure to terminate such a token with the appropriate delimiter may cause much of the following program text to be inadvertently absorbed into the token. If the same delimiter (e.g., a quotation mark) is used at both ends, the situation is even worse (e.g., all the remaining program text may be treated as strings, and all the strings as program text). To limit the effects of delimiter errors, some compilers bound the length of such tokens (e.g., by limiting them to one card).

Some compilers attempt to recover on the lexical level from certain errors detected by syntactic or semantic analysis. For example, if the parser expects the next token to be one of a set of keywords, but finds an identifier instead, it may inquire of a special "spelling correction" module whether the identifier is a plausible misspelling of any of those keywords. Similarly, if a semantic routine detects the use of an undeclared identifier as a variable, it may inquire whether the identifier is a plausible misspelling of any declared identifier. Morgan [1970] claims that up to 80% of the spelling errors occurring in student programs may be corrected in this fashion.

4.2. STATIC SEMANTIC ERRORS

The number of errors detected during semantic analysis depends both on how many restrictions are specified syntactically and on the amount of checking deferred until run-time. Some checking that could, in principle, be done syntactically (e.g., type compatibility of operators and operands) is frequently left to the semantic routines, for grammatical simplicity and for superior diagnostic capability. If the size or speed of the compiler is of more concern than the speed of the target program (e.g., in a student-oriented compiler), such checking may even be postponed until run-time. However, it is generally preferable to detect errors at compile-time if possible, since equivalent checking at run-time may be executed thousands or millions of times.

Errors of declaration or scope are generally detected during semantic analysis. The most common error in this class is the use of an undeclared identifier. Unless "spelling correction" (Sec. 4.1.) removes the error, recovery is accomplished by treating the identifier as though it had been declared with the type required by its current context; further error messages for the same identifier may be suppressed by entering it into the symbol table with a special "error entry" flag.

Multiple declaration of an identifier within a single scope is an error that is easily detected while adding the new entry to the symbol table. It is debatable whether a better recovery is obtained by discarding the old declaration or the new one; flagging it as an error entry can suppress further messages.

To be useful, every variable must be assigned a value somewhere in the program, and its value must be used somewhere in the program. By keeping a "set" flag and a "used" flag with each variable in the symbol table, the compiler can warn the user of useless variables, which probably represent errors and certainly represent inefficient use of memory.

The remaining major opportunity for static error detection is the discovery of type incompatabilities between operators and operands (or formal and actual parameters, or variables and expressions to be assigned to them). How effective a compiler can be here depends almost totally on the language being compiled. Some languages (e.g., BCPL and BLISS) have only a single data type, so no incompatabilities can arise. Others (e.g., APL and SNOBOL) have several types, but allow the type of a variable to change dynamically, forcing type-checking to be postponed to run-time. Still others (e.g., PL/I) define automatic transformations among most of their types, replacing error-detection by type-conversion. However, some languages (e.g., Pascal) combine a rich type structure with strong typing; in these languages thorough type-checking will catch the majority of errors that have escaped detection by other means. (Strong typing requires that the type of every variable, expression, parameter, etc. be calculable at compile-time; it excludes such constructs as pointers that are not restricted to pointing at objects of a single type and formal parameters whose type is not specified.) The security gained by strong typing is particularly important in the integration and maintenance of large programs.

4.3.   *DYNAMICALLY DETECTED ERRORS*

Run-time error checking is done for a variety of reasons. Some kinds of errors can only be effectively detected at run-time. Any checking postponed from compile-time must be done at run-time. It may be desirable to include <u>redundant checking</u> to duplicate checks made by the compiler, particularly if the program must function more reliably than the compiler, hardware, and operating system that support it, or if the cost of undetected errors may be high.

In order to perform dynamic checking, extra information associated with the program and/or data must be preserved and checked for consistency. Some kinds of checking (e.g., subscripts vs. array bounds) require very small overheads and should always be performed, while others (e.g., dynamic type checking) are very expensive with current hardware and must be carefully justified to warrant inclusion.

The value of a variable to which no assignment has yet been made is meaningless. Although the compiler can sometimes detect instances of use before definition, in general these errors must be detected dynamically. Ideally, we would associate an extra flag bit with each variable, indicating whether it contained a valid value, and test it on each reference. Some compilers have reduced the storage overhead of this checking by using a single value (e.g., the largest negative number) to represent "uninitialised" (with luck, perhaps it will not generate too many error messages for valid programs!). Other compilers merely initialise all variables to some standard value (e.g., zero), and ignore these errors. And an unfortunately large number of compilers fail to take even this precaution, leaving the user at the mercy of whatever garbage was previously in memory.

In any context, there is a range of acceptable values for an expression, determined by machine restrictions (e.g., word length), language considerations, and programmer-supplied information (e.g., array bounds). A careful compiler can determine that some expressions will always be in range (and hence need not be checked dynamically), and that some will never be (and hence can be reported as errors at compile-time); however, there will remain a residue whose range must be checked at run-time. In some cases, such as arithmetic overflow, the hardware itself may supply both the bounds and the checking, but in general the burden of saving the bounds and producing the checking code falls on the compiler.

Two types of range errors can have such severe consequences that many otherwise uncritical compilers generate checks for them: array subscripts out of bounds, and <u>case</u> (or computed <u>go to</u>) selectors out of range. The former might otherwise allow an arbitrary location in memory to be overwritten, the latter might cause the transfer of control to an arbitrary location; in either case, determining the source of the error from its symptoms may be exceedingly difficult.

Errors that are not caught by any of the techniques mentioned so far are generally called "logical errors," and have as their symptoms either incorrect output or failure to terminate (infinite looping). The compiler can provide little assistance with valid, but incorrect (i.e., not what the programmer intended) output, unless the programmer has supplied additional tests by which the output may be checked. However, some compilers do attempt to detect infinite looping. The problem of whether an arbitrary program will halt is formally undecidable, but as a practical matter these compilers cause execution to be interrupted after some set number of times through any loop without exiting (obviously, it must be possible to increase this bound for particular programs). This technique may be somewhat more effective than simply relying on an execution time limit imposed externally by the operating system.

Since (with current hardware) many useful forms of dynamic checking incur substantial overheads, many compilers allow the user to specify the amount of checking to be performed. Typically, full checking is specified during program debugging, and minimum checking for the production version of this program. Hoare [1970] has criticised this practice on the grounds that it is only undetected errors in the production version that are harmful. (He likens it to the practice of keeping a fire extinguisher in your car at all times, except when it is being used!) Another problem is that the symptoms of subtle errors may disappear or shift when checking code is added or removed. However, the economic argument is frequently compelling.

4.4. LIMIT FAILURES

Every real compiler has a number of limits that may be consequences either of its design or of the finite resources at its disposal. Thus a compiler might be limited to a parse stack depth of 75 and to 500 entries in its symbol table; less reasonably, it might restrict identifiers to 8 (or 31) characters, or the number of blocks in a program to 255. Sensible compiler-writers will attempt to minimize the number of such limits (the ideal is one: total space used by the compiler), and to ensure that the average user never encounters them.

No matter how large any particular compiler limit is, some user, some day, will encounter it. Since the encounter will come near the end of compiling some large program, it is very important that the compiler react sensibly, and report not only that a limit was exceeded, but which one, and what its value is. Thus _every_ place in the compiler where some limit _may_ be exceeded _must_ contain a check against the limit. (A very useful technique that guards against forgetting such checks is to access each limited resource solely by means of a procedure or macro that contains the check.)

The target program will also be run with limited resources, and it is essential that the compiler produce code to check run-time limits wherever they may be exceeded. If storage is allocated dynamically on a stack or heap, every allocation must be preceded by a test to assure that sufficient memory is actually available. Limit checking may be a substantial portion of the overhead in dynamic storage allocation, but the consequences of omitting it are intolerable, since very large programs will malfunction inexplicably.

4.5. COMPILER SELF-CHECKING

While the compiler-writer should spare no pains to ensure the correctness of his compiler, he should be eternally suspicious of his own accomplishments. Even modules that can "never" receive incorrect input should be error immune (cf. Sec. 2.2.). It is good policy to include tests throughout the compiler that can never fail while the compiler is functioning properly, to provide early warning of compiler malfunctions. (The worst way to find them is by debugging the target code of correct user programs that fail to execute correctly.) Simple consistency checks (e.g., that input is within range, counters never go negative, stacks are never popped when empty, registers are free at appropriate places) have often uncovered subtle errors that would otherwise have remained unnoticed for months or years.

During compiler development it is wise to "instrument" every major module so that its inputs and outputs can be traced at will. If it contains a major data structure (e.g., the symbol table), provision should also be made for dumping its contents, in a readable format, upon request. These self-diagnostic capabilities should not be removed from the production version of the compiler, since their resource consumption is small unless they are used, and they can be invaluable during maintenance.

5. ERROR DIAGNOSIS

It is not sufficient to tell the user that his program contains one or more errors. To a very large extent, a compiler's popularity with its users is determined by its helpfulness in locating and explaining their errors. Since debugging is currently one of the largest single costs of computing, economics indicate that the compiler-writer should invest considerable effort in trying to speed this process.

Good error messages will exhibit a number of characteristics:
- they will be <u>user-directed</u>, reporting problems in terms of what the user has done, not what has happened in the compiler
- they will be <u>source-oriented</u>, rather than containing mysterious internal representations or portions of target text
- they will be as <u>specific</u> as possible

- they will <u>localize the problem</u>
- they will be <u>complete</u>
- they will be <u>readable</u> (in the user's natural language)
- they will be <u>restrained and polite</u>.

The final point is of particular importance. It is all too easy for compiler-writers to forget that the user must be the master, the compiler the servant. The attitude (if not the phraseology) of error messages should always be "Oh worthy master, I have failed to fully understand your intentions," rather than "That does not compute" (or, worse "0C5").

5.1. LOCATING THE PROBLEM

The first thing the user must be told about an error is where the inconsistency was detected. Frequently he can detect and correct an error simply from an indication of the line and symbol at which a problem was found, provided that error detection was not too long delayed (cf. Sec. 3.1.). A visible pointer into the line is superior to a numerical or verbal description of the location. Where the problem involves identifiers or symbols, they should be given explicitly, e.g., "OUTPOT not declared," rather than "undeclared indentifier" or "THEN may not follow IF" rather than "illegal symbol pair."

5.2. DESCRIBING THE SYMPTOM

One of the hardest things to remember in designing error diagnostics is that you don't <u>know</u> what the error was. Two (or more) pieces of information have been found to be inconsistent, but it cannot be said with certainty where the error lies. The safest strategy is to describe the symptom (the detected inconsistency) as clearly as possible before attempting to make any suggestions about the nature of the error.

Symptoms should be described in a positive fashion wherever possible, e.g., "I expected this or this, but found that," rather than "Missing right parenthesis." If the inconsistency involves information from some other part of the program (e.g., a declaration), that information should be displayed, or at least its co-ordinates given.

5.3. SUGGESTING CORRECTIONS

The compiler-writer's knowledge of, and experience with, the language being compiled may indicate that certain kinds of inconsistencies nearly always spring from particular kinds of errors ("characteristic errors"). If he is unable to re-design the language to eliminate these errors, he may nevertheless pass this information on

to the user in the form of suggestions for correcting the error. Such ad hoc
suggestions correspond to the reflex actions of experienced program advisors, in which
a particular message will trigger an automatic query of the form "Have you checked...?"

It is not possible for the compiler-writer to separately anticipate every error that
may lead to an inconsistency and prepare a suitable suggestion for it. Particularly
in the area of syntactic errors, it is probably better to use some simple algorithm
(working on the stack, the input, and the parsing tables) to generate "reasonable"
suggestions for a whole class of inconsistencies than to consider each one separately.

A compiler that does careful repair (see Sec. 3.4.) may use the repaired source text
as a suggested correction. The repaired text will be valid, and "similar" to the
input. Even when it fails to match the user's intent, the repair may be very successful in communicating to the user the nature of the problem and the steps that he should
take to remove it. (The repaired text should be listed anyhow, so the user can understand further messages about the revised program.)

5.4. *LOCALISATION OF ERROR PROCESSING*

All messages about errors should be processed by a central module. Failure to observe
this principle will have numerous undesirable consequences:
- redundant code will be produced throughout the compiler to handle error messages
- subtle inconsistencies in the treatment of errors and formatting of messages
  will creep in
- the adaptability of the compiler will suffer, and changes to error-handling will
  be difficult
- it will not be convenient to collect statistics on the number of error messages,
  nor to suppress duplicate or excessive messages.

The final point deserves further comment. The user should not be bludgeoned with
numerous messages springing from a single error. We have already mentioned some
recovery techniques to minimize duplicate messages (e.g., error entries in the symbol
table). Some compilers suppress all error messages for a line of source text following
the first reported syntactic error. The reason is simple: current syntactic error
recovery/repair techniques are just not good enough to ensure that further messages
really indicate new errors. Most compilers also place a limit on the total number of
error messages they will print, since at some point confidence in the whole recovery/
repair mechanism breaks down.

5.5. *SYNTHESIS AND PLACEMENT OF MESSAGES*

The error-reporting module should have a standard format for messages that is concise

yet distinctive - error messages should stand out on the page. A typical format might
include:
- a pointer to the symbol where the inconsistency was noted
- a series of asterisks or other special characters in the margin to catch the
  eye
- an indication of severity
- a brief description of the symptom
- the count of error messages, and the co-ordinate of the immediately previous
  message.

Other information would be included depending on the particular symptom, such as
- identifiers, symbols, or types involved
- what was expected by the compiler
- suggested corrections.

Gries [1971] discusses techniques for efficiently synthesizing error messages.

There are two reasonable placements for error messages: in the listing at the point
of detection, and following the listing, with the summary information. These placements are frequently, although not necessarily, associated with single-pass and multipass compilation, respectively.

For dealing with individual errors, placement of the message at the point of detection
is certainly more convenient. The location of the message itself establishes the
co-ordinate of the symptom, and it is not necessary to flip back and forth from the
listing to the error messages to find the problem. This placement occurs automatically
in single-pass compilation unless all messages are saved until the end. If it is
desired in multi-pass compilation, listing must be postponed until the completion of
analysis, and the error messages collated into the listing.

Error messages that are collected in the summary information are easier to find, and
are perhaps less likely to be overlooked. It is essential that all messages dealing
with a single statement appear together, and desirable that messages be sorted into
the same order as the statements they refer to. For single-pass compilation this
simply requires a FIFO buffer in which messages are saved, but with multiple-pass
compilation it becomes necessary to collate the messages from the various passes.

5.6.   ERROR LOGGING

Of course the user wants to know at the end of compilation how many error messages
were issued by the compiler. There are also others who may be concerned with statistics
about errors. An instructor in a course may wish to know what kinds of errors his
students are currently making, so he can take corrective action. A programming

manager might want similar statistics, or statistics about the error-proneness of individual programmers. A language designer could try to eliminate the more common errors, if he had accurate statistics about what they were. Finally, the compiler-writer himself may be able to improve the utility of the compiler by monitoring its response to detected errors.

Different uses may require different kinds of error logging. For some, gross aggregates (e.g., 5,842 severe error messages, 10,914 error messages, 7,231 warning messages) may suffice. Others will need classification by point of detection (e.g., 5,914 lexical errors, 10,231 syntactic errors, 7,842 semantic errors), and still others will need the frequencies of each message. For a detailed study of responses to errors, it may be helpful to save every source statement that caused a message, together with the message, or even to "drain" a copy of every program containing a detected error. (This latter is particularly helpful in evaluating changes in the compiler's response to errors.)

5.7. RUN-TIME DIAGNOSIS

The diagnosis of errors detected at run-time should follow the general principles discussed in previous sections. However, these standards can only be achieved with some forethought, and many otherwise excellent compilers abdicate all responsibility in this domain to an operating system totally unequipped to deal reasonably with run-time errors - the result is a cryptic message and a hexadecimal dump.

The fundamental principle that diagnostics must be given in terms of the source, not the target, program, requires (as a minimum) that the symbol table be available at run-time (although not necessarily in main memory). Dumps, when required, should contain variable names and values in source-language form, and should be selective, working outward from the scope in which the error was detected. [Poole 1973]

Traces should also be based on the source program; ideally, a trace will list the source statements as they are executed, but source co-ordinates provide an acceptable substitute. Since they potentially generate so much output, it is particularly important that traces be selective. Some popular techniques are: letting the programmer dynamically start and stop tracing; tracing only particular sections of the program; tracing only major program elements (e.g., procedure calls and returns); only tracing each statement the first N times it is executed (typically N=2 is adequate); and keeping a ring buffer of trace lines, and printing only those executed immediately preceding the detection of the error.

Another useful tool, both in diagnosing actual errors and in detecting inefficiencies, is the "program profile" - a labelling of each statement by its frequency of execution. Zero-frequency statements are either untested or useless. High-frequency statements are candidates for optimization. Satterthwaite [1972] describes the implementation of profile collection for Algol W, as part of what is undoubtedly the best run-time diagnostic package available today.

References

1. Aho, A.V., Johnson, S.C.: LR parsing. Computing Surveys (to appear 1974).
2. Conway, R.W., Wilcox, T.R.: Design and implementation of a diagnostic compiler for PL/I. Comm ACM 16 169-179 (1973).
3. Gordon, H.E.: Paragraphing computer programs: M.Sc. thesis, University of Toronto expected 1974.
4. Graham, S.L., Rhodes, S.P.: Practical suntactic error recovery in compilers. Conference record of ACM symposium on principles of programming languages, Boston, 52-58 (1973).
5. Gries, D.: Compiler construction for digital computers. John Wiley & Sons, Inc. 1971.
6. Hoare, C.A.R.: The use of high level languages in large program construction. In Turski, W.M. (ed.): Efficient production of large programs. Warszawa 1971
7. Holt, R.C., Wortman, D.B.: Structured subsets of PL/I. Computer Systems Research Group Technical Report CSRG-27. University of Toronto 1973.
8. Koster, C.H.A.: Error reporting, error treatment, and error correction in Algol translation, part 1. Second annual conference of Gesellschaft für Informatik, Karlsruhe 1972.
9. Leinius, R.P.: Error detection and recovery for syntax directed compiler systems. Ph.D. thesis, University of Wisconsin, Madison 1970.
10. Morgan, H.L.: Spelling correction in system programs. Comm ACM 13 90-94 (1970)
11. Poole, P.C.: Debugging and testing. In Bauer, F.L. (ed.): Advanced course on software engineering. Springer-Verlag 1973.
12. Satterthwaite, E.: Debugging tools for high level languages. Computer software - practice and experience 2 (1972).
13. Wirth, N.: A programming language for the 360 computers. Journal ACM 15 37-74 (1968).

OPTIMIZATION

W. M. Waite

University of Colorado

Boulder, Colorado, USA

A program is a description of an algorithm given in some language. The task of a translator is to accept this description and to produce a description of an "equivalent" algorithm in another language. Usually the second algorithm is accepted as being "equivalent" to the first if it produces the same results for particular sets of input data. Note that this definition of "equivalence" permits the translator to choose any one of many possible algorithms; it is not restricted to the one which was written down by the programmer. The term optimization is used to denote the attempt by a translator to improve upon the description of the algorithm which was given by the programmer. Optimization is most appropriate when the source language does not provide access to all of the facilities of the target computer.

Work on optimization techniques began in earnest with the original FORTRAN, whose design specifications were frozen in 1954. At that time most programmers wrote in symbolic assembly language (a few still used numeric machine code), and the attention of the FORTRAN group was focused on the challenge of constructing an automatic coding system which could take over many of the tasks of the programmer and still create object programs of competitive efficiency. Backus and Heising [1964] recall that "... the group had one primary fear. After working long and hard to produce a good translator program, an important application might promptly turn up which would confirm the views of the skeptics: this application would be of the sort that FORTRAN was designed to handle and, even though well-programmed in FORTRAN, its object program would run at half the speed of a hand-coded version." The group felt that if one or more such applications appeared, acceptance of FORTRAN would be blocked.

The major design problem which the group foresaw was the inefficiency arising from subscript calculation within a loop, when that calculation involved a multiplication. (In many loops it is possible to compute initial subscript values and then merely to increment them by constants each time around the loop.) Their solution involved partitioning the program into "regions" based on the frequency of execution, and in one twenty-minute compilation on the IBM 704 ten minutes were devoted to region formation [Backus 1964]. This and other types of optimization, although expensive, did enable the FORTRAN compiler to meet the goals of object code efficiency set by its designers. The case for "automatic coding" was thus proved.

As users discovered the ease of coding in higher-level languages, efficiency considerations began to fade into the background. Machine costs have decreased significantly since the early 1960s, while programming costs have risen sharply. Modern programming languages have therefore been designed to increase the efficiency of the programmer, even at the expense of machine efficiency.

1. Classification of Techniques

Any general approach to code optimization is severely limited by undecidability results [Aho 1970] and by the lack of definitive optimality criteria. The

compiler's optimizer therefore provides improvement (relative to some cost function), rather true optimization. In order to avoid undecidable equivalence questions, the improvement is carried out by applying a sequence of equivalence-preserving transformations to the original algorithm [Aho 1973]. Each transformation is based upon information gathered from some region of the program. In this section I shall classify the currently-popular techniques on the basis of the transformations which they perform and the regions which they consider. I shall then summarize the results of a study of actual FORTRAN programs [Knuth 1971], with emphasis upon the relative efficacy of the various optimizations.

1.1.   <u>Transformations</u>.   Optimizing   transformations   [Allen 1972]   can   be dichotomized as <u>machine independent</u> and <u>machine dependent</u>.   Machine independent optimization   involves   manipulation   of the original algorithm independently of its realization.   This includes such operations as:

- Folding and propagation

- Rearrangement

- Redundancy elimination

- Strength reduction

- Frequency reduction

When the values of all operands in an expression are known to the compiler,   that expression   can   be folded (replaced by a single value); when a variable is set to a value known at compile time, that value   can   be   propagated   (substituted   for   the variable)   by   the   compiler.   Although   a   programmer   would not normally write an expression like 1+2 explicitly, constant subexpressions   are   generated   by   certain constructs.   For   example,   the   array   reference   A(I,J,K)   in   FORTRAN yields the following index polynomial [ANSI 1966]:

$$I+d1*J+(d1*d2)*K-d1*(d2+1)$$

Taken together, folding and propagation also enable the user to   increase   both   the readability   and   adaptability   of   his   program   by   <u>parameterization</u> at no cost in execution time: Constants   can   be   expressed   symbolically   to   eliminate   "magic numbers" [Clark 1973], and to localize changes.

Care   must be taken in folding when the translator is running on one computer and producing code for another.   If the precision of the machine on which the translator runs is less than that of the machine on which the program is to execute,   then   the accuracy   of   computations performed at compile time will not be as great as that of the same computations performed during execution.   In general, however,   folding   is an inexpensive optimization which should be performed by most translators.

The usual purpose of rearrangement is to reduce the amount of temporary storage required during the evaluation of an expression. On most machines this has the effect of speeding up the evaluation because it may be possible to compute a value using only registers for temporary storage. However, the rearrangement may be irrelevant for some target computers. For example, on a stack machine such as the Burroughs 5000 or 6000 series, there is virtually no penalty for temporary storage used during expression evaluation. The savings might also be negligible on machines having either large numbers of registers or a high-speed cache memory, because of the relative simplicity of the expressions which occur in practice.

Code is redundant if the value which it computes is already available at the point where the code occurs. Most programmers will not write obviously redundant code unless there are important documentation considerations which make that form preferable in a particular instance. However, constructs such as references to multi-dimensional arrays may generate redundant code without themselves being redundant. Gear [1965] mentions a FORTRAN assignment statement used in the three dimensional Gaus-Seidel iteration of the Laplace equation:

$$A(I,J,K) = (A(I,J,K-1)+A(I,J,K+1)+$$
$$A(I,J-1,K)- A(I,J+1,K)+$$
$$A(I-1,J,K)+A(I+1,J,K))/6.0$$

If d1 and d2 are the first two dimensions of A, this statement generates the expression $I+d1*(J+d2*K)$ (in combination with various constants) seven times.

Strength reduction is the general process of replacing an expensive operation by a cheaper one. When a value is raised to a constant power, for example, it may be possible to replace the exponentiation by a series of multiplications [Bagwell 1970]. The most common use of strength reduction is in the induction variable optimization mentioned at the beginning of this chapter. When the controlled variable of a loop is multiplied by an expression whose value remains constant over the loop, that multiplication may be replaced by an addition.

Most of the expressions which yield to induction variable optimization are generated by references to multi-dimensional arrays. I have given two examples of such references in this section; in each case they would be candidates for strength reduction if J or K were induction variables. Documentation considerations may also lead the programmer to use multiplication by an induction variable explicitly. In this case, strength reduction is possible only if the constant expression has an integer value because the accumulation of roundoff error precludes repeated addition of reals [Forsythe 1969].

Frequency reduction attempts to shift operations from regions of the program which are entered frequently to those which are entered rarely. As with the other transformations, references to multi-dimensional arrays provide most of the expressions moved during frequency reduction. The most important use of this transformation is to remove invariant calculations from loops, on the assumption that the code inside a loop is executed more frequently than that surrounding the loop. This is a reasonable assumption in general, but may be defeated in specific programs. In some cases the program will normally pass through the loop once, only making multiple passes when some unusual situation arises. Here optimization will be waste motion but will not effect the runnning time of the program. A less fortunate situation is the one in which the loop is not traversed at all in the normal case. Here optimization will move the invariant operations from the less-frequently executed body of the loop to the more-frequently executed area surrounding the loop, and the transformation actually produces a degredation of the program's performance.

Machine-dependent optimizations are concerned with the realization of an algorithm on a particular piece of hardware. It is necessary to make a distinction between true machine-dependent optimization and the simple avoidance of stupidity in code generation. Typical machine-dependent optimization techniques include:

- Register allocation
- Special instructions
- Code rearrangement

In each case there are degrees of care which may be taken. I regard elementary precautions against bad code as being the normal task of the compiler writer rather than the province of a discussion on optimization.

Register allocation can be performed on the basis of global flow analysis which provides the code generator with information on the future use of values currently residing in registers, and this type of allocation definitely falls in the province of optimization [Beatty 1974]. The so-called "peephole optimization" [McKeeman 1965], which avoids locally redundant fetches and stores of register contents, is merely an instance of intelligent code generation.

Many machines have special instructions for incrementing the contents of a register or storage location. Picking up situations in which these instructions can be used may or may not be difficult depending upon the language. For example, implementation of the FORTRAN assignment I=I+1 by an "increment storage" instruction requires the analysis of a relatively large subtree of the structure tree. On the other hand, implementation of the ALGOL 68 operator "+:=" by the same machine instruction is simply an example of competent code generation. Special instructions such as "increment storage" have been called idioms by A. D. Hall of Bell Telephone Laboratories. His experience indicates that the proper generation of idioms is an important key to producing good object code for a wide class of minicomputers [Hall 1974].

Code rearrangement is usually concerned with operators which take single-length operands and produce double-length results or vice versa. For example, integer multiplication on many machines requires a single-length multiplicand and produces a double-length product. Conversely, integer division requires a double-length dividend and produces a single-length quotient plus a single-length remainder. If this is the case, then multiplications and divisions should be alternated during the computation of an expression. The multiplication will produce a double-length result which can be immediately used as the double-length dividend in a following division. If this alternation is not observed, then additional register manipulations are usually required [Sheridan 1959, Wilcox 1971].

1.2. Regions. During optimization, the compiler considers some fragment of the program in its entirety. Increasing the size of the fragment increases the amount of information upon which decisions can be based, and hence normally improves the quality of the generated code; it also increases the amount of storage which the compiler must devote to the fragment during optimization. Obviously, a tradeoff based upon the resources available and the normal usage of compiled programs must be made (see Section 1.3.)

The choice of a program fragment is not based solely upon its size, but also upon its structural properties. Particular properties which simplify the analysis are used to define regions, and these regions (rather than arbitrary program fragments) are considered by the optimizer. Region definition may be based upon general properties of programs (control flow, side effects), or upon specific language constructs (DO and for loops, blocks, procedures, etc.) I shall concentrate upon the former here, since the latter merely uses the language constructs to bypass a part of the analysis. (The OS/360 FORTRAN H compiler explicitly ignores the information provided by DO statements in favor of a complete structural analysis of the program [Lowry 1969].)

The set of possible regions is usually first partitioned according to control flow: Local optimization is performed on regions which contain no transfers, while global optimization considers control flow. Most literature on optimization uses inappropriate terminology to express the choice of regions, but I feel that I should not attempt to rectify that inadequacy here. I shall therefore simply present the common name and important characteristics for each kind of region.

An expression is a region which has only a single entry point and contains no control statements, and within which no construct is permitted to have a side effect which alters the value of any element used in the region. This region may or may not correspond to the nonterminal "expression" as defined in the syntax of the language; Figure 1.1 illustrates two cases in which an expression (defined by the ALGOL 60 syntax) contains a function call which alters the value of another element of the same expression.

The control of side effects is a fundamental question in language design. Some people hold strong opinions on this point [Bauer 1961]: "Indeed, the idea of expressions having any effect but defining an actual value is so preposterous that it was not even considered by the ALGOL committee." A softer line appears in Section 6.4 of the FORTRAN Standard [ANSI 1966]: "The evaluation of functions appearing in an expression may not validly alter the value of any other element

```
meansq := (READ(30)↑2+READ(30)↑2)/2.0
```

a) Obtaining two numbers from an input file

```
begin real w;
real procedure SNEAKY(z); value z; real z;
    begin SNEAKY := z+(z-2)↑2;
    w := z+1;
    end
w := 1;
PRINT(SNEAKY(w)+w);
end
```

b) Result depends upon order of evaluation [Hext 1965]

Figure 1.1

Illustration of Side Effects

within the expressions, assignment statement or CALL statement in which the function reference appears." Thus any single expression, assignment statement or CALL statement in FORTRAN may be considered an expression for optimization purposes.

All of the transformations of Section 1.1 except frequency reduction are relevant to optimization within an expression. For a language such as FORTRAN, expression optimization can be carried out locally and the transformations can be applied easily to the tree form of the expression. Thus the cost of this form of optimization is not high.

A basic block is a region which has only a single entry point and in which control statements, if any, follow all computational and input/output statements. Thus all computations of a basic block must be executed if any is, and no extensive analysis is required to determine the order in which the computations will be carried out. The basic block forms the underlying unit for all optimizations using global flow analysis. Figure 1.2 illustrates the definition of a basic block applied to a portion of a FORTRAN program.

All transformations other than frequency reduction are applicable to a basic block, and the analysis techniques are similar to those used for expressions. Consideration of a region larger than a basic block requires the compiler to investigate the flow paths of the source program to determine possible computations. This entails analysis which is fundamentally different from that used within a basic block, where the computation is fixed. The distinction between local and global optimization is thus drawn at the level of the basic block: Local optimization involves transformations within expressions and basic blocks, while global optimization involves transformations upon collections of interconnected basic blocks.

The next obvious region for the compiler to consider is a loop: A set of basic blocks which are connected by transfers in such a way that each block can be reached from every other block. Computations which are invariant within a loop can be made prior to entry rather than during execution of the loop (frequency reduction), and others cannot be made redundant by identical computations outside of the loop. In Figure 1.3a, for example, 2.0*PI*FREQ is invariant within the loop but J+1 is not. As Figure 1.3b shows, the former can be evaluated prior to entry, but the latter

```
        A = B
        IF (X) 1,2,3
1       C = D
2       M = N
        I = J
3       IF (P .LT. Q)   P = Q
```

a) A sequence of FORTRAN statements

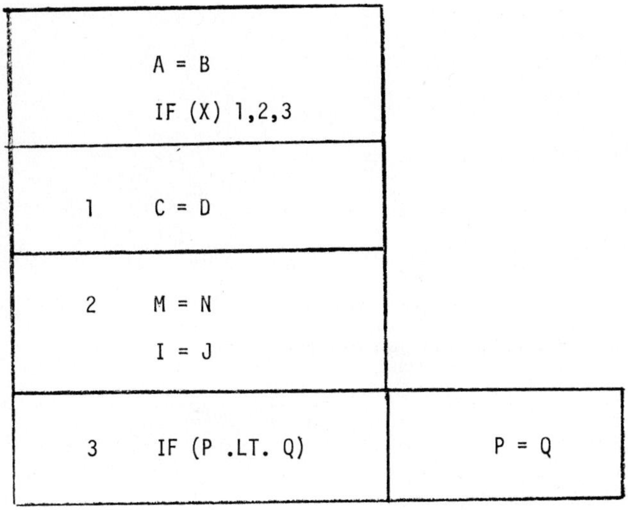

```
┌─────────────────────────────────────┐
│                                      │
│        A = B                         │
│        IF (X) 1,2,3                  │
├─────────────────────────────────────┤
│                                      │
│   1    C = D                         │
├─────────────────────────────────────┤
│                                      │
│   2    M = N                         │
│        I = J                         │
├─────────────────────────┬────────────┐
│                         │            │
│   3    IF (P .LT. Q)    │    P = Q   │
└─────────────────────────┴────────────┘
```

b) Basic blocks in (a)

Figure 1.2

Illustration of Basic Blocks

```
      NP = J+1
      DO 1 I=M,N
      Z(I) = 1.0/(2.0*PI*FREQ*C(I))
 1    J = J+1
```

a) A sequence of FORTRAN statements

```
      NP = J+1
      OMEGA = 2.0*PI*FREQ
      DO 1 I=M,N
      Z(I) = 1.0/(OMEGA*C(I))
 1    J = J+1
```

b) Optimized version of (a)

Figure 1.3

Loop Invariance

cannot be eliminated or replaced by NP.

Loops are chosen as regions not only because frequency reduction is applicable, but also because all of the transformations applied within a loop are independent of the remainder of the program. When the analysis of the loop is complete, the entire region is replaced by a single block which summarizes the results of that analysis; the summary is then used when containing loops are analyzed. Constructs other than loops may have this same property and may therefore be considered as regions for global optimization. Such regions may be identified by some explicit topological property [Cocke 1970] or by a simulated execution of the program [Kildall 1972].

1.3. _Efficacy_. The theoretical aspects of optimization present a host of the easy-to-state, yet moderately challenging, problems so dear to the hearts of Ph.D. candidates. As is usual in such cases, it was a long time before anyone had the idea of studying just how effective these techniques were in improving the performance of real programs. In the summer of 1970, D. E. Knuth and a small group at Stanford analyzed a number of randomly-selected programs from the University and from industry [Knuth 1971]. The final sample consisted of about 11,000 cards from Stanford and over 250,000 from Lockheed Missiles and Space Corporation.

Static measurements on the number of occurrences of different statement types indicated internal consistency but poor agreement between industry and university. Industry had 2.7 times as many comments, and more IF's and GOTO's (possibly indicating more careful checking for erroneous input data.) An analysis of the assignment statements showed that 68% involved simple replacements of the form A = B, with no arithmetic operators present. 13% were of the form A = A op e: The first operand on the right was the same as the variable on the left ("op" is some operator and "e" is an arbitrary expression.)

The complexity of an assignment was rated by defining a cost of one unit for each addition or subtraction, five units for each multiplication and eight units for each division. More than 85% of the assignment statements had a cost of 0 or 1. 2% had a cost of 6 and 3% had a cost of 8, reflecting the use of a single multiplication or division operator. Thus over 90% of the assignment statements probably involved an expression with no more than one operator. Turning to the variables, Knuth and his coworkers found that 58% were unindexed, 30.5% had a single index, 9.5% had 2 and only 1% had 3.

Dynamic checks indicated that in most programs less than 4% of the code accounted for more than 50% of the execution time exclusive of input/output. I/O statements, although they represented only 5% of the code, accounted for more than 25% of the execution time (this figure includes the time spent in the operating system servicing I/O requests.) Thus if optimization were to reduce the execution time of the computational part of a program to 0, we would only see a factor of 4 speedup in the overall execution.

Knuth distinguished four levels of optimization (summarized in Table 1.1), according to the amount of effort required by the compiler to acheive them. He then optimized the most-frequently executed regions of seventeen randomly-selected programs. Table 1.1 shows the minimum, average and maximum increases in speed obtained within these regions at each level of optimization, taken over all seventeen programs. (This optimization does not affect the input/output time.) Notice that the average improvement, even with the most complex kind of optimization, was only a factor of 3.5. By the time the third level had been reached, almost all of the improvement had been obtained. Since the cost of the optimization increases rapidly with level it seems that many of the more esoteric techniques proposed in the literature should be treated merely as curiosities.

The best conceivable optimization (anything goes except a change in the algorithm or data structure) increased the speed of the program by a factor of 4 or more in about half of the 17 cases which Knuth studied in detail. Assuming that the computational part of the program accounts for approximately 75% of the execution time, simple arithmetic shows us that this optimization may gain us a factor of 2 in overall speed - well below the penalty for poor choice of algorithm (which can cost several orders of magnitude.)

The message contained in these statistics is that extensive optimization is probably not justified in a FORTRAN compiler unless the operating environment is quite different from that of Stanford and Lockheed. Note that conclusions regarding other languages cannot be drawn on the basis of this study because other languages may have particular features which must be optimized in order to reduce operating costs to a tolerable level.

Table 1.1

Efficacy of Various Optimizations

Level	Improvement Factor			Transformations
	Min	Avg	Max	
1	1.1	1.4	2.5	Local folding, rearrangement and redundancy elimination. Competent register allocation as discussed in Chapter 3.E.
2	1.1	2.7	9.0	Global folding, rearrangement, strength and frequency reduction.
3	1.1	3.6	9.4	Idioms for the IBM System/360.
4	1.5	4.8	13.1	Any transformation which could conceivably be performed by a compiler of arbitrary complexity. Changes in the basic algorithm or data structures were not allowed.

Notes:

1. Each level includes all optimizations specified for lower levels.

2. The improvement factors are all relative to "classical one-pass compilation techniques" with dedicated registers.

2. Local Optimization

The basic data structure used during local optimization is a directed acyclic graph (DAG). It describes the constraints placed upon the order of evaluation: Descendents of a node must be evaluated before the node itself. Since the definition of an expression precludes side effects which alter the value of any component, disjoint subexpressions may be evaluated in any order.

Optimizing transformations are applied to fold constant subexpressions as the structure tree is being built, and a number which specifies temporary storage requirements is attached to each node. The resulting tree is converted to a directed acyclic graph by identifying common subexpressions, and the graph is flattened into a sequence of elementary actions. This sequence is passed to the code generator, as discussed in Chapter 3.E.

No changes to the overall code generation procedure described in Chapter 3.E are required to accommodate optimization, although the number of operators will increase. We shall see that the register allocation strategies discussed in Chapter 3.E are adequate, and that the operations are performed in the proper order.

2.1. Rearrangement of an expression. Some number (perhaps 0) of anonymous operands must exist simultaneously during the evaluation of a given expression. This number depends upon the order in which the components of the expression are evaluated; the minimum may be determined by applying the following rules [Sethi 1970] to the tree which defines the expression:

a. Attach the number 0 to each leaf.

b. Let j and k be the numbers attached to the sons of a node ($j \leq k$). If $j < k$, attach k to the node, otherwise attach $k+1$.

To see why these rules work, consider an expression with two subexpressions. Suppose that one of the subexpressions is defined by a tree to which we have attached the number j, and the other is defined by a tree to which we have attached the number k ($j < k$). Suppose further that the first subexpression to be evaluated is the one to which k has been attached. This means that, at some point during the evaluation of the subexpression, k anonymous operands are required simultaneously. When the evaluation is complete, only the single result remains. We must preserve this result (which is itself anonymous) during the evaluation of the second subexpression. At some point during this second evaluation, j anonymous operands are required simultaneously. Because we must also preserve the result of evaluating the first subexpression, a total of j+1 values are required simultaneously. Since we have assumed that j<k, j+1 can be no greater than k and the maximum number of anonymous operands which must exist simultaneously at <u>any</u> time during the computation is k. Note that this result requires a particular order of evaluation. If we evaluated the subtree requiring j anonymous operands first, then the entire evaluation would have required k+1 anonymous operands to exist simultaneously. If j=k, the order of evaluation is irrelevant and k+1 operands must exist simultaneously. Figure 2.1 gives several examples of trees whose nodes have been numbered according to these rules.

The temporary storage requirements for a given tree are fixed. (Temporary storage must be available for the maximum number of anonymous operands which can exist simultaneously.) In order to lower the requirement, we must transform the tree into another which yields the same value but has a different structure; this is done by making use of particular properties of the operators. Consider, for example, the expression of Figure 2.1c. We can apply the associativity transformation of Figure 2.2a to obtain the tree of Figure 2.2b, which requires only a single temporary rather than two.

Notice that the tree of Figure 2.2b exhibits less parallelism than that of Figure 2.1c. On a machine like the Control Data 6600, Figure 2.1c might be superior to Figure 2.2b because it makes better use of the multiple arithmetic units. Even in this case, however, I believe that there is a good reason to prefer Figure 2.2b: It provides a canonic structure for the tree which simplifies commutativity transformations. When final code is generated from the tree, Figure 2.2a can be applied in reverse to regain the parallelism.

Although the mathematical properties of an operator include associativity, the fact that computer arithmetic has finite precision may make it non-associative [Knuth 1969]: The associativity axiom for addition states that $(A+B)+C = A+(B+C)$ must hold for all values of A, B and C. Consider a machine which operates upon floating point numbers with a precision of two decimal digits, and assume that the values of A, B and C are -10.0, 11.0 and 0.1 respectively. The value of $(A+B)+C$ is

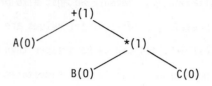

a) A+B*C

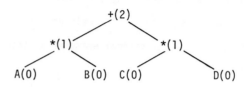

b) A*B+C*D

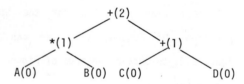

c) A*B+(+D)

Figure 2.1

Temporary Storage Requirements

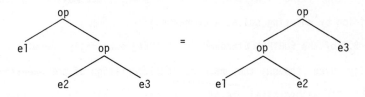

a) General form

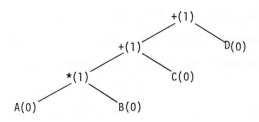

b) Applied to Figure 2.1c

Figure 2.2

Associativity Transformation

1.1, but the value of B+C is 11.0 due to the two-digit precision of the machine and consequently the value of A+(B+C) is 1.0. (This failure may be duplicated for any fixed precision by choosing suitable operands.)

Section 6.4 of the FORTRAN Standard [ANSI 1966] explicitly permits the use of associativity even though the machine implementation of the operators cannot be associative: "If mathematical use of operators is associative, commutative, or both, full use of these facts may be made to revise orders of combination, provided only that integrity of parenthesized expressions is not violated." This statement forces the programmer to insert explicit parentheses where the order of evaluation within an expression is important - as much a documentation aid as an aid to optimization.

Note that this specification requires a semantic action for the production P::=(E): A flag must be set in the root of the tree for E to indicate that its operator is non-associative. This flag simply disables the associativity transformation when it attempts to examine the subtree resulting from the parenthesized expression.

Sheridan [1959] has given the name segment to a subexpression whose operands may be permuted arbitrarily. A sequence of operands linked by occurrences of an operator which is both associative and commutative is obviously a segment. This is not a necessary condition, however, since A-B+C-D is also a segment. (The operands may be permuted arbitrarily by making use of the identity A-B = A+(-B) and the properties of + [Knuth 1969, Frailey 1970, Rohl 1971].)

The optimizer can permute the operands of a segment to fold expressions like I-1+J+2, and to reduce temporary storage requirements: A segment will use less storage if the operand with the highest number attached to it is evaluted first. For example, in Figure 2.3 the operand with the highest number is C*D. When that subexpression is evaluated first, the required storage is reduced from 2 to 1.

At each node, the routine which flattens the tree should traverse the subtree with the largest number first. If the operator of the node is non-commutative this requires that a "reverse" flag be set in the node to indicate that the operands are not in the order given by the programmer. The transducer can then interchange the value descriptors when simlulating the operator (Chapter 3.E). Notice that at the

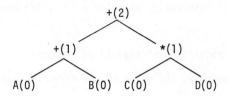

a) A+B+C*D

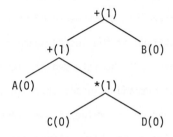

b) A+C*D+B

Figure 2.3

Making Use of Associativity and Commutativity

time the transducer requests simulation of the operator both operands must have been computed. Thus the interchange of value descriptors does not affect the order of computation.

When the operands require equal amounts of temporary storage, other points should be considered. For example, the value of the first operand to be computed is the most likely to end up in memory. This is due to the strategy which we use for generating code: An anonymous operand is maintained in a register as long as possible, but stored into temporary memory when the number of registers is not adequate to the task. Thus the computation of the second operand may use a sufficient number of registers to force the value of the first operand into a temporary storage location. Notice that if we attempted to keep the value of the first operand in a register at the expense of storing some of the intermediate values required during computation of the second operand, we would not be making optimum use of the registers. The intermediate values must necessarily be used before the value of the first operand is used; they should therefore be kept in registers in preference to keeping the value of the first operand.

The hardware implementation of non-commutative operators on many machines favors the use of memory for a particular operand. For example, the IBM System/360 can subtract the contents of a memory location from the contents of a register with a single instruction; two instructions plus a scratch register are required to subtract the contents of a register from a memory location. Thus I would prefer a "reverse subtract" operation in the case where both subtrees of a minus node had the number k (>0) attached to them.

2.2. _Redundant Code Elimination_. A structure tree is converted into a DAG by retaining only one copy of each distinct node; all uses of the subexpression represented by that node are linked to this single copy (Figure 2.4.) The first step in the transformation is to rearrange the descendants of a node into some canonic order. The exact criterion is immaterial provided that it is applied consistently. (In Figure 2.4a I have ordered terminal symbols alphabetically from left to right and placed non-terminals to the right of terminals.) The canonic order is used only during the common subexpression analysis, and does not affect the order in which code is generated for a particular node.

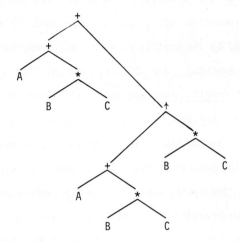

a) Canonical tree for A+B*C(C*B+A)↑(B*C)

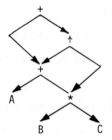

b) Equivalent DAG

Figure 2.4

Relationship Between a Tree and a DAG

We have already seen (Chapter 2.D) that the syntax analyser can report the postfix encounters with nodes of the parse tree by executing a semantic action whenever a reduction takes place. The semantic actions will be executed in the order specified by the postfix form of the expression being analyzed. As these actions are executed, the DAG is created. The data structures used during this process are a _semantic stack_ and the _triples_ representing nodes of the DAG. Before a new triple is generated, the compiler checks all existing triples for a match.

Figure 2.5 shows how this procedure is used to create the DAG of Figure 2.4b. Each step in the process is taken by a semantic action which corresponds to a reduction by the syntax analyser. In the example of Figure 2.5, step 8 recognizes the common subexpression B*C. This recognition requires that the top two elements of the semantic stack be placed in canonic order (i.e. reversed) before the triple is compared with all previously generated triples. Since there is a match with (1), no new triple is generated at this time; (1) is simply placed on the stack as the result of reducing B*C. Another common subexpression is recognized at step 10, which notes that we have encountered a second instance of (2). This requires that (1) was previously recognized as common, but (1) no longer represents a _directly_ common subexpression after recognition of (2). In other words, the common subexpression B*C has been superseded by the larger expression A+B*C. One more instance of B*C is recognized in step 13.

An "expression" for optimization purposes may actually encompass several (syntactic) expressions, and hence redundancy analysis may yield a DAG in which several nodes have no predecessors. Figure 2.6 illustrates this point with a FOR statement from BASIC.

It is possible to argue that the FOR statement of Figure 2.6 does not constitute an expression because the assignment to the control variable has an effect upon the value of the limit. Since there is no standard for BASIC, it is not possible to predict with certainty what the result of this FOR statement will be. (Most BASIC manuals are written for novice programmers and hence do not explore such esoteric points.) The following explanation [GE 1968] is typical: "If the initial, final, or stepping factor values are given as formulas, these formulas are evaluated upon entering the FOR statement. The control variable can be changed in the body of the

$$ABC*+CB*A+BC*\uparrow+$$

a) Postfix form of $A+B*C+(C*B+A)\uparrow(B+C)$

Step	Semantic Stack	Triple Generated
1	A	
2	AB	
3	ABC	
4	A(1)	1: * B C
5	(2)	2: + A (1)
6	(2)C	
7	(2)CB	
8	(2)(1)	
9	(2)(1)A	
10	(2)(2)	
11	(2)(2)B	
12	(2)(2)BC	
13	(2)(2)(1)	
14	(2)(3)	3: ↑ (2) (1)
15	(4)	4: + (2) (3)

b) Construction of the triples

Figure 2.5

Creation of a DAG

JK*L*I = JK*L*I*limit = JK*step =

a) Postfix form of FOR I=J*K*L TO J*K*L*I STEP J*K

Step	Semantic Stack	Triple Generated
1	J	
2	JK	
3	(1)	1: * J K
4	(1)L	
5	(2)	2: * L (1)
6	(2)I	
7		3: = I (2)
8	J	
9	JK	
10	(1)	
11	(1)L	
12	(2)	
13	(2)I	
14	(4)	4: * I (2)
15	(4)limit	
16		5: = limit (4)
17	J	
18	JK	
19	(1)	
20	(1)step	
21		6: = step (1)

b) Construction of the triples

Figure 2.6

A DAG with Several "Roots"

loop; of course, the exit test always uses the latest value of this variable." My interpretation is that the expressions defining the initial value, limit and step size are evaluated before any assignment is made to the control variable; this point of view agrees with that of Lee [1972]. The triples of Figure 2.6b will therefore yield the correct result if (3) is executed last.

Note the treatment of the assignment triples in steps 7, 16 and 21: They do not leave a result on the semantic stack. Sometimes it is appropriate to use the value of an assignment triple as an operand to another triple; this point is covered in Section 2.3.

Once the DAG has been constructed, it must be traversed to yield a sequence of instructions. It is possible to prove the optimality of the sequence generated by traversing a tree [Sethi 1970], but no analogous result holds for DAGs. I shall therefore give a heuristic procedure, adapted from one presented by Aho and Ullman [1973]. The general idea is to traverse the DAG, creating a stack of triple numbers. This stack represents the computations to be performed, in reverse order. The elements are then popped off the stack and passed to the code generator. The procedure is:

a. Set up an empty stack, S, for triple numbers.

b. Choose a triple, not already on S, all of whose ancestors (in the DAG) are on S. Add the number of this triple to S. The procedure terminates if no such triple can be found. (A triple which has no ancestors may be added to S.)

c. If n was the last triple added to S, and one descendent of n is not on S, and all ancestors of that descendent are on S, then add that descendent and repeat step c. Otherwise go to step b.

A convenient way of deciding whether or not all of the ancestors of a particular triple are on S is to include a reference count with each triple in the DAG. This reference count can be computed as the triples are being generated: When a new triple is added to the list, set its reference count to 0 and increment the reference count of each triple which is one of its operands. A triple may be placed on S if and only if its reference count is 0. When a triple is added to S, decrement the reference count of each of its operand triples. Figure 2.7a shows the

	Triple			Count
1:	*	B	C	2
2:	+	A	(1)	2
3:	↑	(2)	(1)	1
4:	+	(2)	(3)	0

a) Reference counts added to the triple list of Figure 2.5

Step	Stack	Resultant Triple List
1	(4)	1: * B C 2 2: + A (1) 1 3: ↑ (2) (1) 0 4: + (2) (3) 0
2	(4)(3)	1: * B C 1 2: + A (1) 0 3: ↑ (2) (1) 0 4: + (2) (3) 0
3	(4)(3)(2)	1: * B C 0 2: + A (1) 0 3: ↑ (2) (1) 0 4: + (2) (3) 0
4	(4)(3)(2)(1)	no change

b) Construction of the stack

Figure 2.7

Flattening the DAG

triple list generated in Figure 2.5 with reference counts added; Figure 2.7b illustrates the generation of a stack from this triple list.

The choice of a triple is fixed at each step in Figure 2.7 by the reference count. The DAG of Figure 2.6 does not have this property (see Figure 2.8). Initially there are three triples with 0 reference counts; presumably any one of them could be placed on S first. In this particular example, however, (3) has a side effect and consequently must be executed last. This means that (3) must be selected as the initial element of S, and the resultant triple list is given in Figure 2.8b.

We must now make a choice between (5) and (6), each of which has a reference count of 0. Since neither has a side effect within this expression, we are free to select either. I would advocate selection of (5). The reason is that its operand, (4), has a reference count of 1 while the operand of (6) has a reference count of 2. This means that if I select (5) I will be able to select its operand as the next element of S. The advantage of selecting an operand immediately after selecting the triple which uses it is that the two computations are linked [Sheridan 1959]: The computed operand value will be used immediately. If I chose (6) in this example, I would have to delay selection of its operand until several other nodes in the DAG had been placed on S. This would mean that the computation of the operand would be remote from its use, and its value might have to be stored in memory instead of being kept in a register.

Once I choose (5) the rest of the selections are fixed: The reference count of (4) is decremented to 0 and hence (4) must be selected according to rule b. This decrements the reference count of (2), which must be selected for the same reason. At this point (6) is the only triple with a 0 reference count, and selection of (1) follows by rule b. The resulting contents of S are shown in Figure 2.8c.

It appears that linkage is the most important property which can be used to determine the next triple to place on S. In more complex expressions, where each immediate operand has a reference count of 1, it may be useful to look at the reference counts of their operands in turn. The search can be continued to any depth, tracing only operands with reference count 1, and will eventually reach either a leaf or a triple whose reference count is greater than 1. The operand

```
1:  *  J      K          2
2:  *  L      (1)        2
3:  =  I      (2)        0
4:  *  I      (2)        1
5:  =  limit (4)         0
6:  =  step  (1)         0
```

a) Reference counts added to the triple list of Figure 2.5

```
1:  *  J      K          2
2:  *  L      (1)        1
3:  =  I      (2)        0
4:  *  I      (2)        1
5:  =  limit (4)         0
6:  =  step  (1)         0
```

b) After placing (3) into the stack

$$(3)(5)(4)(2)(6)(1)$$

c) The complete stack, assuming (5) was chosen at step 2

Figure 2.8

Choices During Flattening

which leads to the longest chain should be selected. Obviously the cost of this strategy increases as the depth of the search increases, and the additional efficiency gained with each step goes down.

In Chapter 3.E (Section 1.3) I noted that a common subexpression value must be given a name because it will be used more than once and thus cannot be modelled by an entry in the transducer's pushdown store. This name must be assigned when the common subexpression is first encountered in the traversal of the DAG, and it must be used for all references to the particular triple which represents the common subexpression. Thus we must expand the description of a triple to include space for a name.

Only those triples which appear as common subexpressions will have names. This fact can be used to delimit the range of a common subexpression (the portion of the program over which its value must be preserved): We are within the range of a common subexpression if and only if the reference count is nonzero and the name is nonnull. We can make use of this property to provide explicit PROTECT and RELEASE commands (Chapter 3.E, Section 4) to the code generator. Upon encountering a node with a nonzero reference count and null name, the traversal algorithm should issue a name and place a RELEASE command for that name onto S. The corresponding PROTECT command is placed onto S just before adding a named node with a 0 reference count. The PROTECT and RELEASE commands are then passed to the code generator when they are taken off the stack as the triples are being evaluated.

This approach (illustrated in Figure 2.9) places the protect operation just after the evaluation of the common subexpression, and places the release operation just before the last computation which uses its value. This is the proper order because the last computation which uses the value should know that that value need not be preserved. (Recall from Chapter 3.E that a release operation does not make the value descriptor vanish immediately.)

2.3. Basic Blocks. The side effects possible within a basic block force us to consider more than just the form of a triple in order to check for common subexpressions. In Figure 2.10, for example, B*C is not a common subexpression because of the assignment to C. The information necessary to account for the side effects can be provided by attaching level numbers to the variables and triples and

Step	Stack	Resultant Triple List					
1	(4)	1:	*	B	C	2	
	RELEASE T1	2:	+	A	(1)	1	T1
		3:		(2)	(1)	0	
		4:	+	(2)	(3)	0	
2	(4)	1:	*	B	C	1	T2
	RELEASE T1	2:	+	A	(1)	0	T1
	(3)	3:		(2)	(1)	0	
	RELEASE T2	4:	+	(2)	(3)	0	
3	(4)	1:	*	B	C	0	T2
	RELEASE T1	2:	+	A	(1)	0	T1
	(3)	3:		(2)	(1)	0	
	RELEASE T2	4:	+	(2)	(3)	0	
	PROTECT T1						
	(2)						
4	(4)	1:	*	B	C	0	T2
	RELEASE T1	2:	+	A	(1)	0	T1
	(3)	3:		(2)	(1)	0	
	RELEASE T2	4:	+	(2)	(3)	0	
	PROTECT T1						
	(2)						
	PROTECT T2						
	(1)						

Figure 2.9

Providing Names for Common Subexpression Values

```
A = B*C

C = D+G

E = B*C

F = A+E
```

Figure 2.10

Side Effects Within a Basic Block

then checking these.

Level numbers are assigned as follows:

a. The level number of a triple is one larger than the largest level number among its operands.

b. The level number of a variable is the number of the triple which last caused its value to change.

(Level number 0 is used to indicate that the value of a variable has not changed in this basic block.) When a new triple is formed, its level number is computed. The triple is redundant if and only if there is an identical triple with the same level number.

The use of level numbers is illustrated in Figure 2.11. (I have eliminated the reference count and name fields from Figure 2.11 in order to save space. These fields would, however, be used in the manner discussed in Section 2.2.) In step 14 the term B*C is reduced. Since the level number of C was reset to 4 at step 10, the level number for this triple would be 6. Although there is an identical triple, (1), its level number is 1. Consequently B*C is not a common subexpression and a new triple must be generated. Once the decision has been made to generate a new triple, we are free to use the value of assignment (4) rather than that of the variable C itself. The necessary information is given by the level number of C, which is equal to the number of the triple that last altered its value (rule b). The level number for triple (4) is 3, not 5, and this value is used to compute the level of the generated triple. Notice that step 19 has a similar effect, using the value of the assignments (2) and (6) in lieu of the variables A and E.

A value is assigned to the variable C in steps 10 and 20. The first of these assignments is irrelevant outside the basic block, since the value is destroyed at step 20. (5) uses the value of (4) rather than the value of C, and therefore the assignment to C is totally redundant. This redundancy can be deduced at step 20 by the fact that the level number of C is not 0. Moreover, the level number of C specifies the triple number of the redundant assignment.

We wish to flag this assignment as being redundant, but not to eliminate it entirely. The reason is that we may discover during code generation that the value cannot be held in a register but must be placed in memory. If this situation

Step	Semantic Stack	Triple Generated

1	A	
2	AB	
3	ABC	
4	A(1)	1: * B C 1
5 (Level of A is reset to 2)		2: = A (1) 2
6	C	
7	CD	
8	CDG	
9	C(3)	3: + D G 1
10 (Level of C is reset to 4)		4: = C (3) 2
11	E	
12	EB	
13	EBC	
14	E(5)	5: * B (4) 3
15 (Level of E is reset to G)		6: = E (5) 4
16	F	
17	FA	
18	FAE	
19	F(7)	7: + (2) (6) 5
20 (Level of C is reset to 8)		8: = C (7) 6

Figure 2.11

Construction of Triples for Figure 2.10

arises, the variable C provides the obvious temporary storage location. Thus an additional temporary need not be assigned by the code generator.

The use of level numbers does not alter the traversal of the DAG in any way. There is no need to select a particular initial node because of a possible side effect; the last triple on the list is always eligible as a starting point.

So far I have discussed only _explicit_ assignments to variables. In most languages, assignments can be made in other ways as well. For example, suppose that an assignment is made to the array element A(I). Since the value of I is not known to the compiler, it has no way of discovering which element of A was altered. Thus it must associate a single level number with the entire array and update that number whenever any element of the array is assigned a value. The compiler cannot generally use the value of the assignment as the value of a particular array element, although this is possible in certain cases.

There are other cases in which the compiler can't even be sure that an assignment has taken place, let alone verify the value assigned [Spillman 1972]. Examples of such "possible assignment" are the side effects which a function call may have on global variables and variables which are arguments to the function. As in the case of array references, the compiler may not use the triple value where the possibly assigned variable appears in subsequent triples. Thus an extra flag is required to distinguish "possible assignments" from explicit assignments in which the triple number may be used in place of the variable.

To handle side effects of function calls, certain triples are treated as "possible assignments" to all global and argument variables. The choice of the triples is determined by the language definition. In ALGOL 60, for example, each function call triple must be regarded as making assignments to all of its argument variables and to all global variables. In FORTRAN, however, the triple making the possible assignment is the last triple of a statement containing a function call.

The effects of a "possible assignment" can be extended through the use of equivalence statements such as those in FORTRAN. In certain algorithms it is useful to establish an equivalence relation between simple variables and selected elements of an array. This makes it easier to access those elements, and allows references to them to be optimized as though they were simple variables. However, when an assignment is made to an arbitrary element of the array the compiler must assume that the values of all of the equivalenced simple variables have been destroyed.

Figure 2.12 illustrates the problem of "possible assignment" with a FORTRAN program. In this example, B*(C+D) is a common subexpression, but A*B*C cannot be a common subexpression because A is an argument variable in the second statement. X*(Y+Z) is common in the assignments to R and S, but the other occurrences of X*(Y+Z) cannot be considered common because the variables X, Y and Z are in COMMON and are thus subject to alteration by the functions ABCF and XYZF. Actually, a more sophisticated analysis could show that X*(Y+Z) would also be common throughout this basic block if the program adhered to the FORTRAN Standard [ANSI 1966]. The reason is that all three of the variables X, Y and Z appear in each assignment statement. According to the excerpt from Section 6.4 of the Standard quoted in Section 1 of this Chapter, neither of the functions can validly alter any of these variables. The analysis required to discover this fact, however, is not usually carried out by a FORTRAN compiler. It is not only expensive, but also it is dangerous. In the second statement, for example, XYZF could alter the values of X, Y and Z without affecting the assignment. The reason is that these variables appear only in an argument expression of the function, and this argument expression must invariably be evaluated before the function is called. The FORTRAN Standard thus provides a specification which is more restrictive than necessary in this situation.

3. Global Optimization

Flow of control within a program can be described by a directed graph which may contain cycles. Each node of the graph corresponds to a single basic block in the program, and each edge represents a direct control path from one basic block to another. A compute point for an expression is a point in the program at which a computation of the expression occurs; a definition point is one at which a new value is assigned to some operand of the expression. If a path through the program graph contains neither a compute point nor a definition point for a particular expression, then it is said to be a clear path with respect to that expression. The value of an expression is available at a point P if every path by which we may arrive at P

$$P = A*B*C+B*(C+D)-ABCF(A)+X*(Y+Z)$$

$$Q = B*(C+D)-XYZF(X*(Y+Z),A)$$

$$R = B*(C+D)-(X*(Y+Z)/(A*B*C))$$

$$S = (X*(Y+Z))/ABCF(A)$$

A, B, C and D are local

X, Y, and Z are in COMMON

Figure 2.12

Possible Assignment

contains a clear subpath from some compute point of the expression to P. Finally, an expression is _live_ at point P if there is a clear path from P to a compute point at which the value is available (if an expression is not live it is _dead._)

Consider the FORTRAN program and corresponding graph shown in Figure 3.1. There are compute points for E*F in the third, fifth and sixth statements of Figure 3.1a; X+E*F has a definition point in the third statement. There is no clear path with respect to E*F from the IF statement to statement 11, because each path contains a compute point for that expression. The value of E*F is available on entry to the basic block beginning with statement 11; it is live at the end of the third and fifth statements, and dead after statement 11.

In this section I shall show how the transformations which we have applied locally can be extended through the use of information regarding availability and liveness, and how these concepts apply to frequency reduction and induction variable optimization. This will allow us to determine the type of flow analysis which is necessary to support global optimization.

3.1. _Redundancy and Rearrangement._ The expression E*F is evaluated in three of the four basic blocks. Figure 3.1b shows that one of these evaluations invariably precedes entry to the basic block which begins at statement 11. Since no new value is assigned to either E or F between the time E*F is evaluated and the time it is used, it need not be re-evaluated in statement 11. Thus this computation is redundant and may be replaced by the name of the value calculated in either of the predecessor blocks. (Recall from Section 2 that the optimizer must give each common subexpression a name by which the code generator may refer to it.)

A particular instance of an expression is redundant if the value of the expression is available at that point. Notice, however, that an expression is available at P only if there is a compute point on _every_ path leading to P, and a clear subpath between that compute point and P. In Figure 3.2, for example, A*B is computed in the third statement of the program but not in statement 10. Thus the value of this expression is unavailable at entry to statement 11 because there is a path to statement 11 which does not contain a compute point of that expression. This in turn means that A*B is dead following its computation in the third statement.

```
      FUNCTION H(A,B,C,D,E,F,G,X,Y)
      IF (A.GE.B) GO TO 10
      X = D+E*F-G
      GO TO 11
10    C = X+E*F/SIN(Y)
11    H = COS(E*F-THETA)
      RETURN
      END
```

a)   A FORTRAN program

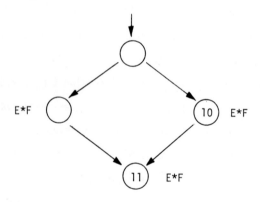

b)   The graph corresponding to (a)

Figure 3.1

Describing the Flow of Control

```
        FUNCTION H(A,B,C,D)

        IF (A.GE.B) GO TO 10

        H = A*B+C

        GO TO 11

10      H = 0.0

11      D = D-A*B

        RETURN

        END
```

a) A FORTRAN program

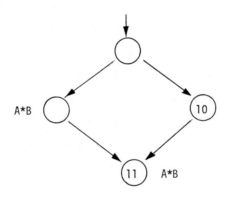

b) The graph corresponding to (a)

Figure 3.2

An Unavailable Expression

Figure 3.3 shows that if E*F is introduced into the entry block of the function all three existing occurrences become redundant; thus the number of occurrences can be reduced from three to one. Earnest [1974] says that it is _profitable_ to insert an expression into a block whenever such an insertion makes the value available at two or more compute points of that expression. Unfortunately this insertion does not necessarily improve the execution speed of the program because it may transfer computations from low-frequency to high-frequency regions. I believe, however, that such problems are minimized by proper region selection.

Local rearrangement of computations cannot introduce error conditions (such as overflow and divide check) unless improper use is made of associativity. The reason is that all computations in a basic block will be executed if any are, a property which is not necessarily shared by any larger region. For example, suppose that A = Q*C, B = Q*A and C≥0 in Figure 3.4. The code of Figure 3.4a will not execute SQRT(Q) if Q<0, while the code of Figure 3.4b always executes SQRT(Q). Thus the profitable rearrangement of Figure 3.4b may introduce an error. It is _safe_ [Earnest 1974] to move an expression which could result in an error if every path leaving the new position leads to a compute point in the original program. This means that the error would have occurred in the original program; the rearrangement has simply moved it to a new position. (Consider the problems of debugging a program which has been subjected to global rearrangement - optimization should only be applied to validated, production software!)

3.2. _Frequency_ _and_ _Strength_ _Reduction_. A loop is represented by a strongly-connected region in the program graph, and an expression is constant within the loop if it has no definition points in the region. Even when an expression has definition points in the region it may be constant, as illustrated by Figure 3.5a. There the variable T is assigned a value which is constant within the loop, and thus remains constant itself. Figure 3.5b shows that this condition is not sufficient, however: T is assigned a constant value at the end of the first iteration, but this value differs from the value which it had on entry. When an expression has a definition point within the loop, then it is invariant if it is dead at each entry to the loop and the value assigned at each definition point is invariant.

```
FUNCTION H(A,B,C,D,E,F,G,X,Y)

T = E*F

IF (A.GE.B) GO TO 10

X = D+T-G

GO TO 11

10    C = X+T/SIN(Y)

11    H = COS(T-THETA)

RETURN

END
```

a) Introduction of a new variable

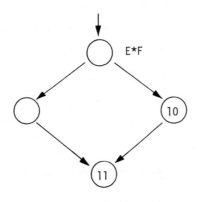

b) Movement of the computation

Figure 3.3

Optimizing Figure 3.1

```
      IF (A .GE. B) GO TO 1
      H = Y+2.7*SQRT(Q)
      GO TO 2
1     IF (C .NE. 0) P = COS(Y)/(2.7*SQRT(Q))
2     H = H+SIN(THETA)
```

a) Source program

```
      T = 2.7*SQRT(Q)
      IF (A .GE. B) GO TO 1
      H = Y*T
      GO TO 2
1     IF (C .NE. 0)  P = COS(Y)/T
2     H = H+SIN(THETA)
```

b) A profitable rearrangement which is unsafe

Figure 3.4

Safety

```
     DO 1 I = J,K
     T = A*B+C
     FI = I
     X(I) = Y(I)+R/T
1    Z(I) = S*T
```

a) Constant expressions with a definition point

```
     T = A*B-C
     DO 1 I = J,K
     FI = I
     X(I) = Y(I)+R/T
     Z(I) = S*T
1    T = A*B+C
```

b) Non-constant expressions

Figure 3.5

Loop Constants

If an expression is invariant over a loop, then it can be evaluated at each entry rather than during execution of the loop. We usually ignore the profitability (Section 3.1) of this move, arguing that it reduces the frequency of execution, but the safety constraint discussed in Section 3.1 must be satisfied.

Aho and Ullman [1973] define an _induction_ _variable_ as one which takes on a sequence of values forming an arithmetic progression (with positive or negative difference) for arbitrary computation paths in a region. The problem of finding all of the induction variables in a region is unsolvable, but several heuristics serve to detect the important cases. One obvious approach is to use language constructs such as DO and _for_ statements to flag the loop control variable, and then ignore other induction variables. Gear [1965] looks for variables which are incremented by constant amounts within the loop; another possibility is to examine the variables which are tested to determine loop termination [IBM 1968].

Linear expressions involving induction variables can be transformed to remove the multiplication from the loop, as illustrated in Figure 3.6. (Such expressions normally arise from references to multi-dimensional arrays subscripted by the loop control variable.) The profitability test is not applied to this transformation because of the expected frequency reduction, and the safety criterion is usually satisfied because the computations do not generate errors.

Note that the strength reduction transformation creates new induction variables. Strength reduction can then be performed anew upon expressions which are linear in these variables. The classic example is the index polynomial of the FORTRAN array reference $A(I,J,K)$ when K is the original induction variable [ANSI 1966]:

$$I+d1*(J-1+d2*(K-1))$$

The expression K-1 is linear, and can be replaced by a single temporary. This temporary is an induction variable, and the coefficient of d1 is a linear function of it. Thus the same transformation can be applied, replacing the coefficient of d1 by another single induction variable. Finally, the entire expression is replaced by a single induction variable. The sequence of transformations is equivalent to rewriting the expression as:

$$K*(d1*d2)+(I+d1*(J-1-d2))$$

This expression is obviously linear in K, but the manipulation required to obtain it

```
      DO 1 I = M1,M2,M3
      ...(K1*I+K2)...
1     CONTINUE
```

a) A linear function of the induction variable

```
      I1 = K1*M1+K2
      I2 = K1*M3
      DO 1 I = M1,M2,M3
      ...(I1)...
1     I1 = I1+I2
```

b) Multiplication removed from the loop

Figure 3.6

Strength Reduction

is not easily taught to a compiler.

3.3. Global Analysis. The optimizations described above require a representation of the program graph and some additional information derived from the basic blocks. Computations within a basic block are defined by lists of triples, as discussed in Section 2. The triples do not specify transfers of control, although they do describe the computations (if any) upon which such transfers are based.

The program graph is most conveniently stored as a list of nodes and a list of edges [Hopcroft 1973]. Each node is represented by a block package [Lowry 1969] containing the following information:

  a. Pointer to the list of edges entering this node.
  b. Pointer to the list of edges leaving this node.
  c. Pointer to the next block package.
  d. Specification of the computation carried out by this basic block.
  e. Additional information as discussed below.

Actual text for the computation is not normally stored in the block package. FORTRAN H [IBM 1968] represents the text for each block as a linear list of quadruples [Gries 1971], with the block package pointing to the first quadruple. (This list is essentially equivalent to the flattened DAG which I discussed in Section 2.) The "additional information" contains summaries of expression and variable usage within the basic block which are relevant for global flow analysis; thus the actual text can reside on backing storage while the graph is analyzed.

Each edge of the graph is represented by an edge package (analogous to the block package) which contains the following information:

  a. Pointer to the next edge entering the same node.
  b. Pointer to the next edge leaving the same node.
  c. Pointer to the next edge package.
  d. Specification of the computation (if any) which causes this edge to be traversed.
  e. Pointers to the block packages for the nodes which this edge connects.

Edges serve as associators [Lang 1968], and hence each edge lies on two lists. This is the purpose of the first two pointers, as shown in Figure 3.7. The computation which causes the edge to be traversed is relevant only when the edge represents a

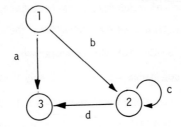

a) A program graph

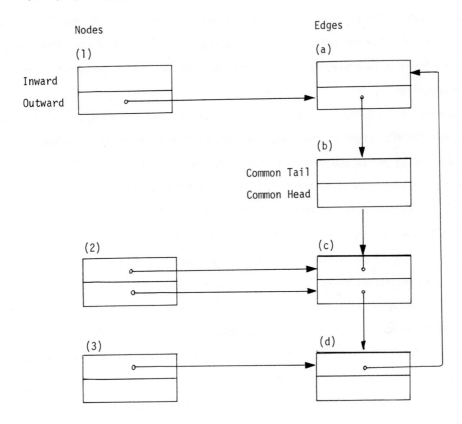

b) Internal representation

Figure 3.7

Storing a Program Graph

conditional transfer of control. In that case, the edge package would contain a pointer to the single triple which summarizes the computation (i.e. a pointer to the root of the tree or DAG for the computation.)

The block and edge packages are built and linked during the first pass over the program text: Space for the first basic block is allocated, and analysis of the text begins. When a jump is encountered in this analysis, space for an edge package and the block package for the target block is allocated and linked. The dictionary specifies the correspondence between labels and block packages, so that new edges can be properly linked to existing block packages. At the end of the first pass the program graph is complete, and the computations carried out by each basic block have been specified.

Section 3.1 explained that the characteristics of the computation which were relevant for rearrangement and redundancy elimination were the relative positions of the definition points and compute points. In a single basic block, there are five possibilities which must be distinguished for each expression -

a. A compute point preceeds any definition points.

b. A definition point preceeds any compute points.

c. A compute point follows any definition points.

d. A definition point follows any compute points.

e. There are neither definition points nor compute points.

Possibilities a and b are opposites, as are c and d; if e is true then none of a-d is true. Three bits are therefore required to express the information which can be derived from the basic block for each expression.

There are many ways to specify the values of the three bits; your choice will depend upon the problem you are trying to solve and the precise algorithm which you are using. For example, consider the problem of determining the block entries at which a particular value is available [Cocke 1970, Allen 1971, Ullman 1973]. Let us express the solution by a single bit for each block:

AVAIL(i)=1 if the value is available on entry to block i.

AVAIL(i)=0 otherwise.

First we assume that the value is available on entry to a block if and only if that block has at least one predecessor. This assumption enables us to initialize

AVAIL(I) for all i.

A value is available on entry to a block only if it is available on exit from <u>all</u> of that block's predecessors. Once we determine that the value is unavailable on exit from some block, no other conditions which we can discover will render that value available to a successor. Thus availability is a fragile flower, which cannot be resurrected once it is destroyed. The boolean <u>and</u> implements this property - if AVAIL is altered only by assignments of the form AVAIL=AVAIL*e, then once it becomes 0 it can never be reset to 1.

If possibility (d) holds for any block, then the value cannot be available on entry to any successor of that block. This suggests that we represent (d) by a 0-bit, KILL, and make a single pass over the edges of the graph setting AVAIL(j)=AVAIL(j)*KILL(i). (Here the edge is directed from block i to block j.) After this pass is completed, we can forget about case (d) entirely and concentrate upon cases (c) and (e). In case (c) the value is unconditionally available on exit, while in case (e) it is available on exit only if it is available on entry. Suppose that case (c) is represented by a 1-bit, GEN. If block j is a successor of block i, and AVAIL(i)=0, then AVAIL(j)=AVAIL(j)*GEN(i). If AVAIL(j) becomes 0 during either the initialization or the first pass, place block j on a stack, S. At the end of the first pass, remove the top block (i, say) from S and perform the assignment AVAIL(j)=AVAIL(j)*GEN(i) for each successor block j. If this assignment changes AVAIL(j) to 0, place block j on S. The process continues until S is empty, and requires O(ne) steps (where n is the number of blocks and e the number of edges [Ullman 1973].)

The limited information required by the availability algorithm was naturally encoded by the GEN and KILL bits. Earnest [1974] presents a composite algorithm for rearrangement and redundancy which makes decisions on the basis of safety and profitability in addition to availability. This algorithm requires the full three bits, and encodes the information as follows:

c(i)=1 if block i contains no definition point for the expression, or if a
   compute point follows all definition points in block i.

d(i)=1 if there is no clear path for the expression through block i.

e(i)=1 if there is no definition point for the expression in block i, or if a compute point precedes all definition points.

(These names are used by Earnest, and should not be confused with cases c, d and e discussed above. If "-" indicates "don't care", then cases a through e are encoded by -11, -10, 11-, 01- and 101 respectively.)

Each bit gives the appropriate summary information for one expression in one basic block. Unfortunately, we need this information for every expression in every basic block in order to complete the analysis. Most of the expressions will turn out to be irrelevant for optimization, but I know of no systematic method of determining which are important. (FORTRAN H [Lowry 1969] retains summary information only about the first 127 simple variables, and then does exhaustive searches for common subexpressions in order to eliminate redundancy.)

The global analysis procedure does not normally attempt to consider the entire program at once. Rather it finds a partition of the basic blocks which covers the graph and has some useful property (e.g. each group of basic blocks is strongly-connected, or has only a single entry point.) It then deduces, for each region of the partition, summary information similar to that used for a basic block. Finally it iterates the process, using a graph whose nodes are the regions. One particularly important aspect of this process is that it makes the loop nesting apparent and allows nests to be optimized in "inner to outer" order. Region formation is well-documented in the literature [Allen 1970, Ullman 1973], and I shall not discuss the mechanics of it here.

Upon completion of "inner to outer" processing, additional information is available about values at region boundaries. This information is then passed into the region, and deposited at the boundaries of nested regions. Eventually it reaches the level of the basic block, where it causes modification of the text. This final modification is what actually performs the optimization (the global analysis merely serves to gather the necessary information); it consists of the normal transformations discussed in Section 2.

References

Aho, A.V., Sethi, R., Ullman, J.D.: A formal approach to code optimization.

SIGPLAN Notices 5, 86-100 (July, 1970).

Aho, A.V., Ullman, J.D.: The theory of parsing, translation, and compiling. Prentice-Hall 1973.

Allen, F.E.: Control flow analysis. SIGPLAN Notices 5, 1-19 (July, 1970).

Allen, F.E.: A basis for program optimization. Information Processing 71, 385-391, North-Holland 1972.

Allen, F.E., Cocke, J.: A catalogue of optimizing transformations. In Rustin, R. (Ed.): Design and Optimization of Compilers. Prentice-Hall 1972.

ANSI: FORTRAN. X3.9-1966, American National Standards Institute 1966.

Backus, J.W., Heising, W.P.: FORTRAN. IEEE Transactions EC-13, 382-385 (1964).

Bagwell, J.T.: Local optimizations. SIGPLAN Notices 5, 52-66 (July, 1970).

Bauer, F.L., Samuelson, K.: Comment in ALGOL Bulletin 10 (1961).

Beatty, J.C.: Register assignment algorithm for generation of highly optimized object code. IBM J. Res. Develop. 18, 20-39 (1974).

Clark, B.L., Horning, J.J.: Reflections on a language designed to write an operating system. ACM SIGPLAN/SIGOPS Interface Meeting, Savannah, 9-12 April 1973.

Cocke, J.: Global common subexpression elimination. SIGPLAN Notices 5, 20-24 (July, 1970).

Cocke, J., Schwartz, J.T.: Programming languages and their compilers: preliminary notes. New York University 1970.

Earnest, C.: Some topics in code optimization. JACM 21, 76-102 (1974).

Forsythe, A.I., Keenan, T.A., Organick, E.I., Stenberg, W.: Computer science: a first course. John Wiley 1969.

Frailey, D.J.: Expression optimization using unary complement operators. SIGPLAN Notices 5, 67-85 (July, 1970).

GE: GE-400 Series Basic Language. CPB-1470 (1968).

Gear, C.W.: High speed compilation of efficient object code. CACM 8, 483-488 (1965).

Gries, D.: Compiler Construction for Digital Computers. John Wiley, 1967.

Hall, A.D.: Private Communication 1974.

Hext, J.B.: Programming Languages and Compiling Techniques. Ph.D. Dissertation,

University of Cambridge 1965.

Hopcroft, J., Tarjan, R.: Efficient algorithms for graph manipulation. CACM 16, 372-378 (1973).

IBM Corp.: IBM system/360 operating system FORTRAN IV (H) compiler program logic manual. Y28-6642-3 (1968).

Kildall, G.A.: Global expression optimization during compilation. Ph.D. Thesis, University of Washington 1972.

Knuth, D.E.: The Art of Computer Programming, Vol. 2: Seminumerical Algorithms. Addison Wesley 1969.

Knuth, D.E.: An empirical study of FORTRAN programs. Software - Practice and Experience 1, 105-133 (1971).

Lee, J.A.N.: A formal definition of the BASIC language. Computer J. 15, 37-41 (1972).

Lowry, E.S., Medlock, C.W.: Object code optimization. CACM 12, 13-22 (1969).

McKeeman, W.M.: Peephole optimization. CACM 8, 443-444 (1965).

Rohl, J.S., Linn, J.A.: A note on compiling arithmetic expressions. Computer J. 15, 13-14 (1972).

Sethi, R., Ullman, J.D.: The generation of optimal code for arithmetic expressions. JACM 17, 715-728 (1970).

Sheridan, P.B.: The FORTRAN arithmetic-compiler of the IBM FORTRAN automatic coding system. CACM 2, 9- (1959).

Spillman, T.C.: Exposing side-effects in a PL/I optimizing compiler. Information Processing 71, 376-381, North-Holland 1972.

Ullman, J.D.: Fast algorithms for the elimination of common subexpressions. Acta Informatica 2, 191-213 (1973).

Wilcox, T.R.: Generating Machine Code for High-Level Programming Languages. Ph.D. Thesis, Cornell University 1971.

CHAPTER 6.

Appendix: HISTORICAL REMARKS ON COMPILER
CONSTRUCTION

F. L. Bauer

Technical University of Munich

Munich, Germany

Historical Remarks on Compiler Construction

D. E. KNUTH [81] has observed (in 1962!) that the early history of cimpiler construction is difficult to assess. Maybe this, or maybe the general unhistorical attitude
of our century is responsible for the widespread ignorance about the origins of compiler construction. In addition, the overwhelming lead of the USA in the general development of computers and their application, together with the language barrier, has
in fact favoured negligence of early developments in Middle Europe and in the Soviet
Union.

Far from being able to give a thorough and complete history of compiler writing - I
hope to find one day the time for doing the immense reading and screening involved in
such an enterprise - I will only try to give a few remarks together with bibliographi-
cal notes, that may help some interested readers to penetrate into the historical work

and to do their own investigations. I should also give the warning that I may be biased: My own attitude to compilers has in the early 60's strongly favoured syntax-controlled analysis over syntax-directed analysis [1], faithful to the economic principle of doing things rather once for all than repeatedly. Moreover, I have been involved myself at some time with the development, and know some parts of it better than others.

Nevertheless, I would venture the hope that historical studies are still considered to be more than digging out material for patent courts and for the entertainment of students, that historical assessment is an indispensable part of science and in particular of a discipline that has keenly called itself "computer science" and is now compelled to live with the claim.

---

[1] In the sense of FLOYD [51]

1.   Prehistorical 'Gedanken-compilers'

Translation is a conversion of sentences from one language to another, which preserves the meaning. A compiler translates descriptions of algorithms from a language suitable for human use to a more hardware-oriented language specifying somehow more elementary actions. In this sense, the problem of 'reading' a complicated arithmetical formula, particularly with the intention to do some calculation according to this prescription means actually a mechanical mental process (which is helped by some drill received at junior highschool). Thus, logicians, looking behind the curtain of obviousness in mathematics, were close to studying the processes of compiling arithmetical and other "algebraic" formulae, totally independent of the existence and use of computers.

The parenthesis-free or 'polish' notation which was introduced by J. LUKASIEWICZ in the late 20's [88], today frequently called prefix notation, was a perfect notation for the output of a compiler as defined above, and thus a step towards the actual mechanization and formulation of the compilation process.

A further step was made 1953 by BURKS, WARREN, WRIGHT [28] in specifying a right-to-left check algorithm for well-formed parenthesis-free Boolean formulae. However, H. ANGSTL, in 1950, had designed a mechanism that solved the problem, see [14].

Mere 'rules of spelling' for the parenthesis-free notation had been formalized and proved by MENGER 1932 and SCHRÖTER 1943 [91], [113] (for formulae with parenthesis in the most general case apparently 1934 by KLEENE [79] and 1941 by CHURCH [36]). In 1950, P. ROSENBLOOM's book [103] already contained a chapter on formal languages, based on work by POST [99] in 1943, and thus the tools for describing even the syntax of the class of arithmetic and other 'algebraic' formulae with parentheses. The aim, however, was mathematical proof theory and the mechanism heavy.

This was only changed when N. CHOMSKY in 1957 introduced very special classes of languages [32], [33], [34], [35]. Mention should also be made of a rather unsuccessful attempt by WELLS in 1947 [125]. All this happened in the realm of logic. An exception is K. ZUSE. Parallel to, but independent of, his pioneering work in hardware and functional design, ZUSE specified in 1945, immobilized by war events in a small bavarian village, an algorithm that determines whether an expression with parentheses is well-formed and tackles already simplification problems like double negation and removal of superflous parentheses. ZUSE writes a program, fully operational as an application example of his Plankalkül [129], [130]. But it only describes a check algorithm, the compilation itself is lacking; there is also no indication in ZUSE's work that he had considered mechanical processing in his Plankalkül, that he had even seen the possibility. [1]

Thus, according to our knowledge, it was H. RUTISHAUSER who was (1951) the first to describe a compilation process both in its full operational detail and in its actual importance [104], [105], [106]. The Z4 computer accessible to RUTISHAUSER was actually not suited to do the compilation, RUTISHAUSER could only perform a Gedankenexperiment, that strongly influenced the design of the Swiss ERMETH [120]. RUTISHAUSER's method was to establish the parentheses level contour map (Klammergebirge) and then to work down level by level, see Fig. 1.

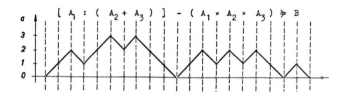

Fig. 1. Parentheses level contour map.
Facsimile from Rutishausers original paper.

2.   The first compilers

RUTISHAUSER has used the term "Automatische Rechenplanfertigung". "Automatic programing" was a similar term, in usage since 1951 [127]. A compiler was originally a program that "compiled" subroutines [126]. When in 1954 the combination "algebraic compiler" came into use [66], [67], or rather into misuse, the meaning of the term had already shifted to the present one. In the german language area, "Übersetzer" was favoured, and language-conscious people like PERLIS [97], [7], used more properly "translator". But in the sloppy way so typical for a wide part of the computer community, compiler became the dominating term.

A number of early compilers in the more trivial sense was presented in 1954 at the US Office of Naval Research Symposium on Automatic Programming. Names to be mentioned are ADAMS and LANING (Comprehensive compiler, Summer Session Compiler) [2], RICE (APS III Comiler) [101], GOLDFINGER (NYU Compiler) [55], BACKUS and HERRICK (IBM 701

---

[1]   KNUTH, in [81], simplifies history too much when merely writing "a complete history of compilers should mention the work of ZUSE ..."

Speedcoding) [8], somebody (Remington Rand A-2 Compiler) [1], BROWN and CARR III (MAGIC I) [27] and GORN [56].

Remarkable was in 1954 the first "algebraic compiler" written [2], [84] by ADAMS, LANING and ZIERLER for the Whirlwind and the proclamation of a universal, machine independent programming language by J. W. CARR III [27]; also a first practical attempt in this direction: APT, a common programming language proposed by B. RICH [102] which is essentially a prefix notation and thus escaped from the more subtle problems of arithmetic formulae.

Restricting the notation was obviously one way to ease the actual compilation process. Among the two trivial ways, suppressing operator precedence (as RUTISHAUSER had done) and requiring full parenthesation, the second one is of particular interest, since there is a simple mechanical way of establishing this form by inserting virtual parentheses (see Fig. 2), which was also in the logicians' folklore, according to KALMAR.

readily. An ingenious idea used in the first FORTRAN compiler was to surround binary operators with peculiar-looking parentheses:

$+$ and $-$ were replaced by $)))+(((($ and $)))-((($

$*$ and $/$ were replaced by $))*(($ and $))/(($

$**$ was replaced by $)**($

and then an extra "$(((($" at the left end "$)))$)" at the right were tacked on. The resulting formula is properly parenthesized, believe it or not. For example, if we consider "$(X+Y)+W/Z$," we obtain

$$((((X)))+(((Y))))+(((W))/((Z)))$$

This is admittedly highly redundant, but extra parentheses need not affect the resulting machine language code. After the above replacements are

Fig. 2. The full parenthesation trick. Faksimile from Knuth's 1962 Survey paper [81].

C. BÖHM [19], in his 1952 Zurich thesis under RUTISHAUSER could therefore restrict his interest to the full parenthesized case; for this case he was first to show that a sequentially working process could be used in place of RUTISHAUSER's process, which worked on the whole formula (see Fig. 3).

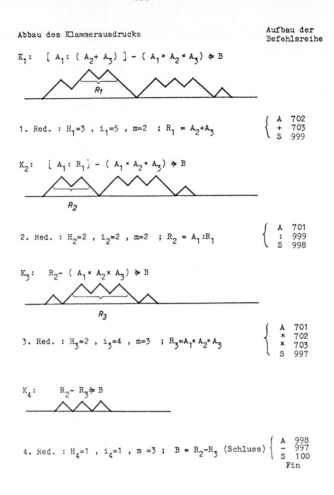

Abbau des Klammerausdrucks

Aufbau der Befehlsreihe

K_1: $[A_1 : (A_2 + A_3)] - (A_1 \times A_2 \times A_3) \nRightarrow B$

R_1

1. Red. : $H_1 = 3$, $i_1 = 5$, $m = 2$; $R_1 = A_2 + A_3$

A	702
+	703
S	999

K_2: $[A_1 : R_1] - (A_1 \times A_2 \times A_3) \nRightarrow B$

R_2

2. Red. : $H_2 = 2$, $i_2 = 2$, $m = 2$; $R_2 = A_1 : R_1$

A	701
:	999
S	998

K_3: $R_2 - (A_1 \times A_2 \times A_3) \nRightarrow B$

R_3

3. Red. : $H_3 = 2$, $i_3 = 4$, $m = 3$; $R_3 = A_1 \times A_2 \times A_3$

A	701
×	702
×	703
S	997

K_4: $R_2 - R_3 \nRightarrow B$

4. Red. : $H_4 = 1$, $i_4 = 1$, $m = 3$; $B = R_2 - R_3$ (Schluss)

A	998
-	997
S	100
Fin	

Fig. 3. RUTISHAUSER's method of layered reduction. Faksimile from [105].

Thus, BÖHM was ahead of the first FORTRAN compiler by SHERIDAN [116], which used the same technique. See also [10], [115]. The other way, suppressing operator precedence and thus requiring sufficient parenthesizing, was used in 1956 by A. J. PERLIS in the IT compiler [97]. He was also able to give a sequential algorithm. Again, BÖHM had already briefly discussed this case. Also, some early attempts by NAMUR in 1954 [92] are outdated by BÖHM.

In the Soviet Union, Ljapunov and Yanov [86], [75], [76] developed, without relation to compilation, in 1957 an algorithmic notation. KANTOROVIC showed in 1957 how a parsed formula can be represented with help of a tree [78] (see Fig. 4).

3.   Sequentially working compilers

In the middle of the 50's, it had become evident that compilation of arithmetical formulae was only a prototype of the general problem of compiling a reasonable programming language. Moreover, machines were still slow and had restricted storage capacity
so that effective compilation methods were sought for, in particular in the pover-
stricken European quarters, where rumours about the size of the FORTRAN system encouraged people particularly to do it better in order to do it at all. Thus compilation techniques were aimed at what would work sequentially for *unrestricted* arithmetic
formulae and thus for the prototype of most general nested and agglomerated structures.

Described in terms of RUTISHAUSER's parentheses level, the simplest possibility is
the following: to proceed until the first closing parentheses is found and then to
work down from there. This was proposed by BOTTENBRUCH 1957 [20], was used by ADAMS
and SCHLESINGER (1958) for the IBM 650 [3] and, as far as we could see, was also
found by ERSHOV in 1958 [43], [41], [42] and used in the "Programming Program" for
the BESM. The GAT Compiler of ARDEN and GRAHAM [5] works also in this way (and shows
other striking parallels with the Russian approach). GARWICK also independently discovered this method, as mentioned in [18], and maybe others. Clearly this method may
proceed farther than necessary, since for RUTISHAUSER's parenthesis levels, full parenthesation is not assumed.

A more sophisticated method proceeds in the parentheses contour map until the first
pair of relative maxima is found, and works down from there (see Fig. 4, the numbering indicates the order). For dyadic operators, this is intuitively the most effective method. It has been found by SAMELSON in 1955 [107] and was used by BAUER and
SAMELSON in 1957 [16] in designing the hardware of a machine accepting 'algebraic
code'.[1]

---

[1] Another early attempt in the direction of 'high level language computers' was made
in the SEAC design, see [117]. In the Burroughs B 5000 [29] and in Ferranti KDF9
[64] design, as well as in microprogrammed machines, to some extent a revival of
the idea of high level language computers can be found.

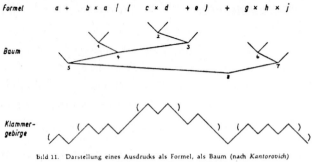

Fig. 4. RUTISHAUSER's parentheses level contour map,
KANTOROVIC's tree and the sequential method
of SAMELSON-BAUER. Facsimile from the BAUER-
SAMELSON 1961 survey paper [18].

It was the basis of the work preparing the GAMM proposals [53], [15] for the Zurich
1958 ALGOL conference and subsequently of the ALCOR compilers for ALGOL, the prototype and the first of which was written 1958 (working in spring 1959) for ALGOL 58
by PAUL for the ZUSE Z22, a small machine with a drum memory of 2000 cells. It was
followed in the compilers for ALGOL 60 by PAUL for the Z22, by SCHWARZ for the ERMETH,
by SEEGMÜLLER for the PERM, by HILL and LANGMAACK for the Siemens 2002, see [109] and
[111]. WEGSTEIN (1959) independently found [124] essentially the same solution, which
was characterized by SAMELSON and BAUER as "left-to-right (or right-to-left) scanning,
deferring symbols just as long as necessary and evoking action as soon as possible"
[16].

The outbreak of ALGOL   stimulated independent, more or less systematic work on a
number of other early compilers, among which we mention from 1959 in the WEGSTEIN
line KANNER [77], in the PERLIS line KNUTH with RUNCIBLE [80],then GORN and INGERMAN
[57], [70]; from 1960 and later FLOYD [46], [47], HUSKEY and WATTENBURG ([68], [69],
[123]) with the NELIAC adherents (see [65]). Apparently, MAUCHLY, HOPPER and Anatol
W. HOLT with the Remington Rand people [118], [45], [119], were also on this road.
The Mercury Autocode people around BROOKER [21], [22], [23], [24], [25], [26], and
some others will be mentioned later at appropriate places. [1])

---

[1])Further material that might be relevant, concerning work by DAHN and by BARTON and
TURNER [12] seems to be difficult to get at.

Almost all the efficient sequential compilation methods [1] had used for intermediate storage of not yet processed parts a 'last in - first out' store, also called 'stack', 'cellar' [2] (from German 'Keller'), 'pushdown store'. RUTISHAUSER had stored intermediate results in a stack-like fashion, (see Fig. 3), but had not stressed at all this point. In fact, such a last in - first out store had already been used by ANGSTL and BAUER in the logical (relay-) computer STANISLAUS designed in 1951 [4], [14], and this experience was the starting point for SAMELSON (1955), to use a "cellar" not only for deferred intermediate results, as needed even with parenthesis-free notation, but also for deferred operations. The principle was independently found elsewhere and other intuitive imaginations were involved, for example a railyard shunt served for DIJKSTRA [38]. General aspects were also taken into account in 1961 by ARDEN, GALLER and GRAHAM [6] describing the MAD compiler, and in 1963 by GREIBACH [61].

In 1959 [109] (an English translation [110] appeared in 1960) [3] BAUER and SAMELSON summarized their technique as applied to a full language and worded it in terms of a transition table with input characters and the state-determining top position of a cellar. In a colloquium with logicians 1960 in Berlin (see [82]), the interpretation as a pushdown automaton, a generalization of a finite state automaton was particularly stressed. This coincided with A. G. OETTINGER's (1961) independent introduction of pushdown automata [93], which originated from earlier considerations of mechanical translation of natural languages. Following OETTINGER's approach, P. C. FISCHER [44] had reached in 1959 about the same mastery of languages with parentheses that may be omitted either in the presence of associative operators or in the presence of operators with hierarchical difference, as the ALCOR group. Pushdown automata were further investigated by SCHÜTZENBERGER [114], the design of the transition table was studied by CONWAY [37] and later by GRIES [62a]. All methods, so far, had been "bottom-up" in modern terminology. Except for OETTINGER's, who apparently had used a top-down parsing ('predictive analysis' of the linguistics) and HUSKEY's. This line will be taken up again in 6.

---

[1] It seems that the NELIAC compilers had not used explicitly a stack (see GRIES, Compiler Construction for Digital Computers. Wiley 1971, p. 153.) but recursive descent (see 6.) instead.

[2] The expression 'cellar' came from a particular set-up of wire lines in the design drawing of STANISLAUS, see below.

[3] See also [17].

4.   "Syntax controlled compilers"

It was obvious that the transition tables of the BAUER-SAMELSON and of the OETTINGER pushdown automaton reflected the structure of the language. The problem of deriving them mechanically from a structural language description, was given to PAUL and solved in his Mainz thesis of 1962 [94], see also [96] and [95] as well as [108]. The generality, however, in which PAUL had attacked the problem, resulted in a complicated process. Nevertheless, later independent attempts to solve this problem for restricted types of language, for example for operator languages with precedence properties of the kind PERLIS had used, by FLOYD in 1963 [48], would have been corollaries of PAUL's results, had those been known. Work in this direction was interpreted as refining the grammar in order to cut off dead-end roads and thus defining deterministic transitions. Results by EICKEL et al. [40] in 1963 were generalized by FLOYD [49], GRAHAM [58], and IRONS [74] in 1964, introducing bounded context grammars. The first paper that actually showed how to construct tables for a (m,n) left-to-right bounded context recognizer was by EICKEL [39][1]. The most general class LR(k) of grammars that could be treated with a   deterministic pushdown automaton, which is allowed to look to all the symbols in the stack and the k symbols to the right, was specified (and shown how to construct the recognizer) by KNUTH. Still, the class is at present somewhat too general to be used unrestrictedly in practice. Here we reach the modern and recent development, as discussed by HORNING in this course.

5.   Compilers based on precedence

The idea to use precedence between adjacent symbols in controlling the recognizer, introduced intuitively by PERLIS 1956 and used also by others, was generalized in the NELIAC compilers and elsewhere to the use of precedence between neighbouring pairs of operators. It led FLOYD in 1963 to introduce precedence grammars, for which a recognizer was easily constructed [48]. FLOYD's operator precedence grammar was paralleled by the simple precedence grammar of WIRTH and WEBER [128], the (1,1)-case of the more general (m,n)-grammars which were also introduced by WIRTH and WEBER, but, according to GRIES, 'the definition was wrong' and was corrected later by him [62].
In 1966, McKEEMAN found a generalization of simple precedence, the (1,2)(2,1) precedence. Again, we reach here the material of this course.

---

[1] GRIES writes, 'the paper is not only hard to read, but also hard to obtain'. The second is not true, several hundred copies have been sent out on request, and copies can still be obtained from the Math. Inst., Techn. Univ. Munich; therefore anyone who wants may find out for himself whether the first assertion is true.

The further development seems to approach (1,1) bounded context and thus to converge. There are in any case deeper connections between: Use of precedence for controlling their pushdown transitions was discussed by BAUER and SAMELSON in 1959 [17]. In 1961, M. PAUL and C. A. PETRI (see [111]) independently found that parts of the ALCOR pushdown automaton transition tables reflect a simple linear ordering of the entry pairs. This was later used in the ALCOR ILLINOIS compiler by GRIES, PAUL and WIEHLE [63].

6.   Syntax-directed compilers

Syntax-directed compilation was in its pure form first proposed by GLENNIE in 1960 [54]. He already treated the algebra of recognition graphs and used it intuitively in order to avoid backup. Parsing by explicit recursive descent was proposed by LUCAS in 1961 [87], describing a simplified ALGOL 60 compiler by a set of recursive subroutines that closely followed the BNF syntax. Clearly, this was top-down analysis, the call-and-return stack of the recursive procedure implementation mechanism [1] serving as a pushdown store, and it was without backup because it contained appropriate tests. It was somehow similar to GRAU's [60], [59] compiler in 1961, using recursive procedures, which is not surprising since both were based on the transition tables for a deterministic pushdown automaton that were in current use in the ALCOR group. As a result, it was more clearly seen in the ALCOR group how pushdown state symbols reflected syntactic states, and this stimulated work on syntax-controlled processor generators. HUSKEY [68], [69] also used recursive descent. Then, in 1961, IRONS described a parsing algorithm [72], [73] driven by tables which described the syntax, but his method was a mixture of top-down and bottom-up. His method needed backup and so did BROOKER's [25], [26], [23]. The idea was fascinating (many papers: WARSHALL [121], REYNOLDS [100], LEDLEY and WILSON [85], INGERMANN [71], CHEATHAM and SATTLEY [31], BASTIAN [13], BARNETT and FUTRELLE [11], WARSHALL and SHAPIRO [122], CHEATHAM [30], SCHORRE [112] followed within a short time) but its practical use was restricted to places that had abundant computer time. KUNO and OETTINGER, in natural language translation, also favoured a 'multi-path syntactic analysis'[83]; a similar idea was used in COGENT by REYNOLDS in 1965 [62].

Several compilers in practical use used top-down parsing with recursive descent: The META compilers of SCHORRE [62], the Burroughs extended ALGOL compiler and the SHARE 7090 ALGOL compiler. The elegance and convenience for the compiler writer was paid for in compile time by the user. While GLENNIE had estimated that 1000 instructions were to be executed in order to produce one machine instruction, PAUL in his ALGOL 60 compiler for the Z22 did it with about 50.

---

[1] A subroutine return stack was proposed in 1952 by W. L. van der Poel [98].

The situation changed, when one learned to do syntax-directed (top-down) parsing without backup. In 1965, FOSTER found the general rule for mechanically transforming a grammar into what was called later LL(1). The publication was delayed until 1968 [52]. Independently, KNUTH, in the Copenhagen summer school 1967, gave a definition of LL(1) - the publication was delayed until 1971. So, techniques for achieving this systematically were first published in 1968 by UNGER [62], while LEWIS and STEARNS [62] in 1968, ROSENKRANTZ and STEARNS [62] in 1969 treated the class LL(k) of grammars that can be parsed top-down without backup by examining at each step all the symbols processed so far and k symbols more to the right. Clearly, LL(k), like LR(k), is an efficient method, and the discrepancy between bottom-up syntax-controlled and top-down syntax-directed methods is no longer of more than historical importance, it has been replaced by competition. Again, we have reached the actualities of this field.

7.   Concluding remarks

The development in the Soviet Union and its neighbours has progressed quite independently from the Western side, and vice versa. An attempt to arrive at a complete and comparative coverage would be very desirable, but I am not even able to give a first approximation in the framework of this course. I would, however, venture the hope that in co-operation with Soviet colleagues such an aim can be approached. Quite generally, I would appreciate to receive additional material, from whatever part of the world, on the history of compilers, and may combine with the thanks to potential contributors the thanks to my colleagues and friends, in particular the lecturers of this course, for their help.

References

[1]   The A-2 Compiler System: Automatic Programming. Computers and Automation 4,
      25-31 (Sept. 1955) and 4, 15-23 (Oct. 1955)

[2]   Adams, Ch. W., Laning, J. H. jr.: The MIT systems of automatic coding: Compre-
      hensive, Summer Session, and Algebraic. Symposium Automatic Programming Digi-
      tal Computers, Office of Naval Research, PB 111 6o7. May 13-14, 1954, p. 3o-33

[3]   Adams, E. S., Schlesinger, S. I.: Simple automatic coding systems. Comm. ACM
      1:7, 5-9 (1958)

[4]   Angstl, H.: Seminar über Logistik. Prof. W. Britzelmayr, Universität München,
      195o

[5]   Arden, B. W., Graham, R. M.: On GAT and the construction of translators. Comm.
      ACM 2:7, 24-26 (1959)

[6]   Arden, B. W., Galler, B. A., Graham, R. M.: The internal organization of the
      MAD translator. Comm. ACM 4, 28-31 (1961)

[7]   Automatic Programming: The IT translator. In: E. M. Grabbe et al. (eds.):
      Handbook of Automation, Computation, and Control 2, 2·2oo-2·228. New York:
      John Wiley and Sons 1959

[8]   Backus, J. W., Herrick, H.: IBM 701 speedcoding and other automatic programming
      systems. Symposium Automatic Programming Digital Computers, Office of Naval
      Research, PB 111 6o7. May 13-14, 1954, p. 1o6-113

[9]   Backus, J. W.: Automatic Programming: Properties and performance of FORTRAN
      Systems I and II. Symposium Mechanisation of Thought Processes, National
      Physical Lab., Teddington, November 24-27, 1958, p. 231-255

[10] Backus, J. W. et al.: The FORTRAN automatic coding system. Proc. AFIPS 1957
      WJCC 11, p. 188-198

[11] Barnett, M. P., Futrelle, R. P.: Syntactic analysis by digital computer. Comm.
      ACM 5, 515-526 (1962)

[12] Barton, R. S.: Another (nameless) compiler for the Burroughs 220. Comm. ACM 4,
      A 11 (1961)

[13] Bastian, A. L. jr.: A phrase-structure language translator. Air Force Cam-
      bridge Res. Labs., Hanscom Field (Mass.), Rep. No. AFCRL-69-549, August 1962

[14] Bauer, F. L.: The formula-controlled logical computer "Stanislaus". Mathema-
      tics of Computation (MTAC) 14, 64-67 (1960)

[15] Bauer, F. L., Bottenbruch, H., Rutishauser, H., Samelson, K.: Proposal for a
      universal language for the description of computing processes. Zürich, Mainz,
      München, Darmstadt (ZMMD-Projekt), April 1958

[16] Bauer, F. L., Samelson, K.: Verfahren zur automatischen Verarbeitung von ko-
      dierten Daten und Rechenmaschine zur Ausübung des Verfahrens. Deutsche Patent-
      auslegeschrift 1094019. Anm.: 30. März 1957; Bek.: 1. Dez. 1960

[17] Bauer, F. L., Samelson, K.: The cellar principle for formula translation. Proc.
      ICIP Paris 1959, p. 154

[18] Bauer, F. L., Samelson, K.: Maschinelle Verarbeitung von Programmsprachen. In:
      Hoffmann, W. (Hrsg.): Digitale Informationswandler. Braunschweig: Vieweg 1962

[19] Böhm, C.: Calculatrices digitales. Du déchiffrage de formules logico-mathé-matiques par la machine même dans la conception du programme (Dissertation, Zürich 1952). Annali Mathematica pura applicata, Ser. 4, 37, 5-47 (1954)

[20] Bottenbruch, H.: Einige Überlegungen zur Übersetzung einer algorithmischen Sprache in Maschinenprogramme. Manuskript, Institut für Praktische Mathe-matik (IPM) der Techn. Hochschule Darmstadt, 1957

[21] Brooker, R. A.: Some technical features of the Manchester Mercury Autocode Programme. Symposium Mechanisation of Thought Processes, National Physical Lab., Teddington, November 24-27, 1958, p. 2o1-229

[22] Brooker, R. A., Morris, D.: An assembly program for a phrase structure language. Computer J. 3, 168-174 (1960)

[23] Brooker, R. A., Morris, D.: Some proposals for the realization of a certain assembly program. Computer J. 3, 22o-231 (1961)

[24] Brooker, R. A., Morris, D.: A description of Mercury Autocode in terms of a phrase structure language. In: Goodman, R. (ed.): Second Annual Review of Automatic Programming. New York: Pergamon 1961

[25] Brooker, R. A., Morris, D.: A general translation program for phrase-struc-ture languages. J. ACM 9, 1-1o (1962)

[26] Brooker, R. A. Morris, D.: A compiler for a self-defining phrase structure language. University of Manchester, England (undated)

[27] Brown, J. H. Carr III, J. W.: Automatic programming and its development on the MIDAC. Symposium Automatic Programming Digital Computers, Office of Na-val Research, PB 111 6o7. May 13-14, 1954, p. 84-97

[28] Burks, A. W., Warren, D. W., Wright, J. B.: An analysis of a logical machine using paranthesis-free notation. Math. Tables and Other Aids to Computation (MTAC) 8:46, 53-57 (1954)

[29] Burroughs B5000. In: Data Processing Encyclopedia. Detroit 1961, p. 5o-55

[30] Cheatham, T. E.: The TGS-II translator-generator system. Proc. IFIP Congr. 65, New York. Washington (D.C.): Spartan 1965

[31] Cheatham, T. E., Sattley, K.: Syntax-directed compiling. Proc. AFIPS 1964 SJCC 25. Washington (D.C.): Spartan 1964, p. 31-57

[32] Chomsky, N.: Syntactic structures. Den Haag: Mouton 1957

[33] Chomsky, N.: On certain formal properties of grammars. Information and Con-trol 2, 137-167 (1959). Addendum: A note on phrase structure grammars. In-formation and Control 2, 393-395 (1959)

[34] Chomsky, N.: Formal properties of grammars. In: Luce, R. D., Bush, R., Ga-lanter, E. (eds.): Handbook of Mathematical Psychology, Vol. 2. New York: John Wiley and Sons 1963, p. 323-418

[35] Chomsky, N., Schützenberger, M. P.: The algebraic theory of context-free languages. In: Braffort, P., Hirschberg, D. (eds.): Computer Programming and Formal Systems. Amsterdam: North-Holland 1963, p. 118-161

[36] Church, A.: The calculi of lambda-conversion. In: Annals of Mathematics Studies No. 6. Princeton (N.J.): Princeton University Press 1941

[37] Conway, M. E.: Design of a seperable transition-diagram compiler. Comm. ACM 6, 396-4o8 (1963)

[38] Dijkstra, E. W.: Making a translator for ALGOL 60. Annual Review in Automatic Programming 3, 347-356 (1963)

[39] Eickel, J.: Generation of parsing algorithms for Chomsky 2 - type languages. Mathematisches Institut der Technischen Universität München, Bericht Nr. 6401, 1964

[40] Eickel, J., Paul, M., Bauer, F. L., Samelson, K.: A syntax-controlled generator of formal language processors. Comm. ACM 6, 451-455 (1963)

[41] Ershov, A. P.: On programming of arithmetic operations (Russ.). Doklady AN SSSR 118:3, 427-43o (1958). (Engl. Transl. in: Comm. ACM 1:8, 3-6 (1958))

[42] Ershov, A. P.: The work of the computing centre of the Academy of Sciences of the USSR in the field of automatic programming. Symposium Mechanisation of Thought Processes. National Physical Lab., Teddington, November 24-27, 1958, p. 257-278

[43] Ershov, A. P.: Programming Programme for the BESM Computer (Russ.). Moskau: Verlag der Akademie der Wissenschaften der UdSSR 1958 und London: Pergamon Press 1960

[44] Fischer, P.. C.: A proposal for a term project for applied mathematics 205. Manuscript, 1959

[45] Flow-Matic Programming System. Remington-Rand Univac Div. of Sperry Rand Corp. New York 1958

[46] Floyd, R. W.: An algorithm defining ALGOL statement analysis with validity checking. Comm. ACM 3, 418-419 (1960)

[47] Floyd, R. W.: An algorithm for coding efficient arithmetic operations. Comm. ACM 4, 42-51 (1961)

[48] Floyd, R. W.: Syntactic analysis and operator precedence. J. ACM 1o, 316-333 (1963)

[49] Floyd, R. W.:Bounded context syntactic analysis. Comm. ACM 7, 62-67 (1964)

[50] Floyd, R. W.: Syntactic analysis and operator precedence. In: Pollack, B.W. (ed.): Compiler Techniques. Princeton (N.J.): Auerbach Publishers 1972

[51] Floyd, R. W.: The syntax of programming languages - a survey. In: Pollack, B. W. (ed.): Compiler Techniques. Princeton (N.J.): Auerbach Publishers 1972

[52] Foster, J. M.: A syntax improving device. Computer J. 11, 31-34 (1968)

[53] GAMM Fachausschuß Programmieren (Hrsg.): Vorschläge für eine algorithmische Schreibweise zur Formelübersetzung. Zürich, Mainz, München, Darmstadt, Oktober 1957

[54] Glennie, A.: On the syntax machine and the construction of a universal compiler. Carnegie-Mellon University, Techn. Report No. 2 (AD-24o512), July 1960

[55] Goldfinger, R.: New York University Compiler System. Symposium Automatic Programming Digital Computers, Office of Naval Research, PB 111 6o7. May 13-14, 1954, p. 3o-33

[56]   Gorn, S.: Planning universal semi-automatic coding. Symposium Automatic Programming Digital Computers, Office of Naval Research, PB 111 6o7. May 13-14, 1954, p. 74-83

[57]   Gorn, S.: On the logical design of formal mixed languages. Moore School of Electrical Engineering, University of Pennsylvania, Philadelphia, 1959

[58]   Graham, R. M.: Bounded context translation. Proc. AFIPS 1964 SJCC 25. Baltimore (Md.): Spartan 1964, p. 17-29

[59]   Grau, A. A.: Recursive processes and ALGOL translation. Comm. ACM 4, 1o-15 (1961)

[60]   Grau, A. A.: The structure of an ALGOL translator. Oak Ridge Nat. Lab., Oak Ridge (Tenn.), Report No. ORNL-3o54, February 9, 1961

[61]   Greibach, S. A.: Inverses of phrase structure generators. Harvard University, Cambridge (Mass.), Ph. D. dissertation, June 1963

[62]   Gries. D.: Compiler construction for digital computers. New York: John Wiley and Sons 1971

[62a]   Gries, D.: Use of transition matrices in compiling. Comm. ACM 11, 26-34 (1968)

[63]   Gries, D. et al.: Some techniques used in the ALCOR-Illinois 7090. Comm. ACM 8, 496-5oo (1965)

[64]   Haley, A. C. D.: The KDF 9 computer system. Proc. AFIPS 1962 FJCC 22. Washington (D.C.): Spartan 1962, p. 1o8-12o

[65]   Halstead, M. H.: Machine independent computer programming. Washington (D.C.): Spartan 1962, p. 37 ff

[66]   Hopper, G. M.: Automatic programming, definitions. Symposium Automatic Programming Digital Computers, Office of Naval Research, PB 111 6o7. May 13-14, 1954, p. 1-5

[67]   Hopper, G. M.: First glossary of programming terminology. Report to the Association for Computing Machinery (ACM), June 1954

[68]   Huskey, H. D.: Compiling techniques for algebraic expressions. Computer J. 4, 1o-19 (1961)

[69]   Huskey, H. D., Wattenburg, W. H.: A basic compiler for arithmetic expressions. Comm. ACM 4, 3-9 (1961)

[70]   Ingerman, P. Z.: A new algorithm for algebraic translation. Reprints of papers presented at the 14th National Meeting of the Association for Computing Machinery, 1959, p. 22·1-22·2

[71]   Ingerman, P. Z.: A syntax oriented compiler... . Moore School of Electr. Engineering. University of Pennsylvania, Philadelphia, April 1963

[72]   Irons, E. T.: A syntax directed compiler for ALGOL 60. Comm. ACM 4, 51-55 (1961)

[73]   Irons, E. T.: The structure and use of the syntax-directed compiler. In: Annual Review in Automatic Programming 3, 2o7-227 (1963)

[74]   Irons, E. T.: 'Structural connections' in formal languages. Comm. ACM 7, 67-
         72 (1964)

[75]   Janov, Y. J.: On the equivalence and transformation of program schemes (Russ.).
         Doklady AN SSSR 113:1, 39-42 (1957). Engl. transl. in: Comm. ACM 1:1o, 8-12
         (1958)

[76]   Janov, Y. J.: On matrix program schemes (Russ.). Doklady AN SSSR 113:2, 283-
         286 (1957). Engl. transl. in: Comm. ACM 1:12, 3-6 (1958)

[77]   Kanner, J.: An algebraic translator. Comm. ACM 2:1o, 19-22 (1959)

[78]   Kantorovich, L. V.: On a mathematical symbolism convenient for performing
         machine calculations (Russ.). Doklady AN SSSR 113:4, 738-741 (1957)

[79]   Kleene, S. C.: Proof by cases in formal logic. Annals of Mathematics 35,
         529-544 (1934)

[80]   Knuth, D. E.: Runcible: Algebraic translation on a limited computer. Comm.
         ACM 2, 18-21 (1959)

[81]   Knuth, D. E.: A history of writing compilers. Computers and Automation 11,
         8-14 (1962)

[82]   Kolloquium über Sprachen und Algorithmen. Berlin, 8. - 11. Juni 1960. Math.
         Logik 7, 299-3o8, 1961

[83]   Kuno, S., Oettinger, A. G.: Multiple-path syntactic analyzer. Proc. IFIP
         Congr. 62, Munich. Amsterdam: North-Holland 1962, p. 3o6-312

[84]   Laning, J. H., Zierler, N.: A program for translation of mathematical
         equations for Whirlwind I. Massachusetts Institute of Technology, Cambridge
         (Mass.), Engineering Memorandum E-364, January 1954

[85]   Ledley, R. S., Wilson, J. B.: Autmatic-programming-language translation
         through syntactical analysis. Comm. ACM 5, 145-155 (1962)

[86]   Ljapunov, A. A.: On logical schemes of programming (Russ.) Problemi Kiber-
         netiki 1, 46-74 (1958). Deutsche Übers. in: Ljapunov, A. A. (Hrsg.): Pro-
         bleme der Kybernetik, Bd.1. Berlin: Akademie Verlag 1962, p. 53-86

[87]   Lucas, P.: The structure of formula-translators. Mailüfterl, Vianna, Austria.
         ALGOL Bulletin Suppl. No. 16, September 1961 und Elektronische Rechenanlagen
         3, 159-166 (1961)

[88]   Lukasiewicz, J.: O znaczeniu i potrzebach logiki matematycznej (On the impor-
         tance and needs of mathematical logic). Nauka Polska 1o, 6o4-62o (1929)

[89]   Lukasiewicz, J.: Elementy logiki matematycznej (Elements of mathematical
         logic). Lecture Notes, 2nd edition (1929) - Warszawa, 1958, PWN, p. 4o

[89a]   Lukasiewicz, J.: Elements of mathematical logic. Oxford: Pergamon Press 1963

[90]   Lukasiewicz, J., Tarski, A.: Untersuchungen über den Aussagenkalkül. C.R.Soc.
         Sci. Lett. Varsovie, Ch. III, 23, 31 (1930)

[91]   Menger, K.: Eine elementare Bemerkung über die Struktur logischer Formeln. In:
         Menger, K. (Hrsg.): Ergebnisse eines mathematischen Kolloquiums 3, (1932).
         Leipzig und Wien: Deutige 1935, p. 22-23

[92]   Namur, P.: Entwurf eines Hochgeschwindigkeits-Rechenautomaten mit Leucht-
         punktabtastung als Grundelement. Technische Hochschule Darmstadt, Disserta-
         tion, November 1964

[93]   Oettinger, A. G.: Automatic syntactic analysis and the push-down store. Proc. Symp. Appl. Math. 12, Providence (R.I.): Amer. Math. Soc. 1961, p. 1o4-129

[94]   Paul, M.: Zur Struktur formaler Sprachen. Universität Mainz, Dissertation D77, 1962

[95]   Paul, M.: A general processor for certain formal languages. Proc. Symp. Symbolic Languages in Data Processing, Rome, 1962. New York - London: Gordon and Breach 1962, p. 65-74

[96]   Paul, M.: ALGOL 60 processors and a processor generator. Proc. IFIP Congr. 62, Munich. Amsterdam: North-Holland 1962, p. 493-497

[97]   Perlis, A. J. et al.: Internal translator (IT), a compiler for the 650. Carnegie Institute of Technology, Computation Center, Pittsburgh 1956. Reproduced by Lincoln Lab. Div. 6, Document 6D-327

[98]   van der Poel, W. L.: Dead programmes for a magnetic drum automatic computer. Applied Scientific Research (B) 3, 19o-198 (1953)

[99]   Post, E. L.: Formal reduction of the general combinatorial decision problem. Amer. J. Math. 65, 197-215 (1943)

[100]   Reynolds, J. C.: A compiler and generalized translator. Applied Math. Div., Argonne Natl. Lab., Argonne, Ill. , 1962

[101]   Rice, H. G.: The APS III compiler for the Datatron 204. Westinghouse Research Lab., Pittsburgh, Manuscript, 1957

[102]   Rich, B.: APT common computer language. Manuscript, Appl. Phys. Lab. Johns Hopkins University, Baltimore (Md.) 1957 and Annual Review in Automatic Programming 2, 141-159 (1961)

[103]   Rosenbloom, P. C.: The elements of mathematical logic. New York: Dover 1950

[104]   Rutishauser, H.: Über automatische Rechenplananfertigung bei programmgesteuerten Rechenmaschinen. Z. angew. Math. Mech. 31, 255 (1951)

[105]   Rutishauser, H.: Automatische Rechenplananfertigung bei programmgesteuerten Rechenmaschinen. Inst. f. Angew. Mathematik ETH Zürich, Mitteil. Nr. 3. Basel: Verlag Birkhäuser 1952

[106]   Rutishauser, H.: Automatische Rechenplananfertigung bei programmgesteuerten Rechenmaschinen. Z. angew. Math. Mech. 32, 312-313 (1952)

[107]   Samelson, K.: Probleme der Programmierungstechnik. Aktuelle Probleme der Rechentechnik. Ber. Internat. Mathematiker-Kolloquium, Dresden November 22-27, 1955. Berlin: VEB Deutscher Verlag der Wissenschaften 1957, p. 61-68

[108]   Samelson, K.: Programming languages and their processors. Proc. IFIP Congr. 62, Munich. Amsterdam: North-Holland 1963, p. 487-492

[109]   Samelson, K., Bauer, F. L.: Sequentielle Formelübersetzung. Elektron. Rechenanlagen 1, 176-182 (1959)

[110]   Samelson, K., Bauer, F. L.: Sequential formula translation. Comm. ACM 3, 76-83 (1960)

[111]   Samelson, K., Bauer, F. L.: The ALCOR project. Proc. Symp. Symbolic Languages in Data Processing, Rome, 1962. New York - London: Gordon and Breach 1962, p. 2o7-217

[112] Schorre, D. V.: A syntax oriented compiler writing language. Proc. 19th ACM Conf. 1964, Philadelphia, D1.3-1-D1.3-11

[113] Schröter, K.: Axiomatisierung der Frege'schen Aussagenkalküle. Forschungen zur Logik und zur Gundlegung der exakten Wissenschaften. Neue Serie Bd. 8, Leipzig 1943

[114] Schützenberger, M. P.: On context-free languages and pushdown automata. Information and Control 6, 246-264 (1963)

[115] Share Assembly Program (SAP). In: Grappe, E. M. et al. (eds.): Handbook of Automation, Computation and Control Vol. 2. New York: John Wiley and Sons 1959, p. 2·165-2·167

[116] Sheridan, P. B.: The arithmetic translator-compiler of the IBM FORTRAN automatic coding system. Comm. ACM 2:3, 9-21 (1959)

[117] Slutz, R. J.: Engineering experience with the SEAC. Proc.AFIPS 1951 EJCC 1. New York: Amer. Inst. Electr. Engineers 1951, p. 9o-93

[118] UNIVAC Generalized Programming. Remington Rand Univac Div. of Sperry Rand Corp., New York 1957

[119] UNIVAC Math-Matic Programming System. Remington Rand Univac Div. of Sperry Rand Corp., New York 1958

[120] Waldburger, H.: Gebrauchsanweisung für die ERMETH. Institut für Angew. Math. an der ETH Zürich, 1958

[121] Warshall, S.: A syntax-directed generator. Proc. AFIPS 1961 EJCC 2o. Baltimore (Md.): Spartan 1961, p. 295-3o5

[122] Warshall, S., Shapiro, R. M.: A general table-driven compiler. Proc. AFIPS 1964 SJCC 25. Washington (D.C.): Spartan 1964, p. 59-65

[123] Watt, J. B., Wattenburg, W. H.: A NELIAC-generated 7090-1401 compiler. Comm. ACM 5, 1o1-1o2 (1962)

[124] Wegstein, J. H.: From formulas to computer oriented language. Comm.ACM 2:3, 6-8 (1959)

[125] Wells, R.: Immediate constituents. Language 23, 81-117 (1947)

[126] Wilkes, M. V.: The use of a floating address system for orders in an automatic digital computer. Proc. Cambridge Philos. Soc. 49, 84-89 (1953)

[127] Wilkes, M. V. et al.: The preparation of programs for an electronic digital computer. Cambridge (Mass.): Addison-Wesley 1951 (1957)

[128] Wirth, N., Weber, H.: EULER: A generalization of ALGOL and its formal definition, Part I. Comm. ACM 9, 13-25 (1966)

[129] Zuse, K.: Über den allgemeinen Plankalkül als Mittel zur Formalisierung schematisch-kombinatorischer Aufgaben. Archiv der Math. 1:6, 441-449 (1948/49)

[130] Zuse, K.: Über den Plankalkül. Elektron. Rechenanlagen 1:2, 68-71 (1959)

A. P. Ershov

Computing Center, Sibirian Branch of the
Academy of Sciences of the USSR, Novosibirsk

Professor A. A. Lyapunov was the first in the USSR who treated programming as a scientific discipline, analysed it as a whole and identified a series of its fundamental concepts. He considered program execution as a discrete sequence of elementary actions performed by operators (we say now statements) extracted by some control process from the program text. Lyapunov introduced some classification of statements and this classification became an important component of the theory. He considered arithmetical operators (assignment statements) which act on data, logical operators (including logical relation evaluation as well as transfers of control), and modification operators which act on other operators of the program. Operator modification was based on an idea of dependence of an operator on some parameter (usually an integer variable). Modification consisted of forming operators (initialization), readdressing operators (a modification according to a regular advancing of the parameter) and restoring an initial form of an operator.

A program text was considered to be formed by two parts: the program scheme which is a string of symbolic names of operators showing the transfers of control and classification of the operators, and operator specifications showing their concrete contents. This partition of a program reflected also two stages of programming: firstly, general planning of an algorithm which resulted in the program scheme including an informal specification of operators (a creative stage) and then a systematic implementation of separate operators from the specification by means of a machine language (a routine stage). A possibility of systematic transformations of a program, aiming at its improvement, was also stressed. This methodology, which was later called "operator method of programming", was first presented by Lyapunov in his course on programming read in Moscow university in 1952/53 and published in [1].

Thinking in terms of the operator method of programming led Lyapunov in 1953 to the formulation of two problems: the problem of formal transformations of program schemata in some abstract formalism and the problem of automatic programming as an algorithmization of implementation of different kinds of operators and memory allocation for all the program. These problems were easily assimilated, mainly by young students who graduated from Moscow University in 1953 and 1954 and composed a first generation of specialists, identifying themselves as professional programmers from the first day of their career. The first problem resulted in classical papers by Yu. I. Yanov [2], and the second one led to a series of "preALGOL" compilers and assemblers implemented in the period of 1955 - 1959.

E. Z. Lubimsky and S. S. Kamynin were those who initiated in the USSR the idea of an integrated compiler in 1954 [3]. A full description of the PP-2 Compiler developed by a team led by Professor M. R. Shura-Bura was published in 1958 [4]. The source language of the PP-2 Compiler preserved the partition of a program text into a scheme and a statement specification, as introduced by Lyapunov. Assignments contained arithmetical operations and some built-in mathematical functions. Expression flattening ignored operation priorities and was performed by a "reduction" method, i.e. replacement in the source string of a programmed term by the symbol of the resulting working cell (repetitive occurences of the term in the expression were identified and substituted, too). Conditions in logical statements were arbitrary Boolean functions of binary variables. The PP-2 Compiler was implemented for the STRELA computer in 1955 and became a prototype for a series of subsequent implementations of compilers for this computer [5].

A parallel project of a compiler for the BESM computer (PP-BESM) was implemented by a team led by A. P. Eršhov in 1955/56. In this compiler a compilation scheme for arithmetical expressions using a construction similar to a stack was implemented (together with L. N. Korolev). It used also operation priorities. A formula was being rewritten into the stack until a programmable term was found there. After its coding (in the form of a three-address instruction) the latter was added to the generated program (with the economization of identical instructions in the reach of a linear component) and the term in the stack was substituted by the symbol of the result. Conditional statements in the source language slightly resembled contemporary case-statements. The most important innovation in PP-BESM were for-statements and subscripted variables. Besides, the program text was not partitioned just being a usual sequential string of statements [6].

Many basic compilation techniques were invented and implemented in these compilers. Starkman developed a method of optimal register allocation when a sequence of operations in an expression is given [7]. Luckovitskaya developed a method of Boolean function implementation as a series of binary checks and jumps [8]. Shura-Bura showed the effectiveness of the use of Boolean vectors as a universal mean of representing subsets of some general enumerated set [9]. Ershov implemented a universal scheme for implementation of nested loops [10], invented hashing functions with application to the elimination of identical expressions and proposed an algorithm of optimal expression flattening which minimizes the number of registers [11]. Shura-Bura developed an effective scheme of procedure calls from a run-time library where for the first time certain methods of dynamic residency of subroutine modules in the working space were implemented [12].

V.S. Korolyuk and Ye.L. Yushchenko in Kiev systematically treated indirect addressing in programming [12'].

Professor L. V. Kantorovich formulated a series of fundamental ideas in programming. He stressed the importance of information flow in the representation of a program, in particular, representation of expressions as trees [13]. He also introduced a concept of structured data as program objects. Corresponding composition rules were called "geometric operations" [14]. Kantorovich considered the execution of a program complex (represented in a form of network of separate modules) as a functioning of some superprogram ("prorab") which determines the sequencing of modules by an analysis of their information and control relations [15]. He introduced the term "modular programming" [16]. Kantorovich's ideas resulted in a series of specialized programming systems implemented by his young Leningrad colleagues [17].

In 1958 first direct contacts between Soviet and Western programmers were established. In August, Alan Perlis visited the USSR with an American delegation and brought, in particular, the draft version of ALGOL 58. In December, at a Symposium at NPL (Teddington) Andrei Ershov met Grace Hopper and John Backus, and presented a talk on the first Soviet compilers [18]. In 1959 main Soviet papers [19] were published in English, and in the USSR a collection of translated papers under the title "Automatic Programming" had appeared. From that time compiler writing in the USSR becomes a real part of the general development line.

Among the papers mentioned, perhaps only Yanov's papers specifically influenced the general development of programming theory in the West. Most of the other papers are just independent reinventions of many basic compilation techniques. But there exists at least one other, less direct but deep influence of this work on the contemporary shape of programming. Soviet programmers are, seemingly, the largest professional community performing major part of production programming in ALGOL and its direct successors.

The lack of an adequate attention to the syntax problems and textual representation of programs in programming languages prevented at the time elaboration of a competing idea of an algorithmic language in the USSR. Nevertheless, a general philosophy of the "Operator method of programming" and accumulated experience on compiler construction brought "proper frequencies" of Soviet programmers into resonance with those of ALGOL authors.

References

Konf-56: Konferenciya "Puti razvitiya sovetskogo matematicheskogo mashinostroeniya i priborostroeniya". Sekciya universalnych cifrovych mashin. Chast' III. Moskva, 12-17 marta, 1956.

Pk/1:   Problemy kibernetiki. Pod redakciej A.A. Lyapunova. Vypusk I. Gosudavstvennoe izdatel'stvo fiziko-matematicheskoj literatury. Moskva, 1958.

GIFML: Gosudarstvennoe izdatel'stvo fiziko-matematicheskoj literatury.

[1.1]   A.A.Ljyapunov, Yu. I. Yanov. "O logecheskih s'hemah programm". Konf-56, 5-8.

[1.2]   A.A. Lyapunov. "O logicheskih s'hemah programm". Pk/1, 46-74.

 [2]   Yu. I. Yanov. "O ravnosil'nosti i preobrazovanijah s'hem programm". DAN SSSR, 113, No. 1 (1957).
          Yu. I. Yanov. "O matrichnyh s'hemah". DAN SSSR, 113, No. 2 (1957)
          Yu. I. Yanov. "O logicheskih s'hemah algoritmov". Pk/1, 75-127.

 [3]   S.S. Kamynin, E.Z. Lyubimskij. ; Avtomatizaciya programmirovaniya". Konf-56, 9-17.

 [4]   S.S. Kamynin, E.Z. Lyubimskij, M.R. Shura-Bura. "Ob avtomatizacii programmirovaniya s pomoshch'yu programmiruyushchej programmy". Pk/1, 135-171.

 [5]   "Sistema avtomatizacii programmirovaniya". Pod redakciej N.P. Trifonova i M.P. Shura-Bury. GIFML, Moskva 1961.

 [6]   A.P. Ershov. "Programmiruyushchaya programma dlya bystrodejstvuyushchej elektronnoj s'chetnoj mashiny". Izdatel'stvo AN SSSR, Moskva, 1958, 116 straniz.

 [7]   V.S. Shtarkman. "Blok ekonomii rabochih yacheek v PP-2". Pk/1, 185-189.

 [8]   E.S. Lyuhovickaya. "Blok obrabotki logicheskih uslovij v PP-2". Pk/1, 172-177.

 [9]   A.A. Lyapunov described his method in § 6 of [1.2].

[10]   Chapter III in the second part and chapter III in the third part of [6].

[11]   A.P.Ershov. "O programmirovanii arifmeticheskih operatorov". DAN SSSR, 118, No. 3 (1958), 427-43o.

[12] M.R. Shura-Bura. "Sistema interpretacii IS-2". V sbornike "Biblioteka stan-
dartnyh podprogramm" pod obshchej redakciej M.P. Shura-Bury. Zavod s'chetno-
analiticheskih mashin. Central'noe byuro tehnicheskoj informacii. Moskva 1961,
5-21.

[12'] E.L. Yushchenko. "Adresnoe programmirovanie". Gostehizdat USSR, Kiev, 1963.

[13]
[14] L.V. Kantorovich, L.T. Petrova, M.A. Yakovleva. "Ob odnoj sisteme programmi-
[15] rovaniya". Konf-56, 3o-36.
[16]

[17] Trudy Matematicheskogo instituta imeni V.A. Steklova LXVI. "Raboty po
avtomaticheskoj programmirovaniyu, chislennym metodam i funkcional'nomu ana-
lizu". Izdatel'stvo AN SSSR, Moskva-Leningrad, 1962.

[18] Symposium on Mechanisation of thought processes". National Physical Laboratory,
Teddington, December 1958.

[19.1] A.P. Ershov. "On programming of arithmetic operations". CACM, August 1958.

[19.2] A.P. Ershov. "Automatic programming in the Soviet Union". Datamation, July/
August, 1959.

[19.3] A.P. Ershov. "Programming programme for the BESM computer". Pergamon Press,
London-Oxford-New York-Paris, 1959.

[19.4] Systems theory research. A translation of "Problemy Kibernetiki. Edited by
A.A. Lyapunov, Vol. 1.

ERROR RECOVERY AND CORRECTION - An Introduction to the Literature

David Gries

Technical University Munich
and
Cornell University, Ithaca, N.Y.

1.   INTRODUCTION

Horning [74, 532-546] contains a good overview of error recovery and correction and it would be senseless to rewrite everything he says in my style. I will therefore limit my remarks to topics not covered by him, and give more details where I think it's necessary. At the end is an annotated list of references, with an index into it to help you find references for a particular kind of parser, etc.

2.   RECOVERY AND/OR CORRECTION

1. When compiling, errors are detected in three places:
    a) during lexical analysis
    b) during syntax analysis
    c) during semantic analysis

There are three possible responses to detected errors. First, we can stop compilation immediately.

Secondly, we can attempt to "recover" from the error, so that the compiler can continue analysis in order to find and report as many errors as possible. The program will _not_ be compiled and executed; the only purpose of error recovery is to find as many source program errors as possible.

Thirdly, we can attempt to "correct" the error, continue compiling,and execute the program. The term "correct" is misleading. What we are really doing is "repairing" the error in some fashion. We transform an illegal program into a legal one, hopefully correcting the users error the way he would. But more often than not we change it to something he _didn't_ intend. Nevertheless, the term "error correction" is in use, and we take it to mean "error correction and/or repair".

Lexical error correction or recovery usually consists of fixing spelling errors or deleting characters which do not occur in the language. This is covered in some detail in Horning [74] and we won't discuss it further.

Semantic error processing is rarely discussed, probably because it hasn't been formalized. It is discussed a bit in Gries [71, 317-320].

We will concentrate here on syntactic error recovery, since that has been the topic of many papers and theses.

3. *MINIMUM DISTANCE ERRORS — THEORETICAL RESULTS*

If we are to formalize error correction and study it, we have to know what an error is. Typically, errors are defined in terms of the minimum number of changes needed to map an incorrect string into a correct one.

Consider three kinds of changes: (1) replace one symbol by another; (2) insert a symbol; and (3) delete a symbol. Given a string x supposedly belonging to a language L, the number of errors in x is the minimum number of changes needed to map x into the language. This has been called the <u>Hamming distance</u> from x to L; or the <u>minimum distance error</u>. The errors in x are then those symbols to be replaced, deleted, or inserted.

It is not clear that this definition of error is the best — whether it leads to error correction which makes sense. It works in many cases and it doesn't work in many cases.

Perhaps a better definition might concern the number of changes in a tree. When an error is detected, a partial syntax tree has already been formed. We might consider the minimum number of changes in this partial syntax tree (and in the prefix parsed so far) to yield a partial tree (and prefix) for which no error is detected. This idea has not been worked on at all.

Finding the minimum distance error corrections is unpractical. Even for regular languages in a left to right parser the distance between the error detection point and error correction point can be unbounded (see e.g. Levy [71,35-36]). Lyon [72] produced an error corrector based on Youngers [67] algorithm which corrected in time $n^3 \log n$ (where n is the length of the string being parsed). Both Peterson [72] and Lyon [74] give correctors based on Earley's [70] parser which uses n^2 storage and n^3 time. But practical error recovery or correction must work in time n or close to it, since programs do get large.

4. *PARSER DEFINED ERRORS*

Most parsers do not do minimum distance error correcting. They do what Peterson [72] calls correcting of <u>parser defined</u> errors. Let w = xbv be a word not in a language L(G). Suppose x is a prefix of L but xb is not. Then b is a <u>parser defined error</u>. It is the first symbol encountered in a left to right scan of w which would cause any parser to report an error.

A language is UL(k) if the location of a parser defined error is at most k symbols from a minimum distance error. It would be nice to work only with a UL(k) language (for some fixed k), for then we could do minimum distance error recovery quite easily; the distance from the error detection point to error correction point would no longer be unbounded. Peterson [72] shows that the problem of determining whether a language is UL(k) for some k is unsolvable.

Thus, minimum distance error correcting is unpractical, and will quite likely remain so.

Simple precedence parsers do not always detect the so-called parser defined errors. At a typical step in the parser, we have

$$\vdash S_1\ S_2\ \cdots\ S_{k-1} <\cdot S_k \doteq S_{k+1} \doteq \cdots \doteq S_\ell \qquad T_1\ T_2\ \cdots\ T \dashv$$

$$\underbrace{\hspace{4cm}}_{\text{stack}} \qquad \underbrace{\hspace{3cm}}_{\text{input to be processed}}$$

The error determined here may fit one of several cases:

1) no relation between S_ℓ and T_1;

2) $S_\ell \cdot> T_1$ but there is no rule $U := S_k \cdots S_\ell$; such that S_{k-1} has a relation with U and U has a relation with T_1;

3) $S_\ell \doteq T_1$ but $S_k \cdots S_\ell T_1$ is not the head of a right part. LR(1), SLR(1), LL(1), etc., parsers usually detect the parser defined errors.

5. *GENERAL IDEA BEHIND ERROR RECOVERY*

When an error occurs, suppose the stack contains

$$\vdash S_1\ S_2\ \cdots\ S_\ell \qquad \text{and incoming symbols are } T_1\ \cdots\ T_m \dashv$$

The usual ways of correcting are

1) insert a terminal between S_ℓ and T_1,
2) replace T_1 by another terminal,
3) delete T_1,
4) change states $S_\ell,\ S_{\ell-1},\ \cdots,$
5) delete a few states $S_\ell,\ S_{\ell-1},\ \cdots,$
6) or a mixture of 1 through 5.

The principal purpose is to create a correct stack - incoming symbol configuration. There are several ways of doing this:

1. <u>Panic mode</u> delete incoming symbols T_1, T_2, ..., until an "important" one is found, e.g. semicolon. Delete states S_ℓ, S_{-1} until a correct configuration is found. This is simply bad.

2. Ad hoc "intuitive" technique. Add "error productions" to the grammar, use other lists generated by the compiler writer, to aid in recovering.

3. Base the recovery solely on the grammar, the parser, the stack $\vdash S_1 ... S_\ell$ and the incoming symbols $T_1 ... T_m \dashv$.

The latter technique is becoming better and more refined. The talk will discuss some of the methods.

6. ANNOTATED REFERENCES

We precede the references by a topical index into the references; this should help you find material you need quickly.

1. Surveys: Elspas, Green and Levitt [71], Gries [75] and Horning [74].

2. Theoretical results on errors, correction: Eggers [72], Hopcroft & Ullman [66], Levy [71], Lyon [72], Lyon [74], Peterson [72], Souza and Schultz [69].

3. Recovery in top-down parsers: Gries [71,322-325], Holt [74], Irons [63].

4. Recovery in precedence parsers: Graham and Rhodes [73], Gries [71], Johns [74], Leinius [70], McKeeman [70], Rhodes [73], and Wirth [68].

5. Recovery in transition matrix parsers: Conway and Wilcox [71], Freeman [63], Gries [68], and Gries [71].

6. Recovery in LR (etc.) parsers: Aho and Johnson [74], James [72], Leinius [70], Levy [71], McGruther [72], and Peterson [72].

7. Recovery when using Feldman's production language: LaFrance [70], LaFrance [71].

8. Recovery when using recursively defined finite automata: Eggers [72], Levy [71].

9. Adaptive correction: James and Partridge [73].

10. Discussions of compilers with error recovery or correction: Conway and Wilcox [71], Conway and Maxwell [63], Freeman [63], Moulton and Muller [67].

11. Spelling error correction: Damerau [64], Freeman [63] and Morgan [70].

* Aho, A.V. and S.C. Johnson. LR Parsing. <u>Computing Surveys 6</u> (June 74), 99-124.

Discusses using extra error productions, along with Leinius' error isolation ideas. The current error symbol is replaced by <u>error</u>. Elements of the stack are then discarded until a state is reached with a parsing action for <u>error</u>. <u>Error</u> is then read and reduced. Finally input is discarded until everything is all right.

* Conway, R.W. and T. Wilcox. Design and Implementation of a Diagnostic Compiler for PL/I. TR 71-107, Sept. 1971, Computer Science Dept., Cornell University.

Describes the overall structure of the PL/C compiler, Cornell's very successful implementation of a subset of PL/I. As its predecessor CORC, the compiler tries to correct and run every program. Syntax analysis is done by the transition matrix technique (see Gries[7]) developed by hand. Syntax correction is also done in an intuitive, heuristic fashion. Error correction methods are not described in detail or formalized.

* Conway, R.W. and W.L. Maxwell. Corc, the Cornell computing language. <u>CACM 6</u> (June 63), 317-321.

Describes in general terms the simple language CORC and the fact that error <u>cor</u>rection is performed. This was perhaps the first compiler which actually tried to correct programs; the authors mention that because of the correction facilities the average number of runs to check out student programs was slightly more than two. No attempt is made to explain the parsing method or the correction method.

* Damerau, F. A technique for computer detection and correction of spelling errors. <u>CACM 7</u> (March 1964), 171-176.

An early paper, not oriented towards compilers, but just to the problem of spelling errors. This work is used as a basis for Morgan's [70] work on spelling correction in compilers. Read Morgan first.

* Earley, J. An efficient context free parsing algorithm. <u>CACM 13</u> (Feb. 1970), 94-102.

An n^3 execution time, n^2 space parser for any context free grammar. n^2 time if grammar is unambiguous.

* Eggers, B. Error reporting, error treatment and error correction in ALGOL translation, part II., <u>2nd Annual Meeting G.I. Karlsruhe,</u> (Oct. 1972).

* Eggers' thesis examines techniques for finding errors in regular expressions, using both a left-right and right -left scan. This is then incorporated into a parser for systems of recursive finite state automata.

* Elspas, B., M.W.Green and K.N. Levitt. Software reliability, Computer 1 (1971), 21-27.

A survey of error recovery methods up to 1971.

* Freeman, D.N. Error correction in CORC: the Cornell computing language. Thesis, Cornell University, September 1963, and Proc. AFIPS FJCC 26, Spartan, NY, 15-34.

This thesis goes into detail on syntactic analysis and correction of a relative-ly simple language CORC (see Conway and Maxwell [1963]). No attempt is made to formalize and generalize either analysis or correction to other languages; only the ad hoc techniques used in CORC are explained.

* Graham, S.L. and S.P. Rhodes. Practical syntactic error recovery in compilers. ACM Symposium principles of prog. languages, Oct. 1-3, 1973, 52-58.

Based on Rhodes 1973 thesis at Berkeley. Uses simple precedence. Upon error de-tection a "condensation" is performed. Possible reductions in the stack are per-formed, then possible parsing to the right of the error point is performed until another error occurs. Thus we are left with a stack

$$\vdash x_1 \ \cdots, \ x_k <\cdot \ y_1 \ \doteq. \ y_2 \ \doteq. \ \cdots \ \doteq. \ y_n \dashv$$

and input $a_1 a_2 \ \cdots \ a_p b_1 \ \cdots$ where a_1 and a_p are the two error points. The sub-strings $y_1 \ \cdots \ y_n$, $y_1 \ \cdots \ y_n a_1 \ \cdots a_p$ and $a_1 \ \cdots \ a_p$ are then compared to the right parts of rules and the best match is chosen as the correction. "Costs" can be assigned to each right part to influence the matching. Seems to work well. The idea of parsing ahead $(a_1 \ \cdots \ a_p)$ before correcting leads to using more in-formation, which is good.

* Gries, D. The use of transition matrices in compiling. CACM 11 (Jan. 1968),26-34.

* Gries, D. Compiler Construction for Digital Computers. Wiley, 1971.

Irons [63] top-down error recovery is discussed on 322-325. A correction mechanism for use with transition matrices is discussed on 325-326. It consists mainly of determining correction at construction time (not when the error is detected, but before compilation), based on the head of the right part at the top of the stack and the incoming symbol. For example, if x is the head of a right part on the stack and T is the incoming symbol, and if there is a rule V::= xzT, a possible

correction is to insert before T a terminal string for z.
Contains a general discussion of recovery on correction of semantic errors.

* Gries, D. Error recovery and correction.

  This manuscript.

* Hext, J.B. Recovery from error. <u>Computers and Automation 16</u> (1967), 29-31.

* Holt, R.C. (unpublished, but discussed in Horning [74, 537-538].

  This discusses correction in a top-down parser (LL(1)). If a wrong input symbol occurs and a terminal symbol is required by the grammar, that symbol is inserted, if a nonterminal is required, one of its alternatives (chosen beforehand by the compiler writer) is inserted. The process continues until repair has been completed and normal parsing can be continued. Horning says it works surprisingly well for a simple strategy.

* Hopcroft, J.E. and J.D. Ullman. Error correction for formal languages. TR 52, Dept. of E.E., Princeton University, Nov. 1966.

  Proves that e-tuple errors, burst errors and types of errors corrected by recurrent codes preserve regular, context free and context sensitive languages. Uses the usual idea of the "Hamming distance" from one string to another. Largely theoretical, it gives no parsing, correction, or recovery algorithms.

* Horning, J.J. What the Compiler should tell the user, in Compiler Construction, Lecture Notes in Computer Science 21, Springer-Verlag, 1974, 526-548.

  Contains general survey of error correction and recovery takes, with pointers to the literature.

* Irons, E.T. An error-correcting parse algorithm. <u>CACM 6</u> (Nov. 63), 669-673.

  This is the first work to appear on automatic error correction/recovery. It is best described in Gries [71]. Based on top-down parsing, it uses the partial tree built so far and the incoming sequence of symbols to determine the correction. The prefix x for which the partial tree has been built is <u>not</u> changed.

* James, E.G. and D.P. Partridge. Adaptive correction of program statements. <u>CACM 16</u> (Jan. 1973), 27-37.

  A technique completely different from others. It uses a syntax tree structure to represent possible input sentences and employs basically a top-down parse. With each node of the tree, may be numbers representing the relative frequency of

involvement in the matching process and various "confidence measures" in determining particular strategies. Some of these numbers change whenever the node is
used in matching, and periodically the tree can be restructured using this information to maintain or improve efficiency and to improve correction of frequent
errors.

* Jones, L.R. A syntax directed error recovery method. CSRG-13, University of
Toronto, 1972.

Describes an error recovery scheme implemented in an LALR parser at Toronto. The
scheme is based on Leinius' work.

* Johns, C.B. The Generation of Error Recovering Simple Precedence Parsers. TR74/
10, 1974, Dept. of Applied Math., McMaster University.

Outlines Leinius' [70] and Rhodes' [73] error recovery for simple precedence parsers
and implements Rhodes' error recovery.

* LaFrance, J.E. Optimization of error-recovery in syntax directed parsing algorithms. SIGPLAN Notices 5 (Dec. 1970), 2-17.

* LaFrance, J.E. Syntax directed error recovery for compilers. TR 459, June 1971,
Computer Science Dept., University of Illinois.

Among other things, contains ad hoc error recovery techniques for Feldman's production language, mainly by adding "error productions" to the production language
program.
Develops a measure of effectiveness of error recovery for a program based on the
number of errors detected, missed and inserted by the recovery procedure, and on
a subjective analysis of each recovery.

* Leinius, R.P. Error detection and recovery for syntax-directed compiler systems.
Thesis, 1970. Dept. of Computer Science, University of Wisconsin.

Peterson [72] states that his error recovery algorithm is equivalent to one given
by Leinius for LR(1) parsers, but that his (Peterson's) needs only the LR(1)
tables to implement it, while Leinius needs the grammar itself. Leinius' thesis
also talks about error recovery in simple precedence parsers.

* Levy, J.P. Automatic Correction of Syntax Errors in Programming Languages.
Thesis.TR 71-116, Computer Science Dept., Cornell University, 1971.

Given fixed k, he shows how to do minimum distance error correction for strings
with up to k errors. Extends this to fixing k local errors in any number of places
in a string. His work is based on making a "backward move" through the string at

the error detection point, then a "forward move" through the string generating all possible corrections,(up to k). While working mainly with languages defined by recursively defined finite automata, he also discusses using SLR(1).

He discusses restrictions to make it practical (for example, finding or defining "beacons" or fiducials), brackets, restricting how deep in the stack the backward move is allowed to look, etc. Not really practical yet.

*   Lyon, G. Least error recognition of mutated context free sentences in time $n^3 \log n$. Sixth Princeton Conference on Inf. Sci. and Systems (1972), 115-118.

Uses Younger's [31] parsing algorithm to achieve the time bound, but only uses replacement of symbols, not deletions or insertions. Younger's algorithm is matrix-oriented and uses much space.

*   Lyon, G. Syntax directed least error analysis for context free languages - a practical approach. CACM 17 (Jan. 1974), 3-14.

This is not really practical; Lyon gives an algorithm for error correction, using Earley's [70] parser, using space n^2 and time n^3. The best theoretical result to date. He also discusses ad hoc constraints to make it practical, including fiducials.
Another kind of constraint is to limit the number of errors allowed in any right hand side. He says that a least error global correction is often worse in reconstructing an original sentence than a constrained, local correction technique.

*   McGruther, T. An approach to automating syntax error detection, recovery and correction for LR(k) grammars. Masters thesis, Naval postgraduate School, Monterey, Calif., 1972.

*   McKeeman, W.M., J.J. Horning and D.B. Wortman. A Compiler Generator, Prentice-Hall, 1970.

The XPL compiler uses "panic node". Upon error detection, scan forward for an important symbol (defined by implementor END, etc.), then discard stack symbols until a legal configuration is found.

*   Morgan, H.L. Spelling correction in system programs. CACM 13 (Feb. 70), 90-94.

Based on earlier work by Damerau [69] and Freeman [63]. Basic idea is to find the closest word making use of the number of letters which match after 1 or 2 transpositions and/or substitutions. Discusses reducing the number of words to match against by using context. For example, when parsing the condition of a conditional statement, misspelled words may be relational operators, but not keywords such as BEGIN, FOR, etc.

* Moulton, P.G. and M.G. Muller, DITRAN - A compiler emphasizing diagnostics.
<u>CACM 10</u> (Jan. 67), 45-52.

Another compiler like CORC or PL/C, which tries to find all syntax errors, is
discussed. There is little discussion on the error recovery methods used.

* Peterson, T.G. Syntax Error Detection, Correction and Recovery in Parsers.
Thesis 1972. Stevens Inst. of Tech., N.J.

He defines the conventional minimum distance error and parser defined error. He
proves that the problem of determining whether a language is UL(k) (whether any
parser defined error is at most k symbols from a minimum distance error,essential-
ly), is unsolvable.
He gives an n^3 minimum distance recovery algorithm based on Earley's [70] parser,
using an "extended grammar" (in one case the grammar went from 4 to 18 productions); in this respect Lyon's [74] algorithm is better.
He gives an error recovery technique for LR(1) and SLR(1) parsers which maps
error configurations into a non-error configuration. This mapping is determined
by a table preconstructed from the original parser and possibly the whole stack
during parsing. His recovery is identical to Leinius [70] but the preconstructed
table can be determined from reduced or compressed parser tables.
He describes a parser-defined-error-corrector for LR(1) and SLR(1) grammars.

* Rhodes, S.P. Practical syntactic error recovery for programming languages.
TR 15, Univ. of Calif., Berkeley, 1973. Thesis.

See Graham and Rhodes [73].

* Smith, W.B. Error detection in formal languages. <u>J. of Comp. and Sys. Sciences 4</u>
(Oct. 70), 385-405.

* Souza, C.R. and R.A. Scholtz. Syntactical decoders and backtracking grammars.
TR A69-9, AD701796, Univ. of Hawaii, Honolulu, HI, 1969.

A parser (pushdown automata) uses backtracking to affect minimum distance correction in exponential time.

* Wirth, N. PL 360 - A programming language for the 360 computers. <u>CACM 15</u> (Jan.
1968), 37-54.

In one section Wirth discusses error <u>recovery</u> with simple precedence. If an empty
relation ⊙ holds between the top of the stack S and the next symbol T, a list of
possible symbols to insert is scanned. If a symbol I is found such that S ∅ I
and I ∅ T, then I is inserted; otherwise T is simply stacked.

If at reduction time no right part of a rule matches the top of the stack, a list of "error productions" (provided by the compiler writer) is scanned. If one matches, a message is printed and it is used. Wirth indicates a possible list of insertion symbols and error productions for PL360, and mentions the possibility of the compiler producing statistical information on errors so that these tables can be changed and expanded.

* Younger, D.A. Recognition and parsing of context free languages in time n^3. Information and Control 10 (Feb 1967), 189-208.